Quick Reference Guide

For a complete guide to chapters and main sections, see table of contents.

Merriam-Webster's
Secretarial
Handbook

Merriam-Webster's
Secretarial
Handbook

THIRD EDITION

Merriam-Webster, Incorporated
Springfield, Massachusetts

Copyright © 1993 by Merriam-Webster, Incorporated
Philippines Copyright 1993 by Merriam-Webster, Incorporated

Library of Congress Cataloging-in-Publication Data

Merriam-Webster's secretarial handbook.—3rd ed.
      p.   cm.
    Rev. ed. of: Webster's secretarial handbook. 2nd ed. © 1983.
    Includes index.
    ISBN 0-87779-236-4
    1. Office practice—Handbooks, manuals, etc. 2. Secretaries—Handbooks, manuals, etc. I. Merriam-Webster, Inc. II. Webster's secretarial handbook.
HF5547.5.W4   1993
651—dc20   93-10632
                                        CIP

Printed and bound in the United States of America

456RMcN989796

THIRD EDITION

CONSULTING EDITOR
Sheryl Lindsell-Roberts

CONTRIBUTORS
Warren M. Bergstein, C.P.A.   Lloyd M. Perell
Valerie McCusker   Catherine Sherwood

GENERAL EDITOR
Mark A. Stevens

SECOND EDITION

CONSULTING EDITOR
Marie G. Seaton

CONTRIBUTORS
Carol C. Jonic   Melvin Morgenstein
George J. Metzler   Donald J. Tate

ASSOCIATE EDITOR
Coleen K. Withgott

FIRST EDITION

CONSULTING EDITOR
Anna L. Eckersley-Johnson

CONTRIBUTORS
W. Arthur Allee   George J. Metzler
Mina M. Johnson   Melvin Morgenstein
Roger Wayne Johnson   Donald D. Scriven
Carol C. Jonic   Jolene D. Scriven
Nathan Krevolin   Donald J. Tate

ASSOCIATE EDITOR
Anne H. Soukhanov

Contents

Preface

This book is a product of Merriam-Webster Inc., publishers of Merriam-Webster dictionaries and reference books, and is characterized by the same thorough research, comprehensive content, and careful editing that have distinguished Merriam-Webster publications for nearly 150 years. A number of carefully chosen specialists—both educators and managers—with experience and expertise in business education and private industry have collaborated with the Merriam-Webster editorial department in each new edition of this work.

Merriam-Webster's Secretarial Handbook, Third Edition, is intended to serve as both a thorough introductory guide to the workings of the modern office and a highly practical day-to-day reference source for both secretaries and executives. Every paragraph of the previous edition has been subjected to review and reconsideration, and major changes have been made throughout the book.

The new chapter on "Desktop Publishing" deals with a subject that barely existed when the previous edition was published but has assumed great importance in the course of a very few years, to the extent that it is now a common secretarial specialization.

The new "Business Etiquette" chapter focuses greater attention on an essential subject that was formerly discussed under different headings and less extensively. Many of the issues it addresses are perennial; however, newer issues of male-female interaction in the workplace that have provoked anxiety and discussion are treated here in some detail as well. (To the extent that the previous edition sometimes implicitly assumed that employers were male and secretaries female, the current revision has tried to remove such implications.)

Two other chapters have been entirely rewritten. "Computers, Word Processing, and Office Equipment" discusses in depth the functions, features, and applications of office computers as well as the purchase of office hardware and software. "Telephones and Telecommunications" deals with the astonishing range of new developments and options in the field, of which the fax machine and electronic mail are only the most obvious.

"A Guide to Business English" has been substantially revised and expanded from the second edition, and now provides the most comprehensive treatment of the use of language available in any secretarial handbook. A section on specific problems of word usage is a new feature of the third edition.

A few subjects have naturally diminished in importance since the last edition was published, generally as a result of advancing technology. Shorthand, once an essential secretarial skill, has become far less so as a result of dictation machines. The greatly increased use of the word processor has resulted in a proportional decrease in the use of the typewriter. Office copying, formerly handled by a number of different methods, is today largely accomplished by the photocopier. A number of similar examples could be mentioned.

The book's interior has been redesigned for greater readability and maximum speed of reference. The Quick Reference Guide on the front endpaper will steer the reader immediately to a variety of frequently sought subjects; the contents listings at each chapter opening provide page references to all the book's major topics; and the detailed index will serve to locate even the briefest significant reference to every point mentioned.

We hope that executives as well as secretaries and other support staff will discover how valuable a resource this book can be. Several chapters, including "A Guide to Business English" and "Travel Arrangements and International Business," should prove equally as useful to the executive as to the secretary, and there are few pages in the entire volume that do not contain material that bears directly on the executive's own functions.

If time does not permit you to read the entire handbook, we recommend that you at least familiarize yourself with the text by skimming through it from front to back. You may be surprised by the quantity and breadth of information it contains.

Like other Merriam-Webster publications, *Merriam-Webster's Secretarial Handbook* is the product of a collective effort. For the first edition, Victor W. Weidman, Vice President, and Dr. H. Bosley Woolf, Editorial Director/Dictionaries, made major contributions during the initial planning stages, and Dr. Mairé Weir Kay and Dr. Frederick C. Mish, Joint Editorial Directors, reviewed the entire manuscript, offered sound advice, and provided invaluable guidance. For the second edition, Dr. Mish again reviewed the manuscript and lent assistance and support throughout the project.

This third edition has greatly benefited from the contributions of numerous members of the Merriam-Webster staff. Georgette B. Boucher prepared the many typed facsimiles. Stephen J. Perrault, Amy K. Harris, and Julie A. York produced a number of new illustrations. James W. Withgott, Thomas L. Coopee, Dr. Mish, Stephen Perrault, Daniel J. Hopkins, Maria A. Sansalone, and Lee Phenner all reviewed chapters in areas of their expertise and offered helpful comments and criticism. E. Ward Gilman, Susan L. Brady, Alexandra C. Horowitz, and Jennifer B. Tufts provided new text for Chapter 6. Robert D. Copeland, Kathleen M. Doherty, and Francine A. Roberts gave useful suggestions and other assistance. Paul F. Cappellano, Jennifer N. Cislo, Jennifer S. Goss, Peter D. Haraty, Joan I. Narmontas, Brett P. Palmer, Donna L. Rickerby, Michael D. Roundy, Katherine C. Sietsema, Linda Picard Wood, and several of the editors listed earlier proofread the text under the direction of Madeline L. Novak. Two freelance editors contributed to the project: Lois J. Principe copyedited the entire manuscript, and Eileen M. Haraty prepared the index. John M. Morse, Vice President and Executive Editor, carefully reviewed the manuscript, contributed to the shaping of several chapters, and improved the text through hundreds of suggestions and emendations.

Merriam-Webster's
Secretarial
Handbook

Career Development

It is appropriate to begin a handbook for secretaries with an overview of what it means to be a member of an extremely competitive profession—a profession that by its very nature must reflect the broadened scope and the heightened competition of today's business world. The secretary is now much more than a receptionist/typist, since an increasing number of executives expect their secretaries to function as administrative assistants who can relieve them of many routine and some specialized tasks. The secretary has always been a vital link between those who make management-level decisions and those who react to and implement the decisions. In the present role of administrative assistant, however, a competent and responsible secretary serves not only as a link between management and staff but also as a key support person for the executive.

Increased Responsibilities and Required Skills

In the past, many secretaries were placed in positions of responsibility without being delegated enough authority to carry out the responsibility. The current faster pace of business and the resulting pressures affecting managers have caused them to rethink the secretarial function and to delegate both more responsibility and more authority to their secretaries. While the qualifications for different job slots vary with the nature of the particular job and the requirements of each executive, the trend today is toward better-educated secretaries who are willing and qualified to perform as many tasks as can be delegated to them. Some of these tasks are specialized and demanding and require good judgment; many of them were once considered administrative or executive functions. Additional responsibilities expected of today's administrative secretary might include the following:

1. Preparing rough drafts of executive communications
2. Editing and signing executive correspondence
3. Composing speeches, memorandums, and reports for the executive

1

4. Composing articles for publication
5. Editing copy prepared by others
6. Consulting reference sources to obtain information needed by the executive
7. Abstracting information from various sources for the executive's use
8. Setting up meetings and conferences and reminding executives of the tasks delegated to them at these meetings
9. Chairing or participating actively in meetings
10. Supervising and training employees
11. Recommending or selecting office equipment systems and supplies for purchase

This administrative expansion of the secretarial function is reflected in the definition of a secretary provided by Professional Secretaries International: "an executive assistant who possesses a mastery of office skills, who demonstrates the ability to assume responsibility without direct supervision, who exercises initiative and judgment, and who makes decisions within the scope of assigned authority."

Another aspect of the changing role of the secretary is the effect of rapid and continual technological developments, especially in office equipment. Rather than eliminating secretaries from the office, technological developments have freed them from many time-consuming routine tasks so that they may be better employed in the more specialized areas of office work. For example, a secretary may now retrieve information from a computerized file without having to leave the workstation. Computers now expedite the processing of written communications and accounting procedures. And highly sophisticated telecommunications equipment and electronic-mail systems facilitate the rapid transmission of both oral and written communications.

Communication   Facility with language has always been a basic requirement not only for transcribing and composing letters, memorandums, and reports but also for oral communication in the office. A secretary's ability to handle telephone calls with ease, give clear instructions to other employees, give accurate messages to the employer, and meet customers and clients graciously is still prized by every employer.

Establishing priorities   It is essential that a secretary be able to organize the work to be done so that the most important tasks are carried out first. Smooth office work flow depends on the secretary's ability not only to handle routine matters but also to set up sensible work priorities, a skill that requires good judgment. The competent secretary knows which matters can be handled with prior approval of the executive, which should be relayed to other executives for action, and which must be sent directly to the executive for whom one works.

Identifying areas for improvement in the office   Attentive secretaries are on the alert for situations that could be improved through the development of new procedures, and they try to come up with concrete suggestions for implementing these improvements.

Bookkeeping   Executives and secretaries share responsibility for accurately maintaining the financial records that are used in the preparation of tax reports. Many changes in payroll procedures have evolved as a result of government regulations. The preparation of numerous and often complex reports by businesses at the behest of governmental agencies also requires the special attention of top-level secretaries. They must know who will need the information, what information will be required, and in what form it should be presented.

Multinational business challenges   An increasing number of major U.S. corporations are international and multinational in character. Since these companies operate throughout the world, the secretaries to the executives of such firms are involved in planning for international travel by the executives. In addition, a competent executive-level secretary tries to become sufficiently familiar with pertinent laws and regulations of particular countries in order to assist a manager in researching, interpreting, and applying them. Other desirable skills include a broad background in the customs and history of the countries with which the executive deals and the ability to speak at least one foreign language.

Communicating and retrieving information   Because of the complex relationships between corporations and government as well as by the global reach of modern business, the secretary needs to be able to acquire, handle, store, retrieve, and understand varied types of information as rapidly and efficiently as possible. The secretary's ability to obtain information from the appropriate files and reference sources can be extremely helpful to the executive. Such information may be acquired manually, mechanically, or electronically. Even in an era of automation, secretaries still use manual techniques for recording data on certain business forms and communications, such as purchase orders, cost tickets, expense accounts, and credit memorandums. Letters are not only important conduits of information but are also one of the many ways in which the corporate image is projected. Reports are also a vital information medium, as they assist in keeping designated persons abreast of past, present, and future management actions.

The handling of data is called *information processing*. In the office, data may be accurately and rapidly obtained through mechanical and electronic means with the aid of word processors, computers, transcribing machines, and microfilm units. These devices can facilitate many tasks, including preparing payroll records, copying personnel records, transcribing dictated letters, and storing, retrieving, and updating information.

The Importance of Self-Improvement

GENERAL AND CONTINUING EDUCATION

Self-evaluation is the first step in self-improvement and is essential if you aspire to a business career. Create a mental balance sheet of your professional assets and liabilities. Then decide how your assets can be further improved and how your liabilities can be reduced or eliminated. For example, if you lack computer skills, take a course in computer literacy. If you work for a corporation that is involved in international business, study a foreign language. You owe it to yourself to envision specific career goals and to take the steps to attain them rather than merely to stay afloat at your job from day to day.

It has already been mentioned that the increasing complexity and worldwide interaction of business, industry, and government have led executives to become more conscious of the value of college-educated secretaries. The well-educated secretary has a broader outlook and a more acute awareness of national and international problems. Many companies offer tuition-refund plans that encourage secretaries to continue their formal education in business schools, community colleges, and universities. Company in-service training programs are conducted at all levels; in addition, many companies cosponsor special educational seminars with professional, managerial, and secretarial associations.

TECHNICAL SKILLS

Executives today emphasize high-level office skills as requisites for secretarial placement and advancement. As a result, some secretaries report that they have had to learn how to carry out specialized office procedures and use sophisticated communications equipment while they are on the job. Firms that administer tests to applicants for office positions frequently include tests of typewriting, spelling, business mathematics, and English usage as well as a personality inventory, a general aptitude test, and an inventory of interest preferences in their evaluations. The following paragraphs examine specific skills and describe ways to improve them.

Shorthand and transcription   Most executives no longer regularly require secretaries to take dictation; however, many secretaries find that shorthand and transcription skills still come in handy. See the Appendix for recommended shorthand texts. Shorthand skills can be acquired by using the progressive speed-dictation cassettes available from commercial publishers. Dictation training tapes may also be prepared by the individuals for whom the secretary works. The normal types of office communications (such as letters, memorandums, reports, legal briefs, and engineering specifications) recorded at varying speeds will provide excellent skill-building practice for the new or inexperienced secretary.

Typewriting and keyboarding   Many companies set down specific typing standards for new employees. The required typing rate varies from 40 to 60 words a minute, with the degree of accuracy dependent on the amount of typing involved in the particular job. If you work for a company that does not have its own secretarial manual, you should carefully read the chapters in this book that contain information on specialized and automated typing and keyboarding, the typing of business letters, special typing projects (such as reports), and writing letters for an executive. You should also practice skill-building exercises and timed-writing exercises to improve your speed. In large offices secretaries should frequently check the company's secretarial manual (usually prepared by the secretarial-services division or the personnel department's training section) for recommended written-communication formats.

Editing and proofreading skills   All secretaries should strive for perfection in editing and proofreading. Proficiency is acquired by being very attentive to details to ensure that meaningful information is conveyed to the reader. One way to check for effectiveness of communication is to read aloud sections that may at first glance seem meaningless.

The need for editing skills will depend greatly upon the person for whom you work. Quite often, simple editing is performed by the employer and is easy to follow. An understanding of the editing guidelines and symbols that are commonly found in general office manuals such as this one will usually suffice.

Business mathematics   One way to review basic business mathematics is to use a programmed-learning text on the subject. After reviewing general arithmetic, such a text will then introduce you to the types of mathematical operations that may be needed in preparing payrolls and insurance registers.

Listening skills You must be able to follow instructions precisely. Therefore, you must listen carefully to oral instructions in order to comprehend them and convey them to others if necessary. In telephone conversations, you need to listen carefully for the name of the caller and the purpose of the call. When taking notes in a conference or at a meeting, cultivate the ability to listen purposefully in order to cull important matters that must be recorded and to screen out extraneous information.

Creativity Professional secretaries with strong imaginative abilities can put them to work in many ways, such as developing interesting and attractive layouts for the office, drafting more efficient forms, and devising innovative ways of working with other members of the office staff. Use initiative in finding original and creative ways to assist the executive.

HUMAN RELATIONS

Good human relations in business require the ability to deal positively with coworkers and supervisors. A good working relationship with the executive is of the utmost importance. Your first responsibility in this area is to understand your employer as an individual. In addition, you must be aware of the particular goals and burdens that are associated with an executive's position. A manager often has to accept heavy responsibilities, make demanding corporate decisions, and work under extreme pressure. Your loyalty both to superior and to company is essential if you and the executive are to work together as a team. You must prove yourself worthy of the employer's confidence and the responsibility for handling confidential and personal material.

A good employer-secretary team will cooperatively develop guidelines to enable the secretary to assume shared administrative responsibility for routine duties, to screen out nonessential from essential interruptions, and to supervise the work of coworkers. In this way, you may proceed to exercise initiative and creativity so as to complement the overall goals, systems, and policies of the firm.

As a secretary, you will need to work well not only with your peers but with all coworkers, regardless of professional level. In doing so, you should display loyalty, dependability, and good judgment.

Many secretaries supervise other employees. This may involve planning and organizing work assignments as well as instructing personnel on acceptable office procedures. Effective supervisors try to foresee unusual situations before they arise. They also should be able to substitute temporarily for a worker who may be unexpectedly absent. One's performance as a supervisor and one's relationships with those being supervised have a great deal to do with building and preserving a smooth-working office organization.

Good working relations must extend to visitors, maintenance personnel on call, delivery people, and messengers. You can be proud of your role in creating and maintaining a high level of goodwill within the organization and promoting a positive corporate image to outsiders.

Upward Mobility

Advancement in a company depends upon the quality of the work you perform, a willingness to acquire additional informal or formal education, and an interest in company operations. The following paragraphs examine various general levels of secretarial work and explain methods of advancement.

SECRETARIAL LEVELS

Pre-secretarial The person who works for a junior executive is more likely to function as a receptionist or a clerk-typist than as a secretary per se. Many duties will center upon people-to-people contacts such as dealing with visitors, handling telephone conversations, and making appointments. A pre-secretarial worker can enhance the likelihood of being promoted to a full secretarial position by performing competently and desiring promotion enough to work for it.

Secretarial A full secretary will find that transcription skills are essential to the position but that additional administrative duties will come as well. Many of these, such as opening and routing the mail, ordering new supplies, daily filing, and answering the telephone, will seem strictly routine; but they represent the first steps in acceptance of individual responsibility, since they are performed with little or no supervision. They merit the utmost care and attention. Other duties that may be assigned to a secretary include typing correspondence and other written communications, setting up travel itineraries, determining the payroll for a section, or handling a petty-cash fund.

In large corporations today, the secretary can lend administrative support to the executive by handling time-consuming tasks such as compiling and organizing information for reports and long memorandums, maintaining confidential files, disseminating information relative to administrative policies, researching data for presentations by the executive, and composing and dictating letters. The title *administrative secretary* is frequently given to the secretary who functions in an administrative-support capacity.

Corporate secretarial The corporate secretary occupies a unique position in business society, reporting directly to the board of directors in theory, but in practice answering to the president or chief executive officer of the company. The corporate secretary holds such important responsibilities as organizing corporate meetings, recording minutes of these meetings, maintaining a record of activities in stocks and bonds, improving stockholder relations, keeping records of trademark information, and handling corporate books, records, and reports. The American Society of Corporate Secretaries, 1270 Avenue of the Americas, New York, NY 10020 (212-765-2620), provides an information and reference service and conducts educational programs for its members.

SPECIALIZED SECRETARIAL POSITIONS

Secretarial employment opportunities are available in specialized fields such as law and medicine as well as in engineering and other technical areas. Secretarial positions may also be secured in other countries through the U.S. Foreign Service or with multinational corporations. Those who plan to enter a particular field often prefer to develop general experience in a business or government office before applying for specialized jobs (for example, in science). Some important specialized secretarial positions are described in this section.

The legal secretary The legal secretary performs varied duties depending on the size and nature of the law firm. A general-practice lawyer handles all types of legal transactions; in a large firm, on the other hand, each lawyer usually specializes in one branch of law. A legal secretary may also be employed by a large corporation. Most large corporations have in-house law departments staffed by lawyers qualified in virtually every field of law needed in the company's operations (such as antitrust law, insurance law, and labor law).

Courts on all levels provide a variety of legal-secretarial positions. One of the most demanding jobs is that of secretary to a judge whose court docket is extremely crowded. Some secretaries are also employed by lawyers who have become members of city councils, state legislatures, or the U.S. Congress.

A knowledge of legal terminology and procedures such as pleadings, deeds, and subpoenas is vital to the competence of a legal secretary, and many community colleges offer courses in these areas. Legal secretaries are called upon to type and format legal documents such as briefs, proxies, wills, rental leases, and abstracts. They may need to hold a notary's commission so that they can notarize papers. In a small law office or partnership, a legal secretary may assume much of the responsibility for managing the routine work of the legal practice. For example, a legal secretary must be constantly alert to the lawyer's calendar that indicates dates for pending cases, current cases, and office appointments. Many legal secretaries also serve as apprentices or paralegal aides as they continue part-time education at a college or law school, and many aspire to obtain certification as a Professional Legal Secretary (PLS). The National Association of Legal Secretaries (International), 2250 East 73rd Street, Suite 550, Tulsa, OK 74136 (918-493-3540) offers this certification to applicants who successfully complete a series of examinations.

The medical secretary   The medical secretary has more opportunities than are available in most other areas of secretarial specialization. With a strong background in medical terminology, medical shorthand, and medical office procedures, you can choose from a wide variety of jobs—in doctors' or dentists' offices, in hospitals and clinics, and in government health departments. But do not overlook such additional possibilities as those in corporations having medical departments or in companies manufacturing medical supplies and pharmaceuticals. If you are also interested in editorial work, investigate research foundations and medical publishers.

The duties of the medical secretary will vary according to the nature and size of the organization and the scope and degree of specialization of the employer. For example, if you work for a large medical insurance company you may be involved with claims for hospitalization benefits. If you work for doctors in a large joint practice, you may make appointments for their patients, transfer patients to other physicians, arrange with cooperating hospitals for the admission of patients, and spend a great deal of time typing and filing medical records. In particular, medical secretaries are responsible for typing case histories and patients' records, receiving payments for medical bills, and ordering office supplies. If qualified, they may also be requested to secure personal medical data from patients, take temperatures and pulse rates, prepare patients for examination, and even sterilize medical instruments.

Preparation for becoming a medical secretary includes instruction in accounting and maintaining financial records adapted to doctors' and dentists' offices, and practice in working with hospital records and insurance forms. Essential qualifications are a sympathy for human problems and an ability to guard confidential matters.

As modern medical offices grow larger and more specialized, the distinction between the medical secretary and the *medical assistant* will increase. A person who enjoys working as a medical secretary may wish to enroll at a school that trains students to become medical assistants. Such preparation provides a thorough background in the basic sciences, laboratory practice, and the fundamentals of patient care. The graduate medical assistant works closely with physicians in obtaining case-history data, conducting laboratory tests such as blood counts, and, when requested, applying and removing surgical dressings. A medical assistant may be expected to operate some of the less formidable equipment in the office. The American Association of Medical Assistants, 20 N. Wacker Drive, Suite 1575, Chicago, IL 60606 (312-899-1500) offers certification as a Certified Medical Assistant (CMA) to those who qualify and pass an examination.

The technical secretary   Technical secretaries specialize in preparing technical correspondence and reports (e.g., for engineering firms). Keyboarding tabulations and chemical and mathematical formulas featuring special characters is a typical task. Knowing the fundamentals of accounting is also necessary for technical secretaries, since they may work with highly complex financial records, such as those associated with research contracts.

If a company deals with classified information, the technical secretary may have to be cleared by the U.S. government to handle such documents, and, if so cleared, will be expected to follow carefully all security regulations imposed by the government.

If you wish to become a technical secretary, you should be well prepared in the physical sciences (such as chemistry and physics) as well as in mathematics and statistics. Familiarity with scientific and engineering terminology and proficiency in recording technical dictation are also required.

The education secretary   Education secretaries are employed by educational systems and organizations. Responsibilities include close contact with students, teachers, parents, librarians, administrators, and the news media. The National Association of Educational Office Professionals (NAEOP), P.O. Box 12619, Wichita, KS 67277 (316-942-4822) provides educational secretaries with a means of further education and opportunities for professional growth. The NAEOP has a certificate program which is highly regarded by educational administrators.

The travel secretary   Travel secretaries can find opportunities with airlines, hotels, travel agencies, and tour agencies. Several perquisites come with such positions, particularly free or reduced travel rates. In order to work successfully in the travel industry, you should be knowledgeable about geography, proficient at reading timetables, and competent at using a computer.

The Foreign Service secretary   Secretaries who qualify for the Foreign Service can seek employment in any of the approximately 230 embassies and consulates in over 150 countries overseas. You need to be a U.S. citizen, be 21 years of age, be able to type 60 words per minute, and have word-processing/computer experience. For more information, write to Recruitment Division (Foreign Service Secretary Program), U.S. Department of State, Box 9317—Rosslyn Station, Arlington, VA 22219, or call 703-875-6820.

The desktop publishing (DTP) specialist   As publishing of brochures, newsletters, and reports is gradually transferred into the office, a wide range of opportunities will be available to secretaries who want to enter the field. The DTP specialist is often drawn from the secretarial ranks. With the coming of sophisticated page-layout programs, scanners, and laser printers, more and more secretaries are expected to extend their knowledge from word processing to desktop publishing. The transition is not necessarily an easy one, as is evidenced by the many poorly designed documents that we see today. However, virtually anyone with an eye for design and the ability to write can be taught to create simple newsletters, brochures, and overhead slide presentations. The duties of the DTP specialist often include coordinating the efforts of writers and graphic designers. If you are called upon for these challenging opportunities, ask your company to let you take advantage of one of the many courses in desktop publishing that are offered by organizations and schools.

The National Association of Desktop Publishers (NADTP), 462 Old Boston Street, Suite 8, Topsfield, MA 01983 (800-874-4113), is dedicated to fostering the growth of the DTP industry. It publishes *The NADTP Journal* and provides a forum for developers and users.

Employment possibilities in other countries   For those interested in private foreign-based employment, the best sources of employment are U.S. corporations that operate internationally. Although knowledge of a foreign language may not be required for a job abroad, such a skill will increase your opportunities for obtaining and holding a good position. (See also "The Foreign Service secretary" above.)

POST-SECRETARIAL OPPORTUNITIES
College graduates aspiring to certain professional and executive jobs frequently find that their best entrance is by way of a secretarial position. This may be the case in such areas as publishing, fashion design, personnel, and television. If office assistants perform satisfactorily, they may be given assignments in, for example, television programming or news writing for a city newspaper.

An increasing number of secretaries are qualifying for positions as personnel directors, production coordinators, editors, advertising executives, office managers, programmers, and systems analysts. Although the career path from secretarial to non-secretarial managerial posts is not common, there is nevertheless a trend toward filling managerial positions by promotion from within a company or industry. Thus, talented individuals entering the secretarial field can realistically aspire to post-secretarial positions at a higher level. They will, however, need a few years' experience to learn the operations of their companies and to prove that they are capable of assuming administrative duties.

PROFESSIONAL CERTIFICATION
The Certified Professional Secretary   In 1951 the National Secretaries Association (International), now called Professional Secretaries International, inaugurated the program for the Certified Professional Secretary (CPS). To qualify as a CPS, you must have several years of verified work experience and must also pass a two-day examination that is given each year in May and November at approved colleges and universities throughout the United States. The CPS examination is based on an analysis of secretarial work, with emphasis on judgment, understanding, and administrative ability gained through education and work experience. The examination tests skills, techniques, and knowledge in the following specific areas:

1. *Behavioral Science in Business*   Principles of human relations and understanding of self, subordinates, peers, and superiors. One's own needs and motivations, the nature of conflict, problem-solving techniques, essentials of supervision and communication, leadership styles, and understanding of the informal organization.
2. *Business Law*   Principles of business law as they apply in day-to-day business practice. Content and implications of the operation of governmental controls on business. History of the development of these controls.
3. *Economics and Management*   Applied economics, principles of management,

and elements of business operations. Management of personnel, finance, production, and marketing.

4. *Accounting* Elements of the accounting cycle. Analysis of financial statements and accounts. Arithmetic necessary for accounting and for computing interest and discounts. Summarizing and interpreting financial data.

5. *Office Administration and Communication* Office management, records management, reprographics, preparing communications, editing.

6. *Office Technology* Business data processing, communications media, advances in office-management technology, records-management technology, and office systems.

Successful candidates are awarded a certificate from the Institute for Certifying Secretaries. The professional status of a secretary holding this certificate is significantly enhanced. Further information on the Certified Professional Secretary rating may be obtained by writing to Professional Secretaries International, 10502 NW Ambassador Drive, P.O. Box 20404, Kansas City, MO 64195 (816-891-6600).

The Certified Administrative Manager Professional recognition in the form of the C.A.M. (Certified Administrative Manager) designation is available to secretaries with supervisory or management-level positions. This program was initiated in 1970 by the Administrative Management Society (AMS) for qualified persons in the area of administrative management. The certification process requires that the individual fulfill the C.A.M. program standards within a ten-year period. Successful candidates must meet the following requirements:

1. Pass C.A.M. examinations in (a) personnel management, (b) financial management, (c) administrative services, (d) information systems management, (e) management concepts, and (f) an in-depth case study
2. Have two years of experience at the administrative management level
3. Have high standards of personal and professional conduct
4. Provide satisfactory evidence of active participation and/or leadership within recent years in voluntary organizations
5. Show evidence of having made contributions to effective administrative management ideas and principles through oral and/or written communications

Candidates who successfully complete the C.A.M. program become members of the Academy of Certified Administrative Managers and are entitled to use the initials *C.A.M.* after their names on letterheads or in signature blocks. Inquiries may be sent to: Director of Educational Programs, Administrative Management Society, 1101 14th St. NW, No. 1100, Washington, DC 20005-5601.

Other secretarial specialties The legal, medical, and education fields have their own certification requirements. See pages 6–8 for further information.

Obtaining Employment

Before seeking out employment agencies or submitting application letters to specific companies, it is wise to make two important decisions about yourself. First, determine what kind of secretarial position you would enjoy. Do you prefer working for a small or a large company? a company specializing in particular products or services? Do you work best alone, or do you prefer close association with others? Could you work overtime if required? Second, analyze your skills. What are your strengths and weaknesses? How can you best focus on your strengths in the search for a job?

The ways in which you can obtain a secretarial position will differ according to your educational background, the contacts you have made during your studies, your professional experience, and your geographical area.

SOURCES OF EMPLOYMENT AND INFORMATION

A Department of Labor study of the primary means through which Americans find jobs came up with the following results:

Source	Percentage
Friends and relatives	48
Direct contact with employers	24
Private employment agencies	1
Public employment agencies	3
Help-wanted ads	5
School placement services	6
Combination of methods	13

It is certainly to your benefit to employ all or most of the possible sources, because you never know which one will work for you. Often the lead that results in a job offer comes from the most unusual and unexpected source.

Private employment agencies   Professional placement agencies place newspaper ads for their employer clients regarding job openings that they need to fill. The agency interviews and screens candidates and then refers the qualified candidates to the prospective employer. If an employment ad says "fee paid," it means that the agency fee will be paid by the agency's client, your prospective employer. Otherwise, you will have to pay the fee if you are selected for the job. Therefore, ask what you might pay the agency when it finds you a job. Try to avoid agencies that insist on a payment from you before the job search begins.

State employment agencies   Many job seekers overlook the free services of state employment agencies, through which you will find many current job openings. Many state employment agencies have computers and printers for your use, and many offer classes on résumé preparation, interview skills, and networking.

Temporary-employment agencies   A survey of the National Association of Temporary Services (NATS) has revealed that two-thirds of those who solicit temporary assignments regard such jobs as a path to full-time employment. If you are unemployed, accepting a temporary assignment can offer you not only a long- or short-term salary but an opportunity to establish new relationships (another form of networking), to shop around for an industry or field you might enjoy, and to explore avenues for full-time employment.

Advertisements   In all likelihood, you will respond to newspaper advertisements. Although you should check the Help Wanted sections of your local newspapers daily, most job openings are advertised on Sundays. In addition to newspapers, many jobs are advertised in professional journals and magazines. Ads may be "blind" or "signed." A blind ad is one that gives a post-office box to which you should respond. Companies place blind ads because they do not want to be bothered with telephone calls. A signed ad gives the name of the company and often the name of someone to contact. If you respond to a signed ad by sending a résumé and do not get a response within about two weeks, it is appropriate to call the company to be certain they received your résumé and to reaffirm your interest in the position.

You should also read the news sections of your local newspaper and be aware of companies that may be expanding or moving into your area; they might be in the market for your skills.

Networking   One of the most effective means of finding a job is through networking. As the term implies, networking means creating a chain of friends, relatives, and professional acquaintances who can link you with other people. Spread the word—tell your relatives, your friends, your neighbors, your attorney, your doctor, and anyone else you know that you are looking for a job. Clubs and professional organizations also provide endless networking opportunities. The more people you speak to, the more your network will expand, and the greater your chances of finding the right position will be. (If you are currently employed and do not want to jeopardize your position, you must naturally exercise discretion.)

Government opportunities   Many jobs are available at federal, state, county, and municipal offices. In fact, the federal government is the largest employer in the United States. Most government positions require that you pass a civil-service exam. You can get more information about government opportunities through state employment services or by contacting the Office of Personnel Management at the various government agencies in which you are interested.

Job fairs   Many companies and employment agencies rely on job fairs to find qualified job candidates. Job fairs are held periodically in most major cities and are advertised in the Help Wanted sections of local newspapers, generally in the Sunday edition.

The hidden job market   It is estimated that 80 percent of job openings are not advertised but are filled through what is known as the hidden job market. Many of these may come to your attention through networking or through your own research efforts. There are many resources at your local and school libraries which can direct you to firms and possible jobs. Some of the most useful are the following:

- Chamber of Commerce directories for local towns and cities.
- State industrial directories.
- *Reference Book of Corporate Management.* New York: Dun's Marketing Services. Annual.
- *The Corporate Directory.* San Mateo, Cal.: Walker Western Research.
- *Thomas Register of American Manufacturers.* New York: Thomas Publishing Co. Annual.
- *Directory of Corporate Affiliations: Who Owns Whom.* Wilmette, Ill.: National Register Publishing Co. Annual, with three supplements.
- *Directory of American Research and Technology.* New York: R. R. Bowker. Annual.
- *National Trade and Professional Associations of the United States.* New York: Columbia Books. Annual.

INTRODUCING YOURSELF

Telephoning a prospective employer's office   When inquiring about a job by telephone, make sure that you call only during the hours specified. Have your background material at hand so that you can respond concisely, coherently, and completely to all questions. One of a secretary's prime responsibilities is the easy handling of telephone calls; thus, the office team will be evaluating your telephone performance from the beginning to the end of the conversation. Project a smile in your voice and a relaxed, confident manner. Since you can never know what kinds of questions will be asked, you must be ready for anything. Keep in mind the following:

1. In your concern about the job, do not forget to say hello and good-bye.
2. Identify yourself at once and state your reason for calling.
3. Use the other person's name in the conversation; if for some reason it has not been mentioned, ask "To whom am I speaking, please?"
4. Give brief, straightforward, complete answers to all questions.
5. Ask the questions that *you* have.
6. Be polite and enthusiastic, but not insincerely so.
7. If you have small children at home, do not try to call when they are in the room making noise, since this would indicate that you aren't well organized.
8. If you discover during the conversation that you really are not qualified for the job or that you do not want to pursue the matter further, say so politely.
9. If the interviewer sounds rushed, ask if you can call at another time, or if the interviewer could call you back at his or her convenience.
10. Do not try to discuss salary matters during an initial telephone conversation.

Sometimes the applicant will receive a call after the employer has reviewed the applicant's résumé. In such cases, the following additional suggestions may be helpful:

1. If you are expecting such a call, don't just answer the telephone with "Hello," but give your name as well.
2. Answer all questions politely and thoroughly. However, do not ramble and waste the caller's time with irrelevancies.
3. If the employer suggests a personal interview, save most of your questions for then. You may, however, mention that you have a question or two that cannot wait, thus showing your interest but not at the expense of the caller's valuable time.
4. Verify your appointment date, time, and location.
5. Let the caller terminate the conversation by saying good-bye first.

The job-application letter   A properly formatted and well-written letter of application will greatly assist in pre-selling you to a prospective employer. This letter should be a concrete indication of your verbal and technical skills and of your general personality and intelligence.

You should type or keyboard the letter on good-quality plain bond paper. Either white or a conservative color like cream or gray is appropriate. Do not use social stationery or letterhead from your present place of employment. Exotic typefaces should be avoided. The Block, Modified Block, and Modified Semiblock stylings are all appropriate (see Chapter 7). The letter ought not to exceed one page. Under no circumstances should you send a photocopied form letter.

Before writing the letter, plan your approach in detail. An outline of the points to be made or a complete draft will assist you. If the letter is solicited (i.e., if you are responding to an advertisement), mention in the first paragraph the specific position for which you are applying and the source of the advertisement. If the letter is unsolicited (i.e., if you are applying on your own initiative), say as much in the first paragraph and indicate why you are interested in working for the particular company or department. Next, focus on and develop your best assets. A concise statement of your technical skills (such as computer skills) may be given, along with mention of any more specialized skills (such as financial record-keeping or a foreign language). Another sentence or even a paragraph expanding on some aspect of your education or previous employment experience not developed fully in the résumé can be included. Finally, the letter should state what kind of response or action is to be taken: whether, for instance, you will expect a call from their office or if you will call the following week. The tone throughout should be straightforward, modest, and sincere. The material should be carefully proofread for grammatical and typographical errors. Keep a copy of the letter for your records. (See the sample job-application letter in Fig. 1.1.)

The résumé   Your résumé (also called *vita, curriculum vitae, CV,* or *personal data sheet*) is the complete statement of your professional advancement and accomplishments to date. As such, it will be a key factor in achieving your employment objectives. Although books have been written on this subject, the elements essential to all well-written résumés can be discussed briefly. These elements are as follows:

1. *Personal identification:* your full name, address, and telephone number (home and/or office), at the top of the résumé.
2. *Employment experience:* each job that you have held listed chronologically from present to past, including the name and address of each business, employment dates, your job title, a *brief* job description if the responsibilities are not obvious from the title itself, and perhaps a concise summary of your special accomplishments in each position if space permits.
3. *Educational background:* a list of the institutions that you have attended, with dates and degrees earned, if any, starting with the highest level (e.g., college) and concluding with high school.
4. *Special skills:* a list of special skills that might be valued by a prospective employer.
5. *References:* the sentence "References will be provided on request."

If you have no previous employment experience, supplement your education category with a list of the business and secretarial courses that you have successfully completed, and list any academic or professional honors that you have been awarded. If you have completed any special free-lance secretarial projects (such as the typing of manuscripts and theses), you can mention them under the heading "Special Projects" following the education section. Optionally, you may begin with a brief "Objective," and you may also include a section for "Professional Associations." Résumés sent to large companies often include a subheading such as "Job Objective: Executive Secretary" to help the personnel department, which may be handling applications for a wide variety of jobs within the company.

The following data should *not* be given on the résumé:

1. *Names and addresses of references.* References should be typewritten separately and should be provided by you at the interview or in an interview follow-up letter.

Fig. 1.1   Job-Application Letter

April 8, 19--

3 Ternure Avenue
Suffern, NY 10901

Ms. Roberta Johns
Lehman Larson, Inc.
5 Astor Place
New York, NY 10003

Dear Ms. Johns:

Your advertisement in The New York Times for an Executive
Secretary in the Marketing Department is of great interest
to me. I have spent five years as Executive Secretary to
the Vice President for Marketing at Marc Bros. and have all
the qualifications you're seeking.

As you can see from the enclosed resume, my background
includes strong computer skills. I have worked extensively
with Microsoft Word and WordPerfect 5.1 and have the primary
responsibility for producing newsletters and overhead slide
presentations. I also have a working knowledge of Lotus
1-2-3 and basic bookkeeping skills. Additionally, I now
supervise two secretaries and help to set up trade shows and
conferences.

Should you find that my background meets your needs, I
would appreciate the opportunity for a personal interview
to discuss the contribution I can make to your company.

Very truly yours,

Ethel Lorenz
Ethel Lorenz

enc.

2. *Salary.* It is best to discuss salary requirements and ranges during the interview itself, since you will not want to undersell yourself ahead of time or possibly price yourself out of a job that you may be unfamiliar with.

3. *Your reasons, if any, for changing jobs.* Since wording can often be misunderstood without personal clarification, it is best to discuss this matter with the interviewer and only if you are asked, rather than committing yourself on paper.

4. *Your reasons for present unemployment, if applicable.* This topic is also tricky and is therefore best dealt with in person or in a telephone conversation, since adequate explanations often require valuable page space that can be better used to highlight your assets.

5. *A photograph.* A photo can work for or against you, depending on the person evaluating your application; hence, it is best not to risk a negative reaction before you have had a chance to present yourself in person.

Your résumé normally should not exceed one page. You should prepare the material first in draft form. Use plain, straightforward English devoid of technical jargon and superlatives. The finished résumé should be printed on plain standard bond paper that matches your letter of application.

Although there are many acceptable résumé formats, the simplest and cleanest treatment is to block all the material flush left. Entries should be single-spaced internally, with double- or triple-spacing between entries, depending on the space available. Capital letters, boldface, or italic type may be used for main and secondary headings. Margins should be balanced on all four sides. (See the sample résumé in Fig. 1.2.)

Professional and personal references   When you prepare a list of references, follow the general format and style that you have used for your résumé. Use the same paper size and color and the same typeface. Head the list "References for [name]." Single-space each entry and double- or triple-space between entries. Include the full name, address, and telephone number of each person who has consented to recommend you. Include at least one supervisor or manager from each former place of employment. Include one former instructor if possible. No unexplained gaps should show up when the résumé and reference list are compared. Personal character references can be listed at the bottom of the sheet, if necessary.

It is important *not* to give a person's name as a reference without first getting permission. Of those who consent, some will write blanket "To whom it may concern" letters of recommendation that you can take with you in sealed envelopes to the interview; others will write directly to each prospective employer; but most will expect the prospective employer to telephone them. (See the sample reference list in Fig. 1.3.) Make sure that you have enough names (generally three or four) to satisfy the office's requirements. Give the prospective employer the reference list when it is asked for, but do not staple it to your résumé.

Application forms and tests   Many offices require applicants to fill out an employment form. Be prepared by bringing a copy of your résumé with you for reference. Follow instructions carefully, print (or type) neatly, and double-check information for accuracy. Be sure to fill in all the blanks, writing "N/A" (for *not applicable*) or a dash on those blanks that are not relevant. Some application forms have a space in which to write the salary you expect. It is better to write a salary *range* rather than a specific amount.

Performance tests for keyboarding/transcription, shorthand, grammar, and math skills, as well as general intelligence tests, are used by many employers.

Fig. 1.2 Résumé

ETHEL LORENZ
3 Ternure Avenue, Suffern, NY 10901
home: (914) 357-1234
work: (212) 987-6543

OBJECTIVE

A challenging Executive Secretarial position that will fully utilize my secretarial and computer skills and experience.

EMPLOYMENT EXPERIENCE

MARC BROS., 70 West 33rd Street, New York, NY 10001
    Position: Executive Secretary to Vice President for Marketing (February 19-- to present)
    Responsibilities: Supervising two junior-level secretaries, producing newsletters and overhead slide presentations on a desktop publishing system, helping to set up trade shows and conferences, telephone communications, and records management.

H&M CONTRACTORS, One Lake Road, Monroe, NY 10960
    Position: Office Manager (October 19-- to February 19--)
    Responsibilities: General office management, light bookkeeping, office correspondence, records management, and telephone communications.

EDUCATION

ROCKLAND COMMUNITY COLLEGE, Suffern, NY
Degree: Associate in Arts
Graduated: June 19--

SUFFERN HIGH SCHOOL, Suffern, NY
Graduated: June 19--

SPECIAL SKILLS

Hardware: IBM PC and Macintosh
Software: Microsoft Word, WordPerfect, and Lotus 1-2-3
Language: Fluency in French

PROFESSIONAL ASSOCIATIONS

Professional Secretaries International
Academy of Certified Administrative Managers

REFERENCES

References will be provided on request.

Fig. 1.3   Job References

```
                        REFERENCES FOR ETHEL LORENZ


        Thomas Sullivan, Vice President
        Marc Bros.
        70 West 33rd Street
        (212) 879-1234



        Karen Amy Karp, Vice President
        H&M Contractors
        One Lake Road
        Monroe, NY 10960



        Dr. Steven Jeffrey Teisch
        7 Mountain Road
        New City, NY 10956
        (914) 352-1234
```

When you take such tests, try to relax. Be sure you understand the instructions, as well as the machine you are working with, *before* you begin the test.

INTERVIEW MANNERS AND APPEARANCE

Since the secretary is frequently the first and the last member of the office team seen by visitors, impeccable manners are required, and an applicant's manners will be carefully observed by the interviewer with this in mind. The following are some of the most important points to remember.

Punctuality   Be on time for your interview. If you do not know exactly where the office is located, get directions beforehand. If the office is in a large city where traffic and parking are a problem, ask a staff member for the best driving or public-transportation route and find out where you can park. This can be done when your appointment is being made. If you are still unsure of the directions, make a dry run in advance to make sure that you know the way. In any event, give yourself plenty of time to get there.

Arrival   When you enter the office, identify yourself to the receptionist or assistant ("I'm Ms. Lorenz, and I have a 4:30 appointment with Ms. Johns"). Be cheerful and polite. If the weather is bad and you need to remove heavy outerwear, find out where to hang it up so that you will not be burdened with coat, scarf, mittens, hat, or the like during the interview.

Dress   In business offices, personal appearance is very important; therefore, you should dress carefully for your interview. Although it may not be necessary to wear a suit, it is essential that the clothing you do wear be clean, pressed, professional, and conservative. Casual attire (such as jumpsuits or jeans) is definitely out of place. Do without cologne or perfume, and, if you are a woman, avoid excessive makeup. Your hair should be clean, combed, and generally neat. Be especially careful that your hands are clean and your fingernails are manicured. A sloppy, unkempt appearance is often taken as an indicator of a sloppy worker.

Cigarettes and gum   Many waiting rooms and private offices are now no-smoking areas. Even where smoking is permitted, it is best not to smoke at all. And never chew gum at an interview!

THE INTERVIEW ITSELF

Learning as much as you can about the company beforehand will provide you with opportunities to ask questions and show your interest in the company. Just as important is *self*-knowledge: awareness of your own abilities and knowledge of your short-term and long-term career goals. Be prepared for unexpected questions. You may be asked why you left a former job or why there are gaps in your educational or professional background. An interviewer may also ask what you think you can contribute to the organization. Self-knowledge gives you a positive, assured attitude that conveys your competence to the interviewer. While it is impossible to offer cut-and-dried guidelines to cover every eventuality, the following paragraphs give general suggestions that will make your experience more positive.

Introductions   When introduced to the staff members, smile, repeat their names ("How do you do, Mr. Lee," or "It's nice to meet you, Ms. Smith"), and appear enthusiastic. Avoid seeming glum or sick (even if you *feel* that way!).

Posture   When sitting, do not sprawl. On the other hand, do not sit rigidly like a store mannequin. Try to relax and enjoy the experience.

Eye contact   Look directly at the interviewer when you are speaking. Avoiding someone's eyes, especially when you are answering questions, can be interpreted as evasiveness. On the other hand, do not stare blankly at the interviewer.

Speech mannerisms   Try to avoid those annoying verbal tics that many people use to cover up pauses or to give themselves time to think of what to say next. Some of the more irritating mannerisms are the use of "ah" or "uh," starting sentences with "Like, . . ." and repeating "you know" or "OK" throughout a conversation.

Asking questions   Don't try to lead the conversation, since the interviewer undoubtedly will have decided what to ask and discuss. Follow the interviewer's lead. You can interject your own questions during appropriate lulls in the conversation, or you can save them for the end, when the interviewer will probably ask if you have any questions.

Listening   Listen carefully to what the interviewer is saying and asking. As Calvin Coolidge once said, "Nobody has ever listened himself out of a job."

Job description and on-the-job training   Be sure that you get a clear idea of just what you will be doing in the office. Understand the expected hours of work and any required overtime. Find out if the employer intends to give you any on-the-job training and, if so, what kind.

Questions you cannot answer   Many people are embarrassed when they discover during an interview that they do not know everything an interviewer expects them to know. If you are asked something that you cannot answer, say so honestly. Sometimes interviewers ask questions that they *know* you cannot answer, just to see whether they will get an honest reaction.

Weaknesses in your skills   If the interviewer mentions a required skill in which you know you are weak, admit it right away. Be prepared to say that you are willing to improve in that area, whether by programmed self-study, by taking a refresher course, or by learning on the job.

Permissible and impermissible interview questions   Most of the interview questions will concern your ability to do the job and how well you will fit into the company. There are several questions the interviewer may ask to get a better understanding of how you think and handle yourself, such as:

- Could you tell me something about yourself?
- What is your greatest weakness? strength?
- What do you like to do when you are away from work? How do you spend your leisure time?
- Why are you changing jobs?
- Where do you see yourself five years from now?
- Why should I hire you?

There are, however, other questions that cannot (or should not) be asked because they are illegal:

- Are you married? single? divorced? living with anyone?
- Do you have young children at home? Who cares for them? Do you plan to have more children?
- Do you have any mental or physical handicaps?
- How much do you weigh?
- Have you ever been arrested? jailed?
- How old are you?
- What is your ethnic background? your religious affiliation?
- Do you own your own home? rent?
- What type of military discharge do you have? (He or she can, however, ask if you have served in the military.)

If you are asked any of these questions, you have a number of options, and only you can decide which one is most appropriate.

- Answer it.
- Respond with your own question: "Is this relevant to the position?"
- Report the interviewer to the Equal Employment Opportunity Commission (EEOC) subsequently, if the questions are persistent or demeaning.

Salary, fringe benefits, and insurance   The interviewer will tell you your base pay and will undoubtedly outline the fringe benefits and insurance provisions. Feel free to bring up any of these topics, including holidays, vacations, and sick leave, if he or she does not (while being careful not to convey the impression that vacations are all you care about).

Sometimes an employment ad that you are responding to will stipulate that the salary is *open* (i.e., open to negotiation). If you have familiarized yourself beforehand with the usual salary range for secretaries in your area, you ought to be able to discuss the issue intelligently. In cases like this, it is even more important to highlight your education, experience, and any specialized skills that you feel would place you as close as possible to the top of the range. And it is usually a good idea to state an amount that is slightly higher than what you actually expect. However, it is bad practice to argue about a salary that you feel is too low. You can ask about the office's raise policy (for example, "What is a standard raise and when are employees considered for them?"). You may also ask about staff promotions if the office is a large one.

If you see that the interview is about to end before the subject of salary has been brought up, you might say, "Oh, by the way, Ms. Johns, what do you feel is a reasonable salary based on your expectations and my qualifications?" or "What will the starting salary be for this position?" or "May I ask what the salary will be?"

The closing   At the conclusion of an interview, the interviewer will often ask if you have any questions. In addition to asking any you may have, it may also be appropriate and beneficial at this point to encourage the interviewer to summarize your qualifications for the position or clear up any concerns, by asking, "What do you see as my strengths for this position?" and "Are there any concerns about my background that I can clear up?"

At the end of the interview, you may be offered a job on the spot or the interviewer may tell you that he or she will get back to you in a week or so, after all other applicants have been interviewed. If you would like a day or two to think about the offer, say so. However, you should set a specific day and hour when you will call the interviewer back. Do not delay your return call more than one or two days. If the interviewer says that you will be called regarding a possible offer, accept this decision politely. Try to get some idea of when you will be contacted so that you will be at home. You might also mention that you need to complete your own plans rather soon.

If your prospects look good or if you have been offered the job, try to get a brief tour of the office suite. Another good idea is to borrow an extra copy of the procedures manual, if there is one, so that you can familiarize yourself with the actual management of the office before your first day on the job.

Let the interviewer end the interview. When he or she stands up, then you may do the same. Shake hands, thank the interviewer for the time spent with you, express your interest in the position, say that the interview has been enjoyable or whatever seems most appropriate, and then say good-bye. Do not forget to say good-bye to the assistant or receptionist on your way out.

THE TELEPHONE INTERVIEW

Most of us who have interviewed for jobs have had the advantage of being able to prepare for a scheduled interview. For the sake of cutting costs, however, many employers now conduct preliminary interviews on the telephone in an attempt to screen candidates. Typically, you will not have advance notice of a telephone interview, and it might not be conducted during normal business hours. It is not unusual for a telephone interview to be conducted in the evening or over the weekend. But there are still certain things you can do to prepare.

Keep a file folder that contains your résumé and other pertinent information near the telephone so that you can discuss your qualifications confidently and accurately. Be certain to inform family members or roommates that you might be getting a business call, in order that the telephone will be answered in a businesslike manner. If you have an answering machine, be sure your recording sounds professional. If the call comes in at an inopportune time, tell the caller that you are not able to speak freely at the moment and that you would like to call back at a time convenient for the interviewer.

Once the telephone interview has started, smile, put yourself in a positive state of mind, and treat it as you would a face-to-face meeting. Take notes, ask questions, and be professional. Before you hang up, be sure you know what the next step will be.

AFTER THE INTERVIEW

If, at the close of the interview, you are told that you are not quite qualified for the position, thank the interviewer for the candid evaluation and be sure to mention that the interview has been a pleasant as well as an informative experience. Say good-bye politely. Do not be needlessly discouraged: appreciate the honest evaluation, work to improve any indicated deficiencies, and keep looking for the right position. Each interviewing experience will bring you added confidence and ease in answering the interviewer's questions.

If the possibility of employment is left open, follow the interview with a thank-you letter. You can use this opportunity to restate your interest in the position or to add anything you omitted during the interview. (See the sample thank-you letter in Fig. 1.4.)

Knowing Your Company

The forward-thinking secretary strives to become an extension of the executive, working with, as much as for, him or her. The executive's job is difficult and challenging. Technological advances have produced far-reaching changes in routine operations. Management continues to become more sophisticated. Forecasting techniques and market analysis have become more complicated as business competition has become more and more acute. The global thrust of modern business continues to broaden the role of the executive.

Most executives would like to turn larger amounts of routine work over to their secretaries. To prepare for such increased responsibilities, you must truly know your company. Become familiar with its corporate structure, products, goals, achievements, and basic advertising and marketing strategies. Become well acquainted with employer-employee relationships as well as with employee benefits. Study the company manuals pertinent to your job thoroughly. Make a real effort to understand the people for and with whom you work, as well as those you may supervise.

If you advance from one level to another, your associations with the key personnel of the company will increase. An opportunity to work with top management is an opportunity to learn much about the operations of the company. Such associations will be stimulating and rewarding. As you work at higher levels and are given greater responsibilities, you will soon know more about the company and its operations than many of the department heads and junior executives do.

In a small business operation, the work can be so varied that it will provide you with broad experience. In a larger enterprise, on the other hand, you may be assigned to a particular department (such as marketing, production, person-

Fig. 1.4 Interview Follow-up Letter

April 8, 19--

3 Ternure Avenue
Suffern, NY 10901

Ms. Roberta Johns
Lehman Larson, Inc.
5 Astor Place
New York, NY 10003

Dear Ms. Johns:

It was a pleasure talking with you yesterday.
I hope you will give me the opportunity to put
my skills and enthusiasm to work for you. I am
excited about the challenges I see ahead with
Lehman Larson and look forward to having the
chance to making a major contribution to its
efforts.

Sincerely,

Ethel Lorenz
Ethel Lorenz

nel, or legal) and may not be likely to gain companywide experience unless the executive for whom you work progresses through various departments and managerial levels. However, a thorough knowledge of one particular aspect of company operations can be invaluable if you later decide to specialize.

It is clear that the secretary is an integral part of the American business team. The pressures on management are acute, and the secretary who can relieve these pressures effectively will probably succeed. The person who will reach the top and remain at the top is the one who will take the time and make the effort to continue to grow in general knowledge, technical skills, and human understanding.

Balancing Career and Family

It has been proved that the people who are the most successful and fulfilled are those who can maintain a delicate balance between career and family. Many of us feel that there are just not enough hours in the day or enough days in the week. However, there are some things that secretary-parents can do to make their lives not only emotionally sustainable but enjoyable.

- Set realistic goals. If you decide to do a major renovation project around the house, do not schedule it while you are trying to tackle a major job at the office.
- Set priorities. Decide what is more important to you, cleaning your house or spending precious time with your family.
- If you are the one primarily responsible for cooking, prepare meals in advance so that cooking does not become a nightly chore. When you are making a meal, prepare double or triple portions and freeze what is left over into meal-size portions.
- Delegate whenever you can. If you are overwhelmed at work, try to share some responsibility with others. And have your family help with household chores so that too much responsibility does not fall on your shoulders.
- Trade time with family and friends when you will entertain each other's children.
- Leave some time for yourself, even if it is just 15 minutes each day or one hour a week. Indulge yourself: take a hot bath, read a book, or go for a walk. Think of it as your time to recharge.
- Last but not least, maintain your sense of humor; it will see you through difficult times.

CHAPTER 2

Office Management

Managing an office encompasses many responsibilities, of which the most important are organizing your workstation, handling supplies, scheduling appointments, and managing your own time. In order to manage the variety of tasks you will be called upon to do and to maintain the smooth-running office your employer expects, you must above all be organized.

Various topics relating to the broad subject of office management are discussed in individual later chapters: for example, organizing meetings (Chapter 4), office mail (Chapter 11), and payroll procedures (Chapter 14).

The Work Environment

YOUR WORKSTATION

Even if you cannot control major office-design decisions, your desk and the office space immediately adjacent to it are yours to organize for maximum efficiency and attractiveness. Your desk is the place to begin. Try this: Sit in your chair and face your working surface. Stretch your arms straight out over it about 6″ above the surface with thumbs together. Now swing them carefully out to each side, making a wide arc, and watch to see what areas of the desk your arms cover. This is the surface on which you should have all of the articles that you work with frequently—and *only* the articles that you work with frequently. The far corners which you cannot reach without effort should be clean and free from clutter and may house your nameplate or even a plant or a small, unobtrusive decorative item or two. A nonglare working surface will be easier on your eyes than glass or shiny plastic.

If your telephone is not installed where it is handy for you to use, request permission to have it moved. Your reference books should be readily available on your desktop or in a drawer or shelf within your "working arc." A lazy Susan can hold several books in a small space.

Have a work organizer of some kind on your desk in which to put papers. It might be an expanding portfolio—an accordion file with heavy separator leaves or metal slots. Separate labeled folders inside would hold dictation to be transcribed, items ready for the executive to sign, reading to be done, projects in progress, or other materials. A folder devoted to pending work is useful, especially if you review it each day and attach a note to each piece of work stating exactly what has to be done with it. It is always a good idea to keep a separate folder for letters that must be signed, marked in some way so that the executive can immediately identify it.

Your computer or typewriter should be protected with a dust cover at the end of each day and cleaned at regular intervals.

Store all loose papers at the day's end *inside* your desk. If they must be left on top of your desk, put them out of sight.

Of equal importance is your organization of the contents of your desk drawers. The large center drawer that holds small things is the one most likely to become jumbled unless you corral loose items in box tops, spray-can tops, or something similar. Sticky tape or a dab of glue will hold the containers in place and keep them in order. Store your stamp pad upside down to keep the ink at the top of the pad and to keep you from jangling the nerves of your coworkers whenever you use a rubber stamp.

OFFICE ATMOSPHERE AND LANDSCAPING

At times you may have to call custodial services to let them know that the office is not being cleaned properly, or leave a polite note on your desk to the cleaners asking them to be a bit more thorough in their cleaning of hard-to-reach areas. Telephone dials and receivers need frequent cleaning; a soaped cotton swab dipped in disinfectant works wonders. Books in bookcases must present a neat appearance—bookends can help. Magazines should be housed in cabinets or boxes, because they tend to slip and create unsightly piles.

Insufficient lighting can cause eyestrain, headache, fatigue—and mistakes. High-intensity light is vital for areas where close work such as proofreading is done. Evenness of illumination, absence of glare, and contrast should be considered. Natural light is always best if it is available. Desks, chairs, and especially visitors' chairs should be placed so that they do not face directly into a light source.

Ventilation is another important environmental factor. Hot, stale, or humid air slows down productivity and contributes to illness. Excessive noise may cause stress and fatigue. Pads under office machines, carpets on the floor, and acoustical tiles on the ceiling can reduce office noise.

No heating, ventilating, or music system pleases everyone. If something seriously out of line occurs—too much heat or cold or a sudden increase in music volume—you must notify the proper department or manager at once.

If you have permission to alter furniture arrangement, arrange the desks so that you do not face another person—not even your employer across a room—since such an arrangement is distracting. You should be able to see visitors easily as they approach, and your desk ought to be so located as to form a natural but not a formidable barrier to the executive's office.

A modern approach to office arrangement is called *office landscaping*, whereby the office becomes a large open space with no walls except movable panels and screens of various heights to give some privacy. Colorful furniture can be assembled in a variety of modules to create whatever working arrangement best suits any particular worker. Carpeting, modern decor, and real or artificial plants should create a pleasing effect. However, a careful study of work flow must be made before remaking the office. Handbooks and textbooks of office management have a wealth of information on office layouts and can instruct you in experimenting with space and furniture templates made to scale. (See Appendix.)

Many companies rent paintings and works of art which may be exchanged for others periodically. If no effort is made by your organization to provide anything but the basic furniture needed to do your job, colorful hangings or art

objects may provide welcome relief from monotony. It should be emphasized, however, that decals, amateur artwork, overly elaborate floral arrangements, pictures drawn by a five-year-old niece, and brightly colored inexpensive
"junque" will make your office appear gaudy and cheap. Your objective should
be to produce a restful and pleasing effect on visitors, employees, and the executive for whom you work, while at the same time retaining a businesslike atmosphere in which you can work efficiently.

Office Supplies

One of your responsibilities will very likely be office supplies and inventory control. A large company may have a purchasing department, in which case your
job would be to fill out an order form and give it to the appropriate person. At a
small company, you may make the purchases yourself from a local office-supply
shop or catalog. In either case, you must keep track of the supplies on hand and
know when and how frequently to reorder. Consider ordering in bulk those
items for which there is a steady demand. It is a good idea to keep a sheet near
the supply area so that employees can write down what they need and what supplies are getting low.

   Office equipment and furnishings are discussed in later chapters. See Chapter
5 for a discussion of purchasing computers, printers, photocopiers, and dictation
equipment. Desktop publishing systems are dealt with in Chapter 10. Telecommunications systems, including electronic mail and fax machines, are discussed
in Chapter 13.

Standard office supplies   The following is a list of some of the items to keep on
hand:

Paper Products
Letterhead and additional sheets of matching stock
Letterhead envelopes
Printer paper
Scratch paper
Gummed note pads
Memo pads
Dictation notebooks
Telephone message pads
Index cards
Manila and mailing envelopes
File folders
Hanging file folders (and tabs)
Calendars
Loose-leaf binders
Paper for office equipment (calculators, fax machines, etc.)
Postage stamps

Desk Supplies
Staplers and staples
Tape and tape dispensers

Pens, felt-tip pens, and pencils
Erasers
Scissors
In and Out baskets
Rulers
Rubber bands
Paper clips
Tacks
Bookends
Letter openers
Ink pads for rubber stamps
Correction fluid

Desk References
Dictionary
Thesaurus
Secretarial handbook
Style manual
ZIP-code directory
Rotary card files
Postal rate chart
Telephone books
Office-supply catalogs

Computer Supplies
Printer ribbons or cartridges
Diskettes
Diskette holders

Dictating Supplies
Cassette tapes
Tape storage unit

Miscellaneous
Toner for copier
First-aid kit
Fire extinguisher
Pencil sharpener
Easels
Maps
Coffee (tea, etc.) supplies

Organizing and storing supplies   If several people have access to your supply cabinet, keeping things in order can be a problem. Labeling the shelves should help, as should grouping similar things together. Items that can spill should be stored on bottom shelves. Paper and other heavy supplies should be stored on lower shelves, with the labels facing the front. Open a ream of paper on the end that has no label; in this way, you will preserve the label so that everyone will know what kind of paper is in the package. (This is also helpful for reordering.)

Smaller items should be on shelves at eye level, stored in labeled boxes; do not allow small loose items to scatter about the shelves. Computer diskettes should be stored in their original packaging at temperatures no lower than 50°F, away from any magnetic field.

Distributing supplies   It is crucial to monitor the distribution of supplies, since they have a tendency to "walk away," especially expensive items such as diskettes. Keep the supplies under lock and key if possible, and maintain a list of the supplies you distribute and to whom they are distributed.

Computerized inventory control   If you are responsible for the inventory in a large office, there are software packages available that can track, follow up, and summarize reports; produce price quotations, invoices, vendor lists, and mailing lables; track purchase orders; and automatically add inventory to the reorder report when items fall below a designated level. Ask your local computer-software vendor for information on such packages.

Recycling paper products   The computer explosion was supposed to create a "paperless office," but if you look around you will realize that offices are using at least as much paper as ever. Approximately 70 to 80 percent of all office paper is waste. Recycling paper products makes both environmental and economic sense. If your company has not started a recycling program, perhaps you can initiate one. Place recycling bins or paper cartons near every desk, photocopier, printer, and bulletin board. Affix a label on each bin that indicates it is for recycling purposes. Enlist the help of the custodial staff. You can arrange collection with a wastepaper broker or with your local municipality if it has a recycling program.
    The following white and colored paper products can be recycled:

- bond paper
- envelopes without windows or self-stick labels
- laser/copy paper (but not the wrapping)
- telephone message slips
- computer paper
- adding-machine paper
- uncoated (nonthermal) fax paper
- newsletters

Such a list should appear on each bin. Newspapers should be put in a separate bin.
    To learn more about paper recycling, contact the American Forest and Paper Association, 1111 19th Street, N.W., Suite 700, Washington, DC 20036 (800-878-8878).

Appointments

CALENDARS AND TICKLER FILES
A daily calendar for your desk, one for the executive's desk, and a small pocket diary for the executive to carry are essential for scheduling appointments. A weekly or monthly desk calendar can also be useful, especially for scheduling far in advance. Regularly scheduled events such as weekly meetings and monthly re-

port deadlines should be penciled in at the beginning of each week or month. The appointment notation should include the name of the visitor and the purpose of the appointment as well as the date and time. It is essential to note all events in order to set priorities and avoid conflicts.

One type of permanent calendar is called a *tickler file* because it tickles your memory. It is designed to remind you of recurring events and deadlines rather than day-to-day appointments, though day-to-day items may also be recorded there. To set up a tickler system you will need the following:

1. A simple $3'' \times 5'' \times 12''$ card file box
2. A set of twelve $3'' \times 5''$ guide cards marked "January" through "December"
3. A set of $3'' \times 5''$ numerical guide cards numbered from 1 through 31 (Using two sets will make filing for subsequent months simpler, but is not necessary.)
4. A supply of $3'' \times 5''$ blank index cards to divide the file into subsequent years
5. A supply of $3'' \times 5''$ tickler cards

Suppose that you begin using the system on January 1. The first guide card in the tickler box will be the "January" card, and it will be followed by guide cards for days 1 through 31. Cards marked "February" through "December" will follow. If you have purchased more than one 31-day set of guide cards, they will follow the second (third, fourth) monthly card. The December set will be followed by index cards labeled for the following year and each year thereafter up to 10 years or more.

Now that the guide cards are in place, the tickler cards—the actual reminders—are ready for filing by day, month, and year. Ticklers for future years are simply filed behind the designated year, to be moved into monthly and daily sections as that year approaches.

After the ticklers for the day have been pulled and distributed, the guide card for that day is placed behind the last daily guide card in the tickler box so that it may begin working forward again. For example, if you began your file in January 1993, on March 7 your tickler card box would be organized from the front as follows:

7–31 daily guide cards

April guide card

1–31 daily guide cards (if two sets have been used)

May guide card

1–6 daily guide cards (if *only* two sets have been used)

June–December monthly guide cards

1994 index card

January–March monthly guide cards

1995, 1996, etc., index cards

When the March 7 tickler cards have been pulled, guide card 7 is placed behind the May 6 ticklers, and ticklers for May 7 will thenceforth be filed behind it. As 1993 ends, the ticklers for early 1994 are filed by the appropriate month and day in turn.

Tickler cards can be of many types and designs. They can either be made in your office and designed to fit its needs, or purchased in sets from suppliers. Cards vary in the amount of information they are designed to contain. Color-coded cards can be assigned to specific deadline matters or to departments within the firm. Colors can also be used to indicate the degree of urgency: orange for critical matters, white for personal reminders such as birthdays and anniversaries, and so on. See the sample card in Fig. 2.1.

Fig. 2.1   Tickler Card

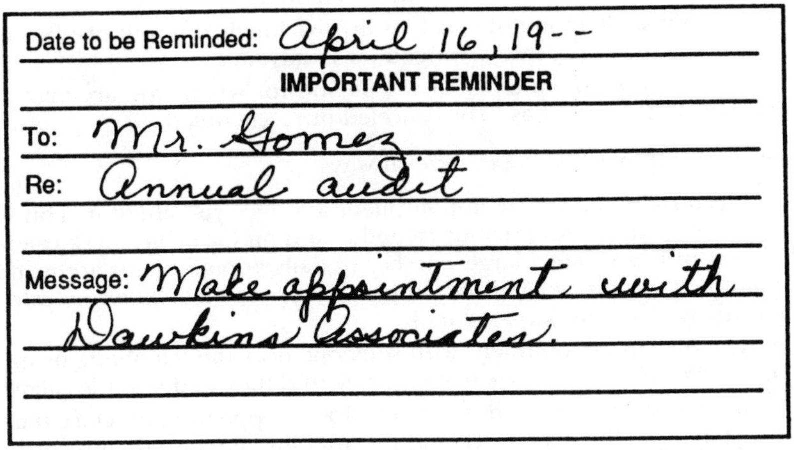

Date to be Reminded: *April 16, 19--*
IMPORTANT REMINDER
To: *Mr. Gomez*
Re: *Annual audit*

Message: *Make appointment with Dawkins Associates.*

SCHEDULING APPOINTMENTS

When making appointments, you will want to keep the following guidelines in mind:

1. Determine in advance those visitors who may see the executive without an appointment, those the executive may not wish to see, and those (such as salespeople) that the executive may prefer to see only during certain hours.
2. Find out the purpose of the appointment. It may be that the visitor would do better to see a person other than your employer. Knowing the purpose of the appointment will also help you decide how long an appointment you ought to schedule. (You may give the visitor these reasons if he or she objects to your inquiries.)
3. Try to avoid scheduling too many meetings in succession.
4. If your employer has been away, don't schedule appointments for the day of return.
5. If you make an outside appointment for the executive, telephone to reconfirm the appointment before he or she leaves the office.
6. Schedule appointments lightly for Monday mornings, Friday afternoons, and days before and after holidays.
7. Allow time in the morning for the set routines of the day to be accomplished before appointments begin.
8. Avoid late-afternoon appointments.
9. Be careful not to make appointments on weekends or holidays! And remember that other faiths have holidays that may not coincide with yours.
10. When you schedule an appointment on your own, be sure to explain that it is subject to the approval of the executive.

11. Suggest a precise time instead of asking an open-ended question such as "When would you like to see Mr. Nichols?"
12. If you know there may be difficulty in keeping an appointment, explain that you will telephone to confirm the date and time.
13. When an appointment is scheduled for someone who is at your desk, type a reminder note for the person with the date and time of the appointment and the office telephone number indicated on it.
14. Call to confirm all appointments that involve luncheons, out-of-town meetings, or meetings that were arranged far in advance.
15. Obtain the telephone number of the person for whom you are making an appointment in case it has to be canceled or rescheduled.

Appointments may be made in several ways:

1. The executive schedules an appointment and tells you about it. You make sure it is recorded both on your calendar and on his or her desk calendar. (In many offices where a large number of daily appointments are made, all appointments are recorded in a separate appointment book or calendar rather than on the desk calendars.)
2. You schedule an appointment with someone over the telephone or in person, check with the executive to confirm it, and then add it to the calendars.
3. Someone writes to secure a definite time for an appointment. Once the time is set, you notify the person seeking the appointment and then record it on the calendars.
4. Your employer may, while conferring with someone, ask that you schedule a future appointment with that person. After doing so, you give the person a written or oral reminder of the appointment and enter it on the calendars.
5. You or your employer may schedule tentative appointments with out-of-town visitors by mail. These should be entered on the calendars in pencil, since they are subject to change.

You may discover, much to your embarrassment, that the executive has scheduled appointments that you know nothing about because he or she has forgotten to tell you about them. Therefore, it is extremely important that you ask the executive each morning to check his or her pocket diary for any appointments you may not be aware of. Be smilingly persistent about this, for your calendar and the executive's *must* coincide. (The two calendars are not duplicates, however; your calendar should include reminders of secretarial tasks that the executive would not want to be bothered with.) As you get to know your employer better, you will be able to screen and classify visitors according to his or her preferences.

Executives need to be reminded of their appointments even though they have a marked calendar before them each day. This may be done by simply giving them cards from the tickler file. Some prefer to be reminded by a typed and detailed list of the day's appointments on their desk when they arrive in the morning. Others prefer that an abbreviated list of the next day's appointments be typed on a 3″ × 5″ card and given to them before they leave in the evening. A quick glance at a typed reminder often is more efficient than reading the handwriting on the daily calendar. Make a copy of the reminder list so that you can check it at the end of the day to delete all appointments that were not kept and insert any that were added. If you do not file appointment books permanently, it is wise to keep these reminder lists as a log of visitors seen and a record of places the executive went during the year. Such records are invaluable for substantiating claims for expenses incurred, trips taken, and charges made, in case of tax audits.

Time Management

Time is a precious commodity that must be managed properly. If there does not seem to be enough time to accomplish all your tasks and you often bring work home that you cannot get done during normal working hours, perhaps you should examine whether you are using your time to best advantage.

Examine how you utilize your hours   Time-study experts suggest keeping a log of your daily activities in half-hour increments. In a few weeks you will start to see patterns emerging.

Combine activities and errands   Perhaps some of your trips and errands can be consolidated. For example, if you make six trips to the photocopier in a normal day, the time normally taken up socializing along the way or waiting in line might be reduced by combining your errands into a couple of trips.

Handle routine tasks efficiently   Are you spending a lot of time opening and distributing the mail? The efficient time manager will not read every letter thoroughly but will merely scan it to determine its importance before routing it to the appropriate person. Are you dealing with a cumbersome filing system? See Chapter 12 for ways to make your system more efficient. Think imaginatively of ways to streamline routine processes. Talk to other secretaries; you might be surprised at how willing they are to share timesaving ideas.

Prepare a "to do" list and set priorities   Each night before you go home, prepare a list of things that need to be done the next day. A desk calendar such as the one shown in Fig. 2.2 can be helpful. Arrange your tasks in order of importance, giving priority to time-sensitive issues. For example, if a client is coming in at 11:00 to sign a contract, be certain the contract is finished by no later than 10:30. Any tasks that are not completed on a given day should be carried over to the next day. It is a good morale booster to start with those routine tasks you like the least. Once those are done, you can look forward to more pleasant tasks and a more pleasant day.

Take on only what you can handle   Although you will want to please the person for whom you work, do not try to be a "supersecretary." If you are overloaded with work, ask for assistance. When you work for more than one person, the pressure can mount if each one needs a job done immediately. If you are unable to get assistance, have those in charge determine which task has priority; you should not have to decide that one person's work is more important than another's. Politely smile and say, "Ms. Passaro has also asked me to do *this* immediately. I would appreciate it if you and she would let me know which project I should work on first."

Avoid distractions and interruptions   If your desk is positioned so that people are constantly walking by and making conversation, consider facing it in another direction. If your desk faces a hallway and people drop in, consider moving it to another location so that you are not so easily seen. If you are working under pressure, you do not have to socialize; politely smile and say something like, "I'd love to sit and chat with you, but I have a 4:00 deadline."

Maintain a sense of order   Keep your desk uncluttered so that you can locate your supplies easily. Replace files when you are finished with them so as not to

Fig. 2.2 Desk Calendar

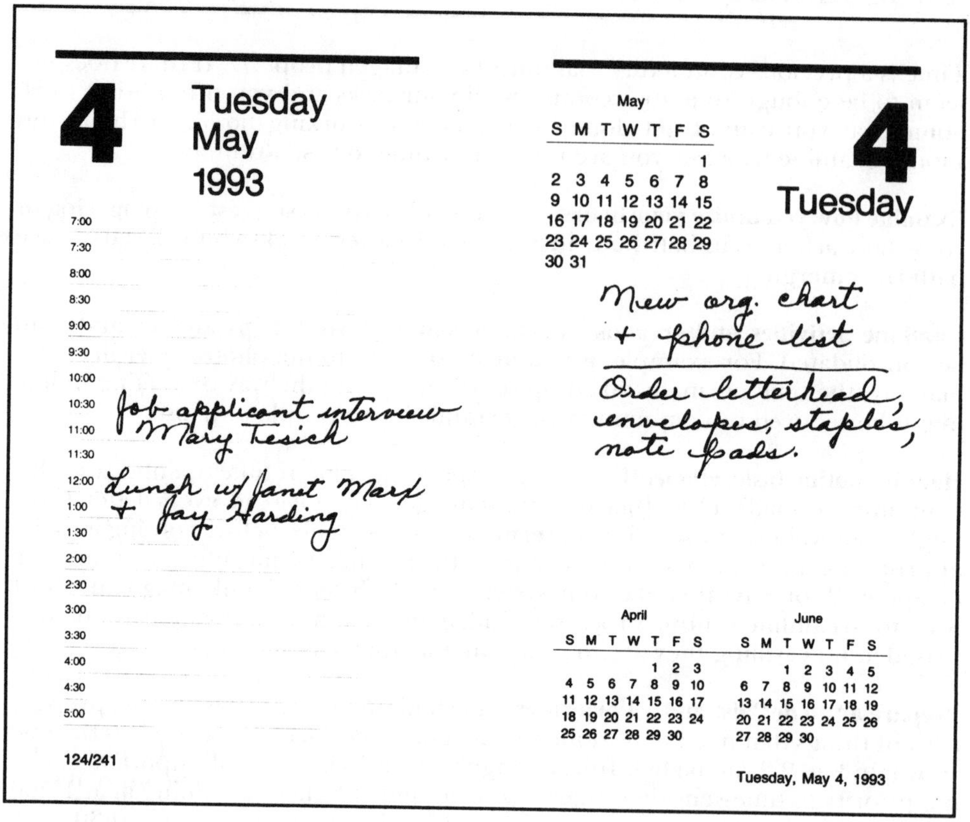

waste time looking for them later. Keep supplies that you use often within easy reach.

Do it right the first time   Much time and energy can be wasted doing a job over. Take the time to do it right the first time.

Let your computer assist you   There are many shortcuts you can take by using your computer if you just know about them. For example, the Mail Merge feature will allow you to produce numerous personalized form letters and mailing labels with minimal labor. Set aside time periodically to study and review the user manual that accompanies your software.

Avoid excessive overtime   Occasionally situations will arise that will keep you from completing important tasks during normal working hours. But overtime should be reserved for extraordinary situations and should not become the norm. Overtime becomes a way of life only if you are not managing your time efficiently or if the work load is genuinely too much for one person. If forthcoming projects are likely to consume excessive amounts of time or if there is to be a period of extended absences because of holidays, vacations, illness, or layoffs, find out about hiring temporary help. Planning in advance for situations that can be anticipated will assure the smooth functioning of your office.

CHAPTER 3

Business Etiquette

The code of professional respect and conduct has always played an important role in the business environment. Business etiquette influences the way we dress, speak, and interact with coworkers and business associates both in and out of the workplace.

With the integration of women into the workplace at every level, male–female stereotypes have fortunately lost much of their power, and that has brought about significant changes in professional etiquette. Business luncheons and dinners are often in mixed company, and men and women accompany each other on business trips and generally intermingle as peers. Some areas of male–female professional relations remain sensitive. But regardless of whether gender differences are involved, business etiquette should be based on good manners, self-control, sublimation of ego, and respect for all coworkers from the cleaning staff to the CEO. (For further reading on office etiquette, see Appendix.)

Dress

What you wear makes a statement about your attitudes, your goals, and your moods. If you want to get ahead in the business world, dress appropriately.

Dress standards vary in different parts of the country. In warmer states such as California and Florida, people tend to dress more simply and casually than their counterparts in New York and Boston. In Washington, D.C., and in the Midwest, dress similarly tends to be more understated than in the Northeast. Some industries, particularly banking, call for more conservative clothing than others. Observe those in your organization whom you admire and whose jobs you would like to have, and pattern your dress after theirs.

BASIC WARDROBE FOR WOMEN
Women often wonder how to maintain their femininity and still move up the corporate ladder. Femininity should have no bearing on one's professionalism

and success. Whether a woman wears a colorful dress or a pinstripe suit and tie, she remains a woman, but should be judged on her merit as if gender differences did not exist.

Your basic wardrobe should contain well-made (not necessarily expensive) suits, blouses, sweaters, and skirts. Strive for quality rather than quantity.

The question often arises as to whether or not a woman should wear pants to the office. Pants go in and out of fashion, so you have to use your own judgment. Again, you can be guided by what other women around you are wearing, the secretaries as well as the executives.

- Avoid clothes that are too tight, too short, or too revealing.
- Hemlines should be guided by fashion and by your own preference. Whatever the fashion, however, do not wear your skirts too short.
- Avoid dressy fabrics such as velvet and satin.
- Do not flaunt designer labels.
- Avoid faddish clothing.
- Stockings with embroidery, seams, or polka dots should not be worn to the office. Suitably professional colors include taupe, off-white, off-black, and gray. It is wise to keep an extra pair of stockings in your desk drawer in the event of a run.
- Shoes should be kept polished and clean and the heels should be in good order. Medium or low heels are appropriate for most situations. If you wear running shoes to work, change into your business shoes as soon as you reach the office.
- The use of accessories differs considerably from one woman to another. They should be understated rather than overstated and should not make you conspicuous. Hats should never be worn in the office. Jewelry should be noiseless and simple; pearls and simple gold or silver are tasteful choices.

BASIC WARDROBE FOR MEN

For male secretaries, proper dress may be somewhat less established. Clothes should be neat, clean, and pressed. A conservative shirt and trousers (not jeans), a restrained tie, and appropriate shoes are the fundamental elements. In some offices a jacket and even a suit may be required.

Introductions

The most important thing to remember about introducing people is to *do* it. Always explain who people are when you introduce them (i.e., their titles and perhaps their general duties). It is not necessary to first introduce a man to a woman; gender no longer has a bearing on who is introduced first.

- Introducing someone in your own company to a peer in another company:

  "Beth, this is Bob Littlehale from Astro. Bob, I'd like you to meet Beth Wolf from our Financial Department."

- Introducing a junior executive to a senior executive:

  "Mr. Teisch, I'd like you to meet Arlene Karp, who joined our group last week. Arlene, this is Mr. Teisch, Vice President for Marketing."

(In regard to the use of titles such as *Mr.* and *Ms.,* be guided by the practice in your company. If the junior person will be expected to work on a first-name basis with the senior person, you might want to say, for example,

"Arlene, this is David Teisch, Vice President for Marketing.")

- Introducing a fellow executive to a customer or client:

"Becki, I'd like you to meet Marv Kostikyan from our Purchasing Department. Marv, this is Becki Gentry from the Human Resources group at Epsilon."

- When someone you know joins your department or group, or whenever you are delegated to show a new employee around, make immediate introductions. It is even appropriate to interrupt social conversation to introduce a newcomer. For example:

"Janice Bergeron, I'd like to introduce you to some of your new colleagues. This is Bill Norman, our assistant marketing director. This is Betty Gau, our creative director, who's been with the firm 25 years this spring. And this is Jean Woods, head of our advertising department and my former boss."

- If you want to make an introduction and cannot remember a person's name, make the introduction anyway. We all suffer from memory lapses at one time or another. You can merely make light of the situation and say something like:

"First I needed glasses, now my memory seems to be failing. I can't recall your first name."

- Some nicknames hang on from childhood and can be embarrassing in business situations. Refrain from using a too-casual nickname when making a business introduction.

BEING INTRODUCED

- People are always flattered when you remember their names. When you are introduced to someone, concentrate on the person's name and repeat it:

"I'm glad to meet you, Dr. White."

Try to form a memory association: perhaps Dr. White has white hair or is wearing a white shirt.

- If you do not hear the person's name, do not be shy about asking that it be repeated:

"I'm sorry, I didn't hear your name. Would you mind repeating it?"

- If you see someone you have met before but do not recall his or her name, say something such as:

"I don't recall your name, but didn't I meet you at the party at the December sales conference?"

- Always extend your right hand for a handshake. The handshake should be firm (not bone-crushing) and should be held for three to four seconds. People tend to think that your handshake matches your character. Look the other individual in the eye and have a smile, or at least a pleasant look, on your face.

Receiving Visitors

Receiving visitors is one of a secretary's daily responsibilities. In a large company, visitors may report to a reception area and you will be advised that they have arrived. In a small company, visitors may report directly to your desk. In any event, it is your responsibility to greet each visitor with a smile and make each one feel welcome. Start with something as simple as: "Good morning, Ms. Allan. I'm Rosa Lopez, Mr. Laurence's secretary. I'll let Mr. Laurence know you're here."

Do not attempt to cope with threatening or abusive visitors. If a person is abusive, threatening, or excessively persistent, get help. Go into your employer's office and make a telephone call or ring for security if your company has such a system.

WELCOMING OUT-OF-TOWN VISITORS

When a guest will be arriving from out of town, you will generally have to make the arrangements. These can range from airplane reservations to entertainment. (See Chapter 15 for detailed information on making travel arrangements.)

General guidelines   Follow these basic steps to ensure a pleasant visit for all out-of-town guests:

- Arrange to have your guest met at the airport, or provide complete information about how to get from the airport to your office. If the guest will be driving, he or she would probably appreciate a map or a full set of instructions. Alternatively, you might want to provide information about taxis, limousines, or other kinds of available ground transportation.
- Arrange for accommodations at a nearby hotel. Determine whether the guest prefers a smoking or nonsmoking room.
- With your employer's approval, arrange for a personal welcome at the desk in the form of a note, flowers, or a small gift.
- Leave the telephone number of a business associate your guest can call after settling in.
- Provide the guest with a schedule of events during his or her stay.
- If the stay is to be lengthy or if your guest is traveling with a spouse, provide a map of the city and brochures with information about local attractions.

MAKING VISITORS FEEL COMFORTABLE

When a visitor enters your office, you should not rise from your chair and make the first move to shake hands unless the visitor is distinguished or elderly. Show visitors where they can hang their hats, coats, or umbrellas. If they have to wait, ask them to have a seat and offer reading material or a beverage. If a visitor wants to converse, let him or her initiate the conversation. Be careful about offering opinions about people or events that are connected with your organization. If a visitor is extremely talkative, you might excuse yourself after a few minutes by saying something like, "You'll have to excuse me—I have a report that must be done by noon."

If a visitor asks to make a telephone call, graciously show him or her to a private telephone if there is one available and make sure he or she knows how to operate it. If no other telephone is available, offer yours and give every indication that you are not listening to the conversation. If the conversation appears to be personal, quietly leave your desk (being sure that the work on it is covered) for the time the visitor is talking.

PRIVILEGED VISITORS

Certain visitors will have privileged access: superiors and their secretaries, peers, immediate staff, and designated relatives. Part of your responsibility will be to learn who these people are. Some executives have an open-door policy and will see anyone at any time.

SPECIAL SITUATIONS

Visitors with an appointment

If your employer is occupied	"Good morning, Mrs. Sikorski. Mr. LaFosse has someone in with him at the moment. He'll be free in about 15 minutes. Won't you have a seat? . . . Can I get you something to read? drink?"
If your employer has been called away briefly	"Mr. LaFosse was called away on an emergency. He'll be back within a half-hour. Would you mind waiting?"
If your employer has been called away and will not be returning	"Mr. LaFosse was called away on an emergency and won't be back until tomorrow. I tried to reach you at your office, but you had already left. Is there anyone else who can help you, or would you prefer to schedule another appointment at your convenience?" . . . "I'm very sorry for any inconvenience this has caused you, but it couldn't be helped."

Visitors without an appointment

If the visitor is someone your employer will wish to see	"Good afternoon, Mr. McCandless. It's nice to see you again. Let me tell Mr. Richards that you're here."
If your employer isn't available	"Mr. Richards has an appointment in five minutes, so I'm afraid he won't be able to see you today. Would you like to schedule an appointment, or is there someone else who can help you?"
If the visitor is soliciting	"Unfortunately, Mr. Richards has a number of charities he contributes to, and he's just not able to undertake any more at this time."

GREETING GROUPS OF VISITORS

If two or more people share a single appointment, make sure you have enough chairs, pencils, notepads, and ashtrays (if smoking is allowed) and that the room is comfortable and conducive to conversation within the group. If they arrive separately, ask each visitor to be seated and to wait for the others before you invite the group into the meeting room. If the visitors do not know each other, graciously introduce them as they assemble.

Telephone Manners

Very often the telephone is the source of a caller's first—and perhaps lasting— impression of you and your company. The telephone can be one of your biggest assets or the bane of your existence.

The ability to handle telephone calls properly is a secretarial quality that exec- utives consider extremely important. The correct use of the telephone can speed business, build goodwill, project the best possible image of your company, ele- vate your office in the eyes of your superiors, and thus be important to your own success. If you learn to recognize frequent callers' voices at once so that you can address them by name, you will gain the reputation of being exceptionally keen.

Knowing your equipment is essential. You must know what each button and switch on your telephone is for and how to use it. You must also be aware that telephone systems have made remarkable technological advances in the past de- cades, providing a wealth of equipment designed for special needs in the office. Telephone company representatives will be glad to answer questions about auto- matic dialers, call forwarding and call pick-up features, special signaling devices, and a wide variety of other options. (See Chapter 13 for further discussion of telecommunications.)

- Develop the habit of picking up a pen and reaching for a pad as soon as the telephone rings.
- Try to pick up no later than the third ring.
- Smile when you answer the telephone. Your voice will be more cheerful.
- When answering, always identify your company, yourself, or your employer: "Good morning, this is the Marric Company (or "this is Kathy Wertalik," or "Ms. Robertson's office"). How may I help you?"
- Hold the handset about 1½″ from your mouth and speak directly into it.
- Do not chew gum or smoke while you are on the telephone, and always keep the radio volume low.
- Unless you are instructed to screen calls, do not say, "May I ask what this concerns?" It can make the caller feel unimportant if he or she is not put through.
- Should a caller ask for someone who is unavailable, you could say, "I'm sorry, she's talking on another line. May I help you or would you care to speak to someone else?" Never say "She hasn't come back from lunch yet" (and it's 3 p.m.), or "He's playing golf today," or "I don't know where she went," or "He isn't in," without elaboration. Courtesy requires that you give correct information, but do not state facts that could lead to a misunderstanding or divulge information you are not authorized to give.
- Understand what constitutes an emergency. Sometimes a call will necessitate interrupting an important meeting, but use good judgment about doing so.
- Before you place a call, be certain you have the information you need. It is rude to put someone you have called on hold while you are thumbing through a file.
- Avoid slang and technical words the caller may not understand.
- If you find you have dialed incorrectly, offer an apology instead of hanging up abruptly.
- If a caller dials you by mistake, never say "Wrong number" and abruptly hang up; instead, say "You've reached the wrong number, I believe." The caller might be a customer who has confused your number with the one above or below it in his or her own listing.

- Always end a call with "Good-bye." Be sure to let the caller hang up first; after the caller has hung up, replace your own handset gently. If the caller persists in talking, you might have to say "I'm sorry, but I have a call on another line," or "I'd like to talk longer, but I'm due at a meeting now," or "Excuse me, but Mr. Nichols has just buzzed for me."

Ask the executive for a priority list for accepting calls. Arranged in descending order of priority, it might look something like this:

1. Internal calls from superiors
2. Calls from customers or clients
3. Internal calls from others
4. Calls from suppliers or salesmen
5. Calls from civic, trade, and service organizations
6. Personal calls

You might want to arrange a buzzer signal to let the executive know of especially urgent calls.

It is helpful to plan for the convenience of other members of the office staff who may answer your phone when you are absent. Write down the greeting favored by your employer and keep it by the phone, together with a list of referral numbers and answers to frequently asked questions.

You may be asked to take dictation over the telephone. Unless you have some kind of hands-free telephone device such as a speakerphone or a telephone shoulder rest, you may have to ask that some things be repeated. It is wise to read the entire dictation back when finished. If you are asked to monitor a telephone conversation and take notes on it, get the main points as you would if you were taking notes at a lecture.

Taking a message   Always take complete and accurate messages. Ask people to spell their names; it is easy to make a mistake. Repeat all numbers, digit by digit if necessary ("Sixteen—that's one–six?").

Telephone message forms are available from stationery and office-supply stores. The form illustrated in Fig. 3.1 contains the following essential information: date, time of day, name and number of caller, message, name or initials of person taking the message, and whether the call is to be returned. Even when there is no message, it is a good idea to record the fact that a call was received.

Putting the caller on hold   Never put a person on hold for more than 30 seconds. If you cannot handle the first call within that time, take a message from the second caller. Clients have been known to change their minds about a sale because of being neglected on the telephone. Before you place someone on hold, ask permission to do so:

"Hello, ABC Company. . . . I'll see if there's someone in the marketing department who can help you. Would you mind if I place you on hold for a few moments?" (Not "Please hold.")

If your phone system plays music while people are on hold, be certain the music is soothing and the volume is pleasing. Remember, music is not a license to keep someone on hold indefinitely.

Finally, if you are disconnected, it is the responsibility of the caller to place the call again. If you placed the long-distance call, ask the operator to give you credit for the call.

Fig. 3.1   Telephone Message Form

```
To      J R S
Date    10/5              Time 11:15   A.M.
                                       P.M.
        WHILE YOU WERE OUT
M       Larry Fisk
of      Transfax
Phone   602      442      4480
        Area Code   Number   Extension
┌───────────────┬───┬───────────────┬───┐
│ TELEPHONED    │ X │ PLEASE CALL   │   │
├───────────────┼───┼───────────────┼───┤
│ CALLED TO SEE YOU │ WILL CALL AGAIN │   │
├───────────────┼───┼───────────────┼───┤
│ WANTS TO SEE YOU  │ URGENT        │   │
├───────────────┴───┴───────────────┴───┤
│        RETURNED YOUR CALL          │   │
└────────────────────────────────────┴───┘

Message
        Call him at Phoenix
        office before 2:00
        (Eastern time.)


                          Operator  MBB
```

Transferring a call   It can be annoying and expensive for a caller to have to repeat a story to several people. If you have to transfer a call, try to connect the caller with the correct party. If you do not know who that might be, take the caller's name and number and be certain that someone returns the call.

Answering machines   Although many people still do not like speaking to answering machines, these machines have become a fact of life. Never hang up on a machine; it is rude. Obviously your call is important—that is why the person has an answering machine. Speak briefly, clearly, and slowly. Leave your name, the date and time of the call, a message, and a number at which you can be reached. If someone does not return your call within a reasonable time, call again; tapes break and mechanical failures do occur, and the person may not have received your message.

When preparing your own recorded message, write down what you want to say and practice saying it. Listen carefully to the message after it has been recorded to be certain it produces the desired effect.

Answering services   If your company uses an answering service, always let the service know where your employer can be reached in an emergency.

Since your business often depends on the service, remember to show your appreciation; a box of candy or a fruit basket is always appreciated during the holidays.

Dealing with an irate caller   We have all had to deal with irate callers, and perhaps have even *been* an irate caller. When people have complaints, they tend to take their frustrations out on whoever answers the phone.

- Stay calm; do not yell back or be rude.
- Politely ask the person to slowly repeat his or her complaint so that you can write it down. Often this will defuse some of the anger.
- Suggest that the caller talk to someone in the organization with greater authority than you. Put the caller on hold and explain the situation to the person who will be receiving the call.

Dealing with a crank or abusive caller   If you receive crank or abusive calls, hang up immediately. Do not answer any questions or reply to offensive comments; this will only encourage the caller. If the calls persist, contact the telephone company.

Men and Women in the Workplace

Even after decades of increasing gender integration in the workplace, office relations between men and women are still frequently the source of friction and misunderstanding. Everything that affects male–female relations in society at large tends to be reflected in the office itself.

In both private and professional life, a man today is not required to hang up a woman's coat, help her with a chair, stand up when she enters a room, or walk curbside. But many men still perform such acts and many women still appreciate them; it is a matter of individual taste and style.

A woman should not assume she has the right to enter an elevator or doorway first, but if a man defers, the woman should be gracious. The same rule holds for leaving an elevator. If a woman enters a revolving door first, she pushes.

After dark, it is proper for a man to escort a woman to her car and be certain she pulls away safely in a parking lot or any area where there is potential danger. This is not chauvinistic; it is simply a safety precaution.

Conversations   Good business etiquette requires that no one should feel excluded from a business conversation or be made uncomfortable because of inappropriate language. If inappropriate language is used in your presence, you should recognize that it may be inadvertent, but politely demur. Something as simple as eye contact can call the offender's attention to your discomfort.

Except when among personal friends, a good conversationalist will avoid gossip, stories in questionable taste, and the topics of health, personal misfortunes, religion, and politics. It is appropriate to make small talk about such topics as current (nonpolitical) events, gardening, books, the environment, pets, the arts, real estate, and travel.

Office romances   Because so much time is spent at work, it may be an ideal place to get to know someone you might like to spend time with outside of the office. For many single people, socializing with coworkers is nonthreatening because of the sense of familiarity and the common base. There is nothing wrong with coworkers meeting, falling in love, and marrying, though you should always try to keep your private life private.

Be very cautious, however, about getting romantically involved with your employer or another executive with whom you have day-to-day dealings. If the relationship does not work out and the daily encounters become uncomfortable, one person may have to leave, and it will probably be you. So think before you act. If it is your policy to keep business and pleasure separate, you can make that known.

Sexual harassment   Sexual harassment may involve offending personal sensibilities, disrespecting coworkers, and abusing power. Though women are by far the more likely objects of such behavior, men are not immune from it.

It is illegal to harass anyone or make anyone in the workplace feel seriously uncomfortable by means of or as a result of sexual aggressiveness. Sexual harassment may simply create a hostile work environment by ongoing reference to the subject of sex through, for example, sexual joking, displaying pornography, or inappropriate touching. An even more serious form of harassment includes all unwelcome advances and requests for sexual favors from a person in a position to threaten you with loss of employment or loss of future promotions or raises if you refuse.

If you are subjected to what you view as abusive treatment or sexual harassment, the first step is to confront the offender, making it plain that you consider the behavior or language inappropriate and offensive. If the person did not realize the impact of such comments or actions, he or she should nevertheless apologize and discontinue the offending behavior. If the person does not stop acting in this manner or simply dismisses your complaint, take the issue to a higher authority, bringing with you a record detailing the nature and date of each offense. In many companies a manager has been delegated responsibility for fielding such complaints. If there is no such person in your company, speak to your boss or supervisor; if he or she is the offender, speak to his or her supervisor. If all else fails and you wish to press charges, there are city, county, state, and federal government offices that can direct your claim.

It would be most unfortunate if fear of being charged with harassment should prevent relaxed, friendly office socializing. Try to be both sensible and firm in judging and dealing with questionable situations.

Business Entertaining

Business entertaining can be conducted anywhere from the hamburger stand to the palatial estate. A firm may choose to entertain new and prospective clients and customers, colleagues, politicians, celebrities, job candidates, or civic leaders, in order to attract or keep business, to return favors, to express gratitude, to celebrate honors or special occasions, or to soothe hard feelings. But however relaxed the atmosphere might be, the purpose of such gatherings is ultimately to conduct business.

The executive dining room   Many business meetings are conducted at a meal in the executive dining room. The meal will either be catered by a private caterer or provided by the dining services of your company. As a secretary, your role may include anything from making the arrangements to participating in the meeting. If you are participating, follow these hints:

- If alcoholic beverages are served, limit yourself to one drink before lunch is served. If the people that you are expected to entertain or interact with are abstaining or likely to abstain, you probably should also. Remember that some companies have a policy of not serving alcoholic beverages during working hours.

- Keep your voice down and maintain the same discipline that you would in the office.
- Do not smoke unless others are smoking.

The restaurant   The host is responsible for making meal reservations, and that responsibility will probably fall upon your shoulders. It is important to keep the occasion in mind when selecting a restaurant, because it is critical to make a good impression without going overboard. Even though business meals are part of an expense account, be aware of budgetary limitations. Once again, your role may include anything from making the arrangements to participating in the meal. If you are invited to the restaurant, be sure to follow these basic guidelines:

- Be on time, as you would for any business appointment.
- Conform to the dress code; wear proper business attire.
- While waiting for guests to arrive, it is appropriate to sit at the bar and order a drink. If you do not drink alcohol, bottled water or a soft drink is a good substitute and is entirely sociable today.
- Use semipersonal stories or getting-to-know-you questions as warmups.
- Order food that is not messy to eat. Do not order more courses than your companions. For example, if no one is ordering dessert, skip it yourself. Skipping a course can sometimes be an indication that people are pressed for time or money.
- Do not leave your handbag on the table.
- Do not take care of personal needs at the table. At an informal meal a woman may perhaps refresh her lipstick quickly at the table, but take care of combing your hair, filing your nails, and applying mascara in the ladies' room.
- If you are in an elegant restaurant, do not ask for catsup.
- Do not smoke unless others are smoking.

Paying the check   If you are paying for the meal, discreetly ask the waiter or maitre d' early in the meal to give the check to you. This is especially important for a woman because the check is traditionally given to a man. Pay by credit card if you have one; it is more discreet than cash. The tip can either be included on the credit card or left on the table.

At a friendly lunch with coworkers, the check is generally split evenly, provided all orders are close in price. If your meal costs substantially more than the others, offer to pay the difference or leave the tip. If one person ordered drinks and others did not, the person who had the drinks should pay that portion of the bill.

Canceling a business meal   Occasionally it is necessary to cancel a scheduled business meal appointment. If so, do it as soon as possible and make sure all invited guests are informed.

Tipping   Tipping is a subject on which the experts often disagree. For instance, some say that a tip should be a reward for good service; others say that if the service is unacceptable, you should tip anyway and complain to the management. In this, and other matters regarding tipping, you have to use your own judgment. The following are general guidelines for tipping. Keep in mind that tips are generally higher in expensive restaurants and in major cities.

Waiter at sit-down meal:	15–20 percent of pretax food charges
Waiter at buffet:	10–15 percent of pretax food charges
Wine steward:	$3–5 per bottle, or up to 15 percent of wine bill
Captain:	5 percent of pretax charges
Bartender:	15–20 percent
Musician who plays requests:	$1–5
Washroom attendant:	$.50–$1
Coat-check attendant:	$.50–$1 per coat
Parking valet:	$1

Theater tickets   When an employer entertains, an evening at the theater is often planned. Order the tickets early, since it may be difficult to get good seats on short notice. Tickets can be ordered from the box office. If time is a factor or the theater is not conveniently located, a ticket agent or telephone service can be helpful. There is generally an additional charge associated with these services, and most major credit cards are honored.

Tickets can either be held at the box office or mailed. When giving theater tickets to your employer, always note on the envelope:

- Date and curtain time.
- Name of show.
- Name and address of theater.
- Seat numbers.

Entertaining business associates at home   When inviting a business associate or coworker to your home socially, be certain that the invitation does not seem to carry an obligation to reciprocate. A good way is to give a valid reason for the invitation.

HOSTING BUSINESS SOCIAL FUNCTIONS

As secretary/assistant to an important executive, you may be called on to host a business social function. In this role you are even more of a representative of your company. Remember—at every moment during the social function, someone will be watching you, and your conduct must be above reproach. Noisy or exuberant behavior at a business-related social function could be damaging to your career.

Your duties will include being gracious to all, remembering names, greeting people whom you know or don't know with equal warmth, circulating to see that no one is neglected, and keeping an eye on details. If the event is held in a hotel facility or a restaurant, your responsibilities will be lighter than if it is a catered function and you are helping with the service. If you are responsible for details, make a checklist that includes the following questions:

1. What place or room is to be used?
2. Have reservations been made in writing, with date and hours of room use confirmed?
3. How many people are expected?
4. Are there any special diet requests?
5. Are name tags to be used? If so, who will provide them?
6. Has the menu been selected?
7. If the function is to be catered, has a letter of confirmation been signed by the caterer?

8. When will the food and beverages be delivered? What number should be called if they are late in arriving? Are arrangements for food storage needed?
9. Where will the food and beverages be delivered?
10. Is there a special theme, or are special decorations to be used? If so, who is responsible?
11. Who will see that tables are properly set up and covered and that all the necessary tableware is in place?
12. Are centerpieces needed for all tables or for the speaker's table?
13. Will bar service be provided? By whom? Are any special arrangements needed?
14. Is there a plan for the disposal of dishes after the meal?
15. Is background music needed?
16. Is a head table needed? How will it be set up? Are place cards to be used? What will be the seating arrangement?
17. Is a receiving line planned? Where? When? Who will be in it?
18. Is entertainment planned? Are there union restrictions?
19. Are out-of-town guests coming? If so, are any of the following needed:
    Hotel reservations?
    Transportation or parking?
    Welcome gifts in rooms?
    Guest cards for local clubs?
    Tickets to local attractions and special events?
    Special activities for spouses? Sightseeing tours?
    Theater or concert tickets?
20. Will the executive need notes for making introductions?
21. Are seating arrangements needed for the group?
22. Have provisions been made for coat checking, or is there a safe place for hanging them?

Your checklist might include one column to list each item or task, a second column for confirmation or fulfillment of the task, a third column for comments or reminders regarding the task, and a fourth column for indicating those tasks that still must be carried out.

A few days before the event, check by telephone to make sure that all is going according to plan, and on the day of the event make a personal on-site check to see if there are any last-minute problems. You must be on guard to spot potential problems and to solve them with mature good judgment and composure.

See Chapter 4 for a detailed discussion of meetings and conferences.

Business Travel

At some point in your career, you will probably have to make business trips. Business trips can be enjoyable adventures or nightmares, depending on how you handle them. Always remember that you are representing your company and conduct yourself accordingly.

Clothing   Bring along appropriate clothing for business hours and after hours. If the trip is to a resort area, avoid wearing bikinis or warm-weather attire that is too revealing. Remember, this is a business trip, not a vacation.

Transportation tipping   The following tips are generally appropriate:

Redcaps:	$1 per bag
Pullman porters:	$2 per person minimum
Hired limousine driver:	10 percent of rental costs
Airport limousine driver:	tipping unnecessary

Hotel tipping   Tips tend to be slightly higher in expensive hotels and in major cities. Tipping should be in line with the service rendered; for example, if a doorman merely opens the door for you, that is far different from standing out in a storm and hailing a taxi.

Doorman:	$1 per bag, $1 or more for hailing taxi
Bellhop:	$1 per bag, $1 for opening room
Room service:	15 percent of meal (pretax)
Chambermaid:	$1–2 per night
Valet:	$2–3 per car
Concierge:	$5–10, depending on how extensive the service is

GENERAL GUIDELINES

- When you are traveling with your employer or a business associate, reservations should permit you to travel together and stay in the same hotel.
- When your days and evenings are heavily scheduled, try to find some time alone to relax.
- If you are traveling alone in a distant city, you might want to do some sightseeing after hours. Ask those you are visiting for suggestions or pick up a guidebook at the hotel.
- Even when working overtime, you must conduct yourself professionally.
- It is appropriate for your employer to invite you to share a meal or entertainment. Being away from home can be lonely. If you accept such an invitation, your employer should be expected to pick up the check.
- If you find yourself in what you think may turn into an embarrassing situation, try to avoid it. Decline the dinner or movie, excuse yourself politely, and go to your room early.
- Never, never become intimate with your employer or with anyone you meet on a business trip.
- If you are sharing a room with a coworker, be discreet in your conversations. Remember, you will still have to face that person back at the office.

Miscellaneous Social Responsibilities

GIFTS

The task of purchasing gifts often falls to the secretary, and it should be done with sensitivity and taste.

If your boss asks you to purchase gifts for his or her spouse's birthday or anniversary, use your discretion. If you feel that such a request is an imposition and not within your area of responsibility, politely say so. Something as simple as "Perhaps you would be able to select something more appropriate than I can" would be sufficient.

If your company is giving a business gift, there should be a good reason for doing so to avoid any hint of impropriety. It is not in good taste to give a gift to someone with whom the firm is negotiating a contract. However, a good reason can be something as basic as an act of friendship or to express gratitude. In order for the gift to have its intended effect, give it on time.

Office collections   In some companies, there is a fund from which gifts can be bought; in others, collections are taken each time there is an occasion. Try not to overdo gift-giving, because some people find it a nuisance or a financial hardship to contribute. Appropriate occasions include a death in the family of an employee, an employee's death or injury, an employee's wedding or the birth of a baby, and an employee's retirement.

Traditional anniversary and birthday gifts   The "new traditional" anniversary gifts are as follows:

1st	Clocks	15th	Watches
2nd	China	16th	Silver hollowware
3rd	Crystal, glass	17th	Furniture
4th	Electrical appliances	18th	Porcelain
5th	Silverware	19th	Bronze
6th	Wood	20th	Platinum
7th	Desk sets	25th	Sterling Silver Jubilee
8th	Linen, lace	30th	Diamond
9th	Leather	35th	Jade
10th	Diamond jewelry	40th	Ruby
11th	Fashion jewelry & accessories	45th	Sapphire
		50th	Golden Jubilee
12th	Pearls or colored gems	55th	Emerald
13th	Textiles, furs	60th	Diamond Jubilee
14th	Gold jewelry		

If a birthday is being observed, the recipient's birthstone may be incorporated in the gift:

January	Garnet
February	Amethyst
March	Bloodstone or aquamarine
April	Diamond
May	Emerald
June	Pearl, moonstone, or alexandrite
July	Ruby
August	Sardonyx or peridot
September	Sapphire
October	Opal or tourmaline
November	Topaz
December	Turquoise or zircon

Food   Food can be a wonderful gift for most occasions and one which is generally appreciated. If the region in which you live is noted for a particular food, it is always a welcome gift to people in other parts of the country. Popular food gifts include jams and jellies, nuts and candy, cheese and crackers, gourmet foods, and flown-in fresh fish or steaks.

Liquor   Although liquor is a popular business gift, it should be given with discretion. You must know whether the recipient drinks, and if so, *what* he or she drinks.

Flowers   Flowers can be delivered in person or ordered over the telephone and sent almost anywhere in the world. They are appropriate when having dinner in someone's home, when extending congratulations, or when someone has been hospitalized.

Personal gifts   If you are giving a business gift from yourself, be aware of the recipient's taste and special interests. Excellent gifts can be found at bookstores, antique shops, museum gift shops, and gourmet food shops, or ordered from catalogs. Gifts should be tastefully wrapped, with a personal message, and should be given in person if possible.

If you want to give your employer a gift during the holidays or at some other appropriate occasion, it does not have to match in value a gift he or she has given you. Avoid cash and gifts of a personal nature. Some appropriate gift ideas for employers are books, bookends, magazine subscriptions, magazine racks, desk accessories, desk calendars, paperweights, home-baked goods, handcrafted objects, picture frames, and foreign dictionaries (for a traveler).

Christmas cards and gifts   Keep an alphabetical listing of the names and addresses of all clients and customers to whom your employer should send holiday cards. When a card is received from a business associate who is not on the list, add the name. Note changes of address as you become aware of them. Order cards that are nondenominational and express such sentiments as "Season's Greetings" or "Good Wishes for the New Year."

About six weeks before Christmas, bring the holiday gift list to your employer's attention. Christmas gifts to clients and business associates should be kept simple, expressing the spirit of the holiday and nothing more. Some popular gifts are wine or liquor, fruit baskets, gourmet food assortments, and special gifts bearing your company logo. When giving gifts to business associates, be aware of their beliefs and customs. For example, it would be in poor taste to give an Arab business associate a bottle of brandy, since devout Muslims refrain from all alcohol.

Gifts of cash are appropriate for service people who do not receive tips throughout the year. Here are some suggested amounts:

Doorman:	$20–30
Elevator operator:	$10–15
Building superintendent:	$20–50
Cleaning person:	one week's pay
Mail carrier:	$10–20
UPS deliverer:	$5–10
Garage attendant:	$15–20 per car

Accepting and acknowledging gifts   Accepting a gift with style means putting a smile on your face and being warm and gracious, whatever the gift. Thank-you notes are a matter of courtesy. If the gift is in good taste and genuinely appreciated, express that enthusiasm in the note. If the gift is in poor taste or inappropriate, merely thank the donor for remembering you.

Gifts for a retiring executive   When an executive retires after having spent many years with a company, the company gift can range from something as simple as a cake and a scrapbook of memorabilia to something as expensive as a trip. A high-level executive may receive a piece of art, or an artist may be commissioned to execute a portrait.

SPECIAL OCCASIONS

Celebrating a company's anniversary   Celebrations generally lead to better morale and increased employee motivation; therefore, many companies enjoy celebrating landmark anniversaries. Some suggestions for an anniversary celebration:

- Draw on the company's history to evoke pride and nostalgia. Most companies have archives from which can be assembled anything from a simple scrapbook to a company book or video.
- Pay tribute to the employees, past and present, and to the customers and clients who put you where you are today.
- Get as much coverage as you can from the press.
- If appropriate, include customers or clients in the celebration.

Retirement of an executive   An executive's retirement may be marked by a private party or a companywide celebration. If you are called on to give a speech, it can be laced with humor and praise. Many companies continue to include retirees in celebrations that occur after retirement.

Death of an executive   When an executive dies, you should notify all employees as soon as possible, give the telephone operator instructions for handling the deceased's telephone calls, and notify the deceased's business associates. Flowers may be sent to the funeral home, the church, or the grave site. Always abide by the wishes of the family and try to determine what is appropriate. For example, when a Jewish person dies, a fruit basket or a donation to a charitable organization in the person's memory is appropriate; flowers are not. If the deceased was a major figure in the firm, a special memorial service may be held.

SOME MISCELLANEOUS DO'S AND DON'T'S

- Always be willing to accept new challenges and to expand your knowledge and skills.
- If you are given directions that are not clear, ask for clarification.
- Cover for your employer when necessary. He or she may be delayed at a meeting and be unavoidably late for an appointment. However, if covering for your employer ever puts you into an uncomfortable situation, do not suffer in silence. Speak to him or her in private about your feelings.
- If you feel you have been treated unfairly, ask to have a private conversation with your employer. Do not yell or harbor grudges.
- Never discuss classified or confidential information with anyone.
- Never smoke, chew gum, or eat your lunch at your desk.
- If you are not busy and choose to read a magazine or book, do so discreetly. Consider putting a file folder around it so that, if a client enters the office, you can close the folder and maintain a professional image.
- Even though it is sometimes lonely at the front, do not entertain personal visitors for long periods of time at or near your desk.

Meetings and Conferences

The scope of your responsibility in assisting with meeting and conference arrangements will vary, depending on the size of the event. A *meeting* or *conference* may be anything from a narrow intraoffice parley to a gathering on a national or international scale. By contrast, the term *convention* regularly and unmistakably refers to large, formal gatherings. Regardless of the magnitude of the event, you will often be assigned duties involving helping to get ready for the meeting, providing services during the meeting, and assisting with post-meeting follow-ups. Flexibility and adaptability will be necessary to cope with the last-minute changes that frequently occur.

Invitations

INVITATIONS TO IN-HOUSE MEETINGS

You will often be responsible for getting the right people together at the right time for business meetings. Executive secretaries frequently say that their most difficult task is to find enough time in the busy schedules of three or four managers to arrange special meetings among them.

When picking a time for an in-house meeting, avoid scheduling it on a religious holiday or early Monday morning or late Friday afternoon. Bear in mind also that people are generally more alert in the morning than in the afternoon.

In-house invitations must be prepared for regular executive meetings, special executive meetings, annual stockholders' meetings (and proxies), and corporate directors' meetings.

Regular executive meetings For weekly or monthly meetings that are on the executives' regular schedules, remind the participants about the meeting by means of an interoffice memorandum or a letter timed to arrive the day before the event. The reminder memorandum should contain the following information:

- Names of the individuals attending or name of the group.
- Day of the week, date, time, and place of the meeting.
- Agenda (including names of persons who are to speak on given topics).

• Any advance preparation required of the participants, or materials they should bring.

See Fig. 4.1. (Additional information on preparing interoffice memorandums may be found in Chapter 8.)

Fig. 4.1   Meeting-Reminder Memorandum

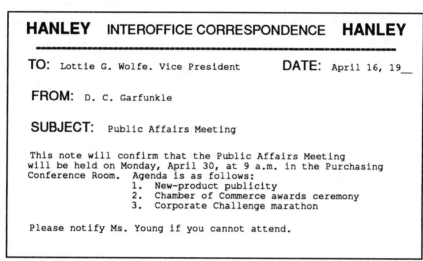

```
HANLEY   INTEROFFICE CORRESPONDENCE   HANLEY
-------------------------------------------------------------

TO: Lottie G. Wolfe. Vice President      DATE: April 16, 19__

FROM: D. C. Garfunkle

SUBJECT: Public Affairs Meeting

This note will confirm that the Public Affairs Meeting
will be held on Monday, April 30, at 9 a.m. in the Purchasing
Conference Room.   Agenda is as follows:
            1.  New-product publicity
            2.  Chamber of Commerce awards ceremony
            3.  Corporate Challenge marathon

Please notify Ms. Young if you cannot attend.
```

You may also telephone executive offices to make a quick check on the availability of officers or managers for regularly scheduled meetings. The person who is chairing the meeting should then be notified of any member's anticipated absence, so that voting on key issues will not be hampered by lack of a quorum.

Special executive meetings   Executives often find themselves in crisis situations that call for fast decision making, and special meetings may be required to deal with these situations. In such situations, you must contact the officers quickly, either in person or by telephone. If the meeting is not to be held immediately, a follow-up written reminder should be sent.

Annual stockholders' meetings (and proxies)   Invitations to or notices of the annual meeting of the stockholders of a corporation must meet certain legal requirements. These formal notices are usually issued in printed form by the corporate secretary. A reply card and a proxy form are routinely mailed with the annual meeting notice about three or four weeks before the event, or as stipulated in the corporate bylaws. If a stockholder is unable to attend, he or she may vote by completing and returning the proxy form.

Corporate directors' meetings   Individual corporate bylaws may stipulate how the directors are to be notified of upcoming meetings. Even if written notification for regular meetings is not required, it is nonetheless advisable. You may also have to notify directors of special meetings by telephoning them. Have a list of the directors' names available for each meeting and indicate on it whether or not they will be present. A printed notification and attendance form such as the one shown in Fig. 4.2 will be a time-saver.

Fig. 4.2   Directors' Meeting Notification and Attendance Form

---

WATERMAN ENTERPRISES, INC.

DIRECTOR'S MEETING

Date:____October 19, 19 –_____   Time: __9:30 a.m._____

Place:_Boardroom_____

Chairperson:_William Waterman, Presiding Officer_____

Board Members	Date Notice Sent	Will Attend	Will Not Attend
Charles France	10/5/ –	X	
Henry G. Johnson	"	X	
Carol Waterman	"	X	
Ralph Knepshield	"	X	
Mark McKallip	"	X	
Myron Klingensmith	"	X	
Andrew Konietzko	"	X	
Harold Rasmussen	"	X	
Roger Wayne Johnson	"		X
William Kiersey	"	X	
Inga Konietzko	"	X	
Elmer Wolfe	"	X	
Laverne Jefferson	"	X	
Leonard Wolfe	"	X	
Rachel Blumenthal	"	X	

Charlotte Davis
Secretary

Total Members to Attend: _14_____
Quorum Assured: _X_ Yes ____ No

Other meetings and conferences   Announcements of other in-house meetings should be distributed two weeks before the meeting date. Meeting notices to be sent to large groups of company personnel are normally printed or duplicated. Your initial task will be to assemble all pertinent data and arrange it in an attractive format. Notices of in-house committee meetings and other routine meetings may be issued on interoffice correspondence paper. Headings such as "Marketing Representatives," "Personnel Staff," or "Department/Division Managers" may be used to address particular groups. Frequently an invitation includes a request that the recipient telephone the chairperson if he or she cannot attend. Depending upon the size of the group and the importance of the event, you may sometimes be requested to send separate letters to specific individuals.

The day of the week, the time of day, the location, and the subject of the meeting must be clearly spelled out. If the participants are to bring any special materials with them, that should be specified. Invitations to seminars, workshops, training sessions, and other specialized in-house business activities may use color and unusual design to gain attention and spark interest.

INVITATIONS TO OUTSIDE CONFERENCES AND OTHER FUNCTIONS
Various styles are used for the announcements of outside business meetings and functions ranging from those for major conventions to those for minor social gatherings.

Outside conferences   Printed invitations designed in an original way are useful in attracting attention and in developing interest in large-scale conferences. In preparing the invitations, be sure to double-check the day of the week, the date, the time of day, the room location, and the names of all participants in the various programs and sectional meetings. No participant should have to telephone the sponsors for vital information inadvertently omitted from these invitations.

Outside professional and community meetings   If your employer is a leader in professional or community affairs, he or she may be asked to send out informal meeting notices, perhaps as part of a newsletter. An illustration of this kind of meeting notice is shown in Fig. 4.3. A self-addressed postal card such as the one

Fig. 4.3   Newsletter Meeting Notice

SECRETARIAL FORUM

JANUARY MEETING

Monday, January 19, 19 --

TOPIC:	"Increasing Office Productivity"
CHAIRPERSON:	Alta Hazelett, Supervisor, Secretarial Services, Arnold Stainless Steel Corporation
PANEL:	Ruth Anderson, Berlin Industries Arline Basarab, Hanley Works, Inc. Cecelia Dul, Tate Products Anthony Bruce, Clarion Mowers, Inc. Paul Gunther, Leechburg Associates Alice Ralph, Latch Insurance Company
PLACE:	Regency Room, Commodore Hotel
TIME:	6:00 p.m. Social 6:30 p.m. Dinner
MENU:	Smorgasbord
COST:	$20.00
RETURN:	Enclosed reservation card by January 12, please

shown in Fig. 4.4 may also be included, so that the participants in the meeting can respond to the invitation quickly. These cards will later serve as the basis for the reservation list (as for a luncheon or dinner meeting).

Fig. 4.4   Reservation Postal Card

```
  PLEASE--Send this reservation card to our Secretary
  on or before Wednesday of next week (9/12).

  __ Yes. I plan to attend the next Forum dinner
     meeting.

  __ Yes, I'll bring ___ guests.
     Guest names: _____

  __ Sorry. I'll miss the Forum this month.


                    Signature _____

                    Company _____
```

Outside social/business functions   You will likely be involved at some time in preparing formal and informal invitations to social/business functions, often as part of a conference. Such invitations are usually extended to executives and their spouses. Reply (R.S.V.P.) cards may be included with the invitation. (Today the reply to a business invitation is rarely handwritten, although handwritten replies are still conventional for formal social invitations.)

For a detailed discussion of international etiquette, see Chapter 15.

USING MAILING LISTS FOR INVITATIONS AND NOTICES
Devise a system for keeping mailing lists current. In most offices, you will keep your mailing lists as word-processing files. Updating can be done rapidly on computer, and mailing labels can be printed out with great speed.

In offices where the only mailings are extremely small, a simple card system may be used. Each card will show the name and address of a regular mailing recipient, and the cards can be arranged by geographical region, by company, or by individual name. However, typing out more than one or two dozen addresses onto labels or envelopes can become very laborious.

Conference Duties

You may be able to contribute greatly to the success of a conference by your work in (1) preparing for the upcoming event, (2) carrying out your duties in the course of the conference, and (3) following up after it is over. It will be necessary to plan ahead for each step of the meeting with appropriate notations on your calendar.

PREPARING FOR CONFERENCES

If you work closely with the executive who is directing or sponsoring a conference, the principal areas of conference preparation in which you may be involved are the following: (1) meeting-site and speaker confirmation, (2) preparing conference materials, and (3) special arrangements for services, including publicity.

Meeting-site and speaker confirmation   If hotel rooms will be needed for conference participants, you should contact the site manager for block reservations. Room size (single or double) and price range should be specified. The site manager should be asked to reserve the appropriate meeting rooms, including both the main auditorium and "break-up" rooms for smaller group sessions. In addition, you should discuss seating plans. (See Fig. 4.5 for an illustration of possible seating arrangements.) If smoking is to be permitted, ashtrays should be provided. A thermos or water pitcher and glasses should be available for the speakers, panelists, or board members. Arrangements for parking and coat checking may also have to be made.

It is a good idea to inspect unfamiliar meeting sites, if possible, to be certain that there is adequate space for the event. Firsthand knowledge of the meeting or conference layout will be helpful in positioning the registration desk, locating needed lighting and electrical outlets for audiovisual equipment, determining whether microphones will be needed, and directing guests to the meeting area. A letter confirming the reservation of all conference facilities should be sent to the site manager. In the case of in-house requests, this may be done by telephone and confirmed by a memorandum.

After the meeting date is set, letters of invitation to speakers may be composed or dictated, unless the executive chooses to telephone the invitations to the speakers. Such invitations should be taken care of as soon as possible. When each invitation is accepted, a follow-up letter requesting information about the speaker's background and experience may be sent. Glossy photographs of the speakers are also frequently requested for inclusion with news releases.

Preparing conference materials   A meeting should never be held without an agenda. An agenda distributed in advance may encourage participants to gather material and ideas to contribute. As the meeting proceeds, the Chair can use the agenda to keep discussions on the subject at hand and then check off each item as it is completed. When there is no agenda, a meeting may lack its necessary focus. An informal agenda is shown in Fig. 4.6. A sample workshop activity sheet and agenda are shown in Fig. 4.7.

Supporting materials such as tables, reports, financial statements, or advertisements may be needed, and you may be asked to prepare copies for the meeting participants. These items are often assembled and distributed in a folder or envelope. Double-check that all names, titles, topics, sections, and meeting times are correct.

When the conference speakers have submitted their résumés or autobiographical sketches, a news release may be prepared. If the firm has a public-relations office, you should forward the information to that department; if the firm does not have such an office, you may be asked to draft a press release. (See Chapter 8 for details on press releases.)

Trip itineraries will be necessary for meetings and conferences held outside the firm. A typical itinerary is shown in Fig. 4.8. Several copies of the itinerary are needed: one for the executive's travel folder, one for the executive's spouse,

Fig. 4.5   Common Seating Arrangements

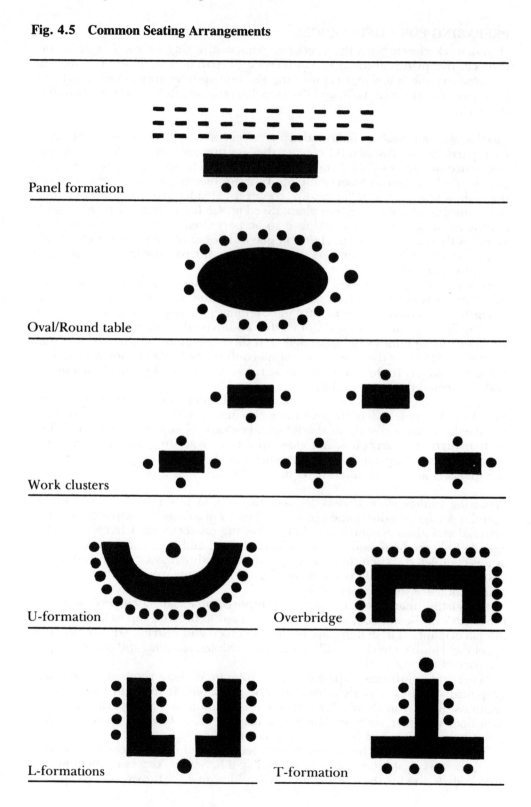

Panel formation

Oval/Round table

Work clusters

U-formation

Overbridge

L-formations

T-formation

Fig. 4.6   An Informal Agenda

```
                         Agenda

Executive Board Meeting--Tues., Oct. 5, 10:00 a.m.


1.  Review of sales figures for whole reference
    line.

2.  New CD-ROM projects.

3.  Marketing strategy for new editions of Smoler
    and Chevigny books.

4.  Possible distribution arrangements with
    different textbook houses.

5.  New-title ideas from sales reps.
```

and at least one office copy. (For a detailed discussion of travel arrangements, see Chapter 15.)

Special arrangements for services   Large-scale conventions and conferences require a wide variety of special services. You may be asked to do any of the following:

Arrange for printing and engraving services.
Organize tours and special events for conferees and spouses.
Arrange for refreshments and meals.
Handle pre-registration and registration arrangements.
Assemble conference folders or packets.
Request audiovisual equipment and materials.
Arrange for translation services (for international conferences).
Mail prework conference materials (to be studied in advance by participants).
Ship supplies and printed materials to conference site.
Arrange for press coverage.
Inform security officers and parking attendants of pertinent conference details.
Prepare meeting file folders.

Assembling all the materials for a complete conference program is a demanding task. You will often have to coordinate the information, type the final copy, and send it to the printer on time. This material usually includes programs, reports, booklets or brochures, name tags, and tickets, among other things. Ban-

Fig. 4.7   A Workshop Activity Sheet

A WORKSHOP IN MULTIMEDIA TRAINING

INTERNATIONAL MANAGEMENT SOCIETY

September 24, 19--

SCHEDULE

8:00 a.m.	Arrive Doyle, Inc.	
8:15 a.m.	Breakfast	Conference Room B
9:00 a.m.	Workshop	Conference Room 6, Education Center
12:30 p.m.	Luncheon	Dining Room
2:00 p.m.	Plant Tour (Optional)	
3:00 p.m.	Departure	

WORKSHOP AGENDA

9:00 a.m.	Welcome	Stella Willins School Department Manager
	Introduction, Management Development Skills Training	Stanley Lindberg Public Relations Manager
10:00 a.m.	Sales Training	Elwin Young Sales Training Supervisor
11:00 a.m.	Service Training	Peter Lawson Service Training Supervisor
12:00 noon	Discussion	All

Fig. 4.8   A Basic Itinerary

ITINERARY
Management Executives' Society Meeting--Hobe Sound, Florida
Bateman Corp. Board Meeting--Chicago, Illinois
April 9-15, 19--

WEDNESDAY, APRIL 9

Lv. Bradley Field	6:45 p.m.	DL #193	(One stop in NY; breakfast served)
Ar. West Palm Beach	11:27 a.m.		

Transportation to Coral Island Club: Perkins Transfer (Courtesy phone near baggage claim area)

Accommodations: Coral Island Club
Hobe Sound, Florida
(505) 546-2751
April 9-12, 19-- (four nights)

Guaranteed for late arrival (American Express).
Confirmation attached.
Check-out time 12 noon.
Secretarial help available: See Ms. Hafey.

SUNDAY, APRIL 13

Lv. West Palm Beach	3:45 p.m.	UA #252	(Snack served)
Ar. O'Hare	5:43 p.m.		

Accommodations: Hotel Grand Monde
562 N. Michigan Ave., Chicago
(312) 123-4567
April 13-14, 19-- (2 nights)

Guaranteed for late arrival (American Express).
Confirmation #66063298.
Check-out time 12 noon.

TUESDAY, APRIL 15

Lv. O'Hare	4:55 p.m.	AA #444	(Dinner served)
Ar. Bradley	8:02 p.m.		Driver at airport to meet flight.

---

quet and special-event tickets should be ready early. Prenumbering tickets will aid in setting up an accounting system later on; special numbering machines may be used for this purpose. Orders for special items (such as award plaques and other engraved pieces) should be placed well ahead of time.

Executives are sometimes accompanied by their families when attending longer conferences, and special activities such as tours or social events may have to be arranged for the families. In these situations, it is helpful to print special brochures for them as well. A spouses' entertainment committee may be established, and a group of hosts and hostesses who are familiar with the city might be made available to assist the guests with information on shopping tours, restaurants, theaters, museums, health clubs, sports events, and other matters of interest. To make these plans, it is important to find out in advance the approximate number of family members who will attend the meeting.

Arrangements must be made with the catering manager for refreshment and meal selection. It is most important to confirm the number of conference participants for coffee breaks, social hours, luncheons, and banquets. For a large banquet, you may have to design the menu itself, perhaps incorporating your firm's logo in the design.

A card system can be a real boon in handling pre-registration information. As reservations and registration fees come in, each conferee's name, title, firm, address, and other important information such as conference-fee payment may be typed on each card. The cards may be grouped and filed by geographical area, by committee, or on some other basis.

After the cutoff date for pre-registration, and usually one week before the meeting, the rooming list of conference participants should be sent to the conference manager.

Arrange for the staffing of the registration desk well in advance. A telephoned reminder to registration assistants the day before the conference will assure that there is no break in attendance at the desk. The organization and placement of the registration desk must be determined. Attractive and readable signs at the desk will enable those registering to find information more quickly; orders should be placed early for signs and other such supplies. The desk may accept registrations by alphabetical divisions, by regions, by countries, or by some other system on the day of the convention.

All conference-related materials should be assembled in packets for the participants. These packets include the program, brochures, reports, and minutes; name tags and tickets for meals and other special events are generally included as well. Individual names may be typed on the packets of those who have pre-registered and paid all necessary fees. These packets should be arranged alphabetically for easy access. Name tags or badges, if not included in the packets, should also be alphabetically arranged. Special program packages will be needed for speakers and honored guests; these packages normally include complimentary tickets to luncheons, banquets, and other special events, as well as badges or name tags.

Arrangements for audiovisual equipment and its operators, if needed, should be made with the site manager, concierge, or another designated person. Some of the most frequently used items include:

Chalkboard	Microphones (floor or lapel)
Easel with large pad of paper	Movie projector (specify size)
Filmstrip projector	Overhead projector
Lectern	Projection screen (specify size)

Simultaneous-translation headsets and control boxes

Slide projector (specify tray design)

Stereo system

Tape recorder (specify cassette size)

Television (specify screen size)

Videocassette recorder

There are many kinds of projectors, so it is vital to determine what type each speaker needs. Find out exactly what kinds of material are to be projected (slides, overhead transparencies, opaque material) in order to confirm the choice of equipment.

Use a reservation request form to order audiovisual aids and other items; the equipment and services can be checked off on such a form. Order stands or dollies of the proper height for the correct placement of the projectors. Ensure that extra projector bulbs and extension cords are provided and that the machines can be replaced or serviced in any last-minute emergency. The person chairing the meeting should be familiar with the location of all electrical outlets and light switches.

Training conferences, such as those for sales personnel, often require the participants to study advance materials. Such prework materials must be mailed to the participants at least two weeks before the event.

General conference supplies, booklets, and other information will have to be shipped to the conference site at least two weeks before the meeting. It will be necessary to call the site manager or concierge and request that the supplies be held for pickup by the chairperson on the conference date. A follow-up letter to this effect would be added insurance against later mix-ups.

Press releases concerning the conference should be prepared for distribution to the news media either before or after the event. (See Chapter 8 for a discussion of press releases.) Arrangements also should be made for any photographs that will be taken during the conference. Summaries of addresses or lectures may be needed for distribution to the media; whenever possible, copies of these summaries should be prepared in advance.

Security guards or other such personnel ought to be alerted about the forthcoming conference, its general agenda, and the locations and times of meetings. They should also be informed if guests requiring extra protection (such as high government officials) will be in attendance. If large numbers of persons are involved, extra parking facilities may have to be made available. Inform parking attendants of the approximate number of meeting participants. It is also helpful to send maps showing various driving routes, along with printed directions, to each participant in advance.

Executive file folders should contain all pertinent information about the conference. A copy of the program, reports, brochures, minutes of previous meetings, correspondence, and other important information should be included. For outside conferences, the folders should contain travel information and the itinerary. The executive file folder should be labeled with the name of the conference, the city, the dates, and any other pertinent information. You will find it useful to have separate file folders relating to arrangements for particular functions in which your employer will take an important part.

Travel-expense sheets or booklets are needed by executives for recording travel and conference expenses. These contain ledger space for expenses such as transportation, personal mileage, taxi fares and fares for other local transport, room, meals (including tips), and business-related telephone calls. There is also space for recording cash advances and the total amount expended from such advances.

DUTIES DURING CONFERENCES

At the actual event, your competence will meet one of its severest tests. In your hands rests the responsibility for the meticulous checking that alone can ensure that all the carefully laid plans are carried through to the letter. Good organization and follow-through are essential to effective conferences.

Checking the in-house meeting room   An early personal visit to the conference room on the day of the in-house meeting will let you make a final check of room arrangements and check to see that all necessary printed materials are available. Since correct lighting and proper heating and ventilation will contribute to the comfort of the participants, these should be double-checked. You should ensure that the room is arranged as desired. Its cleanliness should be checked. Fresh water and glasses should be available for speakers or panelists. Pens, pencils, note pads, and conference folders should be at each place at the conference table for management-level meetings. Check the availability and placement of requested audiovisual equipment and materials.

Checklist of arrangements for outside meetings   Conference-day inspection of the meeting room, audiovisual equipment delivery, and other tasks may be expedited by using a checklist, which you should prepare and give to the catering manager or other designated person for each day of a conference. This list will serve as a summary of items needed for each program as well as of desired food services, menus, and other details. A sample checklist is illustrated in Fig. 4.9.

Fig. 4.9   A Checklist for Conference Arrangements

DAILY CONFERENCE/CONVENTION ARRANGEMENTS CHECKLIST

TO: Catering Manager   KIND OF MEETING: Missouri Bar Association Seminar

FROM: Beatrice Pomerance   MEETING SITE: Kansas Hotel, Kansas City, Mo.
            Administrative Secretary

DATE: October 19, 19 —   MEETING DATES: October 19-21, 19 —

DATE	TIME	AM	PM	ROOM	FUNCTION	ROOM SETUP	NO. OF GUESTS	MENUS/ AUDIOVISUAL AIDS
10/19/19 —	9:00-12:00	AM		McKenzie	Bankruptcy	U-formation Tables for 30	30	1 Lectern 1 Overhead projector 1 Cassette recorder 1 Easel with newsprint paper
	10:30-10:45	AM		McKenzie	Coffee Break	Serving table Self-service	30	Coffee Danish
	12:15-1:15		PM	Kansas Star	Luncheon	5 tables of 6 each	30	French onion soup Trout Meunière Green Beans amandine Butternut squash Apple pie à la mode Coffee/tea
	1:30-4:30		PM	McKenzie	Creditors' rights	6 tables of 5 each	30	Same as 9:00-12:00
	3:00-3:15		PM	McKenzie	Coffee break	Serving table Self-service	30	Coffee Donuts

Greeting conference guests   A pleasant welcome to conference members and guests is extremely important to the positive impression your firm desires to create. Be the epitome of the perfect host when greeting guests and introducing them to one another. If there are only a few guests, you may meet them personally and individually escort them to the meeting room. At a large conference, assistants may direct guests to the coat-check room, the registration desk, and the conference room.

Secretarial services during conferences   The following list identifies some further services that you may have to provide at a conference:

1. Supervise the registration desk. Alert registration-desk personnel as to the identity and the arrival time of speakers and special guests so that badges, programs, and complimentary tickets for luncheons and other events may be presented to them.
2. Provide statistics on the number of participants who will attend each event.
3. Prepare a list of participants with the names and addresses of their companies, to be duplicated and distributed.
4. Take minutes of certain meetings.
5. Handle correspondence requests for conference officers, executives, or special guests.
6. Assemble and prepare information for a conference news sheet. Print and distribute news sheet to participants.
7. Coordinate conference events by transmitting messages and reaching individuals sought by others.
8. Meet media representatives and photographers and direct them to room locations for group pictures and other events. Distribute press releases.
9. Arrange place cards for seating officers and guests on the dais or at the head table for luncheons and banquets.

FOLLOWING UP AFTER CONFERENCES

The follow-up duties after a conference often become your responsibility. You may be asked to perform the following duties at the meeting site:

1. Remove any surplus meeting- or conference-related literature (such as reports or minutes) from the meeting room.
2. Notify the catering manager to collect water glasses and any food-service items from the meeting room.
3. Request that audiovisual equipment be transferred to locked storage areas. For security reasons, await the arrival of authorized representatives to store this equipment.
4. Remove any equipment or materials that have been borrowed or rented and arrange for their prompt return.
5. Return any lost-and-found items to the company receptionist or the appropriate conference authorities.

Upon returning to the office, you will face additional follow-up responsibilities. These should be handled promptly. The success of a meeting often depends on follow-up, and you should try to complete the following tasks within a week after the close of the meeting.

1. *Calendars*   Note on your desk calendar, on the executive's desk calendar, and in a tickler file all dates for further meetings, reports due, and other conference-related information. It may be necessary also to write reminders to committee chairpersons and others charged with follow-up duties.

2. *Correspondence*   Letters of appreciation will have to be written to those officers and chairpersons who assisted with the conference. Letters of congratulation may also be in order for newly elected officers and directors.

3. *Minutes*   Minutes taken at the conference should be transcribed as soon as possible. Particular attention should be paid to specific tasks assigned to conference participants. You will want to remind the executive of any unassigned tasks spelled out in the minutes. Copies of the minutes or meeting summaries may have to be sent to conference participants.

4. *Finances*   Payment for equipment rentals or purchase of supplies should be prompt. Speakers should be given their honoraria and reimbursed for travel expenses as soon as possible. Try to obtain signatures, Social Security numbers, receipts, mileage, and other information necessary for writing checks *before* the meeting is over. Sometimes these payments are made at the close of the meeting.

5. *Meeting of planners*   If a similar conference will be held in the future, those who planned the meeting should discuss ways to improve procedures while the conference is fresh in everyone's mind.

6. *Meeting file*   You should create a file that will contain all records of the conference, including a sample participant's packet. If a similar meeting is planned for the future, the file should also include your own comments on what went smoothly and what could be improved.

Taking Minutes

Serving as recording secretary and taking minutes or notes at meetings and conferences may be a major portion of your responsibility. In a small corporation, you may prepare minutes of stockholders' meetings. In a large company you may be asked to keep minutes of corporate committee meetings.

PREPARING FOR THE MEETING
You should arrive early at the meeting so that you can organize the area where you will be taking minutes. For manual note-taking, you will want a sufficient number of pens, pencils, and notebooks and a supply of paper. For machine shorthand, an adequate supply of paper tape should be on hand. Tape recorders are often used to supplement note-taking when verbatim minutes are required, in which case you will need to have a number of blank cassette tapes of the proper size.

If you are not familiar with the names of the meeting's participants, devise a numbered seating chart so that you can identify by number those who make motions. The presiding officer can give you their names afterward.

The presiding officer and you should discuss the materials that will be needed. Be sure you know which materials you must bring; these might include the minutes books, the bylaws, the membership and committee lists, extra copies of the agenda and printed minutes, and a reference book on parliamentary procedure.

If you are a corporate secretary you will need to take some or all of the following items to the annual stockholders' meeting, directors' meetings, and other special meetings:

Current meeting file (current papers relating to the meeting)

Record of proxies received

Minutes books

Corporate seal

Copy of published meeting notice to stockholders, with a notation of the mailing date

Copy of corporation laws of the state in which the firm is incorporated

Copy of the certificate of incorporation, including amendments

Copy of the corporate bylaws, plus amendments

Meeting regulation information, if any

Blank forms for affidavits, oaths, and other purposes

FOLLOWING MEETING PROCEDURES

Having adequate knowledge of meeting procedures is essential. Reading and referring to previous minutes and talking with secretaries who have taken notes at similar meetings will aid you in your own note-taking. Before a meeting, it is also a good idea to consult the presiding officer about how to have motions or statements clarified or repeated when necessary.

Meetings may be conducted formally or informally. At informal meetings the presiding officer joins in the discussion, and some of the formalities of parliamentary procedure are waived. Such is usually the case in committee meetings. Formal meetings, on the other hand, call for strict adherence to the rules of parliamentary procedure and the bylaws governing the meeting. See the discussion of parliamentary procedure beginning on page 73.

A meeting agenda or order of business may or may not be used at informal meetings; however, it is required for formal meetings, and it is a great help to both the presiding officer and the recording secretary.

The items in an agenda follow a set pattern established by the official group or organization. A comprehensive list of possible agenda items follows.

Agenda (Order of Business)
1. Call to order
2. Roll call or verification of participants present
3. Minutes of the previous meeting (changes/approval)
4. Reading of correspondence
5. Report of treasurer
6. Report of board of directors
7. Report of officers
8. Report of standing committees
9. Report of special committees
10. Unfinished business (from previous meetings)
11. New business (normally items submitted in advance to the presiding officer)
12. Appointment of committees
13. Nominations and elections
14. Program, if appropriate
15. Announcements (including date of next meeting)
16. Adjournment

It is essential to record the following basic facts concerning a meeting:

1. Date, time, and location of the meeting.
2. Name of the presiding officer.
3. Kind of meeting (such as regular, special, board, executive, or committee).

4. Names of members present and absent, for small groups of under 20 persons. A quorum check is needed for larger groups. (Majority representation at stockholders' meetings is usually based upon shares of stock rather than the number of stockholders. Thus, it is necessary to know the number of shares owned by each stockholder.)

5. Order of business as indicated on the agenda.

6. Motions made, their adoption or rejection, how the vote was taken (show of hands, voice, etc.), whether the vote was unanimous, and the names of the originators of the main motions. (It is not necessary to record the names of those who second motions unless requested to do so.)

It is normally unnecessary to record details of discussion. Minutes should concentrate on actions taken, not topics discussed. However, when you need to summarize an important discussion, use one side of your notebook for the main speaker and the other side for incidental speakers. Use paper clips or gummed tags to mark any action that must be taken following the meeting.

Transcribing Minutes

Typing the minutes of any meeting is an important responsibility. Because minutes serve as the official record of a meeting, accuracy is essential. Tape recorders are of great value in checking the precise wording of motions. Though meetings vary in degree of formality, it is always imperative that the wording of minutes be factual, brief, and devoid of editorial comment. Acceptable minutes capture the gist or substance of the meeting and follow the agenda closely; as a rule, a verbatim record is made only of main motions and resolutions.

When your superior is the presiding officer, he or she will frequently want to see a rough draft of the minutes before the final copy is typed. If the minutes are dictated to you by the corporate secretary, you should similarly submit a rough draft for review, because it is essential that there be no errors in the final copy.

Minutes should be typed while the meeting is still fresh in your mind. A little forethought is needed before beginning the actual typing; being well organized will make the task easier and save time and effort. The following items should be assembled:

A copy of the agenda
Attendance information
Previous minutes
Copies of reports and materials distributed
A copy of motions and/or resolutions
A copy of the organization's constitution and/or bylaws
An up-to-date dictionary
Reference books on style and parliamentary procedure
Official stationery and continuation sheets, or plain 20-pound bond paper
Other data pertinent to the minutes

Since the format of the minutes is usually dictated by the organization itself, carefully examine the format of past minutes. Some organizations provide printed stationery designed especially for the first page of the minutes, along with special continuation sheets. Official minutes are frequently printed on 28-

pound bond intended for printing on both sides. If special printed paper is not available, high-quality plain white bond should be used. Minutes are filed in a notebook, either a regulation locking type or an ordinary loose-leaf notebook. Pages are usually numbered sequentially throughout, with an index to facilitate reference to important decisions.

The arrangement of the minutes should closely parallel the agenda or order of business. Common elements include the following:

Name and address of organization or group

Type of meeting

Call to order: time, date, presiding officer

Attendance information: names of individuals, or a statement that a quorum was present

Previous minutes: reading and corrections

Reports: by whom, title, subject

Unfinished business (if any): motions, by whom, votes

Program, including speakers' names and titles

Announcements, including time and place of next meeting

Adjournment, time

See sample minutes in Fig. 4.10. Reports from officers and committee chairs are frequently attached to the minutes as an appendix, and a notation such as "Mr. Hedley read the Finance Committee report, a copy of which is appended to these Minutes" is made in the body of the minutes. Resolutions, especially lengthy ones and ones recorded on printed forms, may be handled in the same manner.

The first rule for typing minutes is to be consistent with the format of previous minutes of the organization. If you are free to adopt your own format, some suggested guidelines for minutes—especially those that are to be typed on plain paper—are as follows:

1. Leave a 2″ top margin.
2. Type the title in capital letters and center it on the page.
3. Center the date two lines beneath the title. Leave two blank lines below the date.
4. Use side headings to provide easy reference. Choice of side-heading style will vary according to organization guidelines; compare the side headings on the sample minutes and meeting summary in Figs. 4.10 and 4.11.
5. Single-space the text paragraphs, unless your organization prefers them double-spaced.
6. Type sums of money in both words and figures when they are mentioned in motions and resolutions.
7. Number each page at bottom center.
8. Provide blank underlines for your signature and the chairperson's.
9. Make the necessary copies for distribution and filing.

Corporate titles and the names of specific entities within a corporation or organization are usually capitalized in minutes; for example, "the Chairman," "the Comptroller," "the Board," "the Company," "the Board of Directors," "Common Stock," "the Corporate Bylaws," "the Annual Meeting of the Corporation." However, lowercase letters are preferred by some executives. Some secretaries type the text of all motions entirely in capital letters in order to facilitate refer-

Fig. 4.10   Minutes of a Board Meeting

117
19-- #4

INTERNATIONAL TRACTORS, INC.
DIRECTORS' MEETING

MINUTES OF APRIL 6, 19--   REGULAR MEETING, NO. 4

A regular meeting of the Board of Directors of
International Tractors., Inc. was held on Thursday,
April 6, 19--. The meeting was called to order by
John E. Wolfe, Chairman, at 10 a.m. in the Founder's
Conference Room of the Corporate Office on Gilpin Road
in Leechburg, Pennsylvania.

PRESENT

Thirteen members of the Board were present:
Pauline Alt, Charles Filip, Glenn France, Robert Hazer,
Joseph Latina, Richard Linamen, Lorraine Perejda,
Ismail Perez, Ethel Rasmusson, Irene Stanick, Elizabeth
Walden, Forest Wolfe, and John Zalesny. These members
constitute a quorum.

ABSENT

One member was absent: Louis Jones.

MINUTES
APPROVED

The minutes of the March 5, 19--, special Directors'
meeting were read and approved.

REPORT OF THE
CHAIRMAN

The chairman reported on the growth in sales during the
last quarter, especially in international business. For that
period, the company enjoyed a 12 percent increase as
compared with a year ago. However, mention was made of
the increasing difficulties in bidding for critical material
supplies against strong and affluent foreign competitors.

A plan for Organizing for Growth was submitted to the
Board for study:

First, decentralize responsibility for sales, marketing,
and accounting from our corporate headquarters into
each operating company.

Next, reinstitute the dual management posts of chairman
and chief executive officer and of president and chief
operating officer. This will assure that undivided attention
will be given to current operations and to future growth.

```
                                                       118
      MINUTES OF APRIL 6, 19--                      19-- #4


      REPORT OF THE          James McKallip, Treasurer, submitted a quarterly
      TREASURER              profit and loss statement, dated March 31, 19--, with
                             a net profit of $12,752,000. The surplus available for
                             dividends is $4,443,000, as determined by a general
                             balance sheet, dated March 31, 19--. These reports
                             were accepted and placed on file.


      ADJOURNMENT             A motion for adjournment was made by Mr. France
                              and seconded by Ms. Stanick. The meeting was
                              adjourned at 11:45 a.m.



      _____        _____
        Charlotte Charpnak, Secretary      John E. Wolfe, Chairman
```

ence to them; for example, "Roger Clark moved THAT THE ORGANIZA-TION DONATE THE SUM OF TWO HUNDRED DOLLARS ($200.00) TO. . . ."

Resolutions are formal expressions of the opinion, will, or intent of the body. Most secretaries follow conventional forms in typing resolutions. Formal resolutions use language such as the following:

> WHEREAS it has become necessary . . . : Therefore be it
> RESOLVED, That . . . ; and be it
> RESOLVED further, That . . . .

An informal resolution might be phrased more simply:

> RESOLVED, That . . . .

CORRECTIONS

Corrections (such as those pointed out at the next meeting) should be written in ink above the line or in the margin. Major corrections and additions may be typed on a separate page and attached, with a note in the margin of the original page drawing attention to the attachment. Never discard the original minutes, no matter how many mistakes they may hold. You may retype a page only if you attach it to the original, uncorrected page.

MEETING SUMMARY

The illustration in Fig. 4.11 is a facsimile of a *meeting summary,* which is a less formal way of recording the business transacted at a meeting. Notice that the word *summary* is typed in capital letters 1" from the top left edge of the page. Since this facsimile illustrates a confidential meeting, the word *confidential* is typed 1" from the top right edge of the page, also in capital letters. The rest of the material is formatted according to the guidelines for normal minutes, except that the signature lines are omitted. Copies of meeting summaries are frequently sent to both those who attended the meeting and those who were absent.

Fig. 4.11   An Informal Meeting Summary

SUMMARY   CONFIDENTIAL

CORCORAN-WREN, INC.

CONSUMER PRODUCTS DIVISION FINANCE COMMITTEE MEETING

October 22, 19--

ATTENDANCE	Messrs. Adams, Bartsch, Carter, and Dann; Ms. Eagleton
TREASURER'S DEPARTMENT	Mr. Adams submitted liquidity forecasts, budget allocations, and figures representing long-term investment transactions. Forty million dollars of cash flow still is not committed for 19-- disbursement, which will result in $45 million of surplus liquidity at year's end if the situation continues.
COMMON STOCK DEPARTMENT	Ms. Eagleton discussed and analyzed current performance and reviewed recent transactions. Cash reserves continue to be held at the 30% level while the Department awaits a more auspicious opportunity to deploy them into stocks.
TRANSACTIONS	All transactions for the period October 1 - November 1 of this year were approved.

Chairing a Meeting

At some point, you may take an active role as the presiding officer of a professional, civic, or community organization. Many firms have organizations of secretaries devoted to developing certain skills, such as their public-speaking ability. Before stepping to the lectern to conduct a meeting, you should be well versed in parliamentary procedure. See the Appendix for further reading.

PLANNING AHEAD

The presiding officer of a meeting usually needs to prepare an agenda to serve as a guide for conducting the meeting. Copies of the agenda may be distributed to the members. The members may contribute topics for the agenda in advance, in accordance with the time limits set down in the bylaws or by mutual agreement of the membership.

The items on the agenda should be carefully thought through by the presiding officer before the meeting. File folders may have to be organized to hold the various reports and other items to be discussed. If one-fifth-cut file folders are used, they may be arranged alphabetically by topic and placed in a small case for easy reference. Being able to locate material quickly at the meeting will result in a well-organized and productive session.

PARLIAMENTARY PROCEDURES

The presiding officer, or Chair, remains impartial in discussions, maintains order by permitting consideration of only one topic at a time, recognizes the rights of members to express themselves, and assures equitable treatment for all members. It is especially important for the Chair to know how to handle the order of business efficiently.

Opening the meeting   To bring the members to attention at the start of the meeting, the Chair usually taps a gavel on the desk and says, "The meeting will now come to order."

Quorum check   The Chair must verify the number of members necessary for a quorum according to the bylaws. If there is no quorum, an attempt may be made to secure one. If the required number of members cannot be found, the only proper action is to fix the time to adjourn and then adjourn.

Reading of the minutes   If a quorum is present, the Chair will then normally say, "The minutes of the previous meeting will be read by the secretary." If copies of the minutes were distributed to the membership in advance, the minutes are not read and the Chair asks, "Are there any additions or corrections in the minutes?"

There should be a pause for membership reflection or response. If there is no response, the Chair continues, "If not, the minutes stand approved [*or* approved as read]." If there is a correction, the Chair may informally direct that it be made. If there is an objection by a member, a formal vote is needed for the correction.

If an error is discovered in the minutes after their approval, an amendment must be made and a vote taken.

Reports   The Chair calls for organization reports in this order:

1. Officers (e.g., vice president, treasurer)
2. Executive board (board of directors)
3. Standing committees
4. Special committees

For example, the Chair might ask, "May we now have the Treasurer's report?" After the report is read or presented, the Chair may state, "The Treasurer's report may now be filed for audit."

Normally, reports of the other officers may be made at the annual meeting or at the end of the term of office. When the report of the executive board is made, action may be taken on it immediately or it may be recalled under new business. (Note that board *minutes* are not read, since they are the property of the board.)

The Chair calls for the appropriate report from an officer, the board, a standing committee, or a special committee by saying, for example, "Will the chairperson of the Ways and Means Committee please present the committee's report?" After the committee chairperson presents the report, a motion is needed to accept or adopt it.

Processing a motion   Following a report, if there is no response in the form of a motion, the Chair may ask, "Is there a motion that this report be accepted?"

Here the Chair may accept only motions that are worded affirmatively. Often rewording is necessary to avoid a negative motion.

One of the members will say, "I move that the Ways and Means Committee report be accepted." Another member will state, "I second the motion." The Chair will then state, "It has been moved and seconded that the Ways and Means Committee report be accepted. Is there any discussion?"

Though the Chair opens the discussion, it is not proper for him or her to enter into the discussion at a formal meeting, except to process the order of business.

Questions from the floor will follow. When there is a lull in the discussion, the Chair should ask, "Is there further discussion?" If no discussion ensues, the Chair then says, "If not, are you ready to put the question?" or "Are you ready to vote?"

If the members are ready, the Chair will usually call for a voice vote: "All those in favor, please signify by saying aye. . . .Those opposed, please signify by saying no." The Chair then states, depending upon the outcome, "The motion is carried" or "The motion is lost." If an accurate count is needed, a show of hands, a rising vote, a roll call, or a ballot vote will be specified instead.

Introducing new business   When the reports are finished the Chair can proceed to introduce an agenda item of new business. Discussion by the membership follows. If a motion is made and seconded, the Chair should restate the motion so that all may hear and understand it. After a reasonable time for discussion, a member may call "Question" or the Chair may say, "Are you ready for the question?" The vote may then be taken.

Types of motions   Main motions are made to present a resolution, a recommendation, or some other proposal for consideration by the members. No other main motion may be brought before the assembly when a main motion is already on the floor.

Subsidiary motions are those that modify the principal or main motion; therefore, such motions must be decided before the main motion. (However, subsidiary motions are considered *after* privileged and incidental motions.) Examples of subsidiary motions include the following:

To postpone indefinitely   The purpose is to dispose of a motion while avoiding a direct vote on the question.

To amend   The purpose is to modify the main motion. (The motion to amend must be germane to the subject which is to be amended.)

To refer to committee   The purpose is to provide for careful consideration of difficult issues by a selected smaller group.

To postpone to a certain day or time   The purpose is to defer action for a definite period.

To limit or extend debate   The purpose is to modify the freedom of debate.

To move the previous question or *call the question*   The purpose is to stop debate at once and prepare to vote.

To lay on the table or *to table*   The purpose is to postpone action on the present order of business in order to make way for more important business.

Incidental motions are those that come incidentally as other motions are being considered. Action must be taken on the incidental motion before the main motion or a subsidiary motion can be considered. Some examples of incidental motions are the following:

To suspend the rules   The purpose is to permit an action that would otherwise be impossible according to the rules that govern the order of business or admission to the meeting. (Such a motion cannot be made to suspend the bylaws or constitution of the organization, however.)

To modify or withdraw a motion   The purpose is to alter the motion or to remove the motion from the floor.

To read a paper   The purpose is to provide for reading a document or motion aloud for the purpose of information.

To object to the consideration of a question   The purpose is to prevent the discussion of a question that is irrelevant or contentious before debate begins.

To appeal a decision from the Chair   The purpose is to call for a vote to reverse the Chair's decision on an issue.

To raise a question (or *point*) *of order*   The purpose is to draw attention to a violation of parliamentary procedure.

Privileged motions relate to matters of urgent importance. These motions are undebatable and take precedence over all questions. Examples include the following:

To call for the orders of the day   The purpose is to demand adherence to the order of business or the program at hand.

To raise a question of privilege   The purpose relates broadly to the rights or privileges of the members of the group. When a member rises to a question of personal privilege and then states his or her complaint and proposes a solution, the Chair must decide if it is in fact a question of sufficient urgency to be considered at that time.

To take a recess   The purpose is to temporarily adjourn the meeting (e.g., for counting ballots).

To fix the time to adjourn   The purpose is to fix the exact time that the meeting shall end.

To adjourn   The purpose is to bring the meeting to a close. Before bringing this motion to a vote, the Chair should be certain that no important items or announcements have been overlooked. All business should cease after an affirmative vote on this motion.

Mastering the complexities of parliamentary procedure is a task that requires both considerable study (using texts such as those listed in the Appendix) and extensive experience of actual meetings.

ADDRESSING AN AUDIENCE

There may be many opportunities for you to speak to groups, large or small.

If you are asked merely to introduce a speaker, obtain information about the speaker's background either by personal request or from published sources. Know the speaker's *current* title, and by all means pronounce his or her name correctly! The best introductions are brief. Avoid a dry listing of all the speaker's accomplishments; select the most pertinent and interesting facts, and project your own enthusiasm without overselling the speaker.

There may also be occasions when you are asked to deliver an address to an audience yourself. Follow these basic guidelines for public speaking:

1. Research your subject carefully in order to be certain of the facts. Have documentation for any information that may be questioned by the audience.
2. Clearly think through in advance what you are going to say. Work with an outline; cards are helpful for this purpose.
3. Practice before a mirror. Be particularly mindful of facial and body expressions and gestures.
4. Time your message to keep it within the specified time limit.
5. Record your message on a tape recorder so that you may check points that might need improvement.
6. Use language that is easy to understand. Keep sentence structure simple and uncomplicated.
7. Maintain poise, stand erect, keep a pleasant expression, be relaxed, and glance around the audience to gain their attention.
8. Speak in a normal, well-modulated voice. Project your voice by directing your comments to the last row of the audience.
9. Pace your rate of speech: it should be neither too fast nor too slow.
10. Pause at appropriate points to allow your audience to absorb your train of thought.
11. Avoid mannerisms such as fumbling with papers or excessive movement of your feet, arms, or hands. If necessary, hold a card or a piece of paper to keep your hands still.
12. Adopt the right frame of mind toward your presentation—one of assurance that you are thoroughly prepared, that you know exactly what you want to say and how you want to say it, and that your message is worthy of the time and attention of your audience.

CHAPTER 5

Computers, Word Processing, and Office Equipment

What we refer to today as word processing is the result of more than a hundred years of technological evolution.

The manual typewriter, which became popular in the late 1800s, was the first major advance in writing technology in centuries and revolutionized the creation of business documents. In the 1930s the first storage mechanism was introduced: a roll of punched paper recorded all the keystrokes used to type a document, and the roll could then be used to produce multiple copies of the same document automatically. Later, it became possible to operate more than one of the paper readers at a time so that text could be merged from different sources. In the 1960s paper tape gave way to the newly developed magnetic tape, which provided much more storage capability and had the added advantage of being reusable. Magnetic tape cartridges (and later magnetic cards) could be erased and reused and were sturdier and easier to handle than paper.

In the 1970s word processing came into its own. The first video-display systems were introduced, allowing the typist to correct or revise material immediately and to view several lines of text on-screen before they were printed. Even with its limited text display, the system increased accuracy and productivity dramatically. At about the same time, magnetic tape and cards were replaced by the floppy diskette, which greatly increased storage capacity and retrieval speed.

Word processing has now evolved into a technologically advanced function that can no longer fairly be called "typing." Word processing is an integral part of almost every office environment, producing print materials ranging from routine memorandums to annual reports. It is performed by managers as well as secretaries, and it exists both as an independent function and as a capability within other computerized tasks such as spreadsheet development. The software advances discussed later in this chapter, coupled with the use of laser printers, have blurred the line between word processing and the newer technology called desktop publishing. (See Chapter 10 for a discussion of desktop publishing.)

We can only speculate on what the future of word processing will be. Voice-driven systems that require no keyboard already exist in prototype form, and pen-based computing is another significant new technology. Other input systems will certainly be developed, as will delivery systems that take the word-processed output beyond the printer. The development of word processing is still in its early stages.

The Work Environment

As Chapter 2 emphasized, your desk and the office space immediately adjacent to it are yours to organize for maximum efficiency and attractiveness. Your immediate work area is defined by the arms-length space surrounding your chair in all directions when you are seated at your word processor. This is the area in which you should have all the articles you work with that relate to word processing.

The open landscape design discussed in Chapter 2 has had a number of positive effects; however, it has also created some problems. The pattern of ceiling lights, which is generally a symmetrical grid for the entire office space, may have no relation to where individual desks and workstations are placed. As a result, you may find that your overhead light is off to the side, while your neighbor may get no direct light at all. To compensate, additional light is often needed, either permanently or just for specific tasks.

Noise is another problem that the open landscape can magnify. Without doors to close, the sound of several impact printers operating all at once can be distracting, if not harmful. If you are sensitive to the noise, there are printer enclosures on the market for virtually every make and model. Laser printers, which are fast replacing impact printers, are almost silent and are ideally suited to the open environment.

In older offices the L-shaped desk arrangement was popular. It consisted of a basic desk and a smaller and somewhat lower typing table attached to the desk at a 90-degree angle. Today, because so many secretaries are working with word processors or computers made up of several component parts, an entire industry has developed to supply customized computer furniture to organize all these parts. The furniture ranges from movable carts, which hold all the devices associated with a computer or word processor, to complete modular systems, which encompass desks, storage shelves, and movable partitions. (In many offices, unfortunately, furnishings have not caught up with technology and the equipment often must be set down wherever it fits.)

For maximum convenience, you should be able to sit at your word-processing equipment and comfortably reach your telephone, your diskettes, and your printer, while still having an accessible flat surface on which to open a manual or other reference book. (If you are connected to a local area network, in which several people share the use of a centralized printer, you will not have to accommodate a printer in your immediate area.)

Keep all foods and liquids far away from word-processing equipment. One spill can result in enormous repair expenses and lost productivity. Avoid placing anything on top of word-processing equipment or adjacent to the many air vents that most devices have. Unblocked ventilation is essential to maintaining the safe operating temperatures required.

Word-processing and computer equipment draws a considerable amount of electricity. Check with your building services department before plugging everything into one outlet. If your screen flickers or the image periodically shrinks while you are working, you may be overloading a circuit.

Ergonomics   As office operations have become increasingly automated, concern for the effects all this automation has on the humans who use it has spawned a new discipline: *ergonomics,* the study of the effects of the physical design of equipment on the physical and emotional well-being of its users. An engineer or designer schooled in ergonomics may be as much concerned with the size and shape of an on/off switch as with whether or not the switch actually works. Can it be reached without the user having to stretch, bend, or risk injury? Is it too large or small to be used conveniently? Is it clearly labeled?

Ergonomics may be thought of as having evolved from the time and motion studies that were popular earlier in the century. However, that movement merely concerned itself with productivity from the employer's standpoint, and we are now looking at office equipment and design from the user's standpoint. Once regarded as an esoteric field, ergonomics has now moved into the mainstream of design. The European Community, for example, established uniform rules in 1992 which made employers responsible for removing health risks from the workplace and required them to be knowledgeable about advances in workstation design.

Specialists in ergonomics have studied the effects of all the various word-processing devices and accessories, examining everything from the color of the components to the shape of the chair. You can profit from the considerable body of knowledge that now exists when selecting or recommending products for your office.

Computer Hardware

Word processing may be performed on either of two types of equipment: a dedicated word processor or a microcomputer, sometimes referred to as a personal computer (PC) even when used only in an office for business purposes.

A *dedicated word processor* is a system designed and sold for one primary application: word processing. A *microcomputer,* on the other hand, is a multifunction system that can be used for a variety of applications depending on the type of software that is installed. Because of their limitations, dedicated word processors are becoming less common; however, the two systems are equally efficient for basic word processing, and in fact they do not differ much in design. For the most part, the description of computer hardware in this chapter applies equally to dedicated word processors and microcomputers.

The computer is a multicomponent system made up of four primary parts:

1. The *computer* itself, which is made up of boards and circuits that process information.
2. The *keyboard,* which is used to enter and format text.
3. The *monitor,* which displays the entered text.
4. The *printer,* which prints the final text on paper.

See the illustration in Fig. 5.1.

Fig. 5.1   Desktop Computer

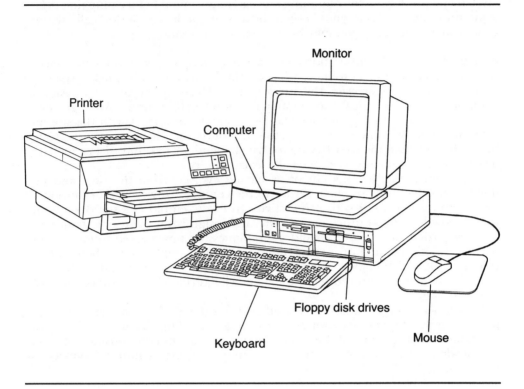

THE COMPUTER

The computer itself depends on a series of *chips*, integrated circuits made from silicon that store and process information. Chips are attached to *boards* inside the computer, which can be removed and replaced only by technicians. The most important board is called the *system board* or *motherboard,* and the most important chip on the system board is the *central processing unit,* or *CPU*. The CPU is the computer's "traffic cop," controlling all the information flowing between the keyboard, the computer itself, the printer, and various other devices you may have connected.

Computer language   A computer does not understand language in the same way that we do. Its language consists of electrical impulses, and it only understands two things: high-voltage impulses and low-voltage impulses. Some people refer to this as "the switch" being "on" or "off." Ultimately, everything must be converted to a pattern of electrical impulses in order for the computer to understand it.

Each electrical impulse is called a *bit,* short for *binary digit.* In the computer's terms, the number 1 represents the switch being on and the number 0 represents the switch being off. Because there are only two possibilities, this is referred to as a *binary system.*

The computer industry has a standardized code in which each keyboard character—every letter, number, and symbol—is represented by a fixed pattern of eight bits, called a *byte.* The code, known as the American Standard Code for Information Interchange, or ASCII (pronounced "as-key"), is recognized and accepted by hardware and software manufacturers. ASCII code actually uses only seven bits to represent a character; the eighth bit may be used for some other purpose by the hardware or software, or it may be ignored. Even so, the code is still described as using eight bits. Here, for example, is the word "HELLO" in ASCII code:

   1001000   1000101   1001100   1001100   1001111

Incidentally, the codes would be different for lowercase letters.

    Each time you press a key on a keyboard, you are sending one byte of electrical impulses to the computer, and the computer is decoding it to display the desired character on the screen.

Computer memory   The computer has two kinds of memory: ROM and RAM. ROM, or *read-only memory,* contains the computer's own internal operating instructions. The computer "reads," or uses, the information in ROM to run itself. The user has no access to anything stored in ROM. RAM, or *random-access memory,* is a temporary work space in which the computer runs your word-processing program and other applications. Unlike ROM, which is permanent memory, anything in RAM is wiped out as soon as you turn off the computer (or experience a power outage). Think of RAM as a desk where you can spread out your work each day but must clean it up at night before leaving.

    Memory, in the computer's terms, is measured in thousands or millions of bytes. A thousand bytes is a *kilobyte,* or K for short. A million bytes is a *megabyte* (Mg). Actually, because of the eight-bit ASCII code, kilobytes and megabytes are multiples of eight, so a kilobyte is really 1,024 bytes, and a megabyte is really 1,048,576 bytes. Here are some common RAM memory capacities. The word equivalents are based on an average of five characters per word.

RAM	*Equivalent to approximately:*
512K	512,000 characters, or 102,400 words
1Mg	1,024,000 characters, or 204,800 words
4Mg	4,096,000 characters, or 819,200 words
10Mg	10,240,000 characters, or 2,048,000 words

Storage   Your word processor would not be of much use if you could not store the documents that you prepare, and reprint or edit them later on. Information is permanently stored on disks, which are magnetized to record the bits making up your document. Computers use two types of disk: *floppy disks,* which are portable, and *hard disks,* which are usually built into the computer itself.

    Floppy disks, so named because they are generally flexible enough to bend, are thin plastic disks. Originally, all floppy disks were 8″ in diameter; today, the standard sizes are 5¼″ and 3½″. The smaller 3½″ disk is sealed in a thicker casing which does not really bend; however, all portable disks are referred to as floppy disks, floppies, or simply diskettes.

    The floppy disk is inserted through a slot into a device called a *disk drive,* which spins the disk and is able to copy information from it (called "reading" the disk) or record new information on it (called "writing to" the disk).

    Information is stored on the disk in sectors, or rings. The disk drive can access any part of the disk without having to go through it sequentially. This is important because information may be stored on a disk in random locations, and the computer must reassemble the information quickly before displaying it on your screen.

Straight out of the box, a floppy disk will fit into any word processor or computer with the correct size of disk drive (3½″ or 5¼″). But it will not work until a simple step, called *formatting*, is carried out. Formatting, which takes only about a minute, customizes the disk for the particular brand of machine in which it will be used. The disk can later be reformatted for use in another computer, but the process erases anything stored on it; be very careful not to reformat a disk unless you are willing to lose all the data on it. Hard disks also need to be formatted, but this is normally done when they are installed in the computer and never again.

Floppy disks require care in handling. They should not be exposed to excessive heat or cold. (Do not leave them in your car, for instance, but they will be safe in the office even if the air-conditioning or heating is turned off over the weekend.) Never touch the surface of the disk, and do not bend it or attach paper clips or anything similar. Use only felt-tip pens when writing on the label. Do not drop it or drop objects on top of it, and avoid forcing it into a disk drive if it will not go in easily. Most important, since the data on the disk is magnetized, keep the disk away from magnets or magnetic fields—for example, telephones—which could scramble the data.

As mentioned, most computers also contain a permanently installed hard disk. The hard disk serves much the same purpose as a floppy disk but stores a great deal more data. Once considered a luxury, hard disks are now generally regarded as essential for storing application programs and the files created with them.

The storage capacity of disks is expressed, as discussed earlier, in kilobytes (K) and megabytes (Mg). Here are some sample storage capacities for the various disks, including the newer high-density (HD) floppy disks:

Disk Type	Storage	Equivalent
3½″ floppy	720K	737,280 bytes or 147,456 words
3½″ HD floppy	1.44Mg	1,474,560 bytes or 294,912 words
5¼″ floppy	360K	368,640 bytes or 73,728 words
5¼″ HD floppy	1.2Mg	1,228,800 bytes or 245,760 words
Hard disk	40Mg	40,960,000 bytes or 8,192,000 words
Hard disk	100Mg	102,400,000 bytes or 20,480,000 words

As hard disks fill up, files tend to become fragmented—that is, broken up and stored on different parts of the disk—which may result in a loss of performance. Special defragmenting software will read and rewrite the entire disk, putting the files back together.

THE KEYBOARD

The keyboard can be detached from the computer itself. The cable should be long enough to allow you to position the keyboard for your maximum comfort and convenience.

There are as many keyboard designs as there are manufacturers of word-processing equipment, but they all have some basic things in common.

The central part of the keyboard, containing the alphabet letter keys, is essentially the same as the traditional typewriter keyboard. In addition, most computer keyboards also have the following:

Cursor control keys These keys, labeled with arrows pointing up, down, left, and right, are used to move the cursor around on the screen. The cursor position represents the precise location where anything you type will appear.

Numeric keypad Most keyboards include a separate section for typing numbers. The keypad, usually placed at the side of the keyboard, looks like a calculator and may have keys allowing for computation as well as input of numbers. (For a complete discussion of how to use the numeric keypad, see Chapter 14.)

Function keys These keys, usually labeled F1 through F10 or higher, are designated to perform different functions for each software program. For example, in one program F3 may be the key that underlines text, while in another program F3 may be used to call up a file from memory. Function keys may appear along the top of the keyboard or at the side.

A typical keyboard is illustrated in Fig. 5.2.

Fig. 5.2 Computer Keyboard

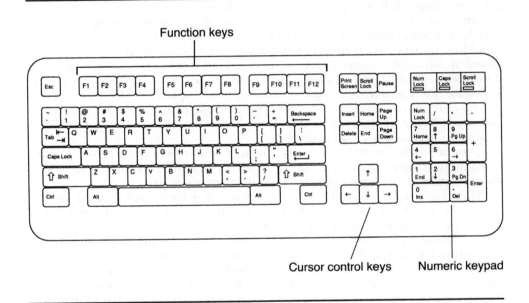

When placed on desktops as they usually are, computer keyboards are generally 3–5″ too high for sustained typing. A special keyboard drawer, which replaces the center drawer of a desk, lowers the keyboard to a more comfortable height and stores it out of the way when not in use.

THE MONITOR

There is much more variation in the types and capabilities of monitors than of keyboards. Your three primary ergonomic concerns about monitors should be ease of positioning adjustment, clarity of image, and absence of glare.

In the early days of word-processing, monitors were fixed in place, and users had to accommodate themselves to the equipment. Today, with an enormous range of monitors available, the user can readily choose a model on which adjustments for convenience and safety can easily be made.

Many monitors have tilt-and-swivel bases that enable you to select the viewing angle you find most comfortable. You may also want a monitor stand to raise the height of the screen so as to avoid neck fatigue.

If space is limited on your desk or if you do not use the monitor all day long, you may want to purchase a monitor arm. A monitor arm suspends the monitor in the air so that it can be raised, lowered, tilted, and swiveled, and pushed out of the way when not in use.

Eyestrain is one of the most common complaints of office workers who spend hours in front of a monitor each day. Monitors vary widely in their ability to deliver a sharp image and to display it without flickering. The screen image is made up of dots, or *pixels,* in much the same way that letters on a dot-matrix printer are made up of dots. The more pixels in the display, the greater clarity you can expect.

Another factor in the screen's comfort level is the color. For example, some people who use a monochrome (one-color) monitor may find that a green or amber display is easier on the eyes than a black-and-white screen. If you have a color monitor, your word-processing program may give you options for text and background display colors. Even if it does not, the program may use different colors to signify different purposes or operations.

Glare from the screen is a problem you can generally handle easily. At the very least, your monitor should have both brightness and contrast controls. You should not have direct sunlight either behind or in front of you when you are seated at the word processor; try to arrange your workstation so that any windows are at angles to you and have blinds or curtains. You can also purchase an anti-glare filter, which fits directly over the screen display.

The effect of radiation coming from computer screens is a controversial topic and a subject of ongoing study. Many people like to use an anti-radiation filter, which also fits easily over the screen.

If you wear glasses, tell your eye doctor that you are working regularly with a video monitor, even if you are not yet experiencing any eyestrain. Your doctor may prescribe tinted lenses or offer special advice about eye care.

When purchasing a monitor, bear in mind that cheap color monitors frequently sold with inexpensive systems display text poorly. A good monitor is a critical part of a word-processing system.

Most monitors will display up to 80 characters, or columns, across the screen. With proportional spacing, in which each character occupies a different amount of space, that number may be smaller. The length of the display varies even more. Most monitors display about half of a standard 11″ page at once; full-page displays are also available, but are more likely to be used for desktop-publishing applications.

Another factor to consider is whether or not the monitor can display graphics. Most word-processing programs allow you to merge graphics and text, but this requires a compatible monitor.

THE PRINTER

The two most common types of printer that can be used with the word processor are impact printers and laser printers. You will probably find both kinds in use in most offices; you may even have both connected to your computer and be able to switch back and forth between them for different purposes.

Impact or dot-matrix printers   The impact or dot-matrix printer prints each character by selecting an arrangement of pins which then strike through an inked ribbon onto the paper. The pin pattern thus resembles the pattern of dots or pixels that makes up each character on your monitor. The greater the number of pins, the higher the quality of the image produced. The most common dot-matrix printers are the 9-pin and 24-pin printers. The better-quality 24-pin printers are sometimes described by their manufacturers as "letter quality" or "near-letter quality." These terms refer to how closely a character produced by the printer resembles one produced by a good electronic typewriter that creates an impression by means of a solid piece of type rather than just a pattern of dots. Printers usually can also be set to produce "draft quality" printing when speed rather than quality is desired.

Dot-matrix printers became popular for a number of reasons. For one thing, they are relatively fast: a dot-matrix printer can print as many as 300 characters per second. And since they work by making impressions, they can print through multilayered forms. They are also flexible enough to handle both standard 8½" paper and 14"-wide computer printouts.

Dot-matrix printers typically use pin-feed paper, which is advanced through the machine by a tractor mechanism. The paper attaches to the tractor by a series of holes along the sides of the sheets; the holes are part of a perforated strip, which can be easily removed after printing. (Cartons of 8½" continuous-form paper are often labeled 9½" because the perforated strip on each side is ½" wide.) Adjusting the paper so that it moves evenly can be tricky, and jams are not unusual, but the dot-matrix printer can be an economical and reliable office workhorse. Many letter quality and near-letter quality printers also offer a single-sheet bypass so that letterhead and envelopes can be fed through without having to remove the continuous-form sheets from the tractor.

Printers do not simply accept one character at a time from the computer and print it; they accept more than they can print at once and store them in temporary memory. As the characters in memory are printed, more are accepted. Dot-matrix printers vary in the amount of memory they have. You may notice that the printer "takes control" of your computer and its memory when printing a document and does not allow it to do anything else.

Laser printers   While a good dot-matrix printer is suitable for most basic office tasks, many companies now rely mainly on the laser printer. Prices have dropped considerably, making the laser printer affordable for small companies and individual business owners.

The laser printer is much like a photocopier. Toner (similar to ink) is housed in a cartridge inside the printer, and electric charges created by the laser beam on the paper attract the toner. Characters are printed in a pattern of dots, but the dots are smaller and in greater density than those produced by a dot-matrix printer—usually 300 dots per inch (DPI). The effect is very close to that of professional typesetting; in fact, many manufacturers talk about "near-typeset quality" when describing the output of their laser printers.

The speed of a laser printer is expressed in the number of pages it can produce per minute. A speed of six to eight pages per minute is common, although expensive lasers can operate much faster. The rated speed of a laser printer describes its performance once it has begun printing multiple copies; the waiting time for the first copy depends to some extent on how full the page is and whether it is straight text or text mixed with graphics.

There are a few drawbacks to laser printers. They can only print one page at a time—no multiple forms—and they cannot accept the oversized paper that a dot-matrix printer can handle. Paper is loaded into cassettes, each of which holds only one size of paper at a time. However, the printer may accommodate two cassettes with a different size in each and may also allow for manual feed of an odd-sized sheet without reloading the cassette. Laser printers also tend to have trouble feeding envelopes smoothly. However, they are becoming more versatile as laser-compatible products flood the market. Adhesive labels that can withstand the heat of the laser are now available, and some manufacturers are offering laser envelopes that feed smoothly through the printer. Other laser products include sheets of rotary address cards, index cards, postcards, and multicolored paper for brochures and mailers.

Some of the most innovative products for the laser printer are directly related to the growth of desktop publishing. In fact, it is the growth of desktop publishing, in which text and graphics are merged, which is largely responsible for the popularity of the laser printer. See Chapter 10 for a discussion of desktop publishing.

The other common type of nonimpact printer is the ink-jet printer, discussed later in this chapter under "Portable Computers."

OTHER HARDWARE

All of the devices that connect to the computer are considered "peripherals." The keyboard, monitor, and printer are the standard peripherals in any word-processing configuration, but there are also a few other devices that may be a part of your system.

The Mouse   The mouse is basically a pointing device. Moving the mouse causes a small, typically arrow- or bar-shaped pointer to make corresponding movements on the computer screen. Using the mouse with appropriate software makes it possible to perform many routine computing tasks more easily and quickly than can be done with just a keyboard. For example, it may be possible to open and close programs and files with a mouse simply by pointing to a small picture (called an *icon*) on the screen and clicking the mouse's button.

Many word-processing programs now allow for at least some use of the mouse, with more and more being adapted to make the mouse useful for almost any task other than typing text. One common use of the mouse is to move the cursor to different places in the text simply by pointing to the desired position and clicking the mouse's button. This is usually much faster than using the arrow keys on the keyboard. The mouse can also be used to select individual words, sentences, and blocks of text to be moved, deleted, or otherwise edited. Many sophisticated programs make it possible to use the mouse for quickly making changes in a document's format—for example, resetting margins and tab stops, choosing a different typeface, or altering the spacing between lines and paragraphs. These are only a few of the functions a mouse can perform.

Some experienced typists find it hard to get used to the mouse because they dislike taking their hands away from the keyboard. Programs designed for use with a mouse do include alternative keyboard methods for the mouse's functions, so it is usually possible to avoid the mouse altogether if you are so inclined. If you spend some time learning to use the mouse, however, you will likely come to feel that it is indispensable for certain tasks.

The modem   A modem enables you to transmit data from one computer to another over ordinary telephone lines. It converts the computer's digital language into the telephone's analog language for transmission. At the other end, a receiving modem converts it back to a digital signal. This is where the modem's name comes from: it is a device that *mo*dulates and *dem*odulates data.

There are two forms of modem: the *internal modem,* a board that fits into a slot in the computer, and the *external modem,* a small box that attaches to the computer cable.

Modems are rated according to the speed at which they transmit data. The measurement is in bits per second, or BPS, sometimes also referred to as the *baud rate*. Here are some common modem speeds:

Modem Speed	Equivalent
1200 BPS	9,000 characters, or 1,800 words per minute
2400 BPS	18,000 characters, or 3,600 words per minute
9600 BPS	72,000 characters, or 14,400 words per minute

In the context of word processing, modems are frequently used to exchange text files between computers. It is not unusual for one person to draft a document, transmit it electronically to someone else who may edit or comment on it, and then return the file to the originator for more work. The electronic transmission may only take seconds, and is far more convenient and economical than exchanging paper, especially across long distances.

There are a number of factors to consider in using modems to exchange files.

1. In addition to word-processing software, both the sender and the receiver must have communications software to drive the modem.

2. The sender and receiver may also need to be using the same word-processing software, so that files loaded at either end preserve the same formatting characteristics (underlines, boldface, type fonts, and so forth). Otherwise, you may have to exchange "text-only" files.

3. Outside third-party vendors, such as electronic mail services, will generally provide for hardware compatibility so that entirely different computers or word processors can exchange files with each other. Differences in software, however, may continue to be a problem. If both parties are transmitting in-house through a local area network (LAN), there should be no problems of hardware or software compatibility.

Every improvement in hardware and software requires a corresponding improvement in transmission capability. If you have a modem, consult your user manual for setup and operating instructions, and do not be surprised or discouraged if you find that you need some technical assistance from the vendor to make it work.

PORTABLE COMPUTERS

Whereas the earliest computers occupied entire rooms, today's word processor or microcomputer is a desktop appliance. With a little effort, you can pick it up and move it around, but it is still hardly portable. Not until the arrival of laptop and notebook computers did true portability become a reality.

The first portable computer was the *laptop computer*—a battery-powered computer, keyboard, and monitor packaged in a briefcase-sized unit that weighed about 20 pounds. The laptop computer soon led to the *notebook computer*, a smaller and lighter version weighing as little as four to six pounds. Advances in the design of chips were responsible for this extraordinary reduction in size. Laptop and notebook computers are available with hard disks, fax modems, and built-in mouse devices, as well as a full range of external devices such as modems, battery chargers, and portable disk drives. They require separate printers, but many vendors offer portable printers as well. The ink-jet printer, which sprays ink on paper, producing a sharper image than those produced by dot-matrix printers, exists in portable as well as nonportable models.

Laptop and notebook computers have tended to be less powerful and more expensive than microcomputers, but with continuing rapid development and cost reduction they can be expected to match the microcomputer soon in both respects.

Computer Supplies and Accessories

SUPPLIES

In many offices, supplies are stored centrally and can only be requisitioned one item at a time as needed. Since word-processing equipment uses a considerable amount of consumable supplies, they should be easily accessible. An adequate supply of blank diskettes is essential, as are labels for them. Extra paper should always be handy for the printer. Individual cut sheets, normally packaged in reams of 500, are easily stored; pin-feed paper for printers with tractors is usually boxed in units of 1000 sheets or more, but the sheets are perforated and any quantity can be easily removed from a large box and stored in a desk drawer. Extra printer ribbons or toner cartridges should also be at hand, especially if your office is given to last-minute rush jobs.

ACCESSORIES

In addition to all the peripheral devices that make up the basic word processor or computer, a range of inexpensive accessories is available to add to your comfort and convenience. Most of these can be purchased at a local computer store or through mail-order catalogs. In a large organization, your purchasing department should be able to help you obtain any of them.

Wrist supports   These useful devices attach to your keyboard and provide a lightweight, comfortable resting place for your hands during prolonged periods of keyboarding. The supports enable you to keep your wrists straight and prevent the fatigue you might otherwise experience when working on long documents. They can also help prevent carpal-tunnel syndrome, an ailment common among long-term users of word processors.

Footrests   Experts on office stress recommend that your knees be higher than your hips when sitting at a keyboard for any length of time. To accomplish this, use a footrest that raises your feet a few inches and lets you adjust the angle of your feet. The footrest reduces the strain on your lower back and aids the circulation in your lower legs.

Copy holder   The tabletop copy stand, familiar in offices for decades, has been improved on by the movable copy holder, which occupies no desk space at all. This device attaches to your desk or to the monitor itself and holds your copy by a clip. It can be raised, lowered, and swiveled so that the copy you are working from is in the most convenient location for you, and can be removed or pushed out of the way when not in use.

Mouse pad   If your word processor or computer uses a mouse, you will want a mouse pad for it. This rubberized pad prevents the mouse from scratching your desk, allows it to move more smoothly, and helps to keep it clean. It also serves to stake out the mouse's territory on the work surface so that it will not tend to be overwhelmed by clutter. Basic mouse pads cost only a few dollars. They can also be purchased with a built-in wrist support.

Power strip   A power strip is basically a heavy-duty extension cord with enough outlets to accommodate all the plugs in your system. The power strip provides two additional features as well. First, it has an on/off switch that controls all the outlets at once, so that you can leave your computer, monitor, and printer permanently switched on and control them through the strip. Some power strips also serve as surge suppressors. Electronic equipment is susceptible to damage from sudden increases in electrical power called "surges" or "spikes," and a surge suppressor will prevent such damage under most circumstances.

Power-backup system   The opposite problem, a loss of power, may be prevented by a power-backup system, which provides emergency power for a period of time ranging from 10 minutes to an hour or more. These systems are considerably more expensive than power strips, and purchasing one may require official approval. Even a momentary power outage can wipe out a considerable amount of work, so if you work in a location where power outages are common you may want to recommend the purchase of a backup system.

Keyboard cover   Word-processing equipment can be susceptible to environmental hazards such as dust particles. The most vulnerable device is your keyboard, because it has so many openings in which dust can accumulate. Fortunately, keyboards tend to be well made, and malfunctions due to dust are not as common as one might assume. Even so, you can contribute to the longevity of these devices by using inexpensive plastic keyboard covers.

Computer tool kit   You may also want to purchase a computer tool kit. These kits include a small vacuum for cleaning keyboards and printers, along with small screwdrivers and other tools for tightening and loosening the cables that connect your devices.

Floor mat   Walking across a carpeted floor, or even just sitting down in an upholstered chair, can cause you to pick up enough static electricity to damage your computer if that is the next thing you touch. Antistatic carpeting is available, but it is costly and not practical if your office is already carpeted. A static-control floor mat under your chair is a convenient and inexpensive alternative. Floor mats also provide a smoother surface for chairs to glide around on, preventing the accidental tipping that can occur if the wheels do not turn smoothly against the carpet.

Chairs   Probably no office furnishing has received as much attention as the chair. Computer stores and catalogs are filled with "ergonomically correct" chairs, some of which look like conventional office chairs while others have strange, futuristic designs. What makes a chair comfortable? According to the experts, it should have these characteristics:

1. It should have an adjustable back support that accomplishes two purposes. First, the lumbar vertebrae at the base of your spine should be supported at all times, no matter how you move around in the chair. Second, your upper back should be supported just below the shoulders.
2. The front edge of the seat should be rounded down (in a so-called waterfall) so that circulation in the thighs is not restricted.
3. The seat height should be adjustable, either manually or by means of a pneumatic cylinder in the post between the seat and the base. Automatic controls should be conveniently accessible from the sitting position. (Chairs on which the seat height is adjusted manually may need to be turned over and the base unscrewed until it extends to the desired height, a cumbersome task that may even require two people.)

4. The chair should both swivel and recline to allow for natural body movements and rest periods, and the angle at which it reclines should be easily
   adjustable.
5. For safety, the chair base should have five radial legs rather than four. This
   design makes the chair sturdier and less likely to tip when moved. The cast-
   ers should turn smoothly.

No matter how comfortable your chair is, do not sit in it all day! Give yourself
frequent rest periods, especially if you are working on a long document and find
yourself in the same position for extended periods of time.

Cables   Because most word processors consist of a collection of components and
devices, or "peripherals," you may find yourself with a thick tangle of connecting
cables and power cords. Besides being unsightly, they may be safety hazards if
not properly stored.

Your office may have modular furniture designed specifically for computers.
This type of furniture typically has features that will largely solve the problem.
The movable partitions that function as walls for each workstation usually contain channels, called "raceways," at the bottom of each panel. Cables fit into the
raceways and are routed to the power source, which may be on the floor, in a
wall, or even overhead behind a suspended ceiling. Desk surfaces may have large
holes at the back through which connecting cables can be run between the various devices in your office. Together, these features will keep most cables safely
stored and out of the way.

If you do not have furniture designed for computers, try to run cables behind
equipment where they are less likely to be accidentally pulled or twisted. Avoid
kinking or crimping the cables, which may affect the smooth operation of the
equipment, and do not put anything down on top of them. You may want to
purchase a supply of self-adhesive plastic cable hooks, which attach to any surface and hold a group of cables together neatly.

If you must run cables across the floor to a power source, try to keep them
close to a wall and away from foot traffic. Consider covering them with an insu-
lated, adhesive cord-cover which will prevent anyone from tripping on them
while guarding the cables from traffic damage.

Computer Software

While some dedicated word processors have their own built-in software, the
trend is toward using off-the-shelf, commercially available software packages
(often referred to as COTS—Commercial Off-The-Shelf—software). These
programs range from the very basic to the highly complex. Most programs offer
more features than any one user would ever need. Prices range widely depending on the programs' sophistication. A *site license*—essentially, a discount for
multiple purchases—may be available if your organization wants many people to
be able to use the same program.

Basically, a word-processing software program consists of one or more disks
containing the program itself. When purchasing, you may have to specify
whether you need 3½″ or 5¼″ disks, although some vendors automatically supply both versions. There will also be a user manual that explains how to use the
program, and possibly separate installation manuals, reference manuals, or even
tutorial manuals as well.

There may also be a licensing agreement that stipulates your responsibilities as a user of the software. Because software files are easily copied from one disk to another, manufacturers are seriously concerned about copyright infringement through the proliferation of "pirated" software. (Recall that software programs are copyrighted in the same way that printed material is.) As a defense, many programs are copy-protected; that is, the files contain an internal program to prevent duplication. Even so, those who would violate the copyright protection of software developers are sometimes able to override those programs and duplicate the files. Protect yourself and your organization from legal problems by avoiding any involvement with pirated software.

The problems related to computer viruses have been well publicized. To minimize the possibility of virus damage, use only commercial software and back up your work systematically. If you think a virus may have penetrated your system, you can use special virus-detection software to locate it.

GETTING STARTED

Some software programs can be run from the original floppy disks, but most programs will need to be installed on the hard disk of a computer. Your manual will contain instructions for installing the program. You may have to copy each individual file, or the program may itself include a built-in installation program that does most of the work for you. Either way, you should not find this a difficult task. You will be instructed to make a set of backup disks first, in case the original disks are lost or damaged. Programs that are copy-protected normally allow you to make one set of backup disks, but no more.

THE WORD-PROCESSING SCREEN

While every program uses different terminology and screen layout, they all share some things in common. In addition to displaying the text that you type, the screen provides certain status information about the document. This information may include any of the following:

- File name
- Length of file, usually in characters
- Page and line on which you are currently working
- Page settings: tabs, margins, etc.
- Current mode (insert or overstrike)

If the program is designed for use with a menu, there may be a menu bar across the top of the screen from which selections can be made by pointing and clicking the mouse's button.

Most full-featured programs make use of the function keys across the top or side of the keyboard to perform certain tasks. Since there are generally more tasks to designate than there are function keys, you may need to use a combination of keys. For example, pressing the Control key (usually labeled "Ctrl") and F6 simultaneously may save a file, while F6 by itself may have an entirely different function. Software programs often include a plastic template that fits on the keyboard and identifies the function of each function key.

STARTING A DOCUMENT

When you begin a new document, the cursor will be in the first position of the document, indicating where the first character you type will appear. The cursor may be a fixed or blinking line positioned either just below or just in front of the next character, or a highlighted box that fully surrounds the character.

The cursor moves with the text as you type. As you progress through the document, you will have occasion to go back and forth making changes; to make those changes, you will need to put the cursor in the right spot. Depending on the program, you may be able to move the cursor in several ways.

1. By using the four arrow keys on the keyboard you can move the cursor up, down, left, or right. Though the cursor normally moves only one position at a time, by holding the key down you may move it rapidly from one end of a line to the other or from the top to the bottom of the page.
2. More sophisticated programs allow you to move the cursor to a specific location with just one or two keystrokes, usually some combination of the Control key and an arrow or function key. You may choose to move to the end of a line (forward or backward), to the start or end of the paragraph, or forward or backward a specified number of characters, words, or pages.
3. The keyboard's Home and End keys, usually located above the arrow keys, can also be used to move the cursor quickly to the beginning ("home") or end of a line and often to make larger movements (such as to the beginning or end of a document) when used in combination with other keys.
4. As mentioned earlier, mouse-driven programs let you move the cursor by simply pointing to the desired location on the screen and clicking the mouse button. This is usually faster than using the keyboard.

Remember that most monitors display somewhat less than a full page at a time. (Word-processing programs generally include a Print Preview feature, however, which allows you to view full pages in a reduced graphics mode before printing.) Full-page monitors are available but are used primarily for desktop publishing. To move around in a lengthy document, you may find it easier to change pages than to move the cursor. Most keyboards contain Page Up and Page Down keys which have the effect of electronically turning the page. Your software may also offer a "scrolling" feature, which lets you move the text continuously up or down until you have located the spot you are looking for, by means of a series of keystrokes or by using the mouse.

BASIC WORD-PROCESSING OPERATIONS

Until you need to add, subtract, or change anything, using a word-processing program is just like typing—you hit a key and the letter or character appears. However, unlike a character typed on paper, the screen display can be changed instantly—and as often as you like—until you are ready to print. Since the finished document is stored on a disk, it can also be kept for editing at a later date and then reprinted.

The word processor performs an automatic carriage return at the end of each line. If you are typing a word with more characters than the line has room for, the program will move the entire word to the beginning of the next line. This feature, called *wordwrap,* is standard with all programs. (What actually happens is that the program looks for a space indicating a break between words. If it runs out of room on a line before the next space is keyed, it treats everything since the last space as a word and moves it to the next line as a unit.) Because of wordwrap, the Return or Enter key on your keyboard is needed only to begin a new line when the previous line ended before reaching the right margin (such as when starting a new paragraph).

The program may also offer an automatic hyphenation feature, in which long words are hyphenated according to standard rules rather than moved in full to the next line.

Word processors generally allow you both to *overstrike*—that is, type over the existing text, automatically deleting it as you do so—and to *insert*—that is, add text *without* losing what is already there. Which of these modes you are in at a given moment may appear at the top or bottom of the screen.

In general, to use any text-editing feature of the program you must perform two steps.

First, identify the text to be affected, usually by *highlighting* it on the screen. Highlighted text will appear either the opposite of its normal color or with a different-colored background surrounding it. Your programs may refer to highlighting as *selecting* or *blocking* the text. There are a number of ways to accomplish it, depending on your software. One method is to use the mouse, holding down one of the buttons and dragging the pointer on the screen across the desired text. Another method requires pressing a function key to start the highlighting process, using the arrow keys to extend it across the desired text, and pressing another key to end the process.

Second, perform the desired operation on the highlighted text, either with a function key, a menu selection, or by typing a special command. Again, the method depends on your program. There is usually a key you can press if you change your mind about an operation you have started. Typically, it is the Escape key (usually labeled "Esc"), but the software program may assign another key instead.

PAGE-SETUP OPTIONS

The following are the most common options available for setting up a page. Others may be available, depending on your program.

Page size   Since the program will automatically paginate for you, it needs to know what size of paper you will be printing on. The standard choices are $8\frac{1}{2}'' \times 11''$ and $8\frac{1}{2}'' \times 14''$.

Page orientation   Most programs will allow you to print either in vertical (sometimes called "portrait") orientation or in horizontal (sometimes called "landscape") orientation. Vertical printing—that is, on an upright page, like the one you are reading—is the normal style, but horizontal is useful for charts, graphics, and other special applications.

Single- and double-spacing   This is another fundamental option available in most programs. The choice between single- and double-spacing can be made for an entire document or for selected sections within a document.

Tabs and margins   There is always an automatic setting for tabs and margins in the program (sometimes called a *default* setting), but you can override the automatic settings for any individual document. This information is generally displayed on the screen.

Page numbering   Most programs provide automatic page numbering, and allow you to specify where the page numbers are to appear. You may also be able to choose between numbering styles, such as Arabic or Roman numerals. (See "Headers and footers," page 95.)

WORD-PROCESSING FEATURES

Some word-processing features affect page setup and appearance, while others affect the arrangement of the text itself. The following features are available in a variety of programs. A few programs may contain all of these features, but most programs will contain only some of them. When selecting a word-processing program or looking to upgrade an existing one, you may want to read through this list and note the features of most use to you, then compare each program you are considering against your list to see how well it will meet your needs.

Append   This feature permits you to take text from one file and add it to another file.

Automatic file backup   Just as you should always back up your files to protect against accidental damage or loss, you should also have a system for saving the previous version of any file you have revised, in case it becomes necessary to have access to the earlier version. Some programs offer a system for automatically saving the previous version.

Boldface   Characters and words can be printed in boldface type for emphasis or to serve as a heading.

Boxes   The ability to create boxes around text, especially when combined with the ability to create horizontal and vertical lines, enables you to design charts, tables, attractive headings, and much else. Boxes can usually be plain, drop-shadowed, or filled with various degrees of shading.

Capitalization   Many programs allow you to select and automatically capitalize any text you have already entered in lowercase. You may also specify that it be set in SMALL CAPITALS.

Centering   Any word, line, or paragraph can be automatically centered between the margins of the document. This is useful for headings, quotations, or any other material that should stand out from the main body of the text.

Columns   This page-layout capability is useful for charts, documentation, and many other applications. It generally permits you to divide your page into a desired number of columns and specify the amount of space between the columns. The most common types of column are newspaper columns, in which the text simply wraps to the top of the next column, and side-by-side columns, in which specific items are lined up directly across from each other.

Copy   Within a file, the Copy feature allows you to select any block of text and duplicate it (see the following "Cut and paste" section). At the directory or menu level of the program, a Copy feature enables you to duplicate an entire file so that an alternative version can be created without losing the original.

Cut and paste   Also called simply *moving copy,* this fundamental feature of all word-processing programs enables you to select any amount of text and move it to another location in the document. The process requires you to "cut" the text after highlighting it, locate the new insertion point with the cursor, and then "paste" it in by using the keys designated by your software. Text that is cut is held in temporary memory until you move it. From temporary memory, it may be pasted into the document multiple times, if desired. If you choose not to paste the text back in—which amounts to deleting it—it will remain in the temporary memory only until you either turn off the computer or displace it by cutting some other text (since there is normally only room for one piece at a time in the temporary memory).

Delete   In the process of editing and correcting, you will probably be deleting text as often as you add it, so this feature is one of the most fundamental capabilities of word processing. Minor deletions are often accomplished by merely backspacing over the last text that was entered. To remove a large block of text, you will have to highlight the entire block and then use whatever method your program requires—function key, Delete key, or a menu choice—to delete it.

Find text   This search feature allows you to specify a word or phrase that occurs anywhere in the document and then have the software locate that spot for you instantly. This is a tremendous time-saver when you are trying to locate something in a long document.

Glossary   This feature enables you to create your own list of frequently used words, phrases, sentences, and paragraphs, and add them to any document with a few keystrokes. Stock sentences and paragraphs, informally known as "boilerplate," can be especially helpful when you need to modify form letters. If your program does not have a glossary function, you can get the same result by storing your boilerplate language as separate files and then loading them into any file as needed.

Graphics   In the early days of word processing, it was a text-only operation. Today, word-processing programs allow you to add, or "import," graphics created through a separate graphics program into your document. Some programs even include a library of useful images that can be placed in a document. This capability has further blurred the lines between word processing and desktop publishing.

Headers and footers   In any document you may need to display repetitive identification at the top or bottom of each page. Typical examples include the name of the document or file, the title of a presentation or proposal, or chapter or section numbers, as well as page numbers. For convenience or attractiveness, you may want these lines to appear as *headers* (that is, lines running across the top of the page, as on the page you are reading) or as *footers* (lines running across the bottom of the page), and your word-processing program should be able to accomplish this for you.

Indexing   This feature automates the job of preparing alphabetical indexes. After you have gone through a lengthy document and highlighted or identified those words or phrases that you want included in the index, the program takes over, pulling together the entire index with appropriate page numbers and formatting.

Justification   This feature controls line width and spacing. Most typed documents have lines of varying length, depending on the number of words in the line. The left margin is flush but the right margin varies, in the style usually called "ragged right." Full justification, also called "right justification," creates equal margins on both sides by inserting extra space as needed between words. Full justification has a more formal look and is desirable for certain kinds of documents, but it is harder to read because of the unequal spacing. Both types of justification are illustrated below.

Ragged right

During the past three years at the Walpole site, Ms. Pestalozzi-Holmes has coordinated the development of CyberWares' systems overview training courses, which were later implemented at our other three plants. She has also coordinated the development of a six-module vendor training program and manual; their success has been a factor in the large retail-sales gains enjoyed by CyberWares' business systems in the last 18 months.

Full justification

During the past three years at the Walpole site, Ms. Pestalozzi-Holmes has coordinated the development of CyberWares' systems overview training courses, which were later implemented at our other three plants. She has also coordinated the development of a six-module vendor training program and manual; their success has been a factor in the large retail-sales gains enjoyed by CyberWares' business systems in the last 18 months.

Kerning   Sometimes the spacing between letters in a word seems too loose or too tight. Increasing or reducing that spacing is called kerning.

Leading   The space between lines on a page is determined by the software and may vary according to the font (that is, the style or design of type) being used and the point size of the letters. The spacing between lines is called leading (pronounced "ledding"). The feature that permits you to increase or decrease the leading is primarily useful for desktop publishing.

Macros   A macro is a miniature computer program you may write by yourself to direct the software to perform one or more repetitive tasks. For example, rather than pressing a series of keys to print, close, and save a file, you could write a macro that would enable you to do all those things with one keystroke. Macros can make word processing much easier, and you should always be alert to the possibility of creating new ones.

Mail merge   The ability to automate large mailings can be one of the great benefits of a word-processing program. This feature allows you to create a document in one file and an address list in another and then merge them to produce personalized letters using each individual's name and address. You will need to embed instructions in the document file telling it where to insert the address and salutation, and you will also have to follow strict rules for formatting the address list so that the information merges correctly.

Pagination   Once you set the page size of a document, the software will automatically begin a new page whenever necessary. If you later edit the document, making it longer or shorter, the system will repaginate for you. You can override this by manually inserting a page break wherever you want one. Page breaks are normally displayed on-screen so that you can always see where they occur.

Password protection Some programs allow you to establish your own access code so that no one else can get into your files. If this is not part of your word-processing program, you can probably purchase a separate program that does the same thing.

Save Every program provides a menu choice or function key for saving a file—that is, placing it permanently on a disk for storage. In addition to saving completed files for later use, work in progress should be saved frequently—ideally, every 15 minutes—to avoid loss from power outages or other malfunctions. Some programs offer a timed Save feature, which automatically saves the file you are working on at specified intervals.

Search and replace This is the advanced version of the Find Text feature described above. In addition to searching for a word or phrase, you can specify another word or phrase to substitute for the original. You can use this feature to make global changes (that is, changes throughout a given document), such as replacing an incorrect name or title wherever it occurs without having to find and retype every instance of it.

Sorting If you ever need to produce documents with long lists that must appear in either numerical or alphabetical order, look for a sorting feature in your word-processing program. This feature allows you, for example, to select a series of entries and sort them by the first character in the entry to create an alphabetical address file or an index, thus freeing you from having to input the text in the correct order and keep rearranging things when a number or an entry changes.

Spell check This is one of the great advantages of word-processing technology, available in many software programs. The spell checker will search for every word from a given document in a built-in list of words, notify you when it fails to find it in its present spelling, and suggest alternative spellings based on near matches with other words. Some programs allow you to add words to the list—for example, technical jargon that may be unique to your industry, and proper nouns—so that all those words will be recognized as correct when you use the spell checker on later documents. One caution: Spell checkers cannot identify a word that is correctly spelled but misused. For example, both "there" and "their" would be accepted by a spell checker, although only one would be correct in the context of a particular sentence.

Styles If you prepare documents containing multiple sections, each with its own characteristics—margins, type font, italics, boldface, or underlining, for example—your word-processing program should offer you the option of creating reusable styles—that is, formats for individual sections. This feature, usually called Styles or Style Sheets, lets you define individual styles, or collections of formatting characteristics, and then apply them to different blocks of text in the document.

Superscript and subscript Various mathematical formulas and chemical notations employ characters printed slightly above or below the regular line of text, which are termed *superscripts* and *subscripts,* respectively. Trademark and registration symbols are also generally written as superscripts or subscripts. Your word-processing program should provide you with the capability to print characters in this way.

Thesaurus   Similar to the spell checker, the built-in thesaurus will look for synonyms and antonyms of any word you select.

Underline   Underlining is useful for highlighting words or phrases for emphasis or for designating subheadings in a document.

Widow and orphan control   In typesetting terminology, a widow is the last line of a paragraph that spilled over to the top of the next page. An orphan is the opposite: the first line of a paragraph at the bottom of a page, when the rest of the paragraph is on the next page. Both are considered unattractive, and many word-processing programs have a feature to prevent them. An additional line of the paragraph from the previous page is brought over to keep the widow company, and the orphan line is moved to the next page to join the rest of its "family."

WORD-PROCESSING APPLICATIONS

While correspondence is still a major word-processing task, today's secretary is involved in producing a much wider range of documents. The following are some examples.

Contracts   Law firms and legal departments of large companies are involved in producing a wide variety of contracts. Personnel departments may also be involved in preparing contracts of employment.

Financial reports   Since financial reports frequently require normal text combined with spreadsheet data (that is, accounting tables and similar material), an integrated software program that provides both spreadsheet and word-processing capability may be used.

Form letters   The availability of Mail Merge features now allows secretaries to do large mailings that in the past had to be handled by specialized mailing houses. The graphics capability of many programs also allows secretaries to design graphically interesting form letters, even if they require boxes, tear-off coupons, and nontext elements.

Instructional material   To support training programs, a large variety of handouts, quick-reference guides, and procedures manuals may be needed. The production of these materials may overlap with desktop publishing.

Presentations   Support materials and handouts are often required for distribution to participants at meetings and presentations.

Proposals   In manufacturing, marketing, and research environments, sales proposals are a common application. Office workers may also prepare proposals for studies they want to undertake or organizational changes they are recommending.

Reports   Progress reports and status reports may be required as part of a special project.

Slides and overhead transparencies   The ability to import graphics, prepare documents in landscape (horizontal) orientation, and use a variety of type fonts now enables secretaries to produce visual aids that could previously have been created only by a graphic-arts department or an outside vendor. There are also specialized presentation software programs available. This application of word processing overlaps considerably with desktop publishing; see Chapter 10 for a further discussion.

SPECIAL CHARACTER SETS

As the world gets smaller, it is no longer sufficient to be able to communicate only with others who speak the same language. The ASCII character set that represents our language in computer terms allows for either 128 characters (in a seven-bit system) or 256 characters (in an eight-bit system). This leaves enough extra spots for the alphabets of some other languages, though not for every language in which we might want to communicate. For example, the 256-character system is adequate for the Hebrew and Russian alphabets, but not for Japanese, Chinese, or Arabic.

Special software programs enable users to produce documents in many other languages. The requirements are complex. Printers must be able both to reproduce the characters of other alphabets and to follow their conventions. (Hebrew, for example, is printed from right to left.) And there must be an easy way to input those characters on standard keyboards. Some programs now allow the user to switch back and forth between languages just by a series of keystrokes.

In addition to the character sets of other languages, many word-processing programs let you reproduce common symbols, scientific and musical notation, and other graphic elements. These special character sets can be accessed by pressing a series of keys. These keys and the character sets differ from one software program to another, so check your user manual to find out which are available and how to access them. The standard ASCII extended character set is shown in Fig. 5.3.

OPTICAL CHARACTER RECOGNITION (OCR)

Recently developed computer technology enables the user to transfer existing printed material directly into a computer file. This requires a *scanner,* a device that conveys the image of the text from a piece of paper to the monitor; optical character recognition (OCR) software then converts it into a word-processing file. (A scanner's success can vary considerably depending on the size, type, and quality of reproduction of the fonts scanned.) Scanners are also used to reproduce photographs and graphic images. They are most widely used for desktop publishing (see Chapter 10).

MANAGING YOUR FILES

If you are doing high-volume word processing, you may sometimes have difficulty locating individual files unless you have a good system in place. There are several steps you can take to set up an efficient file-management system.

1. *Use a file-naming system that makes it easy to identify the file you are looking for.* If you work with an MS-DOS system, you know that file names can be up to eight characters long, followed by a dot with up to three additional characters as an extension. If you do not specify an extension, most programs will supply one of their own, usually identifying the program itself. If you do most of your work with the same program, this will not be very useful, and you will be better off supplying your own extension.

2. *Use a file-storage system that makes it easy to find files.* On an MS-DOS system, you may create subdirectories in which related files can be stored. On a Macintosh, you may create a "folder"—essentially a subdirectory—for re-

Fig. 5.3   ASCII Extended Character Set

Code	Char	Code	Char	Code	Char	Code	Char	Code	Char
0		52	4	103	g	154	Ü	205	═
1	☺	53	5	104	h	155	¢	206	╬
2	●	54	6	105	i	156	£	207	╧
3	♥	55	7	106	j	157	¥	208	╨
4	♦	56	8	107	k	158	₧	209	╤
5	♣	57	9	108	l	159	ƒ	210	╥
6	♠	58	:	109	m	160	á	211	╙
7	•	59	;	110	n	161	í	212	╘
8	▫	60	<	111	o	162	ó	213	╒
9	○	61	=	112	p	163	ú	214	╓
10	◉	62	>	113	q	164	ñ	215	╫
11	♂	63	?	114	r	165	Ñ	216	╪
12	♀	64	@	115	s	166	ª	217	┘
13	♪	65	A	116	t	167	º	218	┌
14	♫	66	B	117	u	168	¿	219	█
15	☼	67	C	118	v	169	⌐	220	▄
16	►	68	D	119	w	170	¬	221	▌
17	◄	69	E	120	x	171	½	222	▐
18	↕	70	F	121	y	172	¼	223	▀
19	‼	71	G	122	z	173	¡	224	α
20	¶	72	H	123	{	174	«	225	β
21	§	73	I	124	|	175	»	226	Γ
22	▬	74	J	125	}	176	░	227	π
23	↨	75	K	126	~	177	▒	228	Σ
24	↑	76	L	127	⌂	178	▓	229	σ
25	↓	77	M	128	Ç	179	│	230	µ
26	→	78	N	129	ü	180	┤	231	τ
27	←	79	O	130	é	181	╡	232	φ
28	∟	80	P	131	â	182	╢	233	θ
29	↔	81	Q	132	ä	183	╖	234	Ω
30	▲	82	R	133	à	184	╕	235	δ
31	▼	83	S	134	å	185	╣	236	∞
32	<space>	84	T	135	ç	186	║	237	ø
33	!	85	U	136	ê	187	╗	238	ε
34	"	86	V	137	ë	188	╝	239	∩
35	#	87	W	138	è	189	╜	240	≡
36	$	88	X	139	ï	190	╛	241	±
37	%	89	Y	140	î	191	┐	242	≥
38	&	90	Z	141	ì	192	└	243	≤
39	'	91	[	142	Ä	193	┴	244	⌠
40	(	92	\	143	Å	194	┬	245	⌡
41	)	93	]	144	É	195	├	246	÷
42	*	94	^	145	æ	196	─	247	≈
43	+	95	_	146	Æ	197	┼	248	°
44	,	96	`	147	ô	198	╞	249	●
45	-	97	a	148	ö	199	╟	250	·
46	.	98	b	149	ò	200	╚	251	√
47	/	99	c	150	û	201	╔	252	η
48	0	100	d	151	ù	202	╩	253	²
49	1	101	e	152	ÿ	203	╦	254	■
50	2	102	f	153	Ö	204	╠	255	
51	3								

lated files. They may be grouped by project, author, department, client, date, or recipient, among other possibilities.

3. *Record the file name on paper copies of the document.* This simple method is often overlooked. At the bottom of the first or last page of the document, type the full file name and subdirectory, if any, in which it is stored. You will save hours of hunting for the file when you need to edit it. One caution: There may be documents on which you would not want this information to appear. For example, if you are sending a personal letter to a customer, you might not want to display codes suggesting that the document is a form letter rather than a personalized one. Instead, handwrite the storage information on your file copy rather than including it on the original.

4. *Print a paper copy of the disk's directory.* Each time you modify anything stored on a floppy disk, print a copy of the directory and store it along with the disk. It is faster than inserting the disk and waiting for the directory to appear on the screen.

5. *Copy the file and edit the copy, not the original.* If you work for people who constantly revise things but do not want the previous versions deleted, be careful to copy the file and edit the copy, not the original. Make sure each version is dated or numbered as part of the file name.

6. *Clean up your files!* On some periodic schedule, go through your files to look for documents that you no longer need to keep. Don't wait until your hard disk is full. Having good records of your files can be especially important here. You may be able to give everyone for whom you do word processing a list of the files you have stored in their names and ask them to identify the ones that are no longer needed. This is an efficient way to handle the task and also takes the responsibility for deleting files off your shoulders.

GETTING HELP

If you use one of the more sophisticated software programs, it probably has features you do not even know about. If you have a problem, here are several resources to consider:

On-line help   Most programs have some kind of help system built into the software. A function key or a click of the mouse can display Help messages that may solve your problem. However, Help messages vary in quality from program to program and may or may not be an improvement over looking something up in the user manual.

User manual   Every word-processing software program comes with a user manual. Take the time to familiarize yourself with the organization of your manual so that you can easily find explanations when you need them. The installation disks for most software contain so-called "readme" files that contain corrections and last-minute additions to the printed manuals. You should consider marking the corrections, at least, in the manual. If the software includes a guided tutorial for first-time users, take advantage of it even if you are already somewhat familiar with the program.

Staff support   In a large organization there may be a software support group staffed by technicians who can help you with the program. If not, ask around to find out who else in the organization uses the same program. Get to know those people and set up your own resource network.

Vendor support   Most software vendors offer telephone support and may even list a telephone number in the user manual. Some vendors provide free telephone assistance indefinitely; others provide it only for a limited time after purchase of the program and then charge for it, usually on an annual contract basis.

User groups   A user group is a loose association of individuals who use the same software program. Informal user groups have sprung up around the country, sometimes promoted by individual software vendors but often organized by the users themselves. The function of the groups is to permit members to call each other with questions when help is needed. Sometimes there is a modest membership fee, and there may even be periodic meetings. Check with your software vendor for information about a user group in your area.

Purchasing Hardware and Software

There is more to purchasing hardware and software than selecting a vendor and comparing prices. Your company must assess its needs and be certain that the equipment purchased today will be useful in the future. Since computer technology is constantly advancing, it is important not to overbuy.

A reliable source of information is a computer users' group, described above. Members are constantly discussing new equipment, and you will get honest answers because the members will not be trying to sell you anything. A local computer dealer can recommend users' groups in your area, or you can call the Boston Computer Society (617-252-0600), the Silicon Valley Computer Society (408-286-2969), or the New York PC Users' Group (212-533-6972).

What to Buy for Business is a newsletter that deals with purchasing office equipment such as copiers, computers, printers, and fax machines. It is published 10 times a year, and each issue is devoted to a different type of equipment. You can order one by calling 800-247-2185, or you may be able to find copies at your local library.

If you are new to computer purchasing, support and documentation are especially critical, as is the reputation of the vendor.

Ask to use the hardware and software yourself before buying, rather than relying solely on a demonstration. A demonstration by an experienced vendor can often make a very complex product appear deceptively simple. Be prepared to spend some time discussing many of the questions below with the vendor, since the answers will not always be readily apparent.

When buying printers, bear in mind that, although the dot-matrix printer can be useful for draft copies and forms, the laser printer is becoming the business standard. However, not all laser printers are of equal quality. Ask to see a sample printout from the printer you are considering, and find out how many pages it will print per minute.

The following checklist can guide you in making purchasing decisions:

- Who will use the equipment, and for what purpose? Word processing? Graphics? Desktop publishing? Spreadsheets? Database management? Telecommunications?
- Will the users require their own equipment, or will the equipment be shared?
- Does the equipment come with detailed, understandable setup instructions?
- Will the vendor provide help in installing the equipment?
- Does the equipment come with at least a one-year guarantee?
- Is there a toll-free number I can call for help?

- Is the software documentation easy to understand? Is there a tutorial I can attend? on-line help? a toll-free number for help?
- Is the keyboard comfortable?
- Is the monitor easy on the eyes?
- Does the monitor tilt to eliminate glare? (A flatter screen generally reflects less glare.)
- Is the memory adequate for my purposes?
- Can the computer be upgraded? At what cost?
- Do I want to connect the computer to a network workstation and access a file server?
- Are there expansion slots?
- How many disk drives do I need?
- Will I need one floppy-disk drive for 5.25″ disks and one for 3.5″ disks?
- Will I require high-density or low-density disks?
- Do I require multitasking (running programs simultaneously)?
- Do I need to run the software in a Windows™ environment?
- Is background printing needed for high-volume output?
- Is security an issue?
- Is a site license available?
- Can the software be run on a network?
- Does the software support multipage documents?
- Can spreadsheets be linked together so that a change in one will be reflected in another?
- What is the vendor's reputation?
- How long has the vendor been in business? Will the vendor be there next year if I have a problem?
- Has the vendor kept abreast of the latest technology?
- How do the prices compare to those of other vendors and mail-order houses?
- Will the vendor install the hardware if necessary?
- Is a maintenance contract available?
- Will the vendor provide repair, or will it be contracted to a third party?
- Will a substitute be made available when equipment is out for repair?
- Will the vendor provide training for software?

Dictation Equipment

While stenography is still in demand, most dictation in the modern office is done on recording media using a dictation machine. There are several benefits to this form of dictation.

- It frees up the secretary to do other work while the material is being dictated.
- It takes pressure off the person doing the dictating. He or she does not need to choose between taking telephone calls or handling other interruptions and continuing to dictate.
- It allows anyone familiar with the equipment to do the transcription. With traditional stenography, there is a greater likelihood that the secretary will

have invented his or her own supplemental shorthand which no one else can read.

TYPES OF DICTATION MACHINES

Three basic types of dictating machines are popular today.

Desktop dictating machine   The desktop dictating machine is probably the most commonly used. The typical unit records on a cassette tape. Standard, mini-, and microcassettes are all used, but the microcassette is the most popular. The machine has a microphone for the dictator to speak into and includes a range of features to control the recording.

Portable recorder   The desktop model is supplemented in many offices by a portable, battery-operated recorder. Some offices provide only the less expensive portables to their employees; others keep a central supply of portables that can be checked out for travel.

Central recording device   The third type of equipment is the central recording device, which is accessed by a telephone. These are not as common as the desktop models, and are only advantageous in a large organization with a transcription department—a modern version of the typing pool, which functions as a service unit to the whole company and relieves the dictator's secretary of any transcription duties.

In addition to recording machines, there is also the *transcription machine*. This is similar to the desktop recorder, but has an earphone or headset instead of the microphone, and a foot pedal to control the playback of the tape.

DICTATION MACHINE FEATURES

Features vary from brand to brand; the following are some you may find on your system or may want on a new system.

Dual track   Some systems use cassettes with two tracks, reserving one of the tracks for instructions by the dictator.

Erase   This feature allows you to erase the entire cassette after all transcription is complete. Some systems include a separate handheld device which simply demagnetizes the tape. (Every office has its own policy about *when* to erase a tape, however.)

Gain control   This feature reduces background noise, one of the most common problems when transcribing from a machine.

Indexing   The transcriber needs to know where each new document begins on a tape and where any special instructions may have been inserted that would help in setting up the document on the word processor. Though older systems use a paper index strip, newer systems provide for audible signals on the tape itself, which identify the end of a document, and instructions to the transcriber, which are not part of the actual text itself. These signals can be picked up during a preliminary scanning of the tape before transcription begins.

Length display   This feature is a lighted display that identifies the length of the recording on the cassette, usually in minutes.

Recall or review   This feature allows you to replay the last few words on the tape each time you restart it. This can help you find the proper starting point so as to assure that no words are lost in the transcription.

Record light   This light lets the dictator know that the machine is actually recording.

Scanning   If the system uses audible signals to mark spots where special instructions occur or where each document ends, it will also have a high-speed scanner to allow the transcriber to quickly find these spots.

Speed control   You may be able to play back a tape at a speed faster than the original recording but still slow enough for you to transcribe.

Voice activation   This feature starts and stops the tape when the dictator starts and stops speaking.

Reprographic Equipment

Reprographic equipment includes any machines used for making copies of documents. In the office environment, it generally refers to photocopiers.

THE PHOTOCOPIER

The photocopier is similar to the laser printer in that its paper is electrostatically charged to attract inklike *toner* to its surface. The toner may be in powder or liquid form and can be refilled as needed right in the office. Photocopiers are classified according to capacity: copies per minute (that is, speed) and copies per month (that is, expected heaviness of use). Here are the typical ranges for standard types of copiers:

Type	*Copies per minute*	*Copies per month*
Low-volume	10–20	2,000–20,000
Medium-volume	20–50	20,000–50,000
High-volume	50–100	50,000–100,000

Low-volume copiers tend to have few special features and may even be desktop models. They are most useful in areas where only a few pages at a time are copied and no large documents have to be collated. Medium-volume copiers are generally equipped with an automatic document feeder and a collator, and are adequate for most routine office copying needs. High-volume copiers, sometimes referred to as high-speed copier-duplicators, often provide two-sided printing and stapling. Their high price makes them economical only in offices where large quantities of reports and other documents are frequently needed.

A significant new product is the printer-copier, a high-speed printer that takes its input directly from the computer, eliminating the need to feed paper originals into the copier.

The weakest aspect of copiers is their potential for paper jams. Most copiers will indicate where the jam has occurred so that office workers can clear it themselves. The potential for jams increases with the length and route of the paper path.

In some offices, for security or budget reasons, you may need an access code to use the copier. This prevents unauthorized use and allows management to track the usage of the copier. The access code is generally for a department rather than an individual, especially where a copier may be used by several different areas and the expenses need to be charged back accordingly.

Features vary by manufacturer and, to an even greater extent, by the volume of work the machine was designed to perform. Some of the more common features are described here.

Automatic document feeder   This is extremely convenient for making even a single copy of an original that is more than a few pages long. The alternative is to keep raising the cover for each successive page of the original. The automatic document feeder, or ADF, usually accommodates 50 or more pages at a time. Another version of this feature, called a semiautomatic document feeder, allows you to manually feed pages into the copier in a continuous stream, one at a time.

Collate   If you frequently need numerous copies of lengthy documents, you will need a copier that can collate for you. Each collated copy is assembled in a separate sorter bin.

Job interrupt   This feature, also known as "memory," allows you to stop a large job in progress so that someone else can use the machine for a quick copy or two. The copier remembers where it was in the original job and resumes copying without mixing up the sequence of pages.

Paper trays   Low-volume copiers generally only accept one tray size at a time, but medium- and high-volume copiers can hold up to three trays, for $8\frac{1}{2}'' \times 11''$, $8\frac{1}{2}'' \times 14''$, and $11'' \times 17''$ (computer-printout size) paper.

Reduction/Enlargement   Most copiers rated for medium or high volume have the ability to make copies that are from roughly 60 percent to 140 percent of the size of the original. Further reductions and enlargements can be made by running the reduced or enlarged copies through the copier again.

Sorter   Copiers that collate have a sorter to collect each collated set of copies. The sorter is a set of shelves that moves up and down to accept copies as they exit from the machine. Medium- and high-volume copiers can collate 10 or more sets at a time.

Stapling   Generally available only on high-volume machines, this feature enables you to produce collated and stapled documents automatically.

Two-side copying   This feature, also known as "duplexing," may be automatic or semiautomatic. If automatic, the copier will print both sides of each sheet before ejecting the copies into the tray or sorter. This is generally possible only on high-volume machines. In the semiautomatic version, the user may have to manually turn over and reinsert the partially printed copies.

OTHER PRINTING PROCESSES

The old-fashioned mimeograph, long favored by schools and nonprofit organizations because of its ease and low cost, is still in use but has very little application in today's office.

Offset printing is still popular in the centralized reprographics departments of many organizations as well as in franchised retail copying shops. Offset is often used for book and magazine printing; it produces higher-quality results than photocopying and can be more economical for printing thousands of copies.

Other Office Equipment

ELECTRONIC TYPEWRITERS

The electronic typewriter occupies a place between the older electric typewriter and the word processor. It can be useful for various tasks—letters and envelopes, forms, memorandums, brief reports, etc.—that do not require advanced features.

Electronic typewriters usually lack a separate monitor or printer. However, a line or two of text just typed may appear on a small electronic display in order to be checked by the typist before printing. They generally have such features as quick correction (of a word or an entire line), wordwrap (automatic carriage return), automatic centering and underscoring, quick tabulation (for creating columns and tables), boldface type, right justification, and automatic letterspacing. The most sophisticated typewriters, with their sizable memory capacities and numerous word-processing features, are almost indistinguishable from actual word processors. Study the accompanying manual carefully until every useful feature is familiar to you.

PAPER SHREDDERS

Paper shredders are used principally as security devices for destroying sensitive documents. Shredders vary in size from compact models that fit on top of wastebaskets to large floor models. Like photocopiers, they are rated according to the volume of work they can handle.

FAX MACHINES

No office-equipment chapter would be complete without mentioning facsimile or fax machines. Fax machines can be used anywhere a telephone jack and an electric outlet are available. With a fax machine, a single source document can be swiftly reproduced in other offices thousands of miles away. Documents, charts, and even pictures can be transmitted or received within a minute or two at the same cost as a telephone call. The quality of the copies is steadily improving, and many machines will print on bond paper. As the cost of equipment and transmission decreases, fax transmission is being used more and more by businesses as an alternative to postal delivery. For a more detailed discussion of fax machines, see Chapter 13.

CHAPTER 6

A Guide to Business English

Effective business communication is a key ingredient in the success of any business, and creating attractively typed material is only one of the factors involved in it. The clarity, grace, and correctness of the writing are also crucial, and ensuring that they are present is often an important responsibility shared by the secretary. For, while the physical appearance of the letter or memorandum will impress a reader at first glance, these other factors will do more to promote effective communication and to create a lasting impression as the reader spends more time with the material.

Clarity and grace are often, to a great extent, the result of observing conventional standards of correctness. Substandard grammar, incorrect spelling, and awkward or contorted sentence structure will be distracting to a careful reader and may lead him or her to undervalue an entire letter or report. Although the person doing the writing or dictating does bear prime responsibility for his or her own grammar and usage, the secretary still should be competent enough in these areas to recognize basic grammatical and stylistic errors. Before typing questionable material, the secretary should research any doubtful points and then tactfully question the originator about them. The following sections have been prepared as a quick but thorough reference tool for just this sort of situation. Further guidance can be obtained by consulting a current book of English grammar, style, or usage (see the Appendix for a list of titles).

Punctuation

Punctuation marks are used to help clarify the structure and meaning of sentences. They separate groups of words for meaning and emphasis; they convey an idea of the variations in pitch, volume, pauses, and intonation of the spoken language; and they help avoid ambiguity. In many cases, the choice of which mark of punctuation to use will be clear and unambiguous. In other cases, the structure of a sentence may allow for several patterns of punctuation. In cases like these, varying notions of correctness have grown up, and two writers might, with equal correctness, punctuate the same sentence quite differently. In this section, wherever more than one pattern of punctuation may be used, each is explained. If there are reasons to prefer one over another, the reasons are presented; however, punctuation frequently requires the exercise of individual judgment and taste.

This section focuses on the general use of punctuation marks. For the punctuation of specific elements in a business letter, see Chapter 7, especially the section on Standard Punctuation Patterns beginning on page 249.

AMPERSAND

The ampersand (&) represents the word *and*. The ampersand is usually used in correspondence only within proper names and abbreviations.

1. The ampersand is used in the names of companies but not in the names of agencies that are part of the federal government.

    American Telephone & Telegraph Co.
    Dow Jones & Company, Inc.
    Occupational Safety and Health Administration
    Securities and Exchange Commission

    In writing corporate names, writers often try to reproduce the form of the name preferred by the company (taken from an annual report or company letterhead). However, this information may not be available and, even if it is available, can lead to apparent inconsistencies in the letter if several corporate names are used. If this is the case, choose one styling, preferably the one with the ampersand, and use it in all corporate names as a substitute for *and*.

2. When ampersands are used with abbreviations in general correspondence, spaces are often left around the ampersand. Writing that makes extensive use of abbreviations, such as technical writing, more commonly omits the spacing.

    Such loans may be available at your bank or S & L.
    The R&D budget looks adequate for the next fiscal year.

3. When an ampersand is used between the last two elements in a series, the comma is omitted.

    the law firm of Shilliday, Fraser & French

APOSTROPHE

1. The apostrophe is used to indicate the possessive case of nouns and indefinite pronouns. For details regarding this use, see pages 160–62.

2. Apostrophes are sometimes used to form plurals of letters, numerals, abbreviations, symbols, and words referred to as words. For details regarding this use, see pages 156–60.

3. Apostrophes mark omissions in contractions made of two or more words that are pronounced as one word.

didn't   you're   o'clock

4. The apostrophe is used to indicate that letters have been intentionally omitted from the spelling of a word in order to reproduce a perceived pronunciation or to give a highly informal flavor to a piece of writing.

"Get 'em while they're hot" was the theme of the ad campaign.
The club's sign will read "Dancin' till three."

Sometimes words are so consistently spelled with an apostrophe that the spelling with the apostrophe becomes an accepted variant.

rock 'n' roll [for *rock and roll*]
fo'c'sle [for *forecastle*]
bos'n [for *boatswain*]

5. Apostrophes mark the omission of digits in numerals.

class of '93   politics in the '90s

Writers who use the apostrophe when writing the plurals of words expressed in numerals usually avoid the use of the apostrophe illustrated in the second example above. Either they omit the apostrophe that stands for the missing figures, or they spell the word out.

80's *or* eighties *but not* '80's

6. Apostrophes are used to produce the inflected forms of verbs that are made of numerals or individually pronounced letters. Hyphens are sometimes used for this purpose also.

86'ed our proposal
OK'ing the manuscripts

7. An apostrophe is often used to add an -*er* ending to an abbreviation, especially if some confusion might result from its absence. Hyphens are sometimes used for this purpose also. If no confusion is likely, the apostrophe is usually omitted.

4-H'er   AA'er   CBer   DXer

8. The use of apostrophes to form abbreviations (such as *ass'n* for *association* or *sec'y* for *secretary*) is avoided in most formal writing.

BRACKETS

1. Brackets enclose editorial comments, corrections, clarifications, or other material inserted into a text, especially into quoted matter.

This was the first time since it became law that the Twenty-first Amendment [outlining procedures for the replacement of a dead or incapacitated President or Vice President] had been invoked.
He wrote, "I am just as cheerful as when you was [sic] here."

2. Brackets enclose insertions that supply missing letters.

"If you can't persuade the P[resident], I'm sure no one can."

3. Brackets enclose insertions that take the place of words or phrases that were used in the original version of a quoted passage.

> The report, entitled "A Decade of Progress," begins with a short message from President Stevens in which she notes that "the loving portraits and revealing accounts of [this report] are not intended to constitute a complete history of the decade. . . . Rather [they] impart the flavor of the events, developments, and achievements of this vibrant period."

4. Brackets enclose insertions that slightly alter the form of a word used in an original text.

> The magazine reported that thousands of the country's children were "go[ing] to bed hungry every night."

5. Brackets are used to indicate that the capitalization or typeface of the original passage has been altered in some way.

> As we point out later, "The length of a quotation usually determines whether it is run into the text or set as a block quotation. . . . [L]ength can be assessed in terms of number of words, the number of typewritten or typeset lines, or the number of sentences in the passage."
> They agreed with and were encouraged by her next point: "In the past, many secretaries have been placed in positions of responsibility *without being delegated enough authority to carry out the responsibility.*" [Italics added.]

The use of brackets to indicate altered capitalization is optional in most situations. It is required only in cases where meticulous handling of original source material is crucial (particularly legal contexts).

6. Brackets function as parentheses within parentheses.

> The company was incinerating high concentrations of pollutants (such as polychlorinated biphenyls [PCBs]) in a power boiler.

7. Brackets are used in combination with parentheses to indicate units contained within larger units in mathematical copy. They are also used in chemical formulas.

$$x + 5[(x+y)(2x-y)] \qquad\qquad NH_4[Cr(NH_3)_2(SCN)_4]\cdot H_2O$$

8. No punctuation mark (other than a period after an abbreviation) precedes bracketed material within a sentence. If punctuation is required, the mark is placed after the closing bracket.

> The report stated, "If we fail to find additional sources of supply [of oil and gas], our long-term growth will be limited."

9. When brackets enclose a complete sentence, the required punctuation should be placed within the brackets.

> [The results of years of anti-inflation policies are slow growth, a slightly higher unemployment rate, and lower consumer prices.]

10. No space is left between brackets and the material they enclose or between brackets and any mark of punctuation immediately following. In typewritten material, two spaces precede an opening bracket and follow a closing bracket when the brackets enclose a complete sentence.

```
Judging from its economic statistics, the country
could stand a dose of reflation.  [The results of
years of anti-inflation policies are slow growth,
a slightly higher unemployment rate, and lower
```

```
consumer prices.]  However, its people seem
determined to stick with austerity.
```

COLON

The colon is a mark of introduction. It indicates that what follows it—whether a clause, a phrase, or even a single word—is tightly linked with some element that precedes it. For information on capitalizing the first word following a colon, see paragraphs 7 and 8 on page 141.

1. **With phrases and clauses** A colon introduces a clause or phrase that explains, illustrates, amplifies, or restates what has gone before.

   > The sentence was poorly constructed: it lacked both unity and coherence.
   > The organization combines a tradition of excellence with a dedication to human service: educating the young, caring for the elderly, assisting in community-development programs.
   > Disk cartridges provide high-density storage capacity: up to 16 megabytes of information on some cartridges.
   > Time was running out: a decision had to be made.

2. A colon directs attention to an appositive.

   > The question is this: Where will we get the money?
   > He had only one pleasure: eating.

3. A colon is used to introduce a series. The introductory statement often includes a phrase such as *the following* or *as follows*.

   > The conference was attended by representatives of five nations: England, France, Belgium, Spain, and Portugal.
   > Anyone planning to participate should be prepared to do the following: spend all day in a conference session, discuss your company's role in the community, and participate in a conference evaluation.

   Opinion varies regarding whether a colon should interrupt the grammatical continuity of a clause (for example, by coming between a verb and its objects). Although many writers avoid this practice and use a full independent clause before the colon, the interrupting colon is common. It is especially likely to be used before a lengthy and complex list, where the colon serves to set the list apart from the normal flow of running text. With shorter or less complex lists, the colon is usually not used.

   > Our programs to increase profitability include: continued modernization of our manufacturing facilities; consolidation of distribution terminals; discontinuation of unprofitable retail outlets; and reorganization of our personnel structure, along with across-the-board staff reductions.
   > Our programs to increase profitability include plant modernization, improved distribution and retailing procedures, and staff reductions.
   > Our programs to increase profitability include the following: continued modernization of our manufacturing facilities; consolidation of distribution terminals; discontinuation of unprofitable retail outlets; and reorganization of our personnel structure, along with across-the-board staff reductions.

4. A colon is used like a dash to introduce a summary statement following a series.

   > Accounting, home computing, tax laws, investments: she discusses them all.

5. **With quotations** A colon introduces lengthy quoted material that is set off from the rest of a text by indentation but not by quotation marks.

> Roy Gaines, executive director of Public Speaking Incorporated, has this to say about speaking to a group:
>
>> The best way to get jitters under control is to prepare thoroughly. Get some experience. Get up on stage a few times. Find out what your audience is interested in, know your subject backward and forward, and do research to brighten your talk with anecdotes, jokes, and examples.
>
> Gaines adds that he often mulls over his own speeches late at night while walking the family dog.

6. A colon may be used before a quotation in running text, especially when (1) the quotation is lengthy, (2) the quotation is a formal statement or is being given special emphasis, or (3) the quotation is an appositive.

> Said Murdoch: "The key to the success of this project is good planning. We need to know precisely all of the steps that we will need to go through, what kind of staff we will require to accomplish each step, what the entire project will cost, and when we can expect completion."
> The inscription reads: "Here lies one whose name was writ in water."
> In response, he had this to say: "No one knows better than I do that changes will have to be made soon."

7. **Other uses** A colon separates elements in page references, bibliographical and biblical citations, and fixed formulas used to express ratios and time.

> *Journal of the American Medical Association* 48:356
> Stendhal, *Love* (New York: Penguin, 1975)
> John 4:10
> 8:30 a.m.
> a ratio of 3:5

8. A colon separates titles and subtitles (as of books).

> *Secrets of the Temple: How the Federal Reserve Runs the Country*

9. A spaced colon is used to join terms that are being contrasted or compared.

> The budget shows an unfavorable difference in research : advertising dollars.

10. A colon punctuates the salutation in a business letter using the mixed-punctuation pattern. (For more on this use of the colon, see pages 249–51.)

> Dear Mrs. Wright: Ladies and Gentlemen:
> Dear Laurence: To whom it may concern:
> Dear Product Manager:

11. A colon punctuates memorandum and government correspondence headings and subject lines in general business letters. (For more on this use of the colon, see pages 324–25, 260–62, and 313–17.)

> TO: VIA:
> SUBJECT: REFERENCE:

12. A colon separates writer/dictator/typist initials in the identification lines of business letters. (For more on this use of the colon, see pages 270–71.)

> WAL:jml
> WAL:WEB:jml

13. A colon separates carbon-copy or blind carbon-copy abbreviations from the initials or names of copy recipients in business letters. (For more on this use of the colon, see pages 271–72.)

   cc:RSP   bcc:MWK
      JES   FCM

14. **With other marks of punctuation** A colon is placed outside quotation marks and parentheses.

   There's only one thing wrong with "Harold's Indiscretion": it's not funny.
   I quote from the first edition of *Business English* (published in 1985):

15. **Spacing** In typewritten material, two spaces follow a colon used in running text, bibliographical references, publication titles, and letter or memorandum headings.

   ```
   The answer is simple:  don't go.
   SUBJECT:  Project X
   ```

16. No space precedes or follows a colon when it is used between numerals.

   9:30 a.m.   a ratio of 2:4

17. No space precedes or follows a colon in a business-letter identification line or in a carbon-copy notation that indicates a recipient designated by initials. Two spaces follow a colon in a carbon-copy notation that indicates a recipient designated by a full name.

   FCM:hg   cc: Mr. Johnson
   cc:FCM

COMMA

The comma is the most frequently used punctuation mark in English. Its most common uses are to separate items in a series and to set off or distinguish grammatical elements within sentences. This section explains the most common aspects of the comma, listed in the following order:

Between Main Clauses	With Compound Modifiers
With Compound Predicates	In Quotations and Questions
With Subordinate Clauses and Phrases	With Omitted Words
	With Addresses, Dates, and Numbers
With Appositives	With Names, Degrees, and Titles
With Introductory and Interrupting Elements	In Correspondence
	Other Uses
With Contrasting Expressions	With Other Marks of Punctuation
With Items in a Series	

1. **Between main clauses** A comma separates main clauses joined by a coordinating conjunction: *and, but, or, nor, for,* and sometimes *so* and *yet.* (For use of commas with clauses joined by correlative conjunctions, see paragraph 24 on page 118.)

   She knew very little about the new system, and he volunteered nothing.
   We will not respond to any more questions on that topic this afternoon, nor will we respond to similar questions at any time in the future.
   His face showed disappointment, for he knew that he had failed.
   The acoustics in this hall are good, so every note is clear.

We have requested this information many times before, yet we have
never gotten a satisfactory reply.

2. When one or both of the clauses are short or closely related in meaning, the
comma is often omitted.

We have tested the product and we are pleased.
We hadn't realized it but none of the shipments were arriving on time.

In punctuating sentences such as these, writers have to use their own judgment. There are no clear-cut rules to follow; however, factors such as the
rhythm, parallelism, or logic of the sentence often influence how clearly or
smoothly it will read with or without the comma.

3. Commas are sometimes used to separate main clauses that are not joined by
conjunctions. This is especially likely if the clauses are short and obviously
parallel.

One day you are a successful corporate lawyer, the next day you are out
of work.
The city has suffered terribly in the interim. Bombs have destroyed most
of the buildings, disease has ravaged the population.

Using a comma to join clauses that are neither short nor obviously parallel is
usually called *comma fault* or *comma splice,* and such constructions should generally be avoided. In general, clauses not joined by conjunctions are separated by semicolons.

4. If a sentence is composed of three or more clauses, the clauses may be separated by either commas or semicolons. Clauses that are short and relatively
free of commas can be separated by commas even if they are not joined by a
conjunction. If the clauses are long or heavily punctuated, they are separated with semicolons, except for the last two clauses, which may be separated by either a comma or a semicolon. Usually a comma will be used
between the last two clauses only if those clauses are joined by a conjunction.
(For more examples of clauses separated with commas and semicolons, see
paragraph 5 under Semicolon on page 137.)

The pace of change seems to have quickened, the economy is uncertain,
the technology seems sometimes liberating and sometimes hostile.
The policy is a complex one to explain; defending it against its critics is
not easy, nor is it clear the defense is always necessary.

5. **With compound predicates** Commas are not normally used to separate the
parts of a compound predicate.

The chairman tried to explain the merger but failed to convince the
stockholders.

However, many writers do use commas to separate the parts of a compound
predicate if the predicate is especially long and complicated, if one part of
the predicate is being stressed, or if the absence of a comma could cause a
momentary misreading of the sentence.

The board helps to develop the financing, new product planning, and
marketing strategies for new corporate divisions, and issues periodic reports on expenditures, revenues, and personnel appointments.
This is an unworkable plan, and has been from the start.
I try to explain to him what I want him to do, and get nowhere.

6. **With subordinate clauses and phrases** Adverbial clauses and phrases that precede a main clause are usually set off (that is, preceded and/or followed) with commas.

> Having made that decision, we turned our attention to other matters.
> To understand the situation, you must be familiar with the background.
> In 1980, the company had its first profitable year.
> In addition, staff members respond to queries, take new orders, and initiate billing.

7. If a sentence begins with an adverbial clause or phrase and can be easily read without a comma following it, the comma may be omitted. In most cases where the comma is omitted, the phrase will be short—four words or less. However, the comma can be omitted even after a longer phrase if the sentence can be easily read or seems more forceful that way.

> In January the company will introduce a new line of entirely redesigned products.
> If the project cannot be done profitably perhaps it should not be done at all.

8. Adverbial clauses and phrases that introduce a main clause other than the first main clause are usually set off with commas. However, if the adverbial clause or phrase follows a conjunction, two commas are usually used: one before the conjunction and one following the clause or phrase. In some cases three commas are used: one before the conjunction and two more to enclose the clause or phrase. Some writers use only one comma to separate the main clauses.

> His parents were against the match, and had the couple not eloped, their plans for marriage would have come to nothing.
> They have redecorated the entire store, but, to the delight of their customers, the store retains much of its original flavor.
> We haven't left Springfield yet, but when we get to Boston we'll call you.

9. A comma is not used after an introductory phrase if the phrase immediately precedes the main verb.

> On the filing cabinet lay a bulging portfolio.

10. A subordinate clause or phrase that follows a main clause or falls within a main clause is usually not set off by commas if it is restrictive—that is, if its removal from the sentence would alter the meaning of the main clause. If the meaning of the main clause would not be altered by removing the subordinate clause or phrase, the clause or phrase is considered nonrestrictive and usually is set off by commas.

> We will be delighted if she decides to stay. [restrictive]
> Anyone who wants his or her copy of the book autographed by the author should get in line. [restrictive]
> Her new book, which was based on a true story, was well received. [nonrestrictive]
> That was a good meal, although I didn't particulary like the broccoli in cream sauce. [nonrestrictive]

11. Commas are used to set off an adverbial clause or phrase that falls between the subject and the verb.

> The weather in the capital, fluctuating from very hot to downright chilly, necessitates a variety of clothing.

12. Commas set off modifying phrases that do not immediately precede the word or phrase they modify.

> The negotiators, tired and discouraged, headed back to the hotel.
> We could see the importance, both long-term and short-term, of her proposal.
> The director, burdened with a tight schedule, expanded her staff.

13. Absolute phrases are set off with commas, whether they fall at the beginning, middle, or end of the sentence.

> Our business being concluded, we adjourned for refreshments.
> I'm afraid of his reaction, his temper being what it is.

14. **With appositives** Commas are used to set off a word, phrase, or clause that is in apposition to (that is, equivalent to) a preceding noun and that is nonrestrictive.

> The sales manager, Mr. Griffith, is in charge of the meeting.
> We were most impressed by the third candidate, the one who brought a writing sample and asked so many questions.

A nonrestrictive appositive phrase or clause sometimes precedes the noun it refers to. It is set off by commas in this position also.

> A cherished landmark in the city, the Hotel Sandburg has managed once again to escape the wrecking ball.

15. Restrictive appositives are not set off by commas.

> Our account manager Andrea Timmons will be in touch with you.

Note that if Andrea Timmons were the firm's *only* account manager, her name would be set off by commas.

16. **With introductory and interrupting elements** Commas set off transitional words and phrases (such as *finally, meanwhile,* and *after all*).

> Indeed, close coordination between departments can minimize confusion during this period of expansion.
> We are eager to begin construction; however, the necessary materials have not yet arrived.
> The most recent report, on the other hand, makes clear why the management avoids such agreements.

When these words are not used to make a transition, no comma is necessary.

> The materials had finally arrived.

17. Commas set off parenthetical elements, such as authorial asides and supplementary information, that are closely related to the rest of the sentence.

> All of us, to tell the truth, were completely amazed by his suggestion.
> The president, now in his sixth year with the company, was responsible for the changes in the staff.

When the parenthetical element is digressive or otherwise not closely related to the rest of the sentence, it is often set off by dashes or parentheses. For contrasting examples, see paragraph 3 under Dash on page 123 and paragraph 1 under Parentheses on page 129.

18. Commas are used to set off words or phrases that introduce examples or explanations.

He expects to visit three countries, namely, France, Spain, and Germany.
I would like to develop a good, workable plan, i.e., one that would outline
   our goals and set a timetable for accomplishing them.

Words and phrases such as *i.e., e.g., namely, for example,* and *that is* are often
preceded by a dash, open parenthesis, or semicolon, depending on the magnitude of the break in continuity created by the examples or explanations.
However, regardless of the punctuation that precedes the word or phrase, a
comma always follows it. For contrasting examples of dashes, parentheses,
and semicolons with these words and phrases, see paragraph 6 under Dash
on page 124, paragraph 2 under Parentheses on page 129, and paragraph 6
under Semicolon on page 138.

19. Commas are used to set off words in direct address.

    We would like to discuss your account, Mrs. Reid.
    The answer, my friends, lies within us.

20. Commas set off mild interjections or exclamations such as *ah* or *oh.*

    Ah, weekends—they don't come often enough.
    Oh, it was quite a meeting.

21. **With contrasting expressions** A comma is used to set off contrasting ex-
    pressions within a sentence.

    This project will take six months, not six weeks.

22. Style varies regarding use of the comma to set off two or more contrasting
    phrases used to describe a single word that follows immediately. Some writ-
    ers put a comma after the first modifier but not between the final modifier
    and the word modified. Other writers, who treat the contrasting phrase as a
    nonrestrictive modifier, put a comma both before and after the phrase.

    The harsh, although eminently realistic critique is not going to make you
       popular.
    The harsh, although eminently realistic, critique is not going to make you
       popular.
    This street takes you away from, not toward the capitol building.
    This street takes you away from, not toward, the capitol building.

23. Adjectives and adverbs that modify the same word or phrase and that are
    joined by *but* or some other coordinating conjunction are not separated by a
    comma.

    a bicycle with a light but sturdy frame
    a multicolored but subdued carpet
    errors caused by working carelessly or too quickly

24. A comma does not usually separate elements that are contrasted through
    the use of a pair of correlative conjunctions (such as *either . . . or, neither . . .
    nor,* and *not only . . . but also*).

    The cost is either $69.95 or $79.95.
    Neither my secretary nor I noticed the error.
    He was given the post not only because of his diplomatic connections but
       also because of his great tact and charm.

Correlative conjunctions are sometimes used to join main clauses. If the
clauses are short, a comma is not added. If the clauses are long, a comma
usually separates them.

    Either you do it my way or we don't do it at all.
    Not only did she have to see three salesmen and a visiting reporter during

the course of the day, but she also had to prepare for the next day's meeting with the president.

25. Long parallel contrasting and comparing clauses are separated by commas; short parallel phrases are not.

> The more I hear about this new computer, the greater is my desire to obtain one for my office.
> "The sooner the better," I said.

26. **With items in a series** Words, phrases, and clauses joined in a series are separated by commas. If main clauses are joined in a series, they may be separated by either semicolons or commas. (For more on the use of commas and semicolons to separate main clauses, see paragraphs 1, 3, and 4 on pages 114–15 and paragraph 5 under Semicolon on page 137.)

> Pens, pencils, and erasers crowded the drawer.
> Her job required her to pack quickly, to travel often, and to have no personal life.
> He responded patiently while reporters shouted questions, flashbulbs popped, and the crowd pushed closer.

NOTE: Practice varies regarding the use of the comma between the last two items in a series if those items are also joined by a conjunction. Sometimes, as in the following example, omitting the final comma (often called the *serial comma*) can result in ambiguity. Some writers feel that in most sentences the use of the conjunction makes the comma superfluous, and they favor using the comma only when a misreading could result from omitting it. Others feel that it is easier to include the final comma routinely rather than try to consider each sentence separately to decide whether a misreading is possible without the comma. Most reference books, including this one, and most other book-length works of nonfiction use the serial comma. In most other kinds of writing, however, practice is evenly or nearly evenly divided on the use or omission of this comma.

> We are looking for a house with a big yard, a view of the harbor, and beach and docking privileges. [with serial comma]
> We are looking for a house with a big yard, a view of the harbor and beach and docking privileges. [without serial comma]

27. A comma is not used to separate items in a series that are joined with conjunctions.

> I don't understand what this policy covers or doesn't cover or only partially covers.
> I have talked to the president and the vice president and three other executives.

28. When the elements in a series are long or complex or consist of clauses that themselves contain commas, the elements are usually separated by semicolons, not commas. For more on this use of the semicolon, see paragraphs 7 and 8 under Semicolon on page 138.

29. **With compound modifiers** A comma is used to separate two or more adjectives, adverbs, or phrases that modify the same word or phrase. (For the use of commas with contrasting modifiers, see paragraphs 22 and 23 above.)

> She wrote in a polished, professional style.
> The office was lit with a hard, flickering light.

30. A comma is not used between two adjectives when the first modifies the combination of the second adjective plus the word or phrase it modifies.

a good used car
a low common denominator

31. A comma is not used to separate an adverb from the adjective or adverb that it modifies.

a truly distinctive manner
running very quickly down the street

32. In quotations and questions A comma separates a direct quotation from a phrase identifying its source or speaker. If the quotation is a question or an exclamation and the identifying phrase follows the quotation, the comma is replaced by a question mark or an exclamation point.

Mary said, "I am leaving on the 12th."
"I am leaving on the 12th," Mary said.
Mary asked, "When are you going?"
"When are you going?" Mary asked.
"I am staying," Mary said, "even if it means missing the reception."
"Don't forget the slides!" Mary shouted.

In some cases, a colon can replace a comma preceding a quotation. For more on this use of the colon, see paragraph 6 on page 113.

33. Commas are not used to set off a quotation that is an integral part of the sentence in which it appears.

Throughout the session his only responses were "No comment" and "I don't think so."
Just because he said he was "about to leave this minute" doesn't mean he actually left.

34. Practice varies regarding the use of commas to set off shorter sentences that fall within longer sentences and that do not constitute actual dialogue. These shorter sentences may be mottoes or maxims, unspoken or imaginary dialogue, or sentences referred to as sentences; and they may or may not be enclosed in quotation marks. (For more on the use of quotation marks with sentences like these, see paragraph 6 under Quotation Marks, Double, on page 134.) The shorter sentence usually functions as a subject, object, or complement within the larger sentence and does not require a comma. Sometimes the shorter sentence will be enclosed in quotation marks like actual quoted dialogue, and in such cases a comma is used to separate it from the text that introduces or identifies it. Where quotation marks are not used, a comma may be inserted simply to mark the beginning of the shorter sentence clearly.

"The computer is down" was the response she dreaded.
He spoke with a candor that seemed to insist, This actually happened to me and in just this way.
The first rule is, When in doubt, spell it out.

When the shorter sentence functions as an appositive in the larger sentence, it is set off with a comma or commas when nonrestrictive and not when restrictive. (For more on restrictive modifiers and appositives, see paragraphs 10, 14, and 15 on pages 116–17.)

He was fond of the slogan "Every man a king, but no man wears a crown."
We had the association's motto, "We make waves," printed on our T-shirts.

35. A comma introduces a direct question, regardless of whether it is enclosed in quotation marks or if its first word is capitalized.

> I wondered, what is going on here?
> The question is, How do we get out of this situation?

36. The comma is omitted before quotations that are very short exclamations or representations of sounds.

> He jumped up suddenly and cried "I've got it!"

37. A comma is not used to set off indirect discourse or indirect questions introduced by a conjunction (such as *that* or *what*).

> Mary said that she was being promoted.
> I wondered what was going on at the main office.
> The clerk told me that the book I had ordered had just come in.

38. With omitted words A comma indicates the omission of a word or phrase, especially in parallel constructions where the omitted word or phrase appears earlier in the sentence.

> Common stocks are preferred by some investors; bonds, by others.

39. A comma often replaces the conjunction *that*.

> The balance sheet looked so bad, we thought surely there would be layoffs.
> The problem is, we don't know how to fix it.

40. With addresses, dates, and numbers A comma is used to set off the individual elements of an address except for ZIP codes; no punctuation appears between a state name and the ZIP code that follows it. If prepositions are used between the elements of the address, commas are not needed.

> Mrs. Bryant may be reached at 52 Kiowa Circle, Mesa, Arizona.
> Mr. Briscoe was born in Liverpool, England.
> The collection was displayed at the Wilmington, Delaware, Museum of Art.
> Write to the Bureau of the Census, Washington, DC 20233.
> The White House is at 1600 Pennsylvania Avenue in Washington, D.C.

Some writers omit the comma that follows the name of a state when no other element of an address follows it, which usually occurs when a city name and state name are being used in combination to modify a noun that follows. However, retaining this comma is still the more common practice.

> We visited their Enid, Oklahoma plant.
>   *but more commonly*
> We visited their Enid, Oklahoma, plant.

41. Commas are used to set off the year from the day of the month. In the middle of a sentence the second comma may be omitted but it is usually retained. (See paragraphs 44–46 below for related examples.)

> On October 26, 1947, the newly hired employees began work on the project.

When only the month and the year are given, the comma is usually omitted.

> In December 1903, the Wright brothers finally succeeded in keeping an airplane aloft for a few seconds.

42. A comma groups numerals into units of three in order to separate thousands, millions, and so on; however, this comma is generally not used in page numbers, street numbers, or numbers within dates. (For more on the styling of numbers, see the section on Numbers, beginning on page 180.)

a population of 350,000	the year 1986
4509 South Pleasant Street	page 1419

43. **With names, degrees, and titles** A comma punctuates an inverted name.

    Sagan, Deborah J.

44. A comma is usually used between a surname and *Junior, Senior,* or their abbreviations. In the middle of a sentence the word or abbreviation is normally followed by another comma; however, this second comma may be omitted. (See paragraph 41 above and paragraphs 45 and 46 below for related examples.)

    Morton A. Williams, Jr.   Douglas Fairbanks, Senior

45. A comma is often used to set off the word *Incorporated* or the abbreviation *Inc.* from the rest of a corporate name; however, many companies elect to omit this comma from their names.

    Leedy Manufacturing Company, Incorporated
    Tektronics, Inc.
    Merz-Fortunata Inc.

    In the middle of a sentence, the word or abbreviation is normally followed by another comma; however, this second comma may be omitted. (See paragraphs 41 and 44 above and paragraph 46 below for related examples.)

46. A comma separates a surname from a following academic, honorary, military, or religious degree or title.

    Amelia P. Artandi, D.V.M.   Robert Menard, M.A., Ph.D.
    John L. Farber, Esq.   Admiral Herman Washington, USN
    Sister Mary Catherine, S.C.

    In the middle of a sentence, the abbreviation is normally followed by another comma; however, this second comma may be omitted. (See paragraphs 41, 44, and 45 above for related examples.)

47. **In correspondence** The comma follows the salutation in informal correspondence and often follows the complimentary close in both informal and formal correspondence. In formal correspondence, a colon follows the salutation. (For more on this use of the colon, see paragraph 10 under Colon on page 113.)

    Dear Rachel,   Affectionately,   Very truly yours,

48. **Other uses** The comma is used to avoid ambiguity when the juxtaposition of two words or expressions could cause confusion.

    Whatever will be, will be.
    To John, Marshall Inc. was a special environment.
    I reviewed the figures that the department had prepared, and altered
        several of them.

49. A comma often follows a direct object or a predicate nominative or predicate adjective when they precede the subject and verb in the sentence. If the meaning of the sentence is clear without this comma, it is often omitted.

    That we would soon have to raise prices, no one disputed.
    A disaster it certainly was.

50. **With other marks of punctuation** Commas are used in conjunction with brackets, ellipsis points, parentheses, and quotation marks. Commas are

not used in conjunction with colons, dashes, exclamation points, question marks, or semicolons. If one of these latter marks falls at the same point in a sentence at which a comma would fall, the comma is dropped and the other mark is retained. For more on the use of commas with other marks of punctuation, see the subheading With Other Marks of Punctuation under the headings for each of those marks of punctuation.

DASH

The dash can function like a comma, a colon, or a pair of parentheses. Like commas and parentheses, dashes set off (that is, precede and follow) parenthetic material such as examples, supplemental facts, or appositional, explanatory, or descriptive phrases. Like colons, dashes introduce clauses that explain or expand upon some element of the material that precedes them. The dash is sometimes considered to be a less formal equivalent of the colon and parenthesis, and it does frequently take their place in advertising and other informal contexts. However, dashes may be found in all kinds of writing, including the most formal, and the choice of which mark to use is usually a matter of personal preference.

The dash exists in a number of different lengths. The most common dash is the *em dash,* which is approximately the width of a capital M in typeset material. In typewritten material, it is represented by two hyphens. The en dash and the two- and three-em dashes have more limited uses which are explained in paragraphs 12–14 on page 125.

1. **Abrupt change or suspension** The dash marks an abrupt change or break in the structure of a sentence.

   > The board of directors seems happy with the change, but the shareholders—there is the problem.

2. A dash is used to indicate interrupted speech or a speaker's confusion or hesitation.

   > "The next point I'd like to bring up—" the speaker started to say.
   > "Yes," he went on, "yes—that is—I guess I agree."

3. **Parenthetic and amplifying elements** Dashes are used in place of other punctuation (such as commas or parentheses) to emphasize parenthetic or amplifying material or to make such material stand out more clearly from the rest of the sentence.

   > Mail your subscription—now!
   > In 1976, they asked for—and received—substantial grants from the federal government.
   > The privately owned consulting firm—formerly known as Aborjaily & Associates—is now offering many new services.

   When dashes are used to set off parenthetic elements, they often indicate that the material is more digressive than elements set off with commas but less digressive than elements set off by parentheses. For contrasting examples, see paragraph 17 under Comma on page 117 and paragraph 1 under Parentheses on page 129.

4. Dashes are used to set off or to introduce defining and enumerating phrases.

   > The fund sought to acquire controlling positions—a minimum of 25% of outstanding voting securities—in other companies.
   > The essay dealt with our problems with waste—cans, bottles, discarded tires, and other trash.

5. A dash is often used in place of a colon or semicolon to link clauses, especially when the clause that follows the dash explains, summarizes, or expands upon the clause that precedes it.

> The test results were surprisingly good—none of the tested models displayed serious problems.

6. A dash or a pair of dashes often sets off parenthetic or amplifying material introduced by such phrases as *for example, namely, that is, e.g.,* and *i.e.*

> After some discussion the motion was tabled—that is, it was removed indefinitely from the board's consideration.
> Sports develop two valuable traits—namely, self-control and the ability to make quick decisions.
> Not all "prime" windows—i.e., the ones installed when a house is built—are equal in quality.

Commas, parentheses, and semicolons are often used for the same purpose. For contrasting examples, see paragraph 18 under Comma on page 117, paragraph 2 under Parentheses on page 129, and paragraph 6 under Semicolon on page 138.

7. A dash introduces a summary statement that follows a series of words or phrases.

> Unemployment, strikes, inflation, stock prices, mortgage rates—all are part of the economy.
> Once into bankruptcy, the company would have to pay cash for its supplies, defer maintenance, and lay off workers—moves that could threaten its long-term profitability.

8. **With other marks of punctuation** If a dash appears at a point in a sentence where a comma could also appear, the dash is retained and the comma is dropped.

> If we don't succeed—and the critics say we won't—then the whole project is in jeopardy.
> Our lawyer has read the transcript—all 1,200 pages of it—and he has decided that an appeal would not be useful.
> Some of the other departments, however—particularly Accounting, Sales, and Credit Collection—have expanded their computer operations.

9. If the second of a pair of dashes would come at a point in a sentence where a period or semicolon should also appear, the period or semicolon is retained and the dash is dropped.

> His conduct has always been exemplary—near-perfect attendance, excellent productivity, a good attitude; nevertheless, his termination cannot be avoided.

10. Dashes are used with exclamation points and question marks. When a pair of dashes sets off material calling for either of these marks of punctuation, the exclamation point or the question mark is placed inside the second dash. If the parenthetic material falls at the end of a sentence ending with an exclamation point or question mark, the closing dash is not required.

> His hobby was getting on people's nerves—especially mine!—and he was extremely good at it.
> When the committee meets next week—are you going to be there?—I will present all of the final figures.
> Is there any way to predict the future course of this case—one which we really cannot afford to lose?

11. Dashes and parentheses are used in combination to indicate parenthetic material appearing within parenthetic material. Dashes within parentheses and parentheses within dashes are used with about equal frequency.

> We were looking for a narrator (or narrators—sometimes a script calls for more than one) who could handle a variety of assignments.
> On this route our trucks cross a number of major rivers—the Hudson, the Delaware, and the Patapsco (which flows through Baltimore)—without paying a single toll.

If the inner parenthetic element begins with a dash and its closing dash would fall in the same position as the closing parenthesis, the closing dash is omitted and the parenthesis is retained, as in the first example above. If the inner element begins with a parenthesis and its closing parenthesis would coincide with the closing dash, the closing parenthesis and the closing dash are both retained, as in the second example above.

12. **En dash** En dashes appear only in typeset material, not in normal typewritten or keyboarded material, and therefore they do not often appear in business correspondence. As a point of information, however, the en dash is shorter than the em dash but slightly longer than the hyphen. It is most frequently used (1) as a replacement for a hyphen following a prefix that is added to an open compound, (2) as an equivalent to "(up) to and including" when used between numbers, dates, or other notations to indicate range, (3) as a replacement for the word *to* between capitalized names, and (4) to indicate linkages, such as boundaries, treaties, or oppositions. In all of these uses, a hyphen can be used in typewritten material.

> pre–Civil War architecture   the New York–Connecticut area
> 1988–89   Washington–Moscow diplomacy
> pages 128–34
> 8:30 a.m.–4:30 p.m.

13. **Long dashes** A two-em dash is used to indicate missing letters in a word and, less frequently, to indicate a missing word. A two-em dash is represented in typewritten material by four hyphens.

> Mr. P—— of Baltimore
> That's b----t and you know it.

14. A three-em dash indicates that a word has been left out or that an unknown word or figure is to be supplied. A three-em dash is represented in typewritten material by six hyphens.

> The study was carried out in ———, a fast-growing Sunbelt city.
> We'll leave New York City on the ------ of August.

15. **Spacing** Practice varies as to spacing around the dash. Some publications and some typists insert a space before and after a dash, others do not. Either practice is acceptable.

ELLIPSIS POINTS

Ellipsis points is the name most often given to periods when they are used, usually in groups of three, to signal an omission from quoted material or to indicate a pause or trailing off of speech. Other names for periods used in this way include *ellipses, points of ellipsis,* and *suspension points.* Ellipsis points are often used in conjunction with other marks of punctuation, including periods used to mark the ends of sentences. When ellipsis points are used in this way with a terminal period, the omission is sometimes thought of as being marked by four periods.

Most of the conventions described in this section are illustrated with quoted material enclosed in quotation marks. However, the conventions are equally applicable to quoted material set as extracts. In the following examples, ellipsis points indicate omission of material. In most cases, the full text from which these omissions have been made is some portion of this paragraph.

1. Ellipsis points indicate the omission of one or more words within a quoted sentence.

    One book said, "Other names . . . include *ellipses, points of ellipsis,* and *suspension points.*"

2. Ellipsis points are usually not used to indicate the omission of words that precede the quoted portion. However, practice varies on this point, and in some formal contexts, especially those in which the quotation is introduced by a colon, ellipsis points are used.

    The book maintained that "the omission is sometimes thought of as being marked by four periods."
    The book maintained: ". . . the omission is sometimes thought of as being marked by four periods."

3. Punctuation used in the original that falls on either side of the ellipsis points is often omitted; however, it may be retained, especially if this helps clarify the sentence.

    According to the book, "*Ellipsis points* is the name most often given to periods when they are used . . . to signal an omission from quoted material or to indicate a pause or trailing off of speech."
    According to the book, "When ellipsis points are used in this way . . . , the omission is sometimes thought of as being marked by four periods."
    According to the book, "*Ellipsis points* is the name most often given to periods when they are used, usually in groups of three, . . . to indicate a pause or trailing off of speech."

4. If an omission includes an entire sentence within a passage, the last part of a sentence within a passage, or the first part of a sentence other than the first quoted sentence, the end punctuation preceding or following the omission is retained and is followed by three periods.

    That book says, "Other names for periods used in this way include *ellipses, points of ellipsis,* and *suspension points.* . . . When ellipsis points are used in this way with a terminal period, the omission is sometimes thought of as being marked by four periods."
    That book says, "*Ellipsis points* is the name given to periods when they are used, usually in groups of three, to signal an omission from quoted material. . . . Other names for periods used in this way include *ellipses, points of ellipsis,* and *suspension points.*"
    That book says, "Ellipsis points are often used in conjunction with other marks of punctuation, including periods used to mark ends of sentences. . . . The omission is sometimes thought of as being marked by four periods."

    The capitalization of the word *The* in the third example is acceptable, even though that word did not begin a sentence in the original version. When the opening words of a quotation act as a sentence within the quotation, the first word is capitalized.

5. If the last words of a quoted sentence are omitted and if the original sentence ends with a period, that period is retained and three ellipsis points fol-

low. However, if the original sentence ends with punctuation other than a period, the end punctuation often follows the ellipsis points, especially if it helps clarify the quotation.

> Their book said, "Ellipsis points are often used in conjunction with other marks of punctuation. . . ."
> He always ends his harangues with some variation on the question, "What could you have been thinking when you . . . ?"

Many writers and editors, especially when writing informally, choose to ignore the distinctions in paragraphs 4 and 5 and instead indicate all omissions by three periods, dropping all terminal periods that may precede or follow an omission.

6. Ellipsis points are used to indicate that a quoted sentence has been intentionally left unfinished. In situations such as this, the terminal period is not included.

> Read the statement beginning *"Ellipsis points* is the name most often given . . ." and then proceed to the numbered paragraphs.

7. Ellipsis points are used to indicate faltering speech, especially if the faltering involves a long pause between words or a sentence that trails off or is intentionally left unfinished. In these kinds of sentences most writers treat the ellipsis points as terminal punctuation, thus removing the need for any other punctuation; however, some writers use other punctuation in conjunction with ellipsis points.

> The speaker seemed uncertain how to answer the question. "Well, that's true . . . but even so . . . I think we can do better."
> "Despite these uncertainties, we believe we can do it, but . . ."
> "I mean . . ." he said, "like . . . How?"

8. Ellipsis points are sometimes used as a stylistic device to catch and hold a reader's attention.

> They think that nothing can go wrong . . . but it does.

9. Each ellipsis point is separated from other ellipsis points, adjacent punctuation (except for quotation marks), and surrounding text by a space. If a terminal period is used with ellipsis points, it precedes them with no space before it and one space after it.

EXCLAMATION POINT

The exclamation point is used to mark a forceful comment. Heavy use can weaken its effect, so it should be used sparingly.

1. An exclamation point can punctuate a sentence, phrase, or interjection.

> This is the fourth time in a row he's been late!
> No one that I talked to—not even the accounting department!—seemed to know how the figures were calculated.
> Ah, those sales figures!

2. The exclamation point replaces the question mark when an ironic or emphatic tone is more important than the actual question.

> Aren't you finished yet!
> Do you realize what you've done!
> Why me!

3. Occasionally the exclamation point is used with a question mark to indicate a very forceful question.

> How much did you say?!
> You did what!?

4. The exclamation point is enclosed within brackets, dashes, parentheses, and quotation marks when it punctuates the enclosed material rather than the sentence as a whole. It should be placed outside them when it punctuates the entire sentence.

> All of this proves—at long last!—that we were right from the start.
> They again contested the figures (for the third time!) and finally prevailed.
> He sprang to his feet and shouted "Point of order!"
> The correct word is "lax," not "lacks"!

5. Exclamatory phrases that occur within a sentence are set off by dashes or parentheses.

> And now our competition—get this!—wants to start sharing secrets.
> The board accepted most of the recommendations, but ours (alas!) was not even considered.

6. If an exclamation point falls at a place in a sentence where a comma or a terminal period could also go, the comma or period is dropped and the exclamation point is retained.

> "Absolutely not!" he snapped.
> She has written about 60 pages so far—and with no help!

If the exclamation point is part of a title, as of a play, book, or movie, it may be followed by a comma. If the title falls at the end of a sentence, the terminal period is usually dropped.

> Marshall and Susan went to see *Oklahoma!*, and they enjoyed it very much.
> His favorite management book is still *Up the Organization!*

7. In typewritten material, two spaces follow an exclamation point that ends a sentence. If the exclamation point is followed by a closing bracket, closing parenthesis, or closing quotation marks, the two spaces follow the second mark. In typeset material, only one space follows the exclamation point.

> ```
> The time is now!  Decide what you are going to do.
> She said, "The time is now!"  That meant we had to
>   decide what to do.
> ```
> The time is now! Decide what you are going to do.
> She said, "The time is now!" That meant we had to decide what to do.

HYPHEN

1. Hyphens are used to link elements in compound words. For more on the styling of compound words, see the section on Compounds, beginning on page 163.

2. A hyphen marks an end-of-line division of a word when part of the word is to be carried down to the next line.

> We visited several showrooms, looked at the prices (it wasn't a pleasant experience; prices in this area have not gone down), and asked all the questions we could think of.

3. A hyphen divides letters or syllables to give the effect of stuttering, sobbing, or halting speech.

    S-s-sammy   ah-ah-ah   y-y-es

4. Hyphens indicate a word spelled out letter by letter.

    p-r-o-b-a-t-i-o-n

5. A hyphen indicates that a word element is a prefix, suffix, or medial element.

    anti-   -ship   -o-

6. A hyphen is used in typewritten material as an equivalent to the phrase "(up) to and including" when placed between numbers and dates. (In typeset material this hyphen is very often replaced by an en dash. For more on the use of the en dash, see paragraph 12 under Dash on page 125.)

    35–40 years   ages 10–15   1988–89

7. Hyphens are sometimes used to produce inflected forms of verbs that are made of individually pronounced letters or to add an *-er* ending to an abbreviation; however, apostrophes are more commonly used for these purposes. (For more on these uses of the apostrophe, see paragraphs 6 and 7 under Apostrophe on page 110.)

    D.H.-ing for the White Sox   a loyal AA-er

PARENTHESES

Parentheses enclose supplementary elements that are inserted into a main statement but that are not intended to be part of the statement. For some of the cases described below, especially those listed under the heading "Parenthetic Elements," commas and dashes are frequently used instead of parentheses. (For contrasting examples, see paragraph 17 under Comma on page 117 and paragraph 3 under Dash on page 123.) In general, commas tend to be used when the inserted material is closely related, logically or grammatically, to the main clause; parentheses are more often used when the inserted material is only incidental.

1. Parenthetic elements Parentheses enclose phrases and clauses that provide examples, explanations, or supplementary facts. Supplementary numerical data may also be enclosed in parentheses.

> Nominations for the association's principal officers (president, vice president, treasurer, and secretary) were heard and approved.
> Although we liked the applicant (her background, training, and experience were excellent), we weren't ready to hire anyone at that point.
> The company shows good earnings ($3.45 a share vs. $3.05 last year), a strong balance sheet, and a good current yield (7.8%).

2. Parentheses enclose phrases and clauses introduced by expressions such as *namely, that is, e.g.,* and *i.e.* Commas, dashes, and semicolons are also used to perform this function. (For contrasting examples, see paragraph 18 under Comma on page 117, paragraph 6 under Dash on page 124, and paragraph 6 under Semicolon on page 138.)

> In writing to the manufacturer, be as specific as possible (i.e., list the missing or defective parts, describe the nature of the malfunction, and provide the name and address of the store where the unit was purchased).

3. Parentheses enclose definitions or translations in the main part of a sentence.

The company announced plans to sell off its houseware (small-appliance) business.

The hotel is located near the famous Paseo del Rio (river walk).

4. Parentheses enclose abbreviations that follow their spelled-out forms, or spelled-out forms that follow abbreviations.

She cited a ruling by the Federal Communications Commission (FCC).

They will study the disposal of PVC (polyvinyl chloride).

5. Parentheses often enclose cross-references.

Telephone ordering service is also provided (refer to the list of stores at the end of this catalog).

The diagram (Fig. 3) illustrates the action of the pump.

6. Parentheses enclose Arabic numerals that confirm a spelled-out number in a general text or in a legal document.

Delivery will be made in thirty (30) days.

The fee is Four Thousand Dollars ($4,000.00), payable to UNCO, Inc.

7. Parentheses enclose the name of a city or state that is inserted into a proper name for identification.

the Norristown (Pa.) State Hospital

the *Tulsa* (Okla.) *Tribune*

8. Some writers use parentheses to enclose personal asides.

It was largely as a result of this conference that the committee was formed (its subsequent growth in influence is another story).

9. Parentheses are used to enclose quotations that illustrate or support a statement made in the main text.

After he had had a few brushes with the police, his stepfather had him sent to jail as an incorrigible ("It will do him good").

10. **Other uses** Parentheses enclose unpunctuated numbers or letters separating and heading individual elements or items in a series within a sentence.

We must set forth (1) our long-term goals, (2) our immediate objectives, and (3) the means at our disposal.

11. Parentheses indicate alternative terms.

Please sign and return the enclosed form(s).

12. Parentheses may be used in combination with numbers for several other purposes, such as setting off area codes in telephone numbers and indicating losses in accounting.

(413) 256-7899

Operating Profits (in millions)	
Cosmetics	26.2
Food products	47.7
Food services	54.3
Transportation	(17.7)
Sporting goods	(11.2)
Total	99.3

13. **With other marks of punctuation** If a parenthetic expression is an independent sentence, its first word is capitalized and a period is placed *inside* the last parenthesis. A parenthetic expression that occurs within a sentence—even

if it could stand alone as a separate sentence—does not end with a period. It may, however, end with an exclamation point, a question mark, a period after an abbreviation, or a set of quotation marks. A parenthetic expression within a sentence does not require capitalization unless it is a quoted sentence.

> The discussion was held in the boardroom. (The results are still confidential.)
> Although several trade organizations worked actively against the legislation (there were at least three paid lobbyists working on Capitol Hill at any one time), the bill passed easily.
> After waiting in line for an hour (why do we do these things?), we finally left.
> The conference was held in Vancouver (that's in B.C.).
> He was totally confused ("What can we do?") and refused to see anyone.

14. If a parenthetic expression within a sentence is composed of two independent clauses, capitalization is avoided and semicolons are usually used instead of periods. Independent sentences enclosed in parentheses employ normal patterns of capitalization and punctuation.

> We visited several showrooms, looked at the prices (it wasn't a pleasant experience; prices in this area have not gone down), and asked all the questions we could think of.
> We visited several showrooms and looked at the prices. (It wasn't a pleasant experience. Prices in this area have not gone down.) If salespeople were available, we asked all of the questions we could think of.

15. No punctuation mark (other than a period after an abbreviation) is placed before parenthetic material within a sentence; if a break is required, the punctuation is placed after the final parenthesis.

> I'll get back to you tomorrow (Friday), when I have more details.

16. Parentheses sometimes appear within parentheses, although the usual practice is to replace the inner pair of parentheses with a pair of brackets. (For an example of brackets within parentheses, see paragraph 6 under Brackets on page 111.)

> Checks must be drawn in U.S. dollars. (PLEASE NOTE: In accordance with U.S. Department of Treasury regulations, we cannot accept checks drawn on Canadian banks for amounts less than four U.S. dollars ($4.00). The same regulation applies to Canadian money orders.)

17. Dashes and parentheses are often used together to set off parenthetic material within a larger parenthetic element. For details and examples, see paragraph 11 under Dash on page 125.

18. **Spacing** In typewritten material a parenthetic expression that is an independent sentence is followed by two spaces. In typeset material, the sentence is followed by one space. In both typewritten and typeset material, a parenthetic expression that falls within a sentence is followed by one space.

```
We visited several showrooms and looked at the
   prices.  (It wasn't a pleasant experience.  Prices
   in this area have not gone down.)  We asked all the
   questions we could think of.
```
> We visited several showrooms and looked at the prices. (It wasn't a pleasant experience. Prices in this area have not gone down.) We asked all the questions we could think of.

PERIOD

1. A period ends a sentence or a sentence fragment that is neither interrogative nor exclamatory.

> Write the letter.
> They wrote the required letters.
> Total chaos. Nothing works.

2. A period punctuates some abbreviations. (For more on the punctuation of abbreviations, see the section on Abbreviations, beginning on page 172.)

a.k.a.	Assn.	Dr.	Jr.	Ph.D.
fig.	in.	No.	e.g.	ibid.
N.W.	U.S.	Inc.	Co.	Corp.

3. Periods are used with an individual's initials. If all of the person's initials are used instead of the name, however, the unspaced initials may be written without periods.

> F. Scott Fitzgerald   J.F.K. *or* JFK

4. A period follows Roman and Arabic numerals and also letters when they are used without parentheses in outlines and vertical lists.

> I. Objectives
>   A. Economy
>   1. Low initial cost
>   2. Low maintenance cost
>   B. Ease of operation
> Required skills are:
>   1. Shorthand
>   2. Typing
>   3. Transcription

5. A period is placed within quotation marks even when it does not punctuate the quoted material.

> The founder was known to his employees as "the old man."
> "I said I wanted to fire him," Henry went on, "but she said, 'I don't think you have the contractual privilege to do that.' "

6. When brackets or parentheses enclose a sentence that is independent of surrounding sentences, the period is placed inside the closing parenthesis or bracket. However, when brackets or parentheses enclose a sentence that is part of a surrounding sentence, the period for the enclosed sentence is omitted.

> On Friday the government ordered a 24-hour curfew and told all journalists and photographers to leave the area. (Authorities later confiscated the film of those who did not comply.)
> I took a good look at her (she was standing quite close to me at the time).

7. In typewritten material, two spaces follow a period that ends a sentence. If the period is followed by a closing bracket, closing parenthesis, or quotation marks, the two spaces follow the second mark.

> `Here is the car.  Do you want to get in?`
> `He said, "Here is the car."  I asked if I should get in.`

8. One space follows a period that comes after an initial in a name. If a name is composed entirely of initials, no space is required; however, the usual style for such names is to omit the periods.

> Mr. H. C. Matthews   L.B.J. *or* LBJ

9. No space follows an internal period within a punctuated abbreviation.

f.o.b. i.e. Ph.D. A.D. p.m.

QUESTION MARK

1. The question mark terminates a direct question.

What went wrong?
"Who signed the memo?" she asked

The intent of the writer, not the word order of the sentence, determines whether or not the sentence is a question. Polite requests that are worded as questions, for instance, usually take periods, because they are not really questions. Similarly, sentences whose word order is that of a statement but whose force is interrogatory are punctuated with question marks.

Will you please sit down.
He did that?

2. The question mark terminates an interrogative element that is part of a sentence. An indirect question is not followed by a question mark.

How did she do it? was the question on everybody's mind.
She wondered, will it work?
She wondered whether it would work.

3. The question mark punctuates each element of a series of questions that share a single beginning and are neither numbered nor lettered. When the series is numbered or lettered, only one question mark is used, and it is placed at the end of the series.

Can you give us a reasonable forecast? back up your predictions? compare them with last year's earnings?
Can you (1) give us a reasonable forecast, (2) back up your predictions, (3) compare them with last year's earnings?

4. The question mark indicates uncertainty about a fact.

Susan O'Hara, advertising vice president(?) of the corporation

5. The question mark is placed inside a closing bracket, dash, parenthesis, or pair of quotation marks when it punctuates only the material enclosed by that mark and not the sentence as a whole. It is placed outside that mark when it punctuates the entire sentence.

What did Andrew mean when he called the project "a fiasco from the start"?
I took a vacation in 1989 (was it really that long ago?), but I haven't had time for one since.
He asked, "Do you realize the extent of the problem [the housing shortage]?"

6. In typewritten material, two spaces follow a question mark that ends a sentence. If the question mark is followed by a closing bracket, closing parenthesis, or quotation marks, the two spaces follow the second mark. In typeset material, only one space follows the question mark.

```
She wondered, will it work?  He said he thought so.
She asked, "Will it work?"  He said he thought so.
```
She wondered, will it work? He said he thought so.

7. One space follows a question mark that falls within a sentence.

Are you coming today? tomorrow? the day after?

QUOTATION MARKS, DOUBLE

The following paragraphs describe the use of quotation marks to enclose quoted matter in regular text, to enclose translations of words, or to enclose single letters within sentences. For the use of quotation marks to enclose titles of poems, paintings, or other works, see the section on Capitals, Italics, and Quotation Marks, beginning on page 140.

1. **Basic uses** Quotation marks enclose direct quotations but not indirect quotations.

> She said, "I am leaving for Frankfurt Monday."
> "I am leaving Monday," she said, "and I'm not coming back until the 1st."
> "I am leaving," she said. "This meeting could go on forever."
> She said that she was leaving.

2. Quotation marks enclose fragments of quoted matter when they are reproduced exactly as originally stated.

> The agreement makes it clear that he "will be paid only upon receipt of an acceptable manuscript."
> As late as 1754, documents refer to him as "yeoman" and "husbandman."

3. Quotation marks enclose words or phrases borrowed from others, words used in a special way, or words of marked informality when they are introduced into formal writing.

> That kind of corporation is referred to as "closed" or "privately held."
> Be sure to send a copy of your résumé, or as some folks would say, your "biodata summary."
> They were afraid the patient had "stroked out"—had had a cerebrovascular accident.

4. Quotation marks are sometimes used to enclose words referred to as words. Italic type or underlining is also frequently used for this purpose. (For more on this use of italics, see paragraph 4 under Other Uses of Italics, pages 155–56.)

> He went through the manuscript and changed every "he" to "she."

5. Quotation marks enclose short exclamations or representations of sounds. Representations of sounds are also frequently set in italic type or underlined. (For more on this use of italics, see paragraph 6 under Other Uses of Italics, page 155.)

> "Ssshh!" she hissed.
> They never say anything crude like "shaddap."

6. Quotation marks enclose short sentences that fall within longer sentences, especially when the shorter sentence is meant to suggest spoken dialogue. Kinds of sentences that may be treated in this way include mottoes and maxims, unspoken or imaginary dialogue, and sentences referred to as sentences.

> Throughout the conference, the spirit was "We can do."
> She never could get used to their "That's the way it goes" attitude.
> In effect, the voters were saying "You blew it, and you don't get another chance."
> Their reaction could only be described as "Kill the messenger."

Some writers omit the quotation marks in sentences whose structure is clear without them. However, in general, quotation marks set the shorter sentence off more distinctly and convey more of the feel of spoken dialogue.

(For the use of commas in sentences like these, see paragraphs 32–34 under Comma on page 120.)

> The first rule is, When in doubt, spell it out.
> They weren't happy with the impression she left: "Don't expect favors, because I don't have to give them."

7. Quotation marks are not used to enclose paraphrases.

> Build a better mousetrap, Emerson says, and the world will beat a path to your door.

8. Direct questions are usually not enclosed in quotation marks unless they represent quoted dialogue.

> As we listened to him, we couldn't help wondering, Where's the plan?
> The question is, What went wrong?
> She asked, "What went wrong?"

As in the sentences presented in paragraph 6 above, style varies regarding the use of quotation marks with direct questions, and writers will often include the quotation marks.

> As we listened to him, we couldn't help wondering, "Where's the plan?"

9. Quotation marks are used to enclose translations of foreign or borrowed terms.

> The term *sesquipedalian* comes from the Latin word *sesquipedalis*, meaning "a foot and a half long."
> While in Texas, he encountered the armadillo ("little armored one").

10. Quotation marks are sometimes used to enclose single letters within a sentence.

> The letter "m" is wider than the letter "i."
> Put an "x" in the right spot.
> The metal rod was shaped into a "V."

However, practice varies on this point. Letters referred to as letters are commonly set in italic type or underlined. (For more on this use of italics, see paragraphs 4 and 5 under Other Uses of Italics on pages 155–56.) Letters often appear undifferentiated from the surrounding text where no confusion would result.

> a V-shaped blade
> He was happy to get a B in the course.
> How many e's are in her name?

11. With other marks of punctuation When quotation marks follow a word in a sentence that is also followed by a period or comma, the period or comma is placed within the quotation marks.

> He said, "I am leaving."
> The packages are labeled "Handle with Care."
> The cameras were described as "waterproof," but "moisture-resistant" would have been a better description.

Some writers draw a distinction, however, between periods and commas that belong logically to the quoted material and those that belong to the whole sentence. If the period or comma belongs to the quoted material, they place it inside the quotation marks; if it belongs logically to the larger sentence, they place it outside the quotation marks. Today the distinction is made by few writers.

The packages are labeled "Handle with Care".
The cameras were described as "waterproof", but "moisture-resistant" would have been a better description.

12. When quotation marks follow a word in a sentence that is also followed by a colon or semicolon, the colon or semicolon is placed outside the quotation marks.

   There was only one thing to do when he said, "I may not run": promise him a larger campaign contribution.
   She spoke of her "little cottage in the country"; she might better have called it a mansion.

13. The dash, question mark, and exclamation point are placed inside quotation marks when they punctuate the quoted matter only. They are placed outside the quotation marks when they punctuate the whole sentence.

   He asked, "When did they leave?"
   What is the meaning of "the open door"?
   Save us from his "mercy"!
   "I can't see how—" he started to say.
   He thought he knew where he was going—he remembered her saying, "Take two lefts, then stay to the right"—but the streets didn't look familiar.

14. **Spacing** One space follows a quotation mark that is followed by the rest of a sentence.

   "I am leaving Monday," she said.

15. In typewritten material, two spaces follow a quotation mark that ends a sentence. In typeset material one space follows.

   ```
   He said, "Here's the car."  I asked if I should get in.
   ```
   He said, "Here's the car." I asked if I should get in.

QUOTATION MARKS, SINGLE

1. Single quotation marks enclose a quotation within a quotation. When both single and double quotation marks occur at the end of a sentence, the period typically falls within *both* sets of marks.

   The witness said, "I distinctly heard him say, 'Don't be late,' and then I heard the door close."
   The witness said, "I distinctly heard him say, 'Don't be late.' "

2. Single quotation marks are occasionally used in place of double quotation marks. This is far more common in British usage.

   The witness said, 'I distinctly heard him say, "Don't be late," and then I heard the door close.'

3. On rare occasions, writers face the question of how to punctuate a quotation within a quotation within a quotation. Standard practice would be to enclose the innermost quotation in double marks; however, this can be confusing, and rewriting the sentence can often remove the need for it.

   The witness said, "I distinctly heard him say, 'Don't you say "Shut up" to me.' "
   The witness said that she distinctly heard him say, "Don't you say 'Shut up' to me."

SEMICOLON

The semicolon is used in ways similar to those in which periods and commas are used. Like a period, the semicolon marks the end of a complete clause, but it also signals that the clause that follows it is closely related to the one that precedes it. The semicolon is also used to distinguish major divisions from the minor pauses that are represented by commas.

1. **Between clauses** A semicolon separates independent clauses that are joined together in one sentence without a coordinating conjunction.

   Some people are natural leaders in their willingness to accept responsibility and delegate authority with intelligence; others do not measure up.
   He hemmed and hawed for an hour or more; he couldn't make up his mind.

2. Ordinarily a comma separates main clauses joined with a coordinating conjunction. However, if the sentence might be confusing with a comma in this position, a semicolon is used in its place. Potentially confusing sentences include those with other commas in them or with particularly long clauses.

   We fear that this situation may, in fact, occur; but we don't know when.
   In a society that seeks to promote social goals, government will play a powerful role; and taxation, once simply a means of raising money, becomes, in addition, a way of furthering those goals.
   As recently as 1978 the company felt the operation could be a successful one that would generate significant profits in several different markets; but in 1981 the management changed its mind and began a program of shutting down plants and reducing its product line.

3. A semicolon joins two statements when the grammatical construction of the second clause is elliptical and depends on that of the first.

   In many cases the conference sessions, which were designed to allow for full discussions of topics, were much too long and tedious; the breaks between them, much too short.

4. A semicolon joins two clauses when the second begins with a conjunctive adverb, such as *accordingly, also, besides, consequently, furthermore, hence, however, indeed, likewise, moreover, namely, nevertheless, otherwise, still, then, therefore,* and *thus.* Phrases such as *by the same token, in that case, as a result, on the other hand,* and *all the same* can also act as conjunctive adverbs.

   Most people are covered by insurance of one kind or another; indeed, many people don't even see their medical bills.
   It won't be easy to sort out the facts; however, a decision must be made.
   The case could take years to work its way through the court system; as a result, many plantiffs will accept out-of-court settlements.

   Practice varies regarding the treatment of clauses introduced by *so* and *yet.* Although many writers continue to treat *so* and *yet* as adverbs, it has become standard to treat these words as coordinating conjunctions that join clauses. In this treatment, a comma precedes *so* and *yet* and no punctuation follows them. (For examples, see paragraph 1 under Comma on page 114.)

5. When three or more clauses are separated by semicolons, a coordinating conjunction may or may not precede the final clause. If a coordinating conjunction does precede the final clause, the final semicolon is often replaced with a comma. (For the use of commas to separate three or more clauses without conjunctions, see paragraph 4 under Comma on page 115.)

Their report was one-sided and partial; it did not reflect the facts; it dis-
torted them.
They don't understand; they grow bored; and they stop learning.
The report recounted events leading up to this incident; it included observations of eyewitnesses, but it drew no conclusions.

The choice of whether or not to use a conjunction, and whether to use a
semicolon or a comma with the conjunction, are matters of personal preference. In general, the semicolon makes the transition to the final clause more
abrupt, which often serves to place more emphasis on that clause. The
comma and conjunction ease the transition and make the sentence seem less
choppy.

6. **With phrases and clauses introduced by** *for example*, *i.e.*, **etc.** A semicolon
is sometimes used before expressions (such as *for example, for instance, that is,
namely, e.g.,* or *i.e.*) that introduce expansions or series. Commas, dashes, and
parentheses are also used in sentences like these. For contrasting examples,
see paragraph 18 under Comma on page 117, paragraph 6 under Dash on
page 124, and paragraph 2 under Parentheses on page 129.

On one point only did everyone agree; namely, that too much money had
been spent already.
We were fairly successful on that project; that is, we made our deadlines
and met our budget.
Most had traveled great distances to participate; for example, three had
come from Australia, one from Japan, and two from China.

7. **In a series** A semicolon is used in place of a comma to separate phrases in a
series when the phrases themselves contain commas. A comma may replace
the semicolon before the last item in a series if the last item is introduced
with a conjunction.

The visitor to Barndale can choose from three sources of overnight ac-
commodation: The Rose and Anchor, which houses Barndale's oldest
pub; The Crawford, an American-style luxury hotel; and Ellen's Bed
and Breakfast on Peabody Lane.
The schedule calls for orientation and planning sessions in the morning;
talks on marketing, long-term investments and tax laws directly after
lunch, and an introduction to computer terminology in the late afternoon.

8. When the individual items in an enumeration or series are long or are sentences themselves, they are usually separated by semicolons.

Among the committee's recommendations were the following: more hospital beds in urban areas where there are waiting lines for elective sur-
gery; smaller staff size in half-empty rural hospitals; review procedures
for all major purchases.

9. A semicolon separates items in a list in cases where a comma alone would not
clearly separate the items or references.

(Friedlander 1957; Ballas 1962)
(Genesis 3:1–19; 4:1–16)

10. **With other marks of punctuation** A semicolon is placed outside quotation
marks and parentheses.

They referred to each other as "Mother" and "Father"; they were the ar-
chetypal happily married elderly couple.

She accepted the situation with every appearance of equanimity (but with some inward qualms); however, all of that changed the next day.

SLASH

The slash is known by many names, including *virgule, diagonal, solidus, oblique,* and *slant.* Most commonly, the slash is used to represent a word that is not written out or to separate or set off certain adjacent elements of text.

1. **In place of missing words** A slash represents the words *per* or *to* when used with units of measure or when used to indicate the terms of a ratio.

40,000 tons/year	9 ft./sec.	a 50/50 split
14 gm/100 cc	price/earnings ratio	risk/reward tradeoff

2. A slash separates alternatives. In this context, the slash usually represents the words *or* or *and/or.*

alumni/ae	introductory/refresher courses
his/her	oral/written tests

3. A slash replaces the word *and* in some compound terms.

   molybdenum/vanadium steel
   in the May/June issue
   1973/74
   in the Falls Church/McLean, Va., area
   an innovative classroom/laboratory

4. A slash is used, although less commonly, to replace a number of prepositions, such as *at, versus, with,* and *for.*

U.C./Berkeley	parent/child issues
table/mirror	Vice President/Editorial

5. **With abbreviations** A slash punctuates some abbreviations.

c/o	A/V	d/b/a
A/R	A/1C	S/Sgt
w/	V/STOL	

   In some cases the slash may stand for a word that is not represented in the abbreviation (e.g., *in* in *W/O,* the abbreviation for *water in oil*).

6. **To separate elements** The slash may be used in a number of different ways to separate groups of numbers, such as elements in a date, numerators and denominators in fractions, and area codes in telephone numbers. For more on the use of the slash with numbers, see the section on Numbers, beginning on page 180.

7. The slash serves as a divider between lines of poetry that are run in with the text around them. This method of quoting poetry is usually limited to passages of no more than three or four lines. Longer passages are usually set off from the text as extract quotations.

   When Samuel Taylor Coleridge wrote in "Christabel" that "'Tis a month before the month of May,/And the Spring comes slowly up this way," he could have been describing New England.

8. **Spacing** In general, no space is used between the slash and the words, letters, or figures separated by it; however, some writers do prefer to place spaces around a slash used to separate lines of poetry.

Capitals, Italics, and Quotation Marks

Words and phrases are capitalized, italicized or underlined (underlining in typed or keyboarded material is equivalent to italics in typeset material), or enclosed in quotation marks in order to indicate that they have a special significance in particular contexts. The section that follows is divided into four parts that describe these contexts. The first part explains the use of capitalized words to begin sentences and phrases. The second explains the use of capitals, italics, and quotation marks to indicate that a word or phrase is a proper noun, pronoun, or adjective. The third and fourth parts explain other uses of capital letters and italics. For other uses of quotation marks, see pages 134–36.

BEGINNINGS

1. The first word of a sentence or sentence fragment is capitalized.

   The meeting was postponed.
   No! I cannot do it.
   Total chaos. Nothing works.

2. The first word of a sentence contained within parentheses is capitalized. However, a parenthetical sentence occurring inside another sentence is not capitalized unless it is a complete quoted sentence.

   The discussion was held in the boardroom. (The results are still confidential.)
   Although we liked the services they could provide (their banquet facilities were especially good), we could not afford to go there often.
   After waiting in line for an hour (why do we do these things?), we finally left.
   He was totally demoralized ("There is just nothing we can do") and was contemplating resignation.

3. The first word of a direct quotation is capitalized. However, if the quotation is interrupted in midsentence, the second part does not begin with a capital.

   The President said, "We have rejected this report entirely."
   "We have rejected this report entirely," the President said, "and we will not comment on it further."

4. When a quotation, whether a sentence fragment or a complete sentence, is syntactically dependent on the sentence in which it occurs, the quotation does not begin with a capital.

   The President made it clear that "there is no room for compromise."

5. The first word of a sentence within a sentence is usually capitalized. Examples of sentences within sentences include mottoes and rules, unspoken or imaginary dialogue, sentences referred to as sentences, and direct questions. (For an explanation of the use of commas and quotation marks with sentences such as these, see paragraphs 34 and 35 under Comma on pages 120–21 and paragraphs 6 and 8 under Quotation Marks, Double, on pages 134–35.)

   You know the saying, "Honesty is the best policy."
   The first rule is, When in doubt, spell it out.
   The clear message coming back from the audience was "We don't care."
   My question is, When can we go?

6. The first word of a line of poetry is usually capitalized.

> The best lack all conviction, while the worst
> Are full of passionate intensity.
> —W. B. Yeats

7. The first word following a colon may be either lowercased or capitalized if it introduces a complete sentence. While the former is the usual style, the latter is also common, especially when the sentence introduced by the colon is lengthy and distinctly separate from the preceding clause.

> The advantage of this particular system is clear: it's inexpensive.
> The situation is critical: This company cannot hope to recoup the fourth-quarter losses that were sustained in five operating divisions.

8. If a colon introduces a series of sentences, the first word of each sentence is capitalized.

> Consider the following steps that we have taken: A subcommittee has been formed to evaluate our past performance and to report its findings to the full organization. New sources of revenue are being explored, and relevant organizations are being contacted. And several candidates have been interviewed for the new post of executive director.

9. The first words of run-in enumerations that form complete sentences are capitalized, as are the first words of vertical lists and enumerations. Numbered phrases *within* a sentence, however, are lowercased.

> Do the following tasks at the end of the day: 1. Clean your keyboard. 2. Clear your desktop of papers. 3. Cover office machines. 4. Straighten the contents of your desk drawers, cabinets, and bookcases.
> This is the agenda:
> Call to order
> Roll call
> Minutes of the previous meeting
> Treasurer's report
> On the agenda will be (1) call to order, (2) roll call, (3) minutes of the previous meeting, (4) treasurer's report . . .

10. In minutes and legislation, the introductory words *Whereas* and *Resolved* either are entirely capitalized or have their first letter capitalized. The word *That* or an alternative word or expression which immediately follows *Whereas* or *Resolved* has its first letter capitalized.

> RESOLVED, That . . . *or* Resolved, That . . .
> WHEREAS, Substantial benefits . . . *or* Whereas, Substantial benefits . . .

11. The first word in an outline heading is capitalized.

> I. Editorial tasks
> II. Production responsibilities
>   A. Cost estimates
>   B. Bids

12. The first word of the salutation of a letter and the first word of a complimentary close are capitalized.

Dear Mary,	Dear Sir or Madam:	Ladies and Gentlemen:
Gentlemen:	Sincerely yours,	Very truly yours,

13. The first word and each subsequent major word following a SUBJECT or TO heading (as in a memorandum) are capitalized.

> SUBJECT: Pension Plans
> TO: All Department Heads and Editors

PROPER NOUNS, PRONOUNS, AND ADJECTIVES

The following paragraphs describe the ways in which a broad range of proper nouns, pronouns, and adjectives are styled—with capitals, italics, quotation marks, or some combination of these devices. In almost all cases, proper nouns, pronouns, and adjectives are capitalized. In many cases, proper nouns are italicized (or underlined in typewritten material) or enclosed in quotation marks in addition to being capitalized. No clear distinctions can be drawn between the kinds of words that are capitalized and italicized, capitalized and enclosed in quotation marks, or simply capitalized.

The paragraphs that follow are grouped under the following alphabetically arranged headings:

Abbreviations	Governmental, Judicial, and Political Bodies	Organizations
Abstractions and Personifications	Historical Periods and Events	People
Academic Degrees		Pronouns
Animals and Plants	Hyphenated Compounds	Religious Terms
Awards, Honors, and Prizes	Legal Material	Scientific Terms
Derivatives of Proper Names	Medical Terms	Time Periods and Zones
	Military Terms	Titles
Geographical and Topographical References	Numerical Designations	Trademarks
		Transportation

1. **Abbreviations** Abbreviated forms of proper nouns and adjectives are capitalized, just as the spelled-out forms would be. (For more on the capitalization of abbreviations, see the section on Abbreviations, beginning on page 172.)

> Dec. [for *December*]   Wed. [for *Wednesday*]
> Col. [for *Colonel*]   Brit. [for *British*]

2. **Abstractions and personifications** Abstract terms, such as names of concepts or qualities, are usually not capitalized unless the concept or quality is being presented as if it were a person. If the term is simply being used in conjunction with other words that allude to human characteristics or qualities, it is usually not capitalized. (For more on the capitalization of abstract terms, see paragraph 2 under Other Uses of Capitals on page 154.)

> a time when Peace walked among us
> as Autumn paints each leaf in fiery colors
> an economy gripped by inflation
> hoping that fate would lend a hand

3. Fictitious names used as personifications are capitalized.

> Uncle Sam   Ma Bell   Big Oil

4. **Academic degrees** The names of academic degrees are capitalized when they follow a person's name. The names of specific academic degrees not

following a person's name may be capitalized or not capitalized, according to individual preference. General terms referring to degrees, such as *doctorate*, *master's degree*, or *bachelor's* are not capitalized. Abbreviations for academic degrees are always capitalized.

E. Terence Ford, Doctor of Divinity
earned her Doctor of Laws degree   *or*   earned her doctor of laws degree
working for a bachelor's degree
Susan Wycliff, M.S.W.
received her Ph.D.

5. **Animals and plants** The common names of animals and plants are not capitalized unless they contain a proper noun as a separate element, in which case the proper noun is capitalized and elements preceding (but not following) the proper noun are usually but not always capitalized. If the common name contains a word that was once a proper noun but is no longer thought of as such, the word is usually not capitalized. When in doubt, consult a dictionary. (For an explanation of the capitalization of scientific names, see paragraphs 67–73 on pages 151–52.)

cocker spaniel	lily of the valley	ponderosa pine
great white shark	Hampshire hog	Kentucky bluegrass
Steller's jay	Bengal tiger	Japanese beetle
Rhode Island red	Great Dane	Brown Swiss
black-eyed Susan	wandering Jew	holstein

In references to specific breeds, as distinguished from the animals that belong to the breed, all elements of the name are capitalized.

Gordon Setter   Rhode Island Red   Holstein

6. **Awards, honors, and prizes** Names of awards, honors, and prizes are capitalized. Descriptive words and phrases that are not actually part of the award's name are lowercased. (For an explanation of capitalizing the names of military decorations, see paragraph 44 on page 148.)

Academy Award	New York Drama Critics' Circle
Emmy	Award
Nobel Prize winner	Rhodes Scholarship
Nobel Prize in medicine	Rhodes scholar
Nobel Peace Prize	

7. **Derivatives of proper names** Derivatives of proper names are capitalized when they are used in their primary sense. However, if the derived term has taken on a specialized meaning, it is usually not capitalized.

Roman architecture	Victorian customs	Keynesian economics
an Americanism	an Egyptologist	french fries
manila envelope	pasteurized milk	a quixotic undertaking

8. **Geographical and topographical references** Terms that identify divisions of the earth's surface and distinct areas, regions, places, or districts are capitalized, as are derivative nouns and adjectives.

Chicago, Illinois	the Great Plains
the Middle Eastern situation	the Mariana Trench
the Southwest	the Riviera

9. Popular names of localities are capitalized.

the Big Apple	the Loop	Hell's Kitchen
the Village	the Twin Cities	the Valley

10. Compass points are capitalized when they refer to a geographical region or when they are part of a street name. They are lowercased when they refer to a simple direction.

back East	West Columbus Avenue
out West	down South
east of the Mississippi	traveling north on I-91

11. Nouns and adjectives that are derived from compass points and that designate or refer to a specific geographical region are usually capitalized.

a Southern accent	a Western crop
Northerners	part of the Eastern establishment

12. Words designating global, national, regional, or local political divisions are capitalized when they are essential elements of specific names. However, they are usually lowercased when they precede a proper name or when they are not part of a specific name.

the British Empire	New York City
the fall of the empire	the city of New York
Washington State	Ward 1
the state of Washington	fires in three wards
Hampden County	Ohio's Ninth Congressional District
the county of Hampden	carried her district

    In legal documents, these words are often capitalized regardless of position.

the State of Washington	the County of Hampden	the City of New York

13. Common geographical terms (such as *lake, mountain, river, valley*) are capitalized if they are part of a specific proper name.

Crater Lake	Hudson Bay	Strait of Gibraltar
the Columbia River	Lake Como	Rocky Mountains
Great Barrier Reef	Ohio Valley	Bering Strait

14. Common geographical terms preceding names are usually capitalized.

Lakes Mead and Powell	Mounts Whitney and Shasta

    When *the* precedes the common term, the term is lowercased.

    the river Thames

15. Common geographical terms that are not used as part of a proper name are not capitalized. These include plural terms that follow two or more proper names and terms that are used descriptively or alone.

the Himalaya and Andes mountains	the Missouri and Platte rivers
the Atlantic coast of Labrador	the Arizona desert
the river valley	the Caribbean islands

16. The names of streets, monuments, parks, landmarks, well-known buildings, and other public places are capitalized. However, common terms that are part of these names (such as *avenue, bridge,* or *tower*) are lowercased when they occur after multiple names or are used alone (but see paragraph 17 below).

Eddystone Lighthouse	Golden Gate Bridge	walking through the park
the San Diego Zoo	on the bridge	
the Pyramids	The Capitol	Rock Creek Park

| Coit Tower | the Dorset Hotel | Fifth Avenue |
| Faneuil Hall | the Dorset and Drake hotels | Fifth and Park avenues |

17. Well-known informal or shortened forms of place names are capitalized.

the Avenue [for *Fifth Avenue*]
the Street [for *Wall Street*]
the Exchange [for the *New York Stock Exchange*]

18. Governmental, judicial, and political bodies Full names of legislative, deliberative, executive, and administrative bodies are capitalized, as are easily recognizable short forms of these names. However, nonspecific noun and adjective references to them are usually lowercased.

United States Congress	the Federal Reserve Board
the Congress	the Fed
the House	the Federal Bureau of Investigation
congressional hearings	a federal agency

Practice varies regarding the capitalization of words such as *department, committee,* or *agency* when used in place of the full name of a specific body. They are most often capitalized when the department or agency is referring to itself in print; in most other cases, these words are lowercased.

The Connecticut Department of Transportation is pleased to offer this new booklet on traffic safety. The Department hopes that it will be of use to all drivers.
We received a new booklet from the Connecticut Department of Transportation. This is the second pamphlet the department has issued this month.

19. The full and short names of the U.S. Supreme Court are capitalized.

The Supreme Court of the United States
the United States Supreme Court
the Supreme Court
the Court

20. Official and full names of higher courts and names of international courts are capitalized. Short forms of official higher-court names are often capitalized in legal documents but lowercased in general writing.

The International Court of Arbitration
the United States Court of Appeals for the Second Circuit
the Virginia Supreme Court
the Court of Queen's Bench
a ruling by the court of appeals
the state supreme court

21. Names of city and county courts are usually lowercased.

the Lawton municipal court	police court
the Owensville night court	the county court
small-claims court	juvenile court

22. The designation *court,* when it applies to a specific judge or presiding officer, is capitalized.

It is the opinion of this Court that . . .
The Court found that . . .

23. The terms *federal* and *national* are capitalized only when they are essential elements of a name or title.

Federal Trade Commission   National Security Council
federal court   national security

24. The word *administration* is capitalized by some writers when it refers to the administration of a specific U.S. president, but is more commonly lowercased. If the word does not refer to a specific presidency, it is not capitalized except when it is a part of the official name of a government agency.

the Truman administration   *or*   the Truman Administration
the administration   *or*   the Administration
the Farmers Home Loan Administration
The running of the White House varies considerably from one administration to another.

25. Names of political organizations and their adherents are capitalized, but the word *party* may or may not be capitalized, depending on the writer's preference.

Tories   Nazis
the Democratic National   the Republican platform
  Committee
the Democratic party   *or*   the Democratic Party
the Communist party   *or*   the Communist Party

26. Names of political groups other than parties are usually lowercased, as are their derivative forms.

the right wing
the liberals
  but usually
the Left
the Right

27. Terms describing political and economic philosophies and their derivative forms are usually capitalized only if they are derived from proper names.

authoritarianism   nationalism   isolationist
democracy   supply-side economics   civil libertarian
fascism *or* Fascism   social Darwinism   Marxist

28. Historical periods and events The names of conferences, councils, expositions, and specific sporting, historical, and cultural events are capitalized.

the Yalta Conference   the Philadelphia Folk Festival
the Minnesota State Fair   the Games of the XXIII Olympiad
the World Series   the San Francisco Earthquake
the Series   the Boston Tea Party

29. The names of some historical and cultural periods and movements are capitalized. When in doubt, consult a dictionary or encyclopedia.

the Augustan Age   the Renaissance   the Stone Age
Prohibition   the Enlightenment   the Great Depression
the fin de siècle   the space age   the cold war *or* the Cold War

30. Numerical designations of historical time periods are capitalized only when they are part of a proper name; otherwise they are lowercased.

the Third Reich   the Roaring Twenties
the seventeenth century   the eighties

31. Full names of treaties, laws, and acts are capitalized.

Treaty of Versailles   The Controlled Substances Act of
1970

32. The full names of wars are capitalized. However, words such as *war, revolution, battle,* and *campaign* are capitalized only when they are part of a proper name. Descriptive terms such as *assault, siege,* and *engagement* are usually lowercased even when used in conjunction with the name of the place where the action occurred.

the French and Indian War   the War of the Spanish Succession
the Battle of the Bulge   the Whiskey Rebellion
the Peninsular Campaign   the American and French revolutions
the second battle of Manassas   the siege of Yorktown
the Meuse-Argonne offensive   the winter campaign
through most of the war

33. Hyphenated compounds Elements of hyphenated compounds are generally capitalized only if they are proper nouns or adjectives.

Arab-Israeli negotiations   French-speaking peoples
East-West trade agreements   Thirty-second Street
an eighteenth-century poet

34. Word elements (such as prefixes and combining forms) may or may not be capitalized when joined to a proper noun or adjective. Common prefixes (such as *pre-* or *anti-*) are usually not capitalized in such cases. Geographical and ethnic combining forms (such as *Anglo-* or *Sino-*) are capitalized; *pan-* is usually capitalized when attached to a proper noun or adjective.

the pro-Soviet faction   post-Civil War politics
Sino-Soviet relations   African-Americans
Pan-Slavic nationalism   Greco-Roman architecture

35. Legal material The names of both plaintiff and defendant in legal case titles are italicized (or underlined in typewritten material). The *v.* (for *versus*) may be roman or italic. Cases that do not involve two opposing parties have titles such as *In re Watson* or *In the matter of John Watson*, which are also italicized. When the person involved rather than the case itself is being discussed, the reference is not italicized.

Jones v. *Massachusetts*
In re Jones
Smith et al. v. Jones
She covered the Jones trial for the newspaper.

In running text, a case name involving two opposing parties may be shortened.

The judge based his ruling on a precedent set in the *Jones* decision.

36. Medical terms Proper names that are elements in terms designating diseases, symptoms, syndromes, and tests are capitalized. Common nouns are lowercased.

Duchenne-Erb paralysis   Parkinson's disease
German measles   Rorschach test
acquired immune deficiency   mumps
  syndrome   herpes simplex

37. Scientific names of disease-causing organisms follow the rules discussed in paragraph 67 on page 151. The names of diseases or conditions derived from scientific names of organisms are lowercased and not italicized.

> a neurotoxin produced by *Clostridium botulinum*
> nearly died of botulism

38. Generic names of drugs are lowercased; trade names should be capitalized.

> a prescription for chlorpromazine
> had been taking Thorazine

39. **Military terms** The full titles of branches of the armed forces are capitalized, as are easily recognized short forms.

> U.S. Marine Corps   the Marines
> the Marine Corps   the Corps

40. The terms *air force, army, coast guard, marine(s),* and *navy* are lowercased unless they form part of an official name or refer back to a specific branch of the armed forces previously named. They are also lowercased when they are used collectively or in the plural.

> the combined air forces of the NATO nations
> the navies of the world
> the American army

41. The adjectives *naval* and *marine* are lowercased unless they are part of a proper name.

> naval battle   marine barracks   Naval Reserves

42. The full titles of units and organizations of the armed forces are capitalized. Elements of full titles are often lowercased when they stand alone.

> U.S. Army Corps of Engineers   the Corps
> the Reserves   a reserve commission
> First Battalion   the battalion
> 4th Marine Regiment   the regiment
> Eighth Fleet   the fleet

43. Military ranks are capitalized when they precede the names of their holders, and when they take the place of a person's name (as in direct address). Otherwise they are lowercased.

> General Colin Powell
> I can't get this rifle any cleaner, Sergeant.
> The major arrived precisely on time.

44. The specific names of decorations, citations, and medals are capitalized.

> Medal of Honor   Purple Heart
> Navy Cross   Distinguished Service Medal

45. **Numerical designations** A noun introducing a reference number is usually capitalized.

> Order 704   Flight 409   Form 2E   Policy 118-4-Y

46. Nouns used with numbers or letters to designate major reference headings (as in a literary work) are capitalized. However, nouns designating minor reference headings are typically lowercased.

> Book II   Table 3   paragraph 6.1
> Volume V   page 101   item 16
> Division 4   line 8   question 21

47. **Organizations** Names of firms, corporations, schools, and organizations and terms derived from those names to designate their members are capitalized. However, common nouns used descriptively or occurring after the names of two or more organizations are lowercased.

    Merriam-Webster Inc.   played as a Pirate last year
    University of Michigan   Kiwanians
    Washington Huskies   American and United airlines

    The word *the* at the beginning of such names is capitalized only when the full legal name is used.

48. Words such as *agency, department, division, group,* or *office* that designate corporate and organizational units are capitalized only when they are used with a specific name.

    while working for the Criminal Division in the Department of Justice
    a notice to all department heads

    Style varies regarding the capitalization of these words when they are used in place of the full name of a specific body; see paragraph 18 on page 145.

49. Nicknames, epithets, or other alternative terms for organizations are capitalized.

    referred to IBM as Big Blue
    the Big Three automakers
    trading stocks on the Big Board

50. **People** The names and initials of persons are capitalized. If a name is hyphenated, both elements are capitalized. Particles forming the initial elements of surnames (as *de, della, der, du, la, ten, ter, van,* and *von*) may or may not be capitalized, depending on the practice of the family or individual. However, the particle is always capitalized at the beginning of a sentence.

    Thomas De Quincey   Gerald ter Hoerst
    Sir Arthur Thomas   Heinrich Wilhelm von Kleist
    Quiller-Couch   the paintings of de Kooning
    James Van Allen   De Kooning's paintings are . . .
    E. I. du Pont de Nemours

51. The name of a person or thing can be added to or replaced entirely by a nickname or epithet (a characterizing word or phrase). Nicknames and epithets are capitalized.

    Calamity Jane   Magic Johnson   Attila the Hun
    Big Mama Thornton   Ol' Blue Eyes   Meadowlark Lemon

52. Nicknames and epithets are frequently used in conjunction with both the first and last name of a person. If it is placed between the first and last name, it will often be enclosed in quotation marks or parentheses. However, if the nickname is in general use, the quotation marks or parentheses are often omitted. If the nickname precedes the first name, it is sometimes enclosed in quotation marks but more often not.

    Earl ("Fatha") Hines   Joanne "Big Mama" Carner
    Mary Harris ("Mother") Jones   Dennis (Oil Can) Boyd
    Kissin' Jim Folsom   Mother Maybelle Carter

53. Words of family relationship preceding or used in place of a person's name are capitalized. However, these words are lowercased if they are part of a noun phrase that is being used in place of a name.

Cousin Mercy   Grandfather Barnes
I know when Mother's birthday is.
I know when my mother's birthday is.

54. Words designating languages, nationalities, peoples, races, religious groups, and tribes are capitalized. Descriptive terms used to refer to groups of people are variously capitalized or lowercased. Designations based on color are usually lowercased.

Latino   Canadians   Ibo   African-American
Caucasians   Muslims
Bushman (nomadic hunter of southern Africa)
bushman (inhabitant of the Australian bush)
black, brown, and white people

55. Corporate, professional, and governmental titles are capitalized when they immediately precede a person's name, unless the name is being used as an appositive.

President Roosevelt   Queen Elizabeth   Senator Sam Nunn
Doctor Malatesta   Professor Kaiser   Pastor Linda Jones
the new pastor, Linda Jones
Chrysler's former president, Lee Iacocca

56. When corporate or governmental titles are used as part of a descriptive phrase to identify a person rather than as a person's official title, the title is lowercased.

Senator Bill Bradley of New Jersey
    but
Bill Bradley, senator from New Jersey

Style varies when governmental titles are used in descriptive phrases that precede a name.

New Jersey senator Bill Bradley   *or*   New Jersey Senator Bill Bradley

57. Specific governmental titles may be capitalized when they are used in place of particular individuals' names. In minutes and official records of proceedings, corporate titles are capitalized when they are used in place of individuals' names.

The Secretary of State gave a news conference.
The Judge will respond to questions in her chambers.
The Treasurer then stated his misgivings about the project.

58. Some writers always capitalize the word *president* when it refers to the U.S. presidency. However, the more common practice is to capitalize the word *president* only when it refers to a specific individual.

It is the duty of the president [President] to submit a budget to Congress.

59. Titles are capitalized when they are used in direct address.

Tell me the truth, Doctor.
Where are we headed, Captain?

60. **Pronouns** The pronoun *I* is capitalized. (For pronouns referring to the Deity, see paragraph 62 below.)

He and I will attend the meeting.

61. **Religious terms** Words designating the Deity are capitalized.

Allah   God Almighty   the Creator
Jehovah   Yahweh   the Holy Spirit

62. Personal pronouns referring to the Deity are usually capitalized. Relative pronouns (such as *who, whom,* and *whose*) usually are not.

> God in His mercy
> believing that it was God who created the universe

63. Traditional designations of apostles, prophets, and saints are capitalized.

> Our Lady   the Prophet   the Lawgiver

64. Names of religions, denominations, creeds and confessions, and religious orders are capitalized, as are adjectives derived from these names. The word *church* is capitalized only when it is used as part of the name of a specific body or edifice or, in some publications, when it refers to organized Christianity in general.

> Judaism   Islamic
> the Church of Christ   the Southern Baptist Convention
> Apostles' Creed   the Baptist church on the corner
> the Poor Clares   the Society of Jesus
> Hunt Memorial Church   Franciscans
> the Thirty-nine Articles of the Church of England

65. Names of the Bible or its books, parts, versions, or editions of it and other sacred books are capitalized but not italicized. Adjectives derived from the names of sacred books are variously capitalized and lowercased. When in doubt, consult a dictionary.

> Authorized Version   Gospel of Saint Mark   Koranic
> Talmud   Old Testament   biblical
> talmudic   Koran   Vedic

66. The names of prayers and well-known passages of the Bible are capitalized.

> the Ave Maria   the Ten Commandments
> the Lord's Prayer   the Sermon on the Mount
> the Our Father   the Beatitudes

67. Scientific terms Genus names in biological binomial nomenclature are capitalized; species names are lowercased, even when derived from a proper name. Both genus and species names are italicized (or underlined in typewritten material).

> Both the wolf and the domestic dog are included in the genus *Canis.*
> The California condor *(Gymnogyps californianus)* is facing extinction.

The names of races, varieties, or subspecies, when used, are lowercased. Like genus and species names, they are italicized.

> *Hyla versicolor chrysoscelis*
> *Otis asio naevius*

68. The New Latin names of classes, families, and all groups above the genus level in zoology and botany are capitalized but not italicized. Their derivative adjectives and nouns in English are neither capitalized nor italicized.

> Gastropoda   gastropod
> Thallophyta   thallophyte

69. The names, both scientific and informal, of planets and their satellites, asteroids, stars, constellations, groups of stars, and other specific celestial objects are capitalized. However, the words *sun, earth,* and *moon* are usually lowercased unless they occur with other astronomical names. A generic term that follows the name of a celestial object is usually lowercased.

| the Milky Way | Sirius | the Moon and Mars |
| Pleiades | Big Dipper | Barnard's star |

70. Names of meteorological phenomena are lowercased.

| aurora borealis | northern lights | parhelic circle |

71. Terms that identify geological eras, periods, epochs, and strata are capitalized. The generic terms that follow them are lowercased. The words *upper*, *middle*, and *lower* are capitalized when they are used to designate an epoch or series within a period; in most other cases, they are lowercased. The word *age* is capitalized in names such as *Age of Reptiles* or *Age of Fishes*.

| Mesozoic era | Quaternary period | Oligocene epoch |
| Upper Cretaceous | Middle Ordovician | Lower Silurian |

72. Proper names forming essential elements of scientific laws, theorems, and principles are capitalized. However, the common nouns *law, theorem, theory,* and the like are lowercased.

| Boyle's law | Planck's constant |
| the Pythagorean theorem | Einstein's theory of relativity |

In terms referring to popular or fanciful theories or observations, descriptive words are usually capitalized as well.

| Murphy's Law | the Peter Principle |

73. The names of chemical elements and compounds are lowercased.

hydrogen fluoride
ferric ammonium citrate

74. The names of computer services and databases are usually trademarks and should always be capitalized. Some names of computer languages are written with an initial capital letter, some with all letters capitalized. Some are commonly written both ways. When in doubt, consult a dictionary.

CompuServe	TeleTransfer	PASCAL *or* Pascal
Atek	PL/1	COBOL *or* Cobol
BASIC	APL	FORTRAN *or* Fortran

75. **Time periods and zones** The names of the days of the week, months of the year, and holidays and holy days are capitalized.

| Easter | Independence Day | June |
| Tuesday | Yom Kippur | Thanksgiving |

76. The names of time zones are capitalized when abbreviated but usually lowercased when written out, except for words that are themselves proper names.

| CST | mountain time |
| central standard time | Pacific standard time |

77. Names of the seasons are lowercased if they simply declare the time of year; however, they are capitalized if they are personified.

My new book is scheduled to appear this spring.
the sweet breath of Spring

78. **Titles** Words in titles of books, long poems, magazines, newspapers, plays, movies, novellas that are separately published, and works of art such as paintings and sculpture are capitalized except for internal articles, conjunctions, prepositions, and the *to* of infinitives. The entire title is italicized (or underlined in typewritten material). Regarding the Bible and other sacred works, see paragraph 65 on page 151.

The Lives of a Cell	*Of Mice and Men*
National Geographic	*Christian Science Monitor*
Shakespeare's *Othello*	the movie *Wait until Dark*
Géricault's *The Raft of the Medusa*	

NOTE: Some writers also capitalize prepositions of five or more letters (such as *about* or *toward*).

79. An initial article that is part of a title is often omitted if it would be awkward in context. However, when it is included it is capitalized and italicized or underlined. For books that are referred to by an abbreviation, the initial article is neither capitalized nor italicized.

> *The Oxford English Dictionary*
> the 20-volume *Oxford English Dictionary*
> the *OED*

80. Practice varies widely regarding the capitalization and italicization or underlining of initial articles and city names in the titles of newspapers. One rule that can be followed is to capitalize and italicize any word that is part of the official title of the paper as shown on its masthead. However, this information is not always available, and even if it is available it can lead to apparent inconsistencies in styling. Because of this, many writers choose one way of writing newspaper titles regardless of their official titles. The most common practice is to italicize the city name but not to capitalize or italicize the initial article.

> the *New York Times*   the *Wall Street Journal*

81. In traditional journalism, and wherever italic type was unavailable, titles have been either capitalized and enclosed in quotation marks or simply capitalized, since this style was simpler and quicker for the typesetter. Even in the modern era of computer typesetting, this practice persists at many newspapers and magazines.

> the Heard on the Street column in the Wall Street Journal
> our review of "The Volcano Lover" in last week's issue

82. The first word following a colon in a title is capitalized.

> John Crowe Ransom: An Annotated Bibliography

83. The titles of short poems, short stories, essays, lectures, dissertations, chapters of books, articles in periodicals, radio and television programs, and novellas that are published in a collection are capitalized and enclosed in quotation marks. The capitalization of articles, conjunctions, and prepositions is the same as it is for italicized titles, as explained in paragraph 78 above.

> Robert Frost's "Dust of Snow"
> Cynthia Ozick's "Rosa"
> John Barth's "The Literature of Exhaustion"
> The talk, "Labor's Power: A View for the Nineties," will be given Friday.
> the third chapter of *Treasure Island*, entitled "The Black Spot"
> Her article, "Computer Art on a Micro," was in *Popular Computing*
> listening to "All Things Considered"
> watching "The Tonight Show"

84. Common titles of book sections (such as *preface, introduction,* or *index*) are capitalized but not enclosed in quotation marks when they refer to a section of the same book in which the reference is made. If they refer to another book, they are usually lowercased.

> See the *Appendix* for further information.
> In the *introduction* to her book, the author explains her goals.

85. Practice varies regarding the capitalization of the word *chapter* when it is used with a cardinal number to identify a specific chapter in a book. Most writers capitalize the word, but some do not.

> See Chapter 3 for more details.
> is discussed further in Chapter Four
> > *but*
> in the third chapter

86. The titles of long musical compositions are generally capitalized and italicized (or underlined in typewritten material); the titles of short compositions are capitalized and enclosed in quotation marks. The titles of compositions identified only by the nature of the musical form in which they were written are capitalized only, regardless of their length.

> Verdi's *Don Carlos*   "America the Beautiful"
> Ravel's "Pavane"   Symphony No. 8 in F Major

87. Trademarks Registered trademarks, service marks, collective marks, and brand names are capitalized.

> Band-Aid   Jacuzzi   Kleenex
> College Board   Velcro   Realtor
> Kellogg's All-Bran Diet Pepsi   Lay's potato chips

88. Transportation The names of individual ships, submarines, airplanes, satellites, and space vehicles are capitalized and italicized (or underlined in typewritten material). The designations *U.S.S., S.S., M.V.,* and *H.M.S.* are not italicized.

> *Apollo 11*   *Enola Gay*
> *Spirit of St. Louis*   M.V. *West Star*

OTHER USES OF CAPITALS

1. Full capitalization of a word is sometimes used for emphasis or to indicate that a speaker is talking very loudly. Both of these uses of capitals are best used very sparingly or avoided altogether in formal writing. Italicizing (or underlining) words for emphasis is more common. (For examples of this use of italics, see paragraph 7 under Other Uses of Italics on page 156.)

> Results are not the only criteria for judging performance. HOW we achieve results is important also.
> All applications must be submitted IN WRITING before January 31.
> The waiter rushed by yelling "HOT PLATE! HOT PLATE!"

2. A word is sometimes capitalized to indicate that it is being used as a philosophical concept or that it stands for an important concept in a discussion.

> Many people seek Truth, but few find it.
> the three M's of advertising: Message, Media, and Management

3. Full capitals or a mixture of capitals and lowercase letters or sometimes even small capitals are used to reproduce the text of signs, labels, or inscriptions.

a poster reading SPECIAL THRILLS COMING SOON
a Do Not Disturb sign
a barn with CHEW MAIL POUCH on the side

4. A letter used to indicate a shape is capitalized.

an A-frame house   a J-bar   V-shaped

OTHER USES OF ITALICS

For each of the uses listed below, italic type is used in typeset material (or where it is otherwise available); in typewritten material, underlining is used.

1. Foreign words and phrases that have not been fully adopted into the English language are italicized. The decision whether or not to italicize a word will vary according to context and the audience for which the writing is intended. In general, however, any word that appears in the main A–Z vocabulary section of *Merriam-Webster's Collegiate Dictionary, Tenth Edition* does not need to be italicized.

> These accomplishments will serve as a monument, *aere perennius*, to the group's skill and dedication.
> They looked upon this area as a *cordon sanitaire* around the city.
> After the banquet, the conferees headed en masse for the parking lot.
> The committee meets on an ad hoc basis.

A complete sentence (such as a motto) can also be italicized. However, passages that consist of more than one sentence, or even a single sentence if it is particularly long, are usually treated as quotations; that is, they are set in roman type and enclosed in quotation marks.

2. Unfamiliar words or words that have a specialized meaning are set in italics, especially when they are accompanied by a short definition. Once these words have been introduced and defined, they do not need to be italicized in subsequent references.

> *Vitiligo* is a condition in which skin pigment cells stop making pigment.
> Another method is the *direct-to-consumer* transaction, in which the publisher markets directly to the individual by mail or door-to-door.

3. Latin abbreviations are usually not italicized, although the traditional practice has been to italicize them, and some writers still do so.

et al.   cf.   e.g.   i.e.   viz.

4. Italic type is used to indicate words referred to as words, letters referred to as letters, or numerals referred to as numerals. However, if the word referred to as a word was actually spoken, it is often enclosed in quotation marks. If the letter is being used to refer to its sound and not its printed form, slashes or brackets can be used instead of italics. And if there is no chance of confusion, numerals referred to as numerals are often not italicized. (For an explanation of the plurals of words, letters, and numerals referred to as such, see paragraphs 17–19 and 23–25 under Plurals on pages 159–60.)

> The panel could not decide whether *data* was a singular or plural noun.
> *Only* can be an adverb, as in the case of "I *only* tried to help."
> We heard his warning, but we weren't sure what "other repercussions" meant in that context.
> You should dot your *i*'s and cross your *t*'s.

He was still having trouble with the /p/ sound.
The first *2* and the last *1* are barely legible.

A letter used to indicate a shape is capitalized but not set in italics.

5. Individual letters are sometimes set in italic type to provide additional typographical contrast. This use of italics is common when letters are used in enumerations within sentences or when they are used to identify elements in an illustration.

    providing information about *(a)* typing, *(b)* transcribing, *(c)* formatting, and *(d)* graphics
    located at point *A* on the diagram

6. Italics are used to indicate a word created to suggest a sound.

    We sat listening to the *chat-chat-chat* of the sonar.

7. Italics are used to emphasize or draw attention to a word or words in a sentence.

    Students must notify the dean's office *in writing* of all courses added or dropped from their original list.
    She had become *the* hero, the one everyone else looked up to.

Italics serve to draw attention to words in large part because they are used so infrequently. The overuse of italics may cause them to lose their effectiveness.

Plurals and Possessives

This section describes the ways in which plurals and possessives are most commonly formed. For some of the questions treated here, various solutions have been developed over the years but no single solution has come to be universally accepted. In these cases, the range of available solutions is described and you must use your own judgment to choose among them.

In regard to plurals, consulting a good dictionary will solve many of the problems that are discussed in this chapter. The best dictionary to consult is an unabridged dictionary, such as *Webster's Third New International Dictionary*. The next best thing is a good desk dictionary, such as *Merriam-Webster's Collegiate Dictionary, Tenth Edition*. Any dictionary that is much smaller than the *Collegiate* will often be more frustrating in what it fails to show than helpful in what it shows.

In giving examples of plurals and possessives, this section uses both *or* and *also* to separate variant forms of the same word. The word *or* is used when both forms of the word are used with approximately equal frequency in standard writing; the form that precedes the *or* is probably slightly more common than the form that follows it. The word *also* is used when one form of the word is much more common than the other; the more common precedes the less common.

PLURALS

The plurals of most English words are formed by adding *-s* to the singular. If the noun ends in *-s*, *-x*, *-z*, *-ch*, or *-sh*, so that an extra syllable must be added in order to pronounce the plural, *-es* is added to the singular. If the noun ends in a *-y* preceded by a consonant, the *-y* is changed to *-i-* and *-es* is added.

However, many English nouns do not follow this general pattern. Most good dictionaries give thorough coverage to irregular and variant plurals, so they are often the best place to start to answer questions about the plural form of a specific word. The paragraphs that follow describe how plurals are formed for a number of categories of words whose plural forms are most apt to raise questions. The symbol → is used here to link the singular and plural forms.

1. **Abbreviations** The plurals of abbreviations are commonly formed by adding -s or an apostrophe plus -s; however, there are some significant exceptions. (For more on forming plurals of abbreviations, see paragraphs 1–5 under Plurals, Possessives, and Compounds on pages 173–74.)

   COLA → COLA's CPU → CPUs bldg. → bldgs.
   f.o.b. → f.o.b.'s Ph.D. → Ph.D.'s p. → pp.

2. **Animals** The names of many fishes, birds, and mammals have both a plural formed with a suffix and one that is identical with the singular. Some have only one or the other.

   flounder → flounder *or* flounders rat → rats
   quail → quail *or* quails monkey → monkeys
   mink → mink *or* minks shad → shad
   caribou → caribou *or* caribous moose → moose

3. Many of the animals that have both plural forms are ones that are hunted, fished, or trapped; those who hunt, fish for, and trap them are most likely to use the unchanged form. The -s form is often used to emphasize diversity of kinds.

   caught four trout a place where fish gather
   but *but*
   trouts of the Rocky Mountains the fishes of the Pacific Ocean

4. **Compounds and phrases** Most compounds made up of two nouns—whether they appear as one word, two words, or a hyphenated word—form their plurals by pluralizing the final element only.

   matchbox → matchboxes city-state → city-states
   judge advocate → judge advocates crow's-foot → crow's-feet

5. The plural form of a compound consisting of an -er noun and an adverb is made by pluralizing the noun element only.

   hanger-on → hangers-on looker-on → lookers-on
   onlooker → onlookers passerby → passersby

6. Nouns made up of words that are not nouns form their plurals on the last element.

   also-ran → also-rans ne'er-do-well → ne'er-do-wells
   put-down → put-downs set-to → set-tos
   changeover → changeovers blowup → blowups

7. Plurals of compounds that are phrases consisting of two nouns separated by a preposition are regularly formed by pluralizing the first noun.

   aide-de-camp → aides-de-camp base on balls → bases on balls
   attorney-at-law → attorneys-at-law man-of-war → men-of-war
   power of attorney → powers of attorney coup d'état → coups d'état

8. Compounds that are phrases consisting of two nouns separated by a preposition and a modifier form their plurals in various ways.

   flash in the pan → flashes in the pan
   jack-in-the-box → jack-in-the-boxes   *or*   jacks-in-the-box
   jack-of-all-trades → jacks-of-all-trades
   stick-in-the-mud → stick-in-the-muds

9. Compounds consisting of a noun followed by an adjective are usually pluralized by adding -s or -es to the noun.

   cousin-german → cousins-german
   heir apparent → heirs apparent
   knight-errant → knights-errant

   If the adjective in such a compound tends to be construed as a noun, the compound may have more than one plural form.

   attorney general → attorneys general   *or*   attorney generals
   sergeant major → sergeants major   *or*   sergeant majors
   poet laureate → poets laureate   *or*   poet laureates

10. **Foreign words and phrases** Many nouns of foreign origin retain the foreign plural. However, most of them also have a regular English plural.

    alumnus → alumni
    beau → beaux   *or*   beaus
    crisis → crises
    emporium → emporiums
     also   emporia
    index → indexes   *or*   indices

    larynx → larynges   *or*   larynxes
    phenomenon → phenomena
    schema → schemata   *also*   schemas
    seraph → seraphim   *or*   seraphs
    series → series
    tempo → tempi   *or*   tempos

    A foreign plural may not be used for all senses of a word, or may be more commonly used for some senses than for others.

    antenna (on an insect) → antennae
    antenna (on a radio) → antennas

11. Phrases of foreign origin may have a foreign plural, an English plural, or both.

    beau monde → beau mondes   *or*   beaux mondes
    carte blanche → cartes blanches
    hors d'oeuvre → hors d'oeuvres

12. **-ful words** A plural -fuls can be used for any noun ending in -ful, but some of these nouns also have an alternative plural with -s- preceding the suffix.

    eyeful → eyefuls
    bucketful → bucketfuls   *or*   bucketsful
    cupful → cupfuls   *also*   cupsful
    tablespoonful → tablespoonfuls   *also*   tablespoonsful

13. **Irregular plurals** A small group of English nouns from their plurals by changing one or more of their vowels.

    foot → feet   man → men   woman → women
    goose → geese   mouse → mice   tooth → teeth
    louse → lice

14. A few nouns have -en or -ren plurals.

    ox → oxen
    child → children
    brother → brethren

15. Some nouns ending in *-f*, *-fe*, and *-ff* have plurals that end in *-ves*. Some of these also have regularly formed plurals.

elf → elves	beef → beefs *or* beeves
knife → knives	staff → staffs *or* staves
life → lives	wharf → wharves *also* wharfs

16. Italic elements Italicized words, phrases, abbreviations, and letters may be pluralized with either an italic or, more commonly, a roman *s*. If the plural is formed with an apostrophe and an *-s*, the *-s* is almost always roman.

> fifteen *Newsweek*s on the shelf
> answered with a series of *uh-huh*s
> a row of *x*'s

17. Letters The plural of letters are usually formed by adding an apostrophe and an *-s*, although uppercase letters are sometimes pluralized by adding an *-s* alone.

> p's and q's
> V's of geese flying overhead
> dot your *i*'s
> straight As

18. Numbers Numerals are pluralized by adding an *-s*, or, less commonly, an apostrophe and an *-s*.

> two par 5s   *or*   two par 5's
> 1970s   *or*   1970's
> in the 80s   *or*   in the 80's
>
> the mid-$20,000s   *or*   the mid-$20,000's

19. Spelled-out numbers are usually pluralized without an apostrophe.

> in twos and threes
> scored two sixes

20. -o words Most words ending in *-o* are pluralized by adding an *-s*. However, some words ending in *-o* preceded by a consonant take *-es* plurals, and some may take either *-s* or *-es*. When in doubt, consult a dictionary.

> alto → altos
> echo → echoes   *also*   echos
> motto → mottoes   *also*   mottos

21. Proper nouns The plurals of proper nouns are usually formed with *-s* or *-es*.

> Bruce → Bruces
> Hastings → Hastingses
> Velázquez → Velázquezes

22. Proper nouns ending in *-y* usually retain the *-y* and add *-s*.

> February → Februarys
> Marys → Marys
> Mercury → Mercurys
>   *but*
> Ptolemy → Ptolemies
> Sicily → The Two Sicilies
> The Rockies

Words that were originally proper nouns and that end in *-y* are usually pluralized by changing *-y* to *-i* and adding *-es*, but a few retain the *-y*.

bobby → bobbies   johnny → johnnies
Jerry → Jerries   Tommy → Tommies
Bloody Mary → Bloody Marys

23. **Quoted elements** Practice varies regarding the plural form of words in quotation marks. Some writers form the plural by adding an -s or an apostrophe plus -s within the quotation marks. Others add an -s outside the quotation marks. Both arrangements look awkward, and writers generally try to avoid this construction.

> too many "probably's" in the statement
> one "you" among millions of "you"s
> a response characterized by its "yes, but"s

24. **Symbols** Symbols are not usually pluralized except when being referred to as characters in themselves, without regard to meaning. The plural is formed by adding an -s or an apostrophe plus -s.

> used &'s instead of *and*'s
> his π's are hard to read
> printed three *s

25. **Words used as words** Words used as words without regard to meaning usually form their plurals by adding an apostrophe and a roman -s.

> five *and*'s in one sentence
> all those *wherefore*'s and *howsoever*'s

When a word used as a word has become part of a fixed phrase, the plural is usually formed by adding a roman -s without the apostrophe.

> oohs and aahs
> dos and don'ts   *or*   do's and don't's

POSSESSIVES

The possessive case of most nouns is formed by adding an apostrophe or an apostrophe plus -s to the end of the word.

1. **Common nouns** The possessive case of singular and plural common nouns that do not end in an *s* or *z* sound is formed by adding an apostrophe plus -s to the end of the word.

   the boy's mother   her dog's leash   the potato's skin
   men's clothing   children's books   the symposia's themes

2. The possessive case of singular nouns ending in an *s* or *z* sound is usually formed by adding an apostrophe plus -s to the end of the word. An alternative approach, although one less widely accepted, is to add an apostrophe plus -s to the word only when the added -s is easily pronounced; if adding the -s is felt to create a word that is difficult to pronounce, only an apostrophe is added.

   the press's books   the index's arrangement
   the boss's desk   the horse's saddle
   the princess's duties   *also*   the princess' duties

   Even those who follow the pattern of adding an apostrophe plus -s to all singular nouns will often make an exception for a multisyllabic word that ends in an *s* or *z* sound if it is followed by a word beginning with an *s* or *z* sound.

   for convenience' sake   for conscience' sake

3. The possessive case of plural nouns ending in an *s* or *z* sound is formed by adding only an apostrophe to the end of the word. One exception to this

rule is that the possessive case of one-syllable irregular plurals is usually formed by adding an apostrophe plus -*s*.

horses' stalls	consumers' confidence
geese's calls	mice's habits

4. **Proper names** The possessive forms of proper names are generally made in the same way as they are for common nouns. The possessive form of singular proper names not ending in an *s* or *z* sound is made by adding an apostrophe plus -*s* to the name. The possessive form of plural proper names is made by adding just an apostrophe.

Mrs. Wilson's store	Utah's capital	Canada's rivers
the Wattses' daughter	the Cohens' house	Niagara Falls' location

5. As is the case for the possessive form of singular common nouns (see paragraph 2 above), the possessive form of singular proper names ending in an *s* or *z* sound may be formed either by adding an apostrophe plus -*s* or by adding just an apostrophe to the name. For the sake of consistency, most writers choose one pattern for forming the possessive of all singular names ending in an *s* or *z* sound, regardless of the pronunciation of individual names (for exceptions see paragraphs 6 and 7 below). Adding an apostrophe plus -*s* to all such names is more common than adding just the apostrophe.

   Jones's car   *also*   Jones' car
   Bliss's statue   *also*   Bliss' statue
   Dickens's novels   *also*   Dickens' novels

6. The possessive form of classical and biblical names of two or more syllables ending in -*s* or -*es* is usually made by adding an apostrophe without an -*s*. If the name has only one syllable, the possessive form is made by adding an apostrophe and an -*s*.

Aristophanes' plays	Achilles' heel	Odysseus' journey
Judas' betrayal	Zeus's anger	Mars's help

7. The possessive forms of the names *Jesus* and *Moses* are always formed with just an apostrophe.

   Jesus' time   Moses' law

8. The possessive forms of names ending in a silent -*s*, -*z*, or -*x* usually include the apostrophe and the -*s*.

Arkansas's capital	Camus's *The Stranger*
Delacroix's painting	Josquin des Prez's music

9. Some writers italicize the possessive ending when adding it to a name that is in italics; however, the ending is usually not italicized.

the U.S.S. *Constitution*'s cannons	the *Mona Lisa*'s somber hues
Gone With the Wind's ending	*High Noon*'s plot

10. **Pronouns** The possessive case of indefinite pronouns such as *anyone, everybody,* and *someone* is formed by adding an apostrophe and an -*s*.

everyone's	anyone's	someone's
everybody's	anybody's	somebody's

Some indefinite pronouns usually require an *of* phrase to indicate possession.

the rights of each	the satisfaction of all
the inclination of many	

11. Possessive pronouns include no apostrophes.

mine	yours	his	hers
its	ours	theirs	

12. Phrases The possessive form of a phrase is made by adding an apostrophe or an apostrophe plus *-s* to the last word in the phrase.

board of directors' meeting
his brother-in-law's sidecar
from the student of politics' point of view
after a moment or so's thought

Constructions such as these can become awkward, and it is often better to rephrase the sentence to eliminate the need for the possessive ending. For instance, the last two examples above could be rephrased as follows:

from the point of view of the student of politics
after thinking for a moment or so

13. Words in quotation marks The possessive form of words in quotation marks can be formed in two ways, with the apostrophe plus *-s* placed either inside the quotation marks or outside them. Both arrangements look awkward, and this construction is best avoided.

the "Today Show" 's cohosts
the "Grande Dame's" escort
but more commonly
the cohosts of the "Today Show"
escort to the "Grande Dame"

14. Abbreviations Possessives of abbreviations are formed like those of nouns that are spelled out. The singular possessive is formed by adding an apostrophe plus *-s* to the abbreviation; the plural possessive, by adding an apostrophe only.

the AMA's executive committee
Itek Corp.'s Applied Technology Division
the MPs' decisions

15. Numerals The possessive form of nouns composed of numerals is made in the same way as for other nouns. The possessive of singular nouns is formed by adding an apostrophe plus *-s*; the possessive form of plural nouns is formed by adding an apostrophe only.

1995's most popular model
the 1980s' most colorful figure

16. Individual and joint possession Individual possession is indicated by adding an apostrophe plus *-s* to each noun in a sequence. Joint possession is most commonly indicated by adding an apostrophe or an apostrophe plus *-s* to the last noun in the sequence, but may also be indicated by adding a possessive ending to each name.

Kepler's and Clark's respective clients
John's, Bill's, and Larry's boats
Bissell and Hansen's law firm
Christine and James's vacation home
or
Christine's and James's vacation home

Compounds

A compound is a word or word group that consists of two or more parts that work together as a unit to express a specific concept. Compounds can be formed by combining two or more words (as in *eye shadow, graphic equalizer, farmhouse, cost-effective, blue-pencil, around-the-clock,* or *son of a gun*), by combining prefixes or suffixes with words (as in *ex-president, shoeless, presorted, uninterruptedly,* or *meaningless*), or by combining two or more word elements (as in *supermicro* or *photomicrograph*). Compounds are written in one of three ways: solid (as in *cottonmouth*), hyphenated *(player-manager),* or open *(field day).*

Permanent compounds are compounds that are so commonly used that they have become permanent parts of the language; many of them are entered in dictionaries. *Temporary compounds* are those created to fit a writer's need at a particular moment; thus, they cannot be found in dictionaries. *Self-evident compounds* are compounds that are readily understood from the meanings of the words that make them up (such as *baseball game* or *economic policy*). Most self-evident compounds are not entered in dictionaries. Writers thus cannot rely wholly on dictionaries to guide them in writing compounds, but must develop an approach for dealing with those that are not in the dictionary.

One approach is simply to leave open any compound that is not in the dictionary. Many writers do this, but there are drawbacks to this approach. A temporary compound may not be as easily recognized by the reader as a compound when it is left open. For instance, if you need to use *wide body* as a term for a kind of jet airplane, a phrase like "the operation of wide bodies" may catch the reader unawares. And if you use the open style for a compound modifier, you may create momentary confusion (or even unintended amusement) with a phrase like "the operation of wide body jets."

Another possibility is to hyphenate all compounds not in the dictionary. Hyphenation gives your compound immediate recognition as a compound. But hyphenating all such compounds runs counter to some well-established American practice, and might thus call too much attention to the compound and momentarily distract the reader.

A third approach is to pattern your temporary compound after some other similar compound. This approach is likely to be more complicated, and usually will not free you from the need to make your own decisions. But it does have the advantage of making your compound less distracting or confusing by making it look like other more familiar compounds. The paragraphs that follow are aimed at helping you to use this third approach.

The symbol + in the following paragraphs can be interpreted as "followed immediately by."

COMPOUND NOUNS

Compound nouns are combinations of words that function in a sentence as nouns. They may consist of two or more nouns, a noun and a modifier, or two or more elements that are not nouns.

1. **noun + noun** Compounds composed of two nouns that are short, commonly used, and pronounced with falling stress—that is, with the most stress on the first noun and less or no stress on the second—are usually written solid.

teapot	cottonmouth	birdbath	handmaiden
catfish	sweatband	handsaw	farmyard

2. When a noun + noun compound is short and common but pronounced with equal stress on both nouns, it is more likely to be open.

bean sprouts	beach buggy
fuel oil	duffel bag

3. Many short noun + noun compounds begin as temporary compounds written open. As they become more familiar and better established, there is a tendency for them to become solid.

data base   *has become*   database
chain saw   *is becoming*   chainsaw
lawn mower   *is becoming*   lawnmower

4. Noun + noun compounds that consist of longer nouns, are self-evident, or are temporary are usually written open.

wildlife sanctuary	reunion committee
football game	television camera

5. When the nouns in a noun + noun compound describe a double title or double function, the compound is hyphenated.

city-state	dinner-dance	player-manager
decree-law	secretary-treasurer	author-critic

6. Compounds formed from a noun or adjective followed by *man, woman, person,* or *people* and denoting an occupation are normally solid.

salesman	saleswoman	salesperson	salespeople
congresswoman	handyman	spokesperson	policewoman

7. Compounds that are units of measurement are hyphenated.

foot-pound	man-hour	light-year
kilowatt-hour	column-inch	board-foot

8. **adjective + noun** Most temporary or self-evident adjective + noun compounds are written open. Permanent compounds formed from relatively long adjectives or nouns are also written open.

automatic weapons	modal auxiliary	modular arithmetic
religious freedom	automatic pilot	graphic equalizer
pancreatic juice	minor seminary	white lightning

9. Adjective + noun compounds consisting of two short words may be written solid when pronounced with falling stress. Just as often, however, short adjective + noun compounds are written open; a few are hyphenated.

shortcut	longhand	redline	blueprint
yellowhammer	highland	drywall	wetland
dry run	bid deal	high gear	long haul
red tape	yellow jacket	red-eye	red-hot

10. **participle + noun** Most participle + noun compounds are written open, whether permanent, temporary, or self-evident

running total	furnished apartment	shredded wheat
whipped cream	nagging backache	whipping boy

11. **noun's + noun** Compounds consisting of a possessive noun followed by another noun are usually written hyphenated or open.

crow's-feet	lion's share	fool's gold
cat's cradle	cat's-eye	cat's-paw
hornet's nest		

Compounds of this type that have become solid have lost the apostrophe.

foolscap	menswear	sheepshead

12. **noun + verb + -er; noun + verb + -ing** Temporary compounds in which the first noun is the object of the verb to which the suffix has been added are most often written open. However, a hyphen may be used to make the relationships of the words immediately apparent. Permanent compounds like these are sometimes written solid as well.

temporary:	gene-splicing	opinion maker	cost-cutting
	risk-taking	career planning	English-speakers
permanent:	lifesaver	copyediting	flyswatter
	data processing	bird-watcher	fund-raising
	lawn mower	penny-pinching	bookkeeper

13. **object + verb** Noun compounds consisting of a verb preceded by a noun that is its object are written in various ways.

clambake	car wash	face-lift	turkey shoot

14. **verb + object** A few, mostly older compounds are formed from a verb followed by a noun that is its object; they are written solid.

tosspot	breakwater	pinchpenny
cutthroat	carryall	pickpocket

15. **noun + adjective** Compounds composed of a noun followed by an adjective are written open or hyphenated.

battle royal	consul general	secretary-general
governor-designate	heir apparent	letters patent
sum total	mayor-elect	president-elect

16. **particle + noun** Compounds consisting of a particle (usually a preposition or adverb) and a noun are usually written solid, especially when they are short and pronounced with falling stress.

downpour	inpatient	outpatient	input
output	throughput	aftershock	overskirt
offshoot	undershirt	crossbones	upkeep

17. A few particle + noun compounds, especially when composed of longer elements or having equal stress on both elements, may be hyphenated or open.

off-season	down payment	off year	cross-fertilization

18. **verb + particle; verb + adverb** These compounds may be hyphenated or solid. Compounds with two-letter particles (*by, to, in, up, on*) are most frequently hyphenated, since the hyphen aids quick comprehension. Compounds with three-letter particles (*off, out*) are hyphenated or solid with about equal frequency. Those with longer particles or adverbs are more often but not always solid.

layup	lead-in	run-on	set-to
sit-in	flyby	letup	pileup
shoot-out	show-off	dropout	turnoff
breakthrough	gadabout	giveaway	follow-through

19. **verb + -er + particle; verb + -ing + particle** Except for *passerby,* these compounds are hyphenated.

hanger-on	diner-out	falling-out	runner-up
summing-up	talking-to	goings-on	looker-on

20. **Compounds of three or four elements** Compounds of three or four elements may be either hyphenated or open. Those consisting of noun + prepositional phrase are generally open, although some are hyphenated. Those formed from other combinations are usually hyphenated.

base on balls	justice of the peace	son of a gun
lily of the valley	jack-of-all-trades	lady-in-waiting
know-it-all	pick-me-up	stick-to-itiveness

21. **letter + noun** Compounds formed from a single letter (or sometimes a combination of them) followed by a noun are either open or hyphenated.

A-frame	B-girl	H-bomb	T-shirt
C ration	D day	I beam	T square
ABO system	J-bar lift	Rh factor	H and L hinge

COMPOUNDS THAT FUNCTION AS ADJECTIVES

Compound adjectives are combinations of words that work together to modify a noun—that is, they work as *unit modifers.* As unit modifiers they should be distinguished from other strings of adjectives that may also precede a noun.

For instance, in "a low, level tract of land" or "that long, lonesome road" the two adjectives each modify the noun separately. We are talking about a tract of land that is both low and level and about a road that is both long and lonesome. These are *coordinate modifiers.* In "a low monthly fee" or "suggested retail price" the first adjective modifies the noun plus the second adjective. In other words, we mean a monthly fee that is low and the retail price that has been suggested. These are *noncoordinate modifiers.* But in "low-level radiation" we do not mean radiation that is low and level or level radiation that is low; we mean radiation that is at a low level. Both words work as a unit to modify the noun.

Unit modifiers are usually hyphenated. The hyphens not only make it easier for the readers to grasp the relationship of the words but also avoid confusion. The hyphen in "a call for more-specialized controls" removes any ambiguity as to which word *more* modifies. By contrast, the lack of a hyphen in a phrase like "graphic arts exhibition" gives it an undesirable ambiguity.

1. **Before the noun (attributive position)** Most two-word permanent or temporary compound adjectives are hyphenated when placed before the noun.

tree-lined streets	fast-acting medication
class-conscious persons	Spanish-American relations
well-intended advice	the red-carpet treatment
a profit-and-loss statement	an input-output device
a trumped-up charge	a risk-free investment

2. Temporary compounds formed of an adverb (such as *well, more, less, still*) followed by a participle (or sometimes an adjective) are usually hyphenated when placed before a noun.

more-specialized controls	a just-completed survey
a still-growing company	a well-funded project
these fast-moving times	a now-vulnerable politician

3. Temporary compounds formed from an adverb ending in *-ly* followed by a participle may sometimes be hyphenated but are more commonly open, because adverb + adjective + noun is a normal word order.

a widely-read feature
but more often
a widely read feature

internationally-known authors
but more often
internationally known authors

4. The combination of *very* + adjective is not a unit modifier.

a very satisfied smile

5. Many temporary compound adjectives are formed by using a compound noun—either permanent or temporary—to modify another noun. If the compound noun is an open compound, it is usually hyphenated to make the relationship of the words more immediately apparent.

the farm-bloc vote
a short-run printing press
a tax-law case

a picture-framing shop
a secret-compartment ring
ocean-floor hydrophones

6. Some open compound nouns are so recognizable that they are frequently placed before a noun without a hyphen.

a high school diploma   *or*   a high-school diploma
a data processing course   *or*   a data-processing course
a dry goods store   *or*   a dry-goods store

7. A proper name placed before a noun to modify it is not hyphenated.

a Thames River marina
a Korean War veteran

a Huck Finn life
a General Motors car

8. Compound adjectives of three or more words are hyphenated when they precede the noun. Many temporary compounds are formed by hyphenating a phrase and placing it before a noun.

spur-of-the-moment decisions
higher-than-anticipated costs

9. Compound adjectives composed of foreign words are not hyphenated when placed before a noun unless they are hyphenated in the foreign language itself.

the per capita cost
a cordon bleu restaurant

an a priori argument
a ci-devant professor

10. Chemical names used as modifiers before a noun are not hyphenated.

a sodium hypochlorite bleach
a citric acid solution.

11. Following the noun (as a complement or predicate adjective) When the words that make up a compound adjective follow the noun they modify, they tend to fall in normal word order and are no longer unit modifiers. They are therefore no longer hyphenated.

arrested on charges that had been trumped up
decisions made on the spur of the moment
They were ill prepared for the journey.

12. Many permanent and temporary compounds keep their hyphens after the noun in a sentence if they continue to function as unit modifiers. Compounds consisting of adjective or noun + participle, adjective or noun +

noun+-*ed* (which looks like a participle), or noun+adjective are most likely to remain hyphenated.

> Your ideas are high-minded but impractical.
> realized that the boy was club-footed
> You were just as nice-looking then.
> metals that are corrosion-resistant
> tends to be accident-prone

13. Permanent compound adjectives are usually written as they appear in the dictionary, whether they precede or follow the noun they modify.

> The group was public-spirited.
> The problems are mind-boggling.
> is well-read in economics

14. Compound adjectives of three or more words are normally not hyphenated when they follow the noun they modify.

> These remarks are off the record.

15. Permanent compounds of three or more words may appear as hyphenated adjectives in dictionaries. In such cases the hyphens are retained as long as the phrase is being used as a unit modifier.

> the plan is still pay-as-you-go   *but*   a plan in which you pay as you go.

16. It is possible that a permanent hyphenated adjective may appear alongside a temporary compound in a position where it would normally be open (such as "one who is both ill-humored and ill prepared"). In such cases, it is best to either hyphenate both compounds or leave both open.

17. When an adverb modifies another adverb that is the first element of a compound modifier, the compound may lose its hyphen. If the first adverb modifies the whole compound, however, the hyphen should be retained.

> a very well developed idea
> a delightfully well-written book
> a most ill-humored remark

18. Adjective compounds that are names of colors may be written open or hyphenated. Color names in which each element can function as a noun (such as *blue green* or *chrome yellow*) are almost always hyphenated when they precede a noun; they are sometimes open when they follow the noun. Color names in which the first element can only be an adjective are often not hyphenated before a noun and usually not hyphenated after.

> blue-gray paint
> paint that is blue-gray   *also*   paint that is blue gray
> bluish gray paint   *or*   bluish-gray paint

19. Compound modifiers that include a number followed by a noun are hyphenated when they precede the noun they modify. When the modifier follows the noun, it is usually not hyphenated. (For more on the styling of numbers, see the section on Numbers, beginning on page 180.)

> five-card stud   10-foot pole   12-year-old girl
> an 18-inch rule   *but*   a 10 percent raise
> a child who is seven years old

20. An adjective that is composed of a number followed by a noun in the possessive is not hyphenated.

> a two weeks' wait   a four blocks' walk

COMPOUNDS THAT FUNCTION AS ADVERBS

1. Adverb compounds consisting of preposition + noun are almost always written solid. However, there are a few important exceptions.

downtown	downwind	onstage	overseas
upstairs	upfield	offhand	underhand

but

in-house
off-line
on-line

2. Compound adverbs of more than two words are usually written open, and they usually follow the words they modify.

every which way	high and dry	off and on
little by little	hook, line, and sinker	over and over

3. A few three-word adverbs are spelled like hyphenated adjectives and are therefore written with hyphens. But many adverbs are written open even if the adjective is hyphenated.

back-to-back (adverb or adjective)
face-to-face (adverb or adjective)
  but

hand-to-hand combat	off-the-cuff remarks
fought hand to hand	spoke off the cuff

COMPOUND VERBS

1. Two-word verbs consisting of a verb followed by an adverb or a preposition are written open.

get together	run around	run across
set to	run wild	put down
break through	strike out	print out

2. A compound composed of a particle followed by a verb is written solid.

upgrade	outflank	overcome	bypass

3. A verb derived from an open or hyphenated compound noun—permanent, temporary, or self-evident—is hyphenated.

blue-pencil	double-check	poor-mouth
sweet-talk	tap-dance	water-ski

4. A verb derived from a solid noun is written solid.

bankroll	roughhouse	mainstream

COMPOUNDS FORMED WITH WORD ELEMENTS

Many new and temporary compounds are formed by adding word elements to existing words or by combining word elements. There are three basic word elements: prefixes (such as *anti-, re-, non-, super-*), suffixes (such as *-er, -ly, -ness, -ism*), and combining forms (such as *mini-, macro-, pseud-, ortho-, -ped, -graphy, -gamic, -plasty*). Prefixes and suffixes are usually attached to existing words; combining forms are usually combined to form new words.

1. prefix + word Except as specified below, compounds formed from a prefix and a word are usually written solid.

precondition	refurnish	suborder	postwar
interagency	misshapen	overfond	unhelpful

2. If the prefix ends with a vowel and the word it is attached to begins with the same vowel, the compound is usually hyphenated.

    anti-inflation   co-owner   de-emphasize

    However, there are many exceptions.

    cooperate   reentry   preempt

3. If the base word to which a prefix is added is capitalized, the compound is hyphenated.

    anti-American   post-Victorian   pre-Columbian   inter-Caribbean

    The prefix is usually not capitalized in such compounds. But if the prefix and the base word together form a new proper name, the compound may be solid with the prefix capitalized.

    Postimpressionist   Precambrian

4. Compounds made with *self-* and *ex-* meaning "former" are hyphenated.

    self-pity   ex-wife

5. If a prefix is added to a hyphenated compound, it may be either followed by a hyphen or closed up solid to the next element. Permanent compounds of this kind should be checked in a dictionary.

    unair-conditioned   non-self-governing
    ultra-up-to-date   unself-conscious

6. In typewritten material, if a prefix is added to an open compound, the prefix is followed by a hyphen. In typeset material, this hyphen is often represented by an en dash. (For more on this use of the en dash, see paragraph 12 under Dash on page 125.)

    ex–Boy Scout   post–coup d'état
    ex–Boy Scout   post–coup d'état

7. A compound that would be identical with another word if written solid is usually hyphenated to prevent misreading.

    a multi-ply fabric   re-collect the money   un-ionized particles

8. A compound that might otherwise be solid may be hyphenated if it could be momentarily puzzling.

    coed *or* co-ed   overreact *or* over-react
    coworker *or* co-worker   interrow *or* inter-row

9. Temporary compounds formed from *vice-* are usually hypenated; however, some permanent compounds (such as *vice president* and *vice admiral*) are open.

10. When prefixes are attached to numerals, the compounds are hyphenated.

    pre-1982 expenses   post-1975 vintages   non-20th-century ideas

11. Compounds created from combining forms like *Anglo-*, *Judeo-*, or *Sino-* are hyphenated when the second element is an independent word. They are written solid when it is a combining form.

    Judeo-Christian   Austro-Hungarian   Sino-Soviet
    Italophile   Francophone   Anglophobe

12. Prefixes that are repeated in the same compound are separated by a hyphen.

    sub-subheading

13. Some prefixes and initial combining forms have related independent adjectives or adverbs that may be used where the prefix might be expected. A temporary compound with *quasi(-)* or *pseudo(-)* therefore may be written open as modifier + noun, or hyphenated as combining form + noun.

> quasi intellectual   *or*   quasi-intellectual
> pseudo liberal   *or*   pseudo-liberal

In some cases (such as *super, super-*), the independent modifier may not have quite the same meaning as the prefix.

14. Compounds consisting of different prefixes with the same base word and joined by *and* or *or* are sometimes shortened by pruning the first compound back to a hyphenated prefix.

> pre- and postoperative care
> anti- or pro-Revolutionary sympathies.

15. word + suffix Except as noted below, compounds formed by adding a suffix to a word are written solid.

> Darwinist   fortyish   landscaper   powerlessness

16. Permanent or temporary compounds formed with a suffix are hyphenated if the addition of the suffix would create a sequence of three identical letters.

> bell-like   will-less   a coffee-er coffee

17. Temporary compounds made with a suffix are often hyphenated if the base word is more than two syllables long, if the base word ends with the same letter the suffix begins with, or if the suffix creates a confusing sequence of letters.

> industry-wide   American-ness   jaw-wards
> umbrella-like   tunnel-like   battle-worthy

18. Compounds made from a number + *odd* are hyphenated whether the number is spelled out or in numerals; a number + *-fold* is solid if the number is spelled out but hyphenated if it is in numerals.

> 20-odd   twenty-odd
> 12-fold   twelvefold

19. Most compounds formed from an open or hyphenated compound + a suffix do not separate the suffix by a hyphen. But such suffixes as *-like, -wide, -worthy,* and *-proof,* all of which exist as independent adjectives, are attached by a hyphen.

> good-humoredness   dollar-a-yearism   do-it-yourselfer
> a United Nations-like agency

Open compounds often become hyphenated when a suffix is added unless they are proper nouns.

> middle age   *but*   middle-ager   New Englandism
> tough guy   *but*   tough-guyese   Wall Streeter

20. combining form + combining form Many new terms in technical fields are created by adding combining form to combining form or combining form to a word or word part. Such compounds are generally intended to be permanent, even though many never get into the dictionary. They are normally written solid.

MISCELLANEOUS STYLING CONVENTIONS

1. Compounds that would otherwise be written solid according to the principles described above may be written open or hyphenated to avoid ambiguity, to ensure rapid comprehension, or to make the pronunciation clearer.

meat-ax *or* meat ax	bi-level	tri-city
re-utter	umbrella-like	un-iced

2. When typographical features such as capitals or italics make word relationships in a sentence clear, it is not necessary to hyphenate an open compound.

a *noblesse oblige* attitude	an "eyes only" memo

Abbreviations

Abbreviations are used for a variety of reasons: to save space, to avoid repetition of long words and phrases, to save time, or simply to conform to conventional usage.

Unfortunately, the contemporary styling of abbreviations is inconsistent and arbitrary. No set of rules can hope to cover all the possible variations, exceptions, and peculiarities encountered in print. The styling of abbreviations—capitalized vs. lowercased, closed-up vs. spaced, punctuated vs. unpunctuated—depends most often on a writer's preference or an organization's policy.

All is not complete confusion, however. Some abbreviations (such as *e.g., etc., i.e., No.,* and *viz.*) are almost always punctuated, while others that are pronounced as words (such as *NATO, NASA, NOW, OPEC,* and *SALT*) tend to be all-capitalized and unpunctuated. Styling problems can be dealt with by consulting a good general dictionary such as *Merriam-Webster's Collegiate Dictionary, Tenth Edition,* especially for capitalization guidance, and by following the guidelines of one's own organization. An abbreviations dictionary such as *Webster's Guide to Abbreviations* may also be helpful.

PUNCTUATION

The paragraphs that follow provide a few broad principles that apply to abbreviations in general. However, there are many specific situations in which these principles will not apply. The section on Specific Styling Conventions, beginning on page 174, contains information on these situations and on particular kinds of abbreviations.

1. A period follows most abbreviations that are formed by omitting all but the first few letters of a word.

bull. [for *bulletin*]	fig. [for *figure*]
bro. [for *brother*]	Fr. [for *French*]

2. A period follows most abbreviations that are formed by omitting letters from the middle of a word.

secy. [for *secretary*]	agcy. [for *agency*]
mfg. [for *manufacturing*]	Mr. [for *Mister*]

3. Punctuation is usually omitted from abbreviations that are made up of initial letters of words that constitute a phrase or compound word. However,

for some of these abbreviations, especially ones that are not capitalized, the punctuation is retained.

GNP [for *gross national product*] PC [for *personal computer*]
EFT [for *electronic funds transfer*] f.o.b. [for *free on board*]

4. Terms in which a suffix is added to a numeral, such as *1st, 2nd, 3d, 8vo,* and *12mo,* are not abbreviations and do not require a period.

5. Isolated letters of the alphabet used to designate a shape or position in a sequence are not punctuated.

T square A 1 I beam V sign

6. Some abbreviations are punctuated with one or more slashes in place of periods.

c/o [for *care of*] w/o [for *without*]
d/b/a [for *doing business as*] w/w [for *wall to wall*]

CAPITALIZATION

1. Abbreviations are capitalized if the words they represent are proper nouns or adjectives.

F [for *Fahrenheit*] Nov. [for *November*]
NBC [for *National Broadcasting* Brit. [for *British*]
  Company]

2. Abbreviations are usually all-capitalized when they represent single letters of words that are normally lowercased. There are, however, some very common abbreviations formed in this way that are not capitalized.

TM [for *trademark*] EEG [for *electroencephalogram*]
ETA [for *estimated time of arrival*] FY [for *fiscal year*]
CATV [for *community antenna* a.k.a. [for *also known as*]
  television] d/b/a [for *doing business as*]

3. Most acronyms that are pronounced as words, rather than as a series of letters, are capitalized. If they have been assimilated into the language as words in their own right, however, they are most often lowercased.

OPEC NATO MIRV NOW account
quasar laser sonar scuba

PLURALS, POSSESSIVES, AND COMPOUNDS

1. Punctuated abbreviations of single words are pluralized by adding *-s* before the period.

bldgs. bros. figs. mts.

2. Punctuated abbreviations that stand for phrases or compounds are pluralized by adding *-'s* after the last period.

Ph.D.'s f.o.b.'s J.P.'s M.B.A.'s

3. Unpunctuated abbreviations that stand for phrases or compound words are usually pluralized by adding *-s* to the end of the abbreviation.

COLAs CPUs PCs DOSs

Some writers pluralize such abbreviations by adding *-'s* to the abbreviation; however, this is far less common.

4. The plural form of most lowercase single-letter abbreviations is made by repeating the letter. For the plural form of single-letter abbreviations that are abbreviations for units of measure, see paragraph 5 below.

cc. [for *copies*]	ff. [for *and the following ones*]
ll. [for *lines*]	nn. [for *notes*]
pp. [for *pages*]	vv. [for *verses*]

5. The plural form of abbreviations of units of measure is the same as the singular form.

30 sec.	24 ml	20 min.	200 bbl.
30 d.	24 h.	50 m	10 mi.

6. Possessives of abbreviations are formed in the same way as those of spelled-out nouns: the singular possessive is formed by adding -'s, the plural possessive simply by adding an apostrophe.

the CPU's memory	most CPUs' memories
Brody Corp.'s earnings	Bay Bros.' annual sale

7. Compounds that consist of an abbreviation added to another word are formed in the same way as compounds that consist of spelled-out nouns.

   a Kalamazoo, Mich.-based company
   an AMA-approved medical school

8. Compounds formed by adding a prefix or suffix to an abbreviation are usually written with a hyphen.

   an IBM-like organization
   non-DNA molecules
   pre-HEW years

SPECIFIC STYLING CONVENTIONS

Paragraphs on the following subjects, arranged alphabetically, describe practices commonly followed for specific kinds of situations involving abbreviations.

A and An	Degrees	Military Ranks and
A.D. and B.C.	Division of	Units
Agencies, Associations,	Abbreviations	Number
and Organizations	Full Forms	Personal Names
Beginning a Sentence	Geographical Names	Saint
Books of the Bible	Latin Words and	Scientific Terms
Company Names	Phrases	Time
Compass Points	Latitude and	Titles
Contractions	Longitude	Units of Measure
Dates	Laws and Bylaws	Versus

1. **A and an** The choice of the article *a* or *an* before abbreviations depends on the sound with which the abbreviation begins. If an abbreviation begins with a consonant sound, *a* is normally used; if an abbreviation begins with a vowel sound, *an* is used.

a B.A. degree	a YMCA club	a UN agency
an FCC report	an SAT score	an IRS agent

2. **A.D. and B.C.** The abbreviations A.D. and B.C. usually appear in typeset matter as punctuated, unspaced small capitals; in typed material they usually appear as punctuated, unspaced capitals.

in printed material: 41 B.C.   A.D. 185
in typed material: 41 B.C.   A.D. 185

3. The abbreviation A.D. usually precedes the date; the abbreviation B.C. usually follows the date. However, many writers place A.D. after the date as well. In references to whole centuries, the usual practice is to place A.D. after the century; the only alternative is not to use the abbreviation at all.

    A.D. 185 *but also* 185 A.D.
    the fourth century A.D.

4. **Agencies, associations, and organizations** The names of agencies, associations, and organizations are usually abbreviated after they have been spelled out on their first occurrence in a text. The abbreviations are usually all-capitalized and unpunctuated.

    EPA   SEC   NAACP   NCAA   USO   NOW

    In contexts where the abbreviation will be recognized, it may be used without having its full form spelled out on its first occurrence.

5. **Beginning a sentence** Most writers avoid beginning a sentence with an abbreviation that is ordinarily not capitalized. Abbreviations that are ordinarily capitalized, on the other hand, are commonly used to begin sentences.

    Page 22 contains . . .   *not*   P. 22 contains . . .
    Doctor Smith believes . . .   *or*   Dr. Smith believes . . .
    OSHA regulations require . . .

6. **Books of the Bible** Books of the Bible are generally spelled out in running text but abbreviated in references to chapter and verse.

    The minister based the sermon on Genesis.
    In the beginning God created the heavens and the earth.—Gen. 1:1

7. **Company names** The styling of company names varies widely. Many writers avoid abbreviating any part of a company's name unless the abbreviation is part of the official name. However, others routinely abbreviate words such as *Company, Corporation,* and *Incorporated.* Words such as *Airlines, Associates, Fabricators,* and *Manufacturing,* however, are spelled out.

    McGraw-Hill Book Company   *or*   McGraw-Hill Book Co.

    An ampersand (&) frequently replaces the word *and* in official company names. For more on this use of the ampersand, see paragraph 1 under Ampersand on page 109.

8. If a company is easily recognizable from its initials, its name is usually spelled out for the first mention and abbreviated in all subsequent references. Some companies have made their initials part of their official name, and in those cases the initials appear in all references.

    General Motors Corp. released its first-quarter earnings figures today. A
      GM spokesperson said . . .
    MCM Electronics, an Ohio-based company . . .

9. **Compass points** Compass points are abbreviated when occuring after street names; these abbreviations may be punctuated and may be preceded by a comma. When a compass point precedes the word *Street, Avenue,* etc., it is usually spelled out in full.

    2122 Fourteenth Street, NW   *or*   2122 Fourteenth Street NW
      or   2122 Fourteenth Street, N.W.
    192 East 49th Street
    1282 North Avenue

10. **Contractions** Some abbreviations resemble contractions by including an apostrophe in place of omitted letters. These abbreviations are not punctuated with a period.

    sec'y [for *secretary*]   ass'n [for *association*]   dep't [for *department*]

    This style of abbreviation is usually avoided in formal correspondence.

11. **Dates** The names of days and months should not be abbreviated in running text. The names of months are not abbreviated in datelines of business letters, but they may be abbreviated in government or military correspondence.

    the December issue of *Scientific American*
    a meeting held on August 1, 1985   *not*   a meeting held on Aug. 1, 1985
    business dateline: November 1, 1985
    military dateline: 1 Nov 1985

12. **Degrees** Except for a few academic degrees with highly recognizable abbreviations (such as *A.B., M.S.,* and *Ph.D.*), the names of degrees and professional ratings are spelled out in full when first mentioned. Often the name of the degree is followed by its abbreviation enclosed in parentheses, so that the abbreviation may be used alone later. When a degree or professional rating follows a person's name, it is usually abbreviated.

    Special attention is devoted to the master of arts in teaching (M.A.T.) degree.
    Julia Ramirez, P.E.

13. Like other abbreviations, abbreviations of degrees and professional ratings are often unpunctuated. In general, punctuated abbreviations are more common for academic degrees, and unpunctuated abbreviations are slightly more common for professional ratings, especially if the latter consist of three or more capitalized letters.

R.Ph.	P.E.	CLA	CMET
Ph.D.	B.Sc.	M.B.A.	BGS

14. The first letter of each element in abbreviations of all degrees and professional ratings is capitalized. Letters other than the first letter are usually not capitalized.

D.Ch.E.	Litt.D.	M.F.A.	D.Th.

15. **Division of abbreviations** Division of abbreviations at the end of lines or between pages is usually avoided.

16. **Full forms** When using an abbreviation that may be unfamiliar or confusing to the reader, many writers give the full form first, followed by the abbreviation in parentheses. In subsequent references, just the abbreviation is used.

    first reference: At the American Bar Association (ABA) meeting in June . . .
    subsequent reference: At that particular ABA meeting . . .

17. **Geographical names** U.S. Postal Service abbreviations for states, possessions, and Canadian provinces are all-capitalized and unpunctuated, as are Postal Service abbreviations for streets and other geographical features when these abbreviations are used on envelopes addressed for automated mass handling.

> *addressed for automated handling:*   1234 CROSS BLVD
> SAYVILLE, MN 56789
> *regular address style:*   1234 Cross Blvd.
> Sayville, MN 56789

18. Abbreviations of states are often used in running text to identify the location of a city or county. In this context the traditional state abbreviations are usually used, set off with commas. In other situations within running text, the names of states are usually not abbreviated.

> John Slade of 15 Chestnut St., Sarasota, Fla., has won . . .
> the Louisville, Ky., public library system
> Boston, the largest city in Massachusetts, . . .

19. Terms such as *street* and *parkway* may be either abbreviated or unabbreviated in running text. When they are abbreviated, they are usually punctuated.

> our office at 1234 Cross Blvd. [*or* Boulevard]
> an accident on Windward Road [*or* Rd.]

20. Names of countries are usually spelled in full in running text. The most common exceptions are the abbreviations *U.S.S.R.* and *U.S.* (see paragraph 22 below).

> Great Britain and the U.S.S.R. announced the agreement.

21. Abbreviations for the names of most countries are punctuated. Abbreviations for countries whose names include more than one word are often not punctuated if the abbreviations are formed from only the initial letters of the individual words.

> | | | |
> |---|---|---|
> | Mex. | Can. | Scot. |
> | Ger. | Gt. Brit. | U.S. *or* US |
> | U.S.S.R. *or* USSR | U.K. *or* UK | U.A.E. *or* UAE |

22. *United States* is often abbreviated when used as an adjective. When used as a noun, it is usually spelled out, or it is spelled on its initial use and then abbreviated in subsequent references.

> U.S. Department of Justice
> U.S. foreign policy
> The United States has offered to . . .

23. *Saint* is usually abbreviated when it is part of the name of a geographical or topographical feature. *Mount, Point,* and *Fort* may be either spelled out or abbreviated, according to individual preference. *Saint, Mount,* and *Point* are normally abbreviated when space is at a premium. (For more on the abbreviation of *Saint,* see paragraph 35 on page 178.)

> | | | |
> |---|---|---|
> | St. Louis, Missouri | St. Kitts | Mount McKinley |
> | Mount St. Helens | Fort Sumter | Point Pelee |

24. Latin words and phrases. Words and phrases derived from Latin are commonly abbreviated in contexts where readers can be expected to recognize them. They are punctuated, lowercased, and usually not italicized.

> | | | | | | |
> |---|---|---|---|---|---|
> | etc. | i.e. | e.g. | viz. | et al. | pro tem. |

25. Latitude and longitude Latitude and longitude are abbreviated in tabular data but written out in running text.

> *in a table:*   lat. 10°20′N *or* lat. 10-20N
> *in text:*   from 10°20′ north latitude to 10°30′ south latitude

26. **Laws and bylaws** Laws and bylaws are spelled in full when first mentioned; in subsequent references they may be abbreviated.

    first reference: Article I, Section 1
    subsequent reference: Art. I, Sec. 1

27. **Military ranks and units** Military ranks are usually given in full when used with a surname only, but are abbreviated when used with a full name.

    Colonel Howe   Col. John P. Howe

28. In nonmilitary correspondence, abbreviations for military ranks are often punctuated and set in capital and lowercase letters. See pages 301–4 for a list of official military abbreviations.

    in the military: BG John T. Dow, USA
                             LCDR Mary I. Lee, USN
                             Col S. J. Smith, USMC

    outside the military: Brig. Gen. John T. Dow, USA
                             Lt. Comdr. Mary I. Lee, USN
                             Col. S. J. Smith, USMC

29. Abbreviations for military units are capitalized and unpunctuated.

    USA   USAF   SAC   NORAD

30. **Number** The word *number,* when used with figures such as *1* or *2* to indicate a rank or rating, is usually abbreviated to *No.*

    The No. 1 priority is to promote profitability.

31. The word *number* is usually abbreviated when it is part of a set unit (such as a contract number).

    Contract No. N-1234-76-57   Publ. Nos. 12 and 13
    Policy No. 123-5-X   Index No. 7855

32. **Personal names** Personal names are not usually abbreviated.

    George S. Patterson   *not*   Geo. S. Patterson

33. Unspaced initials of famous persons are sometimes used in place of their full names. The initials may or may not be punctuated.

    FDR   *or*   F.D.R.

34. When initials are used with a surname, they are spaced and punctuated.

    F. D. Roosevelt

35. **Saint** The word *Saint* is often abbreviated when used before the name of a saint or when it is the first element of the name of a city or institution named after a saint. However, when it forms part of a surname, it may or may not be abbreviated. Surnames and names of institutions should follow the style used by the person or the institution.

    St. Peter   *or*   Saint Peter   St. Cloud, Minnesota
    St. John's University   Saint Joseph College
    Augustus Saint-Gaudens   Louis St. Laurent

36. **Scientific terms** In binomial nomenclature, a genus name may be abbreviated with its initial letter after the first reference to it is spelled out. The abbreviation is always punctuated.

    first reference: *Escherichia coli*
    subsequent reference: *E. coli*

37. Abbreviations for the names of chemical compounds or mechanical or electronic equipment or processes are usually not punctuated.

    OCR   PCB   CPU   PBX

38. The symbols for chemical elements are not punctuated.

    H   Cl   Pb   Na

39. Time When time is expressed in figures, the abbreviations that follow are most often written as punctuated lowercase letters; punctuated small capital letters are also common.

    8:30 a.m.   10:00 p.m.   8:30 A.M.   10:00 P.M.

40. In transportation schedules, *a.m.* and *p.m.* are generally written in capitalized, unpunctuated, unspaced letters.

    8:30 AM   10:00 PM

41. Time-zone designations are usually written in capitalized, unpunctuated, unspaced letters.

    EST   PST   CDT

42. Titles The only courtesy titles that are always abbreviated in written references are *Mr., Ms., Mrs.,* and *Messrs.* Other titles, such as *Doctor, Representative,* or *Senator,* may be either written out or abbreviated.

    Ms. Lee A. Downs
    Messrs. Lake, Mason, and Nambeth
    Doctor Howe   *or*   Dr. Howe

43. Despite some traditional objections, the titles *Honorable* and *Reverend* are often abbreviated.

    the Honorable Samuel I. O'Leary   *or*   the Hon. Samuel I. O'Leary
    the Reverend Samuel I. O'Leary   *or*   the Rev. Samuel I. O'Leary

44. The designations *Jr.* and *Sr.* may be used with courtesy titles, with abbreviations for academic degrees, and with professional-rating abbreviations. They may or may not be preceded by a comma, according to the writer's preference. They are generally only used with a full name.

    Mr. John K. Walker, Jr.
    General John K. Walker Jr.
    The Honorable John K. Walker, Jr.
    John K. Walker Jr., M.D.

45. When an abbreviation for an academic degree, professional certification, or association membership follows a name, it is usually preceded by a comma. No courtesy title should precede the name.

    Dr. Jesse Smith   *or*   Jesse Smith, M.D.   *but not*   Dr. Jesse Smith, M.D.
    Katherine Derwinski, CLU
    Carol Manning, M.D., FACPS

46. The abbreviation *Esq.* for *Esquire* is used in the United States after the surname of professional persons such as attorneys, architects, consuls, clerks of the court, and justices of the peace. It is not used, however, if a courtesy title such as *Dr., Hon., Miss, Mr., Mrs.,* or *Ms.* precedes the first name. (For more on the use of *Esquire,* see pages 306–7.)

    Carolyn B. West, Esq.

47. **Units of measure** Measures and weights may be abbreviated in figure-plus-unit combinations. However, if the numeral is written out, the unit should also be written out.

    > 15 cu ft   *or*   15 cu. ft.   *but*   fifteen cubic feet
    > How many cubic feet does the refrigerator hold?

48. Abbreviations for metric units are usually not punctuated. Abbreviations for traditional units are usually punctuated.

    > 14 ml   12 km   22 mi.   8 ft.   4 sec.   20 min.

49. **Versus** *Versus* is usually abbreviated as *v.* in legal contexts; it is either spelled out or abbreviated as *vs.* in general contexts.

    > *in a legal context:*   *Smith* v. *Vermont*
    > *in a general context:*   honesty versus dishonesty
    >   *or*
    >   honesty vs. dishonesty

Numbers

The styling of numbers presents special difficulties to writers because there are so many conventions to follow, some of which may conflict when applied to particular passages. Your major decision will be whether to write out numbers or to express them in figures, and usage varies considerably on this point.

NUMBERS AS WORDS OR FIGURES

At one extreme of styling, all numbers, sometimes even including dates, are written out. This usage is uncommon and is usually limited to proclamations, legal documents, and some other types of very formal writing. At the other extreme, some types of technical writing, such as statistical reports, contain no written-out numbers except sometimes at the beginning of a sentence.

In general, figures are easier to read than spelled-out numbers; however, the spelled-out forms are helpful in certain circumstances, such as in distinguishing different categories of numbers or in providing relief from an overwhelming cluster of numerals. Most writers follow one or the other of two common conventions combining numerals and written-out numbers. The conventions are described in this section, along with the exceptions to the general rules.

1. **Basic conventions** The first system requires that a writer use words for numbers up to nine and figures for exact numbers greater than nine. (A variation of this system sets the number ten as the dividing point.) In this system, numbers that consist of a whole number between one and nine followed by *hundred, thousand, million,* etc., may either be spelled out or expressed in figures.

    > She performed in 22 plays on Broadway, seven of which won awards.
    > The new edition will consist of 25 volumes, which will be issued at a rate
    >   of approximately four volumes per year.
    > The cat show attracted an unexpected two thousand entries.
    > They sold more than 2,000 units in the first year.

2. The second system requires that a writer use figures for all exact numbers 100 and above (or 101 and above) and words for numbers from one

to ninety-nine (or one to one hundred) and for numbers that consist of a whole number between one and ninety-nine followed by *hundred, thousand, million,* etc.

> The artist spent nearly twelve years completing these four volumes, which comprise 435 hand-colored engravings.
> The 145 seminar participants toured the area's eighteen period houses.
> In the course of four hours, the popular author signed twenty-five hundred copies of her new book.

3. **Sentence beginnings** Numbers that begin a sentence are written out, although some writers make an exception for dates. Avoid spelled-out numbers that are lengthy and awkward by restructuring the sentence so that the number appears elsewhere than at the beginning and may then be written as a figure.

> Sixty-two new models will be introduced this year.
> *or*
> There will be 62 new models introduced this year.
> Nineteen eighty-seven was our best earnings year so far.
> *or*
> 1987 was our best earnings year so far.
> One hundred fifty-seven illustrations, including 86 color plates, are contained in the book.
> *or*
> The book contains 157 illustrations, including 86 color plates.

4. **Adjacent numbers and numbers in series** Generally, two separate sets of figures should not be written adjacent to one another in running text unless they form a series. In order to avoid the juxtaposition of unrelated figures, either the sentence should be rephrased or one of the figures should be spelled out—usually the figure with the written form that is shorter and more easily read. When one of two adjacent numbers is an element of a compound modifier, the first number is often expressed in words, the second in figures. But if the second number is the shorter, the styling is often reversed.

> sixteen ½-inch dowels   twenty 100-point games
> twenty-five 11-inch platters   78 twenty-point games
> By 1997, thirty schools . . .

5. Numbers paired at the beginning of a sentence are usually written alike. If the first word of the sentence is a spelled-out number, the second, related number is also spelled out. However, some writers prefer that each number be styled independently, even if that results in an inconsistent pairing.

> Sixty to seventy-five copies will be required.
> Sixty to 75 copies will be required.

6. Numbers that form a pair or a series referring to comparable quantities within a sentence or a paragraph should be treated consistently. The style of the largest number usually determines the style of the other numbers. Thus, a series of numbers including some that would ordinarily be spelled out might all be written as figures. Similarly, figures are used to express all the numbers in a series if one of those numbers is a mixed or simple fraction.

> The three jobs took 5, 12, and 4½ hours, respectively.
> We need four desks, three chairs, fourteen typewriters, and six file cabinets.

7. **Round numbers** Approximate or round numbers, particularly those that can be expressed in one or two words, are often written out in general writing; in technical and scientific writing they are more likely to be expressed as numerals.

> seven hundred people
> five thousand years
> four hundred thousand volumes
> > *but in technical writing*
> 50,000 people per year
> 20,000 species of fish

8. For easier reading, numbers of one million and above may be expressed as figures followed by the word *million, billion,* and so forth. The figure may include a decimal fraction, but the fraction is not usually carried past the first digit to the right of the decimal point, and it is never carried past the third digit. If a more exact number is required, the whole amount should be written in figures.

> about 4.6 billion years old
> 1.2 million metric tons of grain
> the last 600 million years
> $7.25 million
> $3,456,000,000
> > *but*   200,000 years   *not*   200 thousand years

ORDINAL NUMBERS

1. Ordinal numbers generally follow the styling rules for cardinal numbers. In technical writing, however, ordinal numbers are usually written as figure-plus-suffix combinations. In addition, certain ordinal numbers—for example, those specifying percentiles and latitudinal lines—are usually set as figures.

> the sixth Robert de Bruce   his twenty-third try
> the ninth grade   the 20th century
> the 40th parallel   the 98th Congress
> the 9th and 14th chapters   the 12th percentile

2. The forms *second* and *third* may be written with figures as *2d* or *2nd, 3d* or *3rd, 22d* or *22nd, 93d* or *93rd, 102d* or *102nd*. A period does not follow the suffix.

ROMAN NUMERALS

Roman numerals are generally used in the specific situations described below.

1. Roman numerals are traditionally used to differentiate rulers and popes with identical names.

> Elizabeth II   Innocent X
> Henry VIII   Louis XIV

2. Roman numerals are used to differentiate related males who have the same name. (For more on this use of Roman numerals, see page 312.)

> James R. Watson II   James R. Watson 2nd *or* 2d

Possessives for these names are formed as follows:

> *singular:*   James R. Watson III's [*or* 3rd's *or* 3d's] house
> *plural:*   the James R. Watson IIIs' [*or* 3rds' *or* 3ds'] house

3. Lowercase Roman numerals (i, ii, iii, iv, etc.) are often used to number the pages of a publication that precede the regular Arabic sequence, as in a foreword, preface, or introduction.

4. Roman numerals are often used in outlines and in lists of major headings. An example of an outline is shown on page 189.

5. Roman numerals are found as part of a few established technical terms such as blood-clotting factors, quadrant numbers, designations of cranial nerves, and virus or organism types. Also, chords in the study of music harmony are designated by capital and lowercase Roman numerals. For the most part, however, technical terms that include numbers express them in Arabic form.

blood-clotting factor VII   HIV-III virus
quadrant III   *but*
the cranial nerves II and IX   adenosine $3',5'$-monophosphate
Population II stars   cesium 137
type I error   PL/1 programming language
vii_6 chord

PUNCTUATION AND INFLECTION

The paragraphs that follow provide general rules for the use of commas and hyphens in compound and large numbers, as well as the plural forms of numbers. For specific categories of numbers, such as dates, money, and decimal fractions, see the section on Specific Styling Conventions, beginning on page 185.

1. **Commas in large numbers** In general writing, with the exceptions explained in paragraph 3 below, figures of four digits may be written with or without a comma; the punctuated form is more common. If the numerals form part of a tabulation, commas are necessary so that four-digit numerals can align with numerals of five or more digits.

    2,000 case histories   *or less commonly*   1253 people

2. Whole numbers of five digits or more (but not decimal fractions) use a comma to separate three-digit groups, counting from the right.

    a fee of $12,500
    15,000 units
    a population of 1,500,000

3. Certain types of numbers are treated differently. Decimal fractions and serial and multidigit numbers in set combinations, such as the numbers of policies, contracts, checks, streets, rooms, suites, telephones, pages, military hours, and years, do not contain commas.

    check 34567   2.5544
    Room 1206   the year 1929
    1650 hours   Policy No. 33442

4. **Hyphens** Hyphens are used with written-out numbers between 21 and 99.

    forty-one
    forty-first
    four hundred twenty-two

5. A hyphen is used between the numerator and the denominator of a fraction that is written out when that fraction is used as a modifier. A written-out fraction consisting of two words only (such as *two thirds*) is usually left open, although the hyphenated form is also common. Multiword numerators and

denominators are usually hyphenated. If either the numerator or the denominator is hyphenated, no hyphen is used between them. (For more on fractions, see pages 189–90.)

a two-thirds majority	forty-five hundredths
three fifths of her paycheck	four five-hundredths
seven and four fifths	

6. Numbers that form the first part of a compound modifier expressing measurement are followed by a hyphen, except when the second part of the modifier is the word *percent*.

a 5-foot board	an eight-pound baby
a 28-mile trip	a 680-acre ranch
a 10-pound weight	a 75 percent reduction

7. An adjective or adverb made from a numeral plus the suffix *-fold* contains a hyphen, while a similar term made from a written-out number is closed up. (For more on the use of suffixes with numbers, see page 171.)

    increased 20-fold
    a fourfold increase

8. Serial numbers, such as Social Security or engine numbers, often contain hyphens that make lengthy numerals more readable.

    020-42-1691

9. Numbers are usually not divided at the end of a line. If division is unavoidable, the break occurs only after a comma. End-of-line breaks do not occur at decimal points, and a name with a numerical suffix (such as Robert F. Walker III) is not divided between the name and the numeral.

10. **Inclusive numbers** Inclusive numbers—those which express a range—are separated either by the word *to* or by a hyphen or en dash, which serves as an arbitrary equivalent of the phrase "(up) to and including" when used between dates and other inclusive numbers. (The en dash is explained in paragraph 12 under Dash on page 125.)

pages 40 to 98	the fiscal year 1987–1988
pages 40–98	spanning the years 1915 to 1941
pp. 40–98	the decade 1920–1930

Inclusive numbers separated by a hyphen or en dash are not used in combination with the words *from* or *between*, as in "from 1955–60" or "between 1970–90." Instead, phrases like these are written as "from 1955 to 1960" or "between 1970 and 1990."

11. Units of measurement expressed in words or abbreviations are usually used only after the second element of an inclusive number. Symbols, however, are repeated.

    an increase in dosage from 200 to 500 mg
    ten to fifteen dollars
    30 to 35 degrees Celsius
      but
    $50 to $60 million
    45° to 48° F

12. Numbers that are part of an inclusive set or range are usually styled alike: figures with figures, spelled-out words with other spelled-out words. Similarly, approximate numbers are usually not paired with exact numbers.

from 8 to 108 absences
five to twenty guests
300,000,000 to 305,000,000   *not*   300 million to 305,000,000

13. Inclusive page numbers and dates may be written in full or elided (i.e., shortened). However, inclusive dates that appear in titles and other headings are almost never elided. Dates that appear with era designations are also not elided (see paragraph 14 on page 187).

467–68 *or* 467–468   1724–27 *or* 1724–1727
203–4 *or* 203–204   1463–1510
552–549 B.C.   1800–1801

Elided numbers are used because they save space. The most commonly used style for the elision of inclusive numbers is based on the following rules:

a. Never elide inclusive numbers that have only two digits: 33–37, *not* 33–7.

b. Never elide inclusive numbers when the first number ends in 00: 100–108, *not* 100–08 *and not* 100–8.

c. In other numbers, do not omit the tens digit from the higher number. *Exception:* Where the tens digit of both numbers is zero, write only one digit for the higher number: 103–4, *not* 103–04.

467–68 *or* 467–468   203–4 *or* 203–204
1724–27 *or* 1724–1727   1800–1801
550–602   552–549 B.C.
1463–1510

14. **Plurals** The plurals of written-out numbers are formed by adding *-s* or *-es*.

Back in the thirties these roads were unpaved.
Christmas shoppers bought the popular toy in twos and threes.

15. The plurals of figures are formed by adding *-s*. Some writers prefer to add an apostrophe before the *-s*. For more on the plurals of figures, see paragraphs 18 and 19 under Plurals on page 159, and paragraph 5 under Apostrophe on page 110.

This ghost town was booming back in the 1840s.
The first two artificial hearts to be implanted in human patients were Jarvik-7s.
but also
1's and *7*'s that looked alike

SPECIFIC STYLING CONVENTIONS

The following paragraphs, arranged alphabetically, describe styling practices commonly followed for specific situations involving numbers.

1. **Addresses** Arabic numerals are used for all building, house, apartment, room, and suite numbers except for *one*, which is written out.

6 Lincoln Road
1436 Fremont Street
but
One Bayside Drive

When the address of a building is used as its name, the number in the address is written out.

Fifty Maple Street

2. Numbered streets have their numbers written as ordinals. There are two distinct styling conventions. Under the first, numbered street names from First through Twelfth are written out, and numerals are used for all numbered streets above Twelfth. Under the second, all numbered street names up to and including One Hundredth are spelled out.

> 19 South 22nd Street   145 East 145th Street
> 167 West Second Avenue   122 East Forty-second Street
> One East Ninth Street   36 East Fiftieth
> in the Sixties [streets from 60th to 69th]
> in the 120s [streets from 120th to 129th]

A disadvantage of the first convention is that the house or building number may immediately precede the street number. In these cases, a spaced hyphen may be inserted between the two numbers, or the street number may be written out.

> 2018 - 14th Street
> 2018 Fourteenth Street

3. Arabic numerals are used to designate highways and, in some states, county roads.

> Interstate 91   *or*   I-91   Massachusetts 57
> U.S. Route 1   *or*   U.S. 1   County 213

4. **Dates** Year numbers are written as figures. If a number representing a year begins a sentence, it may be spelled out or the sentence may be rewritten to avoid beginning it with a figure. (For additional examples, see paragraph 3 under Numbers as Words or Figures on page 181.)

> 1988
> 1888–96
> Fifteen eighty-eight marked the end to Spanish ambitions for the control
>   of England.
>   *or*
> Spanish ambitions for the control of England ended in 1588 with the destruction of their "Invincible Armada."

5. A year number may be abbreviated, or cut back to its last two digits, in informal writing or when an event is so well known that it needs no century designation. In these cases an apostrophe precedes the numerals. (For more on this use of the apostrophe, see paragraph 5 under Apostrophe on page 110.)

> He always maintained that he'd graduated from Korea, Clash of '52.
> the blizzard of '88

6. Full dates (month, day, and year) may be written in one of two ways. The traditional style is the month-day-year sequence, with the year set off by commas that precede and follow it. An alternative style is the inverted date, or day-month-year sequence, which does not require commas. This sequence is used in U.S. government publications and in the military.

> *traditional style:*   July 8, 1776, was a warm, sunny day in Philadelphia.
>   the explosion on July 16, 1945, at Alamogordo
> *military style:*   the explosion on 16 July 1945 at Alamogordo
>   Lee's surrender to Grant on 9 April 1865 at Appomattox

7. Ordinal numbers are not used in full dates, even though the numbers may be pronounced as ordinals. Ordinals may be used, however, for a date without an accompanying year, and they are always used when preceded in a date by the word *the*.

> December 4, 1829
> on December 4th   *or*   on December 4
> on the 4th of December

8. Commas are usually omitted from dates that include the month and year but not the day. Alternatively, writers sometimes insert the word *of* between month and year.

> in November 1805   back in January of 1981

9. Once a numerical date has been given, a reference to a related date may be written out.

> After the meeting on June 6 the conventioneers left for home, and by the seventh the hotel was virtually empty.

10. All-figure dating, such as 6-8-95 or 6/8/95, is inappropriate except in the most informal correspondence. It also creates a problem of ambiguity; the examples above may mean either June 8, 1995, or (especially in Britain and Europe) August 6, 1995.

11. References to specific centuries are often written out, although they may be expressed in figures, especially when they form the first element of a compound modifier.

> the nineteenth century
> a sixteenth-century painting   *but also*   a 16th-century painting

12. In general correspondence, the name of a specific decade often takes a short form. Although many writers place an apostrophe before the shortened word and a few capitalize it, both the apostrophe and the capitalization are often omitted when the context clearly indicates that a date is being referred to.

> in the turbulent seventies
>   *but also*
> back in the 'forties
> in the early Fifties

13. The name of a specific decade is often expressed in numerals, usually in plural form. (For more on the formation of plural numbers, see paragraphs 14 and 15 on page 185.) The figure may be shortened with an apostrophe to indicate the missing numerals, but any sequence of such numbers should be styled consistently. (For more on this use of the apostrophe, see paragraph 5 under Apostrophe on page 110.)

> the 1950s and 1960s   *or*   the '50s and '60s
>   *but not*
> the 1950s and '60s   *or*   the '50's and '60's

14. Era designations precede or follow words that specify centuries or numerals that specify years. Era designations are unspaced and are nearly always abbreviated; they are usually typed as regular capitals and typeset as small capitals, and they may or may not be punctuated with periods. Any date that is given without an era designation or context is understood to mean A.D. The two most common abbreviations are B.C. (before Christ) and A.D. (*anno*

Domini, "in the year of our Lord"). The abbreviation B.C. is placed after the date, while A.D. is usually placed before the date but after a century designation.

> 1792–1750 B.C.
> A.D. 35
> the second century A.D.
> between 7 B.C. and A.D. 22

15. **Degrees of temperature and arc** In technical writing, quantities expressed in degrees are generally written as a numeral followed by the degree symbol (°). In the Kelvin scale, however, neither the word *degree* nor the symbol is used with the figure.

> a 45° angle
> 6°40'10"N
> 32° F
> 0° C
> Absolute zero is zero kelvins or 0 K.

16. In general writing, the quantity expressed in degrees may or may not be written out. A figure is usually followed by the degree symbol or the word *degree;* a written-out number is always followed by the word *degree.*

> latitude 43°19"N
> latitude 43 degrees N
> a difference of 43 degrees latitude
> The temperature has risen thirty degrees since this morning.

17. **Enumerations and outlines** Both run-in and vertical enumerations are often numbered. In run-in enumerations—that is, lists that form part of a normal-looking sentence—each item is preceded by a number (or an italicized letter) enclosed in parentheses. The items in the list are separated by commas if the items are brief and have little or no internal punctuation; if the items are complex, they are separated by semicolons. The entire list is introduced by a colon if it is preceded by a full clause.

> We feel that she should (1) increase her administrative skills, (2) pursue additional professional education, and (3) increase her production.
> The oldest and most basic word-processing systems consist of the following: (1) a typewriter for keyboarding information, (2) a console to house the storage medium, and (3) the medium itself.
> The vendor of your system should (1) instruct you in the care and maintenance of your system; (2) offer regularly scheduled maintenance to ensure that the system is clean, with lubrication and replacement of parts as necessary; and (3) respond promptly to service calls.

18. In vertical enumerations, the numbers are usually followed by a period. Each item in the enumeration begins its own line, which is either flush left or indented. Runover lines are usually aligned with the first word that follows the number, and figures are aligned on the periods that follow them. Each item on the list is usually capitalized if the items are syntactically independent of the words that introduce them. However, style varies on this point, and use of a lowercase style for such items is also fairly common. The items do not end with periods unless at least one of the items is a complete sentence, in which case a period follows each item. Items that are syntactically dependent on the words that introduce them begin with a lowercase letter and carry the same punctuation marks that they would if they were a run-in series in a sentence.

Required skills include the following:
1. Shorthand
2. Typing
3. Transcription

To type a three-column table, follow this procedure:
1. Clear tab stops.
2. Remove margin stops.
3. Determine precise center of the page. Set a tab stop at center.

The vendor of your system should
1. instruct you in the care and maintenance of your system;
2. offer regularly scheduled maintenance to ensure that the system is clean, with lubrication and replacement parts as necessary; and
3. respond promptly to service calls.

19. Outlines make use of Roman numerals, Arabic numerals, and letters.

  I. Editorial tasks
    A. Manuscript editing
    B. Author contact
      1. Authors already under contract
      2. New authors
  II. Production responsibilities
    A. Scheduling
      1. Composition
      2. Printing and binding
    B. Cost estimates and bids
      1. Composition
      2. Printing and binding

20. Fractions and decimal fractions In running text, fractions standing alone are usually written out. Common fractions used as nouns are usually written as open compounds, but when they are used as modifiers they are usually hyphenated. Most writers try to find ways to avoid writing out complicated fractions (such as *forty-two seventy-fifths*). For more on written-out fractions, see paragraph 5 on page 183.

21. Mixed fractions (fractions with a whole number, such as 3½) and fractions that form part of a unit modifier are expressed in figures in running text. A *-th* is not added to a figure fraction.

waiting 2½ hours   a ⅞-mile course

When mixed fractions are typewritten, the typist leaves a space between the whole number and the fraction. The space is closed up when the number is set in type. Fractions that are not on the keyboard may be made up by typing the numerator, a slash, and the denominator in succession without spacing.

```
waiting 2 1/2 hours        a 7/8-mile course
```

22. Fractions used with units of measurement are expressed in figures.

¹⁄₁₀ km   ¼ mile

23. Decimal fractions are always set as figures. In technical writing, a zero is placed to the left of the decimal point when the fraction is less than a whole number. In general writing, the zero is usually omitted.

An example of a pure decimal fraction is 0.375, while 1.402 is classified as a mixed decimal fraction.
0.142857

0.2 gm
received 0.1 mg/kg diazepam IV
but
a .12-gauge shotgun

24. A comma is never inserted in the numbers following a decimal point.

25. Fractions and decimal fractions are usually not mixed in a text.

5½ lb. 2⅕ oz.
5.5 lb. 2.2 oz.
but not
5½ lb. 2.2 oz.

26. Money Sums of money are expressed in words or figures, as described in paragraphs 1 and 2 on page 180. If the sum can be expressed in one or two words, it is usually written out in running text. But if several sums are mentioned in the sentence or paragraph, all are usually expressed as figures. When the amount is written out, the unit of currency is also written out. If the sum is expressed in figures, the symbol of the currency unit is used, with no space between it and the numerals.

We paid $175,000 for the house.
My change came to 87¢.
The shop charges $67.50 for our hand-knit sweaters.
The price of a nickel candy bar seems to have risen to more like fifty cents.
Fifty dollars was stolen from my wallet.
forty thousand dollars
fifty-two dollars

27. Monetary units of mixed dollars-and-cents amounts are expressed in figures.

$16.75 $307.02 $1.95

28. Even-dollar amounts are often expressed in figures without a decimal point and zeros. But when even-dollar amounts appear near amounts that include dollars and cents, the decimal point and zeros are usually added for consistency. The dollar sign is repeated before each amount in a series or inclusive range; the word *dollar* may or may not be repeated.

The price of the book rose from $7.95 in 1970 to $8.00 in 1971 and then to $8.50 in 1972.
The bids were eighty, ninety, and one hundred dollars.
or
The bids were eighty dollars, one hundred dollars, and three hundred dollars.

29. Sums of money given in round units of millions or above are usually expressed in a combination of figures and words, either with a dollar sign or with the word *dollars*. (For more on the handling of round numbers, see paragraphs 7 and 8 under Numbers as Words or Figures on page 182.)

60 million dollars
a $10 million building program
$4.5 billion

30. In legal documents a sum of money is usually written out fully, with the corresponding figures in parentheses immediately following.

twenty-five thousand dollars ($25,000)

31. **Percentages** In technical writing, specific percentages are styled as figure plus unspaced percent sign (%). In general correspondence, the percentage number may be expressed as a figure or spelled out. The word *percent* rather than the symbol is used in nonscientific texts.

    technical: 15%
                13.5%
    general: 15 percent
                87.2 percent
                Twenty-five percent of the office staff was out with the flu.
                a four percent increase

32. The word *percentage* or *percent,* used as a noun without an adjacent numeral, should never be replaced by a percent sign.

    Only a small percentage of the staff objected to the smoking ban.

33. In a series or unit combination, the percent sign should be included with all numbers, even if one of the numbers is zero.

    a variation of 0% to 10%

34. **Proper names** Numbers in the names of religious organizations and churches are usually written out in ordinal form. Names of specific governmental bodies may include ordinals, and these are written out if they are one hundred or below.

    Third Congregational Church
    Seventh-Day Adventists
    Third Reich
    First Continental Congress

35. Names of electoral, judicial, and military units may include ordinal numbers that precede the noun. Numbers of one hundred or below are written out.

    First Congressional District
    Twelfth Precinct
    Ninety-eighth Congress   *or*   98th Congress
    Circuit Court of Appeals for the Third Circuit
    United States Eighth Army   *or*   8th United States Army

36. Local branches of labor unions and fraternal organizations are generally identified by a numeral usually placed after the name.

    International Brotherhood of Electrical Workers Local 42
    Elks Lodge No. 61
    Local 98 Operating Engineers

37. **Ratios** Ratios expressed in figures use a colon, a hyphen, a slash, or the word *to* as a means of comparison. Ratios expressed in words use a hyphen or the word *to.*

    a 3:1 chance
    a 6-1 vote
    22.4 mi/gal
    odds of 100 to 1
    a fifty-fifty chance
    a ratio of ten to four

38. **Serial numbers and miscellaneous numerals** Figures are used to refer to things that are numbered serially, such as chapter and page numbers, addresses, years, policy and contract numbers, and so forth.

Serial No. 5274	vol. 5, p. 202
Permit No. 63709	column 2
pages 420–515	Table 16

39. Figures are also used to express stock-market quotations, mathematical calculations, scores, and tabulations.

3⅛ percent bonds	won by a score of 8 to 2
$3 \times 15 = 45$	the tally: 322 ayes, 80 nays

40. Time of day In running text, the time of day is usually spelled out when expressed in even, half, or quarter hours.

> Quitting time is four-thirty.
> The meeting should be over by half past eleven.
> We should arrive at a quarter past five.

41. The time of day is also usually spelled out when it is followed by the contraction *o'clock* or when *o'clock* is understood.

> He should be here by four at the latest.
> My appointment is at eleven o'clock.
> *or*
> My appointment is at 11 o'clock.

42. Figures are used to specify a precise time.

> The meeting is scheduled for 9:15 in the morning.
> Her plane is due at 3:05 this afternoon.
> The program starts at 8:30 in the evening.

43. Figures are also written when the time of day is used with the abbreviations *a.m. (ante meridiem)* and *p.m. (post meridiem)*. The lowercase styling for these abbreviations is most common, but small capital letters are also frequently used. These abbreviations should not be used with the words *morning* or *evening* or the word *o'clock*.

> 8:30 a.m.   *or*   8:30 A.M.
> 10:30 p.m.   *or*   10:30 P.M.
> 8 a.m.   *or*   8 A.M.
> *but*
> 9:15 in the morning
> 11:00 in the evening
> nine o'clock

When twelve o'clock is written, it is helpful to add the designation *midnight* or *noon* rather than *a.m.* or *p.m.*

> twelve o'clock (midnight)
> twelve o'clock (noon)

44. For consistency, even-hour times should be written with a colon and two zeros when used in a series or pairing with any odd-hour times.

> He came at 7:00 and left at 9:45

45. The 24-hour clock system—also called military time—uses no punctuation and is expressed without the use of *a.m., p.m.,* or *o'clock*; the word *hours* sometimes replaces them.

> from 0930 to 1100   at 1600 hours

46. Units of measurement Numbers used with units of measurement are treated according to the basic conventions explained in the first part of this section. However, in some cases writers achieve greater clarity by writing all numbers—even those below ten—that express quantities of physical measurement as numerals.

> The car was traveling in excess of 80 miles an hour.
> The old volume weighed three pounds and was difficult to hold in a reading position.
> *but also in some general texts*
> 3 hours, 25 minutes
> saw 18 eagles in 12 minutes
> a 6-pound hammer
> weighed 3 pounds, 5 ounces

47. When units of measurement are written as abbreviations or symbols, the adjacent numbers are always figures.

   6 cm   67.6 fl oz
   1 mm   4'
   $4.25   98.6°

48. When two or more quantities are expressed, as in ranges or dimensions or series, an accompanying symbol is usually repeated with each figure.

   4" × 6" cards
   temperature on successive days of 30°, 55°, 43°, and 58°
   $400–$500

Parts of Speech

No guide to effective communication can ignore the basic components of writing: the word, the phrase, the clause, the sentence, and the paragraph. Each of these increasingly complex units contributes to the expression of a writer's ideas. Basic to all of them is the word.

Words have traditionally been classified into eight parts of speech: adjective, adverb, conjunction, interjection, noun, preposition, pronoun, and verb. This classification is based mainly on a word's inflectional features, its grammatical functions, and its position within a sentence. On the following pages, the parts of speech are discussed briefly in alphabetical order.

ADJECTIVE

An adjective is a word that describes or modifies the meaning of a noun. Adjectives serve to point out a quality of a thing named, indicate its quantity or extent, or specify a thing as distinct from something else.

Adjectives are often classified by the ways in which they modify or limit the meaning of a noun. The following paragraphs describe, in alphabetical order, the various types of adjectives and also outline situations involving adjectives that are sometimes troublesome for writers.

1. **Absolute adjectives** Some adjectives (such as *prior, maximum, optimum, minimum,* and *first*) normally cannot be used comparatively (see paragraphs 4 and 5 below), because they represent ultimate conditions. These adjectives are called *absolute* or *nongradable adjectives.* Some writers are careful to mod-

ify these adjectives with adverbs such as *almost, near,* or *nearly,* rather than *least, less, more, most,* or *very.*

> an *almost fatal* dose
> at *near maximum* capacity
> a *more nearly perfect* likeness

However, many writers do compare and qualify this type of adjective in order to show connotations and shades of meaning they consider less than absolute.

> a *more perfect* union
> a *less complete* account

When in doubt about the comparability of an absolute adjective, check the definitions and examples of usage given in a dictionary.

2. **Adjective/noun agreement** The number (singular or plural) of a demonstrative adjective *(this, that, these, those)* should agree with that of the noun it modifies.

> *these* kinds of typewriters   *not*   *these* kind of typewriters
> *those* sorts of jobs   *not*   *those* sort of jobs
> *this* type of person   *not*   *these* type of people

3. **Articles** An article is one of three words (*a, an,* and *the*) that are used with nouns to delimit or give definiteness to the application of a noun.

4. **Compared with adverbs** Both adjectives and adverbs describe or modify other words; however, adjectives can only modify nouns, while adverbs can modify verbs, adverbs, and adjectives. For more on the differences between adjectives and adverbs, see paragraph 20 on page 196 and paragraphs 4–6 under Adverb on page 197.

5. **Comparison of adjectives** A gradable adjective can indicate degrees of comparison (positive, comparative, superlative) by the addition of the endings -*er* and -*est* to the base word; the addition of *more, most, less,* and *least* before the base word; or the use of irregular forms.

positive	*comparative*	*superlative*
clean	cleaner	cleanest
meaningful	more meaningful	most meaningful
meaningful	less meaningful	least meaningful
bad	worse	worst

6. The comparative degree is used to show that the thing being modified has more (or less) of a particular quality than the one or ones to which it is being compared. The superlative degree is used to show that the thing being modified has the most (or least) of a quality out of all those things to which it is being compared. The superlative degree is used when there are more than two things being compared.

comparative	*superlative*
prices *higher* than those elsewhere	the *highest* price in the area
a *better* report than our last one	the *best* report so far
the *more expensive* of the two methods	the *most expensive* of the three methods

7. The comparatives and superlatives of one-syllable adjectives are usually formed by adding -*er* and -*est* to the base word. The comparatives and superlatives of adjectives with more than two syllables are formed by adding

more, most, less, and *least* before the base word. The comparatives and super-latives of two-syllable adjectives are formed by either adding *-er* and *-est* to the base word or using *more, most, less,* and *least* before the base word. When in doubt about the inflection of a particular adjective, consult a dictionary.

positive	*comparative*	*superlative*
big	bigger	biggest
narrow	narrower	narrowest
complex	more complex	most complex
concise	less concise	least concise
important	more important	most important
troublesome	less troublesome	least troublesome

8. Some adjectives are ordinarily not compared, because they are felt to represent ultimate conditions (see paragraph 1).

9. **Coordinate and noncoordinate adjectives** Adjectives that share equal relationships to the nouns they modify are called *coordinate adjectives* and are separated from each other by commas.

> a *concise, coherent* essay
> a *hard, flickering* light

10. When the first of two adjectives modifies the noun plus a second adjective, the result is a pair of *noncoordinate adjectives.* Noncoordinate adjectives are not separated by commas.

> a *low monthly* fee
> the *first warm* day

11. **Demonstrative adjectives** A demonstrative adjective, such as *this* or *that,* points to what it modifies in order to distinguish it from others. *This* and *that* are the only two adjectives with plural forms: *these* and *those.*

12. **Descriptive adjectives** A descriptive adjective describes something or indicates a quality, kind, or condition.

> a *sick* pony   a *brave* soldier   a *new* dress

13. **Double comparisons** Double comparisons are considered nonstandard and should be avoided.

> an *easier* method   *not*   a *more easier* method
> the *easiest* solution   *not*   the *most easiest* solution

14. **Incomplete or understood comparisons** Some comparisons are left incomplete because the context clearly implies the comparison. However, the use of incomplete comparisons, especially for making vague claims of superiority such as commonly appear in advertising, is often considered careless or illogical in formal writing.

> *Older* Americans vote in *larger* numbers.
> Get *better* buys here!
> We have *lower* prices.

15. **Indefinite adjectives** An indefinite adjective designates an unidentified or not immediately identifiable person or thing.

> *some* books   *other* hotels

16. **Interrogative adjectives** An interrogative adjective conveys the force of a question.

> *Whose* office is this?   *Which* book do you want?

17. **Nouns used as adjectives** Nouns are frequently used to describe other nouns, and in this way they act like adjectives. For more on the use of nouns as modifiers, see paragraph 7 under Noun on page 204 and the discussion under Compounds That Function as Adjectives on pages 166–68.

18. **Placement within a sentence** Adjectives may occur in the following positions within sentences: (1) preceding the nouns they modify, (2) following the nouns they modify, (3) following the verb *to be* (*am, are, was, were*, etc.) and other linking verbs in the predicate-adjective position, and (4) following some transitive verbs used in the passive voice.

> the *black* hat
> a *dark, shabby* coat
> an executive *par excellence*
> painted the room *blue*
> a hat that is *black*
> food that tastes *stale*
> while I felt *sick*
> a room that was painted *blue*
> passengers found *dead* at the crash site

19. **Possessive adjectives** A possessive adjective is the possessive form of a personal pronoun.

> *her* idea   *my* car   *our* savings plan

20. **Predicate adjectives** A predicate adjective modifies the subject of a linking verb (such as *be, become, feel, taste, smell, seem*) which it follows.

> She is *happy* with the outcome.
> The annual report looks *splendid*.
> The trainee seems *puzzled*.

Because some linking verbs (such as *feel, look, smell, taste*) can also function as active verbs, which can in turn be modified by adverbs, writers are sometimes confused over whether they should use the adverbial or adjectival form of a modifier after the verb. The answer is that an adjective is used if the subject of the sentence is being modified. If the verb is being modified, an adverb is used. (For more examples, see paragraph 5 under Adverb on page 197.)

> *adjective:*   Your memo looks *good*.
>   The colors feel *right*.
>   The copier smells *hot*.
> *adverb:*   They looked *quickly* at each item.
>   He felt *immediately* for his wallet.
>   She felt the corners *carefully* for dampness.

21. **Proper adjectives** A proper adjective is derived from a proper noun. It is usually capitalized.

> *Victorian* furniture   a *Puerto Rican* product   *Keynesian* economics

22. **Relative adjectives** A relative adjective (*which, that, who, whom, whose, where*) introduces an adjectival clause or a clause that functions as a noun.

> at the April conference, by *which* time the report should be finished
> not knowing *which* course she should follow

ADVERB

An adverb is a word or combination of words that typically serves as a modifier of a verb, an adjective, another adverb, a preposition, a phrase, a clause, or a sentence and expresses some relation of manner or quality, place, time, degree, number, cause, opposition, affirmation, or denial. Because of its many roles, the adverb can be one of the most confusing parts of speech.

Most adverbs are adjectives with an *-ly* ending added *(actually, congenially, madly, really)*. There are many exceptions to this pattern, however. Adverbs based on adjectives ending in *-ly (costly, friendly, likely)* do not include an additional *-ly* ending but take the same form as the adjective. In addition, some adverbs do not end in *-ly (now, quite, too)*.

Adverbs answer such questions as: "When?" ("Please reply *at once*"), "How long?" ("This job is taking *forever*"), "Where?" ("She works *there*"), "In what direction?" ("Move the lever *upward*"), "How?" ("The staff moved *expeditiously* on the project"), and "To what degree?" ("The book was *very* popular").

1. **Basic uses** Adverbs modify verbs, adjectives, and other adverbs.

   > She *carefully* studied the balance sheet.
   > She gave the balance sheet *very* careful study.
   > She studied the balance sheet *very* carefully.

2. Conjunctive adverbs join clauses or link sentences. (For more on this use of adverbs, see paragraphs 13–15 under Conjunction on page 202.)

   > You are welcome to join our car pool; *however,* please be ready by 7:00 a.m.
   > He thoroughly enjoyed the symposium. *Indeed,* he was fascinated by the presentations.

3. In addition, adverbs may be essential elements of two-word verbs.

   > Our staff will work *up* the specifications.
   > We can farm them *out* later.

4. **Compared with adjectives** Adverbs but not adjectives modify action verbs.

   > *not:*   He answered very *harsh.*
   > *instead:* He answered very *harshly.*

5. Complements referring to the subject of a sentence and occurring after linking verbs normally take adjectives but not adverbs. (For more examples, see paragraph 20 under Adjective on page 196.)

   > *not:*   He looks *badly* these days.
   >   The letter sounded *strongly.*
   > *instead:*   He looks *bad* these days.
   >   The letter sounded *strong.*
   > *and also:* He looks *good* these days.
   >   He looks *well* these days.

   In the last two examples, either *good* or *well* is acceptable, because both words are here functioning as adjectives in the sense of "healthy."

6. Adverbs but not adjectives modify adjectives and other adverbs.

   > *not:*   She looked *dreadful* tired.
   > *instead:* She looked *dreadfully* tired.

7. **Comparison of adverbs** Most adverbs have three different forms to indicate degrees of comparison: positive, comparative, and superlative. The *positive* form is the base word itself *(quickly, loudly, near)*. The *comparative* form is usually shown by the addition of *more* or *less* before the base word *(more quickly, less quickly)*. The *superlative* form is usually shown by the addition of *most* or *least (most quickly, least quickly)*. However, a few adverbs (such as *fast, slow, loud, soft, early, late,* and *quick*) may also be compared by the addition of

the endings -er and -est to the base word (quick, quicker, quickest). For an explanation of the uses of the comparative and superlative forms, see paragraphs 5 and 6 under Adjective on page 194.

8. As a general rule, one-syllable adverbs use the -er/-est endings to show comparison. Adverbs of three or more syllables use more/most and less/least. Two-syllable adverbs take either form.

fast	faster	fastest
easy	easier	easiest
madly	more madly	most madly
happily	more happily	most happily

9. Some adverbs (such as quite and very) cannot be compared.

10. **Double negatives and similar cases** A combination of two adverbs with negative meaning (such as not, hardly, never, and scarcely) to express a single negative idea should be avoided.

    not: We *cannot* see *hardly* any reason to buy this product.
    instead: We *cannot* see any reason to buy this product.
                We can see *hardly* any reason to buy this product.

11. **Emphasis** Adverbs such as *just* and *only* are often used to emphasize other words. Various emphases can result from the positioning of an adverb in a sentence.

    He *just* nodded to me as he passed.
    He nodded to me *just* as he passed.

12. In some positions and contexts, these adverbs can be ambiguous.

    They will *only* tell it to you.

    It is not clear whether this means that they will only tell it—that is, not put it in writing—or that they will tell no one else. If the latter interpretation is intended, a slight shift of position would remove the uncertainty.

    They will tell it *only* to you.

13. **Placement within a sentence** Adverbs are generally positioned as close as possible to the words they modify, if such a position will not result in misinterpretation.

    unclear: A project that the board would support *completely* occupied her thinking.

    Here it is unclear whether the writer means "would support completely" or "completely occupied her thinking." The adverb may be moved to another position, or the sentence may be rewritten, depending on the intended meaning.

    clear: A project that the board would *completely* support occupied her thinking.
              Her thinking was *completely* occupied with a project that the board would support.

14. When an adverb separates *to* from the verbal element of an infinitive ("hope to really start"), the result is called a *split infinitive*. For a discussion of split infinitives, see paragraph 32 under Verb on page 218.

15. Adverbs sometimes modify an entire sentence rather than a specific word or phrase within the sentence. Such adverbs are referred to as *sentence adverbs*, and their position can vary.

Fortunately they had already placed their order.
They *fortunately* had already placed their order.
They had already placed their order, *fortunately*.

16. Relative adverbs Relative adverbs (such as *when, where, why*) introduce
subordinate clauses. (For more on subordinate clauses, see the section on
Clauses, pages 220–21.)

They met at a time *when* prospects were good.
I went into the room *where* they were sitting.
Everyone knows the reason *why* she did it.

CONJUNCTION

A conjunction is a word or phrase that joins together words, phrases, clauses,
or sentences. Conjunctions may occur in many different positions in a sentence,
although they ordinarily do not appear at the end of a sentence unless the
sentence is elliptical. There are three main types of conjunctions: *coordinating,
correlative,* and *subordinating.* In addition to these three types of conjunctions, the
English language has transitional adverbs and adverbial phrases called *conjunctive adverbs.* These function as conjunctions even though they are customarily
classified as adverbs. A definition and discussion of the three types of conjunctions and of conjunctive adverbs follows. For information about punctuating
sentences with conjunctions, see paragraphs 1–5, 23–24, and 26–28 under
Comma (pages 114–15 and 118–19) and paragraphs 1–5 under Semicolon
(pages 137–38).

Coordinating conjunctions   Coordinating conjunctions (such as *and, but, for, or,
nor, so,* and *yet*) join together grammatical elements of equal weight. The elements may be words, phrases, subordinate clauses, main clauses, or complete
sentences.

1. Coordinating conjunctions are used to join elements, to exclude or contrast,
to offer alternatives, to propose reasons or grounds, or to specify a result.

joining similar elements:	She ordered pencils, pens, *and* erasers.
	Sales were slow, *and* they showed no sign of im- provement.
excluding or contrasting:	He is a brilliant *but* arrogant man.
	They offered a promising plan, *but* it had not yet been tested.
alternative:	She can wait here *or* go on ahead.
reason or grounds:	The report is useless, *for* its information is no longer current.
result:	His diction is excellent, *so* every word is clear.

2. A comma is used before a coordinating conjunction linking coordinate
clauses, especially when these clauses are lengthy. (For more on the use
of commas between clauses, see paragraphs 1–4 under Comma on pages
114–15.)

We encourage applications from all interested persons, *but* we do have
high professional standards that the successful applicant must meet.

3. Coordinating conjunctions should link equal grammatical elements—for
example, adjectives with other adjectives, nouns with other nouns, participles with other participles, clauses with other equal-ranking clauses, and so

on. Combining unequal grammatical elements may result in unbalanced sentences.

> *unbalanced:*   Having become disgusted *and* because he was tired, he left the meeting.
>
> *balanced:*   Because he was tired *and* disgusted, he left the meeting.
> Having become tired *and* disgusted, he left the meeting.

4. Coordinating conjunctions should not be used to string together a series of elements, regardless of their grammatical equality.

> *loose:*   We have sustained enormous losses in this division, *and* we have realized practically no profits even though the sales figures indicate last-quarter gains, *and* we are therefore reorganizing the entire management structure as well as cutting back on personnel.
>
> *tightened:*   Because this division has sustained enormous losses and has realized only insignificant profits even with its last-quarter sales gains, we are totally reorganizing its management. We are also cutting back on personnel.

5. The choice of the right coordinating conjunction is important: the right word will pinpoint the writer's true meaning and intent and will emphasize the most relevant idea or point of the sentence. The following three sentences show increasingly stronger degrees of contrast through the use of different conjunctions:

> He works hard *and* doesn't progress.
> He works hard *but* doesn't progress.
> He works hard, *yet* he doesn't progress.

6. The coordinating conjunction *and/or* linking two elements of a compound subject often poses a problem: should the verb that follows be singular or plural? A subject consisting of singular nouns connected by *and/or* may be considered singular or plural, depending on the meaning of the sentence.

> *singular:*   All loss *and/or* damage [one or the other and possibly both] is to be the responsibility of the sender.
>
> *plural:*   John R. Westlake *and/or* Maria A. Artandi *are* hereby appointed as the executors of my estate. [Both executors are to act, or either of them is to act if the other dies or is incapacitated.]

Correlative conjunctions   Correlative conjunctions are coordinating conjunctions that are used in pairs, although they are not placed adjacent to one another.

7. Correlative conjunctions are used to link alternatives and equal elements.

> *Either* you go *or* you stay.
> He had *neither* looks *nor* wits.
> *Both* typist *and* writer should understand the rules of punctuation.
> *Not only* was there inflation, *but* there was *also* unemployment.

8. Because they link equal grammatical elements, correlative conjunctions should be placed as close as possible to the elements they join. What follows *either* should be parallel to what follows *or;* that is, if a verb immediately follows one of these words, a verb must immediately follow the other.

> *misplaced:*   *Either* I must send a telex *or* make a long-distance call.
> *repositioned:*   I must *either* send a telex *or* make a long-distance call.

9. The negative counterpart to *either . . . or* is *neither . . . nor*. The conjunction *or* should not be substituted for *nor*, because its substitution will destroy the negative parallelism. However, *or* may occur in combination with *no*.

not:	He received *neither* a promotion *or* a raise.
instead:	He received *neither* a promotion *nor* a raise.
	He received *no* promotion *or* raise.

Subordinating conjunctions   Subordinating conjunctions join a subordinate or dependent clause to a main clause.

10. Subordinating conjunctions are used to express cause, condition or concession, manner, purpose or result, time, place or circumstance, and alternative conditions or possibilities.

cause:	*Because* she learns quickly, she is doing well in her new job.
condition or concession:	Don't call *unless* you have the information.
manner:	He looks *as though* he is ill.
	We'll do it *however* you tell us to.
purpose or result:	She routes the mail early *so that* they can read it.
time:	She kept meetings to a minimum *when* she was president.
place or circumstance:	I don't know *where* he has gone.
	He tries to help out *wherever* it is possible.
conditions or possibilities:	It was hard to decide *whether* I should go or stay.

11. The subordinating conjunction *that* introduces several kinds of subordinate clauses, including those used as noun equivalents (such as a subject or an object of a verb or as a predicate nominative).

    Yesterday I learned *that* he has been sick for over a week.

12. In introducing subordinate clauses, subordinating conjunctions deemphasize less important ideas in favor of more important ideas. The writer should take care that the point to be emphasized is in the main clause and that the points of less importance are subordinated.

    We were just coming out of the door *when* the building burst into flames.
    As we were coming out of the door, the building burst into flames.

Conjunctive adverbs   Conjunctive adverbs are transitional adverbs and adverbial phrases that express relationships between two units of discourse (such as two main clauses, two complete sentences, or two or more paragraphs). Though classed as adverbs, they function as conjunctions when they are used as connectives. Some common conjunctive adverbs are listed below.

accordingly	first	incidentally	on the contrary
also	for example	in conclusion	otherwise
anyhow	for instance	indeed	second
anyway	furthermore	in fact	still
as a result	further on	later	that is
besides	hence	likewise	then
consequently	however	moreover	therefore
e.g.	i.e.	namely	to be sure
finally	in addition	nevertheless	too

13. Conjunctive adverbs are used to express addition, to add emphasis, to express contrast or discrimination, to introduce illustrations or elaborations, to express or introduce conclusions or results, or to order phrases or clauses in terms of time, space, or priority.

addition:	This employee deserves a substantial raise; *furthermore,* she should be promoted.
emphasis:	He is brilliant; *indeed,* he is a genius.
contrast or discrimination:	The major responsibility lies with the partners; *nevertheless,* associates should be competent in decision-making.
illustrations or elaborations:	Losses were due to several negative factors; *namely,* inflation, foreign competition, and restrictive government regulation.
conclusions or results:	Government overregulation in that country has reached a prohibitive level. *Thus,* we are phasing out all of our operations there.
time, space, or priority:	*First,* we can remind them that their account is long overdue; *second,* we can say that we must consider consulting our attorneys if they do not meet their obligation.

14. Conjunctive adverbs are usually placed at the beginning of a clause or sentence. When they are placed later in the clause or sentence, they receive additional emphasis.

> The overdue shipment arrived this morning; *however,* we must point out that it was incomplete.
> The overdue shipment arrived this morning; we must point out, *however,* that it was incomplete.

15. The misuse of conjunctive adverbs can lead to a problem known as *comma fault.* When a conjunctive adverb is used to connect two main clauses, a semicolon should be used; a comma will not suffice. (For more on comma fault and punctuation between main clauses, see paragraphs 1–4 under Comma on pages 114–15 and paragraph 5 under Semicolon on page 137.)

comma fault:	The company had flexible hours, *however* its employees were expected to abide by their selected arrival and departure times.
repunctuated:	The company had flexible hours; *however,* its employees were expected to abide by their selected arrival and departure times.

INTERJECTION

Interjections are exclamatory or interrupting words or phrases that express an emotion. Interjections are usually independent clauses that lack grammatical connection with the rest of the sentence. They often stand alone.

1. Interjections may be stressed or ejaculatory words, phrases, or even short sentences.

> Absurd!
> No, no!
> Get out!
> Not now!

2. Interjections may also be so-called "sound" words, such as those representing shouts, hisses, or cries.

> Shh! The meeting has begun.
> Pssst! Come over here.
> Ouch! That hurts.
> Ugh! What a horrible flavor.

3. Emphatic interjections expressing forceful emotions use exclamation points. Mildly stressed words or sentences may be punctuated with commas and periods.

> Fire!
> What an awful time we had!
> *Ah*, that's my idea of a terrific deal.
> *Well, well,* so that's the solution.
> *Oh*, you're probably right.

4. Interjections should be sparingly used, and then only to signal genuine emotion or for strong emphasis.

NOUN

A noun is the name of something (such as a person, animal, place, object, quality, concept, or action). Nouns are used as the subject or object of a verb, the object of a preposition, the predicate after a linking verb, an appositive name, or a name in an absolute construction.

Nouns have several characteristic features. They are inflected for possession; they have number (that is, they are either singular or plural); they are often preceded by determiners (such as *a, an, the; this, that, these, those; all, every; one, two three; his, her, their*); a few still show gender differences (*host/hostess, actor/actress*); and many are formed by adding a suffix (such as *-ance, -ist, -ness*, or *-tion*) to a root or verb form.

1. **Basic uses** Nouns are used as subjects, direct objects, objects of prepositions, indirect objects, retained objects, predicate nominatives, objective complements, and appositives, and in direct address.

subject:	The *office* was quiet.
direct object:	He locked the *office*.
object of a preposition:	The file is in the *office*.
indirect object:	He gave his *client* the papers.
retained object:	His client was given the *papers*.
predicate nominative:	Mrs. Adams is the managing *partner*.
objective complement:	They made Mrs. Adams managing *partner*.
appositive:	Mrs. Adams, the managing *partner*, wrote that memorandum.
direct address:	*Mrs. Adams*, may I present Mr. Bonkowski.

2. **Compound nouns** Because English is not static and unchanging, many of its words undergo styling variations because of the changing preferences of its users. The styling of compound nouns (that is, as open, closed, or hyphenated) is especially subject to changing usage. No set of rules can cover every possible variation or combination; however, some consistent patterns of usage can be seen. For a description of these patterns, see the discussion under Compound Nouns, pages 163–66.

3. **Indefinite articles with nouns** Before a word or abbreviation beginning with a consonant *sound,* the article *a* is used. This is true even if the word begins with a vowel.

a BA degree	a COD package	a door
a hat	a human	a union
a one	a U.S. Senator	

4. Before *h-* in an unstressed or lightly stressed first syllable, the article *a* is generally used, although *an* is more usual in speech whether or not the *h-* is actually pronounced. Either is acceptable in both speech and writing.

a historian   *or*   an historian
a heroic attempt   *or*   an heroic attempt
a hilarious performance   *or*   an hilarious performance

5. Before a word or abbreviation beginning with a vowel *sound,* the article *an* is used. This is true even if the word or abbreviation actually begins with a consonant.

an icicle	an orange	an unknown
an hour	an honor	an nth degree
an FCC report	an MIT professor	an Rh factor

6. **Nominals** Nominals are words or groups of words that function as nouns. Adjectives, gerunds, and infinitives may act as nominals. An example of an adjective used as a noun is the word *good* in the clause "the good die young." Examples of gerunds and infinitives used as nouns are *seeing* in the clause "seeing is believing" and *to see* in the clause "to see is to believe." Noun phrases and noun clauses are also considered to be nominals. For more about gerunds and infinitives, see paragraphs 12 and 14 under Verb on pages 214–15. For information about noun phrases and noun clauses, see pages 219 and 220 respectively.

7. **Nouns used as adjectives** Nouns are frequently used as adjectives by placing them before other nouns, as in *school board* or *office management.* When two or more nouns are frequently combined in this way, they become familiar compounds like *profit margin, systems analysis, money market, box lunch.* Such compounds provide useful verbal shortcuts ("office management" is shorter than "management of an office"). However, care should be taken not to pile up so many of these noun modifiers that the reader has difficulty sorting out their meanings.

| *shorter but unclear:* | Management review copies of the Division II sales department machine parts file should be indexed. |
| *longer but clear:* | Copies of the machine parts file from the Division II sales department should be indexed before being sent to management for review. |

Both of these sentences could be made clearer by hyphenating the compound nouns used as adjectives. (For more about this kind of compound, see the discussion under Compounds That Function as Adjectives, pages 166–68.)

Management-review copies of the Division II sales-department machine-parts file should be indexed.

8. **Plurals** The plurals of nouns are usually produced by adding *-s* or *-es* to the base word, although some nouns have irregular plurals. For more about the formation of plurals, see the discussion under Plurals, pages 156–60.

9. **Possessives** The possessives of nouns are usually formed by adding an apostrophe plus *-s* to singular nouns or just an apostrophe to plural words ending in *-s*. For more about the formation of possessives, see the discussion under Possessives, pages 160–62.

10. **Proper nouns** Proper nouns are nouns that name a particular person, place, or thing. Proper nouns are almost always capitalized. For more about capitalizing proper nouns, see the discussion under Proper Nouns, Pronouns, and Adjectives, pages 142–54.

PREPOSITION

A preposition is a word that combines with a noun, pronoun, or noun equivalent (such as a phrase or clause) to form a phrase that usually acts as an adverb, adjective, or noun.

Prepositions have no inflections, number, case, gender, or identifying suffixes. They can be identified chiefly by their position within sentences and by their grammatical functions. Prepositions may be simple—that is, consisting of only one word (*against, from, near, of, on, out,* or *without*)—or compound—that is, composed of more than one element (*according to, by means of,* or *in spite of*).

1. **Basic uses** Prepositions are chiefly used to link nouns, pronouns, or noun equivalents to the rest of the sentence. A prepositional phrase is usually adverbial or adjectival in function.

    She expected resistance *on* his part.
    He sat down *beside* her.

2. **Conjunctions vs. prepositions** The words *after, before, but, for,* and *since* may function as either prepositions or conjunctions. Their position within the sentence identifies them as conjunctions or prepositions. Conjunctions link two words or sentence elements that have the same grammatical function. Prepositions precede a noun, pronoun, noun phrase, or noun equivalent.

    conjunction: I was a bit concerned *but* not panicky. [*but* links two adjectives]
    preposition: I was left with nothing *but* hope. [*but* precedes a noun]
    conjunction: The device conserves fuel, *for* it is battery-powered. [*for* links two clauses]
    preposition: The device conserves fuel *for* residual heating. [*for* precedes a noun phrase]

3. **Implied prepositions** If two words combine idiomatically with the same preposition, that preposition need not be used after both.

    We were antagonistic [*to*] and opposed *to* the whole idea.
    but
    We are interested *in* and anxious *for* raises.

4. **Position** Prepositions may occur before nouns or pronouns ("*below* the desk," "*beside* them"), after adjectives ("antagonistic *to*," "insufficient *in*," "symbolic *of*"), and after the verbal elements of standard verb + preposition combinations ("take *for*," "get *after*," "come *across*").

5. There is no reason why a preposition cannot end a sentence, especially when it is an element in a common verb phrase.

    His lack of organization is only one of the things I put up *with*.
    What does all this add up *to*?

6. Use of *between* and *among* Despite an unfounded notion to the contrary, the preposition *between* can be used of more than two items. It is especially appropriate to denote one-to-one relationships, regardless of the number of items.

> Treaties established economic cooperation *between* nations.
> This is *between* you and me and the lamppost.

Among is more appropriate where the emphasis is on overall distribution rather than individual relationships.

> There was discontent *among* the peasants.

When *among* is automatically chosen for more than two, the results can sound strained.

> The author alternates *among* quotes, clichés, and street slang.

PRONOUN

A pronoun is a word that is used as a substitute for a noun or noun equivalent, takes noun constructions, and refers to persons or things named or understood in the context. The noun or noun equivalent for which it substitutes is called the *antecedent*.

Pronouns may exhibit the following features: case (nominative, possessive, objective); number (singular, plural); person (first, second, third person); and gender (masculine, feminine, neuter). Pronouns are divided into seven major categories, each with its own function. Each pronoun category is listed and described alphabetically in this section.

Demonstrative pronouns   The words *this, that, these,* and *those* are classified as pronouns when they function as nouns. (They are classified as demonstrative adjectives when they modify nouns.)

1. Demonstrative pronouns point out a person or thing to distinguish it from others of the same type.

   > *These* are the best designs we've seen to date.
   > *Those* are strong words.

2. They also distinguish between a person or thing nearby and one farther away.

   > *This* is my concern; *that* is yours.

3. A potentially troublesome situation occurs when a demonstrative pronoun introduces a sentence, referring back to something previously mentioned. The reference should always be clear.

   unclear: The heir's hemophilia, the influence of an unprincipled faith healer on the royal family, devastating military setbacks, general strikes, mass outbreaks of typhus, and repeated crop failures contributed to the revolution. *This* influenced the course of history.

   clear: The heir's hemophilia, the influence of an unprincipled faith healer on the royal family, devastating military setbacks, general strikes, mass outbreaks of typhus, and repeated crop failures—all these factors contributed to the revolution and thus influenced the course of history.

4. When demonstrative pronouns are used with the words *kind/sort/type* + *of* + noun, they should agree in number with both nouns.

> *not:* We want *these kind* of *pencils.*
> *instead:* We want *this kind* of *pencil.*
> We want *these kinds* of *pencils.*

Indefinite pronouns Indefinite pronouns designate an unidentified or not immediately identifiable person or thing. They are chiefly used as third-person references and do not distinguish gender. Examples of indefinite pronouns are the following: *all, another, any, anybody, anyone, anything, both, each, each one, either, everybody, everyone, everything, few, many, much, neither, nobody, none, no one, one, other, several, some, somebody, someone, something.*

5. Indefinite pronouns should agree in number with their verb. The following are singular and take singular verbs: *another, anything, each one, everything, much, nobody, no one, one, other, someone, something.*

    > *Much is* being done.
    > *No one wants* to go.

6. The indefinite pronouns *both, few, many, several,* and a few others are plural and take plural verbs.

    > *Many were* called; *few were* chosen.

7. Some indefinite pronouns (such as *all, any, none, some*) present problems because they may be either singular or plural, depending on whether they are used with mass nouns or count nouns. (A *mass noun* identifies something not ordinarily thought of in terms of countable elements; a *count noun* identifies things that can be counted.)

    > *with mass noun:* *All* of the *property is* entailed.
    > *None* of the *ink was* erasable.
    > *Some* of the *sky was* visible.
    > *with count noun:* *All* of our *bases are* covered.
    > *None* of the *clerks were* available.
    > *Some* of the *stars were* visible.

8. The pronouns *anybody, anyone, everybody, everyone, somebody, nobody,* and *no one* are singular in form and as such logically take singular verbs. However, because of the plural aspect of their meaning, plural pronoun references to them are common in informal speech.

    > I knew *everybody* by *their* first names.
    > Don't tell *anyone; they* might spread the rumor.

    Even in more formal contexts, such plural pronoun references are used increasingly, especially to avoid sexism in language.

    > We called *everyone* by *their* first *names* [rather than "his first name"].

    For more about avoiding sexism in the use of personal pronouns, see paragraph 22 on page 210.

9. Sometimes an apparently singular indefinite pronoun may take a plural verb if the context makes it seem plural. The following two sentences illustrate how a singular indefinite pronoun may take either a singular or plural verb, depending on how the writer interprets the pronoun *either* (or *neither*):

    > *Either* [*Neither*] of these pronunciations *is* acceptable.
    > *Either* [*Neither*] of these pronunciations *are* acceptable.

    The normal choice of verb would be *is,* because the subject of the sentence is the singular pronoun. However, the plural word *pronunciations,* together with the possibility of interpreting *either* and *neither* to refer alternatively to one or both, permits the writer to choose either a singular or plural verb.

10. The indefinite pronouns *any* and *anyone* are usually followed by *other(s)* or *else* in a comparison of two individuals in the same class.

not:	Helen has more seniority than *anyone* in the firm.
instead:	Helen has more seniority than *anyone else* in the firm.
not:	Our house is older than *any* building on the block.
instead:	Our house is older than *any other* building on the block.

The addition of *else* and *other* in the preceding sentences avoids the logical impossibility that Helen has more seniority than herself or that our house is older than itself. Likewise, it prevents the possible misreading that Helen is not a member of the firm or that our house is not on the block.

11. The antecedent of an indefinite pronoun—that is, the thing it is referring to—must be clearly stated, not implied. A good check for a clear reference is to see if there is an antecedent in the sentence that could be substituted for the pronoun; if there is none, the pronoun should be replaced by a noun or nominal.

unclear:	He's the author of a best-selling book on sailing, even though he's never set foot on *one*.
clear:	He's the author of a best-selling book on sailing, even though he's never set foot on a sailboat.

12. **Interrogative pronouns** The interrogative pronouns *what, which, who, whom,* and *whose,* as well as combinations of these words with the suffix *-ever,* are used to introduce direct and indirect questions.

Who is she?	She asked *whom* the article accused.
He asked me *who* she was.	*Whoever* can that be?
Whom did the article accuse?	We wondered *whoever* that could be.

Personal pronouns   Personal pronouns refer to beings and objects and reflect their person, number, and gender.

13. Most personal pronouns take different forms for the three cases.

	nominative	*possessive*	*objective*
first person singular:	I	my, mine	me
first person plural:	we	our, ours	us
second person singular:	you	your, yours	you
second person plural:	you	your, yours	you
third person singular:	he	his, his	him
	she	her, hers	her
	it	its, its	it
third person plural:	they	their, theirs	them

14. Though a personal pronoun agrees in person, number, and gender with the word it refers to, its case is determined by its function within a sentence. The nominative case is used for a pronoun that acts as a subject of a sentence or as a predicate nominative (but see paragraph 15 below). The possessive case is used for pronouns that express possession or a similar relationship. The objective case is used for pronouns that are direct objects, indirect objects, retained objects, objects of prepositions, or objective complements.

> *You* and *I* thought the meeting was useful.
> My assistant and *I* attended the seminar.

Our new candidate will be *you.*
We all had *our* own offices.
The vice president informed my assistant and *me* about the seminar.
She gave *me* the papers.
Just between *you* and *me,* the meeting was much too long.
I was given *them* yesterday.
That makes our new candidate *her.*

15. The nominative case after the verb *to be* (as in "It is I" and "This is she") is preferred by strict grammarians, but the objective case (as in "It's me") may also be used, especially in spoken English.

The only candidate left for that job may soon be *she* [or *her*].

16. When a personal pronoun follows *than* or *as,* and is the subject of an implied verb, it should be in the nominative case.

He received a bigger bonus than *she* [did].
She has as much seniority as *I* [do].

17. The suffixes *-self* and *-selves* combine only with the possessive case of the first- and second-person pronouns *(myself, ourselves, yourself, yourselves)* and with the objective case of the third-person pronouns *(himself, herself, itself, themselves).* Other combinations (such as "hisself" and "theirselves") are considered nonstandard and should not be used.

18. Personal pronouns in the possessive case (such as *your, their, theirs, its*) do not contain apostrophes and should not be confused with similar-sounding contractions (such as *you're, they're, there's, it's*), which do contain apostrophes.

Put the contract in *its* file.
It's an extensive contract.
Whose turn is it?
Who's going to go?

19. When *I* or *me* is used with other pronouns or other people's names, it should be last in the series.

Mrs. Smith and *I* were trained together.
He and *I* were attending the meeting.
The memorandum was directed to Ms. Montgomery and *me.*

20. Some companies prefer that writers use *we* and not *I* when speaking for their companies in business correspondence. *I* is more often used when a writer is referring only to himself or herself. The following example illustrates the use of both within one sentence:

We [i.e., the company] have reviewed the manuscript that you sent to *me* [i.e., the writer] on June 1, but *we* [i.e., the company] feel that it is too specialized a work to be marketable by *our* company.

21. While the personal pronouns *it, you,* and *they* are often used as indefinite pronouns in spoken English, they can often be vague or even redundant.

vague:	*They* said at the seminar that the economy would experience a third-quarter upturn. [Who exactly is *they*?]
explicit:	The economists on the panel at the seminar predicted a third-quarter economic upturn.
redundant:	In the graph *it* says that production fell off by 50 percent.
lean:	The graph indicates a 50 percent production drop.

22. Forms of the personal pronoun *he* and the indefinite pronoun *one* have long been the standard substitutes for antecedents whose genders are mixed or irrelevant.

    > Present the letter to the executive for *his* approval.
    > Each employee should check *his* W-2 form.
    > If *one* really wants to succeed, *one* can.

    However, many writers today who are concerned about sexism in language recast such sentences to avoid the generic use of the masculine pronoun.

    > Present the letter to the executive for approval.
    > All employees should check *their* W-2 forms.
    > Each employee should check *his or her* W-2 form.

    The phrases *he or she, him or her*, and *his or her* should be used sparingly, however, as they can easily become tiresome. For more on avoiding the generic use of the masculine pronoun, see paragraph 8 on page 207.

23. **Reciprocal pronouns** The reciprocal pronouns *each other* and *one another* are used in the object position to indicate a mutual action or cross-relationship.

    > They do not deal with *one another*.
    > Karen and Rachel spelled *each other* at the convention booth.

24. Reciprocal pronouns may also be used in the possessive case.

    > The two secretaries borrowed *one another's* stationery.
    > The president and his vice president depend on *each other's* ideas.

25. **Reflexive pronouns** Reflexive pronouns express reflexive action or add extra emphasis to the subject of a sentence, clause, or phrase. Reflexive pronouns are formed by compounding the personal pronouns *him, her, it, my, our, them*, and *your* with *-self* or *-selves*. Reflexive pronouns are used when an object or subjective complement refers to the same thing as the foregoing noun or noun phrase.

    > She taught *herself* how to use the DTP system.
    > The chairman isn't *himself* this week.
    > They asked *themselves* if they were being honest.
    > I *myself* am not concerned about the competition.
    > The sales rep told Jim to help *himself* to sample copies.

Relative pronouns   The relative pronouns are *that, what, which, who, whom*, and *whose*, as well as combinations of these with *-ever*. They introduce subordinate clauses acting as nouns or modifiers. While a relative pronoun itself does not exhibit number, gender, or person, it does determine the number, gender, and person of elements that follow it in the relative clause because of its implicit agreement with its antecedent. Consider, for instance, the following sentence:

> People *who are* ready to start *their* jobs should arrive at 8:00 a.m.

In this sentence, the relative pronoun "who" refers to the plural subject "people" and acts as the subject of the relative clause "who are ready to start their jobs." Because it refers to a plural word, it acts like a plural word within its clause and therefore calls for the plural verb "are" and the plural pronoun "their."

26. The relative pronoun *who* typically refers to persons and some animals; *which* refers to things and animals; and *that* refers to persons, animals, and things.

a man *who* sought success
a man *whom* we can trust
Seattle Slew, *who* won horse racing's Triple Crown
a book *which* sold well
a dog *which* barked loudly
a man *that* we can trust
a dog *that* barked loudly
a book *that* sold well

27. *Which,* preceded by a comma, is used to introduce nonrestrictive clauses—that is, clauses that are not essential to the meaning of the nouns they modify. Either *that* or *which* can introduce restrictive clauses—that is, clauses that are needed to define the nouns they follow. However, many writers prefer to use *which* only with nonrestrictive clauses. (For more on restrictive and nonrestrictive clauses, see page 221.)

The paneled doors, *which* cost less, were more popular.
The doors *that* they had ordered were out of stock.

28. Relative pronouns can sometimes be omitted for the sake of brevity.

The man [*whom*] I was talking to is the president.

29. The relative pronoun *what* may be substituted for the longer and more awkward phrases "that which," "that of which," or "the thing which" in some sentences.

stiff: He was blamed for *that which* he could not have known.
easier: He was blamed for *what* he could not have known.

30. The problem of when to use *who* or *whom* has been blown out of proportion. The situation is very simple: standard written English makes a distinction between the nominative and objective cases of these pronouns when they are used as relatives or interrogatives.

nominative case: *Who* is she?
                      Who does she think she is, anyway?
                      She thinks she is the one *who* ought to be promoted.
                      Give me a list of the ones *who* you think should be promoted.
objective case: *Whom* are you referring to?
                      To *whom* are you referring?
                      He's a man *whom* everyone should know.
                      He's a man with *whom* everyone should be acquainted.

In speech, however, case distinctions and boundaries often become blurred, with the result that in spoken English *who* is favored as a general substitute for all uses of *whom* except in set phrases such as "*To whom* it may concern." In speech, then, *who* may be used not only as the subject of the clause it introduces but also as the object of a verb in a clause that it introduces or as an interrogative.

Let us select *who* we think will be the best candidate.
See the manager, Mrs. Keats, *who* you should be able to find in her office.
Who should we tell?

31. *Whom* is commonly used as the object of a preposition in a clause that it introduces.

Presiding is a judge *about whom* I know nothing.
He is a man *for whom* I would gladly work.

However, *who* is commonly used to introduce a question even when it is the object of a preposition.

Who [rarely *whom*] are you going to listen to?
Who [rarely *whom*] do you work for?

32. While in speech the nominative form *who* can often be used in the objective case, the reverse is not true: the objective form *whom* cannot be used in the nominative case in either spoken or written English. Avoid such usages as "*Whom* do you suppose is coming to the meeting?" which result from a mistaken notion that *whom* is somehow always more correct.

33. In formal writing, the relative pronouns *whoever* and *whomever* follow the same principles as *who* and *whom*.

   nominative: Tell *whoever* is going to research the case that . . .
                    He wants to help *whoever* needs it most.
   objective: She makes friends with *whomever* she meets.

In speech, however, as with *who* and *whom*, case distinctions become blurred, and *whoever* is generally used.

   Whoever did she choose?

VERB

A verb is usually the grammatical center of a predicate and expresses an act, occurrence, or mode of being. Verbs are inflected (that is, altered) for agreement with the subject and for mood, voice, or tense.

Verbs exhibit the following features: inflection (e.g., *help, helps, helping, helped*), person (first, second, third person), number (singular, plural), tense (present, past, future), aspect (time relations other than the simple present, past, and future), voice (active, passive), mood (indicative, subjunctive, imperative), and the addition of suffixes (such as *-ate, -en, -ify,* and *-ize*).

Inflection   Regular verbs have four inflected forms, produced by adding the suffixes *-s* or *-es, -ed,* and *-ing.* The verb *help* as shown in the sentence above is regular. Most irregular verbs have four or five forms (for example, *see, sees, seeing, saw, seen*); and one, the verb *be,* has eight *(be, is, am, are, being, was, were, been).* If you are uncertain about a particular inflected form, consult a dictionary that shows the inflections of irregular verbs and inflections resulting in changes in base-word spelling.

   blame; blamed; blaming
   spy; spied; spying
   picnic; picnicked; picnicking

A dictionary should also show acceptable alternative inflected forms for any verbs with such forms.

   bias; biased   *or*   biassed; biasing   *or*   biassing
   counsel; counseled   *or*   counselled; counseling   *or*   counselling
   diagram; diagramed   *or*   diagrammed; diagraming   *or*   diagramming
   travel; traveled   *or*   travelled; traveling   *or*   travelling

All such forms may be found at their respective main entries in *Merriam-Webster's Collegiate Dictionary, Tenth Edition.* There are, however, a few rules that will aid you in determining the proper spelling patterns of certain verb forms.

1. Verbs ending in a silent *-e* generally retain the *-e* before consonant suffixes (such as *-s*) but drop the *-e* before vowel suffixes (such as *-ed* and *-ing*).

arrange; arranges; arranged; arranging
hope; hopes; hoped; hoping
require; requires; required; requiring
shape; shapes; shaped; shaping

A few verbs ending in a silent -*e* retain the -*e* before suffixes beginning with vowels in order to avoid confusion with other words.

dye; dyes; dyed; dyeing [*vs.* dying]
singe; singes; singed; singeing [*vs.* singing]

2. One-syllable verbs ending in a single consonant preceded by a single vowel double the final consonant before suffixes beginning with vowels (such as -*ed* and -*ing*).

brag; bragged; bragging
grip; gripped; gripping
pin; pinned; pinning

3. Verbs of more than one syllable that end in a single consonant preceded by a single vowel and have an accented last syllable double the final consonant before suffixes beginning with vowels (such as -*ed* and -*ing*).

commit; committed; committing
control; controlled; controlling
occur; occurred; occurring
omit; omitted; omitting

The final consonant of such verbs is not doubled when it is preceded by either two vowels or a consonant.

retrain; retrained; retraining
respect; respected; respecting

4. Verbs ending in -*y* preceded by a consonant normally change the -*y* to -*i* before all suffixes except -*ing*.

carry; carried; carrying
marry; married; marrying
study; studied; studying

If the final -*y* is preceded by a vowel, it remains unchanged.

delay; delayed; delaying
enjoy; enjoyed; enjoying
obey; obeyed; obeying

5. Verbs ending in -*c* add a -*k* before a suffix beginning with -*e* or -*i*.

mimic; mimics; mimicked; mimicking
panic; panics; panicked; panicking
traffic; traffics; trafficked; trafficking

6. **Tense, aspect, voice, and mood** Verbs generally exhibit their simple present and simple past tenses by single-word forms (for example, *do, did*).

7. The future tense is expressed by *shall* or *will* or by use of the simple present or present progressive forms in a context that makes the future meaning clear.

I *shall do* it.
He *will do* it.
I *leave* shortly for New York.
I *am leaving* shortly for New York.

8. *Aspect* involves the use of auxiliary verbs to indicate time relations other than the simple present, past, or future tenses. The *progressive tense* expresses ac-

tion in progress or future action. The *present perfect tense* expresses action that began in the past and continues into the present, or that occurred at an indefinite time in the past. The *past perfect tense* expresses action that was completed before another past action or event. The *future perfect tense* expresses action that will be completed before some future action or event.

progressive:	is seeing
present perfect:	has seen
past perfect:	had seen
future perfect:	will have seen

The perfect and progressive aspects can also be combined to produce special verb forms, such as *had been seeing*.

9. *Voice* enables a verb to indicate whether the subject of a sentence is acting (he *loves* = active voice) or is being acted upon (he is *loved* = passive voice).

10. *Mood* indicates manner of expression. The indicative mood states a fact or asks a question ("He *is* here," "*Is* he here?"). The subjunctive mood expresses condition contrary to fact ("I wish that he *were* here"). The imperative mood expresses a command or request ("*Come* here," "Please *come* here").

11. **Transitive and intransitive verbs** Verbs may be used transitively or intransitively. A *transitive* verb acts upon a direct object.

> She *contributed* money.
> He *ran* the store.

An *intransitive* verb does not act upon a direct object.

> She *contributed* generously.
> He *ran* down the street.

As in these examples, many verbs are transitive in one sense and intransitive in another.

Verbals A group of words derived from verbs, called *verbals*, deserve added discussion. The members of this group—the gerund, the participle, and the infinitive—exhibit some but not all of the features of their parent verbs.

12. A gerund is an *-ing* verb form that functions mainly as a noun. It has both active and passive voice. In addition, a gerund has other characteristics of a verb: it conveys action, occurrence, or being; it can take an object; and it can be modified by an adverb. In the following sentences, "typing" and "driving" are gerunds, "data" and "his workers" are their objects, and "daily" and "hard" are adverbs modifying the gerund.

> *Typing* tabular *data daily* is a boring task.
> He liked *driving his workers hard*.

Since gerunds function as nouns, nouns and pronouns occurring immediately before gerunds should generally be in the possessive case.

> She is trying to improve *her typing*.
> We objected to *their telling* the story to the press. [i.e., we objected to the telling]
> We expected the *senator's coming*. [i.e., his arrival]

13. Participles, on the other hand, function as adjectives. They may occur alone ("a *broken* typewriter") or in phrases that modify other words ("*Having broken*

the typewriter, she gave up for the day"). Participles, like gerunds, have active and passive forms.

> *active-voice participial phrase:*   *Having failed* to pass the examination, he was forced to repeat the course.
>
> *passive-voice participial phrase:*   *Having been failed* by his instructor, he was forced to repeat the course.

Participles, unlike gerunds, are not preceded by possessive nouns or pronouns:

> We saw *them telling* their story to the press. [i.e., we saw them as they told]
> We saw the *senator coming.* [i.e., we saw him as he arrived]

14. Infinitives may exhibit active *(to do)* and passive *(to be done)* voice and may indicate aspect *(to be doing, to have done, to have been doing, to have been done).* Infinitives may take complements and may be modified by adverbs. In addition, they can function as nouns, adjectives, and adverbs.

> *noun use:*   *To be known* is *to be castigated.* [subject and predicate nominative]
> He tried everything except *to bypass his superior.* [object of preposition "except"]
>
> *adjectival use:*   They had found a way *to increase profits greatly.* [modifies the noun "way"]
>
> *adverbial use:*   He was too furious *to speak.* [modifies "furious"]

Although *to* forms part of a complete infinitive, it may be merely understood rather than stated.

> He helped [*to*] *complete* the marketing report.

15. **Sequence of tenses** If the main verb in a sentence is in the present tense, any other tense or compound verb form may follow it.

> I *realize* that you *are leaving.*   I *realize* that you *will be leaving.*
> I *realize* that you *left.*   I *realize* that you *will leave.*
> I *realize* that you *were leaving.*   I *realize* that you *may be leaving.*
> I *realize* that you *had left.*   I *realize* that you *must be leaving.*

16. If the main verb is in the past tense, subsequent verbs in the sentence may not use the present tense.

> I *realized* that you *were leaving.*   I *realized* that you *would be leaving.*
> I *realized* that you *left.*   I *realized* that you *could be leaving.*
> I *realized* that you *had left.*   I *realized* that you *might be leaving.*
> I *realized* that you *had been*   I *realized* that you *would leave.*
> *leaving.*

17. If the main verb is in the future tense, subsequent verbs in the sentence may not use the simple past tense.

> He *will see* you because he *is going* to the meeting too.
> He *will see* you because he *will be going* to the meeting too.
> He *will see* you because he *will go* to the meeting too.
> He *will see* you because he *has been going* to the meetings too.
> He *will see* you because he *will have been going* to the meetings too.

18. Most writers try to maintain an order of tenses throughout their sentences that is consistent with natural or real time; that is, present tense is used for present-time matters, past tense is used for past matters, and future tense is

used for matters that will take place in the future. However, there are two common exceptions. First, when the contents of printed material are being discussed, the present tense is normally used.

> In *Etiquette*, Emily Post *discusses* forms of address.
> This analysis *gives* market projections for the next two years.
> In this latest position paper, the Secretary of State *writes* that . . .

Second, in order to convey a sense of immediacy to a particular sentence, the present tense may be used instead of the future.

> I *leave* for Tel Aviv tonight.

19. The sequence of tenses in sentences that express contrary-to-fact conditions is a common problem. The examples below show proper tense sequences.

> If he *were* on time, we *would leave* now.
> If he *had been* [not *would have been*] on time, we *would have left* an hour ago.

20. At one time, *shall* was considered the only correct form to use with the first person in simple future tenses (*I shall, we shall*), while *will* was limited to the second and third persons (*you will, it will, they will*). Today, however, either form is considered correct for the first person, *shall* being slightly more formal than *will*.

> We *shall* give your request special attention.
> We *will* send the agreement out tomorrow.

Subject-verb agreement   Verbs agree in number and in person with their grammatical subjects. At times, however, the grammatical subject may be singular in form but the thought it carries may have plural connotations. Here are some general guidelines for such situations. (For discussion of verb agreement with indefinite-pronoun subjects, see paragraphs 5–9 under Pronoun on pages 207–8. For discussion of verb number as affected by a compound subject whose elements are joined by *and/or*, see paragraph 6 under Conjunction on page 200.)

21. Plural and compound subjects take plural verbs even if the subject is inverted.

> Both dogs and cats *were* tested for the virus.
> Grouped under the heading "fine arts" *are* music, theater, and painting.

22. Compound subjects or plural subjects working as a unit take singular verbs.

> Lord & Taylor *has* stores in the New York area.
> Macaroni and cheese *is* our best-selling product.
> Five hundred dollars *is* a stiff price for a ton.
>   *but*
> Twenty-five milligrams of pentazocine *were* administered.

23. Compound subjects expressing mathematical relationships may be either singular or plural.

> One plus one *makes* [or *make*] two.
> Six from eight *leaves* [or *leave*] two.

24. Singular subjects joined by *or* or *nor* take singular verbs; plural subjects so joined take plural verbs.

> A freshman or sophomore *is* eligible for the scholarship.
> Neither freshmen nor sophomores *are* eligible for the scholarship.

If one subject is singular and the other plural, the verb agrees with the number of the subject that is closer to it.

Either the secretaries or the supervisor *has* to do the job.
Either the supervisor or the secretaries *have* to do the job.

25. Singular subjects introduced by *many a, such a, every, each,* or *no* take singular verbs, even when several such subjects are joined by *and.*

    Many an executive *has* gone to the top in that division.
    No supervisor and no assembler *is* excused from the time check.
    Every chair, table, and desk *has* to be accounted for.

26. The agreement of the verb with its subject ordinarily should not be changed because of an intervening phrase.

    One of my reasons for resigning *involves* purely personal considerations.
    The president of the company, as well as members of his staff, *has* arrived.
    He, not any of the proxy voters, *has* to be present.

27. The verb *to be* agrees with its subject but not necessarily with what follows.

    His mania *was* minimizing payrolls and maximizing profits.
    Women in the work force *constitute* a new field of study.

    The subject following *There is, There are,* etc., must agree in number with the verb.

    There *are* many complications here.
    There *is* no reason to worry about him.

28. Collective nouns—such as *orchestra, team, committee, family*—usually take singular verbs but can take plural verbs if the emphasis is on the individual members of the unit rather than on the unit itself.

    The committee *has agreed* to extend the deadline.
    but also
    The committee *have been* at odds ever since the beginning.

29. The word *number* in the phrase *a number of* usually takes a plural verb, but in the phrase *the number of* it takes a singular verb.

    A number of errors *were* [also *was*] made.
    The number of errors *was* surprising.

30. A relative clause that follows the expression *one of the/those/these* + plural noun takes a plural verb in conventional English, but in informal English it may take a singular verb.

    He is one of those executives who *worry* [also *worries*] a lot.
    This is one of those typewriters that *create* [also *creates*] perfect copies.

31. **Linking and *sense* verbs** Linking verbs (such as the various forms of *to be*) and the so-called "sense" verbs (such as *feel, look, taste,* and *smell,* as well as particular senses of *appear, become, continue, grow, prove, remain, seem, stand,* and *turn*) connect subjects with predicate nouns or adjectives.

    He *is* a vice president.
    He *became* vice president.
    The temperature *continues* cold.
    The future *looks* prosperous.
    I *feel* bad about the loss of jobs.
    He *remains* healthy.

Sense words often cause confusion, since writers sometimes mistakenly use adverbs instead of adjectives following these words.

not: This scent smells nicely.
instead: This scent smells nice.
not: The new formula tastes well.
instead: The new formula tastes good.

32. Split infinitives A split infinitive is an infinitive that has a modifier between the *to* and the verbal (as in "to really care"). Some grammarians disapprove of them, and many people avoid them whenever they can. However, the split infinitive has been around a long time and has been used by a wide variety of distinguished writers. It can be useful particularly if a writer wants to stress the verbal element of an infinitive. For example, in the phrase "to *thoroughly* complete the financial study," placing the adverb immediately before the verbal element strengthens its effect on the verbal. The position of an adverb may actually modify or change the meaning of an entire sentence.

original: He arrived at the office to *unexpectedly* find a new name on the door.
repositioned with new meanings: He arrived at the office *unexpectedly* to find a new name on the door.
                                        He arrived at the office to find a new name on the door *unexpectedly.*

Very long adverbial modifiers that interrupt an infinitive are clumsy and should be avoided or moved.

awkward: He wanted to *completely and without mercy* defeat his competitor.
smoother: He wanted to defeat his competitor *completely and without mercy.*

33. Dangling participles Dangling participles are participles that lack a normally expected grammatical relation to the rest of the sentence. The standard error occurs when the participial phrase with which a sentence begins is immediately followed by a noun or pronoun representing a person or thing different from the one described in the phrase. They are best avoided, as they may confuse the reader or seem ludicrous.

not: Walking through the door, her coat was caught.
instead: While walking through the door, she caught her coat.
              Walking through the door, she caught her coat.
              She caught her coat while walking through the door.
not: Caught in the act, his excuses were unconvincing.
instead: Caught in the act, he could not make his excuses convincing.
not: Having been told that he was incompetent and dishonest, the executive fired the man.
instead: Having told the man that he was incompetent and dishonest, the executive fired him.
              Having been told by his superior that he was incompetent and dishonest, the man was fired.

Participles should not be confused with prepositions that end in *-ing: concerning, considering, providing, regarding, respecting, touching,* etc.

Concerning your complaint, we can tell you . . .
Considering all the implications, you have made a dangerous decision.
Touching the matter at hand, we can say that . . .

Phrases

A phrase is a brief expression that consists of two or more grammatically related words but that does not constitute a clause. (See Clauses section, page 220.)

BASIC TYPES

There are seven basic types of phrases.

1. An *absolute phrase* consists of a noun followed by a modifier (such as a participle). Absolute phrases act independently within a sentence without modifying a particular element of the sentence. Absolute phrases are also referred to as *nominative absolutes.*

    He stalked out, *his eyes staring straight ahead.*

2. A *gerund phrase* includes a gerund and functions as a noun.

    Sitting on a patient's bed is bad hospital etiquette.

3. An *infinitive phrase* includes an infinitive and may function as a noun, adjective, or adverb.

    noun: *To do that* would be stupid.
    adjective: This was an occasion *to remember.*
    adverb: They struggled *to get free* of the mounting debt.

4. A *noun phrase* consists of a noun and its modifiers.

    The second warehouse is huge.

5. A *participial phrase* includes a participle and functions as an adjective.

    Listening all the time with great concentration, she began to line up her options.

6. A *prepositional phrase* consists of a preposition and its object. It may function as a noun, adjective, or adverb.

    noun: *Out of debt* is where we'd like to be!
    adjective: Here is the desk *with the extra file drawer.*
    adverb: He now walked *without a limp.*

7. A *verb phrase* consists of a verb and any other terms that either modify it or complete its meaning.

    She *will have arrived too late* for you to talk to her.

USAGE PROBLEMS

1. Usage problems with phrases occur most often when a modifying phrase is not placed close enough to the word or words that it modifies. The phrase "on December 10" in the following sentence, for example, must be repositioned to clarify just what happened on that date.

    not: We received your letter concerning the shipment of parts on December 10.
    instead: On December 10 we received your letter concerning the shipment of parts.
              We received your letter concerning the December 10 shipment of parts.

2. Dangling participial phrases represent a very common usage problem. For a discussion of dangling participles, see paragraph 33 under Verb on page 218.

Clauses

A clause is a group of words containing both a subject and a predicate. A clause functions as an element of a compound or complex sentence. There are two general types of clauses: the *main* or *independent clause* and the *subordinate* or *dependent clause*. A main clause (such as "it is hot") is an independent grammatical unit and can stand alone. A subordinate clause (such as "because it is hot") cannot stand alone, and must be either preceded or followed by a main clause.

BASIC TYPES

Like phrases, clauses can perform as particular parts of speech within the sentence. There are three basic types of clauses that have part-of-speech functions.

1. The *adjective clause* modifies a noun or pronoun and normally follows the word it modifies.

   Her administrative assistant, *who was also a speechwriter,* was overworked.
   I can't see the reason *why you're upset.*
   He is a man *who will succeed.*
   Anybody *who opts for a career like that* is crazy.

2. The *adverb clause* modifies a verb, an adjective, or another adverb and normally follows the word it modifies.

   They made a valiant effort, *although the risks were great.*
   When it rains, it pours.
   I'm certain *that he is guilty.*
   We accomplished less *than we did before.*

3. The *noun clause* fills a noun slot in a sentence and thus can be a subject, an object, or a complement.

subject:	*Whoever is qualified* should apply.
object of a verb:	I do not know *what his field is.*
object of a preposition:	Route that journal to *whichever department you wish.*
complement:	The trouble is *that she has no ambition.*

ELLIPTICAL CLAUSES

Some clause elements may be omitted if the context makes clear the understood elements.

   I remember the first time [that] we met.
   This typewriter is better than that [typewriter is].
   When [she is] on the job, she is always competent and alert.

PLACEMENT OF CLAUSES

A modifying clause should be placed as close as possible to the word or words it modifies. This placement will ensure maximum clarity and avoid the possibility of misinterpretation. If intervening words impair the clarity of a sentence, it should be rewritten or recast.

awkward: A memorandum is a piece of business writing, less formal than a letter, which serves as a means of interoffice communication.

recast: A memorandum, less formal than a letter, is a means of interoffice communication.

RESTRICTIVE AND NONRESTRICTIVE CLAUSES

Clauses that modify are also referred to as *restrictive* or *nonrestrictive*. Whether a clause is restrictive or nonrestrictive has a direct bearing on sentence punctuation. (For information about punctuating restrictive and nonrestrictive clauses, see paragraph 10 under Comma on page 116.)

1. Restrictive clauses are essential to the meaning of the word or words they modify, and cannot be omitted without the meaning of the sentences being radically changed. They are not set off (that is, preceded and followed) by commas.

   > Men and women who aren't competitive should not aspire to high corporate office.

   In this example, the restrictive clause "who aren't competitive" limits the subject to a certain kind of "men and women," and thus is essential to the meaning of the sentence. If the restrictive clause were omitted, "men and women" would not be limited at all and the sentence would convey an entirely different idea.

   > Men and women should not aspire to high corporate office.

2. Nonrestrictive clauses are not inextricably bound to the word or words they modify but instead merely convey additional information about them. Nonrestrictive clauses may be omitted altogether without radically changing the meaning of the sentence. They are set off by commas when they occur in mid-sentence.

   > Our guide, who wore a green beret, was an experienced traveler.

   In this example, the nonrestrictive clause "who wore a green beret" does not limit the subject to a particular class of guide; it merely serves as a bit of incidental detail. Removal of the nonrestrictive clause does not affect the basic meaning of the sentence.

   > Our guide was an experienced traveler.

Sentences

A sentence is a grammatically self-contained unit that (1) expresses a statement (declarative sentence), (2) asks a question (interrogative sentence), (3) expresses a request or command (imperative sentence), or (4) expresses an exclamation (exclamatory sentence).

BASIC TYPES

Sentences are classified into three main types on the basis of their clause structure.

1. The *simple sentence* has one subject and one predicate (either or both of which may be compound).

    > Paper is costly.
    > Bond and tissue are costly.
    > Bond and tissue are costly and are sometimes scarce.

2. The *compound sentence* is made up of two or more main clauses.

    > I could arrange to arrive late, or I could simply send a proxy.
    > This commute takes 40 minutes by car, but we can make it in 20 by train.
    > A few of the executives had Ph.D.'s, even more had B.A.'s, but the majority had both B.A.'s and M.B.A.'s.

3. The *complex sentence* combines a main clause with one or more subordinate clauses (italicized in the examples).

    > The committee meeting began *when the business manager and the secretarial staff supervisor walked in.*
    > *Although the city council made some reforms,* the changes came so late *that they could not prevent these abuses.*

CONSTRUCTION

Grammatically sound sentences can be constructed by following some general guidelines.

1. Use connectives to link phrases or clauses of *equal* rank. When a connective is used to link phrases or clauses that are not equal, the resulting sentence may sound careless or clumsy, and may even be confusing.

not:	I was sitting in on a meeting, and he stood up and started a long rambling discourse on a new pollution-control device.
instead:	I sat in on a meeting during which he stood up and rambled on about a new pollution-control device.
	I sat in on that meeting. He stood up and rambled on about a new pollution-control device.
not:	This company employs a full-time research staff and was founded in 1945.
instead:	This company, which employs a full-time research staff, was founded in 1945.
	Established in 1945, this company employs a full-time research staff.

2. Create parallel, balanced sentence elements. When clauses having unparallel subjects are linked together, the resulting sentence can be unclear.

nonparallel:	The report gives market statistics, but he does not list his sources for these figures.
parallel:	The report gives market statistics, but it does not list the sources for these figures.
nonparallel:	We are glad to have you as our client, and please call on us whenever you need help.
parallel:	We are glad to have you as our client, and we hope that you will call on us whenever you need help.
in two sentences:	We are glad to have you as our client. We hope that you will call on us whenever you need help.

3. Link sentence elements tightly together. When elements are strung together by loose or excessive use of *and*, the sentence can become too lengthy and may lack any logical flow.

not: This company is a Class 1 motor freight common carrier of general commodities and it operates more than 10,000 tractors, trailers, and city delivery trucks through 200 terminals, and serves 40 states and the District of Columbia.

instead: This company is a Class 1 motor freight common carrier of general commodities. It operates more than 10,000 tractors, trailers, and city delivery trucks through 200 terminals. The company serves 40 states and the District of Columbia.

4. Choose the proper conjunction to link clauses. *And* is used to achieve simple linkage. However, if one clause is being contrasted with another, or if a reason or result is being expressed, a more specific conjunction should be used. (For more on the specific functions of coordinating and subordinating conjunctions, see paragraphs 1–6 and 10–12 under Conjunction on pages 199–201.)

too general: The economy was soft *and* we lost a lot of business.

specific: We lost a lot of business *because* the economy was soft.
The economy was soft, *so* we lost a lot of business.
The soft economy has cost us a lot of business.

5. Avoid unnecessary or unexpected grammatical shifts, which can interrupt the reader's train of thought and needlessly complicate the material.

shifts in verb voice: Any information you *can give* us *will be* greatly *appreciated* and we *assure* you that discretion *will be exercised* in its use.

rephrased: We *will appreciate* any information that you *can give* us. We *assure* you that we *will use* it with discretion.

shifts in person: *One* can use either erasers or correction fluid to remove typographical errors; however, *you* should make certain that *your* corrections are clean.

rephrased: *One* can use either erasers or correction fluid to eradicate errors; however, *one* should make certain that *one's* corrections are clean.
You can use either erasers or correction fluid to eradicate errors; however, *you* should make certain that *your* corrections are clean.

shift from phrase to clause: *Because of the current parts shortage and we are experiencing a strike,* we cannot fill any orders now.

rephrased: *Because of a parts shortage and a strike,* we cannot fill any orders now.
Because we are hampered by a parts shortage and we are experiencing a strike, we cannot fill any orders now.

6. Order the sentence elements rationally and logically. Place closely related elements as close together as possible.

related elements separated: We would appreciate your sending us the instructions on copyediting by mail or fax.

related elements joined: We would appreciate your sending us by mail or by fax the copyediting instructions.
We would appreciate your mailing or faxing us the copyediting instructions.

> We would appreciate it if you would mail or
> fax us the copyediting instructions.

7. Be sure that your sentences form complete, independent units containing both a subject and a predicate.

grammatically incomplete:	During the last three years, our calculator sales soared. While our conventional office-machine sales fell off.
grammatically complete:	During the last three years, our calculator sales soared, but our conventional office-machine sales fell off.
	While our conventional office-machine sales fell off during the last three years, our calculator sales soared.

In dialogue or specialized copy, fragmentation may be used for particular reasons (for example, to attract the reader's attention).

See it now. The car for the Nineties . . . A car you'll want to own.

SENTENCE LENGTH

Sentence length is directly related to the writer's purpose; there is no magic number of words that guarantees a good sentence. An executive covering broad and yet complex topics in a long memorandum may choose concise, succinct sentences for the sake of clarity, impact, fast dictation, and readability. A writer who wants the reader to reflect on what is being said may employ longer, more involved sentences. Still another writer may use a series of long sentences that build up to a climactic and forceful short sentence, in order to emphasize an important point.

SENTENCE STRATEGY

1. **Coordination and subordination** Coordination involves the linking of independent sentences and sentence elements by means of coordinating conjunctions, while subordination involves transforming elements into dependent structures by means of subordinating conjunctions. Coordination tends to promote loose sentence structure; subordination tends to tighten the structure and to emphasize a main clause. (See also paragraph 1 on page 222.)

coordination:	During the balance of 1994, this Company expects to issue $100,000,000 of long-term debt and equity securities *and* may guarantee up to $200,000,000 of new corporate bonds.
subordination:	While this Company expects to issue $100,000,000 of long-term debt and equity securities during the balance of 1994, it may also guarantee up to $200,000,000 of new corporate bonds.

2. **Interrupting elements** Interrupting the normal flow of a sentence by inserting comments can be a useful way to call attention to an aside, to emphasize a word or phrase, to convey a particular tone (such as forcefulness), or to make the prose a little more informal.

His evidence, if reliable, could send our client to prison.
These companies—ours as well as theirs—must show more profits.

This, ladies and gentlemen, is the prime reason for your cost overruns. I trust it will not happen again?

Interrupting elements should not be overused, however, since too many of them may distract the reader.

3. **Parallelism and balance** Parallelism and balance work together to maintain an even, rhythmic flow of thought. Parallelism means a similarity in the grammatical construction of adjacent phrases and clauses that are equivalent, similar, or antithetical in meaning.

> These ecological problems are of crucial concern *to* scientists, *to* businessmen, *to* government officials, and *to* all citizens.
> Our attorneys have argued *that* the trademark is ours, *that* our rights have been violated, and *that* appropriate compensation is required.
> He was respected not only *for his intelligence* but also *for his integrity.*
> The thing that interested me . . . about New York . . . was the . . . contrast it showed between the dull and the shrewd, the strong and the weak, the rich and the poor, the wise and the ignorant. . . .
> —Theodore Dreiser

Balance involves the symmetrical use of two or more parallel phrases or clauses that contain similar, contrasting, or opposing ideas.

> To err is human; to forgive, divine.
> —Alexander Pope
> Ask not what your country can do for you—ask what you can do for your country.
> —John F. Kennedy

4. **Periodic and cumulative sentences** Stylistically, there are two basic types of sentences—the periodic and the cumulative (or loose). The periodic sentence is structured so that its main idea or thrust is suspended until the very end, thereby drawing the reader's eye and mind along to an emphatic conclusion. In the example below, the main point follows the final comma.

> Although the Commission would like to give its licensees every encouragement to experiment on their own initiative with new and innovative means of providing access to their stations for the discussion of important public issues, it cannot justify imposing a specific right of access by government fiat.

The cumulative sentence, on the other hand, is structured so that its main point appears first, followed by other phrases or clauses expanding on or supporting it. In the following example, the main point precedes the first comma.

> The balance must be finely crafted, lest strategists err too much on the side of technological sophistication only to find that U.S. military forces can be defeated by overwhelming mass.

The final phrase or clause in a cumulative sentence theoretically could be deleted without changing the essential meaning of the sentence. A cumulative sentence is therefore more loosely structured than a periodic sentence.

5. **Reversal** A reversal of customary or expected sentence order can be an effective stylistic strategy when used sparingly, because it injects a dash of freshness, unexpectedness, and originality into the prose.

> *customary or expected order:* I find that these realities are indisputable: the economy has taken a dramatic downturn, costs on all fronts have soared, and jobs are at a premium.

reversal: That the economy has taken a dramatic downturn; that costs on all fronts have soared;
that jobs are at a premium—these are the
realities that I find indisputable.

6. **Rhetorical questions** The rhetorical question is yet another device to focus
the reader's attention on a problem or an issue. The rhetorical question requires no specific response from the reader but often merely sets up the
introduction of the writer's own view. A rhetorical question may serve as a
topic sentence in a paragraph, or a series of rhetorical questions may spot-
light pertinent issues.

What can be done to correct the problem? Two things, to begin with:
never discuss cases out of the office, and never allow a visitor to see the
papers on your desk.

7. **Variety** Any kind of repetitious patttern may create monotony. As a means
of keeping the reader's attention, try to maintain a balance of different
kinds of sentences. Use a combination of simple, compound, and complex
sentences in a paragraph, including a variety of short and long sentences.
Vary the beginnings of your sentences so that every sentence in a paragraph
does not begin directly with the subject. Through judicious use of combinations of sentence patterns and the sentence strategies discussed in the preceding paragraphs, you can attain an interesting, diversified style.

Paragraphs

Good paragraphing is a way of controlling the structure of a piece of writing.
While the writer is responsible for the basic paragraphing of his or her material,
the secretary should be able to recognize various kinds of paragraphs and their
functions, as well as the problems that may arise from faulty paragraphing, and
be ready to alert the writer to anything that might detract from the effect of the
communication.

A paragraph is a subdivision in writing that consists of one or more sentences,
deals with one or more ideas, or quotes a speaker or a source. The first line of a
paragraph is indented in reports, studies, articles, theses, and books; in business
letters and memorandums it may or may not be indented, depending on the
style being followed. See Chapter 7 for business-letter styles.

Paragraphs should not be considered as isolated, self-contained units that
can be mechanically lined up without transitions or interrelationship of ideas.
Rather, they should be viewed as components of larger sections that are tightly
interlinked and that interact in the sequential development of a major idea or
cluster of ideas. The overall coherence of a communication depends on this
interaction.

DEVELOPING PARAGRAPHS

Depending on the writer's intentions, paragraph development may take any of
several directions. A paragraph may:

1. Move from the general to the specific.
2. Move from the specific to the general.

3. Exhibit an alternating order of comparison and contrast.
4. Chronicle events in order—from the beginning to the end, or possibly from the end to the beginning.
5. Describe something (such as a group of objects) in a particular spatial order—for example, from near to far, or vice versa.
6. Follow a climactic sequence, with the least important facts or examples described first, leading to the most important facts or examples. Or the facts or issues that are easy to comprehend or accept may be set forth first, followed by those that are more difficult to comprehend or accept. In this way the easier material makes the reader receptive and prepares him or her for the more difficult points.
7. Follow an anticlimactic order, setting forth the most persuasive arguments first so that the reader, having been influenced in a positive way, is carried along by the rest of the argument with a growing feeling of assent.

EFFECTIVE PARAGRAPHING

The following material outlines some ways of building effective paragraphs.

A topic sentence—a key sentence to which the other sentences in the paragraph are related—may be placed either at the beginning or at the end of a paragraph. A lead-in topic sentence should present the main idea of the paragraph and set the tone of the material that follows. A terminal topic sentence should be an analysis, conclusion, or summation of what has gone before it.

A single-sentence paragraph can be used to achieve an easy transition from a preceding to a subsequent paragraph (especially when the paragraphs are long and complex) if it repeats an important word or phrase from the preceding paragraph, contains a pronoun reference to a key individual mentioned in a preceding paragraph, or is introduced by an appropriate conjunction or conjunctive adverb that tightly connects the paragraphs.

1. The very first paragraph should set the tone, introduce the subject, and lead into the discussion. It should be worded so as to immediately attract attention and arouse interest. Opening paragraphs of the following kinds can be effective:

   a. a succinct statement of purpose or point of view
   b. a concise definition of a problem
   c. a lucid statement of a key issue or fact

   Openings of the following kinds, by contrast, can blunt the point of the rest of the material:

   a. an apology for the material to be presented
   b. a querulous complaint or a defensive posture
   c. a rehash of ancient history (such as a word-for-word recap of previous correspondence)
   d. a presentation of self-evident facts
   e. a group of sentences rendered limp and meaningless by clichés

2. The last paragraph should tie together the ideas and points that have been set forth earlier and reemphasize the main thrust of the communication. Effective endings can be of several types:

   a. a setting forth of the most important conclusions drawn from the preceding discussion
   b. a final analysis of the main problems under discussion
   c. a lucid summary of the individual points brought up earlier

    d. a final, clear statement of opinion or position
    e. concrete suggestions or solutions, if applicable
    f. specific questions asked of the reader, if applicable

Endings of the following kinds, by contrast, can reduce the effect of a communication:

    a. apologies for a poor presentation
    b. qualifying remarks that blunt or negate incisive points made earlier
    c. insertion of minor details or afterthoughts
    d. a meaningless closing couched in clichés

3. The following are tests of good paragraphs:

    a. Does the paragraph have a clear purpose, or is it there just to fill up space? Does it simply restate in other terms what has been said before?
    b. Does the paragraph clarify rather than cloud the main ideas of the piece?
    c. Is the paragraph adequately developed, or does it merely raise other questions that it does not attempt to answer? If a position is being taken, are supporting information and statistics essential to its defense included?
    d. Are the length and wording of the paragraphs sufficiently varied, or is the same language used again and again?
    e. Is the sentence structure within each paragraph coherent?
    f. Is each paragraph unified and coherent? Do all the sentences really *belong* there, or do they digress into areas that would have been better covered in another paragraph or omitted altogether? Does each sentence lead clearly and logically to the next?
    g. Are the transitions between paragraphs achieved by transitional phrases that indicate the relationship between them and indicate the direction in which the presentation is moving?

Common Problems in Word Usage

Whether in your own writing or in that of your employer, you will frequently have to decide between alternative words and terms, not to mention alternative spellings, some of which may be more correct or appropriate in given contexts than others. Here are brief discussions (many adapted from *Merriam-Webster's Collegiate Dictionary*) of a number of words and terms that represent usage or spelling problems for many writers.

a, an   In both speech and writing, *a* is used before a word beginning with a consonant ("*a* door," "*a* symphony"). Before a word beginning with a vowel, *an* is usual ("*an* icicle," "*an* operation"), but when the vowel is pronounced like a consonant, *a* is used ("*a* one-time deal," "*a* union"). Before nouns beginning with *h*, *a* is used if the *h* is pronounced ("*a* human," "*a* headache"), except in a few cases where either *a* or *an* can be used ("*a(n)* historic event"), and *an* is used if the *h* is not pronounced ("twice *an* hour").

above   The use of *above* as both a noun ("none of the *above*") and an adjective ("Please refer to the *above* table") has long been established as standard usage.

adapt, adopt   *Adopt* suggests taking something over as it is ("The committee voted to *adopt* a new set of rules"). *Adapt* suggests changing something to meet new needs ("*adapt* a short story for television"). When you start a new job, you'll have to *adapt* to the way your new company does things. You may like one of their procedures well enough to *adopt* it as your own.

adverse, averse   These words are similar in meaning, but *adverse* is the more generally useful word. It is commonly used to modify a following noun ("*adverse* circumstances," "an *adverse* reaction"). *Adverse to* is freely used of things as a predicate adjective ("testimony that was *adverse to* our cause"). When used of people, *adverse to* and *averse to* are essentially the same. A subtle distinction in which *adverse* refers to opinion or intention and *averse* to feelings or inclination is sometimes observed: ("senators *adverse* to the nomination"; "*averse* to long engagements"). *Averse* is very commonly used in negative constructions ("I am not *averse* to hearing myself praised").

affect, effect   These verbs have been getting muddled for about 500 years, but they are not synonyms. There are even two verbs *affect* ("*affected* an air of worldly indifference," "how the news will *affect* the stock market"), and *effect* has been mistakenly put in place of both. *Effect* means approximately "to bring about" ("the steps necessary to *effect* a change in government policy"). If you have doubts about which spelling to use, open up that dictionary and take a look. The nouns are likewise confused, but *effect* is usually the one you'll want, as *affect* is a specialized term in psychology.

aggravate   *Aggravate* is used chiefly in two meanings: "to make worse" ("*aggravated* her shoulder injury," "their financial position was *aggravated* by the market downturn") and "to irritate, annoy" ("The President was *aggravated* by French intransigence"). In a business context you are much more likely to meet the first use than the second. The same is not true, however, for *aggravation*, which means "irritation" more often than not, and *aggravating*, which almost always expresses annoyance.

allusion, illusion   If these words are confused, someone has made a spelling mistake, because the words have nothing in common except their last seven letters. A quick check in your dictionary will dispel all confusion if you aren't sure which word you heard.

almost, most   *Most* is often used like *almost* ("*Most* everyone was there"). This is basically a speech form and is commonly put into advertising copy to create a homey everyday atmosphere. You won't need it in most business writing.

alot, a lot   There are a lot of people who wish that *a lot* were a single word, quicker to write or type, and one space shorter than the two-word form. But most of the people responsible for turning words into print—in books, in magazines, in letters—insist on two words. You might as well resign yourself to two words: you won't have a lot of success in slipping the single word form past their watchful eyes.

alright   Even though the business community has been using the one-word *alright* since the 1920s, the world of publishing has preferred *all right*. *Alright* is only gradually gaining acceptance, and that most often in business publications and newspaper writing. *All right* is still more common in print. You may want to check with the originator of your dictation to see which spelling he or she prefers.

amount, number   *Number* is regularly used with nouns that can form a plural and can be used with a numeral ("a large *number* of orders," "any *number* of times"). *Amount* is mainly used with nouns that denote a substance or concept that can't be divided and counted up ("the annual *amount* of rainfall," "a large *amount* of money"). The use of *amount* with count nouns has been criticized; it is usually used when the number of things can be thought of as a mass or collection ("a substantial *amount* of job offers"), but you'll probably want to avoid it in a business document.

anymore, any more   Although both *anymore* and *any more* are found in written use, in this century *anymore* is more common. *Anymore* is regularly used with negatives ("Don't get out much *anymore*"), to ask a question ("Do you jog *anymore*?") and in the conditional ("If you do that *anymore*, I'll leave"), and sometimes appears in positive constructions ("I'm too old to believe in Santa Claus *anymore*"). The use of *anymore* to mean "now" or "these days" is widespread in speech in all areas of the United States except New England ("Hardly a day passes without rain anymore"), but it is not likely to be needed in a business document.

apt, liable   Both *liable* and *apt* when followed by an infinitive are used nearly interchangeably with *likely* ("He was more *liable* [*likely*] to get tired easily," "The roads are *apt* [*likely*] to be slippery when wet"). This use of *apt* is widely accepted. Some people think *liable* should be limited to situations having an undesirable outcome ("If you speed, you're *liable* to be caught") and it is most often used this way in writing.

as, as if, like   *Like* used as a conjunction in the sense of *as* ("just *like* I used to do") or in the sense of *as if* ("It looks *like* it will rain") has been frequently criticized, especially since its use in a widely publicized cigarette commercial slogan. *Like* has been so used for nearly 600 years, although it was not as common in written works in the past as it has been in the twentieth century. There is no real grammatical basis for objecting to these uses of *like,* but if someone in your office might complain you can avoid confrontation by using *as* or *as if.*

as far as   "*As far as* clothes, young people always know best." This sentence, from a newspaper article, shows *as far as* used as a preposition. Prepositional use developed from the more common conjunction ("*as far as* clothes are concerned") by omission of the following verb or verb phrase, and it is mostly confined to spoken use, although we sometimes find it in journalistic writing. So if you find the preposition in your dictation, you may want to check with the originator to see if he or she really wants it to appear in the final document.

as regards, in regard to, in regards to   The first two, along with their cousins *with regard to* and *regarding,* have been criticized in many handbooks as jargonistic or excessively wordy. You can often replace them with such alternatives as *about* or *concerning,* but if the person writing or dictating a letter prefers the longer phrases, there is no solid reason to change them. *In regards to,* with *regards* pluralized, is a spoken form only and should not be used in a business document except in a direct quotation.

assure, ensure, insure   You can distinguish between these words by using *insure* for money and guarantees ("*Insure* that package before sending it"), *ensure* for things ("Send the package overnight express to *ensure* its arrival in the morning"), and *assure* for people ("I *assure* you that the package will arrive tomorrow morning"). Current American English does reserve *assure* for people, but *insure* is usual for both the other uses; it is perfectly acceptable to write "Send the package overnight express to *insure* its arrival in the morning."

awful   It has been traditional to criticize any use of *awful* and *awfully* that doesn't convey the original sense of being filled with awe. However, *awful* has long been acceptable in the meanings "extremely objectionable" ("What an *awful* color") and "exceedingly great" ("an *awful* lot of money") in speech and casual writing. Use of the adverbs *awful* and *awfully* as intensifiers ("I'm *awful* tired," "he's *awfully* rich") is likewise common in informal prose. You probably won't want to use any of these where a formal tone is called for.

awhile   The use of the adverb *awhile* as the object of a preposition is standard ("After *awhile* I felt better," "For *awhile* she was silent"). But some people are sticklers for the spelling *a while* after a preposition. You may want to check to be sure.

between, among   The notion that *between* can be used only of two items and that *among* must be used for more than two is persistent but unfounded. *Between* is especially appropriate to describe one-to-one relationships, but these need not be of only two items. It can be used when the number is unspecified ("economic cooperation *between* nations"), when more than two items are specifically mentioned ("This is *between* you and me and the lamppost"), and even when only one item is mentioned but repetition is implied ("paused *between* every sentence"). *Among* is more appropriate when the emphasis is not strictly on individual relationships ("discontent *among* the stockholders"). Automatically using *among* when more than two items are mentioned can result in awkwardness and may strain natural idiom ("The movie alternates *among* comedy, philosophy, and drama").

bimonthly, biweekly   These words can cause confusion because they both have two meanings—"twice a week (or month)," and "once every two weeks (or months)." A memo that announces that from now on committee meetings will be biweekly may not be too helpful to the recipients. If you have to draw up such a memo, try to include a hint ("*Biweekly* meetings will be held every Tuesday and Friday"). Or you could skip the *bi*-word altogether and try "every Tuesday and Friday" or "every other Wednesday." Confusion will result if the writer and reader of *biweekly* or *bimonthly* don't both have the same meaning in mind. It's the writer's duty to make sure that there is no confusion.

can, may   Both *can* and *may* are used to refer to possibility ("*Can* the deal still go through?" "It *may* still happen"). Since the possibility of someone's doing something may depend on someone else's agreeing to it, the two words have become interchangeable when they refer to permission ("You *can* [*may*] go now if you like"). Though the use of *can* to ask or grant permission has been common since the last century, *may* is often thought to be more appropriate in formal correspondence. This meaning of *may* is relatively rare in negative constructions, where *cannot* and *can't* are more usual ("They *cannot* [*may not*] use it without paying").

center   The intransitive verb *center* (meaning "to focus") is most commonly used with the prepositions *at, in, on,* and *around. At* appears to be favored in mathematical contexts, while the others are found in a broad range of contexts. Some people object to *center around* as illogical, though it is a standard idiom. If you should need to avoid *center around,* you can use *center on* (or *in*) or try *revolve around.*

complement, compliment   The confusion of these words is purely a matter of spelling, since they have no meanings in common, either as noun or verb. The most frequent mistake is to use the more common *compliment* in place of the less common *complement.* A quick look in a desk-size dictionary, such as *Merriam-Webster's Collegiate Dictionary,* will clear up any doubts as to which word is needed. Take the same precautions for the adjectives *complimentary* and *complementary.*

comprise   The sense of *comprise* meaning "to compose or constitute" ("the branches that *comprise* our government") has been attacked as wrong, for reasons that are unclear. Until recently, it was used chiefly in scientific and technical writing; today, it enjoys literary and business use as well, and this sense of *comprise* has become the most widely used sense. If there's an objector in your office, you may want to choose a safe synonym such as *compose* or *make up.*

consensus   The phrase *consensus of opinion* has been so often claimed to be redundant that many writers avoid it. It is not, in fact, a redundancy, since it uses a sense of *consensus* that means "general agreement." However, you can avoid the phrase by using *consensus* alone in its stead; many writers in fact do so.

contact   The use of *contact* as a verb, especially to mean "get in touch with" ("*Contact* your local dealer"), has long been standard in business use.

data   *Data* has firmly established itself with a meaning independent of its use as the plural form of *datum.* It is used in one of two ways: as a plural noun (like *earnings*), taking a plural verb and plural modifiers (such as *these* or *many*) but not cardinal numbers ("These *data* show that we're out of the recession"); or as an abstract mass noun (like *information*), taking a singular verb and singular modifiers (such as *this, much,* or *little*) ("The *data* on the subject is plentiful"). Both constructions are standard, but many people are convinced that only the plural form is correct, and in consequence the plural form is somewhat more common in print. What you want to avoid is mixing in signs of the singular (like *this* or *much*) when you use a plural verb.

different from, different than   Both of these phrases are standard, in spite of some people's disliking *different than*. Each form has its particular virtues. *Different from* works best when you can take advantage of its preposition *from* ("The new proposal is very *different from* the old one"). *Different than* works best when a clause follows ("very *different* in size *than* it was two years ago"). *Different than* can be used in place of *different from* ("*different than* the old proposal"), but you must rephrase a sentence to change *different than* to *different from* when a clause follows ("very *different* in size *from* what it was two years ago").

disinterested, uninterested   *Disinterested* has basically two uses: an ethical one, in the sense of "unbiased" ("a *disinterested* decision," "*disinterested* intellectual curiosity"), and a neutral one that it shares with *uninterested,* "not interested." Some people object to the neutral use, but it is standard, and may even be chosen for purposes of emphasis ("trying to lecture a wriggling and *disinterested* child") or to suggest a loss of interest, which *uninterested* does not ("became *disinterested* in the subject").

due to   When the *due* of *due to* is clearly an adjective ("absences *due to* the flu") no one complains about the phrase. When *due to* is a preposition ("*Due to* the holiday, our office will be closed"), some people object and call for *owing to* or *because of*. Both uses of *due to* are entirely standard, but if you have an objector in your office, you can use one of the alternatives.

each other, one another   The traditional rules call for *each other* to be used in reference to two ("The two girls looked at *each other* in surprise") and *one another* to be used in reference to three or more ("There will be time for people to talk with *one another* after the meeting"). In actual use, they are employed interchangeably.

enormity   Some people would limit *enormity* to the meaning "great wickedness" and not allow it to be used to denote large size. But the word has many interesting uses. When *enormity* is used to refer to large size, either literally or figuratively, it usually suggests something so large as to be overwhelming ("the *enormity* of the Grand Canyon," "the *enormity* of the problem of the homeless"). *Enormity* can also suggest both great size and deviation from morality ("the *enormity* of our stockpiles of nuclear weapons"). It can emphasize the importance of an event ("the *enormity* of the war") or of its consequences ("the *enormity* of the destruction"). *Enormity* can also suggest a considerable departure from the expected or the normal ("After the hurricane, the *enormity* of the situation set in"). These uses are all perfectly standard.

enthuse   The use or avoidance of *enthuse* is entirely a matter of taste. *Enthuse* is solidly established as standard, especially in journalism. Some may feel it to be a bit informal in a business document ("The sales staff *enthused* about the new promotional materials").

farther, further   *Farther* and *further* have been used more or less interchangeably throughout most of their history, but currently they are showing signs of diverging. As adverbs they are interchangeable whenever spatial, temporal, or metaphorical distance is involved ("lived *farther* [*further*] from town," "The news spread even *farther* [*further*]"). Where there is no notion of distance, *further* is used ("Our techniques can be *further* refined"). *Further* is also used as a sentence modifier ("*Further,* there is no evidence"), but *farther* is not. As adjectives, their use is also diverging, with *farther* taking over the meaning of distance ("the *farther* shore") and *further* the meaning of addition ("needed no *further* invitation").

finalize   *Finalize* occurs most frequently in business and government contexts ("The budget will be *finalized*," "*finalizing* the deal"). See the entry for *-ize* below.

flaunt, flout   *Flaunt* acquired its meaning "to treat with contempt" ("*flaunting* the rules") from confusion with *flout,* which has the same meaning ("*flouting* the rules"). Although this meaning is well established, many people believe it is an error. *Flout* is sometimes used to mean "display ostentatiously" ("*flouted* their wealth"), but the standard term in such contexts is actually *flaunt*. The compromise spelling *flount* is also not standard.

formally, formerly   There is no reason to confuse these words, although they are likely to sound pretty similar in dictated material. *Formally* means only "in a formal way" ("dressed *formally*," "a *formally* constituted committee"). *Formerly* means "at an earlier time" ("B&F Corporation, *formerly* doing business as Binns & Franks"). Notice that you could put *formally* into this last context, but it would not make very much sense. If you are in doubt about meaning, check a dictionary before committing yourself to print.

fortuitous   The sense of *fortuitous* meaning "lucky" ("Our acquisition of the stock at that time was *fortuitous*") is standard, but is sometimes objected to. A newer sense, "coming by a lucky chance" ("There was a *fortuitous* cab at the corner just as the storm broke") is halfway between the "lucky" sense and the original "occurring by chance" sense. Only the original sense is likely to occur in a negative sentence ("Its happening five times in a row cannot have been *fortuitous*").

fulsome   The adjective *fulsome* can present a problem of ambiguity: two of its most frequently used senses mean very different things. In expressions such as "fulsome praise" or "a fulsome tribute," it can be hard to tell whether *fulsome* means "generous in amount, extent, or spirit" or "excessively complimentary or flattering." To avoid misinterpretation, be sure that the context in which you use it makes the intended meaning clear.

good   Both *good* and *well* are acceptable when used to express good health ("I feel *good*," "I feel *well*"). *Good* may also connote good spirits.

The adverb *good* has been much criticized, with people insisting that *well* be used instead. This has resulted in a split in connotation so that *well* is used in neutral informal contexts ("The orchestra played *well* this evening") and *good* in those that are emotionally charged and emphatic ("He hit the ball *good*"). The adverb *good* is mainly a spoken form, and is not likely to be needed in a business document unless in direct quotation.

hanged, hung   In the sense "to suspend by the neck until dead," both *hanged* and *hung* are standard as either the past tense or the past participle. *Hanged* is most appropriate for official executions ("was *hanged*, drawn, and quartered") but *hung* is also used ("ordered the traitor *hung*"). *Hung* is used in all other senses ("was *hung* in effigy," "*hung* the clothes out to dry," "*hung* my head in shame").

hardly   *Hardly* meaning "certainly not" is sometimes used with *not* for added emphasis ("Just another day at the office? Not *hardly*"). *Hardly* is also used like *barely* or *scarcely* to emphasize a minimal amount ("I *hardly* knew her," "Almost new—*hardly* a scratch on it"). When *hardly* is used with a negative verb (such as *can't, couldn't, didn't*) it is often called a double negative, but it is really a weaker negative: "I can't hardly hear you" means that I can hear you, but with difficulty; "I can't hear you" means just what it says. *Hardly* with a negative is a spoken form; you should not need it in a business document, unless you are quoting someone directly.

hone in   This is a recently established term of uncertain origin that some people regard as a mistake for the synonymous *home in*. Because it is so recently established, and has so little to do with the usual meanings of *hone*, you might want to ask, when you meet it, if perhaps *home in* or *zero in* would be more appropriate in a business context.

hopefully   When used to mean "I hope" or "We hope" ("Hopefully, they'll reach an agreement"), as opposed to "full of hope" ("We continued our work *hopefully* and cheerfully"), *hopefully* is often criticized. However, other similar sentence adverbs (such as *frankly, clearly,* and *interestingly*) are accepted by everyone. Despite the objections, this sense of *hopefully* is now in standard use.

I, me   It is all right to use *me* after forms of the verb *be* ("It's *me*"), *than* ("Susan is taller than *me*"), and *as* ("He's as big *as* me"), in absolute uses ("Who, *me*?"), and in emphatic positions ("*Me* too") in speech and in informal or casual contexts. But in more formal contexts many people prefer *I* after *be* ("It was *I* who discovered the mistake") and after *as* and *than* when the first term of the comparison is the subject of the sentence ("Susan is taller than I," "He is as big as I").

imply, infer   Discussions of the proper uses of *infer* and *imply* generally center on logic. But there are no logical problems involved. *Infer* is mostly used to mean "to draw a conclusion, conclude" and is commonly accompanied by *from* ("I *infer* from your comments that you were not pleased with our service"). *Imply* is used to mean "suggest" ("The letter *implies* that our service has not been satisfactory"). The use of *infer* that the fuss is about always has a personal subject and is used like *imply* ("Are you *inferring* that I made a mistake?"). This use is mostly spoken, although it does turn up in letters to the editor, and is not used in logical discourse. It is highly unlikely that you would need or want it in a business document.

importantly   A number of critics have objected to the use of *importantly* to modify a sentence ("More *importantly*, I got my job back"), and have suggested using *important* instead. Either word can be used in this way. *Important* is always used with *more* or *most* ("Second, and most *important*, we must increase our market share"). *Importantly* can be used with or without *more* or *most* ("sticks easily, and just as *importantly*, is easily removed").

irregardless   *Irregardless*, though a real word (and not uncommon in speech), is still a long way from general acceptance. In your business documents, be sure to use *regardless* instead.

its, it's   It's easy to keep these forms separate as each has its own function. *It's* is a contraction of *it is* or *it has*, and *its* is a possessive pronoun ("*It's* been a long time since I've seen *its* equal"). Back in the eighteenth century, people used *it's* for the pronoun. But let's not go back to the eighteenth century. Use *its* for the pronoun and *it's* for the contraction.

-ize   Almost any noun or adjective can be made into a verb by adding *-ize* ("hospitalize," "familiarize," "idolize"). Many technical terms are formed this way ("oxidize," "crystallize") as are verbs of ethnic derivation ("Americanize") and verbs derived from proper names ("bowdlerize," "mesmerize"). People have always complained about new words formed this way and they still do: *finalize* and *prioritize* are two fairly recent ones that have been criticized. Remember that some *-ize* words are special or technical terms regularly used in a particular field or profession. No matter how strange these may seem, they should not be avoided in materials intended for the specialists.

kudo, kudos   *Kudos* was introduced as a singular noun into English from Greek. As it became more popular, it was used in contexts ("She deserves *kudos* for her efforts") where a person unfamiliar with Greek could not tell whether it was a singular or plural. Many people took it to be a plural and used it with a plural verb ("Her kudos are well deserved"), and eventually someone removed the *-s* to make a singular *kudo*. This same sort of word formation has given us such common words as *cherry* and *pea*. The form *kudos* with either a plural or singular verb is still standard, however.

lay, lie   *Lay* has long been used as an intransitive verb meaning "lie" ("tried to make the book *lay* flat," "*lay* down on the job"), but it has been condemned by schoolteachers and grammarians for years. These critics have been largely successful in removing the intransitive *lay* from most formal writing, but it has persisted in the spoken language. Consider most of your business documents as relatively formal writing, and stick to *lie* for intransitive uses there. *Lay* and *lie* have similar but distinct inflected forms. Check your dictionary for the appropriate ones.

lend, loan   Some people still object to the use of *loan* as a verb ("*loaned* me the book") and insist on *lend*. *Loan* is in standard use, however. You should remember that *loan* is used only literally ("*loans* large sums of money"), while *lend* can be both literal ("*lends* large sums of money") and figurative ("Would you please *lend* me a hand?").

less, fewer   The traditional view is that *less* is used for matters of degree, value, or amount, and that it modifies nouns that refer to uncountable things ("less hostility," "less clothing") while *fewer* modifies numbers and plural nouns ("fewer students," "fewer than eight trees"). However, *less* has been used to modify plural nouns for centuries. Today *less* is actually more likely than *fewer* to modify plural nouns when distances, sums of money, and certain common phrases are involved ("less than 100 miles," "less than $2000," "in 25 words or less") and just as likely to modify periods of time ("in less [fewer] than four hours").

like, such as   Should you write "cities *like* Chicago and Des Moines" or "cities *such as* Chicago and Des Moines"? In fact you can use either one, or change the latter to "*such* cities *as* Chicago and Des Moines." These expressions have been subjected to objections so diverse that it is plain there is nothing objectionable about any of them.

literally   *Literally* means "in a literal sense or manner" or "actually" ("took the remark *literally*," "was *literally* insane"). It is also used to mean "in effect" or "virtually" as an intensifier ("She *literally* flew up the stairs," "The performance *literally* brought the house down"). This use is often criticized as nonsensical, but it is not supposed to make sense, only add emphasis. It is often used, however, where no additional emphasis is really needed.

masterful, masterly   *Masterly* means "suitable to or resembling that of a master" ("a *masterly* performance"). *Masterful* has several meanings, one of which is "masterly." It has been argued that since *masterly* has only one meaning, it rather than *masterful* should be used whenever that meaning is intended. However, *masterful* is in reputable use in this sense, so there is no real need to prefer *masterly*.

media   *Media* is the plural of *medium*. With all the references to the mass media today, *media* is often used as a singular mass noun ("The *media* always wants a story"). This singular use is not as well established as the similar use of *data*, and you will probably want to keep *media* plural in most business documents. An exception must be recognized for the world of advertising, in which *media* has long been singular and is sometimes given the plural *medias*.

memorandum   *Memorandum* is a singular noun with two acceptable plurals: *memorandums* and *memoranda*. *Memoranda* is not established as a singular form; if you meet it you'll want to convert it to plural construction, keeping alert for singular modifiers as well as the singular verb.

militate, mitigate   *Militate* means "to have weight or effect" ("Current economic conditions *militate* against expansion at this time"). *Mitigate*, which means "to make less severe," is sometimes used with *against* in place of *militate*. You will want to avoid this use in business documents.

nauseating, nauseous   *Nauseous* is most frequently used to mean "physically affected with nausea" ("The ride made me *nauseous*"), while *nauseating* is used to mean "causing nausea or disgust" ("the *nauseating* violence on TV").

neither   *Neither* is usually followed by *nor* ("*Neither* high winds nor freezing temperatures discouraged the skiers"), although use with *or* is acceptable ("*Neither* he or she knew the answer"). The use of *neither* to refer to more than two nouns, though sometimes criticized, has been standard for centuries ("*Neither* the post office, the bank, nor City Hall is open today").

Traditionally, the pronoun *neither* is used with a singular verb ("*Neither* is ideal"). However, when a prepositional phrase follows *neither*, a plural verb is common and acceptable ("*Neither* of those solutions are ideal").

one   The use of *one* to indicate a generic individual lends formality to writing since it suggests distance between the writer and the reader ("*One* never knows" is more formal than "You never know"). Consequently, *one* is rarely used in informal English. The use of *one* to replace a first-person pronoun ("I'd like to read more but *one* doesn't have the time") is common in British English but may be thought odd or objectionable in American English.

people, persons   *People* is used to designate an unspecified number of persons ("*People* everywhere are talking about the new show"), and *persons* is commonly used when a definite number is specified ("Occupancy by more than 86 *persons* is prohibited"). However, the use of *people* where numbers are mentioned is acceptable nowadays ("Ten *people* were questioned").

per   *Per,* meaning "for each," is most commonly used with figures, usually in relation to price ("$150 *per* performance"), vehicles ("25 miles *per* gallon," "55 miles *per* hour"), or sports ("15 points *per* game"). Avoid inserting words like "a" or "each" between *per* and the word or words it modifies ("could type seventy words *per* each minute").

phenomena   *Phenomena* is the plural of *phenomenon.* Use of *phenomena* as a singular ("St. Elmo's Fire is an eerie *phenomena*") is encountered in speech and now and then in writing, but is not established as standard.

plus   The use of *plus* to mean "and" ("a hamburger *plus* french fries for lunch") or "besides which" ("We would've been on time, but we lost the car keys. *Plus,* we forgot the map") is found in speech and in informal writing, but is not likely to be useful in business contexts.

precede, proceed   The basic idea is that *precede* means "to come or go before" and *proceed* means "to go along." A more specific guide to their meanings can be quickly found in your dictionary. Confusion between the two words is really just a matter of spelling—it's not uncommon to find the tail end of *precede* tacked on to the front end of *proceed.* Your dictionary will keep you straight here too. And while we are on the subject, take note of *procedure*—no double *e.*

presently   The use of *presently* to mean "at the present time" ("I am *presently* working up a report"), while often criticized, is standard and acceptable.

pretty   *Pretty* is used to tone down or moderate a statement ("*pretty* cold weather"). Although it is not restricted to informal writing, it is most commonly found there.

principle, principal   Avoid confusing *principle* and *principal.* *Principle* is only a noun; *principal* is both an adjective and a noun. If you are unsure which noun you need, consult your dictionary.

prior to   *Prior to,* a synonym of "before," most often appears in fairly formal contexts. It is especially useful in suggesting anticipation ("If all specifications are finalized *prior to* system design, cost overruns will be avoided").

proved, proven   Both *proved* and *proven* are past participles of *prove.* Earlier in this century, *proved* was more common than *proven,* but today they appear with nearly equal frequency. As a past participle, either is acceptable ("has been *proved* [*proven*] effective"). *Proven* is more frequent in adjectival use ("*proven* gas reserves").

providing, provided   Although *providing* in the sense of "if" or "on condition that" has occasionally been disapproved ("*providing* he finds a buyer"), both *providing* and *provided* are well established as standard, and either may be used. *Provided* is somewhat more often used.

real   The adverb *real* is used interchangeably with *really* only as an intensifier ("a *real* tough assignment"). This use is very common in speech and casual writing, but you are not likely to need it in a business document.

set, sit   The basic idea with *set* and *sit* is that *set* takes an object ("*Set* the lamp over there") and *sit* does not ("*sat* for an hour in the doctor's office"). But *set* has exceptions: the sun *sets* and so does a hen (intransitive use). So does *sit:* "I *sat* her down by her grandfather" (transitive use). When used of people, intransitive *set* is a spoken use that should not be used in a business document except in direct quotation.

shall, will   *Shall* and *will* are generally interchangeable in present-day American English. In recent years, *shall* has been regarded as somewhat affected; *will* is much more common. However, *shall* is more appropriate in questions to express simple choice ("*Shall* we go now?") because *will* in such a context suggests prediction ("*Will* the prototype be ready next week?").

slow, slowly   Some commentators claim that use of *slow* as an adverb (meaning "slowly") is an error. But there is really not much of a usage problem with *slow* and *slowly* because in actual practice they each have their own use. *Slow* is almost always used with verbs indicating motion or action, and it typically follows the verb it modifies ("a stew cooked long and *slow*"). *Slowly* can be used in the same way ("drove *slowly*"), but it also is used before the verb ("The winds *slowly* subsided"), with adjectives formed from verbs ("the *slowly* sinking sun"), and in places where *slow* would sound inappropriate ("turned *slowly* around").

so   The intensive use of the adverb *so* to mean "very" or "extremely" has been condemned by many commentators but has long thrived especially in speech and informal writing ("He loves her *so*"). No one disapproves of it, though, when it is used in negative contexts ("not *so* long ago") or followed by an explaining clause ("cocoa *so* hot that I burned my tongue").

Use of the conjunction *so* to introduce clauses of result ("The acoustics are good, *so* every note is clear") and purpose ("Be quiet *so* I can sleep") is sometimes criticized, but these uses are standard. In the latter case (when used to mean "in order that"), *so that* is the more common form in formal and business writing ("to cut spending *so that* the deficit will be reduced").

some   When the adverb *some* (meaning "about") is used to modify a number, it is usually a round figure ("*Some* 2000 fans packed the stadium"). It is also used with other numbers, though, as it is more emphatic than the alternatives *about* or *approximately* ("ate some 14 pies to win the contest"). Many people prescribe *somewhat* instead of *some* when used without a number; however, *somewhat* is only a good substitute when *some* modifies an adjective forming a comparison ("I feel *some* better today" or "I feel *somewhat* better today"). It is not a good idea to substitute *somewhat* for *some* automatically in many contexts ("The divorce forced me to mature *some*") because the resulting sentence would be awkward.

such   Some people disapprove of the use of *such* as a pronoun ("*such* was the result") ("have to sort out glass and newspapers and *such*"). All dictionaries, however, recognize it as standard.

that, which, who   In correct usage *that* refers to persons or things ("the man *that* I love," "reading the book *that* she wrote"), *which* refers chiefly to things ("a tree *which* bears apples"), and *who* refers chiefly to persons and sometimes to animals ("the man *who* has everything," "buried my cat, *who* died yesterday"). The notion that *that* should not be used to refer to persons is without foundation; such use is entirely standard.

Although some people say otherwise, *that* and *which* are both regularly used to introduce "restrictive clauses"—clauses that are essential to the description of the word they refer to ("the book *that* [*which*] you ordered is in"). Only *which* is used to introduce "nonrestrictive clauses"—clauses that are not essential to the meaning of the preceding word ("the door, which was painted pink, opened onto the garden").

transpire   Numerous critics have condemned the use of *transpire* to mean "to come to pass" or "occur" ("the events that *transpired* last night"); however, it is firmly established as standard English, in both informal and formal prose.

unique   Much hullabaloo is made of the use of *unique* with words of comparison ("somewhat *unique*," "very *unique*"); critics argue that either a thing is unique or it isn't. This objection is based on the mistaken assumption that there are only two senses of *unique:* "sole," and "unequaled." When *unique* is used in these senses it is not qualified. However, when it is used in its other meanings—"distinctively characteristic" ("a condition *unique* to dogs") or "unusual" ("a very *unique* work of art")—words of comparison and qualification are widespread and standard. This last use is common in advertising copy.

whom   *Whom* continues to flourish, though to many people it seems stilted or dated. It is used as the object of a verb or a preceding preposition ("for *whom* the bell tolls," "not sure *whom* he should hire") and sometimes as the object of a preposition that follows it ("the man *whom* you wrote to"). Uncertainty about whether to use *whom* or *who* has led to mistakenly careful usage ("*Whom* shall I say is calling?").

The following list consists of other frequently confused and misused words. Review the list periodically, and consult your dictionary about any that give you trouble.

access, excess
addition, edition
advice, advise
aesthetic, ascetic
allude, elude
altar, alter
alumnae, alumni
amend, emend
appraise, apprise
ascent, assent
aural, oral
bail, bale
band, banned
bare, bear
bazaar, bizarre
bloc, block
boarder, border
boom, boon
born, borne
brake, break
breadth, breath
bridal, bridle
buy, by
capital, capitol
cite, sight, site
coarse, course
commiserate, commensurate
complacent, complaisant
concert, consort
corespondent, correspondent
council, counsel
councillor, counselor
currant, current
decree, degree
defuse, diffuse
deluded, diluted
denote, donate
desert, dessert
device, devise
died, dyed
disassemble, dissemble
disburse, disperse
discreet, discrete
elicit, illicit
elusive, illusive
eminent, imminent
ethically, ethnically
extant, extend, extent
fair, fare
feat, feet
flair, flare
foreword, forward

foul, fowl
generic, genetic
genteel, gentile
gibe, jibe
guarantee, guaranty
hail, hale
hardy, hearty
healed, heeled
hear, here
hoard, horde
install, instill
jibe, jive
kibbutz, kibitz
lead, led
lean, lien
load, lode
loose, lose
median, medium
might, mite
ordinance, ordnance
pair, pare, pear
palate, pallet, palette
parish, perish
parlay, parley
peace, piece
pedal, peddle
personal, personnel
perspective, prospective, prospectus
pole, poll
pore, pour
portend, portent
pray, prey
preclude, prelude
premier, premiere
prescribe, proscribe
profit, prophet
purser, bursar
raise, raze
reality, realty
rebound, redound
reign, rein
right, rite
role, roll
sheaf, sheath
shear, sheer
stationary, stationery
tack, tact
tail, tale
taught, taut
their, there, they're
threw, through
to, too

toe, tow

track, tract

trooper, trouper

vial, vile

wail, whale

waive, wave

wrap, rap

wreak, wreck

Editing and Proofreading

Basic editing primarily requires checking a manuscript for grammar, spelling, punctuation, stylistic consistency, and factual accuracy, and may also involve moving or even rewriting entire sentences and paragraphs. Such basic editing is often called *copyediting*. Good copyediting requires a firm grasp of English style and usage and a strong sense of organizational logic.

Proofreading, in its narrow sense, is the late-stage correcting of material that has already been typeset—that is, professionally set in type by a typesetter, or compositor. The word means literally the reading and checking of *proofs*—copies of newly typeset material sent back from the typesetter to the editor for correction—against the original manuscript. But the term proofreading is generally used today to mean the final checking of *any* written material.

In the present era of word processors, laser printers, and sophisticated desktop publishing systems, when manuscript may be put in publishable form without leaving the office, the line between copyediting and proofreading has become blurred. However, there is still a distinction to be made between the initial editing done on any letter or manuscript and the final checking for errors in revised and re-keyboarded material.

Both copyediting and proofreading require that you have at hand a good desk dictionary. In addition, it can be very useful to have a style manual (this chapter and Chapters 7–9 should answer most style questions that will arise, but a style manual can help for some kinds of specialized questions), a thesaurus, and possibly other specialized reference books. If your company has its own style guide, the rules stated there must be followed.

The principal difference in marking between copyediting and proofreading is that in formal proofreading (that is, when checking typeset proofs) each error must be marked both where it occurs and in the margin immediately to the left or right. Whereas manuscript for copyediting is normally double-spaced, lines of typeset material are usually set close together, so only small marks can be made within the text. Thus, the margins provide room for larger marks and the insertion of omitted material; just as important, marginal notations make the corrections more visible so that the typesetter will not overlook them.

Figures 6.1, 6.2, and 6.3 show, respectively, a copyedited manuscript page, a table of proofreading marks, and a sheet of proof that has been proofread. (The number of errors in the proof is unrealistically high.) Most of the marks shown within the text area in Fig. 6.1 can be used equally for copyediting and for proofreading, but in formal proofreading each mark must be accompanied in the margin by the mark or notation shown there in the illustration.

When proofreading, move a ruler, an index card, or a blank sheet of paper slowly down the newly set page to keep your eye focused on each successive line, and use your finger to keep your place on the manuscript beside it. Read a few words at a time from the manuscript before immediately reading the same words on the new version or proof. Train yourself to read word by word, or even

Fig. 6.1   A Copyedited Page

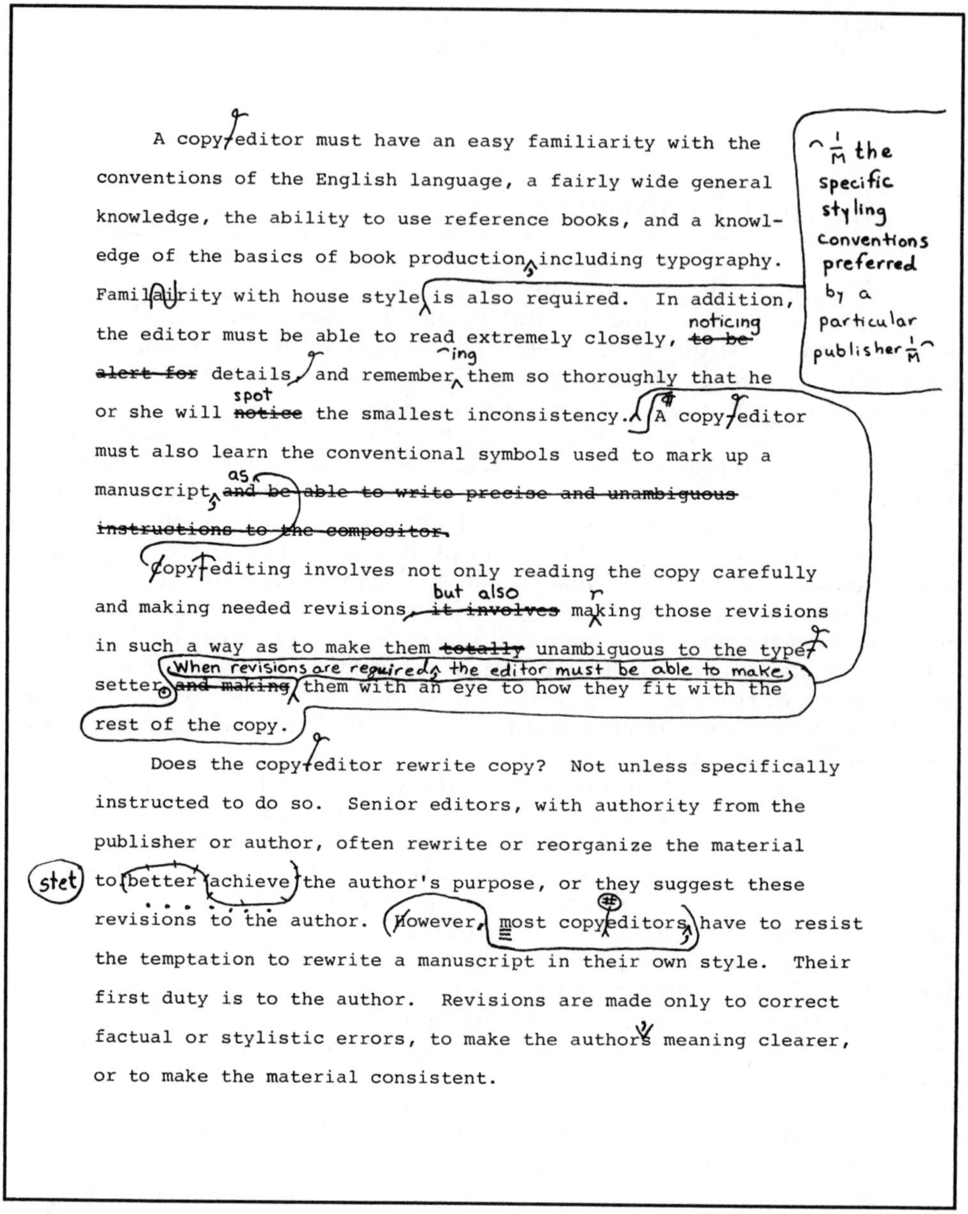

A copy editor must have an easy familiarity with the
conventions of the English language, a fairly wide general
knowledge, the ability to use reference books, and a knowledge of the basics of book production, including typography.
Familiarity with house style is also required. In addition,
the editor must be able to read extremely closely, ~~to be~~
~~alert for~~ details, and remember~ing them so thoroughly that he
or she will ~~notice~~ spot the smallest inconsistency. A copy editor
must also learn the conventional symbols used to mark up a
manuscript, as ~~and be able to write precise and unambiguous~~
~~instructions to the compositor.~~

Copyediting involves not only reading the copy carefully
and making needed revisions, ~~it involves~~ but also making those revisions
in such a way as to make them ~~totally~~ unambiguous to the typesetter, ~~and making~~ When revisions are required, the editor must be able to make
them with an eye to how they fit with the
rest of the copy.

Does the copy editor rewrite copy? Not unless specifically
instructed to do so. Senior editors, with authority from the
publisher or author, often rewrite or reorganize the material
to better achieve the author's purpose, or they suggest these
revisions to the author. However, most copyeditors have to resist
the temptation to rewrite a manuscript in their own style. Their
first duty is to the author. Revisions are made only to correct
factual or stylistic errors, to make the author's meaning clearer,
or to make the material consistent.

[Marginal insertion:] ^ the specific styling conventions preferred by a particular publisher

[Marginal mark:] stet

Fig. 6.2   Proofreaders' Marks

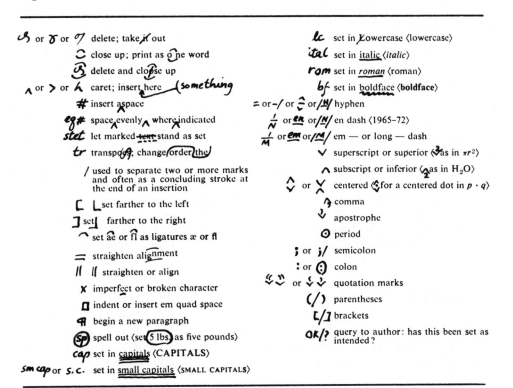

Fig. 6.3   A Proofread Page

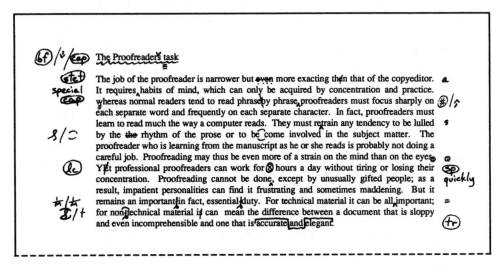

character by character. Otherwise, you will fail to notice omitted words and letters, transposed words and letters, and misspellings in general, since you will tend to unconsciously "correct" them as you read.

After proofreading the printed matter against the original manuscript, go back and reread the later version all by itself for its content as if you were its intended recipient. You may discover important errors, omissions, or repetitions that you missed when doing your more "mechanical" proofreading.

Though word processing has facilitated writing in many ways, it has also facilitated the making of certain kinds of errors. In word-processed manuscripts, be especially alert for unintentional deletions, symbols introduced accidentally, italic and boldface type that runs on past where it should have ended, punctuation that has improperly "wrapped" onto a new line, and material that was not properly deleted at its original location after being moved or after new material was substituted.

There is word-processing software available that offers a variety of grammar- and style-checking features. No software can substitute for human editorial judgment, however, and the problems in existing software are such that you may well be better off without it. The following checklists may be useful as reminders for the copyeditor and proofreader.

COPYEDITING

For the sake of achieving consistency in large manuscripts, consider creating a *style sheet*. A style sheet is primarily an alphabetical list of words and terms that occur in the manuscript for which you have adopted a particular spelling or style. It should also include any special punctuation and capitalization rules, rules for the styling of numbers, etc.

- Check the organization of the document. If there are headings and subheadings, they should by themselves form a coherent outline of the contents.
- Make sure the paragraphing is logical.
- Check the spelling of every word about which you are not absolutely certain.
- Be alert to errors involving similar words (e.g., *it/if/is*) and homophones (*hear/here*).
- Check all proper names. This can be a sensitive area, and errors can slip through very easily.
- Check that list entries are grammatically parallel.
- Check for noun/verb agreement.
- Check all number sequences, particularly numbered lists and numbered footnotes.
- Check *and recheck* any other numbers that are used—they may be extremely important. It may be wise to check any mathematical calculations using a calculator.
- Be sure that all dates are correct.
- Check that all alphabetical lists are in proper alphabetical order.
- Be sure that all punctuation is in place and consistent. Be especially alert to paired punctuation marks—parentheses, quotation marks, dashes, brackets, etc.
- Be sure that capitalization is consistent, particularly in headings, in unusual terms, and in lists and tables.
- Check all bibliographical references for consistency and accuracy.

PROOFREADING

- Check that all headings and other separate elements are consistent in style and properly positioned.
- In letters, check especially that the dateline, reference line, initials, enclosure line, and carbon-copy notation have been included.
- Check that the table of contents is accurate as to both titles and page numbers.
- Check all cross-references.
- Check that all margins are proper.
- Check tables for horizontal and vertical alignment.
- Check that no footnotes have been omitted.
- Check all end-of-line word divisions. (Refer to your dictionary for division points.)
- Be alert for unintentional repetition of small words (*and and, the the,* etc.).
- Check that page numbers are correct. Check all running heads (headers) or running feet (footers).
- Check all headings and captions separately.
- When checking material on which the typesetter has made corrections you have requested, read each corrected line and those above and below against the original.

CHAPTER 7

Business Letter Styles and Formats

This chapter focuses on questions of letter format, the spacing and punctuation patterns that apply specifically to letter-writing, and on the etiquette of letter-writing. For more on punctuation, capitalization, and other mechanics of writing and on grammar and usage, see Chapter 6, "A Guide to Business English."

Business letter styles have changed over the years, and they continue to do so. For example, the open-punctuation pattern and the Simplified Letter have recently gained wide popularity, while the closed-punctuation pattern and the Indented Letter, once considered standard formats, are now little used in the United States. However, writers still have several alternatives available to them. This chapter presents and describes the existing alternative styles. Where there are reasons to prefer one over another, the reasons are explained; however, the choice will often be a question of individual taste, and you may sometimes have to make your own choice among the acceptable styles.

All of the elements of business letter style come together to produce a reflection on paper not only of the writer's ability and knowledge and the typist's competence but also of an organization's total image. Well-prepared business letters reflect a firm's pride and its concern for quality, whereas poorly prepared correspondence can create such a negative impression on its recipients that they may have second thoughts about pursuing business with the firm. This is a special consideration for small businesses. The business letter, then, is actually an indicator of overall organizational style, regardless of the size of the firm. Thus, the impression created by clearly written, logically ordered, and attractively and accurately typed letters can be a crucial factor in the success of any business.

A businessperson may devote more than 50 percent of the workday to correspondence. This includes conceiving the tone and content of outgoing letters and reading and acting on incoming letters. Secretaries spend an even higher proportion of their time on correspondence. And all this time costs money. However, the time and money will have been well spent if both writer and typist keep in mind the following general rules:

1. The stationery should be of high-quality paper with excellent correcting or erasing properties.
2. The typing or keyboarding should be neat and accurate, and any corrections or erasures should be rendered invisible.
3. The elements of the letter (dateline, inside address, message, signature block) should conform in placement and format with one of the generally accepted business letter styles (such as the Simplified, the Block, the Modified Block, or the Modified Semi-block Letter).
4. The language should be clear, concise, grammatically correct, and devoid of padding and clichés.
5. The ideas should be logically presented, and the writer should always keep in mind the reader's reaction.
6. All statistical data should be accurate and complete.
7. All names should be checked for accuracy of spelling and style.

NOTE: Throughout this chapter, wherever lines of type are counted ("six lines from the top," "two lines below," etc.), the number refers to the number of times you must press the Return (or Enter) key. Thus, the number of *blank* lines will always be one less than the number specified.

Paper Selection

Paper and envelope size, quality, and basis weight vary according to application. The table on page 246 lists various paper and envelope sizes along with their uses.

Good-quality paper is essential to the production of attractive, effective letters. Paper with rag content is considerably more expensive than sulfite bond papers; nevertheless, many firms use rag-content paper because it suggests the merit and stature of the company. Since the cost of paper has been estimated at less than five percent of the total cost of the average business letter, it is easy to understand why some companies consider high-quality paper to be worth the added expense—at least for certain types of correspondence. In choosing a good grade of paper, look for paper that meets the following standards:

1. The paper should withstand corrections and erasures without pitting, buckling, or tearing.
2. It should accept even and clear typed characters.
3. It should permit smooth written signatures.
4. It should perform well with carbons and in copying machines.
5. It should withstand storage and repeated handling and retain its color well.
6. It should fold easily without cracking or rippling.
7. It should hold typeset letterhead without bleed-through.

Stationery and Envelope Sizes and Applications

Stationery	Stationery size	Application	Envelope	Envelope size
Standard	8½″ × 11″ *also* 8″ × 10½″	general business correspondence	*commercial* No. 6¾ No. 9 No. 10	3⅝″ × 6½″ 3⅞″ × 8⅞″ 4⅛″ × 9½″
			window No. 6¾ No. 9 No. 10	3⅝″ × 6½″ 3⅞″ × 8⅞″ 4⅛″ × 9½″
			airmail No. 6¾ No. 10	3⅝″ × 6½″ 4⅛″ × 9½″
Executive *or* Monarch	7¼″ × 10½″ *or* 7½″ × 10″	high-level officers' correspondence	*regular* *window*	3⅞″ × 7½″ 3⅞″ × 7½″
Half-sheet *or* Baronial	5½″ × 8½″	extremely brief notes	*regular*	3⅝″ × 6½″

An important characteristic of paper is its fiber direction or grain. Paper grain should be parallel to the direction of the typewritten lines, thus providing a smooth surface for clear and even characters and an easy erasing or correcting surface. Every sheet of paper has a *felt* side, or top side, from which a watermark may be read; the letterhead should be printed or engraved on this side.

The weight of the paper must also be considered when ordering stationery supplies. *Basis weight,* also called *substance number,* is the weight in pounds of a ream of paper cut to a basic size. Basis 24 is the heaviest for stationery; basis 13 is the lightest. The table below illustrates various paper weights according to their specific uses in the office.

Weights of Letter Papers and Envelopes for Specific Applications

Application	Basis weight
Standard (for corporate correspondence)	24 *or* 20
Executive	24 *or* 20
Airmail (for overseas correspondence)	13
Branch-office *or* Salesmen's stationery	20 *or* 16
Form letters	20 *or* 24
Half-sheets	24 *or* 20

In some offices, carbon copies are still made. The paper used for carbon copies is lighter in weight and is available as inexpensive *manifold* paper, a stronger and more expensive *onionskin,* or a lightweight letterhead with the word COPY printed on it.

Continuation sheets and envelopes must match the letterhead sheet in color, basis weight, texture, size, and quality. Therefore, they should be ordered along with the letterhead to ensure a good match.

Letterhead and continuation sheets as well as envelopes should be stored in their original boxes to prevent soiling. A small supply of these materials may be kept in your drawer or near your printer, but it should be arranged carefully so as to protect the materials from wear and tear.

Letter Balance and Letterhead Design

It has often been said that an attractive letter should look like a symmetrically framed picture, with even margins working as a frame for the typed lines, which should be balanced under the letterhead. Many word processors and word-processing packages have functions—such as Print Preview—that can help you prepare letters that are properly spaced and pleasing to the eye. However, regardless of the kind of equipment available to you, the following steps will help you create letters with the desired appearance:

1. Estimate the number of words in the letter or the general length of the message by looking over the writer's rough draft or your own shorthand notes, or by checking the length of a dictated source.
2. Make mental notes of any long quotations, tabular data, long lists, or footnotes, as well as scientific names and formulas that may require margin adjustments, a different typeface, or even handwork within the message.
3. Set the left and right margins according to the estimated letter length: about 1″ for long letters (300 words or more, or at least two pages), about 1½″ for medium-length ones (about 100–300 words), and about 2″ for short ones (100 words or less). Some offices, however, use a standard 6″ typing line for all letters on full-size stationery, regardless of length, because it eliminates the need to reset margins.
4. Remember that the closing parts of a letter take 10–12 lines (2″) or more and that the bottom margin should be at least six lines (1″).
5. Single-space within paragraphs; double-space between paragraphs. Very short letters (up to three sentences) may be double-spaced throughout.
6. Set the margins of any continuation sheets to match those of the first sheet, and carry over at least three lines of the message to the continuation sheet.

Short letters may be typed or printed on half-sheets, on Executive-size stationery, or on full-size stationery with wide margins. Very short letters typed on full-size stationery may create spacing problems. There are three simple ways to handle the extra space:

1. Use the 6″ line but increase the space between the date and the inside address, between the complimentary close and the signature, and between the signature and the transcriber's initials or enclosure notations.
2. Use the 6″ line but double-space. Double-spacing should be used only in very short letters (about six lines or less, or up to three sentences). If a double-spaced letter contains more than one paragraph, indent the paragraph openings.
3. Use a 4″ or 5″ typing line.

LETTERHEAD DESIGN

Letterhead designs vary. Some letterheads are centered at the top of the page, others extend across the top from the left to the right margin, and still others are positioned to the right or left of center. Sometimes a company's name and logo appear at the top of the page and its address and other data at the bottom.

Regardless of layout and design, a typical business letterhead contains some or all of the following elements, including at least items 2, 3, 6, and 7.

1. Logo
2. Full name of the organization
3. Full street address
4. Suite, room, or building number
5. Post-office box number
6. City, state, and ZIP code
7. Telephone number(s), and fax number, if applicable
8. Other data (such as telex or cable references, branch offices, or products or services offered)

The names of particular departments, plants, groups, or divisions may be printed on the letterhead of extremely large or diversified companies or institutions. Large law firms may have the names of their partners and staff attorneys all listed on the letterhead. Elaborate letterhead layouts require especially careful letter planning to avoid an unbalanced look. For example, a letterhead with a long list of names on the left side might be best balanced by use of the Modified Block Letter, where the date, reference numbers, and signature appear on the right side of the page.

High corporate officers frequently use a personalized or executive letterhead. Here the standard company letterhead design is supplemented with the name of the office (such as "Office of the President") or with the full name and business title of the officer (such as "John M. Dennehy, Jr., President") printed or engraved in small letters one or two lines beneath the letterhead at or near the left margin. The officer's business title may appear on the same line as his or her name if space permits and if both name and title are short, or it may be blocked directly below the name. For executive stationery, the letterhead is often not printed but instead engraved on a better grade of paper than that of the standard company stationery. Executive stationery is also smaller than the standard, as shown in the table on page 246. Envelopes should match the paper and should be printed with the executive's name and return address.

If your organization does not have letterhead stationery, you can create a typewritten letterhead. The letterhead you create can include all of the elements found in printed letterhead except for the logo. As in printed letterhead, the essential items are (1) the full name of the company, institution, or group; (2) the full street address; (3) the city, state, and ZIP code; and (4) the telephone and fax numbers. The elements are centered, each on its own line. See Fig. 7.1.

For your own personal correspondence, a letterhead is not required. A three-

Fig. 7.1 Typewritten Letterhead

BELLOWS FALLS HISTORICAL ASSOCIATION
320 Sycamore Street
Bellows Falls, VT 05101

(215) 555-7654

line heading replaces the letterhead: the street address or post-office box number appears on line 1, the city, state, and ZIP code on line 2, and the date on line 3. The heading may be positioned about six lines from the top of the sheet to achieve a good balance, with the longest line flush with the right margin.

Standard Punctuation Patterns

The choice of punctuation pattern, like the choice of letterhead design, is usually determined by the organization. However, it is important that specific punctuation patterns be used with particular letter styles and that these patterns be adhered to for the sake of consistency and speed. The two most common patterns are *open punctuation* and *mixed punctuation*. These patterns have all but totally replaced the older and more complex *closed punctuation* requiring a terminal mark at the end of each element of a business letter.

OPEN-PUNCTUATION PATTERN

Letters using the open-punctuation pattern (see Fig. 7.2) exhibit the following characteristics:

1. The end of the dateline is unpunctuated, although the comma between day and year is retained.
2. The ends of the lines of the inside address are unpunctuated (unless a punctuated abbreviation such as *Inc.* ends a line).
3. The salutation, if used, is unpunctuated.
4. The complimentary close, if used, is unpunctuated.
5. The ends of the signature block lines are unpunctuated.

This pattern is always used with the Simplified Letter (see Fig. 7.27) and is often used with the Block Letter (see Fig. 7.28).

Fig. 7.2   Open-Punctuation Pattern

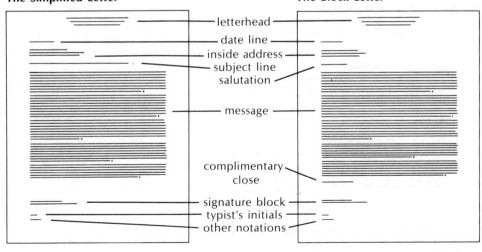

The Simplified Letter   The Block Letter

MIXED-PUNCTUATION PATTERN

Letters using the mixed-punctuation pattern (see Fig. 7.3) exhibit the following characteristics:

1. The end of the dateline is unpunctuated, although the comma between the day and year is retained.
2. The ends of the lines of the inside address are unpunctuated (unless an abbreviation such as *Inc.* ends a line).
3. The salutation ends with a colon.
4. The complimentary close ends with a comma.
5. The end(s) of the signature block line(s) are unpunctuated.

This pattern is used with the Block, the Modified Block, and the Modified Semi-block Letters. (See Figs. 7.28, 7.29, and 7.30.)

Fig. 7.3   Mixed-Punctuation Pattern Illustrated in Three Letter Stylings

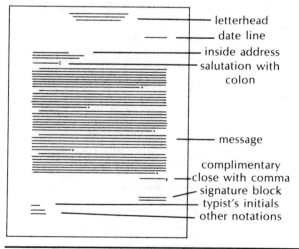

The Block Letter

The Modified Block Letter

— letterhead
— date line
— inside address
— salutation with colon
— message
complimentary close with comma
— signature block
— typist's initials
— other notations

The Modified Semi-block Letter

— letterhead
— date line
— inside address
— salutation with colon
— message
complimentary close with comma
— signature block
— typist's initials
— other notations

CLOSED-PUNCTUATION PATTERN

Although the closed-punctuation pattern is rarely used in the United States today, it is still employed in Europe. This pattern exhibits the following characteristics:

1. The dateline ends with a period.
2. Each line of the inside address ends with a comma, except the last, which ends with a period.
3. The salutation ends with a comma.
4. The complimentary close ends with a comma.
5. Each line of the signature block ends with a comma, except the last, which ends with a period.

This pattern is used chiefly with the Indented Letter. Figure 7.4 provides the only description given in this book of the Indented Letter, which is shown here only because it may occasionally be encountered, especially in foreign correspondence.

Fig. 7.4   Closed-Punctuation Pattern with the Indented Letter

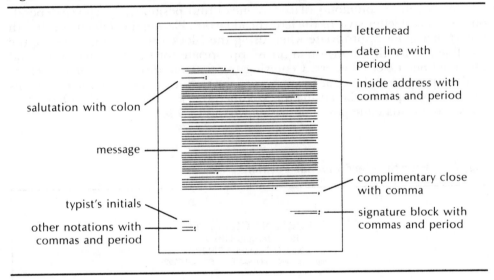

salutation with colon

message

typist's initials

other notations with commas and period

letterhead

date line with period

inside address with commas and period

complimentary close with comma

signature block with commas and period

The Parts of a Business Letter

The various elements of a business letter are listed below in order. Those items with an asterisk are essential elements of any letter regardless of its style; the rest may or may not be included, depending on the style being used and the nature of the letter itself.

*Dateline	Attention line	*Signature block
Reference line	Salutation	Identification initials
Special mailing notations	Subject line	Enclosure notation
On-arrival notations	*Message	Copy notation
*Inside address	Complimentary close	Postscript

Many businesses establish standard letter formats in order to save time, and these company standards should always be followed. However, certain applications of these letter elements will still require an individual decision by the secretary.

DATELINE

The dateline may be typed two to six lines below the last line of the printed letterhead; three lines is recommended as a standard for most letters. Some office manuals specify a *fixed dateline* positioned three lines below the letterhead; extra space can then simply be added as needed below the dateline and elsewhere on the page. Other offices prefer to use a *floating dateline,* which may be typed two to six lines below the letterhead, depending on the letter length, space available, and letterhead design.

The dateline consists of the month, the day, and the year (January 1, 19—), all on one line. Ordinals (1st, 2d, 24th, etc.) should not be used, and the months should not be represented with abbreviations or numerals. However, the day and the month may be reversed and the comma dropped (1 January 19—) in U.S. government correspondence or in British correspondence. The dateline should never overrun the margin.

The dateline is commonly placed in one of four positions; the choice depends on the general letter style or the letterhead layout. Placing the dateline flush with the *left* margin is appropriate when using the Block Letter format. Placing the dateline flush with the *right* margin is appropriate for the Modified Block and Modified Semi-block Letters. Centering the dateline directly under the letterhead or positioning it about five spaces to the right of center are other positions that are appropriate when using the Modified Block or Modified Semi-block formats. All four dateline positions are shown in Fig. 7.5.

Fig. 7.5 Four Standard Dateline Positions

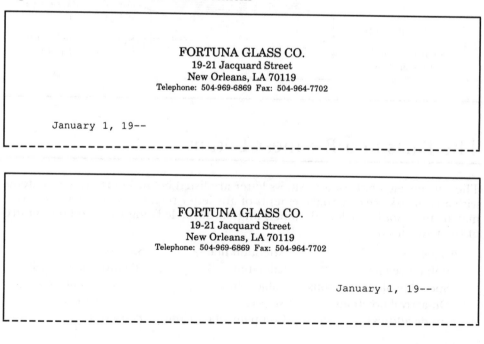

```
                    FORTUNA GLASS CO.
                    19-21 Jacquard Street
                    New Orleans, LA 70119
               Telephone: 504-969-6869  Fax: 504-964-7702




                    January 1, 19--
```

```
                    FORTUNA GLASS CO.
                    19-21 Jacquard Street
                    New Orleans, LA 70119
               Telephone: 504-969-6869  Fax: 504-964-7702




                                  January 1, 19--
```

REFERENCE LINE

A numerical reference line—consisting of a file, correspondence, control, order, invoice, or policy number—is included in a letter when the addressee has specifically requested that correspondence on a subject contain such a line, or when it is needed for your own filing. It may be centered and typed one to four lines below the date; some offices require that it be typed on the line directly above or below the date to make it less conspicuous. In the Block Letter, the reference line should be aligned flush left. In the Modified Block and Modified Semi-block Letters, it may be centered on the page or blocked left or right under or above the dateline (see Fig. 7.6).

Reference line blocked left	*Reference line blocked right*
January 1, 19—	January 1, 19—
X-123-4	X-123-4
or	*or*
X-123-4	X-123-4
January 1, 19—	January 1, 19—

Fig. 7.6 Reference Number Blocked with Dateline to Right of Center, and Centered on Page Four Lines Beneath Dateline

```
                    FORTUNA GLASS CO.
                    19-21 Jacquard Street
                    New Orleans, LA 70119
               Telephone: 504-969-6869  Fax: 504-964-7702



                              January 1, 19--
                              X-123-4
```

FORTUNA GLASS CO.
19-21 Jacquard Street
New Orleans, LA 70119
Telephone: 504-969-6869 Fax: 504-964-7702

January 1, 19--

Your ref: X-123-4

- -

A reference line on the first sheet must be carried over to the continuation sheets. The style of the dateline and reference line on a continuation sheet should match the style used on the first page. For example, if the reference line appears on a line below the date on the first sheet, it should be typed there on the continuation sheet. The following example illustrates a continuation-sheet reference line as used in the Simplified or Block Letter.

Mr. Carlton B. Jones
January 1, 19—
X-123-4
Page 2

The next example illustrates the positioning of a reference line on the continuation sheet of a Modified Block or Modified Semi-block Letter.

Mr. Carlton B. Jones   -2-   January 1, 19—
                                                                 X-123-4

See Figs. 7.14 and 7.15 for continuation-sheet facsimiles.

SPECIAL MAILING NOTATIONS

If a letter is to be sent by any method other than by regular mail, that fact may be indicated on the letter itself as well as on the envelope (see pages 284–91 for details on envelope style). The all-capitalized special mailing notation, such as CERTIFIED MAIL, SPECIAL DELIVERY, or AIRMAIL (for foreign mail only), in all letter styles is aligned flush left about four lines below the line on which the date appears, and about two lines above the first line of the inside address (see Fig. 7.7). While some organizations prefer that these notations appear on the original and on all copies, others prefer that they be typed only on the original. And many omit these notations no matter how the letter is mailed.

Vertical spacing (such as between the dateline and the special mailing notation) may vary with letter length, more space being left for short or medium-length letters.

ON-ARRIVAL NOTATIONS

The on-arrival notations that may be included on the letter itself are PERSONAL and CONFIDENTIAL. The first indicates that the letter may be opened and read only by its addressee; the second indicates that the letter may also be opened and read by any other persons authorized to view such material. These all-capitalized notations are usually positioned four lines below the date-

Fig. 7.7   Special Mailing Notation in Relation to Inside Address and Dateline

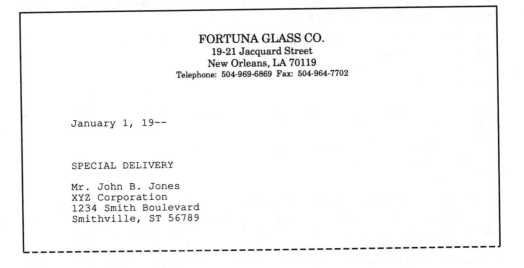

```
                        FORTUNA GLASS CO.
                        19-21 Jacquard Street
                        New Orleans, LA 70119
                   Telephone: 504-969-6869 Fax: 504-964-7702




   January 1, 19--


   SPECIAL DELIVERY

   Mr. John B. Jones
   XYZ Corporation
   1234 Smith Boulevard
   Smithville, ST 56789
```

line and usually two but not more than four lines above the first line of the inside address. They are blocked flush left in all letter styles. If a special mailing notation has been used, the on-arrival notation is blocked one line beneath it. See Fig. 7.8. Spacing between the dateline and the on-arrival notation may be increased to as much as six lines if the letter is extremely brief.

If either PERSONAL or CONFIDENTIAL appears on the letter, it must also appear on the envelope (see pages 284–91 for envelope style).

Fig. 7.8   On-Arrival Notation Position

```
                        FORTUNA GLASS CO.
                        19-21 Jacquard Street
                        New Orleans, LA 70119
                   Telephone: 504-969-6869 Fax: 504-964-7702




   January 1, 19--



   CERTIFIED MAIL
   CONFIDENTIAL

   Ms. Mary T. Dow
   Comptroller
   XYZ Corporation
   1234 Smith Boulevard
   Smithville, ST 56789
```

INSIDE ADDRESS

An inside address typically includes the following elements if the letter is directed to a particular individual:

1. Addressee's courtesy title and full name
2. Addressee's business title, if required
3. Full name of addressee's business affiliation
4. Full address

If the letter is addressed to an organization in general, the inside address typically includes the following elements:

1. Full name of the organization
2. Department name, if required
3. Full address

The inside address is placed about three to eight lines below the date. The inside address in the Simplified Letter is typed three lines below the date. The placement of the inside address in relation to the date may vary according to letter length or organization policy. The inside address is always single-spaced internally. In most of the letters discussed in this book, the inside address is blocked flush with the left margin, as in Fig. 7.9. See pages 274–84 for full-page views.

Fig. 7.9   Inside-Address Style Used with the Block Letter

FORTUNA GLASS CO.
19-21 Jacquard Street
New Orleans, LA 70119
Telephone: 504-969-6869 Fax: 504-964-7702

January 1, 19--

Mr. Joseph R. Rowe
Treasurer
XYZ Corporation
1234 Smith Boulevard
Smithville, ST 56789

A courtesy title (such as *Mr., Ms., Mrs., Miss, Dr.,* or *The Honorable*) precedes the addressee's full name, even if a business or professional title (such as *Treasurer* or *Chief of Staff*) follows the surname. No courtesy title, however, should ever precede the name when *Esquire* or an abbreviation for a degree follows the name.

Before typing the addressee's name, refer to the signature block of previous correspondence from that person to confirm its exact spelling and style. This may also be obtained from printed executive letterhead. A business or professional title, if included, should also match the title used in previous correspondence or in official literature (such as an annual report or a business directory). If an individual holds more than one office (such as Vice President and General Manager) within an organization, the title shown in the signature block of previous correspondence should be copied, or the title of the individual's highest office (in this case, Vice President) may be selected. Business and professional titles should not be abbreviated. If a title is so long that it might overrun the center of the page, it may be typed on two lines with the second line indented two spaces:

Mr. John P. Hemphill, Jr.
Vice President and Director
  of Research and Development

Special attention should be paid to the spelling, punctuation, and official abbreviations of company names. Note, for example, whether an ampersand (&) is used for the word *and*, whether series of names are separated by commas, and whether the word *Company* is spelled in full or abbreviated.

The addressee's title may be placed on the same line as the name, separated by a comma. Alternatively, the title may be put on the second line either by itself or followed by a comma and the name of the organization. Choose a style that will enhance and not detract from the total balance of the letter on the page. The following are acceptable inside-address styles for business and professional titles:

Mr. Arthur O. Brown
News Director
Radio Station WXYZ
1234 Peters Street
Jonesville, ZZ 56789

Dr. Joyce A. Cavitt, Dean
School of Business and Finance
Stateville University
Stateville, ST 98765

Ms. Anna B. Kim, Director
Apex Community Theater
67 Smith Street
North Bend, XX 12345

Mrs. Juanita Casares
President, C & A Realty
Johnson Beach, ZZ 56789

If an individual addressee's name is unknown or irrelevant and the writer wishes to direct a letter to an organization in general or to a unit within that organization, the organization name is put on line 1 of the inside address, followed on line 2 by the name of a specific department, if required.

XYZ Corporation
Consumer Products Division
1234 Smith Boulevard
Smithville, ST 56789

On the other hand, if the addressee's address is unknown and the writer wishes to send a letter in care of a third party, the phrase *In care of* (or *c/o*) is used on line 2 before the name of the third party. (The percentage sign, %, should not be used in formal correspondence as a shortcut symbol for *c/o*).

Street addresses should be typed in full and not abbreviated unless window envelopes are being used. Numerals are used for all building, house, apartment, room, and suite numbers except for *One,* which is written out.

One Bayside Drive   6 Link Road   1436 Fremont Avenue

Numbered street names from *First* through *Twelfth* are usually written out; numerals are usually used for all numbered street names above *Twelfth.*

167 West Second Avenue   One East Ninth Street   19 South 22nd Street

An alternative, more formal convention calls for writing out all numbered streets up to and including *One Hundredth.*

    122 East Forty-second Street   36 East Fiftieth Street

An apartment, building, room, or suite number, if required, follows the street address on the same line with a comma separating the two.

    62 Park Towers, Suite 9   Rosemont Plaza Apartments, Apt. 117

Note that neither the word *Number* nor its abbreviation *No.* is used between the words *Suite, Apartment,* or *Building* and a following numeral.

Names of cities (except those including the word *Saint,* such as *St. Louis* or *St. Paul*) should be typed out in full (e.g., *Fort Wayne, Mount Prospect*). The name of the city is followed by a comma, the name of the state, and the ZIP code. Names of states (except for the District of Columbia, which is always written *DC* or *D.C.*) may or may not be abbreviated. If a window envelope is being used, the all-capitalized, unpunctuated two-letter Postal Service abbreviation, followed by one space and the ZIP code, should be used. If a regular envelope is being used, the name of the state may be typed out in full or the two-letter Postal Service abbreviation may be used; whether abbreviated or not, the state name is followed by one space and the ZIP code. Most firms now use the two-letter Postal Service abbreviations on all inside and envelope addresses. See page 286 for a list of these abbreviations.

An inside address should comprise no more than five lines. No line should overrun the center of the page; lengthy organization names, like lengthy business titles, may be carried over to a second line and indented two spaces from the left margin.

Sometimes a single letter will have to be sent to two persons at different addresses, both of whom should receive an original. In these cases, the inside address should consist of two complete names and addresses separated by a line of space. The names should be in alphabetical order unless one person is obviously more important than the other. For salutations used in letters to multiple addressees, see page 305.

For information about foreign addresses, see pages 287–88.

ATTENTION LINE

If the writer wishes to address a letter to an organization in general but bring it to the attention of a particular individual, an attention line may be typed two lines below the last line of the inside address and two lines above the salutation if there is one. The attention line is usually blocked flush with the left margin; however, some organizations prefer that it be centered on the page. This placement is acceptable in all letters except the Simplified and the Block, in which the attention line must be blocked flush left. This line should be neither underlined nor entirely capitalized. The word *Attention* is not abbreviated. A colon after the word *Attention* is optional unless the open-punctuation pattern is being followed throughout the letter, in which case the colon should be omitted:

    Attention Mr. James Chang   Attention: Mr. James Chang

Even though the attention line routes the letter to a particular person, such a letter is still considered to be written to the organization, so a collective-noun salutation should be used. (See Fig. 7.10.)

Fig. 7.10   Page Placement of an Attention Line in a Block Letter with Open Punctuation

```
                        FORTUNA GLASS CO.
                         19-21 Jacquard Street
                         New Orleans, LA 70119
                   Telephone: 504-969-6869 Fax: 504-964-7702



    January 1, 19--


    XYZ Corporation
    Advertising Department
    1234 Smith Boulevard
    Smithville, ST 56789

    Attention Mr. Jon R. Lee

    Ladies and Gentlemen
```

SALUTATION

The salutation—used with all letter styles except the Simplified—is typed flush with the left margin, two lines beneath the last line of the inside address or two lines below the attention line, if any. Additional space may be added after the inside address of a short letter that is to be enclosed in a window envelope. If the mixed-punctuation pattern is being followed, the salutation is followed by a colon; if open punctuation is being observed, the salutation is unpunctuated. Only in informal personal correspondence is the salutation followed by a comma.

One of the most frequently asked questions today is what salutation to use when addressing an organization or when addressing a person whose name and gender are unknown to the letter-writer. Unfortunately, there are no universally accepted forms to use in these situations. Traditionally the salutation "Dear Sir" has been used when the addressee is a particular individual, and "Gentlemen" has been used when the addressee is an organization or a group of people within it. However, as it has become more and more likely that the recipient may be a woman, many writers have looked for more appropriate salutations. Most have adopted "Dear Sir or Madam" and "Ladies and Gentlemen" as substitutes for "Dear Sir" and "Gentlemen" respectively. Some have used "Dear People," "Dear Person," and "Dear Sir, Madam, or Ms."; however, there is little evidence that these forms are catching on.

The salutation "To whom it may concern" is another way to begin such a letter; however, it is extremely impersonal and is usually used only when the writer is unfamiliar with both the person and the organization that is being addressed, such as when one is addressing a letter of recommendation.

A different type of salutation now being used to solve the problem of addressing a company or a company officer whose name and sex are unknown simply addresses the company ("Dear XYZ Company") or the title or department of the intended recipient ("Dear Personnel Supervisor," "Dear Personnel Department," "Dear XYZ Engineers"). The use of this type of salutation has increased markedly in the past several years.

Occasionally a letter-writer is faced with an addressee's name that gives no clue as to the addressee's sex. Traditionally in these uncertain cases, convention has required the writer to use the masculine courtesy title in the salutation; for example, "Dear Mr. Lee Schmidtke," "Dear Mr. T. A. Gagnon." However, most writers now prefer to express their uncertainty by using such forms as "Dear Mr. or Ms. Schmidtke" and "Dear Lee Schmidtke."

The most convenient way of avoiding the problem of gender is to use the Simplified Letter style (see Fig. 7.27), which eliminates the salutation altogether.

The salutation for a married couple may be written in one of the following ways:

Dear Mr. and Mrs. Hathaway
Dear Dr. and Mrs. Simpson
Dear Dr. and Mr. Singh

For more information about choosing appropriate salutations, including salutations for two or more persons and for people with specialized titles, see pages 291–312.

SUBJECT LINE

A subject line gives the gist of a letter. It must be succinct and should not require more than one line. The subject line serves as an immediate point of reference for the reader as well as a convenient filing aid for the secretaries at both ends of the correspondence.

In the Simplified Letter, which does not include a salutation, the subject line (an essential element) is positioned flush left, three lines below the last line of the inside address. It may be entirely capitalized and not underlined, or the main words may begin with capital letters and every word be underlined. See Fig. 7.11.

If a subject line is included in a letter with a salutation, it is frequently positioned flush left, two lines beneath the salutation, and may be entirely capitalized. See Fig. 7.12. In the Modified Block and Modified Semi-block styles, however, the subject line may be centered or even indented to match the indention of the paragraphs.

Legal correspondence uses the subject line in a variety of positions. Legal correspondence based on letter styles other than the Simplified or Block sometimes centers the subject line and occasionally positions it at the right. A growing number of law offices prefer to position the subject line two lines above the salutation rather than below it.

The subject line may be entirely capitalized, and the word *Subject* may be used to introduce the line. If so, the subject line may also be capitalized headline-style, in which the initial letter of the first word and the initial letter of all other words except coordinating conjunctions, articles, and short prepositions are capitalized. The word *Reference* or its abbreviation, *Re*, are sometimes also used.

SUBJECT: CHANGES IN TRAFFIC ROUTE
Subject: Changes in Traffic Route
Reference: Changes in Traffic Route
Re: Changes in Traffic Route

Fig. 7.11   Page Placement of the Subject Line in the Simplified Letter

```
                        FORTUNA GLASS CO.
                         19-21 Jacquard Street
                         New Orleans, LA 70119
                    Telephone: 504-969-6869  Fax: 504-964-7702




     January 1, 19--


     XYZ Corporation
     1234 Smith Boulevard
     Smithville, ST 56789


     NEW LETTER FORMAT


     We would like to introduce the Simplified Letter to the
     secretaries of XYZ Corporation.  The advantages of this
     new letter format are ....
```

Fig. 7.12   Page Placement of the Subject Line in a Block Letter with Open Punctuation

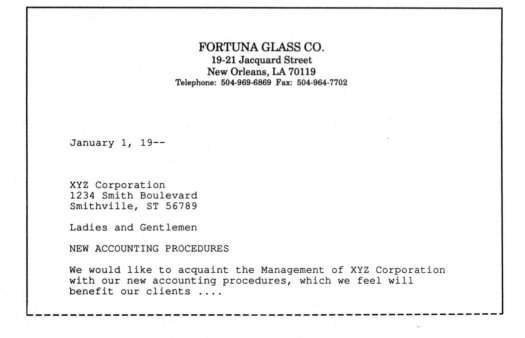

```
                        FORTUNA GLASS CO.
                         19-21 Jacquard Street
                         New Orleans, LA 70119
                    Telephone: 504-969-6869  Fax: 504-964-7702




     January 1, 19--


     XYZ Corporation
     1234 Smith Boulevard
     Smithville, ST 56789

     Ladies and Gentlemen

     NEW ACCOUNTING PROCEDURES

     We would like to acquaint the Management of XYZ Corporation
     with our new accounting procedures, which we feel will
     benefit our clients ....
```

The heading *In re* is now seldom used for general office letters; however, it is often used in legal correspondence. Headings should not be used if you are following the Simplified Letter style.

The subject line should not be confused with the reference line (see pages 253–54), even though the subject line often begins with the word *Reference*. They differ not only in position but also in appearance and purpose: the reference line indicates a numerical classification, whereas the subject line identifies the content of the letter.

MESSAGE

The body of the letter—the message—should begin two lines below either the salutation or the subject line, if there is one, except in the Simplified Letter, where the message is typed three lines below the subject line.

Paragraphs are single-spaced internally. Double-spacing is used to separate paragraphs. If a letter is extremely brief, it may be double-spaced throughout, with indented paragraphs.

The first lines of indented paragraphs (as in the Modified Semi-block Letter) should begin five or 10 spaces from the left margin; five spaces is most common. All other letter styles require flush-left paragraph alignment.

Long quotations should be indented and blocked five to 10 spaces from the left and right margins, with internal single-spacing and top-and-bottom double-spacing so that the material will be set off from the rest of the message. Long enumerations should also be indented: enumerations with items requiring more than one line apiece may require single-spacing within each item, followed by double-spacing between items. Tabular data should be centered on the page. See Fig. 7.13.

Fig. 7.13   Page Placement of Items Inset within the Message

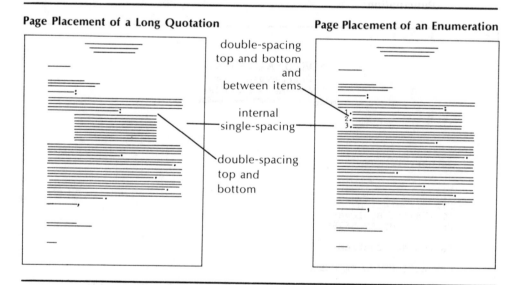

Page Placement of a Long Quotation   Page Placement of an Enumeration

double-spacing top and bottom and between items

internal single-spacing

double-spacing top and bottom

Rules for end-of-line division in business letters include the following:

1. Do not divide a word at the end of the first line.
2. Do not divide a word at the end of the last full line of a letter.
3. Do not divide a person's name from his or her courtesy title.

If a letter is long enough to require a continuation sheet or sheets, at least three message lines must be carried over to the next page. The complimentary close and/or typed signature block should never stand alone on a continuation sheet. The last word on a page should not be divided. Continuation-sheet margins should match those of the first sheet.

At least six blank lines equaling 1″ should be left at the top of the continuation sheet, followed by the continuation-sheet heading. The two most common types of continuation-sheet heading are illustrated in Figs. 7.14 and 7.15. The format shown in Fig. 7.14 is used with the Simplified and Block Letters. The flush-left heading begins with the page number, continues on the next line with the addressee's courtesy title and full name, and ends with the date on the third line. Some companies prefer that the page number appear as the last line of the continuation-sheet heading, especially if a reference number is included.

Another style is illustrated in Fig. 7.15. Here the heading extends across the page, six lines down from the top edge of the sheet. The addressee's name is typed flush with the left margin, the page number is centered on the same line and enclosed with spaced hyphens, and the date is aligned flush with the right margin—all on the same line. This format is often used with the Modified Block and the Modified Semi-block Letters.

Fig. 7.14   Continuation-Sheet Heading for Simplified and Block Letters

```
Page 2
Mr. Henry Doe
January 1, 19--


are continuing to study the problem that you have raised
regarding our new discounting procedures ....
```

Fig. 7.15   Continuation-Sheet Heading for Modified Block and Modified Semi-block Letters

```
Mr. Henry Doe                  -2-              January 1, 19--


are continuing to study the problem that you have raised
regarding our new discounting procedures ....
```

COMPLIMENTARY CLOSE

A complimentary close is used with all letter styles except the Simplified Letter. It is typed two lines below the last line of the message. Its horizontal placement depends on the letter style being used. In the Block Letter, the complimentary close is blocked flush with the left margin (see Fig. 7.16).

Fig. 7.16   Block Letter Format for Complimentary Close, with Open Puncutation

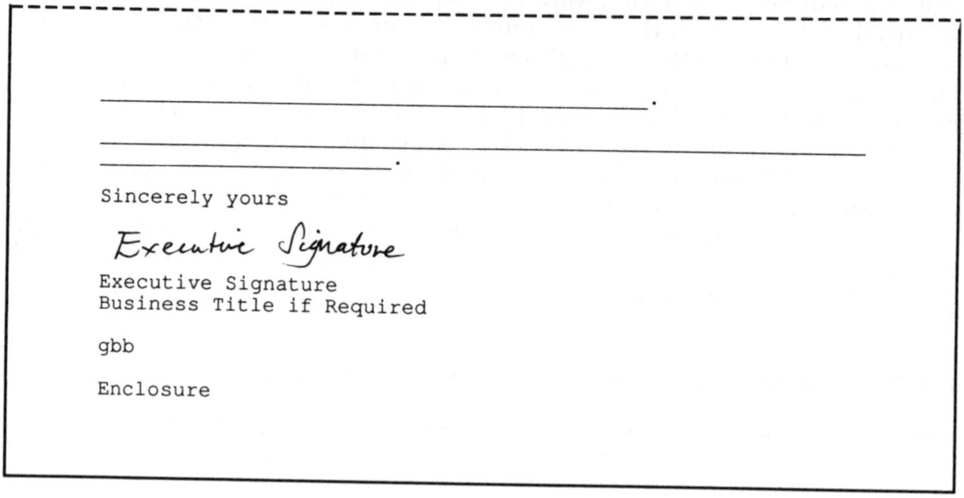

```
Sincerely yours

Executive Signature
Executive Signature
Business Title if Required

gbb

Enclosure
```

In the Modified Block and the Modified Semi-block Letters, the complimentary close may begin at the center or may be aligned directly under the dateline (e.g., about five spaces to the right of center, or flush with the right margin) or under some particular part of the printed letterhead. It should never overrun the right margin. (See Fig. 7.17.)

Fig. 7.17   Complimentary Close Five Spaces to Right of Center, as in a Modified Block Letter, with Mixed Punctuation

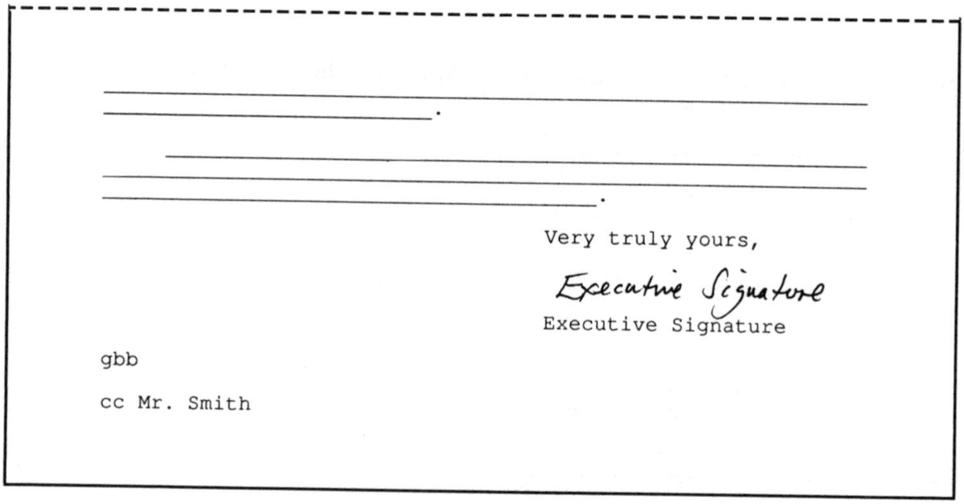

```
                              Very truly yours,

                              Executive Signature
                              Executive Signature

gbb

cc Mr. Smith
```

Only the first word of the complimentary close is capitalized. If the open-punctuation pattern is being followed, the complimentary close is unpunctuated. If the mixed-punctuation pattern is being followed, it ends with a comma.

Always use the complimentary close that is dictated, because the writer may have a special reason for the choice of phrasing. If the writer does not specify a particular closing, you may wish to select the one that best reflects the general tone of the letter and the state of the writer-reader relationship. The table below lists the most commonly used complimentary closes and groups them according to general tone and degree of formality.

Complimentary closes on letters written over a period of time to a particular person may become gradually more informal and friendly; once an informal pattern has been established, they should not revert to a more formal style.

Complimentary Closes for Business Correspondence

General Tone and Degree of Formality	Complimentary Close
Highly formal—usually used in diplomatic, governmental, or ecclesiastical correspondence to show respect and deference to a high-ranking addressee	Respectfully yours Respectfully Very respectfully
Politely neutral—usually used in general correspondence	Very truly yours Yours very truly Yours truly
Friendly and less formal—usually used in general correspondence	Most sincerely Very sincerely Very sincerely yours Sincerely yours Yours sincerely Sincerely
More friendly and informal—often used when writer and reader are on a first-name basis, but also often used in general business correspondence	Most cordially Yours cordially Cordially yours Cordially
Most friendly and informal—usually used when writer and reader are on a first-name basis	As ever Best wishes Best regards Kindest regards Kindest personal regards Regards
British	Yours faithfully Yours sincerely

SIGNATURE BLOCK

The first line of the signature block indicates responsibility for the letter. Either the name of the writer or the name of the organization may appear there. In the former case, the writer's name is typed at least four lines below the complimentary close; in the latter, the organization name is typed all in capital letters two lines below the complimentary close and the writer's name at least four lines below the organization name.

In the Simplified Letter, the name of the writer is typed entirely in capitals, flush left, at least five lines below the last line of the message. If the writer's business title is not included in the printed letterhead, it may be typed on the same line as the name entirely in capitals and separated from the last element of the name by a spaced hyphen. (See Fig. 7.18.) Some organizations prefer to use a comma in place of the hyphen. A combination of the two may be used if the title is complex.

JOHN P. HEWETT - DIRECTOR
JOHN P. HEWETT, DIRECTOR
JOHN P. HEWETT - DIRECTOR, TECHNICAL INFORMATION
  or
JOHN P. HEWETT - DIRECTOR
TECHNICAL INFORMATION CENTER

Fig. 7.18   Page Placement of Signature Block in the Simplified Letter

In the Block Letter, the signature block is aligned flush left at least four lines below the complimentary close. Only the first letter of each element of the writer's name is capitalized, and only the first letter of each major element of the writer's business title and department name, if included, is capitalized. (See Fig. 7.19.) The business title and department name may be omitted if they appear in the letterhead:

If title and dept. needed for identification:	John D. Russell, Director Consumer Products Division
If dept. appears on letterhead:	John D. Russell Director
If both title and dept. appear on letterhead:	John D. Russell

In the Modified Block and the Modified Semi-block Letters, the signature block begins with the name of the writer typed at least four lines below the complimentary close. The beginning of each line in the signature block is aligned

Fig. 7.19   Signature Block in the Block Letter

```
_____
_____ .
_____
_____
_____ .

Very truly yours

Executive Name
Executive's Name, Ph.D.
Business Title if Required

gbb
```

directly below the beginning of the complimentary close (see Figs. 7.20 and 7.21), unless this will result in overrunning the right margin, in which case the signature block may be centered under the complimentary close. Only the first letter of each major element of the writer's name and title (if used) and the department name (if used) is capitalized:

Ms. Joy L. Tate, Director	Ms. Joy L. Tate	Ms. Joy L. Tate
Marketing Division	Director	

If letterhead stationery is being used, the name of the firm should not appear below the complimentary close. If letterhead is not being used, the name of the firm may be typed in capitals on the second line beneath the complimentary close, with the first letter of the firm's name aligned directly underneath and the writer's name typed in capitals and lowercase at least four lines below the firm's name. The writer's title, if needed, is typed in capitals and lowercase on a line directly underneath the signature line. If the company name is long enough to

Fig. 7.20   Signature Block Five Spaces to Right of Center, as in a Modified Block Letter, with Mixed Punctuation

```
        _____ .

              _____
        _____ .

                        Sincerely yours,

                        Alice W. Patterson
                        (Mrs.) Alice W. Patterson
                        Assistant to Mr. Watson

    gbb
```

Fig. 7.21 Complimentary Close and Signature Block Flush Right, as in the Modified Block Letter

```
                                                    Cordially,

                                                    Lee A. Dow

                                                    Lee A. Dow
                                                    Editor

     gbb

     cc Mr. Langley
```

overrun the right margin, it may be centered beneath the complimentary close in the Modified Block and the Modified Semi-block Letters. See Fig. 7.22.

Fig. 7.22 Signature Block When a Printed Letterhead Is Not Being Used

```
Very truly yours,                     Very truly yours,

AJAX VAN LINES, INC.      JOHNSON AEROSPACE ENGINEERING ASSOCIATES

Samuel O. Lescott                     Sidney C. Johnson

Samuel O. Lescott                     Sidney C. Johnson, Ph.D.
Dispatcher                            President
```

The name of the writer should generally be typed exactly as it appears in his or her formal signature. (Since the writer signs the letter only after it has been typed, however, he or she may choose to sign informally—e.g., "Bob"—above the full typed-out name.) (The exceptions to this rule for women are explained below.) If applicable, any academic degrees (such as *Ph.D.*) or professional ratings (such as *P.E.*) should be included after the surname so that the recipient will know the proper form of address to use in the reply.

Typed Signature	*Salutation in Reply*
Francis E. Atlee, M.D.	Dear Dr. Atlee
Ellen Y. Leinsdorf, Ph.D.	Dear Dr. Leinsdorf
Dean of Women	*or*
	Dear Dean Leinsdorf
Carol I. Etheridge, C.P.A.	Dear Ms. Etheridge
or	
Mrs. Carol I. Etheridge, C.P.A.	Dear Mrs. Etheridge

These academic and professional degrees and ratings need not be repeated in the signature line if they are already included in the letterhead, and they are never included in the written signature.

If your employer is a woman, she may choose from a great variety of styles for her typed signature. She may desire that the parenthesized courtesy title "(Ms.)," "(Mrs.)," or "(Miss)" precede the typed signature, in order to let the recipient know which courtesy title to use in future salutations, or to clarify her gender if her name is one (such as Terry, Lee, or Leslie) that might be confused with a man's. If she is unmarried, she may choose to include or omit her middle initial. If she is married, she may nevertheless have kept her maiden name, at least professionally. Or she may use her maiden name followed by her husband's last name, and the two last names may be joined by a hyphen or left open. On the other hand, she may keep only the initial of her maiden name as her middle initial or omit it altogether, or she may use her original middle initial followed by her husband's last name. Though it is extremely rare, she may even use her husband's full name preceded by "Mrs." Any abbreviations of degrees, ratings, or "Esquire" may follow her name just as in men's signatures.

It is the writer herself who determines how her name is to appear in the typed signature—which need not match her actual signature—and it is your responsibility to reproduce it in the exact form she desires.

A woman secretary signing her own correspondence will choose her professional signature and typed signature in a similar way.

A letter may occasionally be written and signed by two individuals. In these cases, it is generally best to place the names side by side, with the first name flush left in block styles or beginning slightly left of center in other letter styles in order to leave enough room for two horizontally aligned signatures. See Fig. 7.23.

Fig. 7.23 Signature Block When Two People Sign a Letter

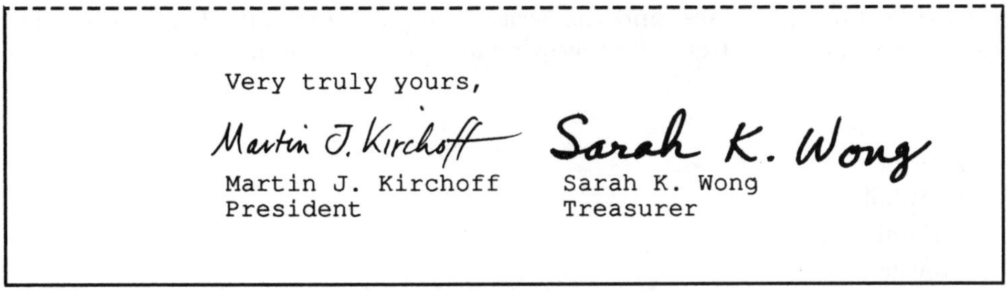
Very truly yours,

Martin J. Kirchoff Sarah K. Wong

Martin J. Kirchoff Sarah K. Wong
President Treasurer

If horizontal positioning is not feasible, the names may be placed one under the other. If you sign a letter for the writer, the writer's name is followed by your initials immediately below and to the right of the surname, or centered under the full name. (See Fig. 7.24.) If you sign a letter in your own name for someone

Fig. 7.24 Signature When Secretary Signs the Writer's Name

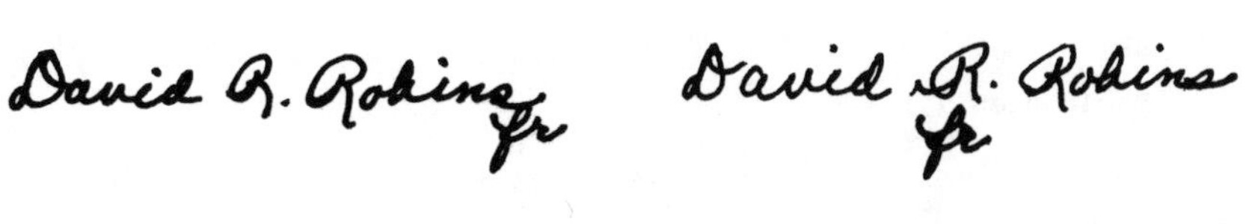

else, that individual's courtesy title and surname only are typed directly below. (See Fig. 7.25.)

Fig. 7.25 Signature Block When Secretary Signs as a Representative

---

Sincerely yours

Lee L. Linden

(Miss) Lee L. Linden
Secretary to Ms. Key

Sincerely yours

Seymour J. Barnes

Seymour T. Barnes
Assistant to Senator Ross

IDENTIFICATION INITIALS

The initials of the typist and sometimes those of the writer are placed two lines below the last line of the signature block and are aligned flush left in all letter styles, as in Fig. 7.26. Most offices formerly preferred that three capitalized initials be used for the writer's name and two lowercase initials be used for the typist's. Today, however, the writer's initials are usually omitted if the name is already typed in the signature block or if it appears in the printed letterhead. In many organizations the typist's initials appear only on office copies for record-keeping purposes, and the writer's initials are omitted unless another individual signs the letter. The following are the most common styles:

hol
hl
FCM/hl
FCM/hol
FCM:hl
FCM:hol

Fig. 7.26 Page Placement of Identification and Enclosure Notations

Sincerely yours

Executive Signature

Executive Signature
Business Title if Needed

gbb

Enclosures (7)

A letter dictated by one person (such as an administrative secretary), typed by another (such as a corresponding secretary), and signed by yet another (such as the writer) may show the writer/signer's initials entirely in capitals, the dictator's initials entirely in capitals, and the transcriber/typist's initials in lowercase; for example, AWM:COC:ds.

ENCLOSURE NOTATION

If a letter is to be accompanied by an enclosure or enclosures, a notation such as one of the following should be aligned flush left and typed one or two lines beneath the identification initials, if any (see Fig. 7.26 above), or one or two lines beneath the last line of the signature block, if there is no identification line. The unabbreviated form *Enclosure* is usually preferred.

Enclosure   Enclosures (3)
enc. *or* encl.   3 encs. *or* Enc. 3

If the enclosures are of special importance, they should be numerically listed and briefly described, with single-spacing between the items.

Enclosures: 1. Annual Report (19—), 2 copies
              2. List of Major Accounts
              3. Profit and Loss Statement (19—)

The following type of notation then may be typed in the top right corner of each page of each of the enclosures:

Enclosure (1) to Johnson Associates letter No. 1-234-X,
dated January 1, 19—, page 2 of 8

If the enclosure is bound, a single notation attached to its cover sheet will suffice.
    When additional material is being mailed separately, a notation such as the following may be used:

Separate mailing: 50th Anniversary Report

COPY NOTATION

Copies of letters and memos, traditionally called *carbon copies,* are now often called *courtesy copies* or simply *office copies.* In some offices, *c* for *copy* or *pc* for *photocopy* is used instead of the traditional *cc* for *carbon copy* or *courtesy copy.*
    A copy notation showing the distribution of courtesy copies to other individuals should be aligned flush left and typed two lines below the signature block if there are no other notations or initials, or two lines below any other notations. If space is very tight, the courtesy-copy notation may be single-spaced below any notations or initials.

cc   cc: Copy to   Copies to

Multiple recipients of copies should be listed alphabetically. Sometimes only their initials are shown.

cc: WPB
      TLC
      CNR

More often, the individual's names are shown and sometimes also their addresses, especially if the writer feels that such information can be useful to the addressee.

cc: William L. Ehrenkreutz, Esq.   cc Ms. Lee Jamieson
     45 Park Towers, Suite 1   Copy to Mr. Javier Linares
     Smithville, ST 56789   Copies to Mr. Houghton
     Dr. Daniel I. Maginnis   Mr. Rhys
     1300 Dover Drive   Mr. Smythe
     Jonesville, ZZ 12345

To save space, the copy notation may group the recipients.

cc   Regional Sales Managers

If the recipient of the copy is to receive an enclosure or enclosures as well, that individual's full name and address as well as a description of each enclosure and the total number of enclosed items should be shown in the carbon-copy notation.

cc: Ms. Barbara S. Lee (2 copies, Annual Report)
     123 Jones Street
     Smithville, ST 56789
     Mrs. Sara T. Torchinsky
     Mrs. Laura E. Yowell

If the first names or initials are given along with the last names, courtesy titles (*Mr., Mrs., Miss,* and *Ms.*) may be omitted.

cc: William L. Ehrenkreutz   cc: W. L. Ehrenkreutz
     Daniel I. Maginnis   D. I. Maginnis

Typists usually leave either one or two spaces between the *cc:* and the names that follow. However, if only one name follows the *cc:* and it is given in all initials, the space or spaces may be omitted.

cc:JBH

If the writer wishes that copies of the letter be distributed without the list of recipients being shown on the original, the blind-courtesy-copy notation *bcc* or *bcc:* followed by an alphabetical list of the recipients' initials or names may be typed on the copies only, either in the same page position as a regular copy notation or in the upper left-hand corner.

Carbon or courtesy copies are not usually signed. The secretary may type the signature, preceded by the symbol */S/* or */s/*, to indicate that the writer signed the original copy.

POSTSCRIPT

A postscript is aligned flush left two to four lines below the last notation (depending on space available). If the paragraphs are blocked flush left, the postscript should also begin flush left; if the paragraphs are indented, the first line of the postscript should also be indented. All postscripts are single-spaced. Their margins conform with the body of the letter. The writer should initial a postscript. While it is not incorrect to head a postscript with the initials *P.S.* (for an initial postscript) or *P.P.S.* (for subsequent ones), these headings are redundant and can be omitted.

Standard Letter Styles

The following pages contain facsimiles of the four most common business-letter formats—the Simplified Letter, the Block Letter, the Modified Block Letter, and the Modified Semi-block Letter (Figs. 7.27–7.30)—followed by facsimiles of the Official Letter Style on Executive letterhead, the Official Letter Style on plain bond, and the Half-sheet (Figs. 7.31–7.33). Each facsimile contains a detailed description of its format and style.

TIME-SAVING CORRESPONDENCE METHODS

An increasing number of business offices rely on time-saving and cost-cutting measures for sending out and replying to routine correspondence. Among these methods are the use of form letters and form paragraphs (see Chapter 8), memorandum forms with detachable reply sections, postal cards, and the writing of marginal notations directly on letters received. The last two methods are discussed below.

Postal cards   Brief messages may be typewritten on standard-size ($5\frac{1}{2}'' \times 3\frac{1}{2}''$) postal cards. A message can be fitted onto the card if you follow these suggestions:

1. Set the margins for a $4\frac{1}{2}''$ writing line, which allows $\frac{1}{2}''$ margins at each side. Plan to leave a $\frac{1}{2}''$ margin at the bottom.
2. Type the date on the third line from the top.
3. Omit the inside address.
4. Leave only one line of space above the salutation.
5. Leave only one line of space above the message.
6. Leave only one line of space above the complimentary close.
7. If necessary, omit one or more of the following: salutation, complimentary close, handwritten signature, identification initials.

Pre-addressed postal cards may also be enclosed with a letter of inquiry to encourage and speed an answer back to your office. You may even type various responses so that the recipient can simply check the appropriate response and mail the card.

Marginal notations   In many business offices, when answering routine queries, the answer to the incoming letter is simply written at the bottom of the letter, a copy is made for the files, and the original is returned to the sender with the reply written directly on it. Frequently a stamped message or sticker is attached explaining that this speedy reply method is for the customer's convenience.

One variation of this procedure is to stamp on your own letter of inquiry, "Reply here to save time. Photocopy for your files." Or you can enclose a photocopy of your original letter with a request that the recipient simply answer in the margin of the copy and return it to you.

Marginal notations save time and cut costs, and they also reduce the number of file copies. However, they should be used only when such informality is appropriate.

Fig. 7.27   The Simplified Letter

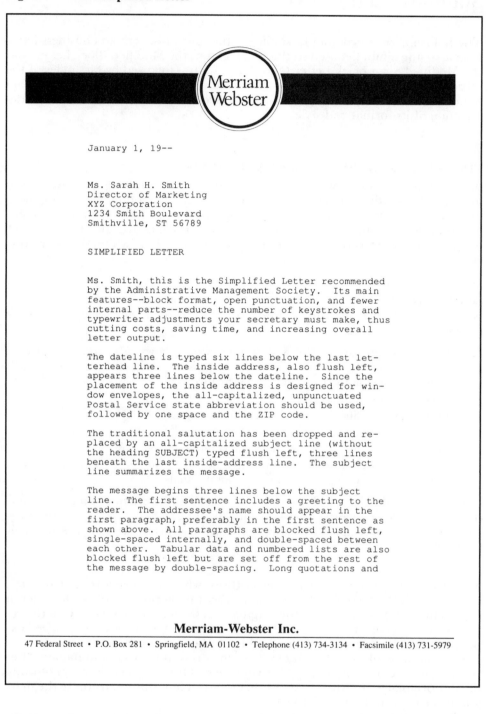

January 1, 19--

Ms. Sarah H. Smith
Director of Marketing
XYZ Corporation
1234 Smith Boulevard
Smithville, ST 56789

SIMPLIFIED LETTER

Ms. Smith, this is the Simplified Letter recommended
by the Administrative Management Society. Its main
features--block format, open punctuation, and fewer
internal parts--reduce the number of keystrokes and
typewriter adjustments your secretary must make, thus
cutting costs, saving time, and increasing overall
letter output.

The dateline is typed six lines below the last letterhead line. The inside address, also flush left,
appears three lines below the dateline. Since the
placement of the inside address is designed for window envelopes, the all-capitalized, unpunctuated
Postal Service state abbreviation should be used,
followed by one space and the ZIP code.

The traditional salutation has been dropped and replaced by an all-capitalized subject line (without
the heading SUBJECT) typed flush left, three lines
beneath the last inside-address line. The subject
line summarizes the message.

The message begins three lines below the subject
line. The first sentence includes a greeting to the
reader. The addressee's name should appear in the
first paragraph, preferably in the first sentence as
shown above. All paragraphs are blocked flush left,
single-spaced internally, and double-spaced between
each other. Tabular data and numbered lists are also
blocked flush left but are set off from the rest of
the message by double-spacing. Long quotations and

Merriam-Webster Inc.

47 Federal Street • P.O. Box 281 • Springfield, MA 01102 • Telephone (413) 734-3134 • Facsimile (413) 731-5979

Ms. Smith
Page 2
January 1, 19--

unnumbered lists should be indented five to ten
spaces from the left and right margins and set off
from the rest of the message by top and bottom
double-spacing.

If a continuation sheet is required, at least three
message lines must be carried over. Continuation-
sheet format and margins must match those of the
first sheet. At least six blank lines are left from
the top edge of the page to the first line of the
heading, which is blocked flush left, single-spaced
internally, and typically composed of the addressee's
courtesy title and last name, the page number, and
the date. The rest of the message begins four lines
beneath the last heading line.

There is no complimentary close in the Simplified
Letter, although a warm closing sentence may end the
message. The writer's name (and business title if
needed) is aligned flush left and typed all in
capitals at least five lines below the last message
line. The Administrative Management Society uses a
spaced hyphen between the writer's surname and
business title; some companies prefer a comma
instead. The writer's department name may be typed
flush left all in capitals, one line below the
signature line.

The identification initials, flush left and two lines
below the last line of the signature block, are the
typist's initials only. An enclosure notation may be
typed on the line below the identification initials
and aligned flush left. A carbon-copy notation may
be typed one or two lines below the last notation,
depending on available space. If only the signature
block and/or typist's initials appear before it, the
carbon-copy notation is typed two lines below.

Executive Signature

EXECUTIVE SIGNATURE - BUSINESS TITLE

gbb
Enclosures (2)

cc Dr. Alice L. Barnes

Fig. 7.28   The Block Letter

Merriam
Webster

January 1, 19--
X-123-4

XYZ Corporation
Sales Department
1234 Smith Boulevard
Smithville, ST 56789

Attention Mr. John Doe

Ladies and Gentlemen

SUBJECT: BLOCK LETTER

This is a facsimile of the Block Letter, all of whose
structural parts begin flush left. It may use either the
open- or the mixed-punctuation pattern; the open pattern is
shown here.

The dateline may be typed two to six lines below the last
letterhead line; here it is placed three lines below the
letterhead. The reference line, if any, is typed flush left
immediately below the dateline.

Placement of the inside address varies according to letter
length; here it is typed four lines below the dateline. If
a window envelope is being used, the all-capitalized,
unpunctuated Postal Service state abbreviations should be
employed, with one space between the state abbreviation and
the ZIP code. If a regular envelope is to be used, the
state name may be typed out in full or abbreviated,
depending on organization preference. An attention line, if
required, is typed two lines below the last inside-address
line.

The salutation is typed two lines below the attention line,
or two to four lines below the last inside-address line.
The salutation is usually "Dear Sir or Madam" or "Ladies and
Gentlemen" if the letter is addressed to an organization,
even if there is an attention line directing the letter to a
particular individual within that organization. If the
letter is addressed to an individual whose name is on line 1
of the inside address, the salutation is "Dear Mr. (or Ms.
or Mrs. or Miss) + surname" or "Dear + first name,"
depending on the writer/reader relationship. A subject

Merriam-Webster Inc.

47 Federal Street • P.O. Box 281 • Springfield, MA 01102 • Telephone (413) 734-3134 • Facsimile (413) 731-5979

XYZ Corporation
Sales Department
January 1, 19--
X-123-4
Page 2

line, all in capitals, may be typed two lines below the
salutation. The subject line is optional.

The first message line is typed two lines below the salutation, or two lines below the subject line if there is one.
The message is single-spaced internally and double-spaced
between paragraphs. At least three message lines must be
carried over to a continuation sheet; the complimentary
close and the signature block should never stand alone. The
last word on a sheet should not be divided. The continuation-sheet heading is typed six lines from the top edge of
the page. Any reference line from the first sheet must be
repeated in the continuation-sheet headings. The message
begins four lines below the last line of the heading.

The complimentary close is typed two lines below the last
message line, followed by at least four blank lines for the
written signature, followed by the writer's name in capitals
and lowercase. The writer's title and/or department may be
included in the typed signature block if they do not appear
in the printed letterhead.

Identification initials will usually be only the typist's.
These initials are typed two lines below the last signature-
block line. The enclosure notation, if used, is typed one
line below the identification line. The carbon-copy notation, if needed, is placed one or two lines below any other
notation, depending on available space.

Sincerely yours

Executive Signature

Executive Signature
Business Title

gbb
Enclosures (2)

cc Mr. Howard T. Jansen

Fig. 7.29   The Modified Block Letter

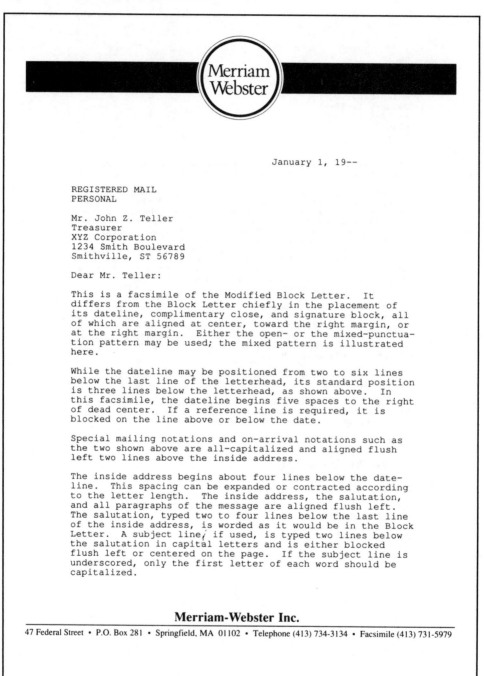

Merriam Webster

January 1, 19--

REGISTERED MAIL
PERSONAL

Mr. John Z. Teller
Treasurer
XYZ Corporation
1234 Smith Boulevard
Smithville, ST 56789

Dear Mr. Teller:

This is a facsimile of the Modified Block Letter. It
differs from the Block Letter chiefly in the placement of
its dateline, complimentary close, and signature block, all
of which are aligned at center, toward the right margin, or
at the right margin. Either the open- or the mixed-punctuation pattern may be used; the mixed pattern is illustrated
here.

While the dateline may be positioned from two to six lines
below the last line of the letterhead, its standard position
is three lines below the letterhead, as shown above. In
this facsimile, the dateline begins five spaces to the right
of dead center. If a reference line is required, it is
blocked on the line above or below the date.

Special mailing notations and on-arrival notations such as
the two shown above are all-capitalized and aligned flush
left two lines above the inside address.

The inside address begins about four lines below the dateline. This spacing can be expanded or contracted according
to the letter length. The inside address, the salutation,
and all paragraphs of the message are aligned flush left.
The salutation, typed two to four lines below the last line
of the inside address, is worded as it would be in the Block
Letter. A subject line, if used, is typed two lines below
the salutation in capital letters and is either blocked
flush left or centered on the page. If the subject line is
underscored, only the first letter of each word should be
capitalized.

Merriam-Webster Inc.

47 Federal Street • P.O. Box 281 • Springfield, MA 01102 • Telephone (413) 734-3134 • Facsimile (413) 731-5979

Mr. Teller   -2-   January 1, 19--

The message begins two lines below the salutation or the
subject line. Paragraphs are single-spaced internally and
double-spaced between each other; however, in very short
letters, the paragraphs may be double-spaced internally and
triple-spaced between each other.

Continuation sheets should contain at least three message
lines. The last word on a sheet should not be divided. The
continuation-sheet heading may be blocked flush left as in
the Block Letter, or it may be laid out across the top of
the page as here. It is positioned six lines from the top
edge of the sheet, and the message is continued four lines
beneath it.

The complimentary close is typed two lines below the last
line of the message. While the complimentary close may be
aligned under some portion of the letterhead, directly under
the dateline, or even flush with the right margin, it often
begins five spaces to the right of dead center as shown
here.

The signature line is typed in capitals and lowercase at
least four lines below the complimentary close. The writer's business title and department name may be included if
they do not already appear in the printed letterhead. All
elements of the signature block must be aligned with each
other and with the complimentary close.

Identification initials are usually only those of the
typist, providing that the writer and the signer are the
same person. These initials appear two lines below the last
line of the signature block. Any enclosure notation is
typed on the line below the identification line, and the
carbon-copy notation, if required, appears one or two lines
below any other notations, depending on space available.

                                        Sincerely yours,

                                        Executive Signature

                                        Executive Signature
                                        Business Title

gbb
Enclosures (5)

cc Ms. Santucci
   Dr. Franklin
   Dr. Mason

Fig. 7.30   The Modified Semi-block Letter

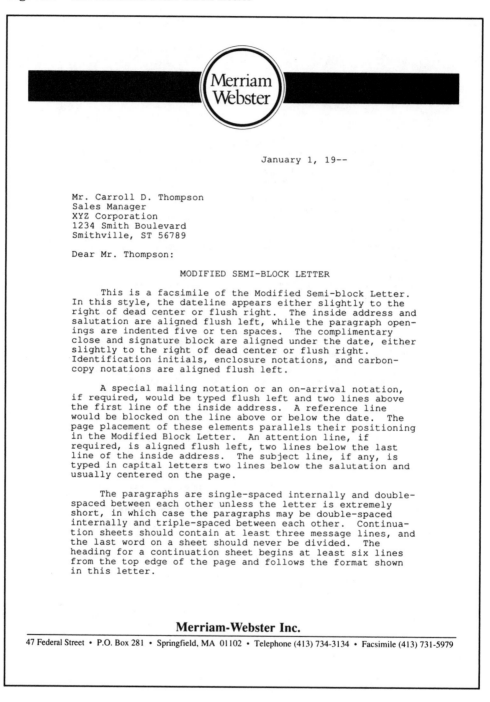

January 1, 19--

Mr. Carroll D. Thompson
Sales Manager
XYZ Corporation
1234 Smith Boulevard
Smithville, ST 56789

Dear Mr. Thompson:

MODIFIED SEMI-BLOCK LETTER

This is a facsimile of the Modified Semi-block Letter.
In this style, the dateline appears either slightly to the
right of dead center or flush right. The inside address and
salutation are aligned flush left, while the paragraph openings are indented five or ten spaces. The complimentary
close and signature block are aligned under the date, either
slightly to the right of dead center or flush right.
Identification initials, enclosure notations, and carbon-
copy notations are aligned flush left.

A special mailing notation or an on-arrival notation,
if required, would be typed flush left and two lines above
the first line of the inside address. A reference line
would be blocked on the line above or below the date. The
page placement of these elements parallels their positioning
in the Modified Block Letter. An attention line, if
required, is aligned flush left, two lines below the last
line of the inside address. The subject line, if any, is
typed in capital letters two lines below the salutation and
usually centered on the page.

The paragraphs are single-spaced internally and double-
spaced between each other unless the letter is extremely
short, in which case the paragraphs may be double-spaced
internally and triple-spaced between each other. Continuation sheets should contain at least three message lines, and
the last word on a sheet should never be divided. The
heading for a continuation sheet begins at least six lines
from the top edge of the page and follows the format shown
in this letter.

Merriam-Webster Inc.

47 Federal Street • P.O. Box 281 • Springfield, MA 01102 • Telephone (413) 734-3134 • Facsimile (413) 731-5979

Mr. Thompson   -2-   January 1, 19--

    The complimentary close is typed two lines below the
last line of the message. The signature line, four lines
below the complimentary close, is aligned with it if possible, or centered under it if the name and title will be
long. In this case, it is better to align both date and
complimentary close about five spaces to the right of dead
center to ensure enough room for the signature block, which
should never overrun the right margin. The writer's name,
business title, and department name (if not already printed
on the stationery) are typed in capitals and lowercase.

    Although open punctuation may be followed, the mixed-
punctuation pattern is quite common with the Modified Semi-
block Letter, and it is the latter that is shown here.

                        Sincerely yours,

                        Executive Signature

                        Executive Signature
                        Business Title

gbb

Enclosures: 2

cc: Dr. Bennett P. Oakley
     Addison Engineering Associates
     91011 Jones Street
     Smithville, ST 56789

    A postscript, if needed, is typically positioned two to
four lines below the last notation. In the Modified Semi-
block Letter, the first line is indented like the message
paragraphs. It is not necessary to head the postscript with
the abbreviation P.S. The postscript should be initialed by
the writer.

                  E. S.

Fig. 7.31   The Official Letter Style on Executive (Monarch) Letterhead

Merriam Webster

Executive Name
Executive Title

January 1, 19--

Dear Ms. Peterson:

This is a facsimile of the Official Letter Style, often used for personal letters written by an executive and other letters typed on his or her own personalized company stationery. The paper size is Executive or Monarch.

The Official Letter Style is characterized by the page placement of the inside address: It is typed flush left, two to five lines below the last line of the signature block or below the written signature.

The typist's initials, if included, are typed two lines below the last line of the inside address. Any enclosure notation appears two lines below the typist's initials, or two lines below the last line of the inside address, also flush left.

A typed signature block is not needed on personalized Executive or Monarch stationery; however, if the writer's signature either is difficult to decipher or might be unfamiliar to the addressee, it may be typed four lines below the complimentary close.

Open punctuation and blocked paragraphs may also be used in this style.

Sincerely,

Executive Signature

Ms. Martha Peterson
490 Jones Street
Smithville, ST 56789

Fig. 7.32   The Official Letter Style on Plain Stationery

```
                                        4400 Ambler Boulevard
                                        Smithville, ST 56789
                                        January 1, 19--

          Dear Bob

          This is a facsimile of a letter typed on plain
          Executive or Monarch stationery.  The basic
          format is the same as that of the Official
          Letter Style.  Block paragraphs and the open-
          punctuation pattern are illustrated here.

          The heading, which includes the writer's full
          address and the date, should be positioned at
          least six lines from the top edge of the page
          and flush with the right margin as shown here.
          The salutation may be positioned two to six
          lines below the dateline.

          The complimentary close is typed two lines be-
          low the last line of the message.  The inside
          address appears flush left, two to five lines
          below the last line of the signature block or
          the written signature.

          The typist's or keyboarder's initials, if in-
          cluded, should be positioned two lines beneath
          the last line of the inside address.  An enclo-
          sure notation or any other notation required
          should be typed two lines below the typist's
          initials or two lines below the last line of the
          inside address if there are no initials.

                                   Sincerely

                                   Executive Signature


          Mr. Robert Y. Owens
          123 East Second Avenue
          Jonesville, ST 45678
```

Fig. 7.33   The Half-sheet

Envelope Addresses

The following information may appear on any envelope regardless of its size. Items 1 and 4 are essential; items 2 and 3 are optional, depending on the requirements of the particular letter.

1. The addressee's full name and full geographical address, typed approximately in the vertical and horizontal center
2. Special mailing notation or notations, typed below the stamp
3. On-arrival notation or notations, typed about nine lines below the top edge on the left side
4. The sender's full name and geographical address, printed or typed in the upper left corner.

The address block on a regular envelope should be no larger than 1½″ × 3¾″. There should be ⅝″ from the bottom line of the address block to the bottom edge of the envelope, which should be free of print. On regular envelopes, the address block usually begins about five spaces to the left of center. It should be single-spaced. Block style should be used. Unusual or italic typefaces should be avoided.

If a window envelope is being used, all address data must appear within the window space, with ¼″ margins between the address and the edges of the window.

POSITION OF ELEMENTS

The elements of the address block should be styled and positioned as shown in the following examples. Though the initial examples below are shown in traditional capital-and-lowercase style, see pages 288–91 for the style now recommended by the Postal Service.

First line   If the addressee is an individual, that person's courtesy title and full name are typed on the first line.

> Mr. Lee O. Idlewild

If an individual addressee's business title is included in the inside address, it may be typed either on the first line of the address block with a comma separating it from the addressee's name, or alone on the next line, depending on the length of title and name.

> Mr. Lee O. Idlewild, President
> Mr. Lee O. Idlewild
> President

If the addressee is an organization, its full name is typed on the first line. If a particular department is specified, its name is typed under the name of the organization.

> XYZ Corporation
> Sales Department

Next line(s)   The full street address should be typed out (although it is acceptable to abbreviate such designations as *Street, Avenue, Boulevard*). In mass mailings that will be presorted for automated handling (see pages 288–91), type all elements of the address block entirely in capital letters and use the unpunctuated abbreviations for streets and street designations that are recommended by the Postal Service. Type the room, suite, or apartment number immediately after the last element of the street address on the same line with it. A building name, if used, goes on a separate line just above the street address.

A post-office box number, if used, is typed on the line immediately above the last line in order to assure delivery to this point. (The box number precedes the station name when a station name is included.) Both street address and post-office box number may be written in the address, but the letter will be delivered to the location specified on the next-to-last line.

Last line   The last line of the address block contains the city, state, and ZIP-code number. Allow one space between the state abbreviation and the ZIP code, which should never be on a line by itself. The ZIP code is mandatory, as are the all-capitalized, unpunctuated, two-letter Postal Service abbreviations. (You may spell the name of a state in full on the letter itself while using the Postal Service abbreviation on the envelope.) See table of abbreviations on page 286.

Two-letter Abbreviations for States and U.S. Dependencies

Alabama	AL	Kentucky	KY	Ohio	OH
Alaska	AK	Louisiana	LA	Oklahoma	OK
Arizona	AZ	Maine	ME	Oregon	OR
Arkansas	AR	Maryland	MD	Pennsylvania	PA
California	CA	Massachusetts	MA	Puerto Rico	PR
Colorado	CO	Michigan	MI	Rhode Island	RI
Connecticut	CT	Minnesota	MN	South Carolina	SC
Delaware	DE	Mississippi	MS	South Dakota	SD
District of Columbia	DC	Missouri	MO	Tennessee	TN
Florida	FL	Montana	MT	Texas	TX
Georgia	GA	Nebraska	NE	Utah	UT
Guam	GU	Nevada	NV	Vermont	VT
Hawaii	HI	New Hampshire	NH	Virginia	VA
Idaho	ID	New Jersey	NJ	Virgin Islands	VI
Illinois	IL	New Mexico	NM	Washington	WA
Indiana	IN	New York	NY	West Virginia	WV
Iowa	IA	North Carolina	NC	Wisconsin	WI
Kansas	KS	North Dakota	ND	Wyoming	WY

When both post-office box number and street address are included in an address, the ZIP code should match the location (usually the post-office box) specified in the line just above.

> XYZ Corporation
> 1234 Smith Boulevard
> P. O. Box 600
> Smithville, ST 56788

If the addressee has included a nine-digit ZIP code on correspondence to you, use it to speed delivery to that address.

Other elements   The on-arrival notations PERSONAL and CONFIDENTIAL must be typed entirely in capital letters, about nine lines below the left top edge of the envelope. Any other on-arrival instructions, such as <u>Hold for Arrival</u> or <u>Please Forward</u>, may be typed in capitals and lowercase, underlined, and positioned about nine lines below the left top edge.

If an attention line is used in the letter itself, it too must appear on the envelope, as the third-to-last line in the address block.

> XYZ Corporation
> Sales Department
> Attention Mr. E. R. Bailey
> 1234 Smith Boulevard
> Smithville, ST 56789

A special mailing notation such as CERTIFIED, REGISTERED MAIL, or SPECIAL DELIVERY is typed entirely in capitals just below the stamp or about nine lines from the right top edge of the envelope. It should not overrun a ½″ margin. (See Fig. 7.34.)

A printed return address may be supplemented by the name of the writer typed in at the top. The return address on a plain envelope should be typed at least two lines below the top edge of the envelope and ½″ from the left edge.

Fig. 7.34   Commercial Envelope Showing On-Arrival and Special Mailing Notations

```
PEREZ & MILBANK, P.C.
99 Main Street
Centerville, ST 34567



            CONFIDENTIAL                    SPECIAL DELIVERY


                    Mr. Joseph P. Brown
                    President
                    WQR Corporation
                    123 Fontaine Street
                    Anywhere, ST 44678
```

See the chart showing stationery and envelope sizes and applications on page 246.

See Chapter 11 for a detailed treatment of mailing procedures.

FOREIGN ADDRESSES

When typing a foreign address, refer to the return address on the envelope of previous correspondence for the correct ordering of the elements. The letter-head on previous correspondence may be checked if an envelope is not available. If neither is available, the address should be typed as it appears in the inside address of the dictated letter. The following guidelines may be of assistance:

1. All foreign addresses should be typed in English or in English characters. If an address must be in foreign characters (such as Russian), an English translation should be inserted between the lines in the address block.

2. Foreign courtesy titles may be substituted for the English, but they are not necessary.

3. The name of the country should be spelled out in capital letters by itself on the last line. Canadian addresses always carry the name CANADA after the name of the province.

4. When applicable, foreign postal-district numbers should be included. These are positioned either before or after the name of the city, never after the name of the country.

Canadian addresses should adhere to the form requested by the Canada Post for quickest delivery through its automated handling system. As shown in the following examples, the name of the city, fully capitalized, is followed by the name of the province, spelled out with initial capitals and lowercase letters on the same line. The Postal Code follows on a separate line. For mail originating in the United States, CANADA is added on a final line. Note that capitalization and punctuation differ slightly in French-language addresses.

Mr. F. F. MacManus	Les Entreprises Optima Ltée
Fitzgibbons and Brown	6789, rue Principale
5678 Main Street	OTTAWA (Ontario)
HALIFAX, Nova Scotia	K1A 0B3
B3J 2N9	CANADA
CANADA	

The Canadian Postal Code consists always of letter-digit-letter, space, digit-letter-digit. Failure to include the correct code number may result in considerable delay in delivery. When space is limited, the Postal Code may be typed on the same line with the province, separated from it by at least two spaces. The following two-letter provincial and territorial abbreviations may also be used when space is limited.

OTTAWA, Ontario   K1A 0B3   *or*   OTTAWA, ON   K1A 0B3

Two-letter Abbreviations for Canadian Provinces, Territories, and Islands

Alberta	AB	Newfoundland	NF	Quebec	PQ
British Columbia	BC	Northwest Territories	NT	Saskatchewan	SK
Labrador	LB	Nova Scotia	NS	Yukon Territory	YT
Manitoba	MB	Ontario	ON		
New Brunswick	NB	Prince Edward Island	PE		

Some foreign corporate abbreviations are shown below.

Foreign Corporate Abbreviations: Some Commonly Used Terms

Language	Type of business	Abbreviation
Danish	Partnership	I/S
	Limited Partnership	K/S
	Limited-liability Company	A/S
	Private Limited-liability Company	Ap/S
Dutch	Private Company	B.V.
	Public Corporation	N.V.
French	Limited-liability Company	SARL
	Corporation	SA
German	Partnership	OHG
	Limited Partnership	KG
	Limited-liability Company	G.m.b.H.
	Corporation	AG
Italian	Corporation	S.p.A.
	Limited-liability Company	S.r.l.
Portuguese	Corporation	SARL
Spanish	Stock Company, Corporation	S.A.
	Company	Cia.
Swedish	Company	AB

ADDRESSING FOR AUTOMATION

To take full advantage of the post office's computerized sorting equipment (including optical character readers that can scan and sort many thousands of pieces of mail an hour), the Postal Service recommends that *all* envelopes be addressed properly for automation. All typescript should be clear and easy to read. The basic procedures in addressing envelopes are as follows:

1. Use rectangular envelopes no smaller than $3\frac{1}{2}'' \times 5''$ and no larger than $6\frac{1}{8}'' \times 11\frac{1}{2}''$. There should be good color contrast between the paper and the type impressions.

2. The address should be single-spaced and blocked (straight left margin). The address must be at least $1''$ from the left edge of the envelope and at least $\frac{5}{8}''$ up from the bottom. The address should be typed entirely in capital letters without punctuation marks. Do not use script, italic, or proportionally-spaced fonts. There should be no print to the right of or below the address.

3. Additional data (such as an attention line, account number, or date) may be part of the blocked address, but positioned above the second-to-last line.

   C REEVES CORP
   ATTN MR R C SMITH

4. If mail is addressed to occupants of multiunit buildings, the unit number should appear after the street address on the same line.

   C REEVES CORP
   ATTN MR R C SMITH
   186 PARK ST ROOM 960

5. The last line of the address should contain the city, state abbreviation, and ZIP code number (see state abbreviations on page 286). No punctuation should be used in the entire address, except the hyphen in a nine-digit ZIP code.

   C REEVES CORP
   ATTN MR R C SMITH
   186 PARK ST ROOM 960
   HARTFORD CT 06106

6. Any post-office box number should be typed on the second-to-last line to assure delivery to this point. Use the ZIP code corresponding to the box number, not to the street address. The box number precedes the station name. (Because of possible confusion in such addresses, consider omitting the street address altogether.)

   C REEVES CORP
   186 PARK ST
   PO BOX 210 LINCOLN STA
   HARTFORD CT 06106

7. At least $\frac{1}{4}''$ should be left between the address and the side and bottom edges of the opening on window envelopes.

A maximum of 22 strokes or positions is allowed on the last line of an envelope address. The Postal Service suggests the following maximum number of positions:

    13 positions for the city
     1 space between the city and state
     2 positions for the state
     1 space between the state and ZIP code
     5 positions for the ZIP code
    ─────────────────────────────────
    22 total positions allowed

Many city names exceed the suggested maximum number of 13 positions. The Postal Service suggests that the abbreviations listed in the following table be used for city and street names and other geographical elements to facilitate mail processing.

Abbreviations for Street Designators and Place-Name Elements

Academy	ACAD	Farms	FRMS	Memorial	MEM
Agency	AGNCY	Ferry	FRY	Middle	MDL
Airport	ARPRT	Field	FLD	Mile	MLE
Alley	ALY	Fields	FLDS	Mill	ML
Annex	ANX	Flats	FLT	Mills	MLS
Arcade	ARC	Ford	FRD	Mines	MNS
Arsenal	ARSL	Forest	FRST	Mission	MSN
Avenue	AVE	Forge	FRG	Mound	MND
Bayou	BYU	Fork	FRK	Mount	MT
Beach	BCH	Forks	FRKS	Mountain	MTN
Bend	BND	Fort	FT	National	NAT
Big	BG	Fountain	FTN	Neck	NCK
Black	BLK	Freeway	FWY	New	NW
Bluff	BLF	Furnace	FURN	North	N
Bottom	BTM	Gardens	GDNS	Orchard	ORCH
Boulevard	BLVD	Gateway	GTWY	Palms	PLMS
Branch	BR	Glen	GLN	Park	PK
Bridge	BRG	Grand	GRND	Parkway	PKY
Brook	BRK	Great	GR	Pillar	PLR
Burg	BG	Green	GRN	Pines	PNES
Bypass	BYP	Ground	GRD	Place	PL
Camp	CP	Grove	GRV	Plain	PLN
Canyon	CYN	Harbor	HBR	Plains	PLNS
Cape	CPE	Haven	HVN	Plaza	PLZ
Causeway	CSWY	Heights	HTS	Point	PT
Center	CTR	High	HID	Port	PRT
Central	CTL	Highlands	HGLDS	Prairie	PR
Church	CHR	Highway	HWY	Ranch	RNCH
Churches	CHRS	Hill	HL	Ranches	RNCHS
Circle	CIR	Hills	HLS	Rapids	RPDS
City	CY	Hollow	HOLW	Resort	RESRT
Clear	CLR	Hospital	HOSP	Rest	RST
Cliffs	CLFS	Hot	H	Ridge	RDG
Club	CLB	House	HSE	River	RIV
College	CLG	Inlet	INLT	Road	RD
Corner	COR	Institute	INST	Rock	RK
Corners	CORS	Island	IS	Rural	R
Court	CT	Islands	IS	Saint	ST
Courts	CTS	Isle	IS	Sainte	ST
Cove	CV	Junction	JCT	San	SN
Creek	CRK	Key	KY	Santa	SN
Crescent	CRES	Knolls	KJNLS	Santo	SN
Crossing	XING	Lake	LK	School	SCH
Dale	DL	Lakes	LKS	Seminary	SMNRY
Dam	DM	Landing	LNDG	Shoal	SHL
Depot	DPO	Lane	LN	Shoals	SHLS
Divide	DIV	Light	LGT	Shode	SHD
Drive	DR	Little	LTL	Shore	SHR
East	E	Loaf	LF	Shores	SHRS
Estates	EST	Locks	LCKS	Siding	SDG
Expressway	EXPY	Lodge	LDG	South	S
Extended	EXT	Lower	LWR	Space Flight Center	SFC
Extension	EXT	Manor	MNR	Spring	SPG
Fall	FL	Meadows	MDWS	Springs	SPGS
Falls	FLS	Meeting	MTG	Square	SQ

State	ST	Ton	TN	Viaduct	VIA
Station	STA	Tower	TWR	View	VW
Stream	STRM	Town	TWN	Village	VLG
Street	STSLP	Trail	TRL	Ville	VL
Sulphur	HR	Trailer	TRLR	Vista	VIS
Summit	SMT	Tunnel	TUNL	Water	WTR
Switch	SWCH	Turnpike	TPKE	Wells	WLS
Tannery	TNRY	Union	UN	West	W
Tavern	TVRN	University	UNIV	White	WHT
Terminal	TERM	Upper	UPR	Works	WKS
Terrace	TER	Valley	VLY	Yards	YDS

Forms of Address

It has already been emphasized that the initial impression created by a letter is vital to the letter's ultimate effectiveness. The proper use of the conventional forms of address is likewise essential, especially since these forms appear in conspicuous areas of the letter: on the envelope, in the inside address, and in the salutation.

The following pages contain a chart of alphabetically grouped and listed forms of address for individuals whose offices, ranks, or professions warrant special courtesy. (For information about choosing complimentary closes, see page 265.) The main categories in the chart are listed below in the order of their appearance.

Clerical and Religious Orders
College and University Faculty and Officials
Diplomats and Consular Officers
Foreign Heads of State
Government Officials—Federal
Government Officials—Local
Government Officials—State
Military Personnel
Miscellaneous Professional Titles

A special chart headed "Multiple Addressees" immediately follows the Forms of Address chart, and a more detailed discussion of special titles and abbreviations (*Doctor, Esquire, Honorable,* etc.) begins on page 306. For the use of gender-neutral salutations, see pages 259–60.

When two or more styles are shown in the Forms of Address chart, the most formal appears first.

Approximately half of the entries are illustrated with a man's name and half with a woman's name. The female equivalent of *Sir* is *Madam* (or *Madame* when the addressee is foreign). The female equivalent of *Mr.* when it immediately precedes a name is *Ms.* (or *Mrs.* or *Miss* if either is known to be preferred by the addressee). The male equivalent of *Madam* standing alone is *Sir.* When *Madam* precedes another title, the male equivalent is *Mr.,* and vice versa. The male equivalent of *Ms.* is *Mr.* The terms *Her Excellency* and *His Excellency* are similarly equivalent.

Lack of space has made it necessary to exclude lower-ranking officials, such as city water commissioners. Addressing these minor officials should present no problem, however. The official's title should appear in the address only if the official *heads* an agency or department; otherwise, only the name of the agency or department is included. The salutation on letters to minor officials should consist simply of courtesy title + surname.

Mrs. Joan R. Zaricki, Chair Smithville School Board	Dear Mrs. Zaricki
Mr. James McPhee Smithville School Board	Dear Mr. McPhee

The substitution of a professional title for the courtesy title is correct only for high-ranking officials such as governors and judges, for military officers, and for certain police and fire officers.

Dear Governor Serafino
Dear Senator Scott
Dear Judge Dvorak
Dear Major Stearns
Dear Chief Rodriguez
Dear Sheriff Robbins
 but also
Dear Mr. Robbins

Military officers retain their highest rank upon retirement and are addressed in the same way as active officers.

Inside-Address Style	*Salutation Style*
Clerical and Religious Orders	
Abbot	
The Right Reverend John R. Smith, O.S.B. (O.F.M., etc.) Abbot of _____	Right Reverend and dear Father Dear Father Abbot Dear Father
Archbishop	
The Most Reverend Archbishop of _____ *or*	Your Excellency
The Most Reverend John R. Smith Archbishop of _____	Your Excellency Dear Archbishop Smith
Archdeacon	
The Venerable The Archdeacon of _____ *or*	Venerable Sir My dear Archdeacon
The Venerable John R. Smith Archdeacon of _____	(same)
Bishop, Catholic	
The Most Reverend John R. Smith Bishop of _____	Most Reverend Sir Your Excellency Dear Bishop Smith
Bishop, Episcopal	
The Right Reverend The Bishop of _____ *or*	Right Reverend Sir
The Right Reverend John R. Smith Bishop of _____	Right Reverend Sir Dear Bishop Smith

Inside-Address Style	*Salutation Style*
Bishop, Episcopal, Presiding The Most Reverend John R. Smith Presiding Bishop	Most Reverend Sir Dear Bishop Dear Bishop Smith
Bishop, Protestant (excluding Episcopal) The Reverend John R. Smith	Reverend Sir Dear Bishop Smith
Brotherhood, member of Brother John, S.J. (O.F.M., O.S.B., etc.)	Dear Brother John
Canon The Reverend John R. Smith Canon of _____ Cathedral	Dear Canon Smith
Cardinal His Eminence John Cardinal Smith	Your Eminence Dear Cardinal Smith
or His Eminence Cardinal Smith *or if also an archbishop*	(same)
His Eminence John Cardinal Smith Archbishop of _____	(same)
or His Eminence Cardinal Smith Archbishop of _____	(same)
Chaplain, college or university—see COLLEGE AND UNIVERSITY FACULTY AND OFFICIALS	
Clergy, Protestant The Reverend Amelia R. Smith	Dear Ms. Smith
or with a doctorate The Reverend Dr. Amelia R. Smith	Dear Dr. Smith
Dean (of a cathedral) The Very Reverend John R. Smith _____ Cathedral	Very Reverend Sir Dear Dean Smith
or Dean John R. Smith _____ Cathedral	(same)
Monsignor, domestic prelate The Reverend Monsignor John R. Smith *or* The Rev. Msgr. John R. Smith	Reverend and dear Monsignor Smith Dear Monsignor Smith

Monsignor, papal chamberlain
The Very Reverend Monsignor John R.
  Smith
	Very Reverend and dear Monsignor
	  Smith
	Dear Monsignor Smith

or The Very Rev. Msgr. John R. Smith	(same)
Mother superior (of a sisterhood) The Reverend Mother Superior Convent of _____	Reverend Mother Dear Reverend Mother My dear Reverend Mother Mary Angelica
or Reverend Mother Mary Angelica, O.S.D. (S.M., S.C., etc.) Convent of _____	(same)

Inside-Address Style	*Salutation Style*
or Mother Mary Angelica, Superior Convent of _____	(same)
Patriarch (of an Eastern Orthodox Church) His Beatitude the Patriarch of _____	Most Reverend Lord Your Beatitude
Pope His Holiness the Pope	Your Holiness Most Holy Father
or His Holiness Pope John	(same)
President, Mormon The President Church of Jesus Christ of Latter-day Saints	My dear President Dear President Smith
Priest, Catholic The Reverend Father Smith	Reverend Father Dear Father Smith
or The Reverend John R. Smith	Dear Father (same)
Priest, president (of a college or university)—see COLLEGE AND UNIVERSITY FACULTY AND OFFICIALS	
Rabbi Rabbi John R. Smith	Dear Rabbi Smith
or with a doctorate Rabbi John R. Smith, D.D.	Dear Dr. Smith
Sisterhood, member of Sister Mary Angelica, S.C. (S.M., O.S.D., etc.)	Dear Sister Dear Sister Mary Angelica

College and University Faculty and Officials

Chancellor Dr. Amelia R. Smith Chancellor	Dear Dr. Smith
Chaplain The Reverend John R. Smith Chaplain	Dear Chaplain Smith Dear Father Smith Dear Mr. Smith
Dean Dean Amelia R. Smith	Dear Dr. Smith Dear Dean Smith
or Dr. Amelia R. Smith Dean	(same)
Instructor Mr. John R. Smith Instructor	Dear Mr. Smith

Inside-Address Style	*Salutation Style*

President
Dr. Amelia R. Smith
President

   or

President Amelia R. Smith

Dear Dr. Smith

Dear President Smith

President, priest
The Very Reverend John R. Smith
President

Dear Father Smith

Professor, assistant or associate
Ms. Amelia R. Smith
Assistant/Associate Professor of _____
   or with a doctorate
Dr. Amelia R. Smith
Assistant/Associate Professor of _____

Dear Professor Smith
Dear Ms. Smith

Dear Dr. Smith

Professor, full
Professor John R. Smith
   or
Dr. John R. Smith
Professor of _____

Dear Professor Smith

Dear Dr. Smith

Diplomats and Consular Officers

Ambassador, American
The Honorable Amelia R. Smith
American Ambassador
   or if in Central or South America
The Honorable Amelia R. Smith
Ambassador of the United States of
   America

Madam
Dear Madam Ambassador

(same)

Ambassador, foreign
His Excellency John R. Smith
Ambassador of _____

Excellency
Dear Mr. Ambassador

Chargé d'affaires ad interim, American
Amelia R. Smith, Esq.
American Chargé d'Affaires ad Interim
   or if in Latin America or Canada
Amelia R. Smith, Esq.
United States Chargé d'Affaires ad
   Interim

Madam
Dear Ms. Smith

(same)

Chargé d'affaires ad interim, foreign
Mr. John R. Smith
Chargé d'Affaires ad Interim of _____

Sir
Dear Mr. Smith

Chargé d'affaires, foreign
Ms. Amelia R. Smith
Chargé d'Affaires of _____

Madame
Dear Ms. Smith

Consulate, American
The American Consulate
   or if in Central or South America
The Consulate of the United States of
   America

Ladies and Gentlemen

(same)

Inside-Address Style	*Salutation Style*
Consul, American (covers all consular grades such as *Consul, Consul General, Vice-Consul,* and *Consular Agent*)	
The American Consul	Sir or Madam
or if in Central or South America	
The Consul of the United States of America	(same)
or if individual name is known	
Amelia R. Smith, Esq.	Madam
American Consul	Dear Ms. Smith
or if in Central or South America	
Amelia R. Smith, Esq.	(same)
Consul of the United States of America	
Consulate, foreign	
The _____ Consulate	Ladies and Gentlemen
or	
The Consulate of _____	(same)
Consuls, foreign (covers all consular grades)	
The _____ Consul	Sir or Madame
or	
The Consul of _____	(same)
or if individual name is known	
The Honorable John R. Smith	Sir
_____ Consul	Dear Mr. Smith
Minister, American	
The Honorable John R. Smith	Sir
American Minister	Dear Mr. Minister
or if in Latin America or Canada	
Minister of the United States of America	(same)
Minister, foreign	
The Honorable Amelia R. Smith	Madame
Minister of _____	Dear Madame Minister
Representative to the United Nations, American	
The Honorable Amelia R. Smith	Madam
United States Permanent Representative to the United Nations	Dear Madam Ambassador
Representative to the United Nations, foreign	
His Excellency John R. Smith	Excellency
Representative of _____ to the United Nations	My dear Mr. Ambassador
	Dear Mr. Ambassador
Secretary-General of the United Nations	
Her Excellency Amelia R. Smith	Excellency
Secretary-General of the United Nations	My dear Madam (*or* Madame) Secretary-General
	Dear Madam (*or* Madame) Secretary-General
Undersecretary of the United Nations	
The Honorable John R. Smith	Sir
Undersecretary of the United Nations	Dear Mr. Smith

Foreign Heads of State

Premier	
His Excellency John R. Smith	Excellency
Premier of _____	Dear Mr. Premier

Inside-Address Style	*Salutation Style*

President of a republic
Her Excellency Amelia R. Smith
President of ———

Excellency
Dear Madame President

Prime minister
His Excellency John R. Smith

Excellency
Dear Mr. Prime Minister

Government Officials—Federal

Attorney General
The Honorable Amelia R. Smith
The Attorney General

Dear Madam Attorney General

Cabinet officer (other than Attorney General)
The Honorable John R. Smith
Secretary of ———
  or
The Secretary of ———

Sir
Dear Mr. Secretary

(same)

Cabinet officer, former
The Honorable Amelia R. Smith

Dear Ms. Smith

Chairman of a (sub)committee, U.S. Congress (styles shown apply to both House of
    Representatives and Senate)
The Honorable John R. Smith
Chairman
Committee on ———
United States Senate

Dear Mr. Chairman
Dear Senator Smith

Chief justice—see SUPREME COURT, FEDERAL; STATE

Commissioner
  if appointed
The Honorable Amelia R. Smith
Commissioner
  if career
Ms. Amelia R. Smith
Commissioner

Dear Madam Commissioner
Dear Ms. Smith

Dear Ms. Smith

Congressman—see REPRESENTATIVE, U.S. CONGRESS

Director (as of an independent federal agency)
The Honorable John R. Smith
Director
——— Agency

Dear Mr. Smith

District attorney
The Honorable Amelia R. Smith
District Attorney

Dear Ms. Smith

Federal judge
The Honorable John R. Smith
Judge of the United States District
  Court of the ——— District
  of ———

Sir
My dear Judge Smith
Dear Judge Smith

Justice—see SUPREME COURT, FEDERAL; STATE

Librarian of Congress
The Honorable Amelia R. Smith
Librarian of Congress

Madam
Dear Ms. Smith

Inside-Address Style	Salutation Style
Postmaster General	
The Honorable John R. Smith	Sir
The Postmaster General	Dear Mr. Postmaster General
President of the United States	
The President	Mr. President
	My dear Mr. President
	Dear Mr. President
President of the United States (former)	
The Honorable John R. Smith	Sir
	Dear Mr. Smith
President-elect of the United States	
The Honorable Amelia R. Smith	Dear Madam
President-elect of the United States	Dear Ms. Smith
Representative, U.S. Congress	
The Honorable Amelia R. Smith	Madam
United States House of Representatives	Dear Representative Smith
or for local address	
The Honorable Amelia R. Smith	Dear Ms. Smith
Representative in Congress	
Representative, U.S. Congress (former)	
The Honorable John R. Smith	Dear Mr. Smith
Senator, U.S. Senate	
The Honorable Amelia R. Smith	Madam
United States Senate	Dear Senator Smith
Senator-elect	
The Honorable John R. Smith	Dear Mr. Smith
Senator-elect	
Senator (former)	
The Honorable Amelia R. Smith	Dear Senator Smith
Speaker, U.S. House of Representatives	
The Honorable Speaker of the House	Madam
of Representatives	
or	
The Honorable Amelia R. Smith	Madam
Speaker of the House of Representatives	Dear Madam Speaker
	Dear Ms. Smith
Speaker, U.S. House of Representatives (former)	
The Honorable Amelia R. Smith	Madam
	Dear Madam Speaker
	Dear Ms. Smith
Special assistant to the President of the United States	
Mr. John R. Smith	Dear Mr. Smith
Supreme Court, associate justice	
Mr. Justice Smith	Sir
The Supreme Court of the United States	Mr. Justice
	My dear Mr. Justice
	Dear Mr. Justice Smith

Inside-Address Style	*Salutation Style*
Supreme Court, chief justice	
The Chief Justice of the United States	Sir
	My dear Mr. Chief Justice
	Dear Mr. Chief Justice
or	
The Chief Justice	(same)
Supreme Court, retired Justice	
The Honorable Amelia R. Smith	Madam
	Dear Justice Smith
Territorial delegate	
The Honorable Amelia R. Smith	Dear Ms. Smith
Delegate of _____	
House of Representatives	
Undersecretary of a department	
The Honorable John R. Smith	Dear Mr. Smith
Undersecretary of _____	
Vice President of the United States	
The Vice President of the United States	Madam
United States Senate	My dear Madam Vice President
	Dear Madam Vice President
or	
The Honorable Amelia R. Smith	(same)
Vice President of the United States	

Government Officials—Local

Alderman	
The Honorable John R. Smith	Dear Mr. Smith
	Dear Alderman Smith
or	
Alderman John R. Smith	(same)
City attorney (includes city counsel, corporation counsel)	
The Honorable Amelia R. Smith	Dear Ms. Smith
Councilman—see ALDERMAN	
County clerk	
The Honorable John R. Smith	Dear Mr. Smith
Clerk of _____ County	
County treasurer—see COUNTY CLERK	
Judge	
The Honorable Amelia R. Smith	Dear Judge Smith
Judge of the _____ Court of _____	
Mayor	
The Honorable John R. Smith	Sir
Mayor of _____	Dear Mayor Smith
Selectman—see ALDERMAN	

Inside-Address Style	*Salutation Style*

Government Officials—State

Assemblyman—see REPRESENTATIVE, STATE

Attorney general
The Honorable John R. Smith   Sir
Attorney General of the State of _____   Dear Mr. Attorney General

Clerk of a court
Amelia R. Smith, Esq.   Dear Ms. Smith
Clerk of the Court of _____

Delegate—see REPRESENTATIVE, STATE

Governor
The Honorable John R. Smith   Sir
Governor of _____   Dear Governor Smith
   or in some states
His Excellency, the Governor of _____   (same)

Governor (acting)
The Honorable Amelia R. Smith   Madam
Acting Governor of _____   Dear Ms. Smith

Governor-elect
The Honorable John R. Smith   Dear Mr. Smith
Governor-elect of _____

Governor (former)
The Honorable Amelia R. Smith   Dear Ms. Smith

Judge, state court
The Honorable John R. Smith   Dear Judge Smith
Judge of the _____ Court

Judge/justice, state supreme court—see SUPREME COURT, STATE

Lieutenant governor
The Honorable Lieutenant Governor   Madam
   of _____
   or
The Honorable Amelia R. Smith   Madam
Lieutenant Governor of _____   Dear Ms. Smith

Representative, state (includes assemblyman, delegate)
The Honorable John R. Smith   Sir
House of Representatives (State   Dear Mr. Smith
   Assembly, House of Delegates, etc.)

Secretary of state
The Honorable Secretary of State   Madam
   of _____
   or
The Honorable Amelia R. Smith   Madam
Secretary of State of _____   Dear Madam Secretary

Senate, state, president of
The Honorable John R. Smith   Sir
President of the Senate of the State   Dear Mr. Smith
   of _____   Senator

Inside-Address Style	*Salutation Style*
Senator, state	
The Honorable Amelia R. Smith	Madam
The Senate of _____	Dear Senator Smith
Speaker, state assembly (house of delegates, house of representatives)	
The Honorable John R. Smith	Sir
Speaker of _____	Dear Mr. Smith
State's attorney	
The Honorable Amelia R. Smith	Dear Ms. Smith
(title)	
Supreme court, state, associate justice	
The Honorable Amelia R. Smith	Madam
Associate Justice of the Supreme Court	Dear Justice Smith
of _____	
Supreme court, state, chief justice	
The Honorable John R. Smith	Sir
Chief Justice of the Supreme Court	Dear Mr. Chief Justice
of _____	
Supreme court, state, presiding justice	
The Honorable Amelia R. Smith	Madam
Presiding Justice _____ Division	Dear Madam Justice
Supreme Court of _____	

Military Personnel

An incomplete listing of address formats for military ranks is shown here. The first entry below describes an appropriate form of address for any member of the armed forces. Abbreviations for each rank and the branches of service using them are shown at individual entries. In actual practice, salutations will differ according to degree of formality. The most formal will often employ the addressee's full title. The salutations shown generally represent a level of formality between the highly formal and the familiar.

For any rank	
full or abbreviated rank + full name +	Dear + *full rank + surname*
comma + abbreviation of the branch of service (USA, USN, USAF, USMC, USCG)	
Admiral [coast guard, navy (ADM)]	
Admiral Amelia R. Smith, USCG (etc)	Dear Admiral Smith
or	
ADM Amelia R. Smith, USCG (etc)	(same)

—a similar pattern is used for **rear admiral** (RADM) and **vice admiral** (VADM), with the full rank given in the salutation line.

Airman [air force (Amn)]	
Airman John R. Smith, USAF	Dear Airman Smith
or	
Amn John R. Smith, USAF	(same)

—a similar pattern is used for **airman basic** (AB) and **airman first class** (A1C), with the full rank given in the salutation line.

Cadet [U.S. Air Force Academy, U.S. Military Academy]	
Cadet Amelia R. Smith	Dear Cadet Smith

Inside-Address Style	*Salutation Style*

Captain [army (CPT); coast guard, navy (CAPT); air force, marine corps (Capt)]

Captain John R. Smith, USAF (etc)	Dear Captain Smith
or	
Capt John R. Smith, USAF (etc)	(same)

Chief petty officer [coast guard, navy (CPO)]

Chief Petty Officer Amelia R. Smith, USN (etc)	Dear Chief Smith
or	
CPO Amelia R. Smith, USN (etc)	(same)

Chief warrant officer [army (CW2, CW3, CW4, CW5); navy, coast guard, air force (CW0-2, CWO-3, CWO-4); marine corps (CWO2, CWO3, CWO4)]

Chief Warrant Officer Amelia R. Smith, USA (etc)	Dear Ms. Smith Dear Chief Warrant Officer Smith
or	
CW4 Amelia R. Smith, USA (etc)	(same)

Colonel [army (COL); air force, marine corps (Col)]

Colonel Amelia R. Smith, USMC (etc)	Dear Colonel Smith
or	
Col Amelia R. Smith, USMC (etc)	(same)

—a similar pattern is used for **lieutenant colonel** [army (LTC); air force, marine corps (LtCol)], with the full rank given in the salutation line.

Commander [coast guard, navy (CDR)]

Commander John R. Smith, USN (etc)	Dear Commander Smith
or	
CDR John R. Smith, USCG (etc)	(same)

—a similar pattern is used for **lieutenant commander** [coast guard, navy (LCDR)], with the full rank given in the salutation line.

Corporal [army (CPL); marine corps (Cpl)]

Corporal Amelia R. Smith, USA (etc)	Dear Corporal Smith
or	
CPL Amelia R. Smith, USA (etc)	(same)

—a similar pattern is used for **lance corporal** [marine corps (L/Cpl)], with the full rank given in the salutation line.

Ensign [coast guard, navy (ENS)]

Ensign John R. Smith, USN (etc)	Dear Ensign Smith Dear Mr. Smith
or	
ENS John R. Smith, USN (etc)	(same)

First lieutenant [army (1LT); air force, marine corps (1stLt)]

First Lieutenant Amelia R. Smith, USMC (etc)	Dear Lieutenant Smith
or	
1stLt Amelia R. Smith, USMC (etc)	(same)

General [army (GEN); air force, marine corps (Gen)]

General Amelia R. Smith, USAF (etc)	Dear General Smith
or	
Gen Amelia R. Smith, USAF (etc)	(same)

—a similar pattern is used for **brigadier general** [army (BG); air force (BGen), marine corps (BrigGen)], **major general** [army (MG); air force, marine corps (MajGen)], and **lieutenant general** [army (LTG); air force, marine corps (LtGen)], with the full rank given in the salutation line.

Inside-Address Style	*Salutation Style*
Lieutenant [coast guard, navy (LT)]	
Lieutenant John R. Smith, USN (etc)	Dear Lieutenant Smith
	Dear Mr. Smith
or	
LT John R. Smith, USN (etc)	(same)
Lieutenant junior grade [coast guard, navy (LTJG)]	
Lieutenant (j.g.) Amelia R. Smith, USCG	Dear Lieutenant Smith
(etc)	Dear Ms. Smith
or	
LTJG Amelia R. Smith, USCG (etc)	(same)
Major [army (MAJ); air force, marine corps (Maj)]	
Major John R. Smith, USAF (etc)	Dear Major Smith
or	
Maj John R. Smith, USAF (etc)	(same)
Master chief petty officer [coast guard, navy (MCPO)]	
Master Chief Petty Officer Amelia R.	Dear Master Chief Smith
Smith, USN (etc)	
or	
MCPO Amelia R. Smith, USN (etc)	(same)
Midshipman [coast guard and naval academies]	
Midshipman John R. Smith	Dear Midshipman Smith
Petty officer first class [coast guard, navy (PO1)]	
Petty Officer First Class John R. Smith,	Dear Petty Officer Smith
USN (etc)	
or	
PO1 John R. Smith, USN (etc)	(same)

—a similar pattern is used for **petty officer second class** (PO2) and **petty officer third class** (PO3).

Private [army (PVT); marine corps (Pvt)]	
Private John R. Smith, USMC (etc)	Dear Private Smith
or	
Pvt John R. Smith, USMC (etc)	(same)

—a similar pattern is used for **private first class** [army, marine corps (PFC)].

Seaman [coast guard, navy (Seaman)]	
Seaman Amelia R. Smith, USCG (etc)	Dear Seaman Smith

—a similar pattern is used for **seaman apprentice** (SA) and **seaman recruit** (SR).

Second lieutenant [army (2LT); air force, marine corps (2ndLt)]	
Second Lieutenant John R. Smith, USA	Dear Lieutenant Smith
(etc)	
or	
2LT John R. Smith, USA (etc)	(same)
Senior chief petty officer [coast guard, navy (SCPO)]	
Senior Chief Petty Officer John R. Smith,	Dear Senior Chief Smith
USCG (etc)	
or	
SCPO John R. Smith, USCG (etc)	(same)
Sergeant [army (SGT); air force, marine corps (Sgt)]	
Sergeant Amelia R. Smith, USAF (etc)	Dear Sergeant Smith
or	
Sgt Amelia R. Smith, USAF (etc)	(same)

Inside-Address Style	*Salutation Style*

—a similar pattern is used for other sergeant ranks, including **first sergeant** [army (1SG); marine corps (1stSgt)]; **gunnery sergeant** [marine corps (GySgt)]; **master sergeant** [army (MSG); air force, marine corps (MSgt)]; **senior master sergeant** [air force (SMSgt)]; **sergeant first class** [army (SFC)]; **staff sergeant** [army (SSG); air force, marine corps (SSgt)]; and **technical sergeant** [air force (TSgt)], with the full rank given in the salutation line.

Sergeant major [army (SGM); marine corps (SgtMaj)]

Sergeant Major Amelia R. Smith, USMC (etc)	Dear Sergeant Major Smith
or	
SgtMaj Amelia R. Smith, USMC (etc)	(same)

Specialist [army (SPC)]

Specialist John R. Smith, USA	Dear Specialist Smith
or	
SPC John R. Smith, USA	(same)

Warrant officer [army (WO1, WO2); navy (WO-1); air force, marine corps (WO)]

Warrant Officer John R. Smith, USA (etc)	Dear Warrant Officer Smith
	Dear Mr. Smith
or	
WO1 John R. Smith, USA (etc)	(same)

Miscellaneous Professional Titles

Attorney

Ms. Amelia R. Smith, Attorney-at-Law	Dear Ms. Smith
or	
Amelia R. Smith, Esq.	(same)

Certified public accountant

Amelia R. Smith, C.P.A.	Dear Ms. Smith

Dentist

John R. Smith, D.D.S. (D.M.D., etc.)	Dear Dr. Smith
or	
Dr. John R. Smith	(same)

Physician

Amelia R. Smith, M.D.	Dear Dr. Smith
or	
Dr. Amelia R. Smith	(same)

Veterinarian

John R. Smith, D.V.M.	Dear Dr. Smith
or	
Dr. John R. Smith	(same)

Multiple Addressees (See also pages 306–312.)

Inside-Address Style	Salutation Style

Two or more men with same surname

Mr. Arthur W. Jones	Gentlemen
Mr. John H. Jones	
or	*or*
Messrs. A. W. and J. H. Jones	
or	Dear Messrs. Jones
The Messrs. Jones	

Two or more men with different surnames

Mr. Angus D. Langley	Gentlemen
Mr. Lionel P. Overton	
or	*or*
Messrs. A. D. Langley and L. P. Overton	Dear Mr. Langley and Mr. Overton
or	*or*
Messrs. Langley and Overton	Dear Messrs. Langley and Overton

Two or more married women with same surname

Mrs. Arthur W. Jones	Mesdames
Mrs. John H. Jones	
or	*or*
Mesdames A. W. and J. H. Jones	Dear Mesdames Jones
or	
The Mesdames Jones	

Two or more unmarried women with same surname

Miss Alice H. Danvers	Ladies
Miss Margaret T. Danvers	
or	*or*
Misses Alice and Margaret Danvers	
or	Dear Misses Danvers
The Misses Danvers	

Two or more women with same surname but
     whose marital status is unknown or irrelevant

| Ms. Alice H. Danvers | Dear Ms. Alice and Margaret Danvers |
| Ms. Margaret T. Danvers | |

Two or more married women with different surnames

Mrs. Allen Y. Dow	Dear Mrs. Dow and Mrs. Frank
Mrs. Lawrence R. Frank	*or*
or	Mesdames
Mesdames Dow and Frank	*or*
	Dear Mesdames Dow and Frank

Two or more unmarried women with different surnames

Miss Elizabeth Dudley	Ladies
Miss Ann Raymond	*or*
or	Dear Miss Dudley and Miss Raymond
Misses E. Dudley and A. Raymond	*or*
	Dear Misses Dudley and Raymond

Two or more women with different surnames but
     whose marital status is unknown or irrelevant

| Ms. Barbara Lee | Dear Ms. Lee and Ms. Key |
| Ms. Helen Key | |

Special Titles, Designations, and Abbreviations

DOCTOR

If *Doctor* or *Dr.* is used before a person's name, academic degrees (such as *D.D.S., D.V.M., M.D.,* or *Ph.D.*) are not included after the surname. The title *Doctor* may be either typed out in full or abbreviated in a salutation, but it is usually abbreviated on an envelope and in an inside address in order to save space. When *Doctor* appears in a salutation, it must be used in conjunction with the addressee's surname.

Dear Doctor Smith
or
Dear Dr. Smith
(*not*   Dear Doctor)

If a woman holds a doctorate, her title should be used in business-related correspondence even if her husband's name is also included in the letter.

Dr. Ann R. Smith and   Dear Dr. Smith and Mr. Smith
   Mr. James O. Smith

If both husband and wife are doctors, one of the following styles may be used:

Dr. Ann R. Smith and   *formal:*
   Dr. James O. Smith   My dear Doctors Smith
The Drs. Smith   *informal:*
The Doctors Smith   Dear Drs. Smith
                                 Dear Doctors Smith

Ann R. Smith, M.D.
James O. Smith, M.D.

Drs. Ann R. and James O. Smith

If two or more doctors are associated in a joint practice, the following styles may be used:

Drs. Francis X. Sullivan and   *formal:*
   Philip K. Ross   My dear Drs. Sullivan and Ross
                                  informal:
Francis X. Sullivan, M.D.   Dear Drs. Sullivan and Ross
Philip K. Ross, M.D.   Dear Doctors Sullivan and Ross
                                  Dear Dr. Sullivan and Dr. Ross
                                  Dear Doctor Sullivan and
                                     Doctor Ross

ESQUIRE

The abbreviation *Esq.* for *Esquire* is often used in the United States after the surnames of professional persons such as attorneys, architects, professional engineers, and consuls, and also of court officials such as clerks of court and justices of the peace. *Esquire* may be written in addresses and signature lines but not in salutations. It is used regardless of sex. Some people, however, object to the use of *Esquire* as a title for a woman professional, and one should follow the recipient's wishes, if they are known, in this regard, using an alternative form such as "Amy Lutz, Attorney-at-Law" or "Edith Asher, P.E."

In Great Britain *Esquire* is generally used after the surnames of people who have distinguished themselves in professional, diplomatic, or social circles. For example, when addressing a letter to a British surgeon or to a high corporate officer of a British firm, one should include *Esq.* after the surname, both on the envelope and in the inside address. Under no circumstances should *Esq.* appear in a salutation in either American or British correspondence. If a courtesy title such as *Dr., Hon., Miss, Mr., Mrs.,* or *Ms.* is used before the addressee's name, *Esquire* or *Esq.* is omitted.

The plural of *Esq.* is *Esqs.,* and it is used with the surnames of multiple addressees.

Carolyn B. West, Esq. American Consul	Dear Ms. West
Samuel A. Sebert, Esq. Norman D. Langfitt, Esq. *or* Sebert and Langfitt, Esqs. *or* Messrs. Sebert and Langfitt Attorneys-at-Law	Gentlemen Dear Mr. Sebert and Mr. Langfitt Dear Messrs. Sebert and Langfitt

Simpson, Tyler, and Williams,
    Esqs.
or
Scott A. Simpson, Esq.
Annabelle W. Tyler, Esq.
David I. Williams, Esq.
	Dear Ms. Tyler and Messrs. Simpson
	    and Williams

British: Jonathan A. Lyons, Esq. President	Dear Mr. Lyons

HONORABLE

In the United States, *The Honorable* or its abbreviated form *Hon.* is used as a title of distinction (but not rank) for elected or appointed (but not career) government officials such as judges, justices, congressmen, and cabinet officers. Neither the full form nor the abbreviation is ever used by its recipient in written signatures, letterhead, business or visiting cards, or in typed signature blocks. While it may be used in an envelope address block and in the inside address of a letter, it is never used in the salutation. *The Honorable* should never appear before a surname standing alone: there must always be an intervening first name, an initial or initials, or a courtesy title. A courtesy title should not be added, however, when *The Honorable* is used with a full name.

The Honorable John R. Smith
The Honorable J. R. Smith
The Honorable J. Robert Smith
The Honorable Mr. Smith
The Honorable Dr. Smith
    not
The Honorable Smith
    and not
The Honorable Mr. John R. Smith

The Honorable may also precede a woman's name:

> The Honorable Jane R. Smith
> The Honorable Ms. Smith

When an official and his wife are being addressed, his full name should be typed out.

> The Honorable John R. Smith   Dear Mr. and Mrs. Smith
> and Mrs. Smith
> *or*
> The Honorable and Mrs. John R.
> Smith

The styles "Hon. and Mrs. Smith" and "The Honorable and Mrs. Smith" should never be used. If, however, the official's full name is unknown, the style is:

> The Honorable Mr. Smith and Mrs. Smith

If a married woman holds the title and her husband does not, her name appears first on business-related correspondence addressed to both persons. However, if the couple is being addressed socially, the woman's title may be dropped unless she has retained her maiden name for use in personal as well as business correspondence.

> *in business correspondence:*
> The Honorable Harriet O.   Dear Mrs. (*or* Governor, etc.)
> Johnson and Mr. Johnson   Johnson and Mr. Johnson
>
> The Honorable Harriet A. Ott   Dear Ms. Ott and Mr. Johnson
> and Mr. Robert Y. Johnson
>
> *in social correspondence:*
> Mr. and Mrs. Robert Y. Johnson   Dear Mr. and Mrs. Johnson
>
> Ms. Harriet A. Ott   Dear Ms. Ott and Mr. Johnson
> Mr. Roger Y. Johnson

If space is limited, *The Honorable* may be typed on the first line of an address block, with the recipient's name on the next line.

> The Honorable
> John R. Smith
> and Mrs. Smith

When *The Honorable* occurs in running text, the *T* in *The* is lowercased.

> A speech by the Honorable Charles H. Patterson, the American Consul in Athens

In informal writing such as newspaper articles, the plural forms *the Honorables* or *Hons.* may be used before a list of persons accorded the distinction. However, in official or formal writing, either *the Honorable Messrs.* may be placed before the entire list of surnames, or *the Honorable* or *Hon.* may be repeated before each full name in the list.

> *formal:*   . . . was supported in the motion by the Honorable Messrs. Alvarez, Goodfellow, and Harrington.
>   . . . met with the Honorable Albert Y. Langley and the Honorable Frances P. Kelley.

informal: ... interviewed the Hons. Jacob Y. Stathis, William L. Williamson, and Gloria O. Yarnell—all U.S. Senators.

JR. AND SR.

The designations *Jr.* and *Sr.* may or may not be preceded by a comma, depending on office policy or writer preference; however, one style should be selected and adhered to for the sake of uniformity.

John K. Walker Jr.   *or*   John K. Walker, Jr.

Jr. and *Sr.* may be used in conjunction with courtesy titles, academic degree abbreviations, or professional rating abbreviations.

Mr. John K. Walker[,] Jr.
General John K. Walker[,] Jr.
The Honorable John K. Walker[,] Jr.
John K. Walker[,] Jr., Esq.
John K. Walker[,] Jr., M.D.
John K. Walker[,] Jr., C.A.M.

MADAM AND MADAME

The title *Madam* should be used only in salutations of highly impersonal or high-level governmental and diplomatic correspondence. The title may be used to address women officials in other instances only if the writer is certain that the addressee is married. The French form *Madame* is recommended for salutations in correspondence addressed to foreign diplomats and heads of state. See the Forms of Address chart for examples.

MESDAMES

The plural form of *Madam, Madame,* or *Mrs.* is *Mesdames,* which may be used before the names of two or more married women associated in a professional partnership or business. It may appear with their names on an envelope and in the inside address, and it may appear with their names or standing alone in a salutation. (See also "Multiple Addressees," page 305.)

Mesdames T. V. Meade and P. A.   Dear Mesdames Meade and Tate
  Tate   Mesdames
Mesdames Meade and Tate

Mesdames V. T. and A. P. Stevens   Dear Mesdames Stevens
The Mesdames Stevens   Mesdames

MESSRS.

The plural abbreviation of *Mr.* is *Messrs.* (short for *Messieurs*). It is used before the surnames of two or more men associated in a professional partnership or business. *Messrs.* may appear on an envelope, in an inside address, and in a salutation when used in conjunction with the surnames of the addressees; however, this abbreviation should never stand alone.

Messrs. Archlake, Smythe, and   Dear Messrs. Archlake, Smythe, and
  Dabney   Dabney
Attorneys-at-Law   Gentlemen

Messrs. K. Y. and P. B. Overton   Dear Messrs. Overton
Architects   Gentlemen

Messrs. should never be used before a compound corporate name formed from two surnames such as *Lord & Taylor* or *Woodward & Lothrop* or a corporate name like *H. L. Jones and Sons.* For the use of *Messrs.* with *The Honorable* and *The Reverend,* see pages 308 and 311.

MISSES

The plural form of *Miss* is *Misses,* and it may be used before the names of two or more unmarried women who are being addressed together. It may appear on an envelope, in an inside address, and in a salutation. Like *Messrs., Misses* should never stand alone but must occur in conjunction with a name or names. (For a complete set of examples in this category, see "Multiple Addressees," page 305.)

Misses Hay and Middleton	Dear Misses Hay and Middleton
Misses D. L. Hay and H. K. Middleton	Ladies
Misses Tara and Julia Smith	Dear Misses Smith
The Misses Smith	Ladies

PROFESSOR

If used only with a surname, *Professor* should be typed out in full; however, if used with a given name and initial or a set of initials as well as a surname, it may be abbreviated to *Prof.* It is therefore usually abbreviated in envelope address blocks and in inside addresses, but typed out in salutations. *Professor* should not stand alone in a salutation.

Prof. Florence C. Marlowe	Dear Professor Marlowe
Department of English	Dear Dr. Marlowe
	Dear Ms. Marlowe
	but not
	Dear Professor

When addressing a letter to a professor and his wife, the title is usually written out in full unless the name is unusually long.

Professor and Mrs. Lee Dow	Dear Professor and Mrs. Dow
Prof. and Mrs. Henry Talbott-Smythe	Dear Professor and Mrs. Talbott-Smythe

Letters addressed to couples in which the wife is the professor and the husband is not may follow one of these patterns:

business correspondence:

Professor Diana Goode and Mr. Goode	Dear Professor Goode and Mr. Goode

business or social correspondence:

Mr. and Mrs. Lawrence F. Goode	Dear Mr. and Mrs. Goode

if wife has retained her maiden name:

Professor Diana Falls	Dear Professor (*or* Ms.) Falls and
Mr. Lawrence F. Goode	Mr. Goode

When addressing two or more professors—male or female, whether having the same or different surnames—type *Professors* and not *Profs.*:

Professors A. L. Smith and C. L. Doe	Dear Professors Smith and Doe Dear Drs. Smith and Doe Dear Mr. Smith and Mr. Doe Dear Messrs. Smith and Doe Gentlemen
Professors B. K. Johns and S. T. Yarrell	Dear Professors Johns and Yarrell Dear Drs. Johns and Yarrell Dear Ms. Johns and Mr. Yarrell
Professors G. A. and F. K. Cornett The Professors Cornett	*acceptable for any combination:* Dear Professors Cornett Dear Drs. Cornett *if males:* Gentlemen *if females:* Ladies *or* Mesdames *if married:* Dear Mr. and Mrs. Cornett Dear Professors Cornett Dear Drs. Cornett

REVEREND

In formal or official writing, *The* should precede *Reverend;* however, *The Reverend* is often abbreviated to *The Rev.* or just *Rev.,* especially in unofficial or informal writing, and particularly in business correspondence where the problem of space is a factor. The typed-out full form *The Reverend* must be used in conjunction with the full name, as in the following examples:

The Reverend Philip D. Asquith
The Reverend Dr. Philip D. Asquith

The Reverend may appear with just a surname only if another courtesy title intervenes:

The Reverend Mr. Asquith
The Reverend Professor Asquith
The Reverend Dr. Asquith

The Reverend, The Rev., or *Rev.* should not be used in the salutation, although any of these titles may be used on the envelope and in the inside address. In salutations, the following titles are acceptable: *Mr. (Ms., Miss, Mrs.), Father, Chaplain,* or *Dr.* See the Forms of Address chart under "Clerical and Religious Orders" for examples. The only exceptions are in letters addressed to high prelates (bishops, monsignors, etc.); see the Forms of Address chart. When addressing a letter to a member of the clergy and his or her spouse, follow the following style:

The Reverend (*or* Rev.) and Mrs. Philip D. Asquith	Dear Mr. (*or with a doctorate,* Dr.) and Mrs. Asquith
The Reverend (*or* Rev.) Marcia Ogden and Mr. James Ogden	Dear Mrs. (Ms., *or with a doctorate,* Dr.) and Mr. Ogden

Two members of the clergy should not be addressed in letters as "The Reverends," "The Revs.," or "Revs." They may, however, be addressed as *The Reverend* (or *The Rev.*) *Messrs.* if both are male, or *The Reverend* (or *The Rev.*) *Drs.* if both have doctorates, or the titles *The Reverend, The Rev.*, or *Rev.* may be repeated be-fore each name.

The Rev. Simon J. Stephens and the Rev. Barbara O. Stephens	Dear Mr. and Mrs. Stephens
Rev. Simon J. Stephens and Rev. Barbara O. Stephens	
The Reverend (*or* Rev.) Messrs. Philip A. Francis and Lanford Beale	Gentlemen Dear Father Francis and Father Beale
The Rev. Philip A. Francis The Rev. Lanford Beale	

In formal lists of names, "The Reverends," "The Revs.," and "Revs." are not acceptable as collective titles. *The Reverend* (or *Rev.*) *Messrs. (Drs., Professors)* may be used if appropriate, or *The Reverend* or *The Rev.* or *Rev.* may be repeated be-fore each name. If the term *clergyman, clergywoman,* or *the clergy* is mentioned in introducing the list, a single title *the Reverend* or *the Rev.* may be used to serve all of the names. While it is true that "the Revs." is often seen in newspapers and elsewhere, it is still not recommended for formal, official writing.

... were the Reverend Messrs. Jones, Smith, and Bennett, as well as ...
Among the clergy present were the Reverend John G. Jones, Mr. Smith, and Dr. Bennett.
Prayers were offered by the Rev. J. G. Jones, the Rev. Mr. Smith, and the Rev. Dr. Bennett.

SECOND, THIRD, FOURTH

These designations after surnames may take the form of Roman numerals (II, III, IV) or ordinals (2nd/2d, 3rd/3d, 4th). There should be no comma between the name and the number.

Mr. Jason T. Cabot III (*or* 3rd *or* 3d)

SEQUENCE OF ABBREVIATIONS AND INITIALS

Initials representing academic degrees, religious orders, and professional rat-ings may appear after a name, separated from each other by commas, in the following order: (1) religious orders (such as *S.J.*); (2) theological degrees (such as *D.D.*); (3) academic degrees (such as *Ph.D.*); (4) honorary degrees (such as *Litt.D.*); (5) professional ratings (such as *C.P.A.*).

Initials that represent academic degrees (with the exception of *M.D., D.D.S.*, and other medical degrees) are not commonly used in addresses, and two or more sets of such letters appear even more rarely. Only when the initials repre-sent achievements in different fields that are relevant to one's profession should more than one set be used. On the other hand, initials that represent earned professional achievements (such as *C.P.A., C.A.M., C.P.S.*, or *P.E.*) are often used in business addresses. When any of these sets of initials follow a name, however, the courtesy title (*Mr., Mrs., Ms., Miss, Dr.*) is omitted.

Nancy Robinson, P.L.S.

Mary R. Lopez, C.P.A.

John Doctorow, M.D., Ph.D.
Chief of Staff
Smithville Hospital

Jordan R. Dodds, J.D., C.M.C.

The Rev. Seamus McMalley, S.J., D.D., LL.D.
Chaplain, Smithville College

Correspondence with Government Agencies

The extensive dealings between government and private industry have made it necessary for civilian contractors to be familiar with government agencies' special correspondence and security procedures. While letter format and security precautions vary with the policies of each government contracting agency and the nature of each contract, the following overview should serve as a general orientation for anyone dealing with government correspondence for the first time.

The two basic aims are to ensure that (1) all material, regardless of its classification, be quickly delivered to its intended addressee and copies of it be readily retrievable, and (2) all classified material be safeguarded according to government guidelines so that unauthorized persons cannot gain access to it.

CORRESPONDENCE FORMAT

Letters to government agencies should conform to the guidelines of the agency with which your firm is working. Letters incorrectly formatted and addressed may be delayed, lost, or even rejected and returned—any of which can result in costly delays or even the loss of a contract, especially when bidding under a deadline is involved.

Correspondence with a nonmilitary government agency may be formatted in any of the generally accepted business-letter styles discussed earlier in this chapter. A subject line and a reference line are always included, since they are necessary for proper intra-agency routing of the letter. The correct forms of address for elected and appointed officials can be found in the Forms of Address chart.

The following general principles are applicable to correspondence directed to the Department of Defense. Most are illustrated in Fig. 7.35.

1. The Modified Block Letter style with numbered paragraphs is recommended.
2. If any section of the letter is classified, the highest classification category for any material therein must be stamped at the top and the bottom of each page. This stamp appears above the printed letterhead and below the last line of the message on the first sheet, and above the heading and below the last notation on all continuation sheets. The CLASSIFIED BY and NATIONAL SECURITY INFORMATION stamps must appear at the bottom of the letterhead sheet.
3. Any special mailing notation is typically typed in capital letters or stamped in the upper left corner of the letterhead sheet and any continuation sheets.
4. The writer's courtesy title and surname, the typist's initials, and the writer's telephone extension (if not already included in the printed letterhead) may be typed in the upper right corner of the first sheet, separated by slashes.
5. The dateline appears flush left about three lines below the letterhead. The date may be styled in either of two ways: "1 January 1995" or "1 Jan 95," for example. The style chosen should be used consistently throughout the letter. For the second style, each of the twelve months may be abbreviated to its first three letters, with no period following.

Fig. 7.35 Letter Style for Department of Defense Correspondence

---

CONFIDENTIAL

Merriam
Webster

CERTIFIED MAIL   Mr. Exec/tp/413-734-4444

```
1 January 19--
76TRANS123


SUBJECT:     Contract AF 45(100)-1147
             Foreign Technology Program
             Life Sciences Translation QC (C)


TO:          Initials or Name of Office
             Name of Applicable Administrator
             Organization
             Geographical Address + ZIP Code


THROUGH:     Applicable Channels
             and Addresses
             Listed and Blocked


REFERENCE:   (a) WXYZ letter ABCD/EF dated 1 December 19--
             (b) EFGH letter IJKL/MN dated 1 November 19--

  1.  This is a typical format for letters directed to the Department of
      Defense.  Styling varies with the agency or department one is
      writing to; thus, a format consensus is shown here.

  2.  In letters containing classified information, the highest
      classification category of any included information must be noted
      at the top and bottom of each page.

      a.  Since the subject of this letter is supposed to be
          CONFIDENTIAL, it is so stamped above the letterhead
          and at the bottom of the page.

      b.  The parenthetical abbreviation (C) for CONFIDENTIAL
          is typed at the end of the subject line.

      c.  Appropriate classification stamps are affixed at the
          bottom of the first page.

  3.  Special mailing notations, if required, are typically typed in the
      upper left corner of the page.
```

CLASSIFIED BY: _____
EXEMPT FROM GENERAL DECLASSIFICATION
SCHEDULE OF EXECUTIVE ORDER 11652
EXEMPTION CATEGORY
DECLASSIFY on

CONFIDENTIAL

NATIONAL SECURITY INFORMATION
Unauthorized disclosure subject to
criminal sanctions.

Merriam-Webster Inc.

47 Federal Street • P.O. Box 281 • Springfield, MA 01102 • Telephone (413) 734-3134 • Facsimile (413) 731-5979

CONFIDENTIAL

CERTIFIED MAIL

Contract AF 45(100)-1147   1 January 19--
Foreign Technology Program   76TRANS123
Life Sciences QC (C)   Page 2

   4.   If the writer's name and telephone number are not on the printed
        letterhead, they may be typed with the typist's initials in the
        upper right corner of the first page.

   5.   The dateline, with the date in inverted form, and the company
        control number are aligned flush left, with the dateline three
        lines below the letterhead.

   6.   The SUBJECT block, sometimes placed after the TO and/or THROUGH
        blocks depending on agency preference, contains the contract
        number, project name, and subject of the letter.

   7.   The TO block is really the inside address. The THROUGH or VIA
        block lists the designated channels through which the letter must
        pass before it reaches the addressee.

   8.   The REFERENCE block lists related material or previous
        correspondence that must be referred to before action can be
        taken.

   9.   The SUBJECT, TO, THROUGH, and REFERENCE blocks are separated by
        triple-spacing, and are internally single-spaced.

  10.   There is no salutation. The message, comprising numbered
        paragraphs and alphabetized subparagraphs, begins two lines below
        the last line in the REFERENCE block.

  11.   Continuation-sheet headings begin six lines from the top edge of
        the page and contain subject data, date, page number, and control
        or reference number. The classification category must be stamped
        at the top and bottom of each continuation sheet.

  12.   There is no complimentary close. The company name is typed all in
        capitals two lines below the last message line, followed four
        lines down by the writer's name, title, and department, if
        necessary, in capitals and lowercase.

  13.   The typist's or keyboarder's initials, if not shown at the top of
        the first page, may appear two lines below the signature block.
        Enclosures should be listed numerically and identified, as should
        carbon-copy recipients. Only external distribution lists appear
        on the original.

MERRIAM WEBSTER INC.

Executive Signature

Executive Signature
Project Manager

Enclosures (1)   (C) 3 copies of Translation
                   Printout dated 30 December 19--

           (2)   1 copy of Contract AF 44(100)-1147

CONFIDENTIAL

6. Companies contracting with the government for a specific project usually assign a control number to files and correspondence related to the project. This reference number should appear on the line below the dateline.

7. The next element of the letter—the SUBJECT block or the TO block, depending on the agency—is typed flush left about three lines below the reference number. The SUBJECT block, shown first in the following facsimile, consists of three lines: (1) the contract number, (2) the name of the program or project, and (3) the subject of the letter, followed by the appropriate security classification—(C) = Confidential, (S) = Secret, or (TS) = Top Secret.

8. The TO block, which is really the inside address, is typed about three lines below the date block or the SUBJECT block. It consists of four lines: (1) the initials or name of the office, (2) the name of the administrator (addressee), (3) the name of the organization, and (4) the geographical address.

9. The THROUGH or VIA block (the caption varies depending on the agency) is typed about three lines below any other blocks that precede it. This block is used in letters that must be sent through designated channels before reaching the addressee. Each agency, office, or individual should be named and addressed as in the TO block.

10. The REFERENCE block is typed about three lines below the last block. It contains a list of material or previous correspondence that the addressee must consult before acting on the letter. The items are numbered or lettered sequentially.

11. The captions SUBJECT, TO, THROUGH, and REFERENCE should not be visible in the window area of a window envelope; only the address in the TO block should be visible. The style of these captions varies: they may be entirely in capitals, they may be in capitals and lowercase, or they may be abbreviated (SUBJ, THRU, etc.). Use the style recommended by the individual agency.

12. There is no salutation.

13. The message begins flush left, two lines below the last line of the REFERENCE block. Paragraphs are numbered consecutively and are single-spaced internally but double-spaced between each other. Subparagraphs are alphabetized, single-spaced internally, and double-spaced between each other. As in a standard outline, if there is a paragraph *1*, there must be a *2*; if there is an *a*, there must be a *b*; and so on.

14. There is no complimentary close.

15. The company name is typed flush left in capital letters two lines beneath the last line of the message. The writer's name is typed in capitals and lowercase at least four lines below the company name, also flush left. The writer's title and department name, if not already on the letterhead, may be included beneath his or her name in capitals and lowercase, also flush left.

16. The typist's initials, if not already included in the top right corner of the first sheet, may be typed flush left, two lines below the last element of the signature block.

17. Enclosures are listed and identified two lines below the typist's initials or the signature block. The numeral styles 1. or (1) may be used. The appropriate headings are *Enclosure(s), Encl.,* or *Enc.* for the Air Force and Navy, and *Inclosure(s)* or *Inc.* for the Army. Classification categories should be noted at the beginning of each applicable enclosure description as shown in enclosure (3) below. Even if enclosures are to be mailed under separate cover, they must be listed on the letter and their classification categories noted.

Enc.: (1) 3 copies of Test Procedure Report
WXYzz dated 1 January 19——
(2) 1 copy of Contract AF 45(100)-1147
(3) (C) 2/c ea. specifications mentioned
in paragraph 7

Some government agencies require that enclosures be noted in a block two or three spaces below the REFERENCE block.

18. The copy notation *cc:* or *Copy to* is typed flush left two lines below any other notations. It includes an alphabetical listing of all individuals not associated with the company who will receive copies. Their addresses should be included. Internal copies should contain a complete list of both the external and internal recipients of copies.

cc: COL John K. Walker
Fort Bragg, NC 28307
(w/enc. (1)—2 copies)

19. Continuation-sheet headings are typed six lines from the top edge of the page, and the message continues four lines beneath the heading. Continuation-sheet headings should include the SUBJECT block data as well as the reference number, the date, and the page number (see facsimile).

20. If the contracting agency must approve the material and return it to the contractor, an approval line must be the last typed item on the page. In this case, two copies of the letter must be enclosed in the envelope.

APPROVED

_____

(addressee's title)

date

This material may be typed two to four lines beneath the last notation and blocked with the left margin.

CLASSIFIED MATERIAL

Both the U.S. government and its civilian contractors are responsible for the security of sensitive material passing between them—responsibility that specifically means the safeguarding of classified material against unlawful or unauthorized dissemination, duplication, or observation. Each employee of a firm that handles or has knowledge of classified material shares responsibility for protecting it while it is in use, in storage, or in transit. The security regulations of the Department of Defense are outlined in DoD publication 5200.1-R, *Information Security Program Regulation,* for sale through the National Technical Information Service, U.S. Department of Commerce, Springfield, VA 22161.

Classification in industrial operations is based on government security guidance. Private-sector management must implement the decisions of the government contracting agency with respect to classified information and material developed, produced, or handled in the course of a project. Management also must designate persons within the firm who will be responsible for assuring that government regulations are followed. Each system and program involving research, development, testing, and evaluation of technical information is supported by its own program security guide.

The following short glossary, adapted from Department of Defense definitions, will introduce the basic concepts of security classification.

Classified information   Official information that requires, in the interest of national security, protection against unauthorized disclosure and has been so designated.

Declassify   To determine that certain classified information no longer requires protection against unauthorized disclosure and to remove the classification designation.

Document   Any recorded information (including written or printed material, data-processing cards and tapes, graphics, and sound, voice, or electronic recordings in any form), regardless of its physical form or characteristics.

Downgrade   To determine that certain classified information does not require as high a degree of protection against unauthorized disclosure as is currently provided, and to change the classification designation to reflect this.

Information   Knowledge that can be communicated by any means.

Material   Any document, product, or substance on or in which information may be recorded or embodied.

National security   A term encompassing both the national defense and the foreign relations of the United States.

Official information   Information owned by, produced for or by, or subject to the control of the U.S. government.

Regrade   To determine that certain classified information requires a different degree of protection against unauthorized disclosure than is currently provided, and to change the classification designation to reflect this.

Upgrade   To determine that certain classified information requires a higher degree of protection against unauthorized disclosure than is currently provided, and to change the classification designation to reflect this.

The following classification categories must be designated on correspondence and other matter by stamps not less than ¼" in height:

Unclassified (U)   For information or material that requires no protection against unauthorized disclosure.

Confidential (C)   For information or material requiring protection because its unauthorized disclosure could cause damage to the national security.

Secret (S)   For information or material requiring a substantial degree of protection because its unauthorized disclosure could cause serious damage to the national security.

Top Secret (TS)   For information or material requiring the highest degree of protection because its unauthorized disclosure could cause exceptionally grave damage to the national security.

The phrases "For official use only" and "Limited official use" should not be used to identify classified information.

The following general marking procedures are required by the government:

1. The overall classification of a document, whether or not permanently bound, or any copy or reproduction thereof must be conspicuously marked or stamped at the top and bottom on the outside of the front cover (if any), on the title page (if any), on the first page, on the last page, and on the outside of the back cover (if any). Each inside page of the document must be marked or stamped top and bottom with the highest classification category applicable to the information appearing there.

2. Each section, paragraph, subparagraph, or part of a document must be marked with the applicable parenthetical classification abbreviation (TS), (S), (C), or (U) when there are several degrees of classified information within the document.

3. Large components of complex documents which may be used separately should be appropriately marked. These components include attachments and appendices to a memorandum or a letter, annexes or appendices to a plan or program, or a major part of a report.

4. Files, folders, or packets for classified documents should be conspicuously marked on both front and back covers with the highest category of classification occurring in documents they enclose.

5. Transmittal documents including endorsements and comments should carry the highest classification category applicable to the information attached to them.

Basic mailing procedures for classified documents are outlined below. (For detailed information on mailing and hand-carrying such documents, see *Information Security Program Regulation.*)

1. Classified material must be enclosed in two sealed opaque envelopes or similar wrappings before it may be mailed through the U.S. Postal Service or a commercial carrier.

2. Both envelopes must contain the names and addresses of the sender and the receiver.

3. The inner envelope must contain the appropriate classification category stamp, which must not be visible through the outer envelope.

4. The classified information should be protected from the inner envelope by being folded inward, or by use of a blank cover sheet.

5. The inner envelope must contain an appropriate classified-material receipt.

6. Confidential material must be sent by CERTIFIED MAIL, and Secret information must be sent by REGISTERED MAIL. Top Secret documents require specialized transit procedures.

7. Classified material should be addressed to an official government agency and not to an individual.

Classified material is downgraded and declassified when the Department of Defense determines that there is no longer any national-security reason for it to be classified. An automatic schedule of downgrading has been set up for the three categories:

1. TOP SECRET will be downgraded automatically to SECRET at the end of the second full calendar year following the year it was originated; downgraded to CONFIDENTIAL at the end of the fourth full calendar year following the year it was originated; and declassified at the end of the tenth full calendar year following the year it was originated.

2. SECRET will be downgraded automatically to CONFIDENTIAL at the end of the second full calendar year following the year it was originated, and de-

classified at the end of the eighth full calendar year following the year it was originated.

3. CONFIDENTIAL will be automatically declassified at the end of the sixth full calendar year following the year it was originated.

Classified documents therefore must be conspicuously marked or stamped to indicate the intended automatic downgrading schedule. This information is typed or stamped on the first or title page of a document immediately below or adjacent to the classification stamp.

Exemptions to the General Declassification Schedule will bear an exemption stamp immediately below or adjacent to the classification stamp on the first or title page (see Fig. 7.35).

Correspondence Composed by the Secretary

Your ability to write routine correspondence can make you a valuable asset to your organization. To the extent that you can perform this quasi-managerial function, you will free the executive for other work. How much correspondence you are entrusted with will depend greatly on your understanding of the executive's responsibilities and his or her confidence in your capacities and judgment.

General Guidelines

Composing a good business letter frequently requires some preparation. If you are responding to a letter, you may want to highlight or underscore significant facts and requests with a felt-tip or ballpoint pen. It may also be helpful to make your own notes in the margin of the previous letter—conference dates, appointments, brochure titles, and so on. To do so, you may have to consult your own tables, reports, printouts, catalogs, reference books, or manuals. Once you have put all the facts together and conceived a clear idea of what you want to say, jot down the topics in order, so as to produce a basic outline of your letter before beginning to write.

TONE

The tone of a communication is usually set in the first paragraph. It may be formal or informal, neutral or biased, friendly or critical, or it may reflect any number of other feelings and attitudes. The tone established is normally maintained throughout the subsequent paragraphs to the end. What kind of tone a writer wishes to establish will depend on several factors. One is the underlying reason why the letter (or memorandum or report) is being written. Another is the personal attitude of the writer toward the reader and the subject matter. Finally, the content itself (for instance, whether it is general or technical) will to some extent determine its tone.

The effect of a communication's tone on its reader cannot be overemphasized. A letter may exhibit attractive stationery, well-ordered layout, clean typing, good sentence structure, correct spelling, smooth flow, and complete and logically presented data—yet if the tone is abrupt or rude, the effect on the reader will be negative.

The reader's point of view and possible responses should never be forgotten, even when the writer is intent on setting forth his or her objectives. Compare the following two approaches, the first of which is abrupt, the second friendly and courteous.

We have seen your article on HDPE pipe in the October 12 issue of *Plastics*. Since our marketing division is preparing a multiclient study on plastic pipe applications, we will need offprints of the following papers you have written on this subject: . . .

We have read with interest your article on HDPE pipe in the October 12 issue of *Plastics*. Our marketing division is preparing a multiclient study on plastic pipe applications—a study that will not be complete without reference to your outstanding research. We would therefore be pleased if you would send us offprints of the following papers you've written on the subject: . . .

A writer's degree of familiarity with the subject matter will not always be shared by the reader. The writer should neither write on too low a level to experts in a given field nor write over the heads of nonexperts. The way information is presented should always be adjusted to the level of the likely reader.

Along with common courtesy and tactfulness, use of the personal pronouns *I*, *we*, and *you* can go far to personalize a communication and make the reader feel more involved in the discussion. Sentence constructions that avoid the use of the personal pronouns, on the other hand, can depersonalize a communication and lessen its impact. Compare the following pair of examples, the first of which is cool and impersonal, the second warm and personal.

Enclosed please find information regarding details of our annual "Get-Acquainted Day" on Thursday, October 2, at which you have agreed to deliver a speech as per our request.

How lucky we are that you said yes to our invitation to appear before a group of new secretaries at our annual "Get-Acquainted Day" on Thursday, October 2! After hearing you speak at the CPS meeting in April, I am convinced that we couldn't find a better speaker.

The effectiveness of your writing can be markedly increased by avoiding padding and clichés. Business-letter clichés—often known as *business static* or *officialese*—have unfortunately become fixtures in the prose of many executives and secretaries who think they are somehow appropriate and desirable. But a busy reader can become impatient at having to wade through superfluous and hackneyed language to get at the gist of a communication.

As you review your letter or memo, be alert for language that sounds stiff, overused, overlong, and redundant or otherwise unnecessary. Consider replacing *at all times* with *always*, *at this point in time* with *now* or *at present*, *due to* (or *in view of*) *the fact that* with *since*, *in the amount of* with *for*, *in view of the foregoing* with *therefore* or *thus*, and so on. In general, choose the shortest words available and delete any that can be omitted. Except when special formality is required, try to adopt a tone that is slightly more formal and concise than your everyday speech. A good book on usage, such as *Webster's Dictionary of English Usage*, can be helpful.

GETTING THE MESSAGE ACROSS

Regard every potential reader of your business letters as a critic of your company. Each communication to a client or potential customer provides an opportunity to epitomize the best in company spirit, service, and helpfulness. Here are some ways to create a positive impression on the reader:

1. Use easy-to-understand language. Short, clear, direct words are easier to read and understand than long words. Use natural language while avoiding casual or slangy expressions. In particular, try to use expressions that your executive uses.

2. Organize your sentences and paragraphs carefully and concisely so that the busy reader can absorb the message on first reading. Coherence and continuity are prime considerations.

3. Give accurate and adequate information. The omission of a single important detail can spell the difference between order and confusion in the reader's mind. The recipient should not have to write back requesting information that should have been included in the initial letter.

4. Avoid ambiguous language. It has often been said that if a statement *can* be misunderstood, it *will* be. By scanning your prose for unintended ambiguity, you can avoid many problems. For example, how would the following statement be interpreted?

    One and two-page photos are needed for this year's annual report.

    How many photos are needed? Is the writer requesting one one-page photo and one two-page photo? Is the recipient expected to supply all the photos needed? Careful rewording will prevent any misunderstanding:

    Please prepare one full-page photo and one double-page photo for use in this year's annual report.

5. Respond to all questions raised. It is a serious omission when you neglect to answer a question raised in previous correspondence. Double-check by rereading the previous correspondence and comparing it with your response.

6. Introduce unfavorable comments with favorable ones. It is tactful to present the positive aspects of a situation before making any negative or unfavorable observations. For example:

    Your kind comments about the usefulness of our *Better Letter Dictation* brochure are greatly appreciated. A complimentary copy is on its way to you. Unfortunately, the demand for copies of the brochure in recent weeks has depleted our supply. However, please feel free to reproduce temporary copies for use by your staff. When our new shipment arrives, we'll speed a dozen copies to you.

Soften your language with euphemisms, if necessary, to avoid a negative tone.

A FRIENDLY CLOSE

Include a pleasant closing thought in the final paragraph, as in this example:

Again, thank you for giving us permission to reprint the article on your company's research in the field of pollution control. This information will provide excellent material for next month's issue of *The Executive*.

Avoid thanking your reader in advance, since it is slightly impertinent to assume beforehand that a request will be honored. Wait until the service is rendered before making an appropriate acknowledgment for it. And compliment the recipient only if he or she has earned the compliment.

The recipient of a letter of request should know exactly what action is expected of him or her by the end of the letter. Any such action should be stated or restated in a clear and friendly manner in the last paragraph.

Proofread the letter for misspelled words, incorrect figures and dates, lack of agreement between subject and verb, misplaced commas, incorrect word division, and other such pitfalls. Check to see that each of the necessary parts or elements of the letter has been included.

When you compose a letter for your employer, there must be an understanding about whose signature is to appear at the end. A good rule to follow is that only letters of general information (conference dates, report titles, etc.) and routine requests may bear your signature unless you have been otherwise instructed. When the executive is away from the office for several days, you may be authorized to sign his or her name on outgoing correspondence. If so, your initials may be written beneath the executive's name, or the letter may be signed with your own name if your name and title are typed in the signature block; see Figs. 7.24 and 7.25 in the previous chapter.

Writing Routine Letters and Memorandums

ROUTINE LETTERS

An expedient way to answer routine letters is through reference to standard response letters. A ring binder with index tabs can be used to file examples of certain types of letters that are frequently written—Acknowledgment, Announcement, Apology, and so on. Such a notebook could also contain a stock of ready-made insertable paragraphs (labeled A, B, C, D, etc.); by referring to these, an executive could delegate to the secretary the task of producing routine request or response letters.

Form letters are sometimes printed in advance, leaving only the date and the inside address, and sometimes other data in the body of the letter, to be filled in by the secretary. Today, however, such letters are commonly kept on a computer disk so that the secretary can easily customize them with a word processor for each individual use, thus giving these letters the appearance of having been newly composed. When numerous form letters must be sent, the word processor's Mail Merge function can be very useful.

MEMORANDUMS

Office memorandums are written for circulation only within the organization (sometimes including corporate branch offices in distant cities). Many companies use printed memorandum forms. Though such forms vary, most contain the four standard headings (TO, FROM, DATE, SUBJECT) followed by space for the message. A memorandum has neither salutation nor complimentary close. It is not usually signed, but it may be initialed by the author. See the sample memorandum in Fig. 8.1.

The memorandum is an efficient way to relay information to all or part of the corporate staff. An office copier can quickly produce multiple copies for wide distribution. A memorandum may also be addressed to a single person. Thus, the TO line may be addressed to one individual, to several individuals, or to a group.

TO: Frances Rummel, Customer Services Supervisor
TO: Department Heads
TO: Administrative Staff, School of Business

It is followed by the FROM line, which includes the name of the writer and often his or her title; the DATE line; the SUBJECT line; and the optional LOCATION (floor, extension, or branch) line.

The SUBJECT line gives the reader an overview or encapsulation of the

Fig. 8.1   Memorandum

──────────────── Metro-Century ────────────────

Memorandum

TO: Sheryl Lansky   Paul DiAngelo
    Charles Cucurullo Desmond Chatworth
    Miche Grenier   George Keynes
    Dolores Alt   Myles Hurd

FROM: Richard Farnsworth, Secretary

DATE: July 15, 19--

SUBJECT: EXECUTIVE ROUNDTABLE MEETING NOTICE

   There will be a meeting of all members of the Executives' Roundtable on Thursday, July 25, at 11 a.m. in the Beacon Room of the Tower Building in Chicago.

   Luncheon will be served at 12:15 p.m.

   If you cannot be with us, please call 247-9521 no later than July 23.

   An agenda is enclosed. You will also find a map with complete travel directions and a description of the parking facilities at the Tower Building.

   It will be a pleasure to welcome all members to this important planning session.

RF:gbb

Enclosures: Agenda
     Map

---

message content, which makes it useful for filing purposes. Examples of typical SUBJECT lines are as follows:

SUBJECT: April Meeting of the Advisory Council
SUBJECT: NEED FOR A NEW ELECTRONIC TYPEWRITER
SUBJECT: Transportation Rates on Iron or Steel Bars

Brevity, courtesy, and factualness are three requirements of office memorandums. The main idea of the message is usually contained in the first sentence, and additional or supporting data may follow. The memorandum may close with a courteous request for action or further information. Sometimes the request may be found at the beginning, and supporting data in subsequent paragraphs.

Sample Letters

This section includes sample business letters that are appropriate for a wide range of situations and occasions. Each letter is preceded by a description of a situation in which it would be written and a description of its elements. Those letters that bear the signature of an executive represent the kinds of letter that a secretary might compose for an executive to sign.

Acceptance of Invitation

SITUATION: Kathleen Simons, president of a small but fast-growing software-development company, has been invited by a professor at a nearby university to speak to his marketing class. The professor particularly wants her to speak at this time because the subject his students are studying at present is one in which she has considerable expertise.

LETTER ELEMENTS: This letter of acceptance does the following:

1. It opens by acknowledging the professor's request and by unambiguously accepting the invitation.
2. It repeats all of the details regarding the invitation. This serves as a way of confirming that the details have been communicated accurately.
3. It mentions the enclosed materials.
4. It closes by expressing appreciation for the invitation and the expectation that the event will be enjoyable.

Fig. 8.2   Acceptance of Invitation

DATAWARE Consultants
1287 West Liberty Avenue
Sacramento, CA 95833
916-937-1212

                                              January 2, 19--

Dr. John C. Thomas
Associate Professor of Marketing
Department of Business Administration
Santa Rosa State College
Santa Rosa, CA 95405

Dear Dr. Thomas:

      Thank you very much for the kind invitation to lead an
upcoming session of your senior seminar. I will be happy to
do so. I understand that the seminar will be held from 2:30
to 5:30 p.m. on March 23 in Milton Hall, Room 1289. The
topic--as you suggested in your letter--will be "Marketing
the Services of the Emerging Growth Company."

      I am enclosing a list of references to recent articles
on the subject that your students may want to acquaint themselves with before the seminar. Since your students are
currently studying this topic, I think that these references
will be valuable aids to them.

      I appreciate your thinking of me, and I look forward to
working with your students.

                              Sincerely,

                              Kathleen C. Simons

                              Kathleen C. Simons
                              President

KCS/gb
Enclosure

Acknowledgment or Deferral

SITUATION: Barbara O'Toole is secretary to Arthur C. Roebling, president of Communications Media Corporation. Mr. Roebling has just received an invitation from Patricia Schmidt, president of the Advertisers Club, to speak at the club's annual awards dinner. However, Mr. Roebling is in Europe on a business trip and therefore cannot reply promptly to the invitation. O'Toole has been instructed to reply to such letters with an acknowledgment letter that is friendly but noncommittal.

LETTER ELEMENTS: This acknowledgment letter does the following:

1. It acknowledges receipt of the letter and thanks Ms. Schmidt for it.
2. It explains the reason for the delay and gives Ms. Schmidt some idea of when she can expect a reply from Mr. Roebling.
3. It closes in a courteous manner.

Fig. 8.3   Acknowledgment or Deferral

Communications Media Corporation/Hawthorne Building/Pierce and Fremont Streets/Houston, TX 7001

CMC
                                                          Telephone (713) 898-7642
                                                                      898-2746

February 15, 19--

Ms. Patricia Schmidt
President, Advertisers Club
P.O. Box 1234
Houston, TX 77040

Dear Ms. Schmidt:

Thank you for your gracious invitation to
Mr. Arthur Roebling to be the speaker at the
annual awards dinner of the Advertisers Club on
May 26, 19--.

Mr. Roebling will be returning from a business trip in Europe next week. On his return, you
can be sure that your letter will receive his
prompt attention.

                         Cordially yours,

                         Barbara O'Toole

                         Barbara O'Toole
                         Secretary to Mr. Roebling

Adjustment or Apology

SITUATION: Thomas Sagarino is president of Sagarino Flower Company. Mr. and Mrs. Edwards, longtime customers of the company, have just called to say that a shipment of roses they had recently received from the company included some that were noticeably wilted. Sagarino believes that the Edwardses have a legitimate complaint. The letter is intended to rectify the current situation and to secure his customers' goodwill and sense of confidence in the company.

LETTER ELEMENTS: The reply to Mr. and Mrs. Edwards does the following:

1. It begins on a friendly and appreciative note by thanking them for calling the situation to the company's attention.
2. It acknowledges the error and explains the measures that will be taken to rectify the situation—in this case, a full refund.
3. It explains the reason for the error, extends an apology, and reassures them that it will not happen again.
4. It expresses appreciation for having them as customers, and closes with a friendly offer of future service.

Fig. 8.4   Adjustment or Apology

Sagarino Flower Company
One Maywell Street
Beverly, MA 01915
Telephone: 617-414-5252

August 15, 19--

Mr. and Mrs. James Edwards
100 Lighthouse Way
Beverly, MA 01915

Dear Mr. and Mrs. Edwards:

Thank you for letting us know about the roses
that arrived at your home in less than perfect
condition. We have enclosed a check refunding
your full purchase price.

An unexpected delay in the repair of our loaded
delivery van, coupled with an unusual rise in
temperatures last Thursday, caused the late delivery of your roses. Please accept our apology and
our assurance that steps will be taken to prevent
this from ever happening again.

During the past fifteen years, it has been our
pleasure to number you among our valued customers.
Customer satisfaction is the goal we strive to
achieve. Please let us know how we may be of
greater service to you.

Yours sincerely,

Thomas Sagarino
Thomas Sagarino
President

gbb

Enclosure: Check

Appointment Confirmation

SITUATION: Dr. Grondahl, the head of a Norwegian publishing firm, will be in the United States for several days and has contacted Charles St. Cyr about a meeting regarding a possible joint project involving yet another firm. Since the discussion will not require much technical material, a lunch meeting seems more appropriate and relaxed than an office meeting. The correspondents have already established that midday on May 2 would be a convenient time for everyone.

LETTER ELEMENTS: The confirmation letter does the following:

1. It specifies the participants, date, time, and location of the meeting.
2. It refers to an enclosed map (directions would often be appropriate as well) and extends other courtesies.

Fig. 8.5   Appointment Confirmation

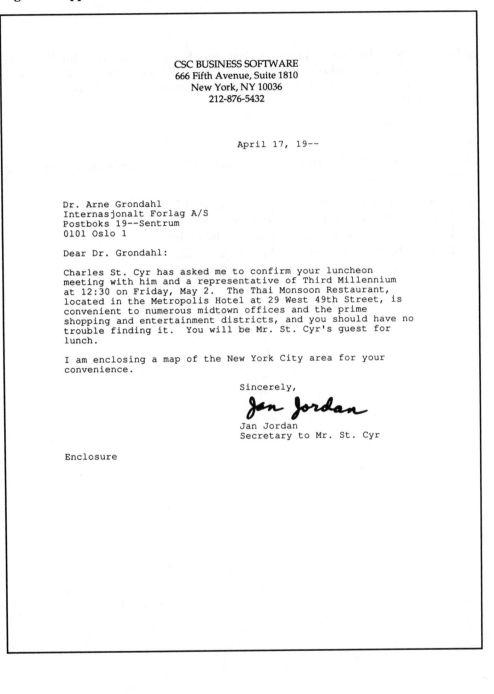

CSC BUSINESS SOFTWARE
666 Fifth Avenue, Suite 1810
New York, NY 10036
212-876-5432

April 17, 19--

Dr. Arne Grondahl
Internasjonalt Forlag A/S
Postboks 19--Sentrum
0101 Oslo 1

Dear Dr. Grondahl:

Charles St. Cyr has asked me to confirm your luncheon
meeting with him and a representative of Third Millennium
at 12:30 on Friday, May 2. The Thai Monsoon Restaurant,
located in the Metropolis Hotel at 29 West 49th Street, is
convenient to numerous midtown offices and the prime
shopping and entertainment districts, and you should have no
trouble finding it. You will be Mr. St. Cyr's guest for
lunch.

I am enclosing a map of the New York City area for your
convenience.

Sincerely,

Jan Jordan

Jan Jordan
Secretary to Mr. St. Cyr

Enclosure

Appreciation

SITUATION: The Chen Lumber Company has received an order from Mr. and Mrs. Sullivan for all the lumber needed to build a new house. The order is considerable, and the president of the company needs a letter of appreciation to the Sullivans.

LETTER ELEMENTS: In order to express the company's appreciation, the letter does the following:

1. It first focuses on the Sullivans, connecting with the excitement they must be feeling at the prospect of building a new house.
2. It expresses personal appreciation for the order.
3. It offers further services that the company might provide.
4. It closes in a friendly but not overly effusive manner.

Fig. 8.6   Appreciation

CHEN LUMBER COMPANY
650 Main Street
Brattleboro, VT 05302
Telephone (802) 643-2101

August 6, 19--

Mr. and Mrs. Gerald Sullivan
68 Cottage Street
Essex Junction, VT 05452

Dear Mr. and Mrs. Sullivan:

Congratulations on your decision to become a new
home owner! Thank you for the confidence you have
shown in us through opening an account and placing
your order at the Chen Company.

It will be a pleasure to supply all the lumber and
millwork needs for your beautiful home. You can
build with confidence knowing that only high-
quality materials and supplies are being used.

Mr. Ralph Fu will be glad to help you with any
aspect of planning or designing your new home.
Please let us know if there is any way in which we
may be of further assistance.

Sincerely,

Larry Chen
President

gbb

Complaint or Request for Adjustment

SITUATION: Helen Davison owns and manages a small marina where she offers repair services to her docking guests. Recently she ordered a bilge pump from her usual parts supplier to replace one in the cabin cruiser of a guest who was staying at her marina. Although the supplier assured her the pump would arrive in seven working days, it did not actually arrive for more than three weeks, by which time the guest had left. Now Davison has discovered that the mounting arms are so badly bent that the pump would be very difficult to install. Her letter to Barry Jacobs, the manager of the parts-supply house, tells him why she is returning the pump and why she wants a full refund.

LETTER ELEMENTS: The complaint to the parts-supply house does the following:

1.   Without being insulting or overly hostile, it gets directly to the point. The details will wait until the next paragraph. The opening tells the credit manager what he can expect, and why.
2.   It goes on to explain the sequence of events, all of which lead in an orderly way to the demand for a full refund.
3.   It does not belabor Ms. Davison's disappointment at not being able to complete the repairs for her guest. It does make clear, however, that she considers the supplier's performance below par in this instance and that she hopes they will try to improve their service.

Fig. 8.7   Complaint or Request for Adjustment

DAVISON'S MARINA
5100 Harbor Drive
Savannah, GA 31419
(912) 333-1111

July 28, 19--

Mr. Barry Jacobs
Manager
Oceanside Supply Company
129 Fulton Boulevard
Jacksonville, FL 32217

Dear Mr. Jacobs:

You will soon be receiving via UPS the Johnson II Bilge Pump I ordered last month. This pump is being returned by me both because it is defective and because it arrived too late to be used in a repair for a customer.

On June 30, three weeks before my guest's scheduled departure, I telephoned Oceanside Supply to order the Johnson Pump and was assured that the pump would arrive within seven working days. The pump actually arrived only after 16 working days, one day after my guest's departure. I had considered keeping the pump in stock for a future repair, but the pump arrived with bent mounting arms that would make installation very difficult and time-consuming, leading to a labor cost that would have to be absorbed by me or my customer. Under these circumstances, I cannot accept this pump, and I am returning it to you with the request that the amount of the purchase price be removed from my account.

Davison's Marina has been a regular customer of Ocean-side Supply for several years, and I must say that we have been quite happy with your service up to now. I hope that in the future you will pay a bit more attention both to customers' needs and your own assurances so that we can all avoid disappointment.

Sincerely,

Helen Davison

Helen Davison
Proprietor

HD:gbb

Condolence or Sympathy

SITUATION: Randolph Parker, president of a textile mill, has heard that Gunnar Caroleen, president of a company that does business with Parker's firm, was recently widowed. The two men have met on business occasions, but not socially. The short letter of sympathy is typed on Executive-size company stationery.

LETTER ELEMENTS: This letter of condolence to a business associate does the following:

1. It is typed on Executive stationery.
2. It begins by offering sympathy simply and straightforwardly on behalf of both Mr. Parker and his staff, since others in his company have dealt with Mr. Caroleen in their work.
3. It offers business-related assistance that Mr. Caroleen might find helpful.

Fig. 8.8   Condolence or Sympathy

PARKER MILLS

2605 Commerce Boulevard
Omaha, NE 68124
Telephone 402-241-7425

Office of the President

September 9, 19--

Dear Gunnar:

My staff and I wish to extend our heartfelt sympathy to you during this period of your bereavement since the passing of your wife, Helen.

Your many friends here at Parker Mills join me in offering assistance with special scheduling of your orders at this time. Please do not hesitate to let us know how we may help.

It must be a comfort to have your family so near. May the memories of your years together sustain you all and bring you strength and peace.

Sincerely,

Randolph Parker

Mr. Gunnar Caroleen
President
Universal Products, Inc.
North Platte, NE 69103

Congratulation

SITUATION: Mary Laurence is an executive at a firm that does business with Ace Precision Tools. Recently, Herbert Duchesne, a longtime friend at Ace, was elevated to a new position. Laurence desires to extend her congratulations in a letter.

LETTER ELEMENTS: This letter of congratulations to a business acquaintance does the following:

1. It is typed on Monarch stationery.
2. It commends him on the honor, giving it its exact title (a courtesy gesture), and reflects on its meaning.
3. It makes additional comments on the nature of the achievement.
4. It closes with personal good wishes.
5. It omits the secretary's initials.

Fig. 8.9   Congratulation

Thor Ball Bearings
888 Atticus Road
Erie, Pennsylvania 16504
Telephone: (814) 299-9400
Fax: (814) 299-9408

Vice President, Personnel

January 3, 19--

Dear Mr. Duchesne:

Yesterday's Erie <u>Recorder</u> announced
the pleasant news of your appointment
as General Manufacturing Manager at Ace
Precision Tools. Congratulations!

It is well known that great strides were
made at Ace Precision Tools while you
were Materials Manager. The recognition
you are now receiving is certainly well
deserved.

Again, you have my sincere congratulations and best wishes for continued
success.

Cordially,

Mary Laurence

Mr. Herbert Duchesne
General Manufacturing Manager
Ace Precision Tools
1408 Lake Avenue
Erie, PA 16509

Credit Cancellation

SITUATION: Seven years ago, Howard Harris, owner of Universal Electrical Service, opened an account with Kelly Electrical Supply Shop. For some time he paid his store's bills within 30 days. For the past several months, however, his payments have been very late, necessitating letters of reminder from Albert Terranova, the credit manager of Kelly Electrical. Universal Electrical is now several months behind in its payments, and Terranova has decided to cancel the account.

LETTER ELEMENTS: In canceling the account, the letter does the following:

1. Before getting to the problem, it commends Mr. Harris for prompt payment in the past. An immediate negative or aggressive approach could prevent such a letter from being read any further, and Terranova wants to avoid that.
2. When it brings up the current problem, it does so as tactfully and politely as possible.
3. Avoiding the negative, it suggests a solution.
4. It offers special assistance.
5. It requests a prompt response, keeping the wording polite but firm.

Fig. 8.10   Credit Cancellation

KELLY ELECTRICAL SUPPLY SHOP
6802 Eastern Highway
Portland, OR 97229
(123) 123-4567

November 5, 19--

Mr. Howard Harris
Universal Electrical Service
4628 Southern Boulevard
Portland, OR 97216

Dear Mr. Harris:

Over the past seven years, we have valued your
account with us and considered it one of our best.
However, with the recent downturn in business, we
have noticed that your practice of discounting
your bills every thirty days has ceased. Your
last payment was ninety days late.

It is imperative that we keep current on our
accounts receivable; therefore, regrettably, it is
necessary to ask you to make future purchases on a
cash-only basis until your account is cleared.

Please accept the enclosed Special Courtesy
Discount card for future cash purchases. It will
entitle you to a ten-percent cash discount to help
you through this transition period.

May we hear from you soon, Mr. Harris.

Very sincerely,

Albert Terranova
Albert Terranova
Credit Manager

AT:gbb

Enclosure

Credit Refusal

SITUATION: Thomas Polani is the office manager for Ardmore Office Products, a retail office-supply store. Margaret Allen, the owner of Interior Enterprises, a newly formed interior-design firm, has placed a sizable order for office equipment and has asked for 120-day credit terms. Interior Enterprises has been a good customer for the past year; however, a review of their financial statement and of the information supplied by credit references indicates that Interior Enterprises is in some financial difficulty. Polani decides to refuse the credit request, but he wants very much to keep Interior Enterprises as a cash customer.

LETTER ELEMENTS: In refusing credit, the letter does the following:

1. It expresses appreciation for the order and for past patronage, letting Ms. Allen know that Mr. Polani sees their business relationship as an ongoing one and that he hopes it will continue in the future.
2. It states that the application for credit has not been accepted. It avoids the word *refuse* and expresses regret that this decision had to be made. At this point, it is neutral in tone and does not criticize or offer advice, which can often seem condescending. Nor does it say anything specific about the financial situation of Interior Enterprises; it simply says that the information provided does not warrant the decision to grant credit.
3. It holds out hope that the decision could be reversed if more information were provided. Most probably, such information is not available; however, it is making clear that Mr. Polani has not come to any negative conclusions about the company.
4. It reminds Ms. Allen that the order can still be filled on a cash basis. It adopts a cheerful tone here to encourage her not to cancel the order.

Fig. 8.11   Credit Refusal

ardmore office products

136 John T. Slocum Street
Jackson, MS 39218
Telephone (601) 999-8115

September 27, 19--

Ms. Margaret Allen
Interior Enterprises
Suite 101
1700 Blandford Road
Jackson, MI 39209

Dear Ms. Allen:

Thank you very much for the order you placed with us
last week. We appreciate your patronage, and we hope we can
continue to serve you in the future.

We have carefully considered your application for
120-day credit terms. We are sorry to say that, on the
basis of the financial information we have seen so far, we
are not able to approve your request. However, if there is
any added financial information that you could send us that
would allow us to reconsider this decision, we would be
happy to do so.

In the meantime, we will be happy to fill this order on
a cash basis, with our customary 3 percent cash discount.

Sincerely,

Thomas Polani
Office Manager

TP/gbb

Employment Refusal

SITUATION: Joseph Forester is personnel director for SportSystems Inc. He has finished considering a group of applicants for a sales position in the store. He has chosen a candidate, and the candidate has accepted. He now needs a letter to the other applicants to tell them that they did not get the job. The same basic text will be used for each letter.

LETTER ELEMENTS: The letter to the unsuccessful applicants does the following:

1.   It briefly thanks the applicants for applying and quickly moves on to the bad news, telling them that they were not selected.
2.   It tells them that their applications are being kept on file in case there is a suitable opening in the near future. This is unlikely to happen, but it might.
3.   It expresses appreciation to them, being extra polite here so as to do nothing to alienate the candidates. After all, they might be potential customers.

Fig. 8.12   Employment Refusal

SportSystems Inc.
10 Ash Grove Road
Webster, Illinois 60069

Telephone: (312) 445-5511
Fax: (312) 461-7091

October 9, 19--

Mr. Walter W. Jaffe
634 Rock River Avenue
Compton, IL 60058

Dear Mr. Jaffe:

Thank you for your letter of October 5. Unfortunately, I
am afraid that there is nothing open at present for someone
with your credentials here at SportSystems.

We will keep your resume on file for future reference.
Thank you for thinking of us, and I wish you success in
finding a suitable position.

Sincerely,

Joseph J. Forester

Joseph J. Forester
Vice President, Personnel

gbb

Follow-up or Reminder

SITUATION: The November executive meeting of Highsmith Laboratories was partly devoted to planning for the coming two years. Tentative goals were proposed, but hard figures were not then available. Samuel Coe, Executive Vice President, needs the promised information soon and has asked his secretary to send a reminder letter to each participant. (Being basically identical, such letters would probably be generated from a single letter in the word processor.)

LETTER ELEMENTS: The follow-up letter does the following:

1. It tactfully reminds the recipient of precisely what is needed, and of any deadlines.
2. It refers to any relevant supporting materials. (In other cases, such materials might actually be sent with the letter.)

Fig. 8.13   Follow-up or Reminder

R. J. HIGHSMITH LABORATORIES INC.
1698 Massachusetts Avenue
Cambridge, MA 02138
617-488-2848

November 25, 19--

Mr. Joseph Sonnenschein
R. J. Highsmith Laboratories, Inc.
4860 South Beach Drive
Palo Alto, CA 94303

Dear Mr. Sonnenschein:

In the wake of the November 18 executive meeting, this
letter is merely intended to remind you that we require
some information from each participant within the next
two weeks in order to complete our near-term prospectus:
(1) proposed new personnel (and salary) requirements
and/or reductions for each separate branch over the next
two years; and (2) expected equipment purchases over the
same period. (You will recall that guidelines and materials for estimating equipment costs were distributed at
the meeting.)

I know how pleased Mr. Coe was with the meeting and the
role of each of you in making it so productive. I hope
to hear from you soon.

With best wishes for
the holidays,

Charlene Daitz

Charlene Daitz
Administrative Assistant
to Mr. Coe

cc: Mr. Lynes
    Mrs. Caswell
    Mr. Kumar

Inquiry or Request

SITUATION: Thomas Domizio is marketing manager for Acme Equipment Company, a company that does a large proportion of its business through its catalog. The company plans to add a line of tractors to the equipment it currently leases, and it has chosen Laprade's Harris Tractors for the purpose. Domizio writes to Harold Thomas, sales manager of Laprade Industries, for specifications that can be used in the upcoming catalog.

LETTER ELEMENTS: The letter of inquiry does the following:

1. It immediately gets to the point, while complimenting the manufacturer on its product.
2. It details the request in an easy-to-read way. It avoids the unhelpful request "Please send me all the information you have on this particular product," instead listing precisely what is needed, set up in such a way that it stands out from the surrounding text.
3. It mentions that the requested information is needed quickly, and explains why.
4. It closes politely.

Fig. 8.14   Inquiry or Request

Acme Equipment Company
42 Grove Street
Rockford, IL 61107
815-327-0605

September 17, 19--

Mr. Harold Thomas
Sales Manager
Laprade Industries
1525 State Street
Cleveland, OH 44140

Dear Mr. Thomas

We are currently planning to add yard and garden tractors to our line of leased equipment. It is my pleasure to announce that we shall feature Harris Tractors.

Would you please send us a complete list of models and specifications for Harris Tractors. It would be helpful to have the following data by September 30:

1. Horsepower/range of job function.
2. Commercial/homeowner equipment.
3. Contract samples/sale terms.

Since the publication date for our catalog is slated for November, your early reply will be appreciated.

Sincerely yours

Thomas Domizio
Marketing Manager

TD:gbb

Meeting Notification

SITUATION: The upcoming meeting of the Coastal Arts Center's board of trustees is three weeks away, and the trustees must be notified. Unless the director desires to send any personal messages or greetings, the secretary will probably generate a set of basically identical letters from a single letter on the word processor.

LETTER ELEMENTS: The notification letter does the following:

1. It specifies the place, date, and time of the meeting.
2. It mentions special agenda items and, if appropriate, any necessary preparation.
3. It refers to relevant materials enclosed.
4. It requests confirmation of attendance.

Fig. 8.15   Meeting Notification

COASTAL ARTS CENTER
781 Santa Maria Blvd.
Los Angeles, California 90027
Tel: (213) 455-5222
Fax: (213) 455-5009

January 12, 19--

Ms. Alessandra Castelnuovo
Director
Secolo Nuovo Galleries,
 Ocean Walk
Newport Beach, CA 92663

Dear Ms. Castelnuovo:

The regular winter meeting of the board of
trustees will be held in the Arts Center
boardroom at 10:00 a.m., Tuesday, February 1.

The tentative agenda and our proposed budget
for FY 19-- are enclosed. Note that the
principal topic will be the new tax laws, on
which our legal counsel will be making a
presentation.

Would you notify me before January 20 as to
whether you will be able to attend.

Yours very truly,

Jasper L. Cozzens
Director

JLC:gbb

Enclosures (2)

Order

SITUATION: Paul Thomas is the purchasing agent of Rodriguez Manufacturing, Inc., a large furniture maker. He has just been informed that the factory has run out of two types of hardware. It is imperative that the stock be replenished as soon as possible. He needs a letter ordering more stock from his supplier.

LETTER ELEMENTS: In ordering replacement stock for the store, the letter does the following:

1. It makes known the store's urgent need for the order. It gives the shipping address that will best facilitate delivery.
2. It lists clearly the quantity, description, and price of the ordered items. Putting the information in table form makes the order as clear as possible.
3. It closes by explaining why prompt delivery of these two items is necessary and by emphasizing that a rush order is needed.

Fig. 8.16 Order

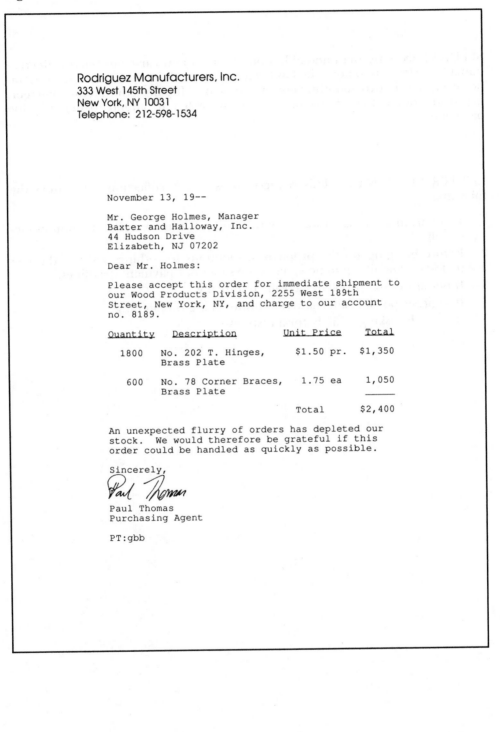

Rodriguez Manufacturers, Inc.
333 West 145th Street
New York, NY 10031
Telephone: 212-598-1534

November 13, 19--

Mr. George Holmes, Manager
Baxter and Halloway, Inc.
44 Hudson Drive
Elizabeth, NJ 07202

Dear Mr. Holmes:

Please accept this order for immediate shipment to
our Wood Products Division, 2255 West 189th
Street, New York, NY, and charge to our account
no. 8189.

Quantity	Description	Unit Price	Total
1800	No. 202 T. Hinges, Brass Plate	$1.50 pr.	$1,350
600	No. 78 Corner Braces, Brass Plate	1.75 ea	1,050
		Total	$2,400

An unexpected flurry of orders has depleted our
stock. We would therefore be grateful if this
order could be handled as quickly as possible.

Sincerely,

Paul Thomas
Purchasing Agent

PT:gbb

Request for Payment

SITUATION: Donna Randall has purchased a new car from Darrow Recreational Vehicles. Up to now, she has been on time with her payments. At present, however, she is two months behind. Francine Hopkins, the credit manager, needs to remind her of the fact and to urge her to attend to her overdue payments.

LETTER ELEMENTS: This request, in essence a collection letter, does the following:

1. It begins in an unusual way, one that will catch its reader's attention immediately.
2. Before bringing up the problem, it mentions something positive, the fact that Ms. Randall, up to now, has always met her payment deadlines.
3. It points out the problem tactfully but firmly.
4. It suggests possible alternatives, without being threatening.
5. It closes by asking politely for a response.

Fig. 8.17   Request for Payment

Darrow Recreational Vehicles
36 Whipple Avenue
Lynchburg, VA 24502
Telephone 303-666-2321 or 686-4897

November 5, 19--

Ms. Donna Randall
61 Endicott Street
Lynchburg, VA 24504

Dear Ms. Randall:

Have you ever had to write a reminder letter? We find
ourselves in that position now.

You have been sending your monthly installments to us
promptly for almost a year. However, we find that your
payments of $260.00 for September 1 and October 1 have
not as yet arrived here.

Perhaps your overdue payments are already on their way
to us. If this is the case, please overlook this letter.
On the other hand, in the event that some difficulty has
arisen, let us know. Perhaps we can offer some helpful
suggestions in order to help you maintain your good credit
rating.

Won't you let us hear from you soon?

Sincerely yours,

Francine Hopkins

Francine Hopkins
Credit Manager

FH/gb

Reservation

SITUATION: A representative of Pineland Paper has researched a number of possible sites for the annual branch manager's conference to be held in three months. Acting on his final recommendation, Robert Anderson is sending a letter to reserve facilities for the conference.

LETTER ELEMENTS: The reservation letter does the following:

1. It opens with a friendly compliment.
2. It restates precisely what rooms and room arrangements will be needed.
3. It requests written confirmation as soon as possible.

Fig. 8.18 Reservation

PINELAND PAPER COMPANY, INC.
608 South Street
Shreveport, LA 71118
Telphone (123) 123-4567

March 20, 19--

Reservations Manager
Willoughby Hotel
674 Dennis Drive
Kansas City, MO 64128

RESERVATIONS FOR BRANCH MANAGERS' CONFERENCE

After seeing your fine facilities last week, our
representative, Howard Martin, has recommended the
Willoughby Hotel as this year's conference site
for our branch managers.

Please reserve your largest three-room executive
suite for June 16 and 17, 19--. We shall need
conference table arrangements using the "U" formation for 20 persons for one room, space for large
product displays in another, and an informal
social meeting room

An early confirmation of this reservation would be
appreciated.

Robert Anderson

ROBERT ANDERSON - MANAGER

RA:gbb

Transmittal

SITUATION: Ms. Forbush has routinely requested a set of trade catalogs from Hudson, a New York publisher, for the use of the buyers for Churchill Bookstores, and the secretary to Hudson's sales manager responds.

LETTER ELEMENTS: The transmittal letter (i.e., the letter that informs its recipient that a package is coming) does the following:

1.   It precisely describes the contents of the package.
2.   It mentions any future mailings that will follow this one.
3.   It provides any necessary instructions for use of the material.

Fig. 8.19   Transmittal

HUDSON PUBLICATIONS, INC.

97 Van Dam Street
New York, NY 10014
(212) 987-6543

April 2, 19--

Ms. Dana Forbush
Wholesale Accounts Dept.
Churchill Bookstores
400 Haddam Way
Chicago, IL 60641

Dear Ms. Forbush:

In response to your letter of March 28, I am sending under
separate cover by UPS a complete set of our wholesale trade
catalogs. The summer editions of catalogs nos. 5 and 9 will
be available in one to two weeks, and I will send them as
soon as they appear.

I have circled the applicable discounts on page xii of
catalog no. 1.

Very truly yours,

Jeffrey Burroughs
Jeffrey Burroughs
Secretary to Mr. Lozano

Special Typing Projects

Preparing a report or manuscript may require considerable time and effort and may call on numerous skills: your research capacity (if you actually participate in writing the report), your command of business English, your ability to proofread and edit, and your grasp of layout and design.

The complexity of the report and the type of printing and binding will depend on the nature of the project, the budget, and the audience. A corporation's annual report, produced for the stockholders, will be more elaborate than a report that will only be distributed internally. (See Chapter 10 for a discussion of desktop publishing.)

Research

There are two kinds of information gathering in the business world: primary research and secondary research. Primary research involves gathering information or data firsthand—by studying company records, by experimentation, or by observation or interviewing. Primary research is often complex, time-consuming, and costly. Secondary research entails the use of databases or printed sources. If information is available from a library or database, it is usually easier and less costly to retrieve than information from primary sources. It is therefore wise to visit libraries and consult databases at the outset of the research in order to avoid needless effort. Although library and database investigation often provides no more than a basis for further research, on occasion it may yield all the needed data. If you are given a role in actually researching for a business report, you will find the following information helpful.

USING A GENERAL LIBRARY

The most expeditious methods of finding information at the library are consulting the library catalog, the available reference works, and the periodical indexes.

The library catalog   The catalogs of all major libraries in the United States are being converted into computerized form. Most have been only partially converted; in these, only the material obtained in recent years is in the computer catalog, and the older holdings are accessible only through the card catalog. When beginning a research project at a particular library, always begin by consulting the reference librarian.

The catalog lists the library's holdings by author's name, title, and subject. Each title is subject-classified by a *call number* which is used to locate it. These call numbers are based on one of two classification systems, the old Dewey decimal system and the newer Library of Congress system:

Dewey Decimal		Library of Congress	
000	General Works	A	General Works
100	Philosophy and Related Disciplines	B	Philosophy, Psychology, Religion
200	Religion	C	History—Auxiliary Sciences
300	Social Sciences		
400	Language	D	History: General and Old World
500	Pure Sciences		
600	Technology (Applied Sciences)	E–F	History: America
		G	Geography, Anthropology, Recreation
700	The Arts	H	Social Sciences
800	Literature	J	Political Science
900	General Geography and History	K	Law
		L	Education
		M	Music
		N	Fine Arts
		P	Language and Literature
		Q	Science
		R	Medicine
		S	Agriculture
		T	Technology
		U	Military Science
		V	Naval Science
		Z	Bibliography and Library Science

Reference works   An unabridged dictionary, such as *Webster's Third New International Dictionary,* will aid you in determining the meanings of terms. Specialized dictionaries in fields such as medicine, law, banking, and chemistry are also available. General encyclopedias such as the *Encyclopaedia Britannica* provide broad information and good points of departure for some investigations, while specialized encyclopedias such as the *Encyclopedia of Banking and Finance* and the *Encyclopedia of Business Information* may be particularly helpful to business people. Biographical directories such as *Who's Who in America, Who's Who of American Women, American Men and Women of Science,* and *Who's Who in Finance and Industry* provide information about distinguished individuals. *Poor's Register of Corporations, Directors and Executives* is another specialized publication that may be of value to businesspeople.

Trade directories such as *Trade Directories of the World, Guide to American Directories, Million Dollar Directory,* and *Thomas Register;* almanacs such as the *World Almanac;* atlases; government publications such as *Current Population Reports;* and business publications such as *Moody's Manuals* and *Standard & Poor's Corporation*

Records are all additional sources of information. A reference librarian can direct you to the appropriate reference works.

Periodical indexes   Periodical indexes list articles published in journals, magazines, and other serials. *Business Periodicals Index, The Wall Street Journal Index,* and *The Reader's Guide to Periodical Literature* are good guides for businesspeople.

NOTE TAKING

To avoid confusion, an orderly research procedure is essential. You must first prepare a working bibliography, and then follow a systematic method of note taking. To accomplish this, you will need two sets of cards.

Bibliography cards   Small 3″ × 5″ cards can be used to record the bibliographic description of each reference. The cards must be numbered sequentially in the upper right corner; your notes will be keyed to their sources by means of these numbers. See Figs. 9.1 and 9.2.

Fig. 9.1   Bibliography Card for a Book

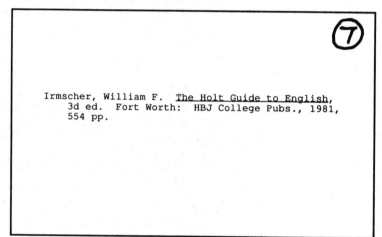

```
                                                         ⑦

     Irmscher, William F.  The Holt Guide to English,
          3d ed.  Fort Worth:  HBJ College Pubs., 1981,
          554 pp.
```

Fig. 9.2   Bibliography Card for a Periodical

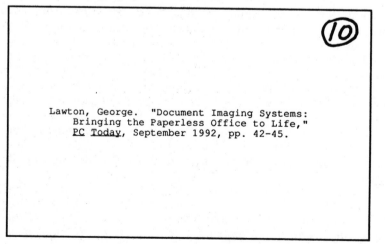

```
                                                         ⑩


     Lawton, George.  "Document Imaging Systems:
          Bringing the Paperless Office to Life,"
          PC Today, September 1992, pp. 42-45.
```

Information or note cards   In addition to the bibliography cards, you will need a set of larger 5″ × 7″ cards to record your findings. Each card should contain four essential pieces of information:

1. *The bibliographical source number*   The information card is keyed to a bibliography card by a code number assigned to the bibliography card. The information card shown in Fig. 9.3, for example, is keyed to the bibliography card in Fig. 9.2.

2. *A heading*   Information cards are most useful when they have a heading that identifies the information on the card. Such headings greatly facilitate later organizing of the notes, especially when there is a large number of cards. In the sample information card, the heading is identical to a heading on the preliminary outline that the researcher should have prepared, and the Roman numeral preceding it comes from the same hypothetical outline.

3. *The page number*   The page number may be needed later for a footnote.

4. *The information*   Information must be accurately recorded, either as an exact quotation or paraphrased in your own words.

Fig. 9.3   Information or Note Card

```
   III.  DIS storage
         p. 44 "Bit-mapped images are often compressed
               in a DIS because of their gluttonous hunger
               for storage space.  A standard 8.5 x 11 inch
               document with 400 words takes 3.74 million
               bits or 467,500 bytes to store in a bit-mapped
               format.  It will take this amount of space
               regardless of the number of words on the
               page."
```

Photocopies   Instead of using cards, you may choose to photocopy your research materials. The photocopy sheets can be keyed to the bibliography cards by code number just like information cards. Making single copies of individual pages for your research purposes is generally permitted under the "fair use" provision of the copyright laws; however, making multiple copies of protected material is not. You may secure additional information about copyright laws by writing for a copy of *General Information on Copyright,* to Copyright Office, Library of Congress, Washington, DC 20559.

COMPUTER-AIDED RESEARCH

Computer searches are often available in public libraries and in companies that have libraries. The process generally involves typing in one or more key words to access a list of reference sources that pertain to the subject (e.g., "micrographics"). This can be a valuable timesaver when you need to locate hard-to-find information or will be reviewing a large number of sources.

Database searches require a computer, a modem, and a subscription to a database service. Through a database service—such as DIALOG, NEXIS, Prodigy, CompuServe, DELPHI, or GEnie—you can read citations, abstracts, books, periodicals, and a host of other sources right on the computer screen. A myriad of databases currently exist, and the list continues to grow. Database services are usually paid for on an hourly basis.

Report Style

Reports, like any other business communications, must be well organized and coherent. Therefore, you should become familiar with conventional styles and formats so that you can be of maximum assistance to the writer during the research, writing, typing, and proofreading stages and avoid asking unnecessary questions.

FORMATS OF BUSINESS REPORTS

The formats of business reports vary widely. A report's format will often bear a direct relationship to its content. Some company manuals offer guidelines for report styling; however, the writer is normally given wide latitude in selecting a format that will best suit the report's purpose. Guidelines concerning four basic kinds of reports—distinguished according to the degree of formality required and the scope of information covered—are presented in this section in ascending order of formality: (1) the memorandum report, (2) the letter report, (3) the short report, and (4) the formal report.

The memorandum report   The memorandum report is an in-house communication that is generally routine and informal. A weekly sales report and a report from an assistant manager to a manager are typical examples. Since the memorandum report is an internal communication, it can be objective and impersonal in tone. The letter openings and closings used on external communications may be omitted, and the report may employ the memorandum format discussed on pages 324–25. Introductory comment is normally very brief. Headings may be used for quick reference and to highlight certain aspects of the report. Though the first draft may be double-spaced for editing, the final draft is usually single-spaced. When in doubt about headings and styling, seek your employer's advice. If you are given a choice, you may alter the styling, within limits, to suit a particular situation.

Use matching plain bond paper for continuation sheets. An appropriate heading for the second page of a two-page report is illustrated in Fig. 9.4. Some writers may wish to have a typed signature line four lines below the end of the report; the signature would then go above this line. Others prefer to initial the report next to their name in the heading. Often the memorandum report is not signed at all.

Fig. 9.4   Memorandum Report Continuation Sheet

```
Memorandum                  -2-              May 14, 19--


A list of the participants for the Sales Training Seminar in
Pittsburgh, Pennsylvania on June 26 is as follows:

                    Pesetsky, Donna
                    Gordon, Sidney
                    Lawson, Peter
```

The letter report   A report in letter format is known as a letter report. The letter-report format is useful for informal reports running to several pages. Letter reports are usually directed to persons or groups outside a company. They are typically used by outside consultants to present analyses and recommendations, and an organization's board of directors often will use a letter report to describe recent changes and developments to its membership. They may contain tables or illustrations that an ordinary letter would not have.

The first page of the letter report is typed on letterhead stationery; matching plain bond paper is used for continuation sheets. The headings on the continuation sheets should be like those on regular letters. A subject line will help to focus attention on the main theme. The body of the report should be interspersed with headings and subheadings for emphasis, clarity, and ease of reference.

The short report   Short business reports differ from memorandum and letter reports in scope and format. The short report may include the following elements: title page; preliminary summary (with emphasis on conclusions and recommendations); authorization information; statement of the problem; findings; conclusions; and recommendations. Tables and graphics may be added if needed.

Either single- or double-spacing is appropriate for the short business report, depending on the company's style or the writer's preference. Headings such as those used in letter reports may be used. In the absence of a specified company format for reports and other manuscripts, use the basic specifications shown in the table on pages 368–69.

The title page contains the title of the report; the name, title, and address of the person to whom it is being submitted; the name, title, and address of its preparer; and the date. Long report titles are divided, centered, and typed in several lines on the upper third of the page. (If possible, each line of the divided main title should be shorter than the line above, so that the title resembles an inverted pyramid.) Extremely brief report titles may be *spread*—that is, typed with a space after each letter and with three or more spaces after each word. Experimenting on scrap paper will help you determine the proper spacing and design.

The formal report   The formal report is distinguished from other types of report by its sophisticated style of presentation, the complexity of its scope and content, and its greater length. A formal report may contain all of the following elements, each of which will be illustrated and discussed in detail:

Cover	List of tables (if any)
Flyleaf	List of figures or illustrations (if any)
Title fly	Synopsis (Summary)
Title page	Body (Text)
Letter of authorization	Endnotes (or Footnotes)
Letter of transmittal	Appendix
Foreword or Preface (optional)	Glossary
Acknowledgments	Bibliography
Table of contents	Index

Some of these elements may be combined; for example, the letter of transmittal may be conflated with the synopsis.

Side-bound reports can use the specifications listed in the table below, with the following exceptions:

1. The left margin should be set at 1½″.
2. Page numbers should be placed at the right margin either ½″ or 1″ from the top of the page or ½″ from the bottom of the page. Alternatively, they may be centered on the text block ½″ from the bottom.

Good-quality bond paper is needed for a formal report. Either single- or double-spacing may be used. The prefatory section of a side-bound report (excluding the title page) is usually paginated with lowercase Roman numerals centered ½″ to 1″ from the bottom. The rest of the report, including the body and all appended sections, is paginated with Arabic numerals positioned at the right margin, generally 1″ from the top or bottom of the page. Additional format suggestions may be found in the following table.

Specifications for Typing Business Reports (Unbound and Top-bound)

Margins	Top, first page	2″
	Top, subsequent pages	1″
	Bottom, all pages	1″
	Left side, all pages	1″
	Right side, all pages	1″
Spacing	Body	Single or double
	Long set-off quotation	Single
	Footnotes or endnotes	Single (but double *between* notes)
Indention	Paragraphs	5 spaces if text is double-spaced; flush left, with line space above, if text is single-spaced
	Long quotations	5 spaces in from left (and sometimes right) margin
	Lists	5 or more spaces in from left and right margins
	Footnotes	Match paragraph indention for first line of footnote
Headings	Primary heads	Flush left, underlined capitals; leave space above and below

	Secondary heads	Flush left, underlined; leave space above and below
	Tertiary heads	Flush left, underlined or italic, followed by period and space; leave space above; text follows on same line
Pagination	Title fly	Assign Roman numeral *i* but do not actually type it
	Title page	Assign Roman numeral *ii* but do not actually type it
	All other preliminary parts— letters, acknowledgments, table of contents, lists of figures and tables, synopsis	Assign Roman numerals starting with *iii*
	Body of report, appendix, bibliography, index	Assign Arabic numerals starting with *1* Center each numeral ½"–1" from bottom of page

Care should be taken to follow a uniform style for the headings and subheadings throughout the report. Many formal reports employ the decimal style of subdividing report topics, but the writer may prefer to use the traditional outline listings of alternate numbers and letters instead. The decimal system is handled in this way:

1. Main heading
   1.1 Subheading
   1.2 Subheading
       1.21 Sub-subheading
       1.22 Sub-subheading
   1.3 Subheading
2. Main heading
   2.1 Subheading
   2.2 Subheading
3. Main heading

The outline system using numbers and letters alternately should be structured as follows:

I. Main heading
   A. Subheading
   B. Subheading
       1. Sub-subheading
       2. Sub-subheading
   C. Subheading
II. Main heading
   A. Subheading
   B. Subheading
III. Main heading

A uniform style for headings and subheadings requires the writer to pay attention to the logic of dividing topics into subtopics. No subheading should appear by itself; that is, you should never create a part 1 without a following part 2, or a section A without a corresponding section B.

Unacceptable	*Acceptable*
A. Dictation procedures 1. Pre-dictation guidelines B. Transcription procedures	A. Pre-dictation guidelines B. Dictation procedures C. Transcription procedures

or

A. Guidelines for better dictation
B. Transcription procedures

or

A. Dictation
   1. Pre-dictation guidelines
   2. Procedures for effective dictation
B. Transcription

Headings and subheadings at a given level should be grammatically similar, or *parallel*. Examples:

Nonparallel	*Parallel*

1. Selecting a topic
2. The outline
3. How to gather information
   a. Primary research
   b. Doing secondary research
	1. Selecting a topic
	2. Writing the outline
	3. Gathering information
	   a. Primary research
	   b. Secondary research

Many software programs have automatic outlining features.

The cover   The cover should adequately protect the report, should be attractive, and should display the title and the author's name. The title may be typed in capital letters either directly on the cover or on a gummed label that is then affixed to it. A very short report without a cover may be stapled. If one staple is used, it should be placed diagonally in the upper left corner.

The flyleaf   A flyleaf is a blank sheet of paper. Formal reports have two flyleaves, one at the beginning and the other at the end. They dress up the report, contribute to its formality, and provide space for written comments.

The title fly   The title fly, if used, contains only the report title, typed in capital letters on the upper third of the page. This title is identical to the one on the title page.

The title page   This page typically contains the title and subtitle, if any; the name, corporate title, department, and/or address of the writer; the name, title, department, firm name, and address of the recipient; and the completion date of the report. If a report does not have a cover and title fly, the title page can be typed on heavier paper and serve as the cover. If the report has a copyright, that fact is recorded on the reverse of the title page. Fig. 9.5 shows the title page of a report.

Letter of authorization   If the writer has received written authorization for the investigation, that memorandum or letter may be included in the report. If the writer has only received oral authorization, this authorization should be cited

Fig. 9.5   Title Page of a Long Report

ER387.171   A
REPORT No.   REVISION

20026-802
QUOTE/WORK ORDER No.

N00024-73-C-5407
CONTRACT/PURCHASE ORDER No.

NAVSEA
CUSTOMER

10/6/—
DATE OF ISSUE

DATE OF REVISION

DATA ITEM COOK

Transportation and Handling

Requirements Report

SIERRA INC.

1200 South Third Street
Sacramento, CA 95853
Tel (619) 555-3867
Fax (619) 555-9022

in the letter of transmittal or the introduction. A typical letter of authorization is shown in Fig. 9.6. (Note that different reports are represented in these examples.)

Letter of transmittal   A letter of transmittal often accompanies a report and may also serve as its preface or foreword. Here the writer conveys to the recipient (of-

ten the person who assigned the report) the purpose, scope, and limitations of
the report, its authorization, the research methods employed, special comments,
acknowledgments, and the main ideas contained therein. The letter usually ends
with an expression of the writer's appreciation for having received the assign-

Fig. 9.6   Letter of Authorization

```
        TO:          Joyce Browning, Assistant Professor
                     Carter Bryce College School of Business

        FROM:        Sarah Leland, Director
                     Secretarial Services Department

        DATE:        April 3, 19--

        SUBJECT:     Report Authorization


                You are hereby authorized to write a research
        study on The Format of Formal Reports.  It is to comprise
        no more than fifty pages and should provide definitive
        information on report writing (selecting a topic, writing
        the outline, and gathering information) and on report
        format.  The study should also provide specific information
        concerning techniques of report writing.

        The completion date of the report is May 29, 19--.

        If you have any questions concerning this investigation, do
        not hesitate to contact me.

                                  S. L.

        gbb

        cc:  Constance Sullivan
```

iii

ment and his or her willingness to provide additional information or answer any questions concerning the report. The tone should be sincere and cordial. The letter of transmittal is typed on letterhead stationery and is signed. A typical letter of transmittal is illustrated in Fig. 9.7.

Fig. 9.7   Letter of Transmittal

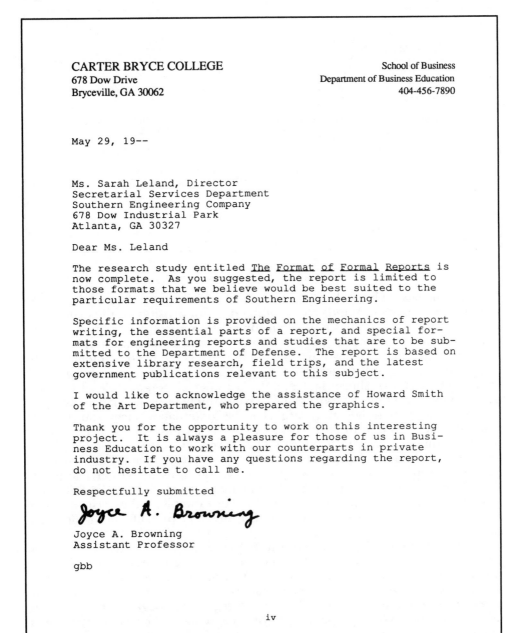

CARTER BRYCE COLLEGE
678 Dow Drive
Bryceville, GA 30062

School of Business
Department of Business Education
404-456-7890

May 29, 19--

Ms. Sarah Leland, Director
Secretarial Services Department
Southern Engineering Company
678 Dow Industrial Park
Atlanta, GA 30327

Dear Ms. Leland

The research study entitled The Format of Formal Reports is now complete. As you suggested, the report is limited to those formats that we believe would be best suited to the particular requirements of Southern Engineering.

Specific information is provided on the mechanics of report writing, the essential parts of a report, and special formats for engineering reports and studies that are to be submitted to the Department of Defense. The report is based on extensive library research, field trips, and the latest government publications relevant to this subject.

I would like to acknowledge the assistance of Howard Smith of the Art Department, who prepared the graphics.

Thank you for the opportunity to work on this interesting project. It is always a pleasure for those of us in Business Education to work with our counterparts in private industry. If you have any questions regarding the report, do not hesitate to call me.

Respectfully submitted

Joyce A. Browning

Joyce A. Browning
Assistant Professor

gbb

iv

Acknowledgments   It is considered proper to acknowledge the individuals, companies, and institutions that assisted in the preparation of the report. Acknowledgments may be made either in the letter of transmittal or in the introduction; however, if there are many acknowledgments a special page may be included. Fig. 9.8 shows the acknowledgment section of a report.

Fig. 9.8   Acknowledgments Section of a Report

```
        ACKNOWLEDGMENTS


        The author is indebted to several individuals who assisted
        in this study.

        Anne Etterman made several trips to the Stevens Engineering
        Company research library to obtain vital information.

        Joseph Brock assisted in the preparation of the graphics.

        Helen Jones edited the manuscript, and Amy Roth typed the
        manuscript.




                                                    J.B.
```

Table of contents   The table of contents is essentially an outline of the report showing its pagination. It indicates major and minor divisions of the material by showing pertinent headings and subheadings. If you use leader lines (periods typed horizontally across the page to connect headings and page numbers) and the periods are spaced, they must align vertically. The table of contents is centered horizontally and vertically on the page, unless the report will be side-bound. The example shown in Fig. 9.9 is a rather elaborate table of contents used in a technical report. Notice that the page numbers are aligned at the right. Notice also how the styling and margins of the continuation sheet (shown at the bottom) match those of the first sheet exactly. The continuation-sheet heading should be simply "Contents (Cont'd)." The second illustration of a table of contents (Fig. 9.10) shows the Roman-numeral outline styling that is followed in the text of the report. This report will be side-bound; thus the larger margin on the left. It should be reemphasized that the table of contents should follow exactly the internal style chosen by the writer. For example, if the decimal system of topic presentation is used within the text, the table of contents should use it as well.

Many word-processing programs can help you generate a table of contents. Consult your user manual to find out how to tag or highlight each heading and subheading so that the program will automatically calculate the page number. If you make changes to the document that affect the page numbering, a recompiling feature in the program will generally regenerate page references in the table of contents. (When preparing a table of contents on the computer, it is wise to insert it at the end of your document so that it will not be included in the pagination.)

Fig. 9.9 Table of Contents in a Long Technical Report Using the Decimal System

CONTENTS

Contents (Cont'd)

Fig. 9.10 Table of Contents Using the Roman-numeral System

CONTENTS

vi

List of illustrations   If the number of illustrations is small, a list of them may be appended to the table of contents. If there are numerous illustrations, a special list may be included on a separate page. The illustration numbers as well as the page numbers should be included in the list. The two partial lists shown in Figs. 9.11 and 9.12 employ the different systems used in their reports. The styling of

Fig. 9.11   List of Illustrations

```
                        ILLUSTRATIONS


       Table

          I.   COMPANY RESOURCES . . . . . . . . . . . . . . .     11

         II.   GENERAL LIBRARIES . . . . . . . . . . . . . . .     16

        III.   SPECIAL LIBRARIES . . . . . . . . . . . . . . .     17

         IV.   TYPES OF GRAPHIC PRESENTATIONS . . . . . . . . .    23



       Figure

          1.   Information Resources . . . . . . . . . . . . .     11

          2.   Report Parts  . . . . . . . . . . . . . . . . .     20

          3.   Placement Guide . . . . . . . . . . . . . . . .     24
```

Fig. 9.12   List of Illustrations in a Long Technical Report

```
                        ILLUSTRATIONS


       Figure  Title                                            Page

       4-1     PERISCOPE MAST ASSEMBLY SHIPPING CONTAINER          8
               NSN 8115-00-691-1458

       4-2     EYEPIECE BOX ASSEMBLY SHIPPING CONTAINER            8

       5-1     LOWER END, PERISCOPE MAST ASSEMBLY WITH            16
               LOWER SEAL PLUG AND GROOVE PROTECTOR INSTALLED

       5-2     PROPER HOISTING METHOD FOR PERISCOPE MAST ASSEMBLY 17

       5-3     EYEPIECE BOX ASSEMBLY (UPPER SECTION)              21
```

the list of illustrations should follow that of the table of contents (e.g., in the use of leader lines).

Synopsis   The synopsis (also called the *abstract, summary, digest, précis, brief, highlights, epitome, scope,* or *introduction*) is a condensation of the entire report. Most busy executives prefer a summarization at the beginning of a report in order to obtain a quick, concise overview of its significant findings. The synopsis usually appears on a page by itself, and it may be either single-spaced or double-spaced. In some offices, additional copies of the synopsis are distributed separately from the report itself, thus permitting wide circulation of the report findings at little cost. Fig. 9.13 shows the format of a one-page synopsis.

Fig. 9.13   Synopsis in a Formal Report

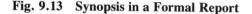

SYNOPSIS

This study concerns the preparation of formal reports in a style suited to the needs of a particular company.

The topic or subject is usually designated in a formal letter of authorization. Before any writing begins, an outline of the report should be carefully constructed and research data must be gathered from primary and/or secondary sources. Only after these data have been thoroughly assimilated can the report itself be written.

The three major sections of the body of a formal report are the introduction, the findings or text, and the final conclusions and recommendations. The ancillary components are the prefatory matter and appendixes.

The writer should be objective (except in the recommendations section), concise, clear, and accurate. The report should be meticulously documented by means of notes or parenthetical references and a bibliography.

The report should be submitted with a letter of transmittal that serves as its preface.

Report body   The body of the report usually includes three parts: a brief introduction, a lengthy general text section, and a final section reporting its conclusions and recommendations. The introduction presents the purpose of the
study, a clear definition of the problems or matters to be considered, the scope of
the study, any limitations imposed on the study, and any pertinent background
information. It should provide a somewhat broader overview than the synopsis.
The body of the text presents all data essential to the study. While the writer may
need to analyze and interpret these data, the material should initially be discussed with as much objectivity as possible. Conciseness, clarity, and complete-
ness should characterize this and all other sections of the report. The conclusions
are derived from the findings of the study. It is imperative that they be relevant
to the findings. As an aid to the reader, the conclusions are often numbered.
The recommendations, including possible courses of action, are derived from
the writer's interpretation of the conclusions and should be closely related to
them. The recommendations are usually numbered. In some formal reports, the
recommendations are placed within the introductory matter and only summarized at the end.

Appendix   Supplementary material is often placed at the end of the report in a
final section called an appendix.

Glossary   Technical terms that might be unfamiliar to the reader should be defined in a glossary. Abbreviations should also be included in the glossary, even if
they are spelled out the first time they appear in the text, as they should be.

Bibliography   The bibliography lists all the sources of information that were
used to compile the report. (See the following "Bibliographies" section for a full
discussion.)

Index   An index may be omitted in short reports, where the table of contents
can serve as an adequate guide. A long report, however, requires an index,
which should be detailed and complete. Every major subject and name should
have its own index entry. An index can be generated electronically in much the
same way as a table of contents.

Two common index styles are the *run-in* and the *indented*. The former requires less space, but the latter is easier for a busy reader to scan quickly. See the
following examples:

Run-in	*Indented*

Inside address: abbre-
  viations in, 33; page
  placement of, 27–28;
  Simplified Letter, 27;
  street address styling
  in, 32–34; ZIP codes
  in, 33. *See also* Letters.
	Inside address. *See*
	  also Letters.
	  abbreviations in, 33
	  page placement of, 27–28
	  Simplified Letter, 27
	  street address styling
	   in, 32–34
	  ZIP codes in, 33

The basic elements of an index are as follows:

1. *Entry*   Each principal entry is typed flush left. Its first letter is usually capitalized; all other words are lowercased, unless they are capitalized in the
   text. In the preceding examples, "Inside address" is a principal entry.
2. *Subentry*   A subentry is a subheading positioned alphabetically with the
   other subentries beneath an entry. A subentry is typically either indented

one or two spaces or run in as in the example on the left above. It enables the reader to locate specific points that are related to or fall within the larger subject encompassed by the entry. A subentry is lowercased unless it is capitalized in the text.

3. *Sub-subentry* A sub-subentry is subordinate to a subentry. Its styling parallels that of a subentry.

4. *Cross-references* Cross-references are devices that direct the reader elsewhere in the index. The two most common types are the *See* and the *See also* cross-references. A *See* cross-reference directs the reader to the entry where the desired information can be found.

> Stationery, quality of. *See* Paper.

A *See also* cross-reference directs the reader from one entry with page references to a related entry that may also be useful.

> Shorthand, 88–92. *See also*
> Stenographic notebook.

Regardless of its positioning within the entry, the cross-reference is followed by a period. If there are multiple cross-references for a single entry, they are separated by semicolons.

> Salutation, 37–40. *See also*
> Courtesy titles; Letters.

Punctuation should be kept to a minimum. Periods are used only before *See* and *See also* and at the end of a list of cross-references. Commas are used between an entry or subentry and any word or words modifying it, and before page references:

> Computers, use of,
> in correspondence, 25

See the index example in Fig. 9.14.

Fig. 9.14   Indented Index

```
Indexes                           Initials
  alphabetical order in, 16. See    abbreviations, 129-33
      also Alphabetical order.      acronyms, 133-35
  capitalization in, 17-20          capitalization of, 140-46
  cards for, 16, 18                 punctuation of, 149-62
  checking copy for, 20          Italics
  cross-references in, 21, 29-30    for aircraft, 172
  double entries in, 21, 22         for emphasis, 173
  entries, definition of, 21        in equations, 180-83
  indentation in, 23-29             for foreign words, 179
  indented styling of, 18-20        in indexes, 24
  italics in, 24                    marking of, 170
  key word choice, 15-18            for movie titles, 145
  page numbers in, 19               quotation marks vs., 179
  run-in styling of, 16-18          for titles, 145-55
  subentries, definition of, 22       in bibliographies, 148-52
  sub-subentries, definition          in footnotes, 146-48
   of, 23
  typing, 34
```

Though indexing is a specialized area that cannot be covered in detail in a book of this type, you should be able to create an adequate index by using care and common sense and by studying actual indexes in books such as this one. Style manuals for writers and editors, such as *Webster's Standard American Style Manual,* usually provide instruction in indexing.

Documenting Sources

The writer of a report may use any of several different methods to indicate the source of quotations or pieces of information borrowed from other works. This crediting of sources, known as *documentation,* is necessary for several reasons: (1) to acknowledge the work of another writer rather than appear to take credit for it oneself; (2) to allow the reader to judge the likely quality of the information in light of what he or she might know about the quality of the source; and (3) to enable the reader to find the source and verify the information or read further on the subject.

Style of documentation has traditionally differed depending on the subject area. Scientific writing generally uses parenthetical references primarily; writing intended for a more general public—which includes most business writing—has tended to use footnotes or endnotes, but parenthetical references are becoming more common. Within the citations themselves, scientific style also differs from nonscientific style.

Some firms will have their own rules or preferences, which may be detailed in a company style manual. If your company has such a manual, the rules in the manual should be followed, as they may conflict with the styles shown here.

FOOTNOTES AND ENDNOTES

The most familiar method of documentation and reference is the use of footnotes or endnotes, along with a bibliography. In this system, superscript numbers in the text refer the reader to short notes either set at the bottom of the page (footnotes) or gathered at the end of the section or the entire report (endnotes). These notes contain full bibliographical information about the works cited, and sometimes also include brief comments about the works or brief discussions of subjects related to the report but not tied to any specific cited work.

Footnotes and endnotes take exactly the same form; they differ only in where they are placed. Endnotes are usually preferred by writers because they are easier to handle (even though they can be slightly less convenient for the reader). However, many software writing programs now make the formatting of footnotes simple and convenient.

Footnote and endnote numbering will generally be consecutive throughout a report; in a long report divided into chapters, the numbering may start over at the beginning of each chapter.

In a carefully documented report, an alphabetically arranged bibliography or list of sources is normally provided at the end of the entire text (and after any endnotes). Since the bibliography will largely repeat information already given in the notes, it may seem unnecessary; however, it can be useful to a reader interested in finding bibliographic information quickly.

Fig. 9.15 shows how footnotes (and their numerical references) appear on a report page. A short typed line, flush left, separates them from the text, and each footnote is single-spaced internally. Fig. 9.16 shows a page of endnotes.

Fig. 9.15 Report Page with Footnotes

that the recent books in the field of business writing all
agree on. As one puts it, "Although some writers apparently
believe that length impresses readers, it is brevity that
readers most appreciate."[5] Another calls for writing that
is "direct, clear, simple, explicit, and to the point," a
goal that "flies in the face of an unfortunate tradition of
pompous, jargon-ridden, sexist language, antiquated and
wordy phrases, and redundancy."[6] Still another observes
that "nobody ever complained that a memo or report wasn't
long enough."[7]

These books agree not only on the goal but also on the
steps needed to realize it. A basic rule is to use short
words: "prefer the smaller word to the larger word when both
say essentially the same thing," as one book expresses it.[8]

---

5. Ray E. Barfield and Sylvia S. Titus, <u>Business
Communications</u> (New York: Barron's, 1992), 14.

6. Gary Blake and Robert W. Bly, <u>The Elements of Business
Writing</u> (New York: Collier-Macmillan, 1991), 35.

7. John Tarrant, <u>Business Writing with Style</u> (New York:
John Wiley, 1991), 130.

8. Blake and Bly, 39.

The basic rules of footnote and endnote form are as follows:

A simple citation of a book or article begins with the author's name (given exactly as it appears on the title page), followed by a comma and the book's or article's full title. Titles of books are italicized or underlined; titles of articles and unpublished works are enclosed in quotation marks but not italicized or under-

Fig. 9.16   Endnotes

```
                          NOTES


   1. Carol J. Loomis, "A Whole New Way to Run a Bank,"
      Fortune, 7 Sept. 1992, 78-79.

   2. Brian J. Cook and John Teresko, "Tomorrow's Industries,"
      Industry Week, 17 Aug. 1992, 31-33.

   3. Allen N. Berger, Kathleen K. King, and James M. O'Brien,
      "The Limitations of Market Value Accounting and a More
      Realistic Alternative," Journal of Banking and Finance
      15, Nos. 4/5 (Sept. 1991), 753-55.

   4. Norman Polmar, The Naval Institute Guide to the Ships
      and Aircraft of the U.S. Fleet, 15th ed. (Annapolis,
      Md.: Naval Institute Press, 1992), 44.

   5. "Eastern Africa," Encyclopaedia Britannica, 15th ed.

   6. Robert L. Hardie, "Long-Term Prospects for the American
      Machine Tool Industry," report prepared for Collins-
      Standiford, Consulting Engineers, Los Angeles, 17 May
      1990.

   7. Encyclopedia of Associations: 1993, 27th ed., ed.
      Deborah M. Burek, vol. 1: National Organizations of the
      U.S. (Detroit: Gale Research, 1992), 745.

   8. W. Szemplinska-Stupnicka and H. Troger, eds.,
      Engineering Applications of Dynamics of Chaos, CISM
      International Centre for Mechanical Sciences Series, No.
      319 (New York: Springer-Verlag, 1991), 299-300.

   9. United States Department of the Army, Uruguay: A
      Country Study (Washington, D.C.: GPO, 1992), 12-15.

  10. Berger, King, and O'Brien, 754.
```

lined. Normally, the first and last words and the first word of any subtitle are capitalized, as are all other words except prepositions, conjunctions, and articles (*a, an,* and *the*).

A book title is followed by its edition number, if any, and its publication data: the city where published, the publisher, and the year of publication, all enclosed in parentheses. The city name is followed by a colon, and the publisher's name is followed by a comma. The publication data are followed by the number of the page or pages where the cited information can be found, usually preceded by a comma and followed by a period. The abbreviations *p.* and *pp.* (for *page* and *pages,* respectively) may or may not be used.

An article title is followed by a comma (placed within the closing quotation marks) and the italicized or underlined title of the magazine, journal, or book in which the article appeared. A journal or magazine citation does not include its publisher or place of publication. However, the issue of the journal must be identified either by volume or by date or both. Scholarly journals are almost always cited by volume number. (A volume corresponds to a year's worth of issues; thus, volume 12 of a given magazine may run from April 1993 through March 1994, volume 13 from April 1994 through March 1995, etc.) This will sometimes be followed by an issue number within that volume. (The issue number is often unnecessary, since serious journals are usually paginated continuously throughout the annual volume, and thus the page number alone will suffice to lead the reader to the cited information.) This will be followed by the date, usually consisting of the month (or season) and year, enclosed in parentheses.

Since popular magazines are not paginated continuously throughout an annual volume, the precise date of the issue must be given. Though popular magazines usually have a volume and issue number printed somewhere inside, these are usually omitted from the citation; the full date is provided instead, set off by commas rather than parentheses. Newspapers are generally treated similarly to popular magazines.

When the name of a book's editor or translator appears on the title page, the name should usually be included in the footnote or endnote. If a book has an editor but no author, the editor's name takes the place of the author's in the citation.

If a work is in more than one volume, that fact should appear in the note. If the volumes are paginated separately, the number of the volume should immediately precede the page number, followed by a colon.

If a book is part of a series, the series name should be included, capitalized like a title but not italicized or underlined.

When citing major reference works, the name of the editor will often be omitted.

If an organization rather than a person is credited as the author on the title page, it should be treated as the author and alphabetized by its first word (excluding *The*). Government publications are usually alphabetized by the name of the government (e.g., "United States," "Delaware," "San Francisco"). Most U.S. government publications are published by the Government Printing Office, which can be abbreviated "GPO."

When referring to a work for the second (third, fourth, etc.) time, the note should include only the author's last name, a shortened version of the title (which may be omitted if it is the only work by the author being cited in the report), and the page reference.

In the sciences, footnotes and endnotes are used far less. When they are used, they observe the style differences listed in the "Bibliographies" section below. However, most science reports will instead employ parenthetical references of the author-date type (see below).

PARENTHETICAL REFERENCES

The alternative system of reference, which is becoming more widely used, employs highly abbreviated bibliographical citations enclosed in parentheses within the text. These parenthetical references direct any reader who needs more information about a source to the bibliography, which is similar in most respects to one that would be used with footnotes or endnotes. Such references can save the time and effort usually required to type footnotes.

If necessary, footnotes or endnotes may be used in addition to parenthetical references, particularly when the writer wants to discuss a peripheral subject briefly, in which case they should be numbered sequentially by themselves.

There are two basic styles for parenthetical references. The *author-date style*, generally used in the sciences, provides the author's last name, the year of publication, and sometimes the page number. The *author-page style*, used in most other areas, provides the author's last name and the page number. In the author-date style, if more than one work by a given author is cited, lowercase letters may be used after the dates (1989a, 1989b, etc.). In the author-page style, if more than one work by a given author is cited in the report, the shortened title of the particular work may be included after the author's name. Fig. 9.17 shows the same report passage as Fig. 9.15 but with the footnotes converted to parenthetical references.

Fig. 9.17   Report Page with Parenthetical References

```
that the recent books in the field of business writing all

agree on.  As one puts it, "Although some writers apparently

believe that length impresses readers, it is brevity that

readers most appreciate"  (Barfield and Titus, 14).  Another

calls for writing that is "direct, clear, simple, explicit,

and to the point," a goal that "flies in the face of an

unfortunate tradition of pompous, jargon-ridden, sexist

language, antiquated and wordy phrases, and redundancy"

(Blake and Bly, 35).  Still another observes that "nobody

ever complained that a memo or report wasn't long enough"

(Tarrant, 130).

     These books agree not only on the goal but also on the

steps needed to realize it.  A basic rule is to use short

words: "prefer the smaller word to the larger word when both

say essentially the same thing," as one book expresses it

(Blake and Bly, 39).  Lists of unnecessarily pretentious
```

BIBLIOGRAPHIES

A bibliography is frequently simply a list of the works cited in the report's notes or parenthetical references. It may also include other works used in the course of research which were not actually cited. An *annotated bibliography* will include brief comments on each work.

Bibliographies are ordered alphabetically by author's name. If no author or editor is cited, the book's title is listed alphabetically as if it were an author's surname.

Bibliography entries are generally identical to initial footnote citations except in the following respects: (1) The author's surname comes first; (2) periods rather than commas separate the elements of the entry; (3) the publication data are not enclosed by parentheses; and (4) page references are used only to locate a complete article (not just the pages cited in a note or reference) within a journal or book.

Scientific bibliographies observe their own set of style rules which differ in several respects from the general style described above. (1) The author's first name is shortened to an initial; (2) all words in titles are lowercased except the first word (and the first word of any subtitle) and proper nouns and adjectives; and (3) article titles are not set off by quotation marks. In addition, in scientific bibliographies the year of publication always immediately follows the author's

Fig. 9.18   Report Bibliography

WORKS CITED

Berger, Allen N., Kathleen K. King, and James M. O'Brien. "The Limitations of Market Value Accounting and a More Realistic Alternative." Journal of Banking and Finance 15, Nos. 4/5 (Sept. 1991), 753-783.

Cook, Brian J., and John Teresko. "Tomorrow's Industries." Industry Week, 17 Aug. 1992, 31-34.

Encyclopaedia Britannica. 15th ed. "Eastern Africa."

Encyclopedia of Associations: 1993. 27th ed. Edited by Deborah M. Burek. Vol. 1: National Organizations of the U.S. Detroit: Gale Research, 1992.

Hardie, Robert L. "Long-Term Prospects for the American Machine Tool Industry." Report prepared for Collins-Standiford, Consulting Engineers, Los Angeles, 17 May 1990.

Loomis, Carol J. "A Whole New Way to Run a Bank." Fortune, 7 Sept. 1992, 76-85.

Polmar, Norman. The Naval Institute Guide to the Ships and Aircraft of the U.S. Fleet. 15th ed. Annapolis, Md.: Naval Institute Press, 1992.

Szemplinska-Stupnicka, W., and H. Troger, eds. Engineering Applications of Dynamics of Chaos. CISM International Centre for Mechanical Sciences Series, No. 319. New York: Springer-Verlag, 1991.

United States. Department of the Army. Uruguay: A Country Study. Washington: GPO, 1992.

name. (In this way, the bibliography's entries are similar to the author-date parenthetical references.)

Study the examples in Figs. 9.18 and 9.19 to see how to deal with a variety of bibliographical problems.

Fig. 9.19   Report Bibliography in Scientific Style

```
                          WORKS CITED


     Banks, A.S., ed. 1992. Political handbook of the world:
     1992. Binghamton, N.Y.:  CSA Publications.

     Broad, W. J. 1992.  Big science squeezes small-scale
     researchers.  New York Times, 29 Dec.:  C1+.

     Gould, S.J., and N. Eldredge.  1977.  Punctuated equilibria:
     The tempo and mode of evolution reconsidered.  Paleobiology
     3: 115-151.

     Holldobler, B., and E. O. Wilson.  1990.  The ants.
     Cambridge, Mass.:  Belknap-Harvard Univ. Press.

     Mayr, E. 1982.  Processes of speciation in animals.  In C.
     Barigozzi, ed., Mechanisms of speciation.  New York:  Alan
     R. Liss:  1-19.

     Nowak, R. M. 1991.  Walker's mammals of the world.  5th ed.
     2 vols.  Baltimore:  Johns Hopkins Univ. Press.

     Preston, R. 1992.  A reporter at large:  Crisis in the hot
     zone.  New Yorker, 26 Oct.:  58-81.
```

Preparing a Press Release

Press releases should be written in "inverted pyramidal form"; that is, the main idea should be set forth first, followed by an exposition of the major details relating to that idea, followed in turn by minor details or supplementary ideas that are not essential to the discussion. Such an article can be cut from the bottom by an editor without deleting essential information. An acceptable release thus contains all the vital information at the beginning: the five *W*'s—who, what, when, where, and why—as well as an important *H*—how.

The article should be factual, interesting, and informative. Since accuracy is very important, you should proofread the article carefully before submitting it for publication. All details, especially numbers and the spelling of names, must be checked and verified.

A press release may be typed on plain 8½″ × 11″ paper or on a special press-release form. Double-spacing is preferred, as it facilitates further editing. Top and side margins are usually 1″ in width; the bottom margin may be somewhat wider to allow for editorial comments. If a preprinted form is not used, the words P R E S S   R E L E A S E are usually typed in spaced capital letters at the top of the page. See the example shown in Fig. 9.20.

Fig. 9.20   Press Release

PRESS RELEASE   MARTENS & McCORMICK

IMMEDIATE RELEASE   156 North LaSalle
                                                 Chicago, IL 60601
                                                 Telephone: 312-998-7654
                                                 Fax: 312-998-0801

                     SECOND QUARTER PROFIT INCREASE

        CHICAGO, August 16--Martens & McCormick, Inc. (AMEX)

today announced that its earnings increased 45% in the

fiscal second quarter to $26.3 million, or 55 cents a share,

from the year-earlier $18.1 million, or 38 cents a share.

        Revenue grew 13% to $1.24 billion from $1.1 billion in

the quarter ended July 31. The increased revenue was at-

tributed to expense controls, including new systems for in-

ventory control, new distribution facilities, and trimming

of payroll.

        Each of Martens & McCormick's four divisions improved

operating performance from a year earlier, with its Lady M

salons turning in the best performance.

        William C. Waite, Chairman of the Board, was quoted as

saying, however, that the level of operating profit increase

was not expected to continue through the fall season.

        Martens & McCormick, Inc., engages in the operation of

leased beauty salons and health clubs in shopping centers

here and abroad. It also owns Carefree, Inc., a distributor

and retailer of beauty and skin care products and services.

                              #####

The heading contains what are called *source data:* the name, address, and telephone number of the individual and/or company issuing the release, and specific release information—for example, "For Release June 26, 19—," or "IMMEDIATE RELEASE."

The title line, centered on the page and typed in capital letters, tells the reader at first glance what the article is about.

The article itself starts with an indented dateline consisting of the city and the date. The city name is typed in capital letters; the date is typed in capital and lowercase letters and is followed by a dash. The name of the state is given only if the city has a very common name or is not well known.

If there is more than one page, the word "MORE" is typed in capital letters at the bottom of the first sheet either in the center or on the right side. Continuation sheets are numbered and feature a brief caption (e.g., "PROFIT INCREASE—2") typed flush with the left margin near the top of the page.

One of the following devices, positioned in the center of the page, signals the end of the release:

# # # # #
-end-
(END)

Desktop Publishing

There have been many important developments in publishing since Gutenberg's movable type in the 1450s began to relieve scribes of the painstaking and tedious task of copying manuscripts by hand. When Benjamin Franklin was setting type manually in the early 1700s, visionaries were thinking to a time when machines could expedite the process, and in 1822 William Church patented a basic type-setting machine. In the 1880s there appeared two inventions, the Linotype and Monotype machines, which cast entire lines of type and individual letters, respectively, from molds that were assembled by using a keyboard. In the mid-1980s, when computers had taken over diverse tasks formerly done manually or mechanically, Paul Brainerd of Aldus Corporation pioneered the concept that publishing could be done from the desktop, beginning another revolution in the publishing industry. Once reserved for the few, publishing is now at everyone's fingertips.

Desktop publishing (DTP) is one of the fastest-growing areas in modern computing. It extends personal computers beyond the realm of word processing and allows the user to produce camera-ready (i.e., ready-for-copying) newsletters, brochures, fliers, advertisements, posters, manuals, and the like, without leaving the office.

In conventional publishing, the author types a manuscript and pastes any necessary artwork in place. The editor then edits it and sends it out for typesetting, and the typeset galleys return for proofreading by the author and editor. These are sent back to the typesetter to be corrected and (usually) pasted up with the artwork into pages. These must again be checked and corrected; errors caught at a late stage can be time-consuming and expensive to correct.

As a desktop publisher, you can be in control of the entire publishing cycle—especially if you are also the author. Most changes that need to be made can be implemented instantly right at your computer, and the endless rounds of mailing manuscript and proofs back and forth and cutting and pasting text and art into pages can be largely eliminated. (There will likely be some projects, however, that are beyond the technical capacities of even an experienced desktop-publishing specialist, and these will probably have to be sent out to a graphic designer.)

Though this chapter will not teach you how to use any particular hardware or software, it will introduce you to the fundamentals of DTP. Refer to the glossary at the end of this chapter for definitions of any unfamiliar terms.

Desktop Publishing Tools

In order to do the job properly, you must have the right tools.

Your desktop publishing system may not include everything you need to complete every assignment. If so, there are outside vendors or service bureaus that will perform particular functions, such as electronic imaging (scanning artwork), laser color copying, and producing 35-mm slides and high-resolution (camera-ready) output from a floppy diskette or data sent from your office by modem. Check under "Computer Graphics," "Desktop Publishing," or "Graphic Designers" in the Yellow Pages.

HARDWARE

Computer. Your primary tool is the computer, which includes the central processing unit, keyboard, disk drive(s), monitor, and mouse. (See Chapter 5 for an extensive discussion of computers.)

Scanner. A scanner converts text and graphic images into a digitized image on your screen, and with the help of OCR software the image is turned into characters that the computer can handle as text. With a scanner you can capture any printed page on your computer for processing. A scanner is not a necessity for most desktop publishing, but for certain tasks it can be extremely useful.

Laser printer. The laser printer lets you produce high-quality printed text; this can either be turned over to a conventional printer (if the job is complex or if large quantities must be printed) or simply duplicated and bound right in the office (for simple jobs and small quantities).

SOFTWARE

Word-processing. Since your text will be created with word-processing software, it will be your first tool. For a detailed discussion of word-processing software, see Chapter 5.

Graphics. There are numerous graphics software packages available to meet almost any DTP need. They vary in sophistication and capabilities, and should be chosen in accordance with your needs. Graphics packages can help you create your own artwork and charts or provide you with public-domain clip art. Fig. 10.1 shows some examples of clip art of the kind available on a typical graphics software package. Though clip art is available in other ways as well, graphics software will help you customize it for your own uses.

Page-layout. This software allows you to take the text you prepared with your word-processing software and the graphics you prepared with your graphics software and turn them into formatted, finished pages. Some word-processing software offers page-layout capabilities.

Communications. This specialized software is necessary only if you will be transmitting your work electronically—to a printer, for example.

Fig. 10.1   Clip Art

Scheduling

Schedule your project to allow ample time for each stage, since there will undoubtedly be delays beyond your control. Give each person involved a copy of the schedule, and be sure that each of them is aware of the due dates. It is essential that all those involved fulfill their obligations if final deadlines are to be met.

To determine how long a project should take, plan the project backwards. Confirm the date on which the project is due and how long the printer needs, and then assign each stage a target date. Certain phases of the project can proceed simultaneously; for example, the artwork can be prepared while the text is being written. See Fig. 10.2 for a sample project schedule.

Contributors often do not realize the effect their delays will have on a schedule. If you find the project is falling behind because of the slowness of others, speak to your supervisor or meet with those involved in order to alter the schedule or determine how time can be made up. Caution your contributors against last-minute changes. Such changes can ripple through an entire document; the addition of one word or phrase can completely alter the page flow, thereby affecting the placement of graphics, the table of contents, and the index.

Get written approval for any revisions that are requested of you, in order to absolve yourself of responsibility. When you submit text or graphics for approval, simply type "Approved by _____" and "Date _____" on the cover of the draft or use a store-bought rubber stamp that provides the same blanks. For more formal and extensive approval routing, see Fig. 10.9.

Typography

Typographic design includes the size and style of type, the length of lines, and the space between lines.

Fig. 10.2   DTP Project Schedule

Due Date		Actual Date	
____/____	Text submitted	____/____
____/____	Edited text returned	____/____
____/____	Revised text submitted	____/____
____/____	Text approved	____/____
____/____	Artwork submitted	____/____
____/____	Artwork approved	____/____
____/____	Page layout submitted	____/____
____/____	Page layout approved	____/____
____/____	Final copy completed	____/____
____/____	Final copy approved	____/____
____/____	Final copy/Film to printer	____/____
____/____	Printed copies delivered	____/____

PARTS OF THE LETTER

In Fig. 10.3 the standard parts of typographic letters are labeled. (See the glossary for definitions of typographic terms.)

UNITS OF MEASURE

Picas and *points* are fixed units of typographic measure. A pica is equal to approximately ⅙"; picas are commonly used to measure the length of a line of type or the depth of a page. (The page of text you are reading is 30 picas wide and 48 picas deep.) A point is ¹⁄₁₂ of a pica. Your software will often ask you to make typographic and format choices using measurements in points or picas.

Fig. 10.3   Parts and Aspects of Typographic Letters

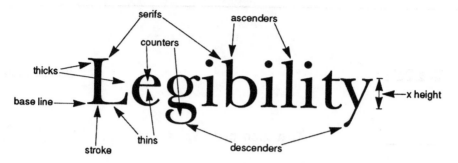

TYPE SIZE

Type size is measured in points. The larger the number of points, the larger the type, as illustrated in the following examples.

Example of 6-point type

Example of 12-point type

Example of 24-point type

Your software will generally allow you to select any size between 4 and 124 points for each available font. The point size of a type font is theoretically measured from the top of the highest ascender to the bottom of the lowest descender. In fact, however, not all typefaces of a given size will actually be the same size. The illustration that follows, in which the two horizontal lines are set 60 points apart, demonstrates the variation among four different "60-point" fonts.

LEADING

All typefaces are designed with enough space above and below so that the descenders on one line do not touch the ascenders on the following line. The amount of space from the base of one line to the base of the next, called leading, can be increased easily using your software. (The text of this book is mostly set in 10-point Baskerville type with 11-point leading, or 10/11—"10 on 11"—Baskerville.)

TYPEFACES

One of the most basic aspects of any typeface is whether it is a serif or sans-serif face.

Serif   Serifs are the tiny trailing lines that finish the strokes of printed letters, as in this text you are reading. Serif typefaces are generally used for normal text because the serifs tend to guide the reader's eye easily (but unnoticeably) across the page. There are many popular serif typefaces, two of which are Times Roman® and Electra®; the roman, italic, and bold fonts of each of these typefaces are shown below.

Times Roman®

abcdefghijklmnopqrstuvwxyz1234567890
ABCDEFGHIJKLMNOPQRSTUVWXYZ

abcdefghijklmnopqrstuvwxyz1234567890
ABCDEFGHIJKLMNOPQRSTUVWXYZ

abcdefghijklmnopqrstuvwxyz1234567890
ABCDEFGHIJKLMNOPQRSTUVWXYZ

Electra®

abcdefghijklmnopqrstuvwxyz1234567890
ABCDEFGHIJKLMNOPQRSTUVWXYZ

abcdefghijklmnopqrstuvwxyz1234567890
ABCDEFGHIJKLMNOPQRSTUVWXYZ

abcdefghijklmnopqrstuvwxyz1234567890
ABCDEFGHIJKLMNOPQRSTUVWXYZ

Sans-Serif   *Sans* is French for "without"; therefore, a sans-serif letter lacks serifs. Sans-serif type is clean and crisp, and thus is often used for posters, scientific material, and headings within documents. Of the many sans-serif typefaces, the two most popular are Helvetica® and Optima®; their roman, italic, and bold fonts are shown below.

Helvetica®

abcdefghijklmnopqrstuvwxyz1234567890
ABCDEFGHIJKLMNOPQRSTUVWXYZ

abcdefghijklmnopqrstuvwxyz1234567890
ABCDEFGHIJKLMNOPQRSTUVWXYZ

abcdefghijklmnopqrstuvwxyz1234567890
ABCDEFGHIJKLMNOPQRSTUVWXYZ

Optima®

abcdefghijklmnopqrstuvwxyz1234567890
ABCDEFGHIJKLMNOPQRSTUVWXYZ

abcdefghijklmnopqrstuvwxyz1234567890
ABCDEFGHIJKLMNOPQRSTUVWXYZ

abcdefghijklmnopqrstuvwxyz1234567890
ABCDEFGHIJKLMNOPQRSTUVWXYZ

Mixing typefaces   Try not to mix several typefaces in the same piece. If you stick with one or two, your printed piece will be more attractive. Many publications use a serif typeface for the text and a sans-serif for headings and subheadings. (This book uses serif typefaces for both headings and text.)

Page Layout

When preparing a page layout, remember that your goals are to draw attention to the printed piece and make it pleasing to the eye and easy to read. You might want to prepare a quick hand-drawn sketch like the one in Fig. 10.4 before you attempt to generate your layout on the computer.

Master page layout   The first step in creating a page layout is to prepare a master page. If there is a common design element that will appear throughout the publication (e.g., a designated number of columns or a horizontal bar at the top of each page), including it on the master page will allow the software to generate it automatically.

The software will ask you to make the following selections:

- Page size (standard, legal, etc.).
- Orientation: portrait (vertical) or landscape (horizontal).
- Margins: top, bottom, left, and right (or inside and outside). If your document will be side-bound (e.g., in a ring binder), allow an extra ½" for the inside margin.
- Number of columns and space between columns (alleys or gutters).
- Number of rows and space between rows.
- Facing pages or single-sided.
- Footers and headers, if any.
- Placement of page number.

Grids   A well-designed piece will have structure, but still offer the flexibility to deviate whenever necessary. Grids, also called *templates,* can provide for structure as well as flexibility.

Grids are invisible rectangular patterns that divide the page area into vertical or horizontal areas. Grids are not rigid and unalterable; they are merely guides. A grid may have as few as two columns or as many as seven or eight. The following are some suggestions for using grids for specific types of design.

Application	Number of Columns in Grid
Reports, manuals, and proposals	1, 2, or 3 columns
Tabloid format, two-column layout with substantial artwork	4 columns
Two-column layout with a third narrow column for headings and quotations	5 columns
Two- or three-column newsletters with artwork	6 columns
Creative layouts	7 or 8 columns

Fig. 10.5 shows some design possibilities based on a five-column grid. Notice how the same grid can be used for a number of different layouts, especially

Fig. 10.4   Page-layout Sketch

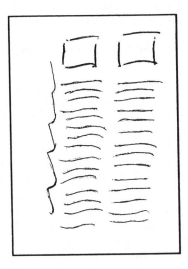

Fig. 10.5   Five-column Grid, with Possible Format Applications

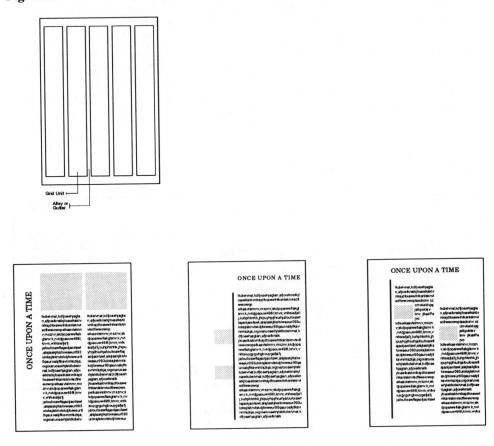

when the text columns are allowed to extend across two or three of the grid columns. Greeking (printed nonsense text) has been used to indicate where the actual text will be placed. Examples such as these can be presented for page-layout approval.

The following suggestions will help to make your layouts eye-catching and easy to follow.

- Never clutter your page. Provide ample white space to shape and frame the content so as to present an elegant and appealing piece.
- If your budget allows, use more than one color. If you are on a limited budget, try shading or an interesting design element instead.
- Consider incorporating borders, boxes, oversized page numbers, and the like, but sparingly. Too much of any single element, or too many different elements, will give the piece a disordered look. Keep it interesting but simple.

When your document is approaching its final form, you should be aware of what will appear on left-hand (even-numbered) and right-hand (odd-numbered) pages. For example, you may want all chapters to begin on right-hand pages; in that case, if Chapter 1 ends on a right-hand page, you must leave the following left-hand page blank so that Chapter 2 will start as a right-hand page.

You can ensure the correct page sequence in several different ways:

1. If your publication has printed page numbers on every page, the printer will not need any further guide. If some pages are blank or unnumbered, their unprinted numbers can be written on the camera copy itself in non-reproducing ("nonrepro") blue ink, or you can indicate that blank pages should be added by means of a note on the last text page preceding them (for example, on page 13 you might simply note "p. 14 is blank").
2. Prepare a *dummy*—that is, a mock-up version of the entire publication, with proofs or photocopies of all text and artwork stripped into place. Most of the dummy pages will often be merely copies of the finished pages generated by your computer, pasted back-to-back, but copies of art not generated on the computer will be pasted in as a guide to the printer.

Fig. 10.6 Production Assembly Sheet

PRODUCTION ASSEMBLY SHEET   sheet __1__ of __2__

TITLE: *Siddons X-42 Copier: User Manual*   no. of pages **32**   no. of halftones **5**
                                                   no. of blanks **4**   no. of copy dot

Even (Left)	Odd (Right)	FIGURE	TABLE	HALFTONE	SPECIAL INSTRUCTIONS
	i				title page
ii					c/r
	iii				contents
iv					blank
	1				Chap. 1 opening
2					
	3			1.1	(X-42 copier) Strip as Indicated
4		1.2			(exploded diagram)
	5				
6					Chap. 2 opening

3. Prepare an *assembly sheet*, which itemizes each page and any artwork that must be specially provided or printed. For many projects, preparing an assembly sheet (or a dummy) may be laborious and unnecessary, but it can be helpful for complex publications. (See Fig. 10.6.)

When sending camera copy to the printer, it will probably be helpful or necessary to fill out a form such as the one shown in Fig. 10.7, which the printer may provide.

Production and routing forms such as those illustrated in Figs. 10.8 and 10.9 may prove useful for important desktop publishing and design projects.

Fig. 10.7 Printing Specifications Form

PRINTING SPECIFICATIONS   Office Control Number _____
Name:

Title:

Number of Pages:

Format Description:

Quantity:

Trim Size: text: ☐ plus bleed
               cover: ☐ plus bleed
               other: ☐ plus bleed

Stock: text:
               cover:
               other:

Ink: text:
               cover:
               other:

Presswork: text: _____ color(s)/_____ side(s);   _____ color(s)/_____ side(s)
               cover: _____ color(s)/_____ side(s);   _____ color(s)/_____ side(s)
               other: _____ color(s)/_____ side(s);   _____ color(s)/_____ side(s)

Artwork: _____ square halftones   _____ line shots   _____ tints
               _____ outline halftones   _____ reverses   _____ strip-ins
               _____ other: _____

Camera Copy: ☐ camera-ready mechanicals   ☐ existing negatives   ☐ other: _____

Lay Up: ☐ per mechanicals   ☐ per dummy   ☐ other: _____

Proof: ☐ blueline   ☐ Color Key   ☐ Cromalin   ☐ other _____

— continued next page —

Figure 10.7   *Continued*

Finishing: ☐ folding:
                 ☐ scoring:
                 ☐ perforating:
                 ☐ punching:
                 ☐ die cutting:
                 ☐ embossing:
                 ☐ other: _____

Binding: ☐ saddle stitch, _____ wires on _____-inch side
                 ☐ perfect bound on _____-inch side
                 ☐ other: _____

Production Schedule:

Special Instructions:

Delivery:

For Further Information, Contact:

Special Conditions:

Courtesy of Promotional Perspectives, Ann Arbor, Michigan.

Fig. 10.8   Creative/Production Checklist

CREATIVE/PRODUCTION CHECKLIST

MARKETING MATERIALS

Project Name: _____   Deadline: _____

P.O. #: _____

Charge to (Code): _____

Artist/Agency: _____

Telephone: _____

Project Description: _____
_____
_____

Special Instructions: _____
_____
_____

Color/Sides: _____

Mailing List (See Attached) _____

Scans: _____   # Halftones: _____

	Item 1	Item 2	Item 3	Total
Dimensions:	_____	_____	_____	_____
Weight:	_____	_____	_____	_____
Paper Stock:	_____	_____	_____	

Mailing Information:

    Class: _____

    Permit Stat: _____

    Business Reply Mail: Letter/Postcard   Indicia to Artist: _____

Photos:
_____
_____
_____

Graphics/Illustrations:
_____
_____
_____

Final Approval: _____   _____
                        Marketing Dept.   Date

Rec'd by Production Mgr: _____   _____
                                 JBH   Date

Fig. 10.9   Routing Form for Desktop Projects

CONCEPT TO MECHANICALS
MARKETING MATERIALS
Direct Mail/Collateral • Packaging • P.O.P.

PROJECT NAME: _____   DEADLINE: _____

1. Internal [Full Review — Copy/Concept] *   Return by: _____
   (Please route in sequence)

____   ____   ____   ____   ____   ____   ____
LPM   CAA   DFM   TLC   JBH   JMM   SEL

> Marketing: Submit photocopies simultaneously to JWW & Corporate Legal for
  review and to TES for input/review. To be returned to SEL by: _____

2. Mechanicals [Full Review]   Return by: _____

____   ____   ____   ____   ____   ____   ____
LPM   CAA   DFM   TLC   JBH   JMM   SEL

3. Final Proof [Blues]   Return by: _____

       ____   ____   ____
       DFM   LPM   SEL

Rec'd by Production Mgr: _____   _____
                                     JBH   Date

Please make comments on reverse side of this sheet.

* Areas of responsibility when proofing:
LPM — Copy & content; mail distribution concerns
CAA — Customer Service concerns; ISBNs, style numbers, prices
DFM — Concept; clarity of the sales message
TLC — Operations/fulfillment concerns
JBH — Production/manufacturing concerns
JMM — Copy editing
JWW — Legal concerns
SEL — Concept, copy, content; Final OK

Printing and Binding

PRINTING

There are several possible methods of printing, and your decision should be based on the type of project, the quality needed, and your budget.

Laser printers   Laser printers often represent the least expensive way to generate copy. Most produce only black-and-white copy; color laser printers are more expensive. The toner cartridges, the available fonts, and the low resolution (usually 300 dots per inch) represent limitations of laser printers; other limitations are the size of the paper they can handle and their slowness in producing substantial quantities.

Your selection of paper should be guided by the nature of the material. Laser paper will provide a higher-quality result than copier paper. For internal memos, reports, and manuals, copier paper will probably be adequate; for sales presentations, financial reports, masters, or pre-press proofs, laser paper should be used. White, bright paper makes the type more legible. Opacity—the paper's ability to keep images on one side of the paper from showing through to the other side—is a consideration when printing on both sides. Paper with a smooth finish provides a uniform transfer of toner, so there is less chance that the printed characters will break up.

Quick print shops   These shops offer good-quality printing, generally at affordable prices. However, many quick print shops cannot handle specialty printing with unusual requirements, and they often must send such work to an outside printer. If your graphic material has heavy ink coverage or fine lines, it may lose some of its quality in the printing. Despite their advertised speed, the service provided by these shops is not necessarily faster than that of other printers. Many are equipped with desktop publishing equipment.

Offset printers   Offset printing companies offer excellent quality, large print runs, four-color print processes, and the highest halftone quality available.

BINDINGS

Newsletter-length publications often require no binding at all, being merely folded in two.

Somewhat longer publications can be bound cheaply and efficiently by means of staples along the spine (sometimes called *saddle-wiring*).

Ring binders are particularly appropriate for materials that are to be saved and accumulated. They require only that the sheets be punched.

Portfolio folders with pockets on the inside covers are another possibility, especially when diverse materials must be assembled.

Plastic report covers, often transparent, hold the pages together with a simple clip on the spine.

More elaborate binding methods requiring special equipment are also available to desktop publishers. Thermal binding machines attach the pages to a cover with a preglued spine by means of a heat process in less than a minute. Plastic comb bindings (particularly desirable for publications that must lie flat when open) can also be attached in the office, using a machine that first punches the holes and then inserts the comb binding element. Most of these binding machines are available for a few hundred dollars.

Commercial bookbinding methods such as sewn, perfect, and notch binding are generally more expensive and will be necessary only for major projects with large budgets.

Desktop Publishing Applications

Desktop publishing can be an ideal means of producing a wide variety of publications. Whatever the project, remember that a fancy design cannot make up for inadequate content. Everything you produce should both be well written and incorporate appropriate and attractive—but not ostentatious—visual elements.

Reports   Reports, whether intended for internal distribution or client/customer distribution, can take many forms and will often include graphs, charts, and art. With DTP programs and equipment, you can produce professional-quality reports with well-integrated art of all kinds.

Brochures   Brochures are useful marketing tools that vary widely in length and quality. DTP can produce effective brochures on a limited budget. Though not usually adequate for elaborate brochures, DTP programs can at least be used to prepare layouts for them.

Corporate communications   Corporate communications can take the form of letters, memos, handbooks, employee forms, handouts, and materials to be distributed outside the corporation. Even if distribution is only internal, well-prepared communications are good for morale and present a positive company image to employees.

Advertising and promotional materials   DTP has proved to be a boon in producing promotional material and advertisements for newspapers, magazines, and trade journals at affordable costs.

Catalogs   Catalog information can often be selected from an electronic database and printed using page-layout software.

Newsletters   More than 100,000 different newsletters are published in the United States by individuals, companies, and civic groups, at costs ranging from almost nothing to thousands of dollars. Desktop publishing equipment can produce typeset-quality text on a shoestring budget. Before you enter the newsletter arena, find a book on the subject (see Appendix, "Further Reading") and gather as many actual newsletters as you can—they are filled with good ideas.

Manuals   Most manuals are substantial or complex enough to require professional printing. However, by producing camera-ready pages for the printer, you can save your company both time and money.

Preparing Presentation Materials

If your organization does not have an in-house art department, the task of planning and creating the visual component of oral presentations may very well fall to you. There is nothing complicated or mysterious about preparing presentation materials, especially if you know how to use the available software packages.

Consider using a presentation software program. Though word-processing software allows you to prepare high-quality charts, presentation software offers much more flexibility, permitting you to design and create 35-mm slides, graphics for overhead projectors, and handouts. Many of these software programs have built-in drawing tools and word-processing components, in addition to a full array of color options and automatic design features. Some programs offer advanced features such as rotating, animation, and resizing. Additionally, such programs may enable you to:

- Write text in the program or import text that was created in a word-processing program.
- Use the internal graphics system to create pie charts, line graphs, bar graphs, and other graphics in black and white or color.
- Use a ready-made template (or automatic format) or create one of your own to give a consistent and professional look to all components of the presentation.
- Integrate transparencies from other presentations so that you do not have to "reinvent the wheel" for each presentation. Many presentations are based on previous ones, and there is obviously a large advantage in being able to integrate and rearrange visual materials that already exist.
- Import data from other programs and other formats. This will let you create slides and transparencies from word processors, spreadsheets, databases, and graphics that have been prepared or scanned.
- Generate your own slides and graphic transparencies. Graphic transparencies for overhead projectors can be produced by placing transparent sheets rather than copy paper in a laser printer and printing them as you would any paper copy. If you have a slide shooter, you can generate your own slides. If not, there are computer graphic services that will produce slides within one or two days after receiving a disk or electronically transmitted data.
- Run your computer as a slide projector. You can create a slide show and set the computer to automatically fade and "wipe" from one slide to another. Synchronized sound is also possible with the proper equipment.

The purpose of a presentation visual is to reinforce and clarify an idea. A presentation can be compared with a magazine article: just as the pictures accompanying the article must be supported by the text, projected images should be used to reinforce the speaker's main points. Visual images can be effectively used to open a presentation, to channel thinking, to emphasize key points, to present numerical or financial information, to show comparisons, and to explain new concepts.

When preparing any visual image, always strive for visibility, clarity, and simplicity. All your charts for a given presentation should have a uniform look. Use both uppercase and lowercase characters for the text; it will be easier to read than all capital letters. Use large type, perhaps 18-point for the text and 24-point for the headings. It is recommended that slide images employ a dark background with light-colored print and that larger transparencies use dark print on a lightly tinted background.

See the sample visuals in Figs. 10.10 and 10.11.

Fig. 10.10   A Sample Overhead Projector Image

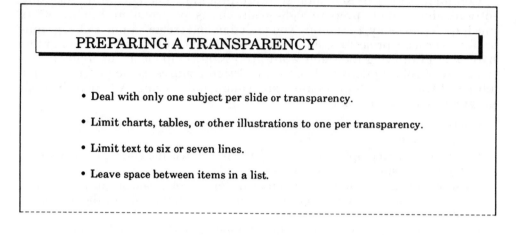

PREPARING A TRANSPARENCY

- Deal with only one subject per slide or transparency.

- Limit charts, tables, or other illustrations to one per transparency.

- Limit text to six or seven lines.

- Leave space between items in a list.

Fig. 10.11   A Sample Slide Image

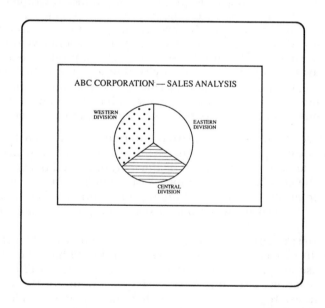

ABC CORPORATION — SALES ANALYSIS

WESTERN DIVISION

EASTERN DIVISION

CENTRAL DIVISION

Desktop Publishing Glossary

The following glossary provides concise definitions of terminology that is commonly encountered in desktop publishing.

AA—see AUTHOR'S ALTERATION

air—see WHITE SPACE

alley   The space between two columns of type.—called also *gutter*

alphabet length   The total width of the 26 lowercase unspaced letters in a particular font. The alphabet length is usually given in points and is used as an indicator of the relative width of the typeface.

artwork   Material (such as a drawing or photograph) prepared for reproduction in printed matter.

ascender   **1**   The part of a lowercase letter (*d*, *f*, *k*, etc.) that rises above the x height of the letter.   **2**   A lowercase character that has an ascender.—compare DESCENDER

ascender height   The height of the highest ascender in a typeface.

author's alteration   An alteration made to typeset copy (as at the galley or page-proof stage) that is not caused by a printer's error.—called also *AA;* compare PRINTER'S ERROR

backbone—see SPINE

back margin   The inside margin of a page.—called also *gutter*

back matter   Matter (such as a bibliography or index) that follows the main text of a book.—compare FRONT MATTER

bad break   **1**   The dividing of a word at the end of a line at an incorrect place within the word.   **2**   The dividing of text between pages in a way that leaves a widow at the top of one page or not enough copy at the bottom of another.

bar graph   A chart showing comparative data by means of vertical rectangles.

base line   An imaginary line on which the body of a typeset letter rests.

binding   Cover and materials that hold a document together.

bleed   Printed image positioned so as to run off the edge of the page after trimming.

block quotation—see EXTRACT

bluelines   Prints in blue ink made from negatives of book pages, used as final proofs.—called also *blues*

blues—see BLUELINES

body   The vertical space that is occupied by a line of type in a given font. The body of a given font is measured from the top of the tallest ascender to the bottom of the deepest descender; however, a line of type can be set on a body that is larger than that actually occupied by the font in order to give the effect of leading between successive lines of type. The 10-point type in this book has a 10-point body, but it is set on an 11-point body.

boldface   **1**   A heavy-faced type. The entry words in this glossary are in boldface type.   **2**   Printing in boldface.—compare LIGHTFACE

box   A rectangular rule usually enclosing text that is to be set apart from the text around it.

broadside cut   An illustration or table laid on its side to fit the page, the left side being at the bottom of the page.

built-up fraction   A fraction whose numbers are set in the same point size as the surrounding text and occupy more than one line of vertical space. The fraction

$\frac{1}{2}$ is a built-up fraction; the fractions $\frac{1}{2}$, ½, and 1/2 are not.—compare CASE FRACTION

bulk   Degree of thickness (not weight) of paper.

bullet   A large dot used to set off items in a vertical list.

camera copy   Material in final form and ready to be photographed and printed.

camera-ready   Ready to be photographed and printed.

cap   A capital letter.

cap height   The height of a capital letter in a typeface.

caption   **1**   The heading especially of an article or document.   **2**   The identification or explanatory comment accompanying a pictorial illustration.

caret   A wedge-shaped mark made on written or printed matter to indicate the place where something is to be inserted.

case binding   Binding in which sewn signatures with end sheets glued on are fastened to a cover with gauze and glue.

case fraction   A simple fraction whose numbers are set one above the other in a smaller type so as to be contained in one line of type. The term *case fraction* can refer to a fraction that takes the form $\frac{1}{2}$ or ½; however, some people use *case fraction* to refer only to a fraction that takes the form $\frac{1}{2}$. The term *piece fraction* is also used to describe both forms of fractions; however, some people use *piece fraction* to refer only to a fraction that takes the form ½.—compare BUILT-UP FRACTION

castoff   **1**   The process of calculating the number of characters in a given manuscript in order to determine the number of pages it will require when printed.   **2**   The result of making a castoff.

character   A letter, symbol, numeral, or mark of punctuation. For some purposes, the spaces between words are also considered characters.

clip art   Copyright-free art designed for graphic applications. Clip art is available in both book and electronic form.

coated paper   Paper with a coating to give it a particular finish.

color separation   The isolation on separate photographic negatives, by the use of filters and scanners, of the parts of full-color artwork that are to be printed in given colors.

comp   A preliminary design (for a cover, advertisement, etc.) intended for review and approval before being prepared in final form for printing.—short for "composition"

composition   The production of type or typographic characters arranged for printing.

condensed   *of a typeface* Having letters that are narrower than those of a typeface not so characterized.—compare EXPANDED

continuous-tone   *of a piece of artwork* Having gradations of tone from dark to light.

copy   Matter that is to be set or photographed for printing.

copyediting   The usually last editing of a manuscript before it is set in type.

copyright page   A page of a book bearing the copyright notice, including the proprietor's name and the date of copyright.

counter   An area within a letter that is wholly or partly enclosed by strokes.

credit line   A line, note, or name that acknowledges the source of an item (such as an illustration).

crop   To trim a piece of art (photograph, etc.) for printing, often by simply marking for the printer the intended borders of the printed image.

crop marks   Marks indicating where a piece of art is to be cropped.

CRT composition Typesetting in which type images are electronically produced and displayed on a cathode-ray tube's screen, from which they are transferred to film or photosensitive paper.

cyan A greenish blue color, one of the four colors used in four-color process printing.

descender **1** The part of a lowercase letter that descends below the base line. **2** A lowercase character that has a descender.—compare ASCENDER

designer A person who makes decisions about typography, layout, and the physical appearance of a publication.

diacritic A mark used with a letter or group of letters to indicate a change in sound value.

dingbat A typographical symbol or ornament.

display Copy (such as a heading) that is set apart from the text in larger type.

drill To make holes in paper to permit insertion into a ring binder.

drop The vertical distance (as on a page) from one typographic or design element to another.

drop folio A page number that is located at the bottom of a page.

dummy **1** A set of model pages, often consisting of text proofs and copies of illustrations pasted in place on paperboard, and usually intended to serve as a guide for page makeup. **2** A bound, unprinted, or only partially printed sample of a planned publication to show its size, shape, and general appearance.

elite A typewriter type providing 12 characters to the linear inch and 6 lines to the vertical inch.—compare PICA

em dash A dash that is as wide as the point size of the type.

em quad—see EM SPACE

em space A space as wide as the point size of the type.—called also *em quad*

en dash A dash that is shorter than the em dash but slightly longer than the hyphen and is used for the hyphen in some situations.

en quad—see EN SPACE

en space A space that is one-half of an em space.—called also *en quad*

epigraph A quotation set at the beginning of a literary work or a division of it to suggest its theme.

expanded *of a typeface* Having letters that are wider than those of a typeface not so characterized.—called also *extended;* compare CONDENSED

extended—see EXPANDED

extract A long quotation that is set off from the text and set in type that is slightly smaller than that of the text.—called also *block quotation*

F&Gs—see FOLDED AND GATHERED SHEETS

facing pages Two successive pages that face each other as in a book lying open.

final proof A proof made by the compositor from the film, usually a negative, that will be sent to the printer to make printing plates from.

flush-and-hang indention—see HANGING INDENTION

flush left Aligned vertically along the left margin.

flush right Aligned vertically along the right margin.

folded and gathered sheets Printed sheets that have been folded into signatures and collected into the correct order for binding.—called also *F&Gs*

folio A page number.

font A set of type all of the same design (in traditional usage, of the same size as well).

footer—see RUNNING FOOT

foot margin   The bottom margin of a page.

format   The page size, margins, fonts, and general makeup of a document.

four-color process   The standard color printing process, which uses four colors of ink (yellow, magenta [red], cyan [blue], and black) to produce a great variety of other colors.

front margin   The outside margin of a page.

front matter   Matter (such as an introduction or preface) that precedes the main text of a book.—compare BACK MATTER

full measure   The full width of the type page or column.

galley or **galley proof**   An early proof of typeset material not yet made into pages. —compare PAGE PROOF

greeking   Nonsense text printed to represent real text when designing page layouts.

grid   Rectangular pattern used to position text and graphics on a page but not intended to appear when the page is printed.

gutter   **1**   The inside margin of a page, or the adjoining inside margins of two facing pages.   **2**   ALLEY.

hair space   A space that is one-fifth of an em, one-sixth of an em, or one-half point in width.—compare THIN SPACE

halftone   A printed image that represents continuous-tone artwork (such as a photograph) through the use of a pattern of dots of varying size.

H & J   Hyphenation and justification.

hanging indention   Indention of all the lines of a passage or index except the first line, which is set flush with the left-hand margin.—called also *flush-and-hang indention*

head or **heading**   A word or series of words often in larger letters placed at the beginning of a passage or at the top of a page or column in order to introduce or categorize.

header—see RUNNING HEAD

headline   **1**   A head of a newspaper story or article usually printed in large type and giving the gist of the story or article.   **2**   Words set at the head of a passage or page to introduce or categorize.

head margin   The top margin of a page.

headnote   A note of comment or explanation that prefaces a text.

hickey   A spot or imperfection on a printed page.

horizontal orientation—see LANDSCAPE ORIENTATION

impose   To arrange (pages) in the proper order and orientation for printing.

imposition   The order or arrangement of imposed pages.

inferior   Relating to or being a subscript.—compare SUPERIOR

italic   A type style whose characters slant upward to the right, as in *"these words are italic."*—compare ROMAN

justify   To align the ends of lines of type at the right and left.

kerning   The adjustment of horizontal spacing between letters.

landscape orientation   Orientation of a page whose width is greater than its height.—called also *horizontal orientation;* compare PORTRAIT ORIENTATION

layout   The final page arrangement of text and art to be reproduced especially by printing.

leaders   Dots or sometimes hyphens (as in a table or index) used to lead the eye horizontally across a space to the right word or number.

leading The distance between lines of type, measured from the base of one line to the base of the next.

legend An explanatory list of the symbols used on a map or chart or in an illustration, or explanatory remarks that accompany an illustration.

letterpress The process of printing from an inked, raised surface, expecially when the paper is impressed directly upon the surface.

letterspacing Insertion of space between the letters of a word.

ligature A printed character (such as *fi*) consisting of two or more letters or characters joined together.

lightface **1** A typeface having comparatively light thin lines. **2** Printing in lightface.—compare BOLDFACE

line drawing A drawing made with a pen or other pointed instrument in solid lines or solid masses.

line graph A graph in which points representing values of a variable for values of an independent variable are connected by a line.

loose-leaf binding A style of binding in which pages with holes punched or drilled through them are held together in such a way as to permit removal and replacement of individual pages.

lowercase Small-letter type used in printing.—compare UPPERCASE

machine-readable Directly usable by a computer.

magenta A deep purplish red, one of the four colors used in four-color process printing.

makeup The arranging of typeset matter, including running heads and illustrations, into pages.

margin The unprinted area of a page.

margin cut A small illustration set within a side margin next to the text.

markup The process of marking on a manuscript all the directions for typesetting.

master proof A set of proofs bearing all corrections and alterations of both the printer and author.

masthead The printed matter in a periodical that gives the title, names of editors, pertinent details of ownership, and advertising and subscription rates.

mechanical A piece of finished copy (representing a page or pages, a book jacket or cover, a brochure, etc.) assembled and mounted, usually on a paperboard sheet, and ready to be photographed for printing.

nut An en space.

offset printing A printing process in which an inked impression from a plate is first made on a rubber-blanketed cylinder and then transferred to paper.

opaque To paint over any translucent areas on a negative that are not wanted on the printing plate.

overlay A transparent sheet containing graphic matter to be superimposed on another sheet.

overrun Extra printed copies.

page proof A proof of typeset material that has been made up into a page.

Pantone Matching System™ An internationally recognized color-matching system. —called also *PMS*

pasteup Camera-ready copy.—called also *mechanical*

PE—see PRINTER'S ERROR

perfect binding A binding process in which collated signatures are trimmed at the back and a glue is applied to the cut and roughened edges. A usually paper cover is then wrapped around the book.

photocomposition   The setting of type directly on film or photosensitive paper for reproduction.

photocopy   A photographic reproduction of graphic matter.

pica   **1**   12-point type.   **2**   A unit of about ⅙ of an inch used in measuring typographical material.   **3**   A typewriter type providing 10 characters to the linear inch and 6 lines to the vertical inch.—compare ELITE

piece fraction—see CASE FRACTION

pie chart   A representation of comparative data by means of a circle divided into wedge-shaped portions.

pixels   Dots on a computer screen that together form the electronic images.

platemaking   The making of printing plates for offset printing.

PMS—see PANTONE MATCHING SYSTEM

point   A unit of typographical measurement that is $\frac{1}{12}$ of a pica (about $\frac{1}{72}$ of an inch) and that is used especially in measuring the vertical size of type or the amount of space between lines of type.

portrait orientation   Orientation of a page whose height is greater than its width. —called also *vertical orientation;* compare LANDSCAPE ORIENTATION

prepress   The process by which individual page negatives are transferred into a printing plate.

pressrun   The number of copies specified to be printed.

printer's error   An error in typeset copy (such as errors caused by incorrect keyboarding or a program malfunction) that is the responsibility of the typesetter. —called also *PE;* compare AUTHOR'S ALTERATION

production   The processes by which a publication is produced. These extend from the completion of the manuscript to the making of the plates from which the pages will be printed.

proof   A copy of typeset text made for examination or correction.

quad   A space in typesetting that is one en or slightly more in width.

ragged left   Unjustified at the left margin.

ragged right   Unjustified at the right margin.

recto   A right-hand page.—compare VERSO

reference mark   A conventional symbol (such as an asterisk or a dagger) or a superior number or letter placed in a text for directing attention to a footnote.

register   Correct alignment of inks on the printed page.

registration marks   Markings that show a commercial printer how to align color negatives for proper printing.

relief   Projection of letters or images from a flat surface.

repro *or* **reproduction proof**   A high-quality, camera-ready, positive print of typeset matter from which a negative is made for making printing plates.

resolution   Overall clarity of detail in a graphic image.

reverse type   White text printed on a colored or shaded background.

right-reading   Having the correct right-to-left orientation.—compare WRONG-READING

river   An irregular streak running through several lines of close-set printed matter and caused by a series of wide spaces that appear to form a continuous line.

roman   Of or relating to a type style with upright characters.—compare ITALIC

rule   A printed straight line or linear design.

runaround   Type set in lines shorter than full measure in order to fit around an illustration.

run back   To transfer text from the beginning of one line to the end of the preceding line.

run down   To transfer text from the end of one line to the beginning of the following line.

run in   To make (typeset matter) continuous without a paragraph or other break.

running foot   A repeated heading (often consisting of the title of the book, chapter, or section) that appears at the bottom of consecutive pages.—called also *footer;* compare RUNNING HEAD

running head   A repeated heading (often consisting of the title of the book, chapter, or section) that appears at the top of consecutive pages.—called also *header;* compare RUNNING FOOT

runover   Typeset material that exceeds the space estimated or allotted.

saddle-stitched—see SADDLE-WIRED

saddle-wired   Secured by a stitch made by driving wire staples through the center fold and clinching them on the inside. This kind of binding is also referred to as being *saddle-stitched,* especially when thread is substituted for the staples.—compare SIDE-STITCHED

sans-serif   A letter or typeface with no serifs.

score   An impression or dent made during the printing process to permit easier folding.

self-cover   **1**   A cover made from the same paper stock as the inside pages.   **2**   A publication having such a cover.

self-mailer   A printed piece that meets post-office requirements for mailing without an envelope.

serif   **1**   Any of the short, trailing lines stemming from and at an angle to the upper and lower ends of the strokes of a printed letter, resembling the beginning or end of a pen stroke.   **2**   A letter or typeface with serifs.

sheet-fed press   A press that prints individual sheets of paper.—compare WEB PRESS

side-stitched   Secured by passing a wire or thread from side to side through a complete book or magazine before covering.—called also *side-wired;* compare SADDLE-WIRED

side-wired—see SIDE-STITCHED

signature   A printed sheet with usually 8, 16, 24, or 32 pages, which is folded, trimmed, and bound with other signatures.

sinkage   The distance from the top of a text page to the first line of text or display type.

small capital   A letter having the form of but smaller than a capital letter.

Smyth sewing   A method of attaching the signatures of books by means of threads passed through the folds.

spine   The back of a bound book that connects the front and back covers.—called also *backbone*

spiral binding   Binding in which a continuous spiral wire or plastic strip is passed through holes at the gutter margin.

stet   An editorial direction, meaning "let it stand," that is used to indicate that words crossed out in copy or proof are to be restored. "Stet" is written in the margin, and heavy dots are placed under the affected words.

stock   Paper to be used for printing, usually identified as to its specific qualities and weight.

strip   To arrange (as negatives) in proper position on a flat.

stroke   One of the lines of a letter of the alphabet.

style sheet   A compilation of detailed style rules (as in regard to punctuation, hyphenation, and abbreviations) to be followed consistently throughout a manuscript.

subheading   A heading of a subdivision (as in an outline or index).

subscript   A distinguishing symbol (such as a letter or number) written immediately below or below and to the right or left of another character.—compare SUPER- SCRIPT

superior   Relating to or being a superscript.—compare INFERIOR

superscript   A distinguishing symbol (such as a letter or number) written immediately above or above and to the right or left of another character.—compare SUB- SCRIPT

tear sheet   A page cut or torn from a publication.

template   A page grid created and intended for repeated use.

text page—see TYPE PAGE

thick   A thick stroke.

thick space   A space that is one-third of an em.—called also *three-to-the-em space*

thin   A thin stroke.

thin space   A space that is one-fourth, or sometimes one-fifth, of an em space. —compare HAIR SPACE

three-to-the-em space—see THICK SPACE

thumbnail   A small sketch of a page.

tint   Percentage of shading on an area of a page (for example, 10 percent black).

title page   A page of a book bearing the title and usually the names of the author and publisher and the place and sometimes the date of publication.

trim marks   Marks placed on a page proof or page negative to show where the edge of the page will be after the printed signatures have been trimmed to their final size.

trim size   The actual size of a book page after excess material required in production has been cut off.

typeface   A particular type design, often including all the standard variants (bold, italic, etc.) of the basic design.

typemark   To specify on the manuscript how type is to be set.

type page *or* **text page**   The area of a page that includes all of the copy measured from the ascender of the top line to the descender of the bottom line. The two terms are usually synonymous; however, the term *type page* is often intended to include the running heads and folios, and the term *text page* to include just the text.

typescript   A typewritten manuscript and especially one that is intended for use as printer's copy.

typesetter   **1**   A person who sets type.   **2**   A device that produces the type from keyboarded instructions.

typesetting   The composing of text for printing, today usually by means of computerized photocomposition.

typography   The style, arrangement, and appearance of typeset matter.

underscore   A line drawn under a word or line to indicate intent to italicize.

uppercase   Capital-letter type used in printing.—compare LOWERCASE

verso   A left-hand page.—compare RECTO

vertical orientation—see PORTRAIT ORIENTATION

web press   A press that prints a continuous roll of paper.—compare SHEET-FED PRESS

weight   Heaviness of paper (20 lb., 50 lb., etc.), as measured for standard 500-sheet reams of 17″ × 22″ sheets.

white space   Intentionally unprinted areas on a printed page.—called also *air*

widow   A single short last line of a paragraph that appears at the top of a printed page or column.

work-and-turn printing   Printing one side of a sheet, turning it over, and printing the other side. Two copies of the pages are produced when the sheet is cut in half.

wrong-reading   Having a reversed right-to-left orientation.—compare RIGHT-READING

WYSIWYG   (pronounced "wizzywig") Literally, "What You See [on the screen] Is What You Get [on paper]"; describes a computer display that exactly reflects the appearance of the document as it will be printed, though at a smaller size.

x height   The height of a lowercase x used to represent the height of the main body of a lowercase letter.

CHAPTER 11

Office Mail and Mail Services

The processing of office mail may be one of your most important responsibilities. Due to its timely nature and its significance as a communication link, all mail must be processed immediately. A system should be established to ensure that both incoming and outgoing mail are handled quickly and efficiently.

Your responsibility for outgoing mail may vary depending on your company. Since each piece of mail should be delivered in the most appropriate and economical way, you must be familiar with the various mail classifications and special services offered by the U.S. Postal Service as well as the alternative delivery services available through other carriers.

Incoming Mail

In large corporations, the mail room receives the mail directly from the carrier or a designated messenger picks it up from the post office. The mail is sorted in the mail room and delivered to the various departments by mail-room messengers. This will usually occur more than once a day. Within the individual departments one person may be assigned to sort the mail further and then deliver it to each executive's secretary, who sorts it in the same manner as in a one-secretary business office. The steps outlined in the following pages apply to mail processing in offices of all sizes.

PRELIMINARY SORTING

It generally saves time to sort mail in piles before opening it, particularly when dealing with large quantities of mail. Mail is commonly sorted at this stage into six categories: top-priority (telegrams and certified, registered, and special-delivery letters), interoffice, first-class, second-class (newspapers and magazines), third-class (circulars, books, catalogs, and other printed materials), and parcels.

OPENING

Unless specifically authorized, you should not open letters marked "Personal" or "Confidential." (If you open such a letter unintentionally, simply mark the envelope "Opened by mistake," initial it, and reseal it with tape.) Second- and third-

416

class mail should be opened neatly; remove all protective covers and flatten any rolled items.

Before slitting open an envelope, tap it to ensure that the contents are not at the top—checks and other important items have been damaged by neglect to do so. Then open each envelope by slitting the top edge with a letter opener or by using a letter-opening machine. The contents must be removed carefully. Be sure that everything is removed from the envelope. Check the enclosure notations on letters; if an enclosure is missing, you should note this on the letter itself. If the letter states that other material is being mailed separately, make a note of it so that you can follow up if it fails to arrive. When practicable, enclosures may be fastened to their letters with paper clips or staples: small enclosures on the front, letter-size enclosures on the back.

Some offices require that envelopes be fastened to letters. If this is not the practice in your office, check to see that the sender's address is on the letter before throwing the envelope away. If anything seems amiss—such as a return address different from that on the letterhead, or a large discrepancy between the postmark date and the date the letter is received—save the envelope. Some experienced secretaries save all the envelopes for the day in order to recheck for missing enclosures, addresses, or other items.

DATING

A hand or automatic date stamp is useful for recording the date and sometimes the time when the mail is received. (Date and time received are often matters of critical importance in law offices, for example.) If you have no date stamp, write "Received" and the date on the letter; in some offices, just the date in numerical form will suffice.

SECONDARY SORTING

The next step is the secondary sorting of opened mail for presentation to the executive. The mail should be arranged by priority so that the executive may deal with the most important mail first. Urgent correspondence (such as telegrams and registered or special-delivery mail) should be placed on the top of the pile. Some offices have special file folders with tabs marked *Urgent, Important, Routine, Information, Advertising, Confidential, Personal,* etc. Identifying the folder labels by color, number, and type of correspondence as in Fig. 11.1 should prove helpful.

Fig. 11.1   Classifications of Executive Correspondence

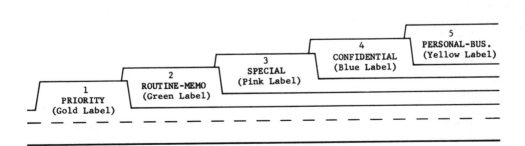

READING

In some offices, you may be asked to read most letters and underline important passages for the executive. Notes to the executive (such as "Refer to file" or "See invoice") may be written in the side margins. When passing mail on to the executive, you should also provide any additional information or material—such as the file of previous correspondence—that the executive may need in responding to the letter. If a piece of mail is to be brought to the attention of several people, it can be circulated with a routing slip (a slip or sheet attached to the correspondence listing those who should see it, each of whom will check off his or her name in turn), or it can be photocopied and distributed. If time is of the essence, photocopying is usually preferable, since routed mail may circulate slowly or get lost.

LOGGING

The final step in handling incoming mail in some offices is making a record of it in a register or log. All important mail should be recorded in this register; items like circulars and ads should not. The following data are usually recorded: the date and time received, the date of the letter itself, the writer, the addressee, a brief description of the subject, and the disposition of the letter. Such a log may also be kept on a word processor. See Fig. 11.2.

Fig. 11.2   Mail Register or Log

REC'D	TIME	DATED	FROM	ADDRESSEE	SUBJECT	DISPOSITION
7/2/–	9 a.m.	7/1/–	Barker Bros.	President	Letter–Info	Reply Sent 7/6
7/2/–	9 a.m.	6/30/–	Acme Corp.	T. Cooke	Price List	Filed 7/2
7/2/–	2 a.m.	6/30/–	R. Dow	S. Smythe	Letter–Appointment	Phone Call 7/2
7/3/–	9 a.m.	7/1/–	Cole, Inc.	Personnel	Seminar Announcement	Referred To T. Cooke 7/4

Outgoing Mail

Your duties in processing outgoing mail will vary according to the size of the business. While a large business office may have a special mailing department, including a messenger service that will relieve its secretaries of some mailing duties, the mail must still be prepared for the mail room. This will usually be your responsibility. In a smaller office, you may have total responsibility for mailing.

CHECKING CONTENTS OF OUTGOING LETTERS

Before sending out your own letters, recheck the following five essential elements.

Addresses   The inside address typed on the letter itself and the address on the envelope should be the same. To reduce the chance of error and to speed up the mailing process, some companies use window envelopes, thus eliminating the need for typing the address on the envelope. If a window envelope is used, it is imperative that the inside address be complete. If the letter is being mailed to a post-office box, the ZIP code of the box number should be used and not that of the street address. Since mail is delivered to the address element on the line immediately above the city and state, be sure that any post-office box number is in that position and the street address, if included, is on the line above. The all-capitalized and unpunctuated two-letter state abbreviations are preferred by the post office. See the table of abbreviations on page 286.

Envelope notations   Two types of notation may appear on an envelope: (1) on-arrival notices such as "CONFIDENTIAL" or "PERSONAL," and (2) mailing-service directions such as "CERTIFIED MAIL" or "SPECIAL DELIVERY," all of which are normally typed entirely in capital letters. Every letter having an at-tention line, a special mailing notation, or an on-arrival notation should also have the same notation on its envelope. On-arrival notations are usually typed four lines below the return address or nine lines below the top edge of the envelope, starting at least ½″ in from the left edge of the envelope. On-arrival notations other than "PERSONAL" and "CONFIDENTIAL" generally appear in the same place, typed in capitals and lowercase letters and underscored (for exam-ple, "Please Forward"). Postal directions or special mailing notations are placed on the same line ½″ from the *right* edge of the envelope and are typed in capital letters. See Chapter 7 for detailed envelope addressing instructions.

An envelope should always include a return address. You may wish to type the sender's name above the preprinted address.

Signatures   It is your responsibility to check all outgoing letters for proper sig-natures. If you are authorized to sign letters with an executive's signature, you must add your initials. A letter may be invalid without a signature in ink.

Enclosures   It is very important that all enclosures cited in the enclosure nota-tion at the bottom of the letter be included with the letter. (Some secretaries type visual reminders, such as three hyphens or periods, in the left margin by each line in which mention is made of the item or items to be enclosed.) It is frustrat-ing for an addressee to receive a letter without the intended enclosure or with the wrong enclosure. Therefore, it cannot be overemphasized that their inclu-sion be double-checked.

If it is necessary to enclose coins or other small objects, they should be taped to a card or inserted in a coin card, and the envelope should be marked "Hand Stamp."

Reference and copy notations   If you are answering a letter that is identified by a reference number, be sure that the number is repeated in the reference line of your reply letter. The copy notation (*cc* or *c*) indicates to whom additional copies of the letter should be sent. Check carefully to see that envelopes have been ad-dressed to the individuals mentioned in regular (*cc*) and blind copy (*bcc*) nota-tions. The blind copy notation appears only on the copies, usually in the upper left corner; however, it may also be placed below the reference and enclosure notations. An extra copy should always be kept for filing.

FOLDING, INSERTING, AND SEALING

The diagrams in Fig. 11.3 depict the correct ways to fold and insert letters.

The following are some suggestions for sealing and stamping envelopes by hand:

Fig. 11.3 Folding and Inserting Letters

Small Envelope

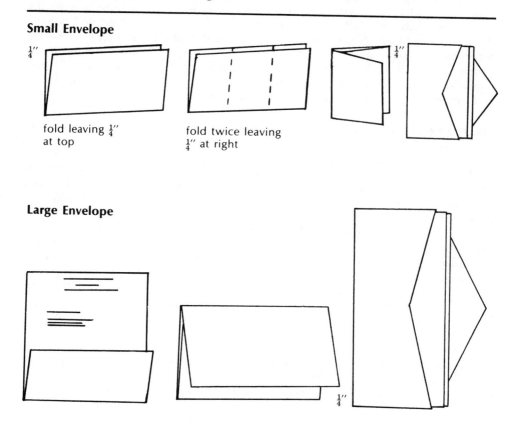

fold leaving $\frac{1}{4}''$ at top

fold twice leaving $\frac{1}{4}''$ at right

Large Envelope

Window Envelope

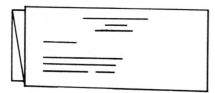

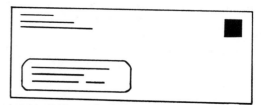

Some stationery has a fold line indicating where to fold for insertion in window envelopes.

Insert so that at least $\frac{1}{4}''$ is left between the side and bottom edges of the address and the window.

1. Use a moist sponge or moistening device. Licking envelopes or stamps is unsanitary and hazardous; you can be cut by the sharp edge of the envelope flap.

2. Moisten envelopes and stamps over a blotter to absorb excess water.

3. A large number of envelopes can be moistened quickly by placing them one behind the other and pressing down the flap of each envelope as it is moistened. See Fig. 11.4.

Fig. 11.4   **Envelopes Aligned for Moistening**

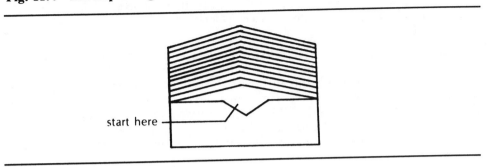

start here

GENERAL POINTERS
Sorting the mail   So that your office will receive faster service, the Postal Service suggests that you or your mailing department handle outgoing mail as follows:

1. Separate the mail. Your mail can skip an entire sorting operation at the post office if you separate it into major categories such as local, out-of-town, state, and precanceled. Each bundle should have a label identifying its category.
2. Use postage meters. When five or more pieces of metered mail are mailed together, they must be faced (arranged so that the address sides all face the same direction) and bundled. The post office will provide the needed printed bands. For large amounts of metered or permit mail, trays will be provided by the post office. Trayed mail should be faced to speed postal sorting and dispatching.
3. Presort your mail by ZIP code. Large mailings are further expedited if sequenced by ZIP-code number from lowest to highest. Mail can be bundled by ZIP-code number if there are 10 or more pieces destined for a single zone.

Mail that must reach its destination the next day requires special separation and sorting. See pages 425–29 for information concerning special mail services.

See Chapter 7 for directions on addressing envelopes for maximum speed of delivery.

When to mail   The Postal Service suggests early mailings to alleviate the usual congestion at the close of the business day. If possible, mailings should be made throughout the day; a single large mailing at the end of the day should be avoided.

ZIP codes   To handle the ever-increasing volume of mail efficiently, the Postal Service relies on the ZIP code—both the standard five-digit number and the more comprehensive number known as ZIP + 4, which consists of the standard ZIP code followed by a hyphen and four digits, such as 03060-1234. The ZIP code encodes the following information:

The first digit identifies one of ten national areas.
The next two digits identify a sectional center facility or the major post office that serves a delivery area.

The next two digits identify a particular post office.

The last four digits of the ZIP+4 are used to further subdivide delivery areas into sectors and segments as small as a city block, a building, or even a firm in a large building.

A piece of mail lacking a ZIP code can be delayed for a day or more. Companies are encouraged to use the ZIP+4 in large mailings in order to save money and speed delivery through the automated processing that the nine-digit code permits. There are rate incentives for companies to use bar codes corresponding to the five- or nine-digit codes. The Postal Service also uses optical character readers (OCRs) that can "read" a ZIP code and apply a bar code. These bar codes allow fast sorting of mail on automated equipment throughout the delivery process.

You can refer to the following basic sources for ZIP-code information:

1. The *National Five-Digit ZIP Code and Post Office Directory* lists all the five-digit numbers in use in the United States. The directory is available at many post offices for purchase. It may also be obtained by writing to: U.S. Postal Service, National Five-Digit ZIP Code Directory Order, National Address Information Center, 6060 Primacy Parkway, Ste. 101, Memphis, TN 38188-0001. For more information, call 800-238-3150, Ext. 640.

2. The *ZIP+4 Code State Directory* is available for purchase from: U.S. Postal Service, ZIP+4 State Directory Orders, at the same address. You must specify which state directories you desire. Many include more than one state. Order forms are available at most post offices. For more information, call 800-238-3150, Ext. 640.

3. Your telephone directory should have a map indicating local postal zones and a complete listing of area ZIP-code numbers.

4. The Postal Service will willingly answer questions concerning ZIP codes. Post offices in many cities have a special telephone listing for ZIP-code information, found under "United States Government, United States Postal Service" in the telephone directory.

Business firms that address mail by computer may use a magnetic computer tape providing ZIP code listings. A subscription to the tape, with quarterly updates, is available through the National Address Information Center (see above).

METERED MAIL

Mail that bears an imprinted meter stamp is called *metered mail*. A postage meter is a useful convenience for many mailers. The postmark, date, and cancellation are imprinted by the meter either directly onto the envelope or onto an adhesive strip that is then affixed to large envelopes or packages. The meter may also seal and stack envelopes. Sophisticated electronic mailing machines can even compute the most efficient way to send a particular piece of mail. Meters are leased or rented from the manufacturer, and the mailer must obtain a meter permit from the post office. Payment for a given amount of postage is made in a lump sum to the post office, and the meter is then limited to that amount in advance. For a fee, a Postal Service representative will set the postage meter at your office. Some of the advantages of metered mail are (1) accurate postage accounting that eliminates the theft of stamps, (2) speedier processing of mail in the office, (3) speedier processing of mail at the post office, since envelopes will already be faced and stamps do not have to be canceled, (4) the option of using personalized meter ads, and (5) reduction in the number of trips to the post office.

Postal Services and Classes of Mail

DOMESTIC MAIL CLASSIFICATION

If your office does not have a mail room, it will be your responsibility to send the mail out efficiently and economically. Since postal rates change frequently, you will need to write or call the post office for a brochure of current rates as well as brochures describing all the various classes of mail, the special services, and the rates for each class or service. The brochures are offered at no charge and contain a wealth of information on mail preparation, wrapping instructions, weight, zones, and rates. Another useful reference is the *Domestic Mail Manual* (DMM), which can be purchased at most post offices. The DMM provides detailed information on every aspect of domestic mail and special postal services, some of which are discussed here.

First-class mail   This category includes handwritten and typewritten messages, bills and statements of account, postcards and postal cards (postal cards are the ones printed by the Postal Service), canceled and uncanceled checks, and business reply mail with a weight of 11 ounces or less. First-class mail is sealed and may not be opened for postal inspection. Within a local area, overnight delivery can ordinarily be expected. Your post office will designate what constitutes your local area. To qualify for overnight delivery, you must deposit letters at a post office by 5 p.m., or at a mail processing facility by 6 p.m. Second-day delivery is standard for other points within specified local states. Third-day delivery is standard for other points within the 48 contiguous states.

Mailable envelopes, cards, and self-mailers can be no smaller than $3\frac{1}{2}'' \times 5''$ and should be at least .007 inches thick (about the thickness of a postal card). To avoid a surcharge on first-class mail weighing less than one ounce, the envelope should not exceed $11\frac{1}{2}'' \times 6\frac{1}{8}'' \times \frac{1}{4}''$. First-class postage is required for cards exceeding $4\frac{1}{4}'' \times 6''$. Large envelopes or packages sent as first-class mail should be stamped "FIRST CLASS" just below the postage area to avoid confusion with third-class mail at the post office. Envelopes with green diamond edging are useful because they immediately identify the contents as first-class mail.

First-class zone-rated (priority) mail   All first-class mail exceeding 11 ounces is rated as priority mail and receives the same treatment as regular first-class mail. Rates are determined by weight and by distance to the delivery zone. The maximum weight for priority mail is 70 pounds, and the maximum size is 108" in combined girth and length.

Second-class mail   This category includes magazines, newspapers, and other periodicals issued at least four times a year. A permit is required to mail such material at the second-class rate.

Third-class mail   This category includes items not required to be mailed first-class, not having a permit as second-class, and weighing less than 16 ounces. It generally consists of circulars, books, catalogs, and other printed materials (such as newsletters, or corrected proof sheets with manuscript copy). Merchandise, farm and factory products, photographs, keys, and printed drawings may all be sent third-class. Much of what constitutes third-class mail is sometimes referred to as "advertising mail" or "direct mail." The two categories of third-class mail are *single-piece* and *bulk*. Bulk mail costs less than single-piece but it requires a permit, a minimum number of separately addressed pieces (more than 200 pieces or more than 50 pounds), and presorted bundling. Third-class mail is usually not sealed, so that it can be opened easily for postal inspection. It is generally slower than other types of mail, including fourth-class.

Fourth-class mail (parcel post)   This category consists mainly of domestic parcel post. Also included in it are special catalog mailings, special fourth-class mailings, and library mailings. It is mostly used to send packages or parcels weighing 16 ounces or more. Parcels may not weigh more than 70 pounds or exceed 108" in combined length and girth. Parcel-post rates are based on weight and delivery distance. Parcels under 16 ounces are usually mailed as third-class, first-class, or priority mail.

Overnight delivery can be expected within the local area if parcels are mailed by 5 p.m. at post offices or receiving platforms. Second-day service can be expected for distances up to 150 miles. Service time depends on the distance the parcel must travel; for example, delivery may require as much as eight days for distances beyond 1,800 miles.

A written message in an envelope may be taped to the outside of a parcel if first-class postage is affixed to the envelope. Another way to include a letter with a package is to enclose the letter in the package, mark "First-Class Mail Enclosed" on the package, and affix first-class letter postage in addition to the fourth-class mailing charge.

It is extremely important to wrap parcels securely—in a strong container with the contents thoroughly cushioned—and to write or type the address legibly. The Postal Service prefers that packages be secured with strong tape rather than twine, which can jam the machines that handle the parcels.

INTERNATIONAL MAIL

This category includes all material destined for foreign countries except overseas military mail—that is, APO (Army Post Office) and FPO (Fleet Post Office) mail.

Since the subject of international mail is too large to cover adequately in this book, you should obtain a copy of the *International Mail Manual* (IMM), which is available for purchase from many post offices, or by mailing an application that can be obtained from your post office, or by calling the Government Printing Office at 202-783-3238. This publication is a valuable reference source for those who must handle large amounts of outgoing mail of this type. It contains detailed instructions for sending mail abroad, including specific information for each country. The Postal Service will also provide, without charge, *International Postage Rates and Fees* in booklet or poster form. This publication includes both an overview of international mail services and specific information about rates and fees.

International mail consists of three categories: postal union mail, parcel post, and Express Mail International Service.

Postal union mail is divided into two classes: *letter* or *LC mail* (from the French, "Lettres et Cartes"), which includes letters, letter packages, aerogrammes, and postcards; and *AO mail* (from the French, "Autres Objets"), which includes printed materials, materials for the blind, books, sheet music, periodicals, and small packets. Aerogrammes, a convenient form of stationery for international correspondence, are discussed under "Special Services." Postal union articles should be addressed legibly and completely. The bottom line of the address must show only the country name, written in full (no abbreviations) and in capital letters. Be sure to use the ZIP code or postal delivery zone if available. It is permissible to use a foreign-language address, provided that the names of the post office, province, and country are in English. The envelopes or wrappers of postal union mail should be marked with the mail classification: "Letter," "Printed Matter," "Printed Matter—Books," "Printed Matter—Sheet Music," and so on. Clearly mark "PAR AVION" (that is, "Airmail") on the front and back of any letter or package for which the airmail rate has been paid. The maximum permissible size for envelopes and packages is 36" in combined length, width, and thickness, with a maximum length of 24". For tubes or rolls, the maximum length is 36", and the length plus twice the diameter must add up to no more than 42".

Registered-mail service and daily airmail service are available to almost all countries. Registered letters and registered letter packages must be sealed. Neither insurance nor certified-mail service is available for postal union mail. Special-delivery service is available to most countries. It is also possible to obtain a return receipt.

Special customs forms for postal union mail must be used for dutiable letter packages, printed material, and all small packets. These are not the same forms that are used for parcel post.

All articles should be correctly prepaid in order to avoid delays. If an article is returned for additional postage, the proper amount should be affixed and the "Returned for postage" notation should be crossed out. Postal union mail is generally returned to the sender if delivery cannot be made.

Parcel post, sometimes known as *CP mail* (from the French, "Colis Postaux"), is available to most countries. It is similar to domestic fourth-class mail. The maximum combined length and girth generally allowed is 79", with a maximum length of 42". Parcels should be packed very securely in strong containers made of good-quality material that will withstand often radical climatic changes and repeated and rough handling. Insurance is available to most countries. Insured parcels must be sealed. Customs declarations describing the contents must be attached to all parcel-post packages. The forms used for parcel post are not the same as those used for postal-union mail.

Express Mail International Service provides fast, reliable mail service to certain countries. Insurance is provided against loss or damage at no extra charge. However, there is no guarantee that the mail will be delivered without delay.

There are private companies licensed by the U.S. government, called *customhouse brokers*, that help importers prepare the customs documents required for imported packages and articles. Other services rendered by brokers include export crating, reforwarding, delivery to and from airports and ocean ports, and bonded warehouse marking and distribution. Through these services, brokers offer savings on import/export charges and expedite delivery.

SPECIAL SERVICES

The special services provided by the Postal Service are listed alphabetically and discussed briefly here.

Aerogramme   This is a combined letter and envelope with imprinted postage which provides an economical means of communicating abroad. An aerogramme can be purchased at any post office and can be registered. It should not contain any sort of enclosure; if it does, it will be subject to the higher airmail letter rate. It should not be sealed with stickers or tape.

Business reply mail A business may wish to pay the postage for those responding to its mail—an important factor when selling by mail. To use the business reply service, submit an application on Form 3614-A (obtainable from your local post office), along with the annual permit fee. The mailer guarantees that the first-class postage and handling charge will be paid for each reply. Postage may be collected when the reply is delivered, although an advance deposit may be required under certain conditions. Above the addressee's name and address should appear the following on three lines: "BUSINESS REPLY MAIL," in capital letters at least 3/16" high; "FIRST-CLASS MAIL PERMIT NO. _____, [CITY], [STATE]," in capital letters; and "Postage Will Be Paid By Addressee." The upper right corner, where postage is usually affixed, must contain the words "No Postage Necessary if Mailed in the United States."

Certificate of Mailing A Certificate of Mailing is used by a mailer to prove that an item was actually mailed. Certificates for individual pieces of mail can be issued for a fee. The post office keeps no record of such certificates.

Certified mail This service provides an initial receipt to the mailer, followed by a record of delivery. The carrier obtains a signature from the addressee on a receipt form, which is kept by the delivering post office for two years. A return receipt will be provided for an additional fee. A sample receipt is shown in Fig. 11.5.

Fig. 11.5   Certified Mail Receipt

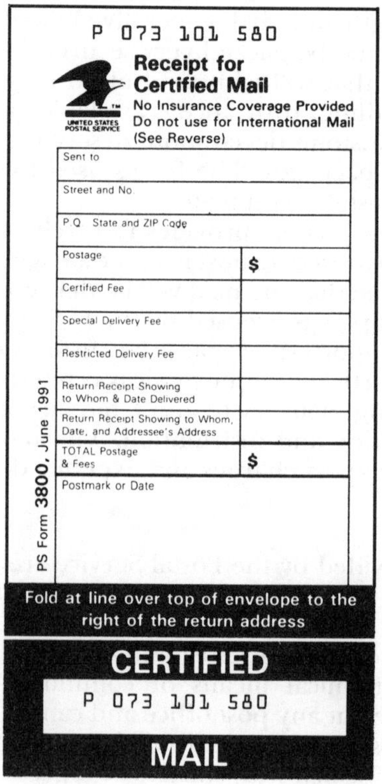

Collect on Delivery   With Collect on Delivery (COD), both the postage and the price of the contents of a parcel or letter are collected from the addressee. The maximum amount that can be collected is $600. The fee charged for COD includes insurance against loss or damage and failure to receive payment. First-, third-, and fourth-class mail and Express Mail can be sent COD, the regular postage being paid in addition to the COD fee. The addressee may not examine the contents of the letter or parcel before paying the charges. Parcels sent must be based upon bona fide orders or on agreement between the mailer and addressee. For an additional fee, the mailer of COD letters or parcels will be notified of nondelivery. First-class mail sent domestic COD may be registered at an additional charge.

Express mail   Express Mail is a fast intercity delivery system linking metropolitan areas in the United States. It is used for the reliable delivery of mail weighing up to 70 pounds and measuring up to 108″ in combined length and girth.

Express Mail Next Day Service requires that your shipment be taken to a post office by the time specified by the postmaster. The post office supplies special packets and address labels for your use. The package will be delivered to the addressee by 12 noon or 3 p.m. the following day, or it may be picked up at the post office as early as 10 a.m. on the next business day. Rates include insurance, a mailing receipt, and a record of delivery at the destination post office. If you are too late for next-day service, you can be assured of Express Mail Second Day Service provided that you post your shipment by 5 p.m. or such later time as your postmaster authorizes. Express Mail shipments can be picked up at your office for an additional charge.

The Postal Service also offers Express Mail Same Day Airport Service between many major airports. To use this service, you must take the shipment to the airport mail-processing facility, and the addressee must pick it up on arrival at the destination airport.

If you have questions about Express Mail, or if you wish to schedule a pickup, call 800-222-1811.

Insured mail   Third- and fourth-class mail can be insured against loss and damage up to $600 if it is properly packaged. Items of greater value should be sent by registered mail. For an additional fee, you may obtain a return receipt as proof of delivery for insured mail exceeding $50 in value. Payment of another fee provides that the mail will be delivered only to the addressee.

Mailgram   The Mailgram is a special mail-via-satellite service offered jointly by the U.S. Postal Service and Western Union. These letter-telegrams are delivered the next business day by U.S. letter carriers to virtually any address within the 48 contiguous states. Small offices can use this service by supplying the Mailgram message to a Western Union office by telephone (toll-free) or in person. Rates are based on 100-word units in the message.

Within larger firms, up to 50 common or variable-text messages can be typed directly from the company's teleprinter into the Western Union computer on a single connection. A basic fee is charged for each message, in addition to the telex/TWX usage charges. (Instructions may be found in the firm's telex/TWX directory.) Mailgrams in volume may be handled by putting mailing lists on computer tape, which can hold up to 10,000 address lines on a single tape. There is a basic fee for each message of 600 characters or less and a fee for each additional 600 characters, plus a minimum charge for each tape. The most economical way to input a Mailgram is from the company's computer directly into Western Union's computer. In this case, a basic fee is charged for each message, in addition to a minimum fee for each tape.

An additional electronic-mail system allows companies to transmit messages from their computers directly to post-office computers, which will then print and deliver as many copies as are requested.

Money orders   Money can be sent through the mail by purchasing postal money orders worth up to $700 each that are redeemable at any post office. International money orders can also be purchased.

Post-office boxes   Boxes and drawers in post offices may be rented. These facilitate the receiving of mail, since mail can be picked up whenever the post-office lobby is open.

Registered mail   Material that has been posted at first-class rates may be registered to protect valuable and important items. Registered mail is kept separate from other mail and is monitored throughout the delivery process. It is therefore the most secure method of mailing. The fee for this service is based on the declared value of the mail, with an indemnity limit of $25,000. The customer is given a receipt at the time of mailing; therefore, registered mail cannot be dropped into a regular collection box. The post office keeps a record of the mailing through the number it has been assigned. Insurance coverage may be purchased to protect against loss or damage. For an additional fee, a return receipt can be sent to the mailer after delivery.

Return receipts   A mailer may request a return receipt that shows to whom and when a piece of COD, express, certified, insured, or registered mail is delivered. If the request is made at the time of mailing, the fee is considerably lower than if the request is made later. The information is mailed to the sender on a card like that shown in Fig. 11.6.

Fig. 11.6   Domestic Return Receipt

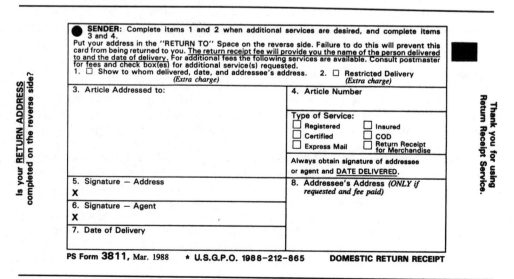

Self-service postal centers   Self-service postal centers are located in convenient places such as post-office lobbies, shopping centers, and automobile drive-ups. They supplement existing postal services by providing around-the-clock service seven days a week. Automatic vending machines dispense stamps, postal cards, stamped envelopes, and minimum parcel insurance. These stamps are sold at face value, unlike those from private vending machines.

Special delivery   This designation virtually assures delivery on the day mail is received at the destination post office, including Sundays and holidays. As soon as the mail is received there, it is delivered by messenger. Special delivery may be used for all classes of mail. Although special delivery does not speed mail transportation from the post office of origin to the destination post office, it does assure rapid delivery from the destination post office to the intended addressee. The mailer must remember that mail cannot be delivered to post-office boxes or on weekends to offices that are closed. Also, some small post offices provide special-delivery service only during post-office hours.

Special handling   This designation assures preferential, separate handling for third- and fourth-class mail and normally speeds its delivery between post offices. It does not ensure speedy delivery after arrival at the destination post office.

FORWARDING, RECALLING, AND TRACING MAIL

All first-class mail is forwarded without charge when the addressee's new address is known. To forward a piece of mail, change the address on the original wrapper and add any required postage. Undeliverable first-class mail will be returned to the sender without charge. To ensure the return of other classes of mail, you must endorse the envelope "Return Postage Guaranteed" and be willing to pay extra postage when the mail is returned to you.

It is wise to purge your mailing lists occasionally to avoid paying consistently for mail that cannot be delivered. To do this, you should print "Forwarding and Address Correction Requested" on each envelope you send out. If the addressee has moved to a known address, the post office will forward the mail and send you the new address. If the mail is undeliverable for any known reason, the post office will tell you the reason. There is a fee for each address correction returned to the sender.

If you ever wish to recall a piece of mail already delivered to the post office, you must fill out a request form at the post office as soon as possible and be prepared to pay all costs of the recall, including telegrams and long-distance telephone calls. You will be notified if the mail has already been delivered. Other post-office forms are available that allow either the sender or the addressee to request lost mail to be traced within a year of the mailing date.

Other Delivery Methods

Shipments to and from business offices are often made by means other than the post office. Shipments are made by air, rail, ship, bus, and truck. Delivery services such as United Parcel Service use all of these methods. Check your local Yellow Pages under "Delivery Services" or "Courier Services" for the names of other parcel delivery services in your area. Before preparing the package, be sure to find out the carrier's regulations concerning size, weight, wrapping, and sealing.

Messenger services may also be called upon to make local, same-day deliveries (as to banks) when the need occurs. Some companies have their own messengers; many others prefer to use the commercial messenger services. These services are also listed in the Yellow Pages.

EXPRESS SERVICE

Air express   Air express is a fast-growing industry. While it is expensive, it is the fastest means of door-to-door pickup and delivery of letters and parcels to most cities in the United States. Air express companies also offer international delivery service. There are many occasions in a business office when quick delivery is essential and it is worthwhile to bear the extra cost.

Bus express   Most bus lines offer a shipping service. This method of delivery is speedy and is especially suitable for delivery to small towns that are not served by airlines. Many items are insurable. The weight limit is 100 pounds per package, and the size limit is $33'' \times 33'' \times 48''$. There is an extra charge for pickup and delivery service.

Railway express   To use rail express service, you must drop off your package for shipping and arrange for someone to pick it up when it reaches its destination station.

FREIGHT SERVICES

Freight, although slower than express, is the most economical way to ship large quantities of material in bulky packages. The various types of freight are railroad, motor, air, and water freight.

INTERNATIONAL SHIPMENTS

As the international business dealings of corporations increase, there is a steadily greater need for international deliveries. Shipments may be made by sea or by air. Since foreign shipments involve special forms and packaging, you must contact international airlines and steamship companies for instructions. They have personnel to assist in preparing the necessary forms and to furnish packing and shipping instructions.

FULL-SERVICE COMPANIES

There are two companies offering several services, including domestic and international air express, that deserve further discussion: United Parcel Service and Federal Express.

United Parcel Service   United Parcel Service (UPS) provides ground and air service within the United States and to over 180 countries worldwide for delivery of letters and packages weighing up to 70 pounds and measuring up to 130″ in combined length and girth, with a maximum length of 108″. You may not use string, cellophane tape, or masking tape. All packages are automatically insured against loss or damage up to $100. Higher insurance protection may be obtained for an additional charge, up to a maximum of $25,000. For information on service, rates, and restrictions, and to order the service guides, contact your local UPS office.

Domestic ground and air service is available to any address in the United States and Puerto Rico. There are two types of air service.

UPS Next Day Air® Service guarantees delivery of letters and packages on the next business day to all addresses in the 48 contiguous states, Puerto Rico, the island of Oahu in Hawaii, and some locations in Alaska. Most of these deliveries, including those to major metropolitan areas, are made by 10:30 a.m., and many others by noon. Other Hawaiian islands may require an extra day; rural Alaska may require one or more additional days. Saturday deliveries can also be scheduled for an additional charge.

UPS 2nd Day Air® Service guarantees delivery of packages on the second business day, except in rural Alaska, which may require one or more extra days.

Special services include address correction, COD service, delivery confirmation service (which provides proof of delivery), and Call Tag service (which allows for return of merchandise previously delivered by UPS from anywhere in the 48 contiguous states). Hazardous materials may not be shipped anywhere by air, nor by ground service to Canada. Some such materials may be shipped by domestic ground service.

UPS service to Canada includes ground service to any address in the 10 provinces, and Air Express service to all of Canada, including the Yukon and the Northwest Territories.

Export documentation is required for shipments to Puerto Rico and Canada, except for UPS Next Day Air letters to Puerto Rico and UPS Air Express letters to Canada.

International service consists of two door-to-door service levels: UPS Worldwide Express service, which serves more than 180 countries and generally provides delivery of letters and packages in two business days, and UPS Worldwide Expedited service, which provides precisely scheduled delivery of packages to major cities in Europe and Asia within four business days. Export documentation is required for all packages. For information on international shipments, including customs brokerage information, call the UPS International Information Center at 800-782-7892.

Federal Express   Federal Express provides fast delivery of letters and packages up to 150 pounds, and measuring up to 130" in combined length and girth, with a maximum length of 108", within the United States and to more than 170 countries worldwide. Freight service is also available for larger and heavier packages. Automatic insurance against loss or damage is provided up to $100, with additional coverage available up to a maximum of $25,000. For information regarding domestic shipping, call 800-238-5355. For international shipping, call 800-247-4747.

The *Federal Express Service Guide,* in two volumes, provides details of services, packaging requirements, customs clearance, and related matters. Volume 1 deals with domestic service, Volume 2, with international deliveries. An overview of some Federal Express services follows.

Domestic services include FedEx® Priority Overnight Service, which provides delivery of letters and packages by 10:30 a.m. or by noon to most locations in the United States. FedEx® Standard Overnight Service offers delivery by 3 p.m. or 4:30 p.m. to most areas. Economy Two-Day℠ Service provides delivery of packages by 4:30 p.m. (5 p.m. within Alaska and Hawaii) on the second business day. With FedEx® Overnight Freight Service, packages weighing from 150 to 500 pounds per piece can be delivered by the next business day within the 48 contiguous states. FedEx® Two-Day Freight Service provides delivery by 4:30 p.m.

on the second business day to the 48 states and Anchorage, Alaska. Approval must be obtained in advance for freight shipments exceeding 500 pounds. Dangerous-goods delivery is offered anywhere in the United States, with some restrictions. Other special services include COD service, proof of performance, and volume discounts.

International services include International Priority® Service, which provides scheduled door-to-door delivery, including customs clearance, on one to three days. Export documentation is required for international shipments. Dangerous goods can be shipped to some locations. Consult the *Service Guide* for further information on international service, including extensive freight and cargo services.

ELECTRONIC MAIL

Electronic mail (E-mail) refers to computer-based message systems that send digitally encoded documents directly from terminal to terminal and whose messages are displayed on a cathode-ray tube (CRT) terminal, with the option of a printed hard copy. Through electronic-mail systems, urgent correspondence can be transmitted in a matter of seconds to most major cities around the world. For a detailed discussion of electronic mail, see Chapter 13.

Records Management

If you are an administrative secretary, you must be familiar with all records containing information that the executive may need. This information may take the form of a letter, a memorandum, or a directive; it may be in microform, on cards, on computer tape, or in a reference book. It may be stored in filing cabinets of various types, on open shelves, in a central storage center, in an inactive storage center, in a computer center, or in the company library.

Basic Modes of Storage

Despite the proliferation of computers, it is estimated that paper still accounts for 95 percent of all the filing in the United States. Paper records do have distinct advantages: they are affordable, they are the most acceptable legal form of record, they are reassuring to people who desire to retain physical evidence, and they are difficult to alter.

The need to control the flow of paper is compelling. *Records management* is the broad term that denotes the systematic control over the creation, maintenance, retention, protection, and preservation of records. *Filing* may be defined more narrowly as the arrangement and storage of recorded information according to a simple and logical sequence so as to facilitate future retrieval. *Indexing* refers to systems of classifying items so that they can be retrieved when needed.

In an efficient records-management program, only records of long-term value are kept in storage. A record may have administrative, historical, legal, or research value. Records that are needed for day-to-day or long-term decision making are of administrative value. Financial records must be retained not only for administrative decision making but also for government tax reports. Firms interested in compiling or maintaining corporate history, either for their own needs or for public, university, or private libraries, will wish to preserve those records in which important company-related events have been chronicled. The company legal counsel identifies the records that must be kept for the company's own protection; deeds, long-term contracts, and articles of incorporation or charters are examples of records with long-term legal value. Records that might be of assistance to researchers in various areas of a company's operations are also important and should be kept over the long term. In dealing with this material, the records administrator should be guided by top management.

All other records are of short-term value and are usually kept in an organization's central records center, if there is one, or in an executive office. The dates on which these records should be destroyed are usually officially determined. Guidelines are established by top management, individual executives, legal counsel, and the records manager regarding which records can be destroyed immediately after action has been taken on them, which should be retained for a specified time and then destroyed, and which should be kept indefinitely. Your responsibility is to know the proper storage location of each type of record that is retained and the length of time it is to be kept.

STORAGE OF RECORDS

Your workstation will usually house vertical or lateral filing cabinets. Other means of storage such as open shelves, card files, microfilm, and computer tape are likely to be found in central records. Only the records necessary for day-to-day operations—records used at least once a month—should be kept in the office. All other material is generally considered inactive and should be moved to central storage, from which it can be retrieved by request when needed.

Vertical and lateral cabinets   Vertical storage cabinets may be from two to five drawers in height. Each drawer should be labeled to indicate its contents and should also contain file guides to provide quick reference and adequate physical support for the folders. Each drawer should have from 20 to 25 guides. Letters should be filed left side down in folders, with the most recent letters at the front of each folder. No folder should contain more than 50 sheets of paper.

The order of the guides and folders in a typical drawer is shown in Fig. 12.1: main guide, individual folders, "Out" guides or folders, special name guides, permanent cross-reference guides, and a miscellaneous folder at the end of the section for material not yet considered active. (Some records managers think miscellaneous folders should not be used at all. If they are used, no more than five pieces on a given subject should be allowed to accumulate there before an individual file is set up.)

In vertical cabinets, hanging folders may be used. The sides of hanging folders have hooks which enable the folders to hang from a frame inserted in the file drawer. Hanging folders can hold larger numbers of records than regular folders and the tab may be moved to different positions.

Many information managers are of the opinion that within a few years the vertical filing cabinet will have become passé. Lateral filing cabinets generally permit speedier storage and retrieval. The length of the cabinet lies against the wall and the drawers pull out only about one foot. The fronts of the folders face the left side of the drawer. The back ledge of the cabinet may be moved to accommodate either letter-size or legal-size folders. Like vertical cabinets, lateral cabinets may be from two to five drawers in height.

Open-shelf storage   Open shelves have become popular because of the savings in space over normal cabinets (up to 50 percent) and the quick and easy reference they offer for highly active files. Only where there is neither air-conditioning nor

Fig. 12.1   Guide and Folder Arrangement for Cabinet Files

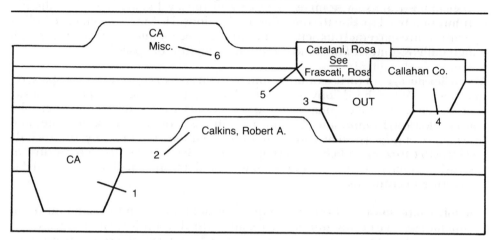

1. *Alphabetical caption guide*   The guide tabs usually are positioned on the left.
2. *Individual account folder*   Most account correspondence and data regarding a company's clients are kept in such folders.
3. *Out guide*   "Out" guides or substitution cards, with tabs at center right, record the identity and location of folders that have been removed.
4. *Special name guide*   Special guides can be inserted at the far right for very active accounts that have more than one folder or that require special handling.
5. *Permanent cross-reference guide*   These guides direct the user to a folder at another location.
6. *Miscellaneous folder*   These folders, placed at the end of each letter-caption category, hold material not yet of sufficient quantity to require an individual folder.

air filtration would the use of open-shelf storage be questionable, since dust and humidity can be harmful to records. Open shelves are sometimes constructed on tracks for movability, requiring less floor space and making filing and retrieving even easier.

Card cabinets   Information for basic reference can be filed in card cabinets of various sizes. The most common card sizes are $3'' \times 5''$, $4'' \times 6''$, $5'' \times 8''$, and $6'' \times 9''$. The most sophisticated card cabinets are those in automatic retrieval units. (See the following section on "Automated systems.")

Visible card cabinets   Visible card cabinets are small desktop cabinets with numerous flat traylike drawers. Racks in these drawers hold cards (usually $6'' \times 4''$ or $8'' \times 5''$) in an overlapping arrangement that permits very rapid access. They are commonly used for indexes to the location and status of other records.

Automated systems   An automated storage and retrieval system offers the advantages of optimum convenience, rapid retrieval, concentration of vast amounts of file material in a small amount of floor space, and superior control over records. Automated units are rotating, electronically driven carriers up to 30 feet high which present the operator with the desired tray at the touch of a button. Some machines can automatically sort and retrieve individual cards or files, thus reducing the handling of cards and files and protecting them against excessive wear. Card index storage and retrieval systems are especially adaptable to mechanized units. Automated storage and retrieval systems also handle microfilm and are adaptable to computer applications. However, mechanized filing operations are extremely expensive and thus are economical only for users with a high daily volume of filing and a minimum amount of space.

Microfilm storage   The use of microfilm has markedly reduced storage space requirements. When hard copy is converted to microfilm, only two percent of the space taken up by the original material is necessary for the microfilm. Microfilm can be filed on 16-mm. and 35-mm. rolls in color or in black and white, and housed in cartridges or magazines. Other microfilm forms, or *microforms,* include jackets, tab cards, microfiche, and strip holders. (See pages 450–53 for a further discussion of microforms.) Storage cabinets, binders, and small tubs are available for storing microforms.

Computer tape storage   Computer tapes can hold a tremendous amount of information, save large amounts of space, and afford fast information retrieval. A special closed cabinet or a rack kept in a closed area can be used to store these tapes. There are also storage boxes designed so that the tapes slide forward as one is taken out, thus facilitating retrieval. The tapes are indexed, and a record is kept of the location of each tape so that information can be located fast.

Tickler files   Tickler files—described in detail in Chapter 2—usually use 3″ × 5″ cards and contain reminders for following up projects or meetings. When the tickler file takes the form of a tub file on wheels instead of a card file, guides and folders (12 guides for the months and 31 folders for the days) are arranged in a similar way. Letters that need following up are placed in folders behind the dates or months on which action must be taken. Special folders are also available with sliding tabs that indicate the dates on which action should be taken.

FOLDERS, LABELS, AND GUIDES

Folders   Plain file folders come in a variety of shapes and sizes. A set of folders will normally include equal numbers of folders with tabs at the left, center, and right, permitting the user to stagger them in the file for maximum tab visibility. On "⅓ cut" folders, the tabs are one-third the width of the entire folder; on "⅕ cut" folders, one-fifth the width; and so on.

End- or side-tabbed folders are designed for use in lateral file cabinets or on open shelves. Accordion or expandable file folders (sometimes secured with string) are used to hold a large number of documents; they may have tabs on either the top or the side. Ring folders have two-pronged fasteners that securely attach the records, which must be punched before filing. Folders also may be purchased with several attached inserts, each with its own fastener, or with plain dividers.

Hanging folders, as described earlier, hang from racks inserted in (or built into) the file drawer, by means of hooks at either end of the top of the folder. Since they slide easily along the rack and do not sag even when full, they permit easy access to their contents. They are stronger but more expensive than standard folders.

Folders are commonly made of four types of material:

Manila. The most common and least expensive folder material. Available with wax or Mylar coating for extra durability, and available in various colors (though "manila" frequently refers only to sand-colored folders).

Kraft. Heavier; brown; quite durable; does not soil easily. More expensive than manila; should be used only for folders subjected to much wear and tear.

Pressboard. Expensive, durable material; more suitable for guides than for folders.

Vinyl or other plastic. Very durable, thus suitable for holding papers of permanent value, but quite expensive. Very smooth in texture, hence slippery and not good for stacking. Available in a variety of colors.

Labels   All folders that are not preprinted should be identified with pressure-sensitive (self-adhesive) labels typed neatly and consistently. The caption should be typed as close as possible to the top of the label for greatest visibility. Runovers are usually indented, and sub-captions are blocked with the caption. If the label includes both an index number and a name, adequate space should separate the two. The primary indexing units should precede any secondary units.

6.78   Schwartz, Howard M., Inc.
       Footwear Division

Color-coded labels marked with letters or numbers provide an excellent system for files, because one can instantly see if a file is out of sequence by noticing that the colors do not match. A color system may work in one of several ways. A particular color may denote the first two or three letters of a name (e.g., "Co" in Fig. 12.1); labels may be used to indicate each large grouping of files; or a single color may be used for a given year.

Guides   To expedite filing and retrieving, guides should be placed throughout the files to separate the cards or folders into groups. In card files, one guide should be placed after every 25 cards.

When purchasing guides, remember that durability and visibility are the most important considerations. The tab on each guide should project far enough above the folders to be completely visible. In straight numeric files, new guides must be added regularly; in alphabetic files, the guides are usually permanent. Guides should be made of pressboard or vinyl. Pressboard is generally preferable because most records need heavy guides for support; vinyl guides are satisfactory for card files. Since guides are sold in sets based on the size of the files, consider potential growth in your files when purchasing guides.

"Out" guides, special name guides, and permanent cross-reference guides should also be used. Guides may be color-coded like labels to differentiate alphabetic and numeric sections or divisions.

COMPANY LIBRARIES

Many organizations have libraries that house records of historical value as well as reference books and other materials. Be aware of the functions and availability of the types of records and information that are kept in such libraries, including what types of document are *restricted*—that is, available only to authorized persons. For instance, the project notebooks of scientists in an industrial firm may be available only to members of its research and development division, even though they may be stored in the general library. Government contracts, including classified documents and confidential papers, will need to be stored in vaults or cabinets with locks or combinations that meet government security specifications. If you handle this kind of document you will be briefed on the procedures required by the Department of Defense.

Types of Filing Systems

A knowledge of the various commonly used filing systems and their advantages and disadvantages is essential. Each system is designed for specific office requirements, and you need to know not only when to use a particular system but how to use it most effectively.

SELECTING A SYSTEM

The most important questions that must be asked before purchasing a system are these: (1) How is the information to be requested? (2) Under what name, subject, or code number will it be found? (3) What is the means of access to it?

Filing by name is the most obvious and most widely used method. Numbers came into use to accommodate very extensive files and as an aid to securing confidentiality. Today numbers and color codes are widely recognized as useful for speedy filing and retrieving, and the use of numbers has also facilitated the storage and retrieval of information with computer systems.

ALPHABETIC FILING SYSTEMS

Ever since spindles were used for storing and records were simply piled in desk drawers or on desktops, alphabetical filing by surname has been used. When several individuals have the same surname, the alphabetization extends to the first name or initial, and then to the middle name or initial. If a further breakdown is necessary, a city, state, or street name may be used. Fig. 12.2 shows a section of an alphabetic file.

Subject filing   When the name of the individual is less important than the subject of the record, the subject becomes the filing unit for reference. The most important subject name becomes the first unit, and the main guide with that title should have its tab on the far left. Subheadings should have their own guides, with tabs at center left. See Fig. 12.3.

A subject system is difficult to set up because it may require considerable judgment to determine the most important subjects and the proper subject headings. The subject headings can be best selected by producing an outline. After the outline has been approved by those who selected the headings, it must be given to all those using the records center. Subheadings can be cross-referenced back to primary headings for faster reference.

An important element in the subject system is the *relative index*. Because of the difficulty in deciding which subjects should be considered primary, requests may be made for an item under a different heading. For example, you might not know where material relating to employees' annual leave has been filed; however, by looking under *Annual Leave* in a relative index, you could see that the material is filed under *Personnel*. By the same token, if you needed to find a file on office furniture, you could see by looking under *Office Furniture* in the relative index that the material is filed under *Supplies*. An index of this sort also prevents the unnecessary creation of a new heading when an appropriate one is already available. Thus, a relative index—a list of all possible subjects that could be used or sought—is a must in subject filing, as well as a time-saver in some other filing systems.

Fig. 12.2   Guide and Folder Arrangement in an Alphabetic File

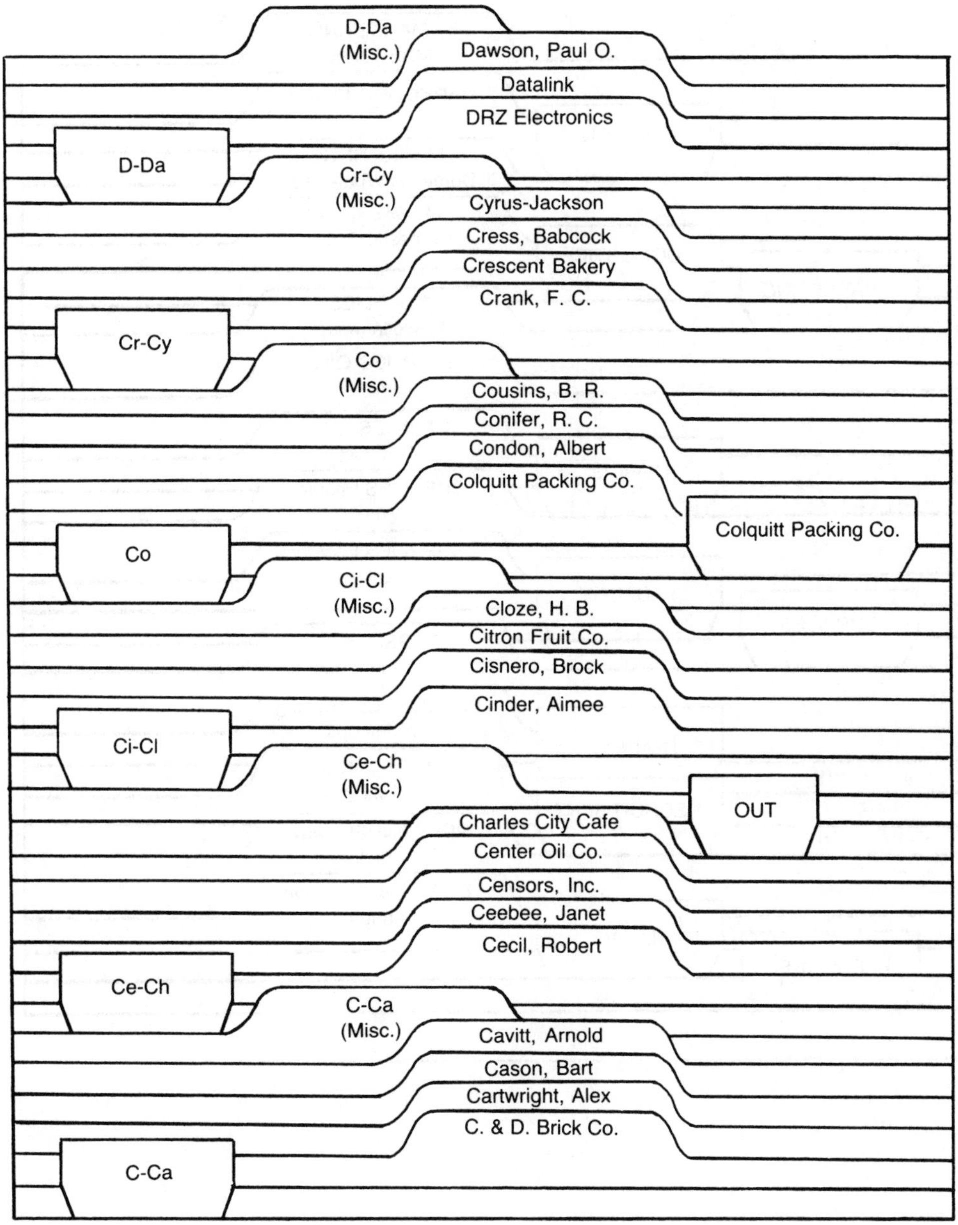

D-Da
(Misc.)

Dawson, Paul O.

Datalink

DRZ Electronics

D-Da

Cr-Cy
(Misc.)

Cyrus-Jackson

Cress, Babcock

Crescent Bakery

Crank, F. C.

Cr-Cy

Co
(Misc.)

Cousins, B. R.

Conifer, R. C.

Condon, Albert

Colquitt Packing Co.

Colquitt Packing Co.

Co

Ci-Cl
(Misc.)

Cloze, H. B.

Citron Fruit Co.

Cisnero, Brock

Cinder, Aimee

Ci-Cl

Ce-Ch
(Misc.)

OUT

Charles City Cafe

Center Oil Co.

Censors, Inc.

Ceebee, Janet

Cecil, Robert

Ce-Ch

C-Ca
(Misc.)

Cavitt, Arnold

Cason, Bart

Cartwright, Alex

C. & D. Brick Co.

C-Ca

Fig. 12.3   Subject File

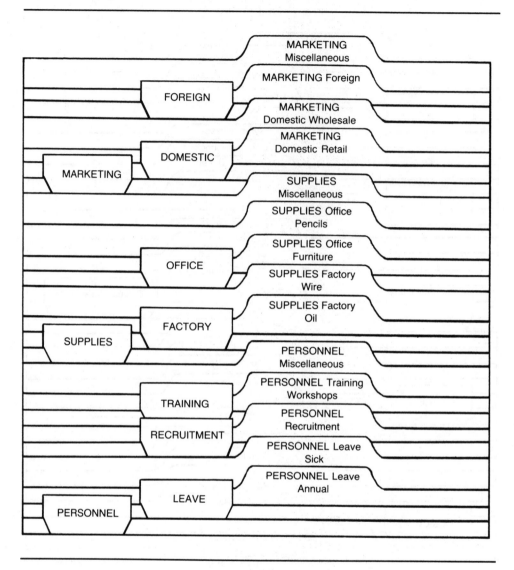

A lengthy relative index may take the form of a card file; a short one may be a simple list such as the following. Whatever form the index takes, it must be kept current to be useful.

Annual Leave
  See PERSONNEL Leave
    Annual

Domestic Marketing
  See MARKETING Domestic

Factory Supplies
  See SUPPLIES Factory

Foreign Marketing
  See MARKETING Foreign

Furniture
  See SUPPLIES Office
    Furniture

Leave
  See PERSONNEL Leave

MARKETING

Office Furniture
  See SUPPLIES Office
    Furniture

Office Supplies
  See SUPPLIES Office

Oil - Factory
  See SUPPLIES Factory
    Oil

Pencils
  See SUPPLIES Office
    Pencils

PERSONNEL

Personnel Recruitment
  See PERSONNEL Recruitment

Personnel Training
  See PERSONNEL Training

Recruitment
  See PERSONNEL Recruitment

Retailing
  See MARKETING Domestic
    Retail

Sick Leave
  See PERSONNEL Leave
    Sick

SUPPLIES

Training
  See PERSONNEL Training

Wholesaling
  See MARKETING Domestic
    Wholesale

Wire - Factory
  See SUPPLIES Factory
    Wire

Workshops
  See PERSONNEL Training
    Workshops

Geographic filing   When the location of a correspondent or subject is of more importance to the user than a name or subject, the geographic system of filing may be preferred. The geographic system is primarily helpful to mail-order companies interested in sales activities in different regions, for example, and to utility companies concerned with the locations of their installations and customers. In such a file, the main guide tabs may show state names, and the secondary guides may indicate cities within each state. When it is evident that a record may be requested under more than one title, a cross-reference procedure is necessary. For example, a company might be operating in more than one city, in which case the main office would be the geographic filing entry. For information about the Hodges Foundry in Lake City, Pennsylvania, a cross-reference might be placed under *Pennsylvania, Lake City, Hodges* to refer the searcher to the main-office location under *Pennsylvania, Pittsburgh, Hodges.*

Combination subject filing   Variations of subject filing are the *subject-numeric system,* in which numbers are assigned to a subject outline; the *duplex numeric system,* in which a combination of numbers is used; the *alphanumeric system,* in which a combination of letters and numbers is used; and the *decimal system.* In all of these variations, an outline is built from the most important subject headings, and numbers or letters are assigned to primary, secondary, third-level, and fourth-level entries. Examples of each of these systems are shown in the following table.

Subject-Numeric System

COMMUNICATIONS

1	Telegraph–Telephone
1-1	Rates–Charges
2	Mail
2-1	Registered–Insured
2-1-1	Receipts

FORMS

1	Design–Development
1-1	Standards
2	Distribution

MEETINGS

1	Local
1-1	Federal agencies
1-1-1	Bureau of Economics
2	National
3	International

Duplex Numeric System

1	COMMUNICATIONS
1-1	Telegraph–Telephone
1-1a	Rates–Charges
1-2	Mail
1-2a	Registered–Insured
1-2a-1	Receipts
2	FORMS
2-1	Design–Development
2-1a	Standards
2-2	Distribution
3	MEETINGS
3-1	Local
3-1a	Federal agencies
3-1a-1	Bureau of Economics
3-2	National
3-3	International

Alphanumeric System

A	ADMINISTRATION
A1	COMMUNICATIONS
A1-1	Telegraph–Telephone
A1-1-1	Rates–Charges
A1-2	Mail
A1-2-1	Registered–Insured
A1-2-1-1	Receipts
A2	FORMS
A2-1	Design–Development
A2-1-1	Standards
A2-2	Distribution
A3	MEETINGS
A3-1	Local
A3-1-1	Federal agencies
A3-1-1-1	Bureau of Economics
A3-2	National
A3-3	International

Decimal System

100	ADMINISTRATION
110	COMMUNICATIONS
111	Telegraph–Telephone
111.1	Rates–Charges
112	Mail
112.1	Registered–Insured
112.11	Receipts
120	FORMS
121	Design–Development
121.1	Standards
122	Distribution
130	MEETINGS
131	Local
131.1	Federal agencies
131.11	Bureau of Economics
132	National
133	International

NUMERIC FILING SYSTEMS

A second filing system is the *numeric system*. The straight numeric system is used by attorneys, physicians, and others who require that records be continually added for new customers, patients, or clients. Files are numbered in the order they are created, in strict numeric sequence. New records are first kept in a separate alphabetic file in *Miscellaneous* folders; when five records about an individual or firm have accumulated, an individual folder is made up and a number is assigned to it.

Numeric system components   A numeric filing system has the following four parts:

1. An *accession register* that houses a record of the numbers assigned.
2. A *cross-index card file* (relative index) that indicates whether correspondence

is located in miscellaneous or individual numbered files; it is a complete list of correspondents, which could include addresses for a mailing list.

3. The *individual numeric folders* that hold only active records and those to which numbers were sequentially assigned; they are kept separate from the miscellaneous folders.

4. The *miscellaneous alphabetic folders* that hold only those records that are not yet active.

The accession register, in either book form or card form, is a complete list of correspondents in numeric order. If the person desiring a record cannot remember its number, the cross-index card file (relative index), which is arranged alphabetically by correspondent, will furnish the number assigned or indicate that the information is filed in the miscellaneous file.

Terminal-digit system   The *terminal-digit system* is a useful variant of the numeric system which automatically spreads out recent files through the whole system. It is often used by hospitals and insurance companies. The difference between this system and the straight numeric system is that the numbers are read from right to left. The first two numbers at the right are considered primary, the next two numbers (third and fourth from the right) are secondary, and the remaining numbers are tertiary. To find policy no. 61534, therefore, you would look under the 34 section of the file first, then under the 15 portion of that section, and finally under the 6 in the 15 section. A file drawer would thus show the following numbers in this order, from front to back:

61534
41734
17034
98534
30135
10235
20235

The terminal-digit system is easy to work with because filing accuracy is improved and locating folders becomes quicker and easier. Terminal-digit filing is especially convenient when large numbers of recent files are used frequently by more than one person.

PHONETIC FILING SYSTEM

A third system, used only in certain environments, is called the *phonetic system.* It is used in large hospitals, Social Security offices, police departments, and motor-vehicle departments, where a very large number of records (especially in card form) is used, where calls for records come over telephones or intercoms (that is, when names are only heard and not seen), and where retrieval must be quick. The employee translates the name heard into a letter-and-number code without knowing exactly how the name is spelled, and by means of this code the record can be located rapidly.

CHRONOLOGICAL FILING SYSTEMS

The tickler system described in Chapter 2 is an example of a chronologically arranged filing system. Another type is a *chronological* or *reading file,* which consists of copies of every piece of correspondence or other information sent out of the office. This file must be read and culled periodically to ensure that correspondence has been answered or followed up. Chronological files do not replace other filing systems, but they can be a useful supplement.

HINTS FOR LOCATING MISPLACED PAPER FILES

- Look on your employer's desk. If you do not find it there, ask your employer if it may be in his or her briefcase.
- Check inside the file folders in front and in back of where you expected to find the missing one; sometimes folders are inadvertently slipped into one another.
- If you use an alphabetic filing system, check different spellings of the name. If you use a numeric filing system, check different numerical arrangements (e.g., straight numeric instead of terminal-digit). If you use a geographic filing system, look under similar names in other geographic locations. And if you use a subject filing system, check under a related heading.

SUMMARY

Alphabetic files shorten retrieval time because information can be located directly without the use of a separate index. However, misspelled names and errors in alphabetizing can cause retrieval problems. A more serious problem with alphabetic files is the difficulty in planning for expansion; the secretary must leave enough space in the cabinets in the appropriate alphabetic sequences to accommodate future files. Both problems can be solved by use of a numeric filing system. The terminal-digit system has rapidly gained popularity because new folders can be distributed quickly and evenly. However, numeric files are also subject to misfiling, and the maintenance of numeric files is time-consuming because they require an accession register and a cross-index card file. Consult your company's records manager or an outside records expert for assistance in setting up the system that will be most efficient for your office.

Setting up Filing Systems

CENTRALIZED AND DECENTRALIZED FILES

Information storage can be either centralized or decentralized. Centralized storage means that all records of any kind are kept in a central storage area, and authorized personnel charge out records and other resource materials at this location. Certain departmental records may be retained within the department itself for 30–60 days or even a year before being forwarded to the central storage area. Other records are sent on as soon as they are no longer needed by a particular department on a daily or monthly basis. The advantages of a centralized filing system are the following:

- It locates files in a central area accessible to all staff.
- It ensures uniform opening, maintenance, and closing procedures and permits supervision of files.
- It makes optimum use of space.
- It frees the secretary for other assignments.

In a decentralized system, all records are kept in individual departments within an organization. Any records that must be preserved after having served their purpose in the departments are sent to an inactive storage center. In a decentralized system, you have complete control over your own files. Your office or workstation will usually have vertical or lateral file cabinets. The advantages of a decentralized filing system are the following:

- Files are close to the user and more quickly retrieved.
- Familiarity with the files results in fewer misfiled documents.
- Inactive and nonessential materials may be eliminated or transferred by the person most familiar with the file contents.

SELECTING A SYSTEM AND EQUIPMENT

If you know how filed materials will be requested, it will be easy to recommend a filing system appropriate for your office. If records are asked for by name, the alphabetic system should be used. If they are requested by subject, the subject system or a variation of it should be used. If location is the most important factor, the geographic system should be used. If your office requires a filing system in which cases or patients are referred to by number (perhaps for the sake of confidentiality), a numeric system should be used. In organizations where records are usually requested by telephone, the phonetic system may be used.

Before actually setting up the files, you must determine what equipment and supplies will be needed: file cabinets, guides, folders, staplers (no paper clips should be used in storing papers), two-hole punches (if ring folders are used), desk trays (to hold incoming materials and materials to be filed), filing shelves (to attach to a file drawer or an open shelf to hold material to be filed), filing stools, sorters, and so on. (Sorters are racks consisting of open compartments, in which materials to be filed or distributed are sorted temporarily.)

SOURCES OF ASSISTANCE

If your company has a records-management program, the records administrator is the person to consult about establishing a filing system. If a companywide program is not in effect, you may wish to consult secretaries in similar offices elsewhere. However, the most efficient source would be an outside consultant familiar with the particular types of records being analyzed. If you consider the value of an expert's advice and the resultant time savings, you will realize that retaining such a consultant is often well worth the cost. In large cities, records consultants are listed in the Yellow Pages. They may also be sought through office supply and equipment firms that employ consultants.

Steps in Filing

The primary issue in handling records is determining whether they need to be filed at all—that is, whether the record can be destroyed immediately after its information has been disseminated or whether it should be retained for a certain period of time. Retention schedules—set up with the cooperation of the records administrator, top management, legal counsel, and department heads—are a necessity in maintaining control over records. A retention schedule lists categories of records, the department or division responsible for the originals, retention periods, the place where the records are to be stored, microfilming instructions where relevant, and sometimes an indication of the method of destruction.

Documents should be filed daily to reduce the chance of their being misplaced. Procedures to be observed when preparing for the storage of records include the following:

1. Read or scan the document.
2. Be sure that a *release mark* (initials, date, or stamped code), indicating that the document is ready for storage, appears on it.
3. If your system permits it, place a numerical file code or a name or subject code in an upper corner of the document to indicate where the material should be stored. (Some records administrators prefer to do this themselves.)
4. Place on the document another code that will indicate how long it must be retained. (Again, some records administrators prefer to do this themselves.)
5. Check to see whether the record needs cross-referencing. If it might be called for by a title other than the one it is filed under, write "X" in the margin and prepare a cross-reference index card for it. (See "Cross-references," below.)
6. Arrange the material in the order in which it will be stored.
7. Prepare any necessary follow-up notations for a tickler file.
8. Remove paper clips to eliminate bulk and prevent damage to the documents. Mend torn pages and smooth out wrinkles.
9. Place documents in the proper sections of the folder, left side down, with the most recent records toward the front.
10. If certain documents are too large to fit in the folder, insert a cross-reference sheet that refers readers to a special area for oversized documents.

Approximately 25 percent of the records crossing your desk each day can probably be destroyed or recycled immediately or passed on to some other person for disposition.

Reading, scanning, and coding   Look for the most important name or subject, and underscore or circle it in pencil, or write or code it onto the letter if it is not mentioned in the text itself. The code will include numbers or letters or both, depending on the filing system being used. (See page 442.) Care should be taken to select the proper code or subject heading. Some records administrators prefer that the secretary not code records that are being sent to central records, as the records personnel will be more familiar with the storage categories. You can, however, always code the records that you will store yourself.

Indicate to the filing personnel that the record is ready to be filed by initialing it or by stamping it "File" or "Release," typically in the upper right corner.

Retention codes   As a help to the filing personnel, each document should be marked with a code indicating the retention period of the material (30 days, 60 days, one year, etc.). The retention schedule will indicate whether the records are then to be transferred to inactive storage, microfilmed, or placed in computer storage in accordance with established company policy.

Cross-references   Too few offices use any cross-referencing procedure, which can be essential to quick retrieval. When a record might be called for under titles other than the one under which it is filed, a cross-reference sheet should be filed under the possible title, referring searchers to the proper storage location. For example, when correspondence is filed under the legal name of a married woman, a cross-reference sheet should be filed under her husband's name, and vice versa. Cross-reference sheets (or cards) may contain only two lines; for example, "Furst, Mrs. Adam H./*See* Furst, Carrie M." ["Matthews, Carrie"; "Matthews-Furst, Carrie"; etc.] Cross-referencing is also useful when the filing name of departments or government bureaus might not be readily recalled, when a company has offices with different addresses, or when a periodical is filed under its name but a cross-reference under its publisher's name might be helpful. Cross-reference sheets are most easily identifiable in the files if they are of a distinctive color.

When five cross-references have accumulated, a permanent cross-reference guide should be inserted. This should be similar to a regular guide, but the tab should contain the same information as a cross-reference sheet.

In large and complex systems, cross-reference guides may be duplicated in an easily accessible card file. In numeric filing systems, these cross-reference cards for alternative titles would simply be placed in alphabetical order with the cards already in the cross-index file box. In an alphabetic filing system, a special cross-reference card box or a loose-leaf notebook would be required.

Follow-up   If an executive expects to want to see a given record in the near future, you or the executive should indicate on the record the date when it should be returned. If the record is being sent to the records center, you or the records personnel should add a card to the tickler file as a reminder.

Indexing Systems

Indexing systems are used to determine how a record is to be filed so that it can be found when needed. There are many different kinds of indexing systems. Whichever your office chooses, the most important rule is to be consistent by treating each piece of information in the same manner. A respected and authoritative source for indexing rules is *Rules for Alphabetical Filing,* published by the Association of Records Managers and Administrators (ARMA). This publication and others on technical records management may be obtained by writing to ARMA, 4200 Somerset Drive, Suite 215, Prairie Village, KS 66208. ARMA recommends rules for three classifications: (1) names of individuals, (2) names of business establishments, and (3) governmental/political designations.

INDEXING NAMES OF INDIVIDUALS
The following guidelines should be used to alphabetize individual names:

1. Alphabetize the names of individuals by surname + given name or initial + middle name or initial.

    Jones, M. Arthur
    Jones, Mary Ann
2. Alphabetize letter by letter to the end of the surname, then the given names and initials.

    Morison, John A.
    Morison, John Thomas
    Morrison, John Andrew
3. Treat hyphenated or compound names as one word.

Fitzgerald, Marcia	Foster-Brown, James	Vandalla, James
Fitz Smith, Patrick	Fosteri, Arnold	van der Meer, Howard
		Van Dyne, Helen

4. Disregard titles such as *Dr., Mrs., Captain,* or *Senator* when alphabetizing. However, these designations may be included to provide additional identifying information.

> Nyhus, Lloyd (Dr.)
> Smith, Walter (Senator)

5. Treat religious titles (such as *Reverend* and *Sister*) similarly.

> Raphael, Mary (Sister)
> Smith, John (Reverend)

However, if only one unit of the name is known *(Father Smith, Sister Mary),* the religious title becomes an indexing unit.

6. Alphabetize abbreviated elements (such as *St.*) as if they were spelled out *(Saint).*

> St. Peter, Joanne
> Saint-Simon, Paul
> Sarris, Eleanor

7. Disregard designations such as *Jr., Sr.,* or *2nd* in filing.

> Smith, John T. (Sr.)
> Smith, John Thomas (Jr.)

8. Use the legal signature of a married woman when filing. Her husband's name may be cross-referenced if desired.

> Poulet, Marie Anne (Mrs. Paul Poulet)

9. File "nothing" before "something" if initials are used for a given name.

> Peters, J.
> Peters, J. G.
> Peters, John

10. Arrange surnames having the prefixes *de, La,* and *Mac* just as they are spelled.

> MacDougal, John
> Mbasdeken, John
> McDover, Mary

11. If you are uncertain which name is the surname, file under the last name given and provide a cross-reference for any other possible surname.

> Hop, Chin Sing [with cross-references at *Chin* and *Sing*]
> Hope, Genevieve Carson [with a cross-reference at *Carson*]

INDEXING NAMES OF ORGANIZATIONS OR BUSINESSES

When indexing the names of organizations or businesses, rules similar to those just described are observed. For example, in a company name beginning with the full name of an individual, the name is inverted so that the surname appears first. In the name *Ted Corvair, Inc.,* the first unit becomes *Corvair* and the second unit becomes *Ted.* When no complete name of an individual is used—for example, *Corvair Construction Company*—the company name is indexed as it is ordinarily written. Companies operating under two different names are indexed under the name used most often and cross-referenced under the other name. Compound words and hyphenated names are treated as single units. Compound geographical names are treated differently, however. *The Palo Alto Trust* would be filed under *Palo* as first unit, *Alto* as second unit, and *Trust* as third unit; the initial *The* should be ignored (but any *internal* articles, prepositions, or conjunctions would have been included as elements for alphabetization). Punctuation is also ignored: *Smith's Grocery* would be alphabetized as *Smiths.*

Single letters in names such as those used in radio or television stations are treated as separate units; thus, *KXYZ* would be filed near the beginning of the *K* section. Names of companies beginning with numbers in figure form are filed in numerical order at the front of the entire file. If the numbers are spelled out, however, the name is filed alphabetically. For example, *21st Century Corp.* would be filed in the front section of the complete files, while *One Main Street* would be filed alphabetically under the *O*'s. Names of foreign firms are filed as they are normally written unless elements of them are identifiable as surnames, in which case they are treated like their English counterparts.

Schools named for their geographical location are indexed by the geographical name; for example, *Tulsa, University of.* In an alphabetical listing, *Tulsa Junior College* would follow *Tulsa, University of.* (Since *Tulsa* is the only unit that precedes the comma, the rule of "nothing before something" applies.)

INDEXING GOVERNMENTAL AND POLITICAL ENTITIES

When indexing government correspondence, use the most important word. Many companies file according to the rule that the first three units are always *United States Government*, followed by the name of the department, bureau, or commission. The same approach is taken with states and cities: the official name of the state is used first (e.g., *Texas, State of* or *Virginia, Commonwealth of*), followed by the applicable department, bureau, or division within the state government. Military installations are first filed under *United States Government* and then under the name of the installation (fort, station, base, etc.). Foreign governments are treated like states and cities; a record from a department of the government of South Korea would be filed first under *Korea, Republic of (South Korea)* and then under the department's name.

Although the alphabetization rules provided here are widely observed, you must primarily follow any particular indexing system used by your organization. The records manager should be able to brief you on the company's guidelines.

Controlling Documents in Storage

No matter how or when records are stored, a system for controlling their location and movement must be established and observed by all personnel. If there is no control, records may be missing when they are needed or may fall into the wrong hands. When you have accepted a record for safekeeping, every precaution must be taken to protect that record so that it will be available when needed. A simple method of protecting company records is to permit only authorized personnel to withdraw material from the files.

CHARGE-OUT PROCEDURES

Removal of a record from the files should not be permitted until it has been properly charged out. A record can be charged out to a person who officially requests it for a specific length of time using a special form. This requisition, which should include a description of the record (including whatever information appears on the label or tab), the date of release, and the person's signature, can often also serve as a charge-out form. The form should be inserted into a pocket on the Out guide. If only one record is removed, then an Out guide or substitution card can replace the charged-out record in the file. Consider using an Out folder rather than a guide when an entire folder has been charged out; the Out folder will serve to hold new records that arrive temporarily.

An "On Call" guide may replace the Out folder. The On Call guide directs the filing personnel to send the folder on to the person listed on the guide itself when the folder is returned. Only when the material is back in its place can the Out or On Call guide be removed for reuse.

A control procedure such as this is absolutely essential. Some companies allow records to be kept out for only a few hours; others, for a week or more. In any case, a policy should be determined and adhered to by all members of the organization.

CONFIDENTIAL AND CLASSIFIED MATERIALS

Special precautions must be exercised when confidential or classified documents are in your possession or stored in the records center. In addition to the normal protection just mentioned, an organization can use a safe or a built-in vault large enough for holding storage equipment. Another method of protecting confidential or classified documents is to duplicate or microfilm the material and then give it to an attorney or a bank for safekeeping.

Private firms with government contracts to manufacture, distribute, or store classified government materials or products are required by the Department of Defense to assign special control numbers to any classified documents kept on company premises, as well as communications (such as letters and memorandums) regarding these contracts or projects. Although the responsibility for maintaining records for these classified documents will be in the hands of a special department within the firm, you must be aware of the necessity for control numbers and any other identification that may be placed on classified documents. The Department of Defense typically classifies documents as *Top Secret, Secret,* or *Confidential.* The national-security regulation warning against unauthorized disclosure of classified material is also stamped or typed on the document.

In addition to following special storage procedures for such documents, take care not to leave classified documents uncovered on desks. Be sure that the documents have cover pages and that they are kept in drawers or locked areas when not being used. Classified documents may not be released to a person unless proof has been furnished that the individual is cleared to handle the documents. Other possible precautions include using red-bordered envelopes indicating that classified information is within, hand-carrying documents instead of using interoffice mail, and retaining receipts signed by those charging out the materials. See Chapter 7 for a detailed discussion of classified documents.

Micrographics and Electronic Storage

MICROFILM STORAGE SYSTEMS

Microfilm—a method for miniaturizing records on film—is a useful medium for indefinitely storing important file material such as legal documents, financial records, and library resources. The initial cost of a microfilm system is high, but savings start to accumulate after a few years. The cost of microfilming a record is approximately equal to that of storing it in an inactive file for 10 years.

Microfilm should be considered when records that the firm wishes to retain but that are rarely charged out expand to take up too much space. Microfilm has many advantages:

1. It is difficult to alter.
2. It offers protection against water and heat damage.

3. If maximum security is needed, microfilm can be stored easily in fireproof vaults.
4. Duplicate microfilm files can be maintained off the premises at little extra cost, to guard against destruction of vital information.
5. It is adaptable to computer systems.
6. It can be integrated with an automatic storage and retrieval system, which can provide highly efficient automation and control when a substantial amount of microfilm is being handled.
7. Most important, it saves space and ultimately money, requiring as little as two percent of the space needed to store equivalent hard-copy records, and freeing the filing staff from much of its sorting, retrieval, and filing duties.

Microfilm also has several disadvantages:

1. A special viewer is required to read it.
2. Microfilm records containing handwritten documents are hard to read.
3. It is difficult to update microfilmed client records.
4. It is expensive to produce paper copies from the film.

Material is easily and speedily converted to microfilm by photographing hard copy of any size manually or automatically. When documents are generally of the same size and can be placed in a logical or sequential order, the process takes little time. Microfilm clerks prearrange the records, remove any fasteners, and, if necessary, attach records of unusual size to $8\frac{1}{2}'' \times 11''$ sheets for automatic feeding.

Types of microfilm   The various forms in which microfilm may be used are microfiche and ultrafiche; roll film; tab-punch or aperture cards; and microfilm strips.

Microfiche takes the form of individual card-sized pieces of film. A card generally consists of strips of microimages cut into pieces and set in rows; a single card may contain 100 or more images. It is easily mailed to a customer (for example, a distributor, for the purpose of updating pages of catalogs with parts and prices) or circulated throughout a company for the fast dissemination of a large amount of information. *Ultrafiche* is similar to microfiche but has an even greater number of smaller images on the card. Documents frequently referred to are best filmed on micro- or ultrafiche because search and retrieval time is much faster. Furthermore, with the use of modern equipment, the updating of microfiche is greatly simplified, with resultant savings in time and money.

Roll film, being cheap to produce but somewhat inconvenient to use, is normally used for records that will be referred to infrequently. For information that is sought more frequently, a roll can be placed in a *cartridge*, enabling the user to load a reader quickly without touching the film. Microfilm in reels can be converted to the more expensive microfiche later if necessary.

A 35-mm. microfilm (of such things as engineering drawings) can be stored on a *tab-punch* or *aperture card*. The keypunched card has identifying information concerning the drawing, and the drawing (reduced to approximately $1\frac{1}{2}'' \times 2''$) is attached to the card by a special machine. The punch cards are easily inserted into a reader. (Such readers are standard desk equipment in offices where this system is used continually.)

Microfilm strips can be stored in a special plastic *film jacket* with horizontal pockets. The film is inserted into the jacket by use of a special instrument that can also pull out a micro unit and substitute an updated one. As many as 100 pages can be stored in one jacket. Jacketed microfilm is used for catalogs of parts, student records, medical records, or similar records containing detailed information. It can be especially useful for storing telephone numbers, credit ratings, rate tables, ZIP codes, and similar data. The strip holder is easily inserted into a reader for viewing.

Computer output microfilm   Microfilming was formerly accomplished exclusively by means of special cameras. Today microfilm is frequently produced as computer output microfilm (COM), a process in which data stored in a computer are transferred directly to film instead of being printed out on paper. COM affords speedy retrieval of information (through computer-assisted retrieval or CAR), considerable savings in computer time, easier distribution of information via film instead of printouts, high-quality copy, a great savings of storage space, and elimination of paper-handling bottlenecks such as collating, bursting, and binding.

COM technology picks up data from magnetic tape and transfers it to the recorder by scanning the data page by page. A camera transfers the pages onto microfilm at speeds of several thousand pages per hour. The COM film is then processed in the usual way into roll film, microfiche, or aperture cards. Hard copies can easily be provided, and extra copies of the microfiche can easily be duplicated at low cost.

If a company does not feel that having this equipment would be economical, especially if it would not be kept in use continually, service centers for various companies can be contracted to do specific COM processing jobs. Information required for updating the output can be furnished to the centers daily, and the updated material can be picked up the next day.

The administrative secretary should become acquainted with this aspect of records handling and keep up-to-date on the technological advances that are reducing costs and making possible more efficient handling of records.

ELECTRONIC STORAGE SYSTEMS

As computer systems continue to improve, the link between computers and microforms becomes ever tighter. We will soon see reader-scanners that can transmit micrographic data anywhere in the world via computers, fax machines, and laser printers. The bar code will play a key role in increasing productivity.

Disk storage   The most widely used means of electronic storage is the computer disk. Data stored on the computer can be sorted and resorted alphabetically, numerically, geographically, or by subject. Files can be sorted without replacing or disrupting the original.

Data can be stored on both the hard disk and floppy disks. However, if all your files are stored on the hard disk, you will eventually use up a lot of memory; therefore, it is often recommended that floppy disks be used as the primary storage medium.

Records-management software   Records-management software responds to an organization's need for tracking file activity in instances where the current systems have become too cumbersome or the volume of activity has become too large. There are three kinds of records-management software available:

- Highly specialized programs that are developed to meet specific company needs.
- Database software that a user can tailor to meet specific needs.

• Off-the-shelf programs that range from single applications to integrated packages that address complex reporting tasks.

Optical disks   The electronic imaging industry was spawned with the invention of the laser optical disk. The disk offers a high-density, long-lasting alternative to storage. There are two types of imaging systems: archival systems, intended for long-term storage, and integrated systems, which provide instant access to documents.

Transferring and Eliminating Files

An active record is one that is referred to at least once a month. Other records are regarded as inactive and should be considered for transfer unless they must be kept in their present location for administrative or security reasons.

TRANSFERRING RECORDS

Records that are no longer useful should be sent to central records or to an inactive storage area. You or the records personnel will be responsible for preparing material for transfer. Transfer boxes, transfer forms, and instructions for labeling should be available from the storage center. Transfer boxes will generally accommodate either letter- or legal-size papers. (Guides are not transferred.) Transfer forms should indicate which records are scheduled to be moved, their codes, inclusive dates or series, and the length of time that the records are to be kept in the inactive area. The transfer boxes and transfer forms should have labels and identification that conform to the requirements of the records administrator.

If a special transfer code is assigned to the transferred files, that code should also be noted on all pertinent index cards. You may even want to move these cards to a separate file box for inactive or transferred files. Whether you take an active part in the transfer or not, you must be aware of the various methods of transfer and storage and the specific transfer process. You need to know where every record in the office is and, if it is not accessible within 30 seconds, what has happened to it. Is it being used by someone in the office? Has it been transferred to the records center on a certain date with a specific location code? Was it transferred to the records center for a definite length of time for storage? Or was it destroyed on a certain date?

Periodic transfer   Files are often transferred at the end of a specified time (for example, six months or a year); this is called *periodic transfer* or *purging*. In small offices, inactive material can be kept in the less accessible bottom and top drawers of a cabinet, or every other cabinet may be reserved for inactive records. Even if inactive material is kept in separate cabinets, difficulty may arise when requested material has to be retrieved from a place where it is not expected to be. And since the material is often transferred out of the office to the inactive area at the end of a designated period, this difficulty can become pronounced.

Continuous transfer   A more effective method is *continuous transfer*. You or the records personnel should set aside time every few weeks to look through the records and pull those that are ready for transfer. This will allow a continuous flow of inactive records out of the active space to provide space for new records, thereby precluding the need to purchase more filing equipment.

RETENTION SCHEDULES

A retention schedule is a form that lists specific kinds of records—from machine repair records and purchase orders to formal legal instruments—and specifies how long each type of record should be kept. It also provides instructions for disposal—whether the papers are to be transferred to inactive or archival storage, destoyed, microfilmed, or placed in computer storage. The retention schedule is generally drawn up by the records administrator and is approved by departmental managers, the company attorney, and a representative of top management. (Retention of medical records is generally determined by state law.) Copies of the schedule should be in the hands of everyone involved in the handling of company information. The secretary should have a copy of this schedule and be aware of any changes that have been made in it.

RECORDS DISPOSAL

The retention schedule may also provide for disposal or destruction of records. Some records that are no longer valuable can simply be discarded in a wastebasket or recycled. Others may need to be shredded, either at your desk or in the records center. Still others may carry instructions for disposal by other means, such as burial or chemical decomposition. The retention schedule could also require that certain records be microfilmed before the originals are discarded.

The destruction of confidential or classified company records must be witnessed by the records administrator and, in some cases, a representative of top management. Signed forms must indicate that the records were destroyed and that proper approval for destruction was given beforehand. Companies having government contracts, and especially contracts with the Department of Defense, must be very careful when disposing of miscellaneous paper in connection with classified documents, since such paper must be destroyed in a manner that renders the information absolutely unreadable. Classified documents, as well as those which have been declassified but still need to be destroyed, must be disposed of by prescribed methods. Refer to the Department of Defense Manual *Information Security Program Regulation* (obtainable from the Superintendent of Documents, P.O. Box 371954, Pittsburgh, PA 15250-7954) for detailed instructions.

CHAPTER 13

Telephones and Telecommunications

This chapter covers the practical and technical aspects of telephone and telecommunications services commonly found in businesses, including telegraphic services, fax machines, electronic mail, and data networks.

As a secretary you will need to know how to operate some of the telecommunications equipment found in your office. The more you understand about telephones, telecommunications, and computers, the more valuable you will be to your employer. In most businesses, technology is underused because no one really understands the full range of its available practical uses. Consult your user manual, ask the technical staff, or, if necessary, contact the supplier or the account representative who sold the equipment or service to your company.

The field of telecommunications can be confusing today, since it is often hard to distinguish a piece of equipment from a system from a service. For example, telephone companies sell services that provide most of the functions of a PBX system. There will often be several ways to obtain the same function.

As features have multiplied, the design and choice of telephone systems have become important but difficult. You will naturally have to adapt to the system chosen, though you may be able to suggest features that should be included. If some of the features discussed in this chapter are not available in your office today, they probably will be in a few years. (For a discussion of telephone manners, see Chapter 3.)

Telephone-Company Services

Telephone-company services have expanded immensely with the thorough computerization of the telephone networks. This has allowed for more flexible direct dialing and the introduction of many new features designed for business use. The dialing methods for basic services are fairly uniform, but the set of available features varies to some extent based on your region and your long-distance carrier.

455

WHO ARE YOUR PHONE COMPANIES?

Most phone customers today deal with two or three phone companies. Your local company bills you for your basic line charges and all your local calls. That company is usually part of a Regional Bell Operating Company (RBOC). There are seven RBOCs in the United States: NYNEX, Bell Atlantic, Bell South, Ameritech, US WEST, Southwestern Bell, and Pacific Telesis. These companies are sometimes called the "Baby Bells," since they represent the breakup of the domestic-services portion of AT&T. In some areas, the RBOC is also the local telephone provider. (In Minneapolis, for example, US WEST is both the regional and local provider.) In a few areas, there is a regional provider that, for historical reasons, is not considered an RBOC. (Connecticut, for example, is served by SNET, which was never a part of AT&T.)

Local calls are those made within your local calling area. If your local provider is also an RBOC or other regional provider, you will be able to get long-distance service from that provider within a somewhat wider area.

To make most long-distance calls, you must have a long-distance carrier. There are many long-distance carriers, of which the largest are currently AT&T, MCI, and Sprint.

Some businesses have more than one long-distance carrier, usually as a cost-saving measure. Computerized programs can be installed in business phone systems to automatically dial each call out through the carrier that has the least-expensive rates for a given area code. However, since all the long-distance carriers offer volume discount rates, it is often more economical to rely on a single carrier.

For residential customers, long-distance and local charges appear on separate portions of the same phone bill. However, for business accounts, the long-distance bill is usually sent by itself directly from the long-distance carrier.

DOMESTIC LONG-DISTANCE CALLING METHODS

Domestic means primarily the United States, but domestic calling procedures also apply to Canada and most of the Caribbean islands. See Fig. 13.1, which shows time zones and area codes for most of North America.

For domestic long-distance calls, dialing direct is the easiest method. However, you may want to make a charge call if you are out of your office, or an operator-assisted call if you need special assistance.

Domestic direct dialing   If you are making a long-distance call within your area code, dial 1 + seven-digit number. If you are making a long-distance call outside your area code, dial 1 + area code + seven-digit number.

Domestic operator-assisted calls   You will need to use operator assistance if you wish to make a collect call, a person-to-person call, or a bill-to-third-number call. Within your area code, dial 0 + seven-digit number; outside your area code, dial 0 + area code + seven-digit number. The operator will come on the line and ask you what kind of assistance you need. If you simply want to reach your local operator without predialing a number, dial 0; if you wish to reach your long-distance operator, dial 00.

Domestic information   For information within your local calling area, dial 411. For calls within your area code that are not considered local, dial 1 + 411. For long-distance information, dial 1 + area code + 555-1212.

Fig. 13.1   Area Codes and Time Zones in North America

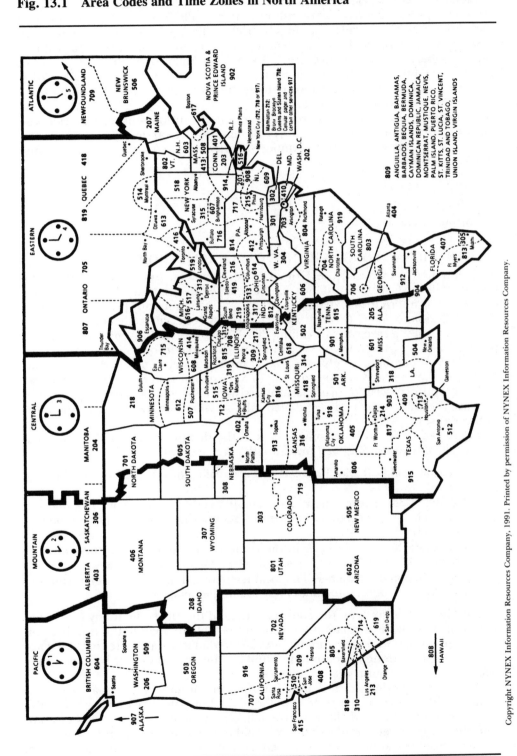

Domestic calling-card calls   Calling cards—that is, credit cards issued to customers by telephone companies for use in making calls from locations other than their home or office—will sometimes be useful. Dial 0 + area code (when needed) + seven-digit number, then wait for the computer tone and enter your calling-card number. For a long-distance call normally billed by your local provider, you will need to enter the calling-card number from that provider. For a long-distance call typically billed by your long-distance carrier, use the calling-card number of your long-distance carrier.

If the phone you are calling from does not use your long-distance carrier, you must first dial the five-digit code of your long-distance carrier, then immediately dial 0 + area code + seven-digit number. The five-digit codes of the major long-distance carriers are:

AT&T   10288
MCI   10222
Sprint   10333

INTERNATIONAL LONG-DISTANCE CALLING METHODS

As mentioned previously, the United States, Canada, Bermuda, Puerto Rico, and most of the Caribbean islands can be reached by domestic dialing. All other countries use international dialing methods. AT&T's annually published *International Telecommunications Guide* lists every country code, city code, and time zone. You can request a free copy by calling 800-874-4000. The international table on pages 524–32 of this book contains much of the same information.

It is becoming increasingly easy to dial international numbers directly. However, if you are unfamiliar with dialing to a particular number or to a particular country, you may wish to use operator assistance. Several less-developed countries are not able to accept direct-dialed calls, so you must always use an operator in those cases.

There can be up to four components in the dialing sequence of an international call, and you should be familiar with each of them.

1. **International Call Dial Prefix** If you are dialing direct, you must begin by dialing 011.
2. **Country Code** Every country has a country code that is two or three digits long. (The only exception is the United States, whose country code has only one digit.)
3. **City Code** Most major cities in the world (except those within the United States and Canada) have city codes that are one to five digits long.
4. **Local Telephone Number** The local telephone numbers of foreign countries vary in length, sometimes even within the same country.

You should first look up the country code and the city code, if any (see pages 524–32). With this information, you should be able to analyze the number you have been given and better understand how to dial it. Please note that if a 0 appears at the beginning of the phone number, this typically must be dialed only *within* the foreign country.

If you are experienced in dialing international numbers, you may feel comfortable making the call yourself; if not, dial the long-distance operator. Tell the operator the country and city you are dialing and the number as it was given to you. Before the operator places the call, make sure you understand—and write down—exactly what digits will be dialed, and which represent the country code, which represent the city code (if needed), and which represent the local telephone number, so that you will be able to place similar calls yourself the next time. Do not hesitate to ask questions.

When you make an international call, either direct-dialed or operator-assisted, you may have to wait for 30–45 seconds before the receiving phone begins to ring. The tone and spacing of rings varies from country to country; sometimes the ring may sound similar to our busy signal. If you are at all confused by what you hear, make an operator-assisted call and ask the operator to stay on the line and interpret the sound you are hearing.

International direct dialing   To dial an international call directly, dial 011 + country code + city code (if needed) + local number. For example, if you are calling Geneva, you will need the country code for Switzerland (41) and the city code for Geneva (22). You would then dial 011 + 41 + 22 + local number.

International operator-assisted calls   You will need operator assistance to make a collect call, a person-to-person call, or a bill-to-third-number call. Dial 01 + country code + city code (if needed) + local number, and the operator will come on the line. If you want the operator to dial the number for you, dial 00 for your long-distance operator.

International information   To reach an information or directory-assistance operator in a specific country, dial 00 to contact your long-distance operator. Tell the long-distance operator the country, the city, and the name of the party you want to reach. The operator will then contact an English-speaking operator in that country to get the information on your behalf. Make sure you are clear and specific when you give the operator instructions. Unless you are confident you have been given the right number, you should request that the operator place the call for you, so that, if you have been given the wrong number, you can more easily get credit for the call.

International calling-card calls   To place an international calling-card call, dial 01 + country code + city code (if needed) + local number. An operator will then come on the line and ask for your international calling-card number.

Receiving international calls   You may at some time need to give instructions on how to dial your own number to someone in another country. A person in Canada, Bermuda, Puerto Rico, and most of the Caribbean islands can call the United States by simply dialing 1 + area code + seven-digit number. From anywhere else, the person will need to dial the international dialing prefix + 1 + area code + seven-digit number. International dialing to the United States is very similar to domestic dialing, since 1 happens to be our country code and we use area codes instead of city codes.

SPECIAL BILLING NUMBERS

There are many special billing number services, ranging from WATS and 800 number services to the newer 900 services.

WATS services   Wide Area Telecommunications Service, usually known as WATS services, are outbound reduced-rate lines. WATS services can be limited to a given state, the entire United States, or particular countries. The term WATS was originally used by AT&T for specific lines that were billed at less-expensive rates. However, now WATS basically refers to a business-wide volume discount plan for long-distance savings.

800 numbers   Most 800 numbers are used to provide for toll-free calling by customers, prospective customers, and employees outside the office.

Inbound 800 numbers are numbers that are free to the caller; the business that owns the 800 number pays the bills. The 800 number can be a dedicated line (sometimes called an inbound WATS number) or an 800 number that is simply assigned to a regular number. An 800 number may be available only to local callers, to callers within the state, or to callers in several "bands" or areas within the United States, and 800 numbers are also available for international inbound calls.

900 numbers   Most 900 and 976 numbers are used to provide prerecorded messages, for which callers pay at rates often much higher than for regular phone calls. However, many companies also use 900 numbers staffed by operators as a way of charging for customer services. Since these numbers are so widely used for non-company-related personal purposes, most telephone companies offer subscriber companies the option of blocking employee access to 900 numbers.

TELEPHONE SERVICE FEATURES
The following is a list of some of the more common features available directly from your phone company. These features can be obtained as ancillary services to your regular phone subscription.

Call forwarding   This feature lets you program your phone to redirect incoming calls to another phone (and, when desired, to return them to the original phone).

Call waiting   With this feature, a short tone will let you know when someone is trying to call you while you are on the phone. You can quickly press down on the switch hook, putting your original conversation on hold, in order to talk to that person.

Conference calling   Conference or three-way calling is available as an option from your phone company. Even if you do not subscribe to this feature, most local or long-distance carriers can still arrange special conference calls. Consult your local phone book or your long-distance carrier on how to arrange a conference call.

Voice mail   In a voice mail system, calls to an employee's number are recorded if the employee cannot answer the phone. He or she can retrieve the messages from any telephone by dialing a given number and entering a personal identification code. Most larger companies now buy or lease voice mail systems. However, many phone companies offer simple voice mail systems to their customers. These may be preferable to answering machines, since there is less concern over power failures and broken message tapes, and messages can be taken if the caller is busy with another conversation.

TELEPHONE LINES
There are several types of telephone lines and trunks available for business use.

Telephone lines and trunks   Business lines are usually associated with individual telephones. Trunks—that is, channels used as common arteries for communications traffic between switchboards or other switching devices—are associated with PBX telephone systems (see page 463). The term *T-1 line* is often used for what is basically a trunk line.

Foreign exchange service   Foreign exchange (FX) service provides you with a telephone number in a service area other than your office, effectively giving you unlimited calling for a flat rate into a specified town, area, or state other than your own. It is also available for international locations. If you call a specific locale frequently, this service may be more economical than toll calls. FX service can also be two-way, allowing incoming calls within a distant area to be answered in your office.

Tie-line service   Full-time point-to-point service can be provided by leasing a tie line. Tie lines are used primarily to connect two or more telephone systems that are in constant communication, such as a home office and a plant, or a sales office and a distributor.

In addition to the features and services that have been discussed, a number of new, high-speed services are emerging. These include Integrated Services Digital Network (ISDN), which will allow for high-speed transmission of both data and voice over a standard telephone line. This will make possible expanded features for telephones and a vast increase in transmission capacity.

Telephone Equipment and Systems

There is a vast range of telephone equipment and systems to support today's businesses. As mentioned, it is sometimes hard to differentiate a piece of equipment from a system from a telephone-company service. Some equipment features must be supported by the phone company or the local phone system in order to operate.

You should consult the user manuals for your telephone equipment in order to learn how to use all of the various features. If a manual has been misplaced, you can obtain another from the manufacturer. Do not assume that you need an extensive technical background to understand telecommunications and other office equipment. By consulting user manuals and exercising common sense, you can learn enough about such equipment to be quite comfortable using it day to day.

Telephone systems such as the PBX support numerous features and functions. Take the time to meet the person who selected your company's telephone system and the person who maintains it in order to learn about all its capabilities. If there is no one knowledgeable within your organization, you can call the company that supplied the system and talk to one of their representatives.

TELEPHONE EQUIPMENT FEATURES

The following are brief descriptions of common types of telephone equipment and typical equipment features. You may use some of this equipment in your office, and you may deal with other employees who communicate using devices such as mobile or cellular phones and beepers.

Multi-button telephone   The multi-button telephone may have six, 10, 20, or even 30 buttons with which to route calls to other phones in the office. Multi-button telephones are typically used in small business offices to place, answer, transfer, and screen calls.

Electronic telephone   This is a multi-button telephone that incorporates many extra features, such as push-button dialing, electronic tone ringing, and multiple-line pickups. One major advantage of electronic sets is that they can operate with a much smaller telephone wire than the multi-button phone.

Line-status indicator   This device, which is built into most multi-button and electronic telephones, shows which of the lines connected to the telephone are busy.

Automatic call distributor (ACD)   This device is used by mail-order firms, hotels, airlines, and other companies that deal extensively with call-in customers. A taped message informs the caller that he or she is in a queue and that the call will be answered by the next available operator.

Voice-response system   Voice-response systems are used in many customer-service businesses. The caller is usually given a taped message and a menu of choices from which to select to receive further information by pressing various buttons on the telephone. Typically, the caller is given the choice of staying on the line or pressing 0 for an operator if he or she wishes to speak to a live person. A touch-tone phone is usually required to participate in this system. (Most new rotary telephones have a touch-tone function that can be activated when needed.)

Answering machine   Small offices may use answering machines to answer calls during lunch or after hours. Voice mail, however, is becoming increasingly popular as an alternative to answering machines.

Voice mail system   Many companies have installed their own voice mail systems. Some systems are very simple; others offer a large number of features. Most voice mail systems will give the name of the person being called, often with a personal greeting, and then allow the caller to leave a message. Messages can usually be received by the employee from his or her office phone or by calling in from outside the office. Voice mail systems will usually take messages if the individual being called is busy with another call. Frequently they can redirect messages to others within the office. Some systems will even allow for one message to be broadcast to every voice "mailbox" within the office.

If your employer lets you receive calls for him or her directly, you may have the option of taking a message yourself or transferring the caller to the voice mail system to leave a message. You may also wish to leave messages in your employer's voice mailbox if you both find that it is a convenient way to communicate while either of you is away from the office. For example, if your employer is traveling in a different time zone, you could place a call to your employer's voice mailbox to make sure he or she gets an important message before or after work hours. Always identify yourself clearly and speak slowly and distinctly when leaving a message in a voice mail system (or an answering machine).

Speakerphone   A speakerphone is also referred to as a hands-free telephone, since it allows you to talk while leaving both your hands free for other activities. It also permits more than one person in the room to participate in the call. (Be cautious when speaking to someone who uses a speakerphone—there may be other people in the room.)

Prestored telephone numbers   Many phones allow you to prestore frequently dialed numbers, so that you can then push a specific button or a simple code to have the number automatically dialed for you.

Flash button   Pushing a flash button is the equivalent of quickly pressing the switch hook. (The switch hook itself can be unreliable.) This feature is useful for such services as call waiting.

Beeper   Many business people and professionals now carry beepers. The simplest beepers merely beep or flash a light to tell the individual carrying the beeper to call his or her office. The standard models, however, allow the caller to leave a telephone number, which is then displayed on the beeper. When you call a beeper number, you typically will only hear a short computer tone when the beeper service picks up your call. You should then press in your phone number (or the number you wish the beeper holder to call) and hang up. (You may want to include the area code if you think the beeper holder may be out of your immediate area.) An additional service permits the caller to leave not only a phone number but also a short message. An operator will take the message and it will be printed out on the beeper's display panel.

Cellular or mobile phone   Cellular and mobile phones—that is, wireless phones that can be carried anywhere—are increasing in popularity. They are especially valuable to sales and repair people. Some cellular phones can be reached from anywhere in the contiguous United States, others only within a smaller geographic area. When you dial a cellular-phone number, you may receive a recorded message saying that the phone is not within the reach of the cellular base that transmits the calls; if so, you can only keep trying the number until the phone owner returns to the region. Many cellular phone owners also use voice mail so that they can pick up messages that arrived when they were out of range.

TELEPHONE SYSTEMS
A wide variety of telephone systems are offered today by many manufacturers. The range of products extends from small key telephone systems to multi-line, computer-controlled PBX systems for large corporations. Generally, telephone systems can be broken down into three categories: (1) key telephone systems, (2) hybrid telephone systems, and (3) PBX systems.

Key telephone systems   These systems provice several line-status indicators. They are usually found in small offices that use multi-button, multi-line telephones with a private interoffice communications arrangement and signaling capability.

Hybrid telephone systems   Hybrid systems are basically key systems with extra features similar to those found in PBX systems. For example, specially designed telephones may be used to place and answer calls and perform functions such as transferring and forwarding calls and making conference calls. A central answering switchboard is usually provided with hybrid systems.

PBX systems   Private Branch Exchange, or PBX, systems are telephone exchanges serving an individual organization and having direct connections to a public telephone exchange. They are used in offices that require over a hundred telephones. PBX systems include a central console where an operator answers incoming calls. Direct dialing to a specific extension is also available. PBX systems are either analog or digital in design; analog systems are designed primarily for voice transmission, while digital systems also allow for high-speed data and facsimile transmission and teleconferencing services.

SPECIAL FEATURES OF TELEPHONE SYSTEMS

The wide variety of telephone systems on the market and the many special features they offer provide an opportunity for selecting a system that best suits your company's needs. Stored-program electronic switching and the use of computers and detailed message accounting techniques enable these systems to offer a wide range of features and options. Along with the standard inbound and outbound direct dialing, an office telephone system may incorporate any of the following special features:

Abbreviated (speed) dialing   This enables you to program your telephone to accept a short numeric code in place of dialing the full telephone number. Some systems allow systemwide speed dialing for all users.

Automatic call back   With this feature, the caller is informed whenever a certain office phone that was previously busy is now free. On first finding that the line is busy, the caller must dial a code before hanging up the phone; as soon as the called phone is no longer busy the caller's telephone rings, and when the caller picks up the telephone the called party's telephone will automatically ring.

Call detail reporting   This cost and management system automatically records information—the number called and the call's duration—for every call placed through the company's telephone system.

Call forwarding   This feature automatically reroutes incoming calls from one number to another, once you have dialed a forwarding code and the forwarding number.

Call pick-up   This enables you to answer an incoming call directed to another telephone.

Call transfer   With this feature you may transfer an incoming or outgoing call to another party without the assistance of an operator.

Camp on busy   This allows the calling party to be put on hold until the called party hangs up, and then have his or her call automatically placed through. A short tone on the called party's line may notify him or her that a call is waiting.

Centralized attendant service   This system permits PBX systems serving several locations to be answered at a single location.

Conference call   This option allows the telephone user to add a third party in the middle of a conversation without the assistance of an operator.

Least-cost routing   This feature automatically routes outgoing long-distance calls through the PBX to the least-expensive long-distance carrier or trunk group and steps the call up to the second-least-expensive route when the primary routes are busy.

Outgoing trunk queuing   With this queuing feature, a call dialed when all outgoing trunks are busy will automatically be put through as soon as a trunk is free.

Remote access to PBX system   This allows callers to dial a telephone number and authorization code from any telephone outside the PBX system and gain access to designated trunks within the PBX system for outgoing calls.

Traffic analysis   This feature automatically gathers trunk loading statistics to assist in determining the number of facilities needed to handle the call load of a company or department.

Telegraphic Services

Telegraphic services are quickly being replaced by fax machines and overnight courier services. However, many of them still may be useful in specific situations. Telegraphic services include telegrams, cablegrams, Mailgrams, Priority Letters, and telex services. Telex services are still used by many international businesses when the telex itself can serve as a document or where phone systems are not modernized enough to handle fax transmissions reliably.

All of these telegraphic services are available through Western Union. If you do not have a telex machine, Western Union will send a telex for you. Many local companies also offer these services; they can be found in the Yellow Pages.

If your company uses telexes frequently, it may have a telex machine. If the company receives telexes only occasionally, you may want to set up your fax machine to receive telexes. The major long-distance companies have telex and electronic-mail services that allow for this capability.

You can also send telegrams, cablegrams, Mailgrams, and Priority Letters from a computer if you have telex and electronic-mail service from a major service provider.

Telegrams, cablegrams, Mailgrams, and Priority Letters   Each of these four types of messages can be sent by either going directly to your local Western Union office or phoning in your message.

Telegrams, more commonly used in the past, are still used to some extent today. Telegrams can be sent almost anywhere in the continental United States within a few hours.

Cablegrams   Cablegrams are international telegrams, which can be sent to almost every country in the world. If the company you are sending to has a registered cable code, use that code as the cablegram address.

Mailgrams   The Mailgram was developed jointly by Western Union and the U.S. Postal Service. A Mailgram can be sent anywhere in the United States, Puerto Rico, Guam, the U.S. Virgin Islands, or Canada. Mailgrams are usually delivered in the next business day's mail. A business reply envelope can be included in a Mailgram to ensure a quick response.

Priority Letters   A Priority Letter is a lower-cost alternative to a Mailgram. It can be sent anywhere in the continental United States within two days. There are also services that can deliver hundreds or thousands of Mailgrams or Priority Letters.

Telex   There are two kinds of telex services, domestic and international. Domestic telexes, those sent only within the United States, are used very rarely; most telex transmissions today are international.

Most telex numbers include an *answerback,* a code (usually an alphanumeric sequence that repeats the telex number and adds an abbreviation of the country or the company name) that the receiving system sends back when it accepts the telex message. Thus, if you include an answerback as part of the telex address, you can be sure when you have reached the right telex number.

All international telex calls require a country code, which precedes the telex number. These serve the same purpose as telephone country codes but are not identical to them. A list of telex country codes should be available from your telex service company.

If you do not know the telex number of a company you want to reach, call your telex service company.

An international telex or cablegram message may contain uppercase letters, numbers, and the following punctuation only: period, colon, comma, apostrophe or single quotation mark, hyphen, parentheses, and slash.

The Electronic Office

Today's office is steadily acquiring new technologies for high-speed communications. Most offices now have facsimile (fax) machines, and many are using different forms of electronic mail. Local area networks (LANs) are linking office computers, allowing users to share software and data files within an office. Wide area networks (WANs) and other public and private data networks are linking companies over large distances. The electronic office can save time and increase productivity, but it also requires that you keep up with rapidly changing technology.

FACSIMILE (FAX) MACHINES

Facsimile, or fax, machines are almost as common in businesses today as telephones. For certain kinds of material, they have replaced overnight couriers, first-class mail, local messengers, and even the telephone as the means of choice for communicating rapidly.

Fax machines work by scanning your document and creating a digitized "bit map" of the information. That information is then sent over telephone lines, and the receiving fax machine prints a copy of the image by reading the digitized map.

When a fax machine calls up another fax machine, they go through a process called "training" or "handshaking." The sending machine also typically prints out a company identification (if it has been programmed into the machine), along with the time, date, and page number, and these appear as headers on each page.

Here are several suggestions for preparing and sending documents by fax:

1. Prepare a cover sheet. It should include the name of the recipient and the number of pages being sent. (The cover sheet itself will usually be included in the number of pages.) If the recipient is in a large organization, it is useful to include his or her department and personal phone number. You should also include your company's fax number and the sender's name and phone number, so that the recipient can call if the fax is not received clearly or pages are missing. If your company does not have a cover sheet form for sending faxes, it would be very useful to create one. See the sample cover sheet in Fig. 13.2.

Fig. 13.2   Fax Cover Sheet

Facsimile Transmission

Merriam
Webster

Merriam Webster Inc.

47 Federal Street   Fax: 413-731-5979
P.O. Box 281   Telephone: 413-734-3134
Springfield, MA 01102   Telex: 981608 (MWEBSTER)

Company:	FAX #:
Attention:	
From:	
Number of pages (including this page):	Date:
Please let us know if all pages are NOT received	

Message:

2. Number the pages you are sending. This will make it easier for the recipient to make sure he or she has received all of the pages. Also, since some fax machines just drop received pages on a table or floor, numbering the pages will help the recipient put the received document in the correct order.

3. If you are concerned about the clarity of the received document—especially if there is small type, pictures, or graphics—you may want to test the transmittal quality by using the machine's copy function before you send your document. Most fax machines allow you to produce a copy of your document that will match the quality of the image that will arrive at the receiving fax machine. If the document you are sending is not clear, you may want to send it in "Fine" mode, available on most fax machines. Documents scanned in finer detail take two to three times longer to transmit.

4. Do not use colored paper or other color on a document without first testing it with the copy function. Even transparent highlighters can block out type.

5. Do not use correction tape or correction fluid, since this may damage your fax machine. If either has been used on the original, photocopy it and use the copy in the fax machine.

6. Make sure you have removed any staples or paper clips before sending your document.

7. If your document is of an irregular size, make a photocopy of it to insert in the machine. The receiving fax machine should, however, be able to accommodate both letter- and legal-size pages.

8. If you have to send more than three to five pages, stay at the fax machine until all the pages are sent. Stack the pages loosely in the machine. You may

carefully add several pages to your stack after the first few pages have been sent; however, never add more pages when the last page is in process. If you are sending a particularly long fax (more than 10–12 pages), you may want to break up the document into more than one transmission. If so, clearly explain what you are doing on the first cover sheet, and include subsequent cover sheets that repeat the explanation.

When you receive a fax, you should check to see that you have received all the pages and that they are readable. If there are pages missing or if some of the document is unreadable, the sender should be notified immediately. You can either place the call yourself or ask the recipient in your organization whether he or she wants to call. Always make sure received faxes are delivered quickly; faxes should be handled with the same urgency as telephone messages.

Faxes printed on thermal paper fade in a few months and become difficult, if not impossible, to read. Thus, if a received fax on thermal paper needs to be filed, you should copy it first. (If your fax machine prints on ordinary paper, you will not need to copy received faxes.)

Many fax machines can prestore commonly used fax numbers, and many will also automatically redial a number if it is busy. (Even when using these features, however, always check the number displayed.)

When sending an international fax, remember that the country you are dialing is probably in a different time zone. Many companies turn off their fax machines at night; thus, if you are having trouble reaching an international fax number, try dialing it during the normal business hours of that country.

You may be able to send faxes from a computer. Some companies have installed "fax boards" in their computers, so that once a document is typed it can be sent directly from the computer.

If you frequently need to send the same fax to many locations, you will want to use the "fax broadcast" feature available on many fax machines.

If you work for an employer who travels frequently, remember that most hotels have a fax machine with which guests can send and receive faxes. You can find out if a hotel offers this service, and the fax phone number, by calling the hotel directly. If you have had trouble reaching your employer by phone, you can even send your own messages to the hotel fax machine.

If you do not have a fax machine, you can use a fax service company. Look in the Yellow Pages under "Facsimile Transmission Service." Most will allow you to both send and receive faxes at their locations. They will typically call you when a fax has arrived for you, and you must then go and pick it up. Make sure that anyone who sends you a fax clearly indicates your name, company, and phone number on the fax.

When the information being sent is confidential, you will need to use your judgment about using a fax machine for delivery, since many fax machines are shared. If you are concerned, you should ask your employer. An alternative means of delivery, such as overnight courier, may be better. One possible method is to ask the recipient to stand by the receiving fax machine as you are sending the document to be sure that it is not seen by others. Some companies have "executive" fax machines or other fax machines that are specially monitored.

ELECTRONIC MAIL

Electronic mail (E-mail) provides a means of data communications between computers. Electronic mail can be on private systems or public networks, or be specialized for a particular function such as Electronic Data Interchange (EDI).

Some of the key characteristics of the various types of electronic-mail systems are explained in the following pages.

Private electronic-mail systems   Many larger companies have electronic-mail systems as part of their computer systems. Some electronic-mail systems are on LANs, while others are on minicomputer or mainframe computer systems.

Electronic-mail systems let users send messages created on their computers to one or more electronic "mailboxes" belonging to other individuals in the company that have access to the mail system. A system administrator is usually responsible for registering system users and for maintaining the system, and he or she should be able to teach new users how to use the system and provide a directory of companywide mailbox addresses.

If you are an electronic-mail user, you will usually have a sign-on identification code as well as a mailbox address. Often the mailbox address will be your name or a code similar to your name. You should check your mailbox periodically to see if you have received an electronic message. When sending a message for your employer, you may need to use his or her sign-on identification. If you use your own sign-on identification to send a message for your employer, be very clear in the message about who it is from, since many mail systems will automatically attach the name of the person whose sign-on identification is being used to the message itself. If someone has asked you to read his or her mailbox, you must sign on as that individual. Make sure you transfer or save the mailbox messages to a computer file or printer.

Many private electronic-mail systems can only be used at one location. However, in large companies the electronic mail systems can usually be networked over a variety of communications avenues so that employees in different parts of the country or the world can communicate with each other. Some private electronic-mail systems are also linked into public electronic-mail systems so that users can have access to individuals outside of their company.

Public electronic-mail systems   There are several major providers of electronic-mail systems in the United States, including AT&T, MCI, Sprint, and CompuServe. These systems provide electronic mail through your office computer. If you are connected through a minicomputer or a mainframe computer to one of these public systems, the technical division within your company will have made all the connections for you.

You will need communications software and a modem to equip a personal computer to use a public electronic-mail system. You can obtain such communications software from your electronic-mail provider or use one of several available brands. A modem is needed to enable your computer to dial up the electronic-mail system so that it can connect with the host computer.

Most public electronic-mail systems can send not only electronic messages but also telexes, messages to fax machines, and computer letters that are delivered through the postal service. Through AT&T you may also send telegrams, cablegrams, Mailgrams, and Priority Letters.

When you send a message through public electronic-mail service, you should be able to obtain notification that the message was delivered. The service should also provide you with a daily summary report of sent messages.

You should not assume that you can send a regular word-processing file through an electronic-mail system, since it could only be read by someone with the same word-processing program. Instead, you must send what are known as *ASCII* ("as-key") or *text files*. You create an ASCII or text file by taking the document you have created in your word-processing program and following the procedures found in your word-processing manual for saving documents as ASCII or text files. (This has the added advantage of eliminating style and formatting from the file.)

However, some electronic-mail systems will let you send word-processing or other computer files such as spreadsheets. This type of service is called File Transfer. File Transfer should only be used when the recipient of the file has the same kind of application program. You would not use this method for sending regular messages, but only for sending a document that another individual needed to work on. This process is the equivalent of giving a file on a disk to another individual to work on.

When you receive messages in a mailbox, you can save them in a computer file or by printing them out. If you want to edit the file in your word-processing program, you will have to consult your word-processing manual on how to edit an ASCII or text file.

There are many private and public electronic-mail systems available, each of which was designed independently. The result is that it may be difficult for these systems to "talk" to each other. During the 1980s, an international committee devised a set of rules to enable electronic-mail systems to interconnect with each other by using the same technical rules or "protocols." As more private and public electronic-mail systems start using these interfaces, electronic mail will become more far-reaching.

The same international committee realized that if a truly universal electronic-mail network was to become a reality, electronic-mail users would need to know who has electronic mailboxes and what their addresses are. Accordingly, it devised a set of rules for creating an automated directory of all electronic-mail addresses.

Unfortunately, a universal directory has not actually been developed yet. For the most part, you still must get mailbox addresses directly from the individuals with whom you want to communicate. Some public electronic-mail users are starting to put their mailbox addresses on their business cards. If your public electronic-mail service does not provide an on-line directory to its subscribers, you may be able to call the service for directory information.

EDI   Electronic Data Interchange, or EDI, is a specialized form of electronic mail, most commonly used for orders, order acknowledgments, invoices, and payments. EDI is based on a set of rules created by national and international committees to allow groups doing business together to automate the ordering process.

Without EDI, most manufacturing or distribution and retail companies generate a flow of paperwork that gets input into different computers. There is paperwork involved in creating an order, shipping an order, creating an invoice, and acknowledging payment, and much of the information on these forms—the invoice number, the item being ordered, the recipient of the order, and so on—is repeated. EDI systems allow this information to be input directly into a local computer and then sent to other computers for processing. Since common information does not have to be input again, both time and money are saved. The EDI process relies on special software to handle the EDI electronic forms and a specialized communications carrier to transmit the data over a network.

DATA NETWORKS
There are a variety of public and private networks designed to support the transmission of data. The following are some of the more common data networks used by businesses.

Packet-switching networks Telephone networks are primarily designed for voice transmission, although they are able to carry data as well. Packet-switching, or X.25, networks were designed for data transmission only. These networks divide data into small packets, each consisting of a header (stating the node and connection point to which the packet is to be delviered), the data itself, an error-detection mechanism, and an end-of-packet identifier. Computers connected to packet networks have both a network identifier and a network address.

Wide area networks Wide area networks, or WANs, are set up privately, usually to provide high-speed data transmission within a company that has several locations while bypassing the telephone networks. Most of these networks are based on satellite communications. Telephone companies, however, are beginning to offer switched data channels at very high speeds, using a technology called *wideband* or *broadband switching*.

Local area networks (LANs) LANs, as mentioned earlier, are internal networks that connect personal computers within a company location, usually by means of cables. The LAN systems are installed on centralized personal computers called *servers*. They permit the personal computers that are connected to share a range of resources, including software, high-speed laser printers, high-speed hard disks for storage, and communications links via shared modems to other LANs or mainframe computers. In this way, high-quality and often costly resources can be used by many employees within a company.

Many software companies provide LAN versions of their software; a company can thus buy a single copy for their LAN system, and all users can have access to it. In some cases, users can work on the same database file at the same time, thereby efficiently dividing the work load of updating a large database file. With a LAN, all users within a company can have the advantages of high-quality printers. If more than one user wants to print at the same time, the LAN will create a print queue, whereby the next document waiting in line will automatically start printing when the first is finished. Electronic mail, for easy user-to-user message sending, is also a frequent feature on LANs.

Most organizations with LANs have an LAN administrator, who handles the technical problems involved in installing and operating the system and is also usually responsible for connecting computers to the LAN and registering LAN users.

Simpler systems—sometimes called *peer-to-peer networks*—can be put together on a very small scale to link two, three, or four individuals, and printer-sharing devices are widely used. An employee with an amateur talent for computers can often organize such simple networks.

CHAPTER 14

Basic Accounting and Bookkeeping Systems

This chapter will introduce you to the features of various record-keeping systems in use today. A general understanding of accounting and bookkeeping terminology will help you to assist the executive in managing the operations of the firm. You may be called upon to type financial reports, proofread reports produced by others, or set up systems or documents to record important transactions. These records or reports are maintained and produced using sophisticated computer programs, other data-processing operations, and, particularly in small firms, various manual bookkeeping systems.

This chapter will guide you through some of these systems. An appropriate place to begin is to look at modern automated applications often used today. Once you are familiar with the available equipment and associated technology, you will be prepared to deal with the multitude of reports, statements, and forms that it can generate.

Automated Accounting

The terms *automation* and *data processing* are often used interchangeably. They both refer to the systematic handling of business information with a minimum of manual involvement. You will be involved in the gathering of the data that will enter the system, referred to as *input,* and the processing of the data produced by the system, known as *output.* Once data are retrieved from the system, a variety of facts will be available to present to management for speedy decision making.

DATA PROCESSING

It is likely that you will deal with programmers, computer operators, data-entry specialists, word-processing department personnel, and systems analysts at one time or another. Therefore, you should be familiar with basic computer technology and the various possible types of input and output.

With the help of data-processing equipment, insurance companies can review millions of insurance policies overnight for appropriate billing and updating the next morning, and can process claims and remit appropriate payments to policyholders with minimum loss. Large corporations can handle payrolls for thousands of employees within a matter of hours. Airlines can process passengers with minimal delay, including ticketing, seat selection, and baggage handling. Department stores can track cash collections, inventory merchandise, and generate purchase and sales data for individual departments and units.

Complex automated machinery capable of processing millions of transactions with impressive speed and accuracy is thus available. With so much information available, you must be able to decide how to use it for maximum efficiency.

The use of computers in business today is extremely widespread. However, computer technology is also expensive, and it has taken some time for smaller firms to equip themselves; thus, you may still encounter some older forms of data processing. The most common of the older systems still used today are the following:

1. *Automated data processing (ADP)*   Data are processed by automatically operated mechanical or electronic equipment.
2. *Integrated data processing (IDP)*   Equipment such as accounting machines and typewriters are provided with special attachments to transfer data to magnetic tape for further processing.
3. *Keypunch machine*   Data are processed by the use of punch cards on equipment that can sort, count, merge, select, match, duplicate, perform arithmetic operations, and generate printed reports. It often takes a second machine or group of machines to perform such operations as sorting, verifying, interpreting, and printing.

COMPUTERS

Though computers are discussed at length in Chapter 5, the following review will serve as an introduction to their role in accounting and bookkeeping.

The older forms of data-processing equipment are generally being replaced by electronic data processing (EDP) systems. Such systems involve computers, which offer the most advanced means of processing data. These machines perform arithmetic and decision-making operations at tremendous speeds and with great accuracy and can provide executives with up-to-the-minute reports in attractive formats.

Hardware   A computer system has the following capacities:

> **Input**   Converts information from punch cards, magnetic tapes, or disks into a form for computer processing. Terminals containing keyboard equipment are also used as input devices in interactive systems. These are systems in which a terminal located either close to or distant from a computer is used to communicate with that computer. Computer personnel refer to this process as on-line data processing.

Control	Interprets instructions and directs all computer operations.
Storage	Retains instructions and data.
Arithmetic	Adds, subtracts, multiplies, divides, and compares; selects the sequence of processing operations.
Output	Provides results of operations in the form of printed reports and documents or as data on punch cards, magnetic tape, magnetic disks, microfiche, and cathode-ray tubes.

Software   This term is used to describe the instructions that guide a computer. There are four kinds of software:

Disk operating systems	These systems coordinate the interaction between the hardware and other software, including the transfer of information and data between the memory in the system unit (internal memory) and the disk drives (external memory).
Computer program languages	Programs are written in a variety of ways, but computers must convert these forms into their own languages. Examples of program languages are COBOL (Common Business Oriented Language), FORTRAN (Formula Translation), BASIC (Beginner's All-purpose Symbolic Instruction Code), and RPG (Report Program Generator). COBOL and RPG are used widely for business purposes.
Operating environments	Operating environments are programs that change the way an individual interacts with the computer. These programs provide easy-to-use screen displays that allow users to link various programs or work on several projects at one time.
Application programs	Application programs include word processing, spreadsheets, database-management programs, accounting programs, special publishing programs, and programs that provide the user with options to change graphics and special design.

The personal-computer keyboard   In order to use the personal-computer applications just discussed, you need to be able to get the information into the computer. The primary method of doing so is by using a keyboard, which is set up much like a typewriter keyboard. You will see a few familiar keys:

Enter (Return) key	This key may be used to start a new line of text, but is used primarily to enter instructions into the computer.
Shift key	This key works just as it does on the typewriter. You can use it to type capital letters or the upper symbols on dual-use keys (such as $, %, :, and &) and other punctuation and symbols.
Tab key	This key serves the same purpose as it does on the typewriter.

Less familiar may be the 10-key numeric keypad, arrow keys, and function keys:

Number Lock key	When you press this key in the On position, the 10 keys on the right of the keyboard become available to enter numbers and perform calculator functions.

Arrow keys	When the Number Lock key is in the Off position, these keys move the cursor around on the screen.
Cursor	Wherever this blinking mark is positioned is where the next character you type will appear.
Backspace key	You can use this key to correct errors.
Function keys	Function keys change their function for each application and provide a fast way to accomplish various tasks. You will find them to be remarkable in what they can do to save you time.
Control (Ctrl) key and Escape (Esc) key	These keys, like the function keys, serve many purposes depending on the software you are using.

Spreadsheets   A spreadsheet, sometimes called an electronic worksheet, consists of a grid with rows and columns. Spreadsheets are used especially when compiling the potential effect of varying decisions. When you change individual values, the effects of the change are automatically calculated throughout the spreadsheet in each programmed column and row throughout the spreadsheet. A sample spreadsheet is illustrated in Fig. 14.1.

Fig. 14.1   Spreadsheet

	A	B	C	D	E	F	G
1							
2			ABC CORPORATION				
3			SALES ANALYSIS - TOTAL DOLLARS				
4							
5							
6		YEAR 1	YEAR 2	YEAR 3	YEAR 4	YEAR 5	
7							
8	EASTERN DIVISION	646,185	634,324	672,885	381,384	805,629	
9							
10	CENTRAL DIVISION	551,265	452,695	100,258	365,985	258,741	
11							
12	WESTERN DIVISION	652,145	352,147	258,147	265,987	258,965	
13							
14	TOTAL	1,849,595	1,439,166	1,031,290	1,013,356	1,323,335	

There are several factors to consider when selecting a spreadsheet program:

- *Functions*   A spreadsheet program should contain the functions that will match the user's needs.
- *Speed*   The speed of the calculations of a worksheet is an essential consideration.
- *Capacity*   Newer features such as WYSIWYG, which add to the amount of information that can be accessed by a user, are being developed constantly.
- *Output*   The quality of the output from a spreadsheet program is critical to the neatness and presentability of information.
- *Ease of learning/use*   In general, the more recently a spreadsheet program was created, the easier it is to learn. However, the ability to learn a new program depends on the individual, and a prospective user should thoroughly sample a spreadsheet before deciding whether or not to purchase it.

- *Graphics*   Since graphs are an excellent way to illustrate a point, the graph features of a spreadsheet program should enable the user to quickly set up a graph in any section of the spreadsheet.
- *Price*   The cost of spreadsheet programs do not vary that much, so it should not be the most important consideration. More important than price is efficiency: a spreadsheet that is user-friendly and highly efficient is worth its weight in gold.
- *Hardware and software requirements*   The user should investigate how much support is needed for the system to adapt to and handle a new spreadsheet program.

AUTOMATION AS AN AID TO PROFESSIONALS

The ability of computers to retrieve information quickly makes them valuable tools for attorneys, physicians, engineers, educators, and other professionals. Enormous quantities of information can be stored in miniature devices for ready access in printed form. This contrasts sharply with conventional filing systems, which require much space and equipment and expensive clerical time.

SPECIAL EQUIPMENT

Accounting and calculating machines, as well as computer terminals that resemble typewriters and are usually attached to a monitor for viewing, can be provided with attachments to create tapes as by-products of their operations. Teleprinters and teletypewriters are console printers that transmit messages— including handwritten messages—over long distances.

SERVICE BUREAUS

Small and medium-sized firms that do not have computers may contract with service bureaus to process their records. This may be less expensive than owning or renting a computer. Service bureaus provide reports, statements, and documents promptly in whatever form is stipulated.

TIME SHARING

Because computers can be very expensive, some firms purchase time from computer owners instead of purchasing or leasing their own equipment. Other companies may require computer time that their own overburdened computers cannot provide. Time sharing may be desirable for the time seller as well as the time buyer, because it provides income during periods when the computer is not being utilized.

Data Processing with Computers and Calculators

The term *data processing* is not limited to computer programs, expensive equipment, and reports printed on special paper. The daily typewriting and routine arithmetic calculations performed in offices are also forms of data processing. This section describes the calculating machines that you will find in typical offices to process data.

Most desk calculators perform only arithmetic operations: addition, subtraction, multiplication, and division. Other calculating machines may be quite complex: they can perform both arithmetic and logical operations, and they may have the ability to store and retrieve data from machine-readable files. Many of today's calculators are, in fact, nearly indistinguishable from small computers. The major differences between computers and electronic calculators are that computers have larger memories, the ability to make decisions and branch to alternative programs, and the ability to repeat operations a controlled number of times.

ELECTRONIC CALCULATORS

Electronic calculators are much smaller and faster than their predecessors, the manual and electric adding machines. They enable you to perform rapidly all arithmetic functions as well as sequential operations, which are often stored in the calculator's memory. Some calculators print on paper tape while standard models display figures on a digital-readout window.

Electronic printing calculators   Printing calculators are useful for accounting purposes when complex addition or multiplication problems must be verified for accuracy. Electronic printing calculators have a 10-key numeric keyboard for entering the values 0 through 9; numbers and totals are printed on a paper tape. Some models have a digital display window as well. Separate keys are available for the four basic arithmetic functions. Many calculators have additional function keys that allow such operations as the automatic calculation of percentages and square roots. A separate key may facilitate chain arithmetic operations, such as repeated multiplications with different multiplicands. An additional key will allow a constant value to be stored in the machine's memory in order that it can be used in separate calculations.

Electronic display calculators   The electronic display calculator has a digital-readout window for displaying numbers and totals, but no printing capability. Numbers are displayed as they are entered, and totals are displayed as they are calculated. Since the display calculator provides no audit tape or printed record, the operator can only verify these values one by one on the display window. The display calculator is similar in most other respects to the printing calculator. Display calculators are usually less expensive than printing calculators and have few moving parts, resulting in fewer service calls and lower maintenance costs. The low cost of these machines often makes it more economical to discard a broken one than to have it repaired. While the printing calculator usually draws its power from a standard electrical outlet, most display calculators use standard or rechargeable batteries.

Programmable electronic calculators   A programmable calculator can store a complex program in its memory and be directed by a series of instructions to perform sequential calculations automatically. You merely feed the instructions into the calculator, enter any values required, and start the calculation series. These instructions are often called a program. Programs may be recorded on strips of magnetic tape, which are inserted into the calculator whenever the program is required. The use of a program relieves the operator from having to make several repeated calculations in a logical sequence.

Calculator vendors usually have "libraries" containing several routines or programs commonly used in business. In fact, the library often comes with the calculator at no additional cost. Additional programs are available for a small fee. Customized programs designed especially for particular office operations may also be acquired from most vendors. A common arrangement provides for a specific number of customized programs to be delivered with the calculator and additional programs to be prepared at a later date for a specific fee. Some business offices have staff members who are able to write programs for these calculators.

Common features of electronic calculators   In addition to its 10 number keys and its function keys for the four basic arithmetic functions, all electronic calculators contain a number of other keys.

All electronic calculators have a memory, divided into three separate parts: (1) keyboard memory, (2) operating memory, and (3) storage memory. The keyboard memory (sometimes called *keyboard register*) contains the number entered from the keyboard. The operating memory handles addition, subtraction, multiplication, and division. The storage memory retains data that may be recalled in the future.

The following keys, found on most calculators, may be used to make changes in numbers stored in these three memory registers:

Clear Entry (CE)	This key is used to erase a number entered in error. It will erase any number entered into the machine if it is depressed before striking the arithmetic function key.
Clear Memory (CM, MC)	This key erases only the storage memory.
Clear (C)	The Clear key normally erases the keyboard and operating memories but not the storage memory. However, on a calculator that does not have a Clear All key, this key will erase all three sections of memory.
Clear All (CA)	This key will erase the keyboard, operating, and storage memories. It should be depressed before beginning each new calculation in order to clear all previous totals and numbers from the calculator.
Memory Plus (M+)	This key will add the number entered on the keyboard to whatever value is in the storage memory.
Memory Minus (M−)	This key will subtract the number entered on the keyboard from the value in the memory.
Memory Recall (MR, RM)	This function recalls the value in the storage memory in order that it may be displayed or used in an arithmetic calculation, without changing or erasing the value.
Total (T, =, *)	This key will cause the total to be displayed or printed.

The following function keys execute complete calculations:

Round Off (R/O)	This key will round off calculated answers to a selected decimal position. Some calculators have a Round Off switch that may be set to round off all calculations; others have a key for rounding off a given figure.
Constant (K)	The Constant key permits the calculator to use a given value in separate arithmetic operations, usually for repeated multiplication or division. An example is the calculation of a chain of discounts when each discount is identical (5%—5%—5%).
Percent (%)	The Percent key will either give you your answer as a percentage rather than a decimal fraction (e.g., $2 \div 5 = 40\%$, rather than .4) or calculate a percentage relationship and give the answer as a non-percentage (e.g., $60 \times 5\% = 3$).
Percent of Change (% CHG)	This key is usually found only on large calculators. If you enter the base number, depress the Percent-of-Change key, and then enter a second number, the calcu-

lator will automatically show both the amount of change and the percent of change between the base number and the second number.

Some calculator keyboards may have as many as 10 function keys, each of which will automatically perform arithmetic calculations or sequential processing steps that are frequently used in business offices. One example of such a program is the calculation of a number of different chain discounts. A long series of discounts can be recorded as a program, and the entire program can be used by merely pressing one function key. Another example of a program initiated by a function key is the calculation of payroll values. The payroll program can be stored on a cassette tape, and the individual function keys can be used to calculate overtime pay, withholding tax, and Social Security tax. Each deduction requires several arithmetic steps, which the program automatically carries out in the proper sequence.

Verification of arithmetic   Since it is so easy to press the wrong key when entering numbers, you should always verify all your arithmetic. The paper output tape produced by printing calculators makes verification easy by listing each entry as well as the total; many printing calculators will also print a sign representing the arithmetic function applied to each entry. Verifying a calculator's paper tape simply involves comparing each entry on the tape with the number you intended to enter and checking off each correct entry. Verifying arithmetic on a display calculator requires that you repeat the entire input procedure until at least two consecutive final totals are identical.

Hand position for the numeric keyboard   Since you will often have to enter many numbers into a calculator, your operating speed is important. Practice will help anyone develop the skill necessary for touch operation of the keyboard. Like typewriters, calculators have a "home row," with the index, middle, and ring fingers resting on the 4, 5, and 6 keys. The 5 key normally contains a bump or depression to assist in locating the home row by touch. Each of the fingers moves independently from its home-row position straight up to reach the top row of keys and straight down to reach the bottom row. The thumb is used for the zero key.

The numeric keypad on the computer   When you have a computer at your desk, there is little need for a separate calculator. When the Num Lock key is in the On position, you can use the 10-key numeric keypad on the right side of the keyboard to enter numbers and perform all the functions of a calculator. However, if you fail to turn on the Num Lock key, the keys will serve different functions or move the cursor, and you could find yourself typing on the wrong area of your worksheet. Save your data regularly so as to avoid needless destruction of this kind.

Rounding numbers   Most calculators are designed so that any calculated answer completely fills a memory register, often providing an answer with more numbers than are needed by the operator. Thus, an eight-digit-calculator will calculate answers to eight digits, regardless of the operator's need. Some calculators automatically suppress terminal zeros to the right of the decimal point, even though they are calculated and retained in the machine's memory.

When a calculator rounds off numbers through use of the R/O key or switch, it goes through essentially the same process that you can perform without a calculator:

1. Delete all digits beyond four decimal places.
2. When the rightmost, or *test*, digit is 5 or more, add 1 to the digit immediately to its left.
3. Discard the test digit.
4. Repeat steps 2 and 3.

Problem	Round 457.75614 to two decimal places (i.e., two places to the right of the decimal point, or hundredths).	
Solution	1. Delete the digits beyond four decimal places.	457.7561
	2. Since the test digit (1) is less than 5, do not change the digit to its left.	
	3. Delete the test digit.	457.756
	4. Since the new test digit (6) is larger than 5, add 1 to the digit to its left. Discard the test digit. Your answer is:	457.76
Problem	Round $756.42276 to the nearest cent.	
Solution	1. Delete the digits beyond four decimal places.	756.4227
	2. Since the test digit (7) is greater than 5, add 1 to the digit to its left.	756.4237
	3. Delete the test digit.	756.423
	4. Since the new test digit (3) is less than 5, do not change the digit to its left. Discard the test digit. Your answer is:	756.42

CALCULATING PERCENTAGES

Business mathematics employs percentages rather than fractions in expressing relationships between numbers. A percentage is a fraction expressed in hundredths; for example, $1/2 = 50/100 = 50\% = .50$. A few commonly used business fractions with their decimal equivalents are shown in the table on page 481. Invoices typically show a percentage of the total amount due as deductible for prompt payment. Examples of common business discount percentages with their decimal equivalents are shown in the table on page 482. This table also includes the *complement* of each decimal equivalent. The use of complements in calculating chain discounts is explained on pages 482–83.

Calculating a simple percentage   The percentage relationship can be calculated electronically by pressing the % key on your calculator rather than the = key after entering a problem. Percentage can be calculated mentally in the following way:

Percentage Amount = Base Number × Percentage

Problem	What is 9% of $647?	
Solution	1. Convert 9% to a decimal by simply placing a decimal point two places from the right (.09).	
	2. Multiply the base number by the decimal percentage ($647 × .09). Your answer is:	$58.23

Table of Common Fractions with Decimal Equivalents

Fraction	Decimal equivalent	Fraction	Decimal equivalent	Fraction	Decimal equivalent
½	.5	⅟₇	.1429	⅟₁₂	.0833
		²⁄₇	.2857	⁵⁄₁₂	.4167
⅓	.3333	³⁄₇	.4286	⁷⁄₁₂	.5833
⅔	.6667	⁴⁄₇	.5714	¹¹⁄₁₂	.9167
		⁵⁄₇	.7143		
¼	.25	⁶⁄₇	.8571	⅟₁₆	.0625
¾	.75			³⁄₁₆	.1875
		⅛	.125	⁵⁄₁₆	.3125
⅕	.2	⅜	.375	⁷⁄₁₆	.4375
⅖	.4	⅝	.625	⁹⁄₁₆	.5625
⅗	.6	⅞	.875	¹¹⁄₁₆	.6875
⅘	.8			¹³⁄₁₆	.8125
		⅑	.1111	¹⁵⁄₁₆	.9375
⅙	.1667	²⁄₉	.2222		
⅚	.8333	⁴⁄₉	.4444		
		⁵⁄₉	.5556		
		⁷⁄₉	.7778		
		⁸⁄₉	.8889		

Calculating the percentage of change   Sometimes it is important to know the percentage that represents the relationship between two amounts. This relationship is called the *change* or *difference* between them. The following formula and examples may help illustrate this calculation, which can also be done by using the % CHG key on your calculator.

Percentage of Change = Amount of Change ÷ Base Amount

Problem	Profits last year were $5000; profits this year were $8500. What is the percentage representing the increase?	
Solution	1. Calculate the *amount* of change by subtracting the smaller from the larger ($8500 − $5000 = $3500).	
	2. Divide the amount of change by the base (first) amount ($3500 ÷ $5000).	.7
	3. Convert this figure into a percentage by moving the decimal point two places to the right. Profits increased by 70%.	70%
Problem	Sales last month were $1500; sales this month were $950. What is the percentage representing the decrease?	
Solution	1. Subtract the smaller figure from the larger ($1500 − $950 = $550).	
	2. Divide by the base amount ($550 ÷ $1500).	.3666
	3. Round off and convert into a percentage. Sales decreased by 37%.	37%

CALCULATING CHAIN DISCOUNTS

Discounts are normally expressed as percentages. A *chain discount* is a series of discounts which are calculated separately. Each discount in the chain (series) is applied to the remaining, reduced amount. The following example illustrates the procedure for calculating the net invoice amount after a chain of discounts has been applied to the beginning invoice amount.

Net Invoice Amount = Invoice Amount − (Invoice Amount × Discount)

Problem	Calculate the net invoice amount for a $1000 invoice with a 5%–3%–2% chain discount.	
Solution	1. Calculate 5% of the opening amount ($1000×.05 = $50), and subtract that figure from the opening amount ($1000 − $50).	$950
	2. Calculate 3% of the new figure ($950×.03 = $28.50) and subtract ($950 − $28.50).	$921.50
	3. Calculate 2% of this latest figure ($921.50×.02 = $18.43) and subtract ($921.50 − $18.43).	$903.07
	The net invoice amount is $903.07.	

Calculating chain discounts with reciprocals   You may prefer to combine chain discounts into a single value that may be multiplied by the invoice amount to obtain the net invoice amount. Using reciprocals (also called *complements*) can be helpful in this procedure.

A reciprocal is calculated by subtracting the discount percentage from 100 (or in decimal form, 1.00). For example, the reciprocal of 5% is 95% (100 − 5 = 95), and the reciprocal of .15 is .85 (1.00 − .15 = .85). The table below shows the reciprocals of several common discount amounts.

Chain discounts may be combined by multiplying discounts by each other in

Table of Representative Decimal Equivalents with Reciprocals

Percent	Decimal equivalent	Reciprocal
.5 (½ of 1%)	.005	.995
1.0	.01	.99
2.0	.02	.98
2.5	.025	.975
3.0	.03	.97
4.0	.04	.96
5.0	.05	.95
7⅛	.071	.929
7¼	.073	.927
7½	.075	.925
7¾	.0775	.9225
10.0	.10	.90
12.0	.12	.88
12½	.125	.875
15.0	.15	.85
20.0	.20	.80
85.0	.85	.15
90.0	.90	.10

order to obtain a single discount, and then by applying the single discount to the invoice amount. The following example illustrates the use of reciprocals in combining chain discounts:

Net Invoice = (Reciprocal × Reciprocal) × Invoice Amount

Problem   An invoice for $500.00 provides for chain discounts of 10% and 5%. Calculate the net invoice amount.

Solution   1. Calculate, in decimal terms, the reciprocals of 10% (.90) and 5% (.95).
2. Multiply these two figures (.90 × .95 = .855).
3. Multiply the result by the invoice figure (.855 × $500). $427.50

The net invoice amount is $427.50.

CALCULATING MERCHANDISE MARKUP

The basic calculation for retail sales firms is the application of a markup percentage to either the cost or the selling price of merchandise. These two methods of calculating markup are usually designated as (1) calculating selling price with markup based on cost, and (2) calculating selling price with markup based on selling price.

Markup based on cost   This method of calculating the markup involves multiplying the cost of the merchandise by the markup percentage desired and then adding the calculated markup amount to the cost:

Selling price = Cost + (Markup percentage × Cost)

Problem   When an article costs the retailer $20 and the desired markup percentage is 40%, what is the selling price?

Solution   1. Calculate the markup by multiplying the retailer's cost by the decimal percentage ($20 × .40 = $8).
2. Add this figure to the original cost ($8 + $20). $28

The selling price is $28.

Markup based on selling price   This method of calculating the markup is somewhat more complicated. Since the selling price is 100% of the amount we wish to calculate, the cost to the retailer plus the markup must equal 100%. For example, if the markup is to be 40% of the selling price, then the cost must be 60% of the selling price: Selling price (100%) = Markup (40%) + Cost (60%). The selling price is determined by dividing the cost by its percentage relationship to the selling price (Selling price = Cost ÷ .60). The following example illustrates.

Selling price = Cost ÷ Cost's percentage of selling price
Markup = Selling price − Cost

Problem   When an article costs the retailer $30 and the desired markup is 20% of the *selling price,* what is the selling price?

Solution   1. Since the markup will be 20% of the selling price, the remaining percentage will represent the cost to the retailer (100% − 20% = 80%).
2. The selling price equals the cost to the retailer divided by the percentage of the selling price that this cost represents ($30 ÷ .80). $37.50

The selling price is $37.50.

Banking

Bank services include checking accounts, collection of notes, loans, and money orders. Business activities are so intertwined with banking that you must be aware of how these services are used by their firms. As a secretary, you will often be called on to perform such duties as writing checks, depositing funds, paying bills, and arranging travel finances.

CHECKING ACCOUNTS

A checking account is opened at a commercial bank upon deposit of funds and the completion of bank forms listing the bank's rules and regulations. A signature card must be completed containing the signature(s) of anyone empowered to sign checks for the firm. The depositor is known as the *drawer*, the bank is the *drawee*, and the company or individual to whom a check is made out is the *payee*. A check made out to "Cash" can be cashed by anyone in possession of it.

Ordinarily, banks do not pay interest on checking accounts. However, individuals, sole proprietorships, and partnerships (but not corporations) may open NOW checking accounts. These accounts earn the same interest as passbook savings accounts in most commercial banks. NOW accounts usually require the maintenance of minimum balances to avoid the imposition of service charges.

Deposit slips   Funds deposited in the bank are accompanied by a deposit slip in duplicate listing the types and amounts of money being deposited. This money may include coins, bills, checks, and money orders. Interest coupons may also be included. The duplicate is retained by the depositor after the bank has verified the deposit.

Checkbooks   A company's checkbook usually contains three checks to a page, with prenumbered stubs attached to the perforated prenumbered checks. Information about the check—date, payee, amount, and reason for the disbursement—is written on the stub before filling out the check, thus assuring a permanent record of the payment. In lieu of stubs, some checkbooks contain carbonized paper so that a copy of each check is made automatically when the check is written. In larger companies checks are printed by computers, which store information about the checks internally for quick reference.

Writing checks   Checks may be typed, printed, or written in ink. The signature should be written or printed in facsimile. Erasures and deletions are not permitted. If an error is made, the word "Void" should be written on both the stub and the check. The symbols at the bottom of the check are printed in magnetic ink; through the magnetic ink character recognition (MICR) system, computers process large numbers of checks quickly and efficiently. The MICR system is also used to process deposit slips, loan coupons, and other source documents used in banking. There are now computer software programs that are capable of writing each check and doing all related record-keeping simultaneously.

Voucher checks   Checks may be printed with attached stubs that contain information about the checks. The stubs (vouchers) are used by the payees for recording and reference purposes.

Overdrafts   Despite the best intentions, company checks may occasionally be written for sums greater than the amount on deposit. As a courtesy, the bank may honor an overdrawn check and ask the company to deposit sufficient funds to cover it. On the other hand, it may refuse to honor the check. Since this can cause embarrassment to the company, overdrafts should be treated seriously, and good relations with the bank should be cultivated. A dishonored check may be returned to the depositor with a bank notice indicating the reason for its return—usually "NSF" (Not Sufficient Funds). An overdrawn check may be redeposited if the depositor has accumulated sufficient funds to cover the check.

Stop payments   Should a depositor want to stop payment on an issued check, the bank must be notified immediately. Although a check may be stopped by telephoning the bank, the bank must receive a follow-up written request within 14 days or the stoppage will lapse. The bank cannot stop a check if it has already been cleared. Stop payments are usually requested on stolen or lost checks and on checks that contain errors.

Checkwriters   These machines write check amounts so that they are difficult to change. They also reduce the time it takes to write checks.

Check endorsements   In order to negotiate a check, the payee must endorse it on its reverse side. When endorsed *in blank,* only the payee's name appears as the endorsement. This may be done by a payee who is a private individual, but it is a dangerous practice because the bearer of the endorsed check can cash it or negotiate it further. A *full* or *special* endorsement contains the name of the company or person to whom the check is being given ("Pay to the order of Samuel Howard") followed by the original payee's signature. Only the new payee can negotiate the check further. A *restrictive* endorsement indicates the condition of endorsement and limits the negotiability of the check, such as "For Deposit Only—Jennifer Novatt." The words "For Deposit Only" followed by the payee's signature mean that the check is to be deposited in the payee's bank account and cannot be negotiated again. Checks made out to a business rather than to an individual must be deposited by the payee company and may not be cashed or negotiated. In all cases, it is advisable to write or stamp the depositor's account number below the endorsement. Banks encourage stamped endorsements and often provide signature stamps to their depositors.

BANK STATEMENTS AND BANK RECONCILIATIONS

Depositors receive monthly statements from their banks which indicate the previous month's beginning balance, deposits made and checks paid during that month, other charges or additions, and the ending balance. Because it is likely that certain transactions have not been entered on both the bank's and the depositor's books by the closing date of the statement, their respective end-of-period balances will not coincide. A *bank reconciliation statement* may have to be prepared, indicating the reasons for the disparity. The statement is prepared by the computer, an accountant, or a bookkeeper. Any discrepancies between the bank statement and the depositor's records should be reported to the bank immediately. Banks will send more frequent statements if a depositor requests them and if the volume of checks and deposits is large enough to justify them. For a fee, the bank will help in balancing the depositor's checkbook by providing an accurate record of accounts.

Canceled checks   These are checks that have been paid by the bank and are returned in the envelope containing the bank statement. Many banks are developing systems that eliminate the return of canceled checks, but they will supply them to depositors upon request.

Outstanding checks   If a depositor's check has not cleared the bank by the end of the previous month, it is considered outstanding. After a reasonable time, the depositor should trace the status of any outstanding check.

Deposits-in-transit   Depositors may enter receipt amounts in their records that do not reach the bank as deposits by the closing date of the bank statement and are therefore not included on the bank statement. Such deposits are said to be late or in transit.

Bank service charges   Banks may charge depositors for services such as the collection of notes and stop payments. These charges are listed on the bank statements. Banks also charge for the volume of canceled checks and deposits. However, these charges can be offset by the average balance maintained in the account; consequently, depositors with low average balances sustain charges while those with higher balances generally do not.

Bank memos   Deductions and additions indicated on bank statements are sometimes explained in debit and credit memos sent along with the statement to the bank customer.

OTHER BANK SERVICES AND FEATURES

You should be acquainted with the variety of services offered by banks. Such information is invaluable in helping you assist a busy executive.

Cashier's check   A bank customer who does not have a checking account may purchase a cashier's check—also known as a *treasurer's check* or an *official check*—from the bank by paying the amount of the check plus a service charge. The check is written by the bank on its own funds and is used like an ordinary check, but the payee recognizes that it is guaranteed.

Bank draft   Similar in purpose to a cashier's check, a bank draft is a check written by a bank on funds it has in another bank. The customer pays for the amount of the draft plus a service charge. Bank drafts are used mainly for transactions with foreign banks.

Sight and time drafts   These instruments are often used when a seller is not certain of a buyer's credit rating. The seller gives the bank both the draft and a bill of lading prepared by a transportation company that specifies the nature of the merchandise sold. Upon payment of the draft, the buyer receives the bill of lading from the bank, presents it to the transportation company, and receives the goods. The bank then remits the payment to the seller. If the draft is payable at the end of a certain time period, it is called a *time draft;* if it is payable when presented, it is knoiwn as a *sight draft.*

Personal money order   For customers requiring small sums, banks sell money orders similar to those sold by post offices. These bank money orders are negotiable and serve the same purpose as business or personal checks.

Certified check   Should a payee require guaranteed payment, a bank will certify that a depositor's account contains sufficient funds to pay for the check. The amount is subtracted from the depositor's balance when the check is written, and the check is stamped "Certified."

Short-term checking account   A depositor can open a temporary checking account for a particular purpose and close it as soon as that purpose has been accomplished.

Bank discounting   If a company needs to secure cash in exchange for a draft or note it is holding, it may offer the instrument to a bank for discounting. After deducting a specified percentage, the bank gives the company the remainder and collects on the instrument from the debtor when it comes due.

Foreign payments   Firms doing business in foreign countries may send funds through banks in the form of cable money orders, bank drafts, mail payments, and currency.

Safe-deposit box   A firm or an individual may rent a safe-deposit box from a bank for the storage of valuable papers and other items.

Transportation bill processing   A firm can arrange for the bank to pay its freight bills by having transportation companies send their bills directly to the bank, and the firm will receive monthly statements from the bank showing the amounts paid.

Lockbox   For a fee, the bank may handle all steps of a business's accounts-receivable collections: mail pickup, processing, and deposit of payments. The depositor will receive daily reports of the amounts credited to its checking account.

Miscellaneous services   Night-drop facilities (which enable businesses to deposit receipts any time of the day or night), automatic tellers (which allow depositors to conduct transactions without the aid of a teller and at times when the bank is closed), and banking by mail are additional conveniences. Banks also provide special payroll processing help, wire transfer of funds to other banks, dividend collections, and other services.

BANK INVESTMENT SERVICES

You should be aware of the proliferation of investment and personal banking opportunities offered by banks to businesses and individuals. The more common ones are listed here.

Certificates of deposit   Banks pay interest on short-term deposits (a minimum of 14 days) to customers who do not want cash to lie idle. The bank issues a promissory note to the depositor which is redeemed at the end of the time period.

Commercial paper   This consists of short-term promissory notes issued by large corporations for up to six months' duration. Banks act as agents for the sale of the notes, for which they receive a service fee. The notes are in minimum denominations of $25,000.

Treasury bills   The federal government sells these obligations through commercial banks and Federal Reserve Banks. They can be purchased in denominations of $10,000 for time periods of up to one year. Most bills are purchased for 30, 60, 90, or 180 days. The bills are discounted at prevailing interest rates at the time of purchase. Banks charge a modest fee for this service, but Federal Reserve Banks do not charge a fee.

Treasury notes   These are federal-government obligations of more than one year's duration. They are not discounted at the time of purchase, and interest is paid on them every six months. They may be purchased in $5,000 denominations.

Cash Transaction Records

Accounting for cash is an extremely important part of a firm's financial record-keeping system. Controls must be devised to protect receipts and to account for payments. Responsibilities for handling cash must be assigned to personnel in a way that minimizes the opportunities for theft and collusion.

CASH RECEIPTS AND PAYMENTS

Although specific procedures for the receipt and payment of cash depend on the nature of a company's business, there are fundamental rules to which most enterprises adhere. The rules are devised either by the accounting firm that audits the company's books or by the company's internal accounting department.

Types of cash   Most people consider cash as being coins and currency only. From an accounting viewpoint, however, cash also includes checks, money orders, bank drafts, and bank deposits.

Accounting for cash receipts   Firms that do business with consumers use cash registers for cash sales. Some registers record sales and sales-tax information on paper tapes. Other registers are tied to computers to provide automatic cash totals, sales distribution information, and inventory updating. Universal Product Code (UPC) markings and optical character recognition (OCR) symbols on merchandise enable retailers to exercise greater control over cash receipts through the use of devices at checkout counters that record sales information automatically.

Cashiers must be trained to operate their registers properly and to make change correctly. Procedures must be devised for periodic daily collections of cash from the registers. Cash received by mail is usually in the form of checks or money orders, but occasionally currency and coins are included. Personnel responsible for opening the mail should prepare lists of the receipts, which are used for making bank deposits and accounting entries. Whether cash is put into a register or received by mail, those who handle the cash should not make the accounting entries in the firm's books. This separation of functions is an effective means of minimizing the chances of collusion and theft. Recording of cash receipts is made in a cash-receipts journal, which may be a book in which entries are made by hand, a form used on an accounting machine, or a magnetic tape on a computer.

Accounting for cash payments   Except for very small amounts, firms generally make payments by check. As with cash receipts, personnel responsible for authorizing payments should not sign checks. All checks should be supported by invoices or other documents explaining the disbursements. Cash payments are recorded in a *cash-payments journal,* also called a *cash-disbursements journal* or a *check register.*

Cash short and over   Rapid cash-register transactions frequently cause cashiers to make errors in giving change. An end-of-day shortage in cash receipts (as compared with the amount on the register's tape) is considered an expense, while an overage is listed as income.

Cash basis vs. accrual basis of accounting   Professionals and many small businesses maintain their accounting records on a cash basis. This involves recording expenses and income only when cash is paid or received. Larger firms use the accrual basis, which provides for charging expenses and listing income during the period in which they occur, regardless of when cash is paid or received. The choice of basis used may, of course, have a significant effect on a firm's reported net income or loss.

PETTY-CASH FUND

Since it is impractical to pay small expenses by check, firms maintain petty-cash funds. Items such as carfare, postage, and small quantities of office supplies are paid from the fund. To start the fund, a check is written and cashed. The cash is kept in a locked office drawer or box and is maintained by a designated person (frequently the secretary). The amount of the fund depends on the size of the business and the frequency of small payments. A disbursement from the fund is recorded on a petty-cash receipt, which indicates the date, receipt number, employee's name, amount, and purpose of the expenditure. It also contains the signature of the person receiving the money. (See Fig. 14.2.) The receipts are kept in the petty-cash box, so that at all times the total of cash and receipts equals the original amount. When a bill has been paid out of petty cash, it is attached to the petty-cash receipt. When the fund is low, a check is cashed to restore it to its starting amount. The petty-cash receipts are given to the accounting department for entry in the financial records.

Fig. 14.2   Petty Cash Receipt

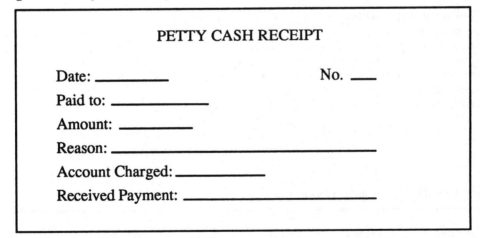

TRAVEL FUNDS

You must be certain that sufficient funds are available to the executive for use on foreign or domestic.trips. Your advance preparations may include visits to banks and offices to secure cash substitutes (or foreign money denominations if the trip involves leaving the country) and documents.

Letter of credit   When a business traveler needs funds in a foreign country, he or she presents a letter of credit to a designated bank and the amount received is listed on the document. Letters of credit are available from the firm's bank. They contain the name of the person who will be requesting the funds and the maximum amount (usually quite large) that can be secured. This amount is deducted from the company's bank account. Domestic companies often use letters of credit in transactions with foreign firms.

Traveler's checks   For smaller amounts, traveler's checks can be purchased at banks, Western Union offices, American Express offices, and some travel agencies. They come in denominations of $10, $20, $50, and $100 and cost approximately $1 for each $100 purchased. However, some banks give free traveler's checks to certain depositors and other customers. The checks must be signed at the time of purchase by the person who will use them, and again when they are cashed.

Express money orders   These may be purchased by you and either given or sent to the traveling executive, who is designated as the payee. As with regular checks, the traveler may either cash the money orders or transfer them to other parties.

Foreign currency   Banks sell foreign money in packages for the use of travelers in foreign countries.

Expense record   Since business expenses are deductible for income-tax purposes, the traveler should maintain careful records. The firm's accounting department supplies the proper expense record forms and uses them upon the traveler's return to make appropriate entries in the books.

Voucher system   Although all business organizations require controlled cash accounting systems, the opportunity for fraudulent practices is greater in larger firms. A voucher system, whereby all debts are listed as soon as they arise, is used by some firms to eliminate the possibility of unauthorized payments. Vouchers are numbered forms containing details about each debt and subsequent payment. The bill comes into the purchasing department and is sent out for approval before payment. A voucher controls the entire procedure.

Payroll Procedures

All business organizations are required to conform to federal and state payroll laws and to maintain accurate payroll records. Federal and state tax forms must be filed showing employee names, amounts earned, and payroll deductions. Management frequently requires information about payroll costs and taxes, and employees must be paid promptly and accurately. Since executives are often involved in payroll matters, you must be able to provide them quickly with pertinent data. A knowledge of payroll laws and procedures is therefore essential.

TYPES OF COMPENSATION

An employee is one who works for a business firm and is subject to the company's directions and supervision. An employee is distinguished from an independent contractor who performs services for a company but is not directly under its control. Payroll laws relate to employees only.

Salary   This term is generally used to describe compensation for administrative-level employees whose pay is determined on a monthly or annual basis and who are paid in monthly, semimonthly, or biweekly increments.

Wages   Employees who work on an hourly or piecework basis are said to receive wages. Such employees may be skilled or unskilled. Many people use the terms *salary* and *wages* interchangeably.

Commissions   Salespeople whose compensation is based wholly or in part on their sales totals receive commissions on those sales and are considered employees.

GROSS PAY AND NET PAY

The total salary, wages, or commissions earned is called *gross pay*. For those paid on an hourly basis, gross pay is computed by multiplying the hours worked by the hourly rate. For example, someone who makes $8 an hour and works 30 hours earns gross pay of $240. If an employee works more than 40 hours during a week (overtime), the federal Fair Labor Standards Act requires that payment be made at the rate of time-and-a-half for all hours above 40. The following case illustrates the computation of gross pay where overtime is involved.

Irv Harold earns $10 an hour and worked 42 hours during the week of February 8. The computation is as follows:

Hours Worked		*× Rate of Pay*	=	*Gross Pay*
Total	40	× $10.00	=	$400.00
Overtime	2	× 15.00	=	+ 30.00
				$430.00

Net pay, or *take-home pay*, is determined by subtracting certain payroll deductions from gross pay. If Mr. Harold's deductions came to $100, his net pay would be $330.

PAYROLL DEDUCTIONS

While some types of payroll deductions vary from company to company, there are some that are common to all business organizations. They are:

1. **FICA (Federal Insurance Contributions Act)** This term is used more frequently by accountants and payroll departments than the term *Social Security*. The FICA rate is set by Congress and has been changed several times over the years. FICA deductions support the Old-Age, Survivors, and Disability Insurance (OASDI) program and the Medicare program. The actual deduction for an employee can be determined from FICA tax tables supplied by the government or purchased from stationers, or by multiplying gross pay by the current FICA rate. Each year, Congress sets a tax rate and the maximum amount of gross pay from which FICA taxes are to be deducted. The law also requires employers to match the taxes deducted from employees' pay by remitting a like amount.

2. **Federal Withholding Taxes (FWT)** This term refers to the federal income taxes that employers must withhold from their employees' salaries or wages as the money is earned.
3. **State and City Withholding Taxes (SWT/CWT)** In most states and a few cities, additional taxes are withheld to support local programs.

Federal Unemployment Insurance Tax (FUTA)   This tax is used for the administration of unemployment-insurance programs. Employers are required to pay the tax. The employer files an annual Federal Unemployment Tax Return (Form 940) by January 31 of the year following the taxable year. This form lists information about the unemployment-insurance taxes the company has paid to the state and federal government, and also provides for the computation of any additional tax due to the federal government.

State Unemployment Insurance Tax (SUTA)   The funds accumulated from this tax are used to pay unemployment-insurance benefits. Merit-rating plans reduce the taxes for employers with stable payrolls. The form is filed quarterly, and its contents vary with the state. Other data that are usually required on this form include employees' names, Social Security numbers, taxable wages, and tax computation. As with federal unemployment insurance, most states tax the employer only.

Workers' compensation insurance   Qualifying employers pay an estimated premium for this insurance, which is adjusted upward or downward at the end of the year. The insurance rate depends on the type of work performed by the employees.

Other deductions   Further deductions may be made for union dues, U.S. Savings Bonds, health insurance, loans, pension funds, company stock purchase plans, and charitable contributions.

PAYROLL SYSTEMS

You should familiarize yourself with the different methods by which payrolls are processed. The payroll system that a particular company, organization, or institution uses is usually geared to the number of its employees and the complexity of the payroll itself.

Computers   High-speed computers can process payrolls in an amazingly short time. The system may also generate printouts (and other media such as magnetic tape) of payroll registers, employee earnings records, employee checks, and payroll tax forms. Computers can also maintain journals, ledgers, schedules, and other records that are essential to the firm's operations.

Service bureaus   Your company may have its payroll data processed by a private service bureau.

One-write (pegboard) systems   Using this method, payrolls can be processed by hand in such a manner than an employee's earnings record, payroll register line, and check are produced simultaneously. A pegboard aligns the three records and carbon interleaves. When the check and check stub are written, for example, the information transfers itself via carbon or chemically treated carbonless paper onto the earnings record and the payroll register. Since the forms are standard, the user is permitted great flexibility in determining if any additional copies should be made. Each time a payroll check is written, a different earnings record may be inserted between the check and the payroll register.

Since the check, earnings record, and payroll register are all posted at the same time as the check is prepared, the accountant can be satisfied that, once the payroll register is balanced, the check and the earnings record have been posted properly. Pegboard systems thus save a great deal of time and ensure the accurate transfer of information. They are used to record cash, sales, and purchase transactions as well as payroll transactions. A one-write system is illustrated in Fig. 14.3.

TAX FORMS

Employers are required to file certain payroll forms at different times of the year. Information on the forms is derived from the payroll register.

Federal Tax Deposit (Form 501)   This form is filed at a commercial bank along with funds withheld for FICA and FWT whenever these amounts plus the employer's FICA contributions amount to more than certain specified amounts.

Employer's Quarterly Federal Tax Return (Form 941)   Amounts remitted with Forms 501 plus amounts not yet remitted are summarized on Form 941, which is filed during the month following the payroll quarter. The form also contains a record of the employer's federal tax liabilities and deposits.

Transmittal of Income and Tax Statement (Form W-3)   Income taxes withheld and listed on Forms 941 are summarized on Form W-3. The form is accompanied by copies of W-2 forms for all employees.

Wage and Tax Statement (Form W-2)   This statement is sent by employers to employees no later than January 31 of each year; it lists the previous year's gross pay, federal income taxes withheld, FICA taxes withheld, and total FICA wages paid. Where state income taxes are deducted, an additional copy is sent. By April 15 employees must file their federal income tax form along with a copy of the W-2 statement. If an employee leaves the firm during the year, a W-2 form must be sent to him or her within 30 days of the last payment of wages, not at the end of the calendar year.

Employee's Withholding Allowance Certificate (Form W-4)   This form is completed by the employee and filed with the employer at the time of employment. It lists the number of exemptions to which the employee is entitled and becomes the basis for the employer's use of FWT tables. A new form is filed when the employee's exemptions change.

PAYROLL RECORDS

Some companies design their own payroll forms to conform to computer or accounting-machine specifications. Other firms use standard records that can be purchased from stationery suppliers.

Time cards   These cards are used to maintain records of employee arrival and departure times and as an indication of the amount of time spent by employees on specific work assignments.

Fig. 14.3   A One-write (Pegboard) System for Payroll

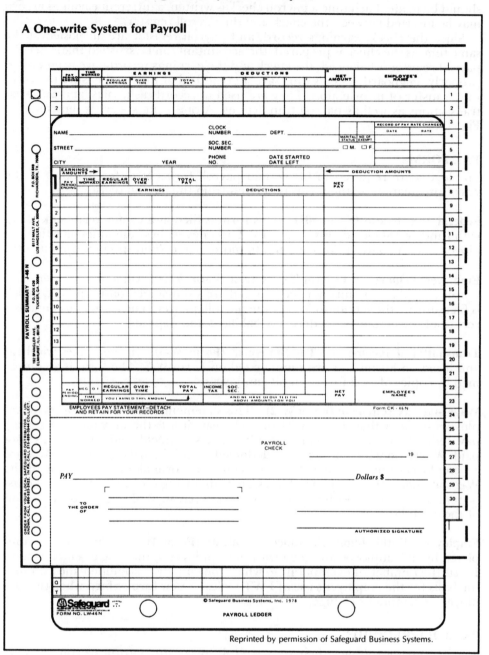

Reprinted by permission of Safeguard Business Systems.

Payroll register Information is copied from the time cards onto a payroll register, which also includes employees' names, the number of exemptions claimed, pay rates, gross pay with overtime pay listed separately, taxable earnings for FICA and unemployment-insurance computations, deductions, net pay, and check numbers. The register includes all employees who work during a payroll period. A sample payroll register is shown in Fig. 14.4.

Fig. 14.4 Payroll Register

PAYROLL REGISTER

PAYROLL PERIOD: JANUARY 8-14, 19__

NAME	NO. EX.	HRLY RATE	HRS. WKD	REG.	OVERTIME	TOTAL	FICA	FWT	MED.	STATE	CITY	TOTAL	NET PAY	CHK NO.
Gross, Avi	2	11.25	40	$450.00	$0.00	$450.00	$27.90	$44.00	$6.53	$25.51	$9.15	$113.09	$336.92	65
Norris, Neil	1	15.54	40	$621.60	$0.00	$621.60	$38.54	$102.00	$9.01	$40.53	$17.90	$207.98	$413.62	66
Rodriguez, Iris	3	22.00	40	$880.00	$0.00	$880.00	$54.56	$102.00	$12.76	$67.84	$27.10	$264.26	$615.74	67
Van Sant, Nell	2	16.00	36	$576.00	$0.00	$576.00	$35.71	$62.00	$8.35	$35.43	$15.25	$156.74	$419.26	68
Kostos, Arlene	1	15.00	38	$570.00	$0.00	$570.00	$35.34	$85.50	$8.27	$37.05	$15.96	$182.12	$387.89	69
Josephson, Jennifer	1	25.00	28	$700.00	$0.00	$700.00	$43.40	$115.00	$10.15	$77.00	$30.00	$275.55	$424.45	70
TOTAL				$3,797.60	$0.00	$3,797.60	$235.45	$510.50	$55.07	$283.36	$115.36	$1,199.74	$2,597.88	

Employee earnings record The federal Wages and Hours Law requires employees to maintain an individual record for each employee. The employee earnings record contains the employee's name, address, Social Security number, number of exemptions claimed, date of birth, marital status, rate of pay, hours worked, earnings, deductions, net pay, check numbers, and year-to-date earnings. An example is illustrated in Fig. 14.5.

Fig. 14.5 Employee Earnings Record

NAME GROSS, AVI   S.S. # 002-45-9011

ADDRESS 106 Minnie Street   DATE OF BIRTH 5-Jun-1973

Brooklyn NY 11203   MARITAL STATUS Married

NO. EX. 2   HRLY RATE $11.30

LINE NO.	WEEK ENDED	HOURS WORKED	REG	OVERTIME	TOTAL	FICA	MEDICARE	STATE	CITY	FICA	FWT	MED	STATE	CITY	TOTAL	NET PAY	CHK NO.	YTD
						TAXABLE EARNINGS				**DEDUCTIONS**								
1	7-Jan	41	$450.00	$11.30	$461.25	$461.25	$461.25	$461.25	$461.25	$28.60	$46.00	$6.69	$25.83	$9.60	$116.72	$344.53	22	$461.25
2	14-Jan	40	$450.00	$0.00	$450.00	$450.00	$450.00	$450.00	$450.00	$27.90	$44.00	$6.53	$25.51	$9.15	$113.09	$336.92	65	$450.00
TOTAL			$900.00	$11.30	$911.25	$911.25	$911.25	$911.25	$911.25	$56.50	$90.00	$13.21	$51.34	$18.75	$229.80	$681.45		$911.25

The Employer's Tax Records

Every business organization pays taxes, but not all companies pay the same types of taxes. Taxes are imposed by all levels of government: federal, state, and local. Records must be maintained for information on which tax rates are based, and completed tax forms must be available for ready reference. Accounting journals, ledgers, business papers, and report forms are designed by accountants, office managers, forms design specialists, and systems analysts. Record books and other forms can also be purchased from stationers and printers in preprinted bound or loose-leaf stylings.

The typing of tax-return forms will occasionally be your responsibility. Care must be taken to see that all figures are correct, that all required signatures have been affixed, that payments due are included, and that the forms are mailed on time.

THE FEDERAL INCOME TAX

While corporations and individuals pay federal income taxes and must file annual tax returns, proprietorships and partnerships do not. However, single owners and partners must report business profits on their personal income tax returns. In addition, partnerships are required to file informational returns annually. (Some states require corporations and individuals to pay state income taxes.) You must always maintain confidentiality when dealing with tax returns.

IMPACT OF DECISION MAKING ON TAXES

Business decisions often affect a company's tax liability. For this reason, tax planning is an essential part of a firm's policies. Accountants, tax specialists, and attorneys provide advice to boards of directors, corporate officers, and proprietors on a fee or retainer basis. You will often need to be available to supply necessary information to these consultants.

THE SALES TAX

Most states and many cities impose sales taxes on tangible personal property sold at retail as well as on services furnished at retail. Although this means that consumers are charged the tax, business concerns act as tax collectors by remitting the taxes collected to the government. This tax-collecting responsibility requires companies to maintain sales records that include sales-tax collections. Depending upon the requirements of the particular state or city, sales-tax reports are filed monthly or quarterly along with the remittances.

THE PROPERTY TAX

Local governments impose property taxes on businesses according to the latter's assessed property values. Once its budget needs for the year have been determined, the government establishes a tax rate. The assessed valuation for each business is then multiplied by the tax rate to arrive at its tax liability. Accurate records of business property holdings must be maintained to assure the establishment of fair assessed values.

Financial Statements

Since businesses are organized on a for-profit basis, owners and managers must be able to evaluate their financial operations through the preparation and analysis of statements for varying time periods. The statements are prepared by accountants and may be used by a number of people in the firm for different purposes.

OFFICE BUDGETS

As a key employee, you should be able to provide office cost data. You might even be asked to help in the preparation of the office budget. Budgets are effective only if they are controlled through proper record-keeping. If funds in one category are running low, it may be necessary to shift funds from another category. Situations may arise in which funds are eliminated because of cancellation of an expense category. Periodic statements of budget expenditures will enable you to judge how well the office is adhering to budget allowances.

Office cost elements include personnel, equipment, and supplies. With proper record maintenance and with an awareness of prior years' expenses, a budget can be developed to reflect the new year's plans. Though not every expense can be anticipated, you should attempt to allow for all foreseeable needs, and contingency funds should be included to provide for unexpected expenditures.

THE INCOME STATEMENT

A company determines its profits (or losses) by means of a financial report called an *income statement*. Prepared by an accountant, the income statement provides management with information about its income and expenses. The income statement is also a key document for decision making by stockholders, creditors, and lending institutions.

Time period   Although the income statement can be prepared monthly, quarterly, or semiannually, a formal statement for income-tax purposes and for the corporation's annual report is prepared at the end of the fiscal year.

Components   For a service business, two basic elements appear in the income statement: income and expenses. For a trading concern, the additional element "cost of goods sold" is required. Manufacturing firms also include the element "cost of goods manufactured."

Format   The simple income statement in Fig. 14.6 shows how the profit for the year 19— was calculated for Bert and Meri's Tavern. The heading specifies the type of statement and the time period. The Expenses section lists a variety of expenses normally incurred by a restaurant. The last line indicates the amount of profit for the year.

The next illustration (Fig. 14.7) shows an income statement for a trading company. The "Cost of Goods Sold" section shows the goods on hand on the first day of the year ($422,200), additional purchases of goods made during the year ($435,100), the total amount of goods available for sale during the year ($857,300), the goods on hand on the last day of the year ($376,200), and the cost of goods sold. The gross profit is the profit before deducting expenses.

Analysis   It is more valuable to analyze financial statements using percentages than dollars. For example, it is more useful to say that Bert and Meri's net profit

Fig. 14.6   Income Statement

Bert and Meri's Tavern
Income Statement
for the Year Ended December 31, 19___

Income:		$117,820.
Expenses:		
Salaries	$74,450.	
Rent	8,540.	
Supplies	15,590.	
Utilities	2,210.	
Services	610.	
Miscellaneous	1,150.	
Total Expenses		102,550.
Net Profit:		$15,270.

---

is 13 percent of its income than that the net profit is $15,270 of the $117,820 income. It is easier to compare net profits of different years by using percentages; similarly, we can make better judgments about expense trends by comparing them in percentage terms.

Tax impact   Since corporations pay income taxes on net profits, they constantly analyze their expenses in order to minimize their tax liability. Stockholders receive dividends from net profits and must report the dividends on their personal income tax returns.

THE BALANCE SHEET

This statement shows the financial condition of a business at a particular time. Accountants prepare balance sheets to enable management and stockholders to assess the financial health of their business. Balance sheets are also of interest to creditors and tax agencies.

Components   Three basic elements appear on a balance sheet:

1. *Assets:* items owned by a business.
2. *Liabilities:* amounts owed by a business.
3. *Equity:* the value of the business—that is, the difference between assets and liabilities.

Fig. 14.7   **Income Statement for Trading Concern**

Susan Hersch Office Supplies
Income Statement
for the Year Ended December 31, 19___

Sales		$710,600.
Cost of Goods Sold:		
Merchandise Inventory —1/1	$422,200.	
Add: Purchases	435,100.	
Goods Available for Sale	857,300.	
Less: Merch. Inv. —12/31	376,200.	
Cost of Goods Sold		481,100.
Gross Profit on Sales		229,500.
Operating Expenses:		
Salaries	$77,500.	
Rent	8,500.	
Supplies	6,200.	
Advertising	4,600.	
Depreciation	8,800.	
Miscellaneous Expenses	3,200.	
Total Expenses		108,800.
Net Profit before income taxes		$120,700.

Format The statement in Fig. 14.8 shows how the components of a balance sheet are presented for convenient reading by those who may not understand accounting. The assets appear on the left. The liabilities and stockholders' equity, representing claims by creditors and stockholders on the firm's assets, are listed on the right. The asset "Cash" includes checks and money orders. The asset "Accounts Receivable" shows how much the company's customers owe; the liability "Accounts Payable" shows how much the firm owes to its creditors.

Fig. 14.8 Balance Sheet

Lady Jeanette Inc.
Balance Sheet
December 31, 19___

Assets			Liabilities	
Cash		$ 4,300.	Accounts Payable	$12,580.
Accounts Receivable		28,250.	Loans Payable	26,000.
Inventory		54,360.	Taxes Payable	3,220.
Office Equipment	17,280.		**Equity**	
Less Accum. Deprec.	(3,420.)		Robin Jeanette, Capital	50,000.
Net Office Equipment		13,860.	Retained Earnings	8,970.
Total Assets		$100,770.	**Total Liabilities and Equity**	$100,770.

Analysis Accountants use ratios to provide management with useful information. For example, Lady Jeanette Inc. has assets in cash, accounts receivable, merchandise, and office supplies totaling $100,770, compared to $41,800 in liabilities, which indicates how well the company is able to meet its current debts: the ratio $100,770 : $41,800 shows that almost $2.50 could be available quickly to pay each $1 of current debt. Other ratios enable management to project future activities.

STATEMENT OF ACCOUNT

A statement of account is sent by a company to its customers monthly to record the transactions for the month and indicate outstanding debt. The next illustration (Fig. 14.9) shows that Harwood Music (the customer) owed $1,512.85 on June 1, paid that balance on June 11, and then incurred additional debt through purchases amounting to $215.12 and $304.81 on June 15 and June 28. The closing balance due on June 30 was $519.93.

Fig. 14.9   Statement of Account

Statement

Sam's Guitar Workshop   To: Harwood Music Co.
67 Main Street   99 Little Town Rd.
Middletown, CT 06457   Jamestown, RI 02835

Date	Explanation	Charges	Credits	Balance
June 1	Opening Bal.			$1,512.85
11	Payment		$1,512.85	00.00
15	Sale	$215.12		215.85
28	Sale	304.81		519.93

Corporations and Securities

A corporation is organized under a charter issued by a state. Although stockholders are the corporation's owners, business policies and decisions are made by a stockholder-elected board of directors. Decisions made by the board of directors are recorded in a minutes book, and accountants rely on these minutes for making entries in the financial records.

Large corporations issue an annual report reviewing the year's activities. In addition to an income statement and balance sheet, the report lists other financial statements and measurements of performance such as earnings per share (of stock), dividends per share, and stockholders' equity per share.

STOCKHOLDERS' RIGHTS
Depending on the class of stock owned, a stockholder may possess the following rights:

1. To vote.
2. To share in the distribution of earnings.
3. To purchase shares of new stock issues so that the same fractional ownership will be maintained (preemptive right).
4. To share in the distribution of assets if the corporation goes out of business.

CAPITAL STOCK
Corporations sell stock to secure operating funds. Ownership of stock is represented by stock certificates, each certificate representing a number of shares owned. An updated record of stockholders' names and number of shares owned is maintained in a stockholders' ledger.

Common stock   This class of stock often carries all the four rights just mentioned. Since voting rights are usually provided, those who own a sufficient number of common shares can control the corporation. It is also the class of stock that rises or falls in price most rapidly.

Preferred stock   This class of stock receives dividends (distributions) from earnings before common stock does. In the event a corporation is liquidated and goes out of business, it entitles its holders to a share of the assets before holders of common stock. However, a preferred stockholder does not usually have the right to vote.

Dividends   These are distributions of corporate profits to stockholders, usually on a quarterly or annual basis. Dividends may be given in the form of cash or additional stock. Only the board of directors has the right to declare dividends.

Market prices of stock   Stock is bought and sold through stockbrokers on stock exchanges. Stock prices are affected by corporate earnings, the condition of the nation's economy, government policies, world problems, and other factors. People and institutions trade stock in the hopes of making profits and also in order to receive dividends.

Stock-market tables   Information about stock is published in newspapers and financial publications. For each stock shown in the tables, the data usually include (1) the highest and lowest prices at which the stock has sold during the year; (2) dividend information, including amount of annual dividend in dollars per share, percentage of yield, and ratio of price to earnings; (3) daily sales volume; (4) the high, low, and last prices for the day; and (5) the net price change for the day.

BONDS

Corporations may secure additional funds by issuing bonds. A bond is a written promise by a corporation to repay a loan to a creditor at a specific rate of interest at certain time intervals. Most corporate bond interest payments are made semiannually. Bonds are long-term (e.g., 10-, 20-, 30-year) obligations and sell in minimum denominations of $1,000.

Types of bonds   Secured bonds, such as *collateral trust bonds, chattel mortgage bonds,* and *real-estate mortgage bonds,* provide bondholders with claims on specific corporate property in the event of default on bond payments. Unsecured bonds, called *debenture bonds,* are based on the general credit of the corporation. *Registered bonds* provide for bondholders' names to be listed with the corporation, whereas *coupon (bearer) bonds* do not. Bonds that come due at one time are called *term bonds,* while those that mature at different dates are known as *serial bonds. Callable bonds* give the corporation the right to redeem the bonds before maturity, and *convertible bonds* allow bondholders to exchange their bonds for corporate stock.

Bond interest rate   The interest rate printed on the bond certificate is called the *contract, nominal,* or *coupon rate.* The actual rate at which a bond is sold is known as the *market* or *effective rate.* Market rates are affected by conditions similar to those that affect stock prices. For a particular bond issue, the contract and market rates may be the same or different, depending on business conditions.

Bond redemption   Bonds may be redeemed by the corporation at maturity or, in the case of callable bonds, as specified in the bond indenture (contract), whenever it is to the corporation's advantage. The corporation may also repurchase its own bonds in the open market.

PROMISSORY NOTES

As defined by the Negotiable Instruments Law, a promissory note is a promise in writing to pay a sum of money to a payee or a bearer of the note upon demand or at a fixed or determinable future time. A note is an important medium of exchange and may be used for short- or long-term purposes. The person who promises the money is called the *maker* of the note, and the one to whom the note is made out is known as the *payee*. To the maker it is a *note payable,* while the payee considers it a *note receivable.* A note is negotiated by delivery when it is made out to "Bearer" rather than to a specific payee. When a payee's name is written on the note, it is negotiated by endorsement. Note forms can be purchased from commercial stationers.

CHAPTER 15

Travel Arrangements and International Business

A large increase in business-related travel, especially international travel, has been one of the results of the intensely competitive global market. Consequently, the secretary's role has been extended in yet another direction. But no longer is it enough just to make plane reservations and prepare itineraries. You now must have a fairly broad understanding of what types of trade and travel information are needed for various kinds of business trips, know where to obtain current information quickly, and be able to extract the essential data for the executive. In short, you must be able to expedite a business trip from the initial planning stages through the post-trip follow-up. Good secretarial support during all stages of a trip can sometimes mean the difference between success and failure.

Executives must be kept informed of developments in the countries with which they may be dealing. They must also have an understanding of foreign cultures and social structures in order to establish and maintain friendly working relationships with their foreign counterparts. A secretary who can supply in-depth information about the society and customs of these countries can be of great value to the executive and the company. An awareness of the economic relationships between the U.S. government and other governments is also desirable. Finally, knowledge of at least one foreign language could be one of your most important qualifications.

This chapter provides an overview of domestic and multinational travel and business and the secretary's expanded role in facilitating and supporting them.

Setting Up a Trip

A successful foreign business trip requires careful preparations carried out methodically. Even if your firm has an in-house travel department, you yourself should know what information will be needed and where it may be obtained. You should know *in advance* the following:

1. *Office policies and procedure*
   - Whether travel arrangements are to be made by an in-house travel department, a travel agent, or you and the executive.
   - The procedure for making a formal travel request.

- The procedure for requesting cash advances and/or prepayment or reimbursement of expenses.
- How to coordinate office schedules in the executive's absence.
2. *The executive's personal preferences and needs*
   - Means of transportation—specific carrier, class, time of day, meal service, and special services.
   - Hotel accommodations—chain affiliation, required facilities, smoking or nonsmoking room, and special arrangements.
   - Entertainment and sightseeing.
   - Ground transportation services.
   - Amount of leisure time.
   - Personal interests.
   - Medical problems.
3. *Methods for keeping records of the trip*
   - Portable dictation equipment, telephone communication, secretary's attendance, outside clerical assistance, or dictation upon return.

Although gathering and organizing this information may involve a great deal of time, the result will make the investment worthwhile.

In addition, you must determine the following:

- Purpose of the trip, departure and return dates, and number of people traveling.
- Most convenient and expedient means of transportation, mileage, and estimated travel time.
- Hotel most completely equipped and closest to trip activities.
- Arrangements and facilities for meetings.
- Forms to be completed before departure.
- Availability of necessary supplies (dictation equipment, reference books or research facilities, files, handout materials, etc.) and services (clerical, reproduction, etc.).
- Allocation of free time and designated activities.
- Additional arrangements for family and traveling companions.
- Notes on climate, time zones, and accepted modes of dress.

COMMERCIAL TRAVEL AGENCIES

Reputable travel agencies are staffed with skilled employees who can assist international and domestic travelers at no additional cost to the traveler. A call to a travel agent will save time and assure a minimum of confusion from the beginning to the end of the trip. Travel agents make travel reservations, issue tickets, recommend hotels and make hotel reservations, arrange for car rentals, and assist in obtaining passports and visas. They sometimes give additional help with incidentals such as tickets for the theater or sporting events. They have at their fingertips data about airline flight schedules and prices, air distances and travel times to principal cities around the globe, luggage limitations, and air freight.

The selection of a travel agent may be based on personal recommendations, established reputation, or spot usage. Once an agent has been chosen, try to use the same agent to arrange all trips, so that he or she can become familiar with the traveler's habits and a rapport can develop between you.

Names of accredited travel agencies are available from the American Society of Travel Agents (ASTA), 1101 King Street, Alexandria, VA 22314. You can also get a list of Certified Travel Agencies in your area by sending a self-addressed, stamped envelope to the Institute of Certified Travel Agents, 148 Linden Street,

P.O. Box 56, Wellesley, MA 02181. Once you have determined the names of a few agencies you may be interested in using, consider asking the following questions: Do you specialize in business travel? What businesses in the area are using your services? Are you associated with ASTA and are your agents certified?

Have all necessary information at hand before calling the agent, and be courteous and friendly yet completely candid about the executive's desires. Be ready to supply the following information:

1. The executive's name, office address, and home and office telephone numbers.
2. The desired dates and times of departure and return.
3. The executive's travel preferences—first-class or coach, smoking or non-smoking, etc.

The agent will provide confirmation, suggest an acceptable method of payment, tell you the check-in time and the estimated time of arrival, and arrange either to send the tickets to you or have you pick them up.

IN-HOUSE TRAVEL DEPARTMENTS

Many companies have in-house travel departments that monitor travel requests and provide a detailed tracking system of monies spent. Some companies have special policies regarding returning frequent-flyer awards to the company, and this too can be monitored by an in-house travel department.

ELECTRONIC RESERVATION SYSTEMS

Regardless of whether you are making reservations through a commercial travel agency or an in-house travel department or on your own, there are computer services such as Prodigy and CompuServe through which you can make reservations and obtain tickets. The *Official Airline Guide* (Official Airline Guides, 2000 Clearwater Dr., Oak Brook, IL 60521; 800-323-3537) has an Electronic Edition (OAGEE). The following services are literally at your fingertips by means of a computerized travel service: latest flight information, ticketing arrangements, credit-card arrangements, meal selections, seating preferences, hotel and motel reservations, restaurant information, banquet and conference facilities, weather conditions in cities throughout the world, and travel tips.

MAKING TRAVEL ARRANGEMENTS DIRECTLY

If you make travel reservations without the help of an agent, preparation is more complex. It involves obtaining and keeping current the appropriate schedules and brochures from airlines, bus lines, railroads, travel clubs, motor clubs, and various travel agencies. If you make extensive arrangements directly with airlines, keep the current copy of the *Official Airline Guide,* available by subscription at the address above. The guides are published in both domestic and international editions.

Know the full particulars of the trip before making any reservations. Contact the chamber of commerce, convention bureau, or tourism office of the destination city for brochures and special information. Another source of information is the local newspaper of the destination city, where you can find special-events calendars, weather reports, and service and facility advertisements.

Most of the major airlines, hotels, and car-rental agencies have toll-free numbers. If you do not have access to a directory of toll-free 800 numbers, call the toll-free information number, 800-555-1212, for the listing you need.

Airline reservations   If you do not rely on an agent for airline reservations, a call to the airline will provide information about its schedules and rates. Reservations and even seat assignments may be made instantly. You can confirm flights and sometimes make hotel reservations through the airline, but you should always confirm hotel reservations yourself. Clip the special service announcements and schedules that are often published in newspapers. Allot enough time between connecting flights. Inquire specifically as to (1) methods of payment, (2) how to pick up the ticket, (3) check-in time at the airport, and (4) space available for carry-on luggage.

Most major airlines have private clubroom facilities in the larger airports. An annual membership charge enables the club member to avoid the turmoil of a busy airport, find a quiet place to work during layovers, change reservations if necessary, and obtain seat assignments well in advance of the gate's opening. Information about such facilities is available from ticket agents and flight attendants.

Railroad travel   Rail travel is limited to certain cities at certain times of the day and is feasible only when time and access to Amtrak terminals are available. Rail travel generally requires more time than the executive is likely to have, but some people prefer to travel by train. You can obtain a schedule for Amtrak trains as well as for connecting or commuter lines from the nearest Amtrak station. A call to a ticket agent will answer any additional questions. If the executive will be driving to the station, provisions for parking must be made. The National Railway Publications Co., 424 West 33 Street, New York, NY 10001, and the Thomas Cook Travel, 4435 Main Street, Suite 150, Kansas City, MO 64111, offer timetables, fares, and a host of other information regarding railroad travel.

Automobile travel   In some instances the executive may choose to travel by automobile. Membership in an automobile or oil-company travel club provides guides and maps, towing and repair service, and detailed road trip plans. If the executive prefers to rent a car, the type of car and rate should be guaranteed with the agency. You should determine the method of payment, special discounts available, insurance requirements, and driver's-license stipulations. The executive's arrival time should be relayed to the rental agency so that no unnecessary delays are encountered at the destination. Some car-rental agencies use the term "unlimited mileage" to indicate that the driver pays a set amount for a designated period of time, regardless of the number of miles the car is driven. The term "drop-off charges" refers to the fee the driver must pay when the car is rented at one location but returned to another.

Hotel reservations   It is essential to make hotel reservations as soon as the dates of the trip are definite, since hotels in major cities may be fully booked several weeks in advance. *The Hotel & Motel Red Book*, published by the American Hotel and Motel Association, 1201 New York Avenue, NW, Washington, DC 20005, provides descriptions of selected hotels and motels throughout the United States. Reservations are normally made by telephone and confirmed in writing. When making hotel reservations, you should provide the name, address, and telephone number of the guest and your own name for reference. You should also specify whether the traveler will desire a smoking or nonsmoking room. Many hotels hold reservations only until a certain hour, usually 6 p.m. You may frequently hold a reservation beyond that hour by guaranteeing payment whether or not the guest arrives. To guarantee a room, you will need to give the name and address of the firm or the number and expiration date of a major credit card.

Advise the hotel by telephone as to the executive's preferences and inquire about a guarantee that such accommodations will be available. Find out about valet and laundry services, barber/hairdressers, masseurs, health clubs, and shoe shining and repair facilities, and make notes of these services on the itinerary. It may be desirable to make advance appointments for certain services. Request written confirmation of all hotel reservations, including arrival and departure dates, guarantee, room rates, and tax. In addition, ask about check-out times, payment procedures, credit and check-cashing privileges, fax machine availability, meeting facilities, and other needed services.

An understanding of hotel meal plans is helpful when making reservations. The American Plan (AP) includes all meals; the Modified Plan (MP) includes breakfast and dinner; the Breakfast Plan (BP) includes breakfast only; the Continental Plan (CP) includes a breakfast of coffee, tea, juice, muffins, and rolls; and the European Plan (EP) includes no meals.

Ask about complimentary limousine service from the airport or railway station and the comparative rates and times of other means of ground transportation. The clerk should also be able to tell you how to find ground transportation upon arrival if arrangements cannot be made beforehand. There may be a direct telephone line to the hotel from the baggage-claim area of the airport, for example, or an agent at a desk or curbside, or posted notices of available transportation.

SPECIAL ARRANGEMENTS

The executive with health problems may have to wear appropriate identification, carry medication, and arrange for access to a local physician. Provision for special diets or storage facilities may also have to be made.

THE TRAVEL FOLDER

File all notes on the various arrangements in one folder to facilitate the preparation of an itinerary and appointment schedule. When the arrangements are completed, mark a deadline on the calendar for receipt of confirmations. If confirmations are not received by that date, a follow-up phone call must be made.

The itinerary   An itinerary is invaluable in guiding an executive through a hectic day in a distant city. The itinerary should be logically and neatly arranged so that he or she can review it at a glance and accomplish the trip's purpose as easily as possible. It should include a brief description of activities, with dates and times; departure and arrival times, with airports or train stations specified; hotel names and addresses, and confirmed reservations (official confirmations are usually attached); and social engagements, with comments as to dress. A detailed itinerary may also contain pertinent information about individuals, reference to files or reports and correspondence, reminders to reconfirm flight reservations and meeting arrangements, and comments on climate and social amenities. A simple itinerary is illustrated in Fig. 4.7.

In preparing the itinerary, confer with the executive and make careful notes about desired dates and times of departure and return, the time needed for each meeting or appointment, and any need for free time to relax or attend to personal matters. The traveler should be told the details of any flight—what meals will be served, whether the flight is nonstop, the distance between terminals if a change of planes is involved, and the approximate distance between the airport and the hotel. Errors in planning can result in costly delays and needless confusion.

Travel agents also provide itineraries, but these are usually in the form of a printout from a computerized reservation service and thus should be carefully reviewed and supplemented with additional appointments and information. In some cases a separate appointment schedule is advisable, with notes for each meeting—participants, papers needed, and so on. After the draft itinerary is approved by the executive, the final itinerary is typed and filed in the travel folder, and copies may be distributed as needed within the office.

The travel checklist   The final step is to assemble all the necessary materials and equipment. The following checklist may be helpful:

_____ tickets
_____ frequent-flyer number
_____ hotel/motel information
_____ car-rental confirmation
_____ traveler's checks
_____ passport, visa, international driving permit
_____ medical prescriptions
_____ vaccination certificate
_____ itinerary
_____ names, addresses, and phone numbers of business associates at destination
_____ agenda and advance publicity for conferences/meetings
_____ all necessary files
_____ speeches, reports
_____ slides or transparencies
_____ business cards
_____ company letterhead and envelopes
_____ gummed note tags, paper clips, manila folders, etc.
_____ laptop computer
_____ portable fax machine
_____ portable dictating equipment, extra tapes
_____ reference books for destination city and country

CANCELING A PLANNED TRIP

When a planned trip is canceled, you must notify all parties as quickly as possible. Transportation and hotel arrangements should be canceled promptly by telephone, and a follow-up letter should confirm the cancellation. Meeting arrangements should be canceled with the concierge, catering manager, or meeting coordinator.

If the tickets have been prepaid, application for a refund (accompanied by the unused tickets if you have them) is made directly to the carrier or travel agent. If hotel accommodations have been paid for in advance, apply for a refund to the hotel by letter promptly after telephoning the cancellation. If hotel reservations are guaranteed, *prompt* cancellation is crucial to avoid charges. If any payment has been made by charge card, application for credit should be made through the carrier, the hotel reservations clerk, or the travel agent. Be sure that the correct credit has been allowed on the monthly statement.

INTERNATIONAL TRAVEL

Passports and Visas   To find information about passports, look in the telephone directory under "United States Government," or contact Passport Services, Bureau of Consular Affairs, 1425 K Street, NW, Washington, DC 20524 (202-647-0518). If a passport is required, a person can apply at a passport agent's office or through a clerk of a federal court, a clerk of a state court of record, a judge or clerk of a probate court, or a designated postal clerk. Passport agencies are located in Boston, Chicago, Honolulu, Houston, Los Angeles, Miami, New Orleans, New York, Philadelphia, San Francisco, Seattle, Stamford (Connecticut), and Washington, D.C.

All U.S. citizens generally need passports to leave and reenter the United States and to enter most foreign countries. Even though a passport is not required by U.S. law for travel to North, South, and Central America or adjacent islands except for Cuba, it is still recommended. Travelers who visit countries in these areas without a passport should carry personal identification (such as a driver's license or an employee ID card) and a birth certificate or some other documentary evidence showing U.S. citizenship. Information about passport requirements for travel to and from specific countries can be obtained from the embassies or consulates of these countries. The pamphlet *Your Trip Abroad* is available from the Superintendent of Documents, P.O. Box 371954, Pittsburgh, PA 15250-7954. Another pamphlet, *Foreign Entry Requirements*, is available from Consumer Information Center, Pueblo, CO 81009.

The traveler should apply early for a passport, preferably several weeks before the planned departure. To apply for a first passport, the traveler should present a completed passport application at one of the issuing offices. A second passport can be applied for by mail if the conditions stated on the application are met. Several items are needed for filing an application for a passport:

1. **Evidence of citizenship**   A previously issued passport provides this evidence. A first-time applicant must provide an original birth certificate with an embossed seal, a certificate of naturalization, a baptismal certificate, voter-registration certification, or if all these are lacking, other evidence such as insurance papers.

2. **Two passport photos taken within six months of the date of application**   Photos should be 2″×2″, front view and full-faced. Color shots are acceptable.

3. **Proof of identity**   Personal identity must be established to the satisfaction of the person executing the application. If the applicant is personally known by the executor, no further identification is required. Items generally accepted for identification are a previously issued U.S. passport, a driver's license, a certificate of naturalization or citizenship, or a government (federal, state, or municipal) card or pass. Social Security cards and credit cards are not acceptable.

Business firms contracting with U.S. government agencies to carry out missions abroad should check with the contracting agency about special requirements for passports.

New passport applications may be made by mail if the applicant has held a U.S. passport for not more than eight years before the date of application. Passports are valid for five years from the date of issuance unless they are specifically limited by the Secretary of State. Lost or stolen passports should be reported immediately to the Passport Services office or to the nearest American consular office. Stolen passports should also be reported to local police authorities. Every precaution should be taken to prevent loss or theft of passports, for there may be considerable delay before a new passport can be issued.

A visa is permission granted by the government of a country for an alien to enter that country and remain there for a specified period of time. Visas are usually stamped in passports. Visas should, when possible, be obtained well in advance from the nearest embassy or consular office of the country or countries to which one is going. The addresses of foreign consular offices in the United States may be obtained by consulting *The Congressional Directory* or telephone directories for larger cities.

Because visa policies change, up-to-date information should be obtained before each trip. Even in countries not requiring visas, the traveler should carry evidence of U.S. citizenship and personal identification.

International driving permits Some countries will not honor U.S. driver's licenses and require local licenses in the native language. The American Automobile Association (AAA) recommends that anyone renting a car in a foreign country inquire about an international driving permit. For more information, you can call the AAA collect at 407-444-7883.

Vaccinations and required immunizations Up-to-date information about required immunizations must be obtained before any trip to a foreign country. Details concerning the immunizations and other disease-prevention measures recommended or required for travel to all areas of the world can be obtained from local, county, or state health departments. The countries that the executive intends to visit should be determined well in advance of the trip, since entry into and exit from some countries require special immunizations. The World Health Organization now recommends that most countries no longer require from travelers a certificate of vaccination against smallpox. Several countries require certificates showing that travelers have been vaccinated against cholera and yellow fever. For return to the United States, a smallpox certificate is required only if in the preceding days the traveler has visited a country in which smallpox has broken out. Required immunizations must be recorded on approved forms— International Certificates of Vaccination—available through most local health department offices. Exemptions from immunizations can be obtained if a physician thinks certain immunizations should not be given on medical grounds, in which case the traveler should be given a signed and dated statement of these reasons written on the physician's stationery. If smallpox and cholera shots are given by a private physician, the physician must give the traveler an official written statement confirming that the shots have been given. Yellow-fever shots can be given only by a local, county, or state health department. Allowing ample time for a traveler to complete all necessary shots before departure is of the utmost importance. You should call the health department to arrange for the executive's shots, since certain shots may be given only on specific days of the week.

The publication *Health Information for International Travel*, which contains information about required immunizations for different countries as well as many useful suggestions for coping with travel conditions, can be obtained from the Superintendent of Documents, P.O. Box 371954, Pittsburgh, PA 15250-7954.

Medical help overseas It is wise for the traveler to take a few emergency items such as aspirin, decongestants, bandages, first-aid cream, and antidiarrheal medication. In some countries there are problems with water or disease that the traveler should be aware of. Most major hotels have a doctor on call and have arrangements with a nearby hospital or clinic, but before traveling overseas it might be wise to contact (1) your personal physician; (2) the International Association for Medical Assistance to Travelers (IAMAT), 417 Center Street, Lewiston, NY 14092 (716-754-4883), a nonprofit organization that accepts donations; or (3) International SOS Assistance, Inc., P.O. Box 11568, Philadelphia, PA 19116 (215-244-1500).

Legal help overseas   If a legal problem should arise during foreign travel, the traveler should contact a law firm that is experienced in such matters as customs or immigration violations and driving infractions. International Legal Defense Counsel, 111 S. 15th Street, 24th floor, Philadelphia, PA 19102, is staffed with attorneys experienced in overseas legal matters.

Luggage   For international travel, check about luggage requirements and excess-weight charges with the airline on which the passenger will be traveling. Passengers are generally allowed two checked bags and one carry-on piece; however, size limits and the amount of under-seat space available for carry-on luggage vary with the airline.

Unless an excess valuation is declared before departure, the airline's maximum liability for baggage and claims on such baggage will be strictly limited; the passenger should inquire about liability limitations. Claims for damage must be filed in writing within seven days, and claims for loss or delay must be filed within 21 days.

Customs declarations   Travelers should pay special attention to duty-free imports and items that must be declared. Articles acquired abroad and brought into the United States are subject to duty and internal revenue tax; however, as a returning resident, a traveler is allowed certain exemptions from duties on items obtained abroad. Articles totaling $400 (based on fair retail value in the country where they were purchased) may be entered duty-free; this may include only small amounts of liquor, cigarettes, and cigars. Failure to declare an article may lead to its seizure and forfeiture, and to an additional liability equal in amount to the value of the article in the United States. If in doubt about whether an article is dutiable, the article should be declared and the customs inspector should be asked about it. The understatement of an article's value or the misrepresentation of its nature may lead to seizure and forfeiture. Duty must be paid even if an article is seized. The original invoice or bill of sale must reflect the true value of the article.

Detailed pamphlets on customs regulations, including *Customs Hints for Returning U.S. Residents*, are available from the Office of Public Information, U.S. Customs Service, 1301 Constitution Ave., NW, Washington, DC 20229 (202-927-5580), as well as from the Superintendent of Documents.

Film and recordings   Before departure, the traveler should register cameras, tape recorders, computers, and other articles that can be readily identified by serial numbers or other markings. All foreign-made articles are subject to duty each time they are brought into the United States unless the traveler has acceptable proof of prior possession. Certificates of registration can be obtained at the nearest customs office. If such certificates for any reason cannot be obtained, one can use bills of sale, insurance policies, or purchase receipts as proof of prior possession.

Exposed film that a traveler has purchased abroad may be released without examination by customs if it is not to be used for commercial purposes and if it does not contain objectionable matter. Developed or undeveloped U.S. film exposed abroad is duty-free and need not be listed in customs exemptions. Motion-picture film to be used for commercial purposes is, however, dutiable when returned to the United States. Foreign film purchased abroad as well as prints developed there are subject to duty, but they may be included in customs exemptions. U.S.-manufactured film may be mailed to the United States in the mailing envelopes obtainable from film manufacturers or processing laboratories. The outside wrapper should be marked "Undeveloped photographic film of U.S. manufacture—Examine with care."

International customs and amenities   The American executive who conducts business abroad should be familiar with the business and social customs of the host countries so as not to risk offending those with whom he or she confers or negotiates. Acceptable behavior is often based more on experience, instinct, and a feel for good manners than on written protocol. Although social practices and behavior in homes and restaurants do vary from country to country, tact, subtlety, courtesy, and geniality are always in order. Foreign business executives, and particularly those whose educational ties are European, are impressed if a visitor understands the cultural heritage and language of their country. The American executive going abroad should therefore take the time and make the effort to become well informed about the countries that will be visited and to brush up on the languages of these countries.

The American who is invited to a foreign business associate's home for an evening should take the invitation seriously, even though such an occasion is likely to be strictly social. The American executive who can talk intelligently about the arts and world affairs will make a favorable impression. If an executive is a guest in a foreign colleague's home, a small present might be given to the host or hostess. The guest should be discreet about choosing gifts; certainly the selection should not be ostentatious. Flowers are generally appropriate. No gift should be taken if one is a guest at a private club; however, if the entertainment is a golf game, the guest might present the host with golf balls imprinted with the company name and its logo.

Business behavior is as important and as varied as social behavior in different countries; for example, Austrians are formal in their business associations, but less so than Germans. Shaking hands is a polite gesture when greeting or leaving throughout Europe. In some countries, visiting cards are exchanged among executives. In some, business is conducted during lunch; in others, it is not. Business hours differ from country to country, and from summer to winter. For example, office hours in Italy are customarily from 8:00 a.m. to 1:00 p.m. and from 4:00 p.m. to 7:00 p.m.; in Denmark, summer hours are from 8:30 a.m. to 3:00 p.m., but winter hours are from 9:00 a.m. to 5:00 p.m. Banking hours also vary from country to country. Punctuality is important in many countries; in fact, delays of more than five minutes in some countries might be considered rude. In other countries, meetings customarily begin late.

Local customs for making appointments and for dress also should be adhered to. The American practice of making spur-of-the-moment appointments by telephone is looked upon with disapproval in many countries. Foreign business people are accustomed to receiving requests for appointments by letter well in advance; such a letter should contain the visitor's corporate title and specify the reason for the meeting. While Americans make a habit of working lunches, European luncheons are more frequently a time for building personal relationships than for discussing business.

Executives should be familiar with the dress conventions of the countries they visit. A dark business suit may be the masculine uniform in one country, but more casual attire may be acceptable in another. Some countries have strong notions about female attire; for example, pants are considered inappropriate in many countries. It is the traveler's responsibility to be informed on social and business customs before embarking on a trip. You should try to provide background material for the executive so that he or she will be an exemplary representative of both company and country abroad.

For more about cultural and business customs in individual countries, contact their embassies or consulates, many of which have brochures or booklets on the subject. Almost all travel guides deal with these issues as well.

Worldwide holidays   Holidays in foreign countries can affect the American executive's travel and appointment schedule. You can help the executive by supplying a list of holidays observed in the countries that will be visited. Holidays should also be included in the itinerary. For instance, Muslim, Christian, and Jewish holidays all might affect the schedule of an executive traveling in the Middle East. Indeed, there are very few days in the year when there is no holiday somewhere in the world. American travelers also must consider U.S. holidays when scheduling appointments with U.S. government representatives and American business people stationed overseas.

In the Western nations, New Year's (Jan. 1) and Christmas (Dec. 25) are always observed, Easter Monday and Boxing Day (Dec. 26) are almost always observed, and Labor Day (May 1) and Good Friday are widely observed.

Holiday schedules for a given country may vary from year to year, dates may be changed by law, new holidays may be added, and established holidays may be renamed, curtailed, or dropped altogether. When in doubt about a holiday in a particular country, telephone the consulate or embassy of that country. You may also consult the international division of a large bank or call the U.S. Department of State. A very useful booklet is the *World Holiday and Time Guide*, published annually by J.P. Morgan & Co., 60 Wall Street, New York, NY 10260; every firm engaged in international business should keep the current edition on hand.

Holidays occurring on Saturdays and especially Sundays are often celebrated on the preceding Friday or the following Monday. Avoid scheduling appointments on days which may be affected.

The celebration of some holidays often begins at noon or 1 p.m. on the day preceding. Sometimes stores, banks, and offices will remain closed until about noon of the day following the holiday.

In Israel, banks, government offices, and businesses are closed on Saturday. Most Israeli holidays follow the Jewish religious calendar.

Countries in which the Muslim religion is predominant (Saudi Arabia, Egypt, Indonesia, Jordan, Tunisia, Morocco, Pakistan, etc.) observe religious holidays which are based on the lunar calendar and are therefore variable. Banks and other offices are usually closed on Friday but are open on Saturday and Sunday. Some other countries (such as Guyana and Nigeria) observe both Muslim and non-Muslim holidays. Some Asian countries observe holidays based on the Buddhist and other Eastern religious calendars.

In some countries such as France and Italy, business activity is sharply curtailed in July and August when people go on vacation. It is therefore wise to avoid traveling in these countries on business during the summer months unless one is sure that one's business colleagues will not be on vacation. The practice of taking long weekends is also customary in many countries; you may have to inquire if foreign business associates will be in their offices on Friday. In Muslim countries, business is generally conducted on Saturday and Sunday but not on Friday.

Time differences   The world is divided into 24 standard time zones (some of these are further divided into half-zones), beginning at the International Date Line. This line approximates the 180° meridian in the Pacific Ocean between Asia and Hawaii. It is here that one day officially ends and another begins: for example, when it is Monday morning in Tokyo, it is still Sunday in the United States. On the opposite side of the globe is the prime or zero meridian, which passes through Greenwich, England, and marks Greenwich Mean Time, the standard by which other times are reckoned.

The United States lies within seven of the 24 standard time zones, from the westernmost point of Alaska to the East Coast. The standard time-zone numbers increase from west to east, starting at the International Date Line. Remember that the earth turns toward the east and that the sun rises earlier in the east than in the west. Thus, the farther east from the United States, the later in the day it is. When it is 8 a.m. Monday on the West Coast, it is 11 a.m. on the East Coast. It is even later (5 p.m.) in much of Europe, and still later—Monday evening— in India. Even farther east, in Siberia, it is already early Tuesday morning—all while it is still Monday morning on the West Coast of the United States.

The chart on pages 524–32 shows the comparative standard times of major countries of the world.

Many countries observe daylight saving time during the spring and summer. The dates of change from standard time differ from those in the United States, however, and the traveler should check with foreign embassies or consulates or see the *World Holiday and Time Guide* to find out what these dates are.

Expense account records   Reimbursable and tax-deductible items are key listings in any record of business expenses. Forms for recording expense records can be prepared by the forms designers and analysts in corporations, and must comply with Internal Revenue Service requirements. Conditions and record-keeping rules underlying deductions on federal income-tax returns for travel, entertainment, and gifts are set forth in the Internal Revenue Service's pamphlet *Travel, Entertainment, and Gift Expenses*. Copies can be obtained from the Superintendent of Documents, P.O. Box 371954, Pittsburgh, PA 15250-7954.

Business people bringing home gifts from abroad must be able to substantiate the following information: cost, date of purchase, description, reason for giving it, and information about the recipient including name, title, and occupation.

Metric equivalents   Many secretaries in multinational firms must work with metric measures. A table of metric measures with their U.S. equivalents is shown on page 533. In the first part of the table, nonmetric units are listed on the left and their metric equivalents on the right. In the second part, metric units are listed on the left, with their nonmetric equivalents on the right. (In the "Weight" portion of the table, *Avoirdupois* refers to standard American measure, *Troy* refers to the measure commonly used for precious metals, and *Apothecaries'* is the measure traditionally used for drugs.)

Background Research

Executives who travel and work in foreign countries frequently need a great deal of background information before going abroad, as do executives in the United States who work with those in other countries. Economics, marketing, management, language, culture, politics, history, and geography are all important facets of this background. A knowledge of the changing international policies of the United States and other nations is also vital, because foreign relations can affect the operations of multinational firms.

Company, city, and university libraries house source materials (such as federal government publications) on these subjects. A description of especially useful reference works appears on the following pages.

INDEXES

Using indexes is a practical way to identify periodicals in print and to research topics discussed in them. Finding the headings under which articles are listed can be difficult until one becomes comfortable with the system of topical indexing that these books employ. Librarians can assist researchers in finding the required headings in these indexes. Some of the most useful indexes are listed here, together with brief descriptions of their scope and utility.

Business Periodicals Index (Bronx, N.Y.: H. W. Wilson).   This monthly publication indexes English-language periodicals in the fields of accounting, banking, labor, and management; it also includes listings for specific businesses, industries, and trades. The heading "Multinational" will direct the researcher to more specific subheadings.

International Executive (Glendale, Ariz.: American Graduate School of International Management).   This index contains references to over 200 periodicals and highlights material that is basic to international business operations. Books and articles are listed with descriptive notes. *International Executive* is published three times a year.

Monthly Catalog of United States Government Publications (Washington, D.C.: Government Printing Office).   This catalog lists current publications (particularly those originating in the Commerce Department), many of which are of interest to executives in multinational firms. Instructions for ordering publications are included.

New York Times Index (New York: New York Times Co.).   This index covers only articles from the *New York Times*. Refer to "Economic Conditions and Trends (General)" for general material on world conditions and especially conditions in underdeveloped areas and for information on private foreign investments. See "Foreign Aid" for general material on government. Refer to "Commerce" for news about continents, groups of countries, or specific countries. Other headings that may prove helpful are "United Nations," "Agriculture," and "Labor."

Predicasts F&S Index Europe (Cleveland, Ohio: Predicasts).   This monthly index covers company, product, and industry information from over 750 financial publications, business-oriented newspapers, trade magazines, and special reports. It is divided into three sections: Industries and Products, Countries, and Companies.

Reader's Guide to Periodical Literature (Bronx, N.Y.: H. W. Wilson).   This index covers virtually all the major periodicals in the United States. The "Multinational" heading is followed by subheadings such as "Corporations—International." Relatively few are strictly business-oriented; however, many general periodicals carry articles of interest to business people.

Social Sciences Index (Bronx, N.Y.: H. W. Wilson). This publication, though not primarily oriented to business, does index some periodicals (such as *Asia, Business History Review, Far Eastern Economic Review, Foreign Affairs,* and *The Journal of Economic History*) that are important to the internationally-minded executive.

Ulrich's International Periodicals Directory (New York: R. R. Bowker). This is a yearly index of the names of over 100,000 periodicals in print throughout the world. Under the heading "Business and Economics" are the headings "Chamber of Commerce Publications," "International Commerce," and other pertinent topics.

Wall Street Journal Index (New York: Dow Jones). This index covers only articles in the *Wall Street Journal,* separating corporate news from general information. The researcher interested in a foreign country should look under its name. The International Monetary Fund and the World Bank are specifically indexed.

TRAVEL GUIDES

Travel guides—also important sources of information because of their frequent updating—are likely to be especially valuable to those who travel on a regular basis. The following annotated list is a representative sampling of these books.

Fielding's Europe, by Joseph Raff (New York: William Morrow). This annual guide contains information on travel preparations, money and prices, food, hotels, tipping, and the attitudes of Europeans toward tourists.

Fodor's Europe (New York: David McKay). This guide, updated annually, contains historical sketches of each country as well as information about its people, art, food and drink, and weather. A tourist's vocabulary in 12 European languages is included.

Michelin Red Guides (Greenville, S.C.: Michelin Travel Publications). These guides rate hotels, motels, and dining service in various European countries. They include maps, tables of distances between cities, and points of interest.

South American Handbook (New York: Prentice Hall Press). Updated annually, this is an extensive guide to South America including Mexico, Central America, and the Caribbean countries. It includes detailed information on weather, government, roads, and other matters beyond the normal tourist information.

The Wall Street Journal Guides to Business Travel, by Eugene Fodor (New York: David McKay). These four guides—*Europe, The Pacific Rim, USA and Canada,* and *International Cities*—written solely for the business traveler are updated annually. They cover topics ranging from import/export regulations and the location of major banks to tipping customs.

ENCYCLOPEDIAS AND ATLASES

Encyclopedias can be helpful to the researcher, particularly the *Encyclopaedia Britannica,* which contains articles the length of short books on many of the world's nations.

Atlases may also be helpful. The major atlases, all of which offer an enormous amount of textual information in addition to finely detailed maps, are the *Times Atlas of the World,* 9th ed. (New York: Times Books, 1992), the *Britannica Atlas* (Chicago: Encyclopaedia Britannica, 1991), the *National Geographic Atlas of the World,* 6th ed. (Washington, D.C.: National Geographic, 1990), and the *New International Atlas,* Anniversary Ed. (Chicago: Rand McNally, 1991). However,

Rand McNally and other publishers also publish numerous small, portable atlases with good-quality maps.

STATISTICAL REFERENCES

Three useful statistical sources of interest to executives in multinational firms are:

Commodity Year Book (New York: Commodity Research Bureau).   This annual publication includes an appraisal of trends in supply, demand, and prices for the 110 basic commodities. For example, the treatment of copper includes information on world copper production starting with 1961 and world smelter production for the major copper-producing countries, U.S. imports from and exports to selected countries, and refined copper stocks outside the United States. The statistical data are preceded by a brief discussion of the particular commodity market for the year. Both agricultural and mineral commodities are included.

Direction of Trade Statistics (Washington, D.C.: International Monetary Fund). This monthly volume reports statistics on exports and imports. Values of trade are given in U.S. dollars. Not all countries of the world are included in each issue.

Foreign Trade Reports: Highlights of U.S. Export and Import Trade (Washington, D.C.: U.S. Bureau of the Census).   This is a monthly compilation of statistical data on U.S. exports and imports, prepared by the Bureau of the Census and the Department of Commerce. Statistics are grouped under headings such as individual commodities by unit of quantity, for all methods of transportation collectively, as well as separately for water and air shipments. Data concerning each commodity for the current year and month and for the previous year and month are included. Cumulative amounts for prior years and months are also shown.

PAMPHLETS

Background Notes A series of pamphlets published by the Bureau of Public Affairs of the U.S. Department of State (available from the Superintendent of Documents, Government Printing Office, Washington, DC 20402).   These periodically updated pamphlets offer the reader a quick look at various countries and territories. Each pamphlet contains information on a country's land, people, history, government, political situation, economy, and foreign relations, as well as a map and a brief bibliography.

PERIODICALS

Secretaries who do research for executives can find information pertinent to multinational business in a variety of periodicals. Some of the periodicals that will assist executives in keeping up-to-date with international business and economics are listed here. For other periodicals devoted to foreign business, and for information about ordering any of these periodicals, consult *Ulrich's International Periodicals Directory* (available in the reference section of most city libraries).

Business America (Washington, D.C.: International Trade Administration, U.S. Department of Commerce).   This biweekly publication is the principal news publication of the Department of Commerce. It includes current reports from the Foreign Service, listings of worldwide business opportunities, and articles on topics such as the economies of foreign countries.

Business International (New York: Business International Corp.).   This weekly report is addressed to managers of worldwide business and industrial operations. Topics such as personnel and labor, foreign trade, government and politics, the European Community, and economic conditions in specific countries are covered in short articles.

Business Week (New York: McGraw-Hill Publications).   This important weekly business-news magazine discusses current business topics and related subjects.

The Commercial and Financial Chronicle (Arlington, Mass.: National News Service).   This is a weekly newspaper which, in addition to articles on business topics, features a digest of market letters, offering its readers a digest of financial news from these financial publications, a list of sales and purchases of stock by officers of firms, stock-exchange records, and listings of securities offered by the U.S. government and its agencies.

The Economist (London: Economist Newspaper).   *The Economist* is a weekly magazine that not only deals with business and economics but also contains thorough coverage of world events. Its primary function, however, is to provide its readers with current economic and business news of Europe and America.

Finance and Development (Washington, D.C.: International Monetary Fund and International Bank for Reconstruction and Development).   This quarterly journal is published in English, French, Chinese, Spanish, German, and Portuguese. Its articles reflect the changing global economic scene, explain the workings and the policies of the Fund and the Bank, and discuss activities of the Fund such as assistance to countries in short-term balance-of-trade difficulties. Another section of the journal offers reviews of books on topics such as exchange and trade controls, international trade policies, and international monetary reform.

Financial Times (London: Financial Times).   This daily British equivalent of *The Wall Street Journal* typically contains coverage of bank base rates, company news, foreign-exchange quotations and rates, international company news, labor news, mining news, the state of the money market, overseas markets and news, stock-exchange reports, and world trade news.

Forbes (New York: Forbes, Inc.).   This magazine, published biweekly, carries articles on domestic and foreign business and presents its viewpoint on investments, discussing past performance of and outlook for specific firms.

Fortune (New York: Time, Inc.).   This biweekly magazine typically carries articles related to domestic and foreign business operations, firms, and executives. The "Fortune Directory" of the largest industrial corporations, commercial-banking companies and life-insurance companies, and utilities companies are useful features.

IMF Survey (Washington, D.C.: International Monetary Fund).   This weekly briefly summarizes articles pertaining to organizations such as the European Community, the Inter-American Development Bank, and the International Monetary Fund. It also contains articles on individual countries of the world and on commodities.

Nation's Business (Washington, D.C.: Chamber of Commerce of the United States).   Articles in this monthly relate strictly to the domestic business scene.

Survey of Current Business (Washington, D.C.: Bureau of Economic Analysis, U.S. Department of Commerce).   This monthly publishes current business statistics (monthly and annual) under headings such as "General Business Indicators," "Commodities," "Prices," "Labor Force," "Employment," and "Earnings," and articles on topics such as balance of foreign payments and foreign trade.

The Wall Street Journal (New York: Dow Jones).   This daily (except Saturday and Sunday) newspaper primarily covers current financial and business news in areas such as foreign trade, investments, stocks, bonds, and commodity markets. Coverage of foreign business news is limited.

UN Chronicle (New York: United Nations Publications).   This periodical, is-sued 11 times a year, summarizes the activities of the United Nations and its specialized agencies, including the Economic Commission, which concerns it-self with Latin America, Western Asia, and other areas of the world. It contains articles on monetary systems, multinational corporations, and the International Monetary Fund (IMF).

International Trade

To increase its awareness of expanding foreign markets and to obtain assistance in developing these markets, private enterprise can look to the U.S. Department of Commerce, the U.S. Department of State, and the Chamber of Commerce of the United States as well as to commercial banking institutions. For American firms, the international scene involves more than just exports: it also includes cooperative ventures, consulting agreements, and joint developmental projects with foreign corporations and foreign governments. Government assistance pro-grams are varied and specialized, but taken together they represent a planned program of great importance to American business.

The concept of international trade has broadened to encompass international service industries. The problems related to the sale of services are similar to those encountered in exporting products. The most important service industries are accounting, advertising, banking, construction and engineering, franchising, health services, insurance, shipping, and tourism.

Secretaries in firms that have never exported their services or products can play an important role in helping to develop foreign markets for their firms by collecting information on procedures for conducting business abroad and on sources of assistance, development of overseas markets, and ways of financing exports. This material can be invaluable to executives interested in penetrating foreign markets. Secretaries in firms already active in these markets can lend valuable assistance by keeping up-to-date on developments related to world trade.

The secretary who is involved in the international business of a company should be able to find answers to questions about the markets and products of the countries that the company does business with, including such questions as the following:

Is the country industrialized? evolving into an industrialized nation?

What is its standard of living?

What is its level of education?

What is its official language? What other languages are used?

How tolerant is the country of foreign products?

Are there religious and social influences to be considered regarding particular products?

What types of customer reside in this country?

How big is the market for our type of product?

How many of this type of product are now sold?

Who sells these products?

What share of the market do they control?

How do our competitors' products differ from our own?

What kind of service for specific products will be needed?

How can marketing strategies be developed?

The discussion that follows provides basic information on international trade and suggestions on how to obtain further information.

U.S. DEPARTMENT OF COMMERCE

The Department of Commerce offers assistance to multinational corporations and to firms desiring to compete in foreign markets. Through the Department's many district offices, aid is available to companies that are launching new programs abroad or expanding their existing programs. You should turn to these offices for more detailed information and assistance.

The International Trade Administration (ITA) of the Department of Commerce works in several ways to help Americans benefit from world trade. First, it strengthens and promotes America's international trade, investment, and sales with the following services:

Counseling the business community on the benefits of exporting, how to get started, how to find buyers and distributors, and how to compete for foreign government contracts.

Staging overseas commercial exhibitions of U.S. products and conducting trade missions, catalog exhibitions, and sales seminars abroad to introduce U.S. manufacturers to foreign buyers.

Maintaining a corps of Foreign Commercial Service Officers around the world to gather information on commercial and industrial trends for the benefit of the U.S. business community.

Publishing commercial and marketing information on the world's regions and countries.

Providing local business communities with information and assistance on exporting and investing abroad.

Operating the Worldwide Information and Trade System (WITS), a computerized international marketing system that links U.S. and foreign commercial services with the Washington headquarters.

Second, the ITA helps to develop and maintain an effective U.S. trade policy through activities such as the following:

Identifying key issues affecting America's international commerce and trade.

Implementing and monitoring tariff and nontariff agreements with our trading partners.

Analyzing international regulations and practices affecting foreign investment.

Third, the ITA tries to control certain export or import practices that adversely affect the United States by doing the following:

Investigating complaints of dumping to determine their validity.

Determining if foreign governments are subsidizing their exports to us.

Administering our export control laws and statutory programs involving exports of certain items.

The Foreign Commercial Service (FCS) of the Department of Commerce is a component of the Foreign Service. Promoting U.S. trade and facilitating U.S. investment are its primary responsibilities. To pursue its mission, the FCS has about 130 offices in almost 70 countries, some of them in foreign-trade centers and some in U.S. embassies and consulates. Foreign Commercial Service officers work directly with foreign governments, business representatives, and individuals interested in increasing and continuing trade.

Export Development Offices (EDOs), maintained by the Department of Commerce, are the principal export promotion facilities abroad. These offices, found in major commercial cities worldwide, cooperate with the Foreign Commercial Service and the Department of State, including consulates. Some of their important services are initial market research, assistance with shipping and customs, and the mounting of exhibits. Export Development Offices organize trade fairs, solo exhibitions, trade seminars, and special promotions. To help the exporter participate in such trade promotions, EDOs will provide office space, design and construct exhibits, advise on shipments to the site, unpack and set up displays, and provide basic utilities and housekeeping services, lounges and meeting rooms, appropriate hospitality, and market counseling.

A *Basic Guide to Exporting,* published by the International Trade Administration, is sold by the Superintendent of Documents. This guide should be in the library of any secretary involved in international trade. It tells the potential exporter what is needed to establish a profitable international trade and how to get assistance in doing so. In addition to explaining the basics of establishing export programs, it directs readers to additional sources of information in the government and the private sector. It includes an extensive glossary of terms used in international trade and a bibliography of export reference publications.

U.S. DEPARTMENT OF STATE

The Department of State plays an important part in developing international trade. It negotiates treaties and agreements that affect commerce and trade. It also handles commercial and economic functions in countries with little commercial activity. In all countries that have U.S. embassies, American businesspeople can get assistance from the Economic/Commercial Officers who brief them and introduce them to firms, individuals, and government officials. Those who are anticipating such assistance should write to foreign service posts at least two weeks before leaving the United States.

Assistance within the United States is available from Country Desk Officers in the Department of State. These officers brief representatives of American firms on the political and economic climate in the countries they represent. Write to [country] Desk Officer, Department of State, Washington, DC 20520, for assistance.

U.S. FOREIGN SERVICE POSTS

American consulates are located around the world. Americans traveling and working abroad can go to them for assistance in business and personal matters. The table on pages 524–32 shows the sites of all U.S. embassies, legations, and consulates, along with other important cities. The addresses of these embassies, consulates, and legations may be found in the current edition of *Key Officers of Foreign Service Posts: Guide for Business Representatives,* available from the Superintendent of Documents.

THE U.S. CHAMBER OF COMMERCE

The Chamber of Commerce of the United States, a private organization, perceives private enterprise as a key contributor to world economic development. It believes that U.S. businesspeople abroad have a dual role, as unofficial ambassadors and as corporate representatives. The Chamber helps business executives adapt to the demands of this dual role, and it cooperates with the government agencies responsible for international policies and programs. It advocates a freer international flow of goods, services, and capital. The International Group of the Chamber of Commerce contributes to the Chamber's formulation of policies in major international trade, investment, energy, and monetary issues. Other activities of the International Group are the following:

Analyzing legislation that affects American business abroad and preparing testimony on bills before Congress.

Maintaining close contact with key congressional staff and Executive Branch officials on matters that affect international business.

Providing active support for an improved and expanded national export promotion program.

Producing a variety of reports, surveys, and other publications (including audiovisual materials) on important international economic questions.

Inquiries related to multinational corporations and global business should be sent to the Chamber of Commerce of the United States, Washington, DC 20062.

FINANCING EXPORTS

In addition to developing foreign trade for American firms, U.S. government agencies facilitate the financing of the sale of goods and services to foreign buyers. Such financing is accomplished in cooperation with commercial banks. To reduce the risk for American exporters, credit insurance is available through the U.S. government in association with the insurance industry. Many exporters, however, obtain direct financing through the numerous U.S. banks that have qualified international banking departments, with experts in different kinds of commodities and transactions. Through correspondent relationships with foreign banks, they provide direct channels to overseas customers of American companies.

The Export-Import Bank of the United States   This organization is an independent agency of the U.S. government that participates in financing America's exports by offering direct loans to overseas purchasers of American goods and services. It cooperates with commercial banks in the United States and abroad in providing financial arrangements that help U.S. exporters offer credit to their overseas buyers, provides export credit guarantees to commercial banks which in turn finance export sales, and offers export credit insurance.

INTERNATIONAL TABLE

The following table lists every nation in the world (in 1993), along with a number of colonies, territories, and other possessions.

Each entry includes the languages predominantly spoken in the country (the official language or languages are listed first) and the name of the country's currency.

The time differential between the United States and each country listed, based on eastern standard time, appears in a separate column. To obtain the time in a given country, add the figure opposite the country's name in the time-differential column to the hour where you are, always remembering to allow for any time-zone difference between your office and eastern standard time. Thus, if it is 4:00 p.m. in your office in Los Angeles, it will be 4:30 a.m. in Afghanistan, since the total differential will be 12½ (that is, 9½ + 3) hours. At the same time, it will be 6:00 p.m. in Costa Rica, since the total differential will be only two hours (that is, the −1 in the time-differential column indicates that the difference will be one hour less than Los Angeles's normal differential with eastern standard time).

Daylight saving time—which in America prevails basically from April through October—effectively moves a country one time zone eastward, thus diminishing the positive time-differential figures by an hour and increasing the negative figures by an hour with respect to countries that do not observe daylight saving time. Daylight saving time is observed by most of the temperate-zone nations in the Northern Hemisphere (though it rarely extends past September). It is generally not observed by countries in the tropical zone. In the temperate-zone nations of the Southern Hemisphere, it is generally observed in reverse. Daylight saving time may thus account for additional differences of an hour, or even two hours, especially when calling countries outside of Europe.

In the right-hand column are listed some of the countries' principal cities. The cities in normal roman type represent the sites of *all* the U.S. embassies and consulates worldwide (1993). The first city listed is always the capital; except when printed in italics, it is also the site of the U.S. embassy or chief consular office. All the other cities listed, except those in italics, have U.S. consular offices.

The dialing code for each country appears in parentheses after its name. If the initials "A.C." (for "Area Code") precede the code, it may be dialed exactly like an area code within the United States. If no code appears after the country's name, the country cannot be dialed direct. Each city's dialing code, if any, appears after the city's name; where no number appears, no code is needed. For instructions on international dialing, see pages 458–59.

Several currency names—in particular, *franc, peso, dinar, pound, rupee, shilling,* and *dollar*—are each used in more than one country for currencies that are not in fact identical in value. Except where indicated, the currency is that of the individual country only. However, the CFA franc (CFA stands for Communauté Financière Africaine, or African Financial Community) and the East Caribbean dollar are genuinely international currencies.

Country and dialing code	Languages	Currency	Time diff.	Cities and dialing codes
Afghanistan	Pashto, Dari Persian	Afghani	9½	*Kabul*
Albania (355)	Albanian	Lek	7	Tirana (42)
Algeria (213)	Arabic, French, Berber	Dinar	6	Algiers (2), Oran (6)
American Samoa [U.S.] (684)	English	U.S. dollar	−6	Pago Pago
Andorra (33)	Catalan, Spanish, French	French franc, Spanish peseta	6	*Andorra la Vella* (628); embassy: Barcelona, Spain
Angola (244)	Portuguese	Kwanza	6	*Luanda* (2)
Antigua and Barbuda (A.C. 809)	English	East Caribbean dollar	1	St. Johns
Argentina (54)	Spanish	Peso	2	Buenos Aires (1), *Córdoba* (51), *Rosario* (41)
Armenia (7)	Armenian, Russian	Dram	9	Yerevan (885)

Country and dialing code	Languages	Currency	Time diff.	Cities and dialing codes
Aruba [Neth.] (297)	Dutch	Guilder	1	*Oranjestad* (8)
Australia (61)	English	Dollar	13, 14½, 15	Canberra (6), Adelaide (8), Brisbane (7), Melbourne (3), Perth (9), Sydney (2)
Austria (43)	German	Schilling	6	Vienna (1), Salzburg (662)
Azerbaijan (7)	Azerbaijani, Russian	Manat	9	Baku (8922)
Azores [Port.] (351)	Portuguese	Portuguese escudo	4	Ponta Delgada (96), *Madalena* (92)
Bahamas (A.C. 809)	English	Dollar	0	Nassau
Bahrain (973)	Arabic, English	Dinar	8	Manama
Bangladesh (880)	Bengali [Bangla], English	Taka	11	Dhaka (2)
Barbados (A.C. 809)	English	Dollar	1	Bridgetown
Belarus (7)	Belorussian, Russian	Ruble	8	Minsk (0172)
Belgium (32)	Flemish, French, German	Franc	6	Brussels (2), Antwerp (3)
Belize (501)	English, Spanish	Dollar	− 1	Belize City (2)
Benin (229)	French	CFA franc	6	Cotonou
Bermuda [U.K.] (A.C. 809)	English	British pound	1	Hamilton
Bhutan (975)	Dzongkha, Nepali, English	Ngultrum	10½	*Thimbu;* consulate: New Delhi, India
Bolivia (591)	Spanish, Quechua, Aymara	Boliviano	1	La Paz (2), *Santa Cruz* (33), *Cochabamba* (42)
Bosnia and Herze-govina (387)	Serbo-Croatian	Dinar	6	*Sarajevo* (71)
Botswana (267)	English, Tswana	Pula	7	Gaborone (31)
Brazil (55)	Portuguese	Cruzeiro	1,2	Brasília (61), Belém [Pará] (91), Belo Horizonte (31), Manaus (92), Porto Alegre (512), Recife (81), Rio de Janeiro (21), Salvador [Bahía] (71), São Paulo (11)
Brunei (673)	Malay, English, Chinese	Dollar	13	Bandar Seri Begawan (2)
Bulgaria (359)	Bulgarian	Lev	7	Sofia (2)
Burkina Faso (226)	French	CFA franc	5	Ouagadougou
Burma—see Myanmar				
Burundi (257)	French, Kirundi	Franc	7	Bujumbura
Cambodia (855)	Khmer, French	Riel	12	Phnom Penh (23)

Country and dialing code	Languages	Currency	Time diff.	Cities and dialing codes
Cameroon (237)	English, French	CFA franc	6	Yaoundé, Douala
Canada (no code needed when dialing from United States)	English, French	Dollar	−3, −2, −1, 0,1, 1½	Ottawa (613), Calgary (403), *Edmonton* (403), Halifax (902), *Hamilton* (519), Montreal (514), Québec (418), Toronto (416), Vancouver (604), *Winnipeg* (204)
Cape Verde (238)	Portuguese	Escudo	4	Praia
Central African Republic (236)	French	CFA franc	6	Bangui
Chad (235)	French, Arabic	CFA franc	6	N'Djamena (51)
Chile (56)	Spanish	Peso	1	Santiago (2)
China (86)	Mandarin Chinese	Yuan	13	Beijing (1), Chengdu (28), Guangzhou [Canton] (20), Shanghai (21), Shenyang [Mukden] (24), *Tianjin [Tientsin]* (22)
Colombia (57)	Spanish	Peso	0	Bogotá (1), Barranquilla (58)
Commonwealth of Independent States—see individual countries				
Comoros (269)	Arabic, French	CFA franc	8	Moroni
Congo (242)	French	CFA franc	6	Brazzaville
Costa Rica (506)	Spanish	Colón	−1	San José
Côte d'Ivoire (225)	French	CFA franc	5	Abidjan or *Yamoussoukro*
Croatia (385)	Serbo-Croatian	Kuna	6	Zagreb (41)
Cuba	Spanish	Peso	0	Havana
Cyprus (357)	Greek, Turkish, English	Pound	7	Nicosia (2)
Czech Rep. (42)	Czech	Koruna	6	Prague (2)
Denmark (45)	Danish	Krone	6	Copenhagen
Djibouti (253)	French, Arabic	Franc	8	Djibouti
Dominica (A.C. 809)	English	East Caribbean dollar	1	*Roseau;* embassy: Bridgetown, Barbados
Dominican Republic (A.C. 809)	Spanish	Peso	0	Santo Domingo
Ecuador (593)	Spanish, Quechua	Sucre	0	Quito (2), Guayaquil (4)
Egypt (20)	Arabic	Pound	7	Cairo (2), Alexandria (3)
El Salvador (503)	Spanish	Colón	−1	San Salvador
England—see United Kingdom				
Equatorial Guinea (240)	Spanish	CFA franc	6	Malabo (9)

Country and dialing code	Languages	Currency	Time diff.	Cities and dialing codes
Eritrea (291)	Amharic	Birr	8	Asmara (4)
Estonia (372)	Estonian, Russian	Kroon	7	Tallinn (2)
Ethiopia (251)	Amharic	Birr	8	Addis Ababa (1)
Fiji (679)	English, Fijian	Dollar	17	Suva
Finland (358)	Finnish, Swedish	Markka	7	Helsinki (0)
France (33)	French	Franc	6	Paris (1), Bordeaux (56), *Lyon* (7), Marseilles (91), Strasbourg (88)
French Guiana [Fr.] (596)	French	French franc	1	*Cayenne;* consulate: Fort-de-France, Martinique
Gabon (241)	French	CFA franc	6	Libreville
Gambia (220)	English	Dalasi	5	Banjul
Georgia (7)	Georgian, Russian	Ruble	9	Tbilisi (8832)
Germany (49)	German	Deutsche Mark	6	Berlin (30), Bonn (228), *Cologne [Köln]* (221), *Essen* (201), Frankfurt (69), Hamburg (40), Leipzig (341), Munich [München] (89), Stuttgart (711)
Ghana (233)	English	Cedi	5	Accra (21)
Gibraltar [U.K.] (350)	English	British pound	6	*Gibraltar*
Greece (30)	Greek	Drachma	7	Athens (1), Thessaloniki [Salonika] (31)
Greenland [Denm.] (299)	Danish	Danish krone	1,2,4	*Godthaab* (2)
Grenada (A.C. 809)	English	East Caribbean dollar	1	St. George's
Guadeloupe [Fr.] (590)	French	French franc	1	*Basse-Terre*
Guam [U.S.] (671)	English, Chamorro	U.S. dollar	15	Agaña
Guatemala (502)	Spanish	Quetzal	− 1	Guatemala City (2)
Guinea (224)	French	Franc	5	Conakry (4)
Guinea-Bissau (245)	Portuguese	Peso	5	Bissau
Guyana (592)	English	Dollar	2	Georgetown (2)
Haiti (509)	French, Creole	Gourde	0	Port-au-Prince
Honduras (504)	Spanish	Lempira	− 1	Tegucigalpa
Hong Kong [U.K.] (852)	English, Chinese	British pound	13	Hong Kong
Hungary (36)	Hungarian [Magyar]	Forint	6	Budapest (1)
Iceland (354)	Icelandic	Króna	5	Reykjavik (1)
India (91)	Hindi, English	Rupee	10½	New Delhi (11), Bombay (22), Calcutta (33), Madras (44)

Country and dialing code	Languages	Currency	Time diff.	Cities and dialing codes
Indonesia (62)	Bahasa Indonesia	Rupiah	12	Djakarta (21), Medan (61), Surabaya (31)
Iran (98)	Persian [Farsi]	Rial	8½	*Teheran* (21)
Iraq (964)	Arabic	Dinar	8	*Baghdad* (1)
Ireland (353)	Irish, English	Pound	5	Dublin (1)
Israel (972)	Hebrew, Arabic	Shekel	7	Tel Aviv (3) or Jerusalem (2), *Haifa* (4)
Italy (39)	Italian	Lira	6	Rome (6), Florence (55), Genoa (10), Milan (2), Naples (81), Palermo (91), *Turin* (11), *Venice* (41)
Ivory Coast—see Côte d'Ivoire				
Jamaica (A.C. 809)	English	Dollar	0	Kingston
Japan (81)	Japanese	Yen	14	Tokyo (3), Fukuoka (92), Kyoto (75), Nagoya (52), Naha (988), Osaka (6), Sapporo (11), *Yokohama* (45)
Jordan (962)	Arabic, English	Dinar	7	Amman (6)
Kazakhstan (7)	Russian, Kazakh	Ruble	10,11	Alma-Ata (3272)
Kenya (254)	Swahili, English	Shilling	8	Nairobi (2), Mombasa (11)
Kiribati (686)	English, Gilbertese	Australian dollar	17	*Tarawa*
Kuwait (965)	Arabic, English	Dinar	8	Kuwait
Kyrgyzstan (7)	Kirghiz	Som	11	Bishkek (3312)
Laos (856)	Lao, French, English	Kip	12	Vientiane (21)
Latvia (371)	Latvian, Russian	Ruble	7	Riga (2)
Lebanon (961)	Arabic, French	Pound	7	Beirut (1)
Lesotho (266)	English, Sesotho	Loti	7	Maseru
Liberia (231)	English	Dollar	5	Monrovia
Libya (218)	Arabic	Dinar	7	*Tripoli* (21)
Liechtenstein (41)	German	Swiss franc	6	*Vaduz* (75); embassy: Zurich, Switzerland
Lithuania (370)	Lithuanian, Russian	Litas	7	Vilnius (2)
Luxembourg (352)	French, German	Franc	6	Luxembourg
Macao [Port.] (853)	Portuguese, Chinese	Patacá	13	*Macao;*
Macedonia (389)	Macedonian	Denar	6	*Skopje* (91)
Madagascar (261)	Malagasy, French	Franc	8	Antananarivo (2)
Malawi (265)	English, Chichewa	Kwacha	7	Lilongwe, *Blantyre*
Malaysia (60)	Malay, Chinese, English	Ringgit	13	Kuala Lumpur (3)

Country and dialing code	Languages	Currency	Time diff.	Cities and dialing codes
Maldives (960)	Dhivehi	Rufiyaa	10	*Malé;* embassy: Colombo, Sri Lanka
Mali (223)	French, Bambara	CFA franc	5	Bamako
Malta (356)	Maltese, English, Italian	Lira, Pound	6	Valletta/Floriana
Marshall Islands (692)	Marshallese, English	U.S. dollar	17	Majuro (9)
Martinique [Fr.] (596)	French	French franc	1	Fort-de-France
Mauritania (222)	Arabic, French	Ouguiya	5	Nouakchott
Mauritius (230)	English, French, Creole, Hindi	Rupee	9	Port Louis
Mexico (52)	Spanish	Peso	−1, −2, −3	Mexico City (5), Ciudad Juárez (16), Guadalajara (3), Hermosillo (62), Matamoros (891), Mazatlán (69), Mérida (99), Monterrey (83), Nuevo Laredo (871), Tijuana (66)
Micronesia, Federated States of (691)	English	U.S. dollar	16	Kolonia
Moldova (7)	Romanian, Russian	Leu	8	Kishinev [Chisinau] (2)
Monaco (33)	French	French franc	6	*Monaco* (93); consulate: Marseille, France
Mongolia (976)	Mongolian	Tugrik	12,13, 14	Ulan Bator (1)
Morocco (212)	Arabic, French	Dirham	5	Rabat (7), Casablanca (2)
Mozambique (258)	Portuguese	Metical	7	Maputo (1)
Myanmar (95)	Burmese	Kyat	11½	Yangon [Rangoon] (1)
Namibia (264)	English, Afrikaans, German	Dollar	7	Windhoek (61)
Nauru (674)	Nauruan, English	Australian dollar	17	*Yaren;* embassy: Canberra, Australia
Nepal (977)	Nepali	Rupee	10½	Kathmandu (1)
Netherlands (31)	Dutch	Gulden	6	The Hague ['s Gravenhage] (70), Amsterdam (20), *Rotterdam* (10)
Netherlands Antilles [Neth.] (599)	Dutch	Dutch gulden	1	Willemstad (9)

Country and dialing code	Languages	Currency	Time diff.	Cities and dialing codes
New Zealand (64)	English, Maori	Dollar	17	Wellington (4), Auckland (9), *Christchurch* (3)
Nicaragua (505)	Spanish	Córdoba	−1	Managua (2)
Niger (227)	French, Hausa	CFA franc	6	Niamey
Nigeria (234)	English, Hausa	Naira	6	Lagos (1), Kaduna (62)
Northern Ireland—see United Kingdom				
Northern Mariana Islands [U.S.]	English	U.S. dollar	14	
North Korea	Korean	Won	14	*Pyongyang*
Norway (47)	Norwegian	Krone	6	Oslo (22)
Oman (968)	Arabic, English	Rial	9	Muscat
Pakistan (92)	English, Urdu	Rupee	10	Islamabad (51), Karachi (21), Lahore (42), Peshawar (521)
Palau [U.S.] (680)	English	U.S. dollar	14	Koror
Panama (507)	Spanish, English	Balboa	0	Panama City
Papua New Guinea (675)	English, Pidgin English, Motu	Kina	15	Port Moresby
Paraguay (595)	Spanish, Guaraní	Guaraní	2	Asunción (21)
Peru (51)	Spanish, Quechua	Sol	0	Lima (14)
Philippines (63)	Pilipino, English	Peso	13	Manila (2), Cebu (32), *Quezon City* (2)
Poland (48)	Polish	Zloty	6	Warsaw (22), Krakow (12), Poznan (61)
Portugal (351)	Portuguese	Escudo	5	Lisbon (1), *Oporto* (2)
Puerto Rico [U.S.] (A.C. 809)	Spanish, English	U.S. dollar	0	San Juan
Qatar (974)	Arabic, English	Riyal	8	Doha
Réunion [Fr.] (262)	French, Creole	French franc	9	*Saint-Denis*
Romania (40)	Romanian, Hungarian [Magyar], German	Leu	7	Bucharest (1)
Russia (7)	Russian	Ruble	8,9,10, 11	Moscow (095), St. Petersburg (812), Vladivostok
Rwanda (250)	French, Kinyarwandu	Franc	7	Kigali
St. Kitts and Nevis (A.C. 809)	English	East Caribbean dollar	1	*Basseterre;* embassy: St. Johns, Antigua
St. Lucia (A.C. 809)	English	East Caribbean dollar	1	*Castries;* embassy: Bridgetown, Barbados
St. Vincent and the Grenadines (A.C. 809)	English	East Caribbean dollar	1	*Kingstown*

Country and dialing code	Languages	Currency	Time diff.	Cities and dialing codes
San Marino (39)	Italian	Italian lira	6	*San Marino* (549); embassy: Florence, Italy
São Tomé and Principe (239)	Portuguese	Dobra	5	*São Tomé;* embassy: Libreville, Gabon
Saudi Arabia (966)	Arabic	Riyal	8	Riyadh (1), Dhahran (3), Jidda (2)
Scotland—see United Kingdom				
Senegal (221)	French	CFA franc	5	Dakar
Serbia-Montenegro (381)	Serbo-Croatian	Dinar	6	Belgrade (11)
Seychelles (248)	Creole, English, French	Rupee	9	Victoria
Sierra Leone (232)	English	Leone	5	Freetown (22)
Singapore (65)	Chinese, Malay, Tamil, English	Dollar	13	Singapore
Slovakia (42)	Slovak	Koruna	6	Bratislava (7)
Slovenia (386)	Slovene	Tolar	6	Ljubljana (61)
Solomon Islands (677)	English	Dollar	16	Honiara
Somalia	Somali, Arabic	Shilling	8	*Mogadishu*
South Africa (27)	Afrikaans, English	Rand	7	Pretoria (12), Cape Town (21), Durban (31), Johannesburg (11)
South Korea (82)	Korean	Won	14	Seoul (2), *Inchon* (32), Pusan (51), *Taegu* (53)
Spain (34)	Spanish	Peseta	6	Madrid (1), Barcelona (3), Bilbao (4), *Valencia* (6)
Sri Lanka (94)	Sinhalese, Tamil, English	Rupee	10½	Colombo (1)
Sudan	Arabic, English	Dinar	7	Khartoum
Suriname (597)	Dutch, Sranan Tongo, English	Gulden	1½	Paramaribo
Swaziland (268)	Swazi, English	Lilangeni	7	Mbabane
Sweden (46)	Swedish	Krona	6	Stockholm (8)
Switzerland (41)	German, French, Italian	Franc	6	Bern (31), *Basel* (61), *Geneva* (22), Zurich (1)
Syria (963)	Arabic	Pound	8	Damascus (11)
Taiwan (886)	Mandarin Chinese	Dollar	13	*Taipei* (2), *Kaohsiung* (7)
Tajikistan (7)	Tajiki, Russian	Ruble	11	Dushanbe (3772)
Tanzania (255)	Swahili, English	Shilling	8	Dar es Salaam (51)
Thailand (66)	Thai, Chinese, English	Baht (Tical)	12	Bangkok (2), Chiang Mai (53), Songkhla (74), Udorn (42)
Togo (228)	French, Ewé	CFA franc	5	Lomé

Country and dialing code	Languages	Currency	Time diff.	Cities and dialing codes
Tonga (676)	Tongan, English	Pa'anga	18	*Nuku'alofa;* embassy: Suva, Fiji
Trinidad and Tobago (A.C. 809)	English	Dollar	1	Port-of-Spain
Tunisia (216)	Arabic, French	Dinar	6	Tunis (1)
Turkey (90)	Turkish	Lira	7	Ankara (4), Adana (71), Istambul (1), Izmir (51)
Turkmenistan (7)	Turkmenian, Russian	Manat	10	Ashkhabad (3632)
Tuvalu (688)	Tuvaluan, English	Australian dollar	17	*Funafuti*
Uganda (256)	English, Swahili	Shilling	8	Kampala (41)
Ukraine (7)	Ukrainian, Russian	Karbovanets	8	Kiev (044)
United Arab Emirates (971)	Arabic, Persian [Farsi], English	Dirham	9	Abu Dhabi (2), Dubai (4)
United Kingdom (44)	English	Pound	5	London (71, 81), Belfast, Northern Ireland (232), *Birmingham* (21), Edinburgh, Scotland (31), *Glasgow, Scotland* (41), *Manchester* (61)
Upper Volta—see Burkina Faso				
Uruguay (598)	Spanish	Peso	2	Montevideo (2)
U.S. Virgin Islands [U.S.] (A.C. 809)	English	U.S. dollar	1	*Charlotte Amalie*
Uzbekistan (7)	Uzbek, Russian	Ruble	10,11	Tashkent (3712)
Vanuatu (678)	Bislama, French, English	Vatu	16	*Vila;* embassy: Port Moresby, Papua New Guinea
Vatican City (39)	Italian, Latin	Italian lira	6	All points: (6)
Venezuela (58)	Spanish	Bolivar	1	Caracas (2), Maracaibo (61)
Vietnam (84)	Vietnamese, French, English	Dong	12	*Hanoi* (4), *Ho Chi Minh City* (8)
Virgin Islands—see U.S. Virgin Islands				
Western Samoa (685)	Samoan, English	Tala	−6	*Apia;* embassy: Wellington, New Zealand
Yemen (967)	Arabic	Dinar, Rial	8	San'a (1)
Yugoslavia—see Serbia-Montenegro				
Zaire (243)	French	Zaire	6,7	Kinshasa (12), Lubumbashi (222)
Zambia (260)	English	Kwacha	7	Lusaka (1)
Zimbabwe (263)	English	Dollar	7	Harare (4)

Nonmetric-to-Metric Weights and Measures

WEIGHT
Avoirdupois

ton		
short ton	20 short hundredweight, 2000 pounds	0.907 metric ton
long ton	20 long hundredweight, 2240 pounds	1.016 metric tons
hundredweight (cwt)		
short hundredweight	100 pounds, 0.05 short ton	45.359 kilograms
long hundredweight	112 pounds, 0.05 long ton	50.802 kilograms
pound (lb, lb avdp also #)	16 ounces, 7000 grains	0.454 kilogram
ounce (oz, oz avdp)	16 drams, 437.5 grains, 0.0625 pound	28.350 grams
dram (dr, dr avdp)	27.344 grains, 0.0625 ounce	1.772 grams
grain (gr)	0.037 dram, 0.002286 ounce	0.0648 gram

Troy

pound (lb t)	12 ounces, 240 pennyweight, 5760 grains	0.373 kilogram
ounce (oz t)	20 pennyweight, 480 grains, 0.083 pound	31.103 grams
pennyweight (dwt also pwt)	24 grains, 0.05 ounce	1.555 grams
grain (gr)	0.042 pennyweight, 0.002083 ounce	0.0648 gram

Apothecaries'

pound (lb ap)	12 ounces, 5760 grains	0.373 kilogram
ounce (oz ap)	8 drams, 480 grains, 0.083 pound	31.103 grams
dram (dr ap)	3 scruples, 60 grains	3.888 grams
scruple (s ap)	20 grains, 0.333 dram	1.296 grams
grain (gr)	0.05 scruple, 0.002083 ounce, 0.0166 dram	0.0648 gram

CAPACITY
U.S. liquid measure

gallon (gal)	4 quarts (231 cubic inches)	3.785 liters
quart (qt)	2 pints (57.75 cubic inches)	0.946 liter
pint (pt)	4 gills (28.875 cubic inches)	0.473 liter
gill (gi)	4 fluid ounces (7.219 cubic inches)	118.294 milliliters
fluid ounce (fl oz)	8 fluid drams (1.805 cubic inches)	29.573 milliliters
fluid dram (fl dr)	60 minims (0.226 cubic inch)	3.697 milliliters

U.S. dry measure

bushel (bu)	4 pecks (2150.42 cubic inches)	35.239 liters
peck (pk)	8 quarts (537.605 cubic inches)	8.810 liters
quart (qt)	2 pints (67.201 cubic inches)	1.101 liters
pint (pt)	½ quart (33.600 cubic inches)	0.551 liter

British imperial liquid and dry measure

bushel (bu)	4 pecks (2219.36 cubic inches)	0.036 cubic meter
peck (pk)	2 gallons (554.84 cubic inches)	0.0091 cubic meter
gallon (gal)	4 quarts (277.420 cubic inches)	4.546 liters
quart (qt)	2 pints (69.355 cubic inches)	1.136 liters
pint (pt)	4 gills (34.678 cubic inches)	568.26 cubic centimeters
gill (gi)	5 fluid ounces (8.669 cubic inches)	142.066 cubic centimeters
fluid ounce (fl oz)	8 fluid drams (1.7339 cubic inches)	28.412 cubic centimeters
fluid dram (fl dr)	60 minims (0.216734 cubic inch)	3.5516 cubic centimeters

LENGTH

mile (mi)	5280 feet, 1760 yards, 320 rods	1.609 kilometers
yard (yd)	3 feet, 36 inches	0.9144 meter
foot (ft, ')	12 inches, 0.333 yard	30.48 centimeters
inch (in, ")	0.083 foot, 0.028 yard	2.54 centimeters

AREA

square mile (sq mi, mi^2)	640 acres, 102,400 square rods	2.590 square kilometers
acre	4840 square yards, 43,560 square feet	0.405 hectare, 4047 square meters
square yard (sq yd, yd^2)	1296 square inches, 9 square feet	0.836 square meter
square foot (sq ft, ft^2)	144 square inches, 0.111 square yard	0.093 square meter
square inch (sq in, in^2)	0.0069 square foot, 0.00077 square yard	6.452 square centimeters

VOLUME

cubic yard (cu yd, yd^3)	27 cubic feet, 46.656 cubic inches	0.765 cubic meter
cubic foot (cu ft, ft^3)	1728 cubic inches, 0.0370 cubic yard	0.028 cubic meter
cubic inch (cu in, in^3)	0.00058 cubic foot, 0.000021 cubic yard	16.387 cubic centimeters

Metric-to-Nonmetric Weights and Measures

WEIGHT

metric ton (t)	1,000,000 grams	1.102 short tons
kilogram (kg)	1,000 grams	2.2046 pounds
hectogram (hg)	100 grams	3.527 ounces
dekagram (dag)	10 grams	0.353 ounce
gram (g)	1 gram	0.035 ounce
decigram (dg)	0.10 gram	1.543 grains
centigram (cg)	0.01 gram	0.154 grain
milligram (mg)	0.001 gram	0.015 grain

CAPACITY

		cubic	*dry*	*liquid*
kiloliter (kl)	1,000 liters	1.31 cubic yards		
hectoliter (hl)	100 liters	3.53 cubic feet	2.84 bushels	
dekaliter (dal)	10 liters	0.35 cubic foot	1.14 pecks	2.64 gallons
liter (l)	1 liter	61.02 cubic inches	0.908 quart	1.057 quarts
cubic decimeter (dm³)	1 liter	61.02 cubic inches	0.908 quart	1.057 quarts
deciliter (dl)	0.10 liter	6.1 cubic inches	0.18 pint	0.21 pint
centiliter (cl)	0.01 liter	0.61 cubic inch		0.338 fluid ounce
milliliter (ml)	0.001 liter	0.061 cubic inch		0.27 fluid dram

LENGTH

kilometer (km)	1,000 meters	0.62 mile
hectometer (hm)	100 meters	328.08 feet
dekameter (dam)	10 meters	32.81 feet
meter (m)	1 meter	39.37 inches
decimeter (dm)	0.1 meter	3.94 inches
centimeter (cm)	0.01 meter	0.39 inch
millimeter (mm)	0.001 meter	0.039 inch

AREA

square kilometer (sq km, km²)	1,000,000 square meters	0.3861 square mile
hectare (ha)	10,000 square meters	2.47 acres
square centimeter (sq cm, cm²)	0.0001 square meter	0.155 square inch

VOLUME

cubic meter (m³)	1 cubic meter	1.307 cubic yards
cubic decimeter (dm³)	0.001 cubic meter	61.023 cubic inches
cubic centimeter (cu cm, cm³, cc)	0.000001 cubic meter	0.061 cubic inch

Appendix: Further Reading

GENERAL

Kaliski, Burton S. *Office Management.* New York: Harcourt Brace Jovanovich, 1986.

The Prentice-Hall Creative Secretary's Letter. Newsletter (biweekly). Published by Bureau of Business Practice, BBP Department AM, 24 Rope Ferry Road, Waterford, CT 06386.

The Secretary. Magazine (9 issues/year). Published by Professional Secretaries International, 10502 N.W. Ambassador Drive, P.O. Box 20404, Kansas City, MO 64195-0404.

Tilton, Rita S., et al. *Secretarial Procedures and Administration.* 9th ed. Cincinnati: South-Western, 1987.

ACCOUNTING

Fess, Philip E. *Accounting Principles.* 16th ed. Cincinnati: South-Western, 1989.

Lee, Nanci. *Elementary Accounting.* Hinsdale, Ill.: Dryden Press, 1981.

Meigs, Walter B. and Robert F. *Accounting: The Basis for Business Decisions.* 6th ed. New York: McGraw-Hill, 1984.

Nickerson, Clarence B. *Accounting Handbook for Non-Accountants.* 2d ed. New York: Van Nostrand Reinhold, 1983.

BUSINESS WRITING

Barfield, Ray E., and Sylvia S. Titus. *Business Communications.* Hauppauge, N.Y.: Barron's, 1992.

Blake, Gary, and Robert W. Bly. *The Elements of Business Writing.* New York: Collier-Macmillan, 1991.

Tarrant, John. *Business Writing with Style: Strategies for Success.* New York: John Wiley, 1991.

DATA PROCESSING

Carter, Juanita E., and Darroch F. Young. *Electronic Calculators: A Mastery Approach.* 2d ed. Boston: Houghton Mifflin, 1985.

Mandell, Steven L. *Principles of Data Processing.* 3d ed. St. Paul: West, 1984.

Robichaud, Beryl, et al. *Introduction to Data Processing.* 3d ed. New York: McGraw-Hill, 1983.

DESKTOP PUBLISHING

Beach, Mark. *Editing Your Newsletter*. 3d ed. Portland, Ore.: Coast to Coast, 1988.

Duff, Jon M. *Introduction to Desktop Publishing*. Englewood Cliffs, N.J.: Prentice-Hall, 1989.

Parker, Roger C. *Looking Good in Print*. 2d ed. Alexandria, Va.: Tools of the Trade, 1992.

Weiner, Ed. *Desktop Publishing Made Simple*. Garden City, N.Y.: Doubleday, 1991.

Williams, Patricia A. *Creating and Producing the Perfect Newsletter*. Glenview, Ill.: Scott, Foresman, 1989.

DICTIONARIES AND WORD GUIDES

Gifis, Stephen H. *Law Dictionary*. Rev. ed. Hauppauge, N.Y.: Barron's, 1983.

Merriam-Webster's Collegiate Dictionary, Tenth Edition. Springfield, Mass.: Merriam-Webster, 1993.

Merriam-Webster's Collegiate Thesaurus. Springfield, Mass.: Merriam-Webster, 1988.

Merriam-Webster's Medical Desk Dictionary. Springfield, Mass.: Merriam-Webster, 1993.

Webster's Instant Word Guide. Springfield, Mass.: Merriam-Webster, 1980.

ETIQUETTE

Axtell, Roger E., ed. *Do's and Taboos around the World*. 2d ed. New York: John Wiley, 1990.

Baldridge, Letitia. *Letitia Baldridge's Complete Guide to Executive Manners*. Ed. Sandi Gelles-Cole. Rawson-Macmillan, 1985.

Phillips, Linda. *Concise Guide to Executive Etiquette*. Garden City, N.Y.: Doubleday, 1990.

Post, Elizabeth L. *Emily Post on Business Etiquette*. New York: HarperCollins, 1990.

GRAMMAR, STYLE, AND USAGE

The Chicago Manual of Style. 13th ed. Chicago: University of Chicago Press, 1982.

Irmscher, William F. *The Holt Guide to English: A Comprehensive Handbook of Rhetoric, Language, and Literature*. 3d ed. New York: Harcourt Brace Jovanovich, 1981.

Keithley, Erwin, and Marie E. Flatly. *A Manual of Style for Business Letters, Memos, and Reports*. 4th ed. Cincinnati: South-Western, 1988.

Keithley, Erwin, and Margaret H. Thompson. *English for Modern Business*. 6th ed. Homewood, Ill.: Richard D. Irwin, 1990.

Merriam-Webster's Guide to Business Correspondence. Springfield, Mass.: Merriam-Webster, 1988.

Merriam-Webster's Standard American Style Manual. Springfield, Mass.: Merriam-Webster, 1985.

Sabin, William A. *The Gregg Reference Manual*. 7th ed. New York: McGraw-Hill, 1992.

Skillin, Marjorie E., et al. *Words into Type*. 3d ed. Englewood Cliffs, N.J.: Prentice-Hall, 1974.

Webster's Dictionary of English Usage. Springfield, Mass.: Merriam-Webster, 1989.

HUMAN RELATIONS

Chapman, Elwood N. *Supervisor's Survival Kit: Phase One Management.* 5th ed. New York: Macmillan, 1990.

Imundo, Louis V. *The Effective Supervisor's Handbook.* New York: AMACOM, 1990.

Kossen, Stan. *Supervision.* 2d ed. St. Paul: West, 1991.

LETTERS, MEMOS, AND REPORTS

Brown, Leland. *Effective Business Report Writing.* 4th ed. Englewood Cliffs, N.J.: Prentice-Hall, 1985.

Gilsdorf, Jeanette. *Business Correspondence for Today: Letters, Memos and Short Reports.* Englewood Cliffs, N.J.: Prentice-Hall, 1989.

Poe, Roy W. *The McGraw-Hill Guide to Effective Business Reports.* New York: McGraw-Hill, 1986.

Poe, Roy W. *The McGraw-Hill Handbook of Business Letters.* New York: McGraw-Hill, 1991.

The Random House Book of Contemporary Business Letters. New York: Random House, 1989.

MAIL

U.S. Postal Service publications. Washington, D.C.: Government Printing Office.
   Domestic Mail Manual.
   Domestic Postage Rates, Fees, and Information.
   International Mail Manual.
   International Postage Rates and Fees.
   National ZIP Code and Post Office Directory.

MEETINGS AND PARLIAMENTARY PROCEDURE

Burleson, Clyde W. *Effective Meetings: The Complete Guide.* New York: John Wiley, 1990.

Eisner, Will. *Robert's Rules of Order.* New York: Bantam, 1986.

Jones, Garfield. *Parliamentary Procedures at a Glance.* New York: Penguin, 1990.

Schwartzman, H. B. *The Meeting: Gatherings in Organizations and Communities.* New York: Plenum, 1989.

Sturgis, Alice F. *The Standard Code of Parliamentary Procedure.* 3d ed. New York: McGraw-Hill, 1988.

Weissinger, Suzanne S. *A Guide to Successful Meeting Planning.* New York: John Wiley, 1991.

OFFICE LANDSCAPING

Duffy, Francis. *The Changing Workplace.* New York: Van Nostrand Reinhold, 1991.

Rappoport, James, et al., eds. *Office Planning and Design Workbook.* New York: John Wiley, 1991.

OFFICE MACHINES

Kutie, Rita C., and Joan L. Rhodes. *Procedures for the Electronic Office.* Englewood Cliffs, N.J.: Prentice-Hall, 1988.

Lord, Kenniston W., Jr. *Office Automation Systems Handbook*. Blue Ridge Summit, Pa.: TAB Books, 1988.

McKenzie, Jimmy C., and Robert J. Hughes. *Office Machines: A Practical Approach*. 3d ed. Englewood Cliffs, N.J.: Prentice-Hall, 1989.

RECORDS MANAGEMENT

Borko, Harold, and Charles L. Bernier. *Indexing Concepts and Methods*. New York: Academic Press, 1978.

General Services Administration. *A Guide to Record Retention Requirements*. Washington, D.C.: Government Printing Office. Annual.

Krevolin, Nathan. *Filing and Records Management*. Englewood Cliffs, N.J.: Prentice-Hall, 1986.

Rules for Alphabetical Filing as Standardized by ARMA. Prairie Village, Kan.: Association of Records Managers and Administrators.

Stewart, Jeffrey R., Jr., et al. *Filing Systems and Records Management*. 3d ed. New York: McGraw-Hill, 1981.

SECRETARIAL SPECIALTIES

Adams, Dorothy, and Margaret A. Kurtz. *The Legal Secretary: Terminology and Transcription*. New York: McGraw-Hill, 1980.

Bruno, Carole A. *Legal Secretary's Standard Desk Book*. Englewood Cliffs, N.J.: Prentice-Hall, 1986.

The Career Legal Secretary. Rev. ed. St. Paul: West, 1991.

Curchack, Norma, Herbert F. Yengel, and Katherine H. Hannigan. *Legal Typewriting*. 2d ed. New York: McGraw-Hill, 1981.

Diehl, Marcy O., and Marilyn T. Fordney. *Medical Typing and Transcription: Techniques and Procedures*. 3d ed. Philadelphia: Saunders, 1991.

Jean Priest and Associates Staff. *The Effective Education Secretary*. Palm Springs, Cal.: ETC, 1989.

Rudman, Jack. *Legal Secretary*. Syosset, N.Y.: National Learning Corp., 1991.

Smith, Patsy C. *Medical Typewriting*. 2d ed. New York: McGraw-Hill, 1983.

Webster's Legal Secretaries Handbook. Springfield, Mass.: Merriam-Webster, 1981.

Webster's Medical Secretaries Handbook. Springfield, Mass.: Merriam-Webster, 1979.

SHORTHAND AND TRANSCRIPTION

Leslie, Louis A., and Charles E. Zoubek. *Gregg Shorthand for the Electronic Office*. Parts I and II. New York: McGraw-Hill, 1984.

Meyer, Lois, and Ruth Moyer. *Machine Transcription in Modern Business*. 2d ed. New York: John Wiley, 1982.

Zoubek, Charles E., and Gregg Condon. *Gregg Shorthand Dictionary: Centennial Edition*. New York: McGraw-Hill, 1989.

TELECOMMUNICATIONS

Bodine, Madeline. *Using the Telephone More Effectively*. New York: Barron's, 1991.

Connell, Stephen, and Ian A. Galbraith. *Electronic Mail: A Revolution in Business Communications*. Boston: G. K. Hall, 1986.

Quinn, Gerald V. *The Fax Handbook*. Blue Ridge Summit, Pa.: TAB Books, 1989.

WORD PROCESSING

Ellis, Bettie H. *Word Processing: Concepts and Applications*. 2d ed. New York: McGraw-Hill, 1986.

Simcoe, Annell L., et al. *Keyboarding for the Automated Office: Intensive Course*. Englewood Cliffs, N.J.: Prentice-Hall, 1986.

Taylor, Helen W., et al. *Word Processing Applications*. Englewood Cliffs, N.J.: Reston-Prentice-Hall, 1986.

INDEX

A

A or *an,* use of, 174, 204, 228
AA (author's alteration), 407
Abbot, forms of address for, 292
Abbreviated dialing, 464
Abbreviations, 172–180. *See also* Initials
  a or *an* with, 174
  academic degrees and professional
    ratings, 143, 176, 179, 312–313
  A.D. and B.C., 174–175, 187–188
  in addresses, 247–258
  a.m. and *p.m,* 179, 192
  with ampersand, 109, 175
  with apostrophe, 110
  beginning sentences, 175
  Bible books, 175
  Canadian provinces, 288
  capitalization of, 142, 173
  compass points, 175
  in compound words, 174
  and contractions, 110, 176
  copy notations, 114, 271–272, 419
  corporate names, 122, 175, 289
  corporate names, foreign, 288 (table)
  courtesy titles, 179, 306–312
  dates, 176, 313
  division of, 176
  geographical and topographical
    names, 176–177
  of *Honorable,* 179, 307–309
  with hyphen, 129, 174
  indefinite articles before, 174, 204
  inflected forms of, 110
  in inside address, 257–258
  Latin words and phrases, 132, 155,
    177, 178
  latitude and longitude, 177
  laws and bylaws, 178
  measures and weights, 174, 180, 193
  military ranks and units, 178
  of *number,* 178
  ordinals, 182
  organizational names, 175
  within parentheses, 130, 176
  with period, 132, 133, 172–173
  personal names, 178
  of phrases, 172–173
  plural forms, 157, 173–174

  possessives, 162, 174
  and Postal Service, 176–177, 258,
    285–286, 288, 290–291
  of proper nouns and adjectives,
    142, 173
  punctuation of, 132, 133, 172–173, 176
  purpose of, 172
  of *Reverend,* 179, 311–312
  of *Saint,* 177, 178
  scientific terms, 178–179
  with slash, 139, 173
  of states (two-letter), 176–177,
    285–286 (table), 419
  of street designators (two-letter),
    176–177, 285, 290–291 (table)
  time and time zones, 152, 179
  of *United States,* 177
  variations in styling of, 172
  of *versus,* 147, 180
  weights and measures, 174, 180, 193
Above, use of, 228
Absolute adjectives, 193–194
Absolute phrases, 117, 219
Abstract. *See* Synopsis
Abstracting of information, 2. *See also*
  Research
Abstractions, capitalization of, 142
Academic degrees
  abbreviations, 143, 176, 179
  capitalization of, 142–143, 176
  and forms of address, 306, 312–313
  punctuation with, 122
  with typed signature, 268
Academy of Certified Administrative
  Managers, 10
Access code, 106
Accession register, 442–443
Accounting, 10, 472–501
  automated, 472–483
  and banking, 484–488
  cash basis vs. accrual basis, 489
  cash transaction records, 488–489
  electronic calculators, use of, 478–483
  financial statements, 497–501 (illus.)
  and medical secretary, 7
  payroll procedures, 490–495 (illus.)
  pegboard system, 492, 494 (illus.)
  petty-cash fund, 489
  tax records, 493–496